AF901302

ASSER International Sports Law Series

For further volumes:
http://www.springer.com/series/8858

R. C. R. Siekmann

Introduction to International and European Sports Law

Capita Selecta

T·M·C·ASSER PRESS

Springer

Prof. Dr. R. C. R. Siekmann
International and European Sports Law
Erasmus University Rotterdam
Erasmus School of Law
Burg. Oudlann 50
3062 PA Rotterdam
The Netherlands

ISSN 1874-6926
ISBN 978-90-6704-851-4 ISBN 978-90-6704-852-1 (eBook)
DOI 10.1007/978-90-6704-852-1

Library of Congress Control Number: 2012935673

© T.M.C. Asser press, The Hague, The Netherlands, and the author 2012

Published by T.M.C. Asser Press, The Hague, The Netherlands www.asserpress.nl
Produced and distributed for T.M.C. Asser Press by Springer-Verlag Berlin Heidelberg

No part of this work may be reproduced, stored in a retrieval system, or transmitted in any form or by any means, electronic, mechanical, photocopying, microfilming, recording or otherwise, without written permission from the Publisher, with the exception of any material supplied specifically for the purpose of being entered and executed on a computer system, for exclusive use by the purchaser of the work. The use of general descriptive names, registered names, trademarks, etc. in this publication does not imply, even in the absence of a specific statement, that such names are exempt from the relevant protective laws and regulations and therefore free for general use.

Printed on acid-free paper

Springer is part of Springer Science+Business Media (www.springer.com)

Series Information

Books in the *ASSER International Sports Law Series* chart and comment upon the legal and policy developments in European and international sports law. The books contain materials on interstate organisations and the international sports governing bodies, and will serve as comprehensive and relevant reference tools for all those involved in the area on a professional basis.

The Series is developed, edited and published by the ASSER International Sports Law Centre in The Hague. The Centre's mission is to provide a centre of excellence in particular by providing high-quality research, services and products to the sporting world at large (sports ministries, international—intergovernmental—organisations, sports associations and federations, the professional sports industry, etc.) on both a national and an international basis. The Centre is the co-founder and coordinator of the Hague International Sports Law Academy (HISLA), the purpose of which is the organisation of academic conferences and workshops of international excellence which are held in various parts of the world. Apart from the Series, the Centre edits and publishes *The International Sports Law Journal.*

Series Editors
Prof. Dr. Robert C. R. Siekmann, Director Asser International Sports Law Centre
e-mail: r.siekmann@asser.nl

Dr. Janwillem Soek
e-mail: J.soek@asser.nl

M. A. van der Harst LL.M.
e-mail: m.van.der.harst@asser.nl

Editorial Office
ASSER International Sports Law Centre
T.M.C. Asser Institute
P.O. Box 30461
2500 GL, The Hague
The Netherlands
www.sportslaw.nl

Erasmus Universiteit Rotterdam

Foreword

The interlocking rings of the Olympic Movement also constitute a suitable emblem of Robert ("Rob") Siekmann's unique linkage of scholarship, editorial leadership, organizational activity, global outreach. and practical counsel in advancing international sports law. It is entirely appropriate that his base of operations is in the world's international law capital, The Hague (and more recently nearby Rotterdam), for Professor Siekmann himself serves as a kind of capital of scholarly developments. He is liked and respected throughout the world of international sports law.

The essays in this book span an impressive array of topics that Professor Siekmann has either addressed in his own scholarship, published as an Asser Institute book, edited in the seminal International Sports Law Journal (ISLJ) that he founded and of which he is Editor-in-Chief, discussed at sports law meetings, or offered expert advice on, often to institutions of the European Union. It is difficult to think of any significant topic of sports law concerning which Professor Siekmann has not been pivotal. It is also difficult to think of more significant issues surrounding the sports arena today than those covered by the lectures in this collection.

Professor Siekmann is well-respected as an expert on European, especially Dutch football. One of the undersigned, however, based as he is in the United States, has attempted to deflect his attention from the world's premier sport by reminding Professor Siekmann of such exotic alternatives on the playing field and in legal practice as North American-style football and baseball. It is a tribute to his intellectual curiosity and generosity that he eagerly acknowledges their place on his agenda for the progressive development of international sports law. The other of the undersigned adds only that Dutch football is the most graceful, elegant and imaginative version of the game to be found on the European continent.[1] Professor Siekmann's scholarly work is similarly and firmly in the same tradition of grace, elegance and imagination.

---

[1] Cf., David Winner, Brilliant Orange—The Neurotic Genius of Dutch Football (2000).

As traditional distinctions fade between amateur and professional athletes and between private and public law, Professor Siekmann's enthusiasm for professional, club-organized football never obscures the clarity of his larger vision encompassing non-professional sports activity and the merger of public and private processes of law. For evidence, one need only turn to his own scholarship, the pages of the ISLJ that he edits, and the numerous books for whose publication he has been responsible at the Asser Institute. He is truly a leader and an inspiration. We are delighted and honored to be given the opportunity to pay tribute to Rob Siekmann by providing this Foreword.

Salem and Oxford, December 2011

J. A. R. Nafziger
Thomas B. Stoel Professor of Law
Willamette University College of Law
Salem Oregon
USA

S. Weatherill
Jacques Delors Professor of European Law
Law Faculty and Somerville College
University of Oxford
London
UK

Preface

Je gaat het pas zien als je het doorhebt[1]

Johan Cruyff

This book is an introduction to sports law, in particular International (worldwide) and European (EU) sports law. The opening contribution is the starting and departure point for all others. It is the full text of the author's inaugural lecture on 10 June 2011 on *What is Sports Law?*, when he was officially appointed Professor of International and European Sports Law at the School of Law of Erasmus University Rotterdam. The Introductions and Conclusions (Summaries) of all articles where applicable are put in the perspective of the sports law doctrine that is developed and proposed in the inaugural lecture. And in the articles on European Sports Law (ESL) the sport specificity test is applied where applicable. In the 'sports betting' article a new, systematic method of jurisprudential analysis is presented and applied by this author, which in principle might be used for studying also other, non-EU jurisprudence.

Capita selecta in the book's subtitle also means *miscellanea*, not only in the meaning of the main themes dealt with in the book, but also regarding the emphases made and the examples given in individual contributions. So, for example the EU competition law side of sports betting is dealt with, but not the aspects of organized crime, sporting fraud and match-fixing that accompany sports betting and which now is an emerging theme in sports law. A crucial legal aspect of international football transfers ('buy-outs') is discussed, but not the specific role and function of agents with regard to transfers. And also the very special issue of sports taxation is not incorporated in this book. *Lex Olympica*, the law of the Olympic Games, does not get a separate treatment, but is represented via the 'sports boycotts' article and the 'passport shopping' theme in the 'sport and

---

[1] 'You will see it not until you have grasped it' is the title of a Dutch book (2004) by Pieter Winsemius (subtitle: *Over Cruijff en leiderschap* ['About Cruyff and Leadership']).

nationality' contribution. Sports image rights are not treated, although the ASSER International Sports Law Centre (hereafter: AISLC) in The Hague, the 'legal capital of the world,' produced a country studies book on the subject as was the case with players' agents, sports betting and other topics. Nevertheless, most relevant, 'hard core' aspects and themes are covered in the book, which is based on more than ten years of theoretical and practical experience on the part of the author in this field, in his capacity of the AISLC's Director (editor in cooperation with Dr. Janwillem Soek, of the *Asser International Sports Law Series* of book publications and of *The International Sports Law Journal* (ISLJ); project manager of applied research reports and studies for, in particular, the European Commission, mostly in the form of comparative legal country studies; organizer of conferences at home and abroad—the most recent addition being the annual conference of the Hague International Sports Law Academy (HISLAC) which was established in Djakarta (Indonesia), September 2010; and individual, private fundamental research). The 'comparative sports law' article represents a good example of what the Centre in cooperation with learned colleagues at home and abroad such as Professor Stefaan van den Bogaert (Leiden University) accomplished in the area of applied research. See for example also, on G-14 and EPFL in the 'Social Dialogue' article, or on the EU non-nationals issue in the 'sport and nationality' article. In the 'competition law and sport' article there is an—anonimised—example of the Asser legal advisory services included which was delivered by Professor Parrish (United Kingdom) (*Dutch Equestrian case*). The author himself was directly involved as a disciplinary arbitrator in the *Dutch Billiard* case (see the article on 'anti-doping law in sport').

In this book association football ('soccer') is the sport that is by far most on the agenda. It is the largest sport in the world, most popular all over the globe. It may be described as a *perpetuum mobile*: the elite football in Europe is a day-to-day commercialised and professionalised industry, which makes it a perfect subject of study from a EU Law perspective. The institutional 'Big Four' of global sports governing (judicial) bodies are specifically represented in this book: IOC, FIFA, CAS and WADA, to which for Europe UEFA must be added. American Sports Law is not treated in this publication, nor the sports laws of other regions in the world.

The way of writing and composing the articles can be characterised further as follows. First, the method of *close reading* was systematically used. It means that primarily the presentation of material is based on what the law, the jurisprudence and other documents of a legal nature exactly provide for. See for example, in particular the 'sport specificity' and 'sports betting' contributions in this book. Secondary comments and learned opinions were not systematically studied, also because the international sports law literature is very diversified and varied. There are leading authors like Professor Jim Nafziger (USA) for the universal, global part of sports law, and Professor Steve Weatherill (UK) for the EU sports law part, but there is only one issue that was and still is hotly debated worldwide in academic sports law circles and where one may find some line of developing reasoning over the years. That is—not very surprisingly—the fundamental topic of what sports law is, where it consists of. In European Sports Law the hotly debated topic remains the core issue of 'sport specificity,' that is the sporting exceptions which are acceptable under EU Law.

Secondly, with regard to European Sports Law, the European Commission's White Paper of Sport (2007) and its 2011 follow-up, the so-called 'White Paper plus' ('Developing the European Dimension in Sport') turned out to be of crucial importance, because both documents most neutrally and objectively describe the *status juris* (and of policy) in European Sports Law, in particular *re* freedom of movement and competition law issues. So, in some cases the Commission's authority was heavily relied on by this author (see for example: on sport specificity; on TV rights in the 'competition law' article; the Social Dialogue in sport article).

Prof. Dr. R. C. R. Siekmann

Contents

Abbreviations

AALS	The Association of American Law Schools
ACT	Association of Commercial Television
AER	Association of European Radios
AIGCP	Association Internationale des Groupes Cyclistes Professionnels
AISLC	ASSER International Sports Law Centre
CAS	Court of Arbitration for Sport
CC	Civil Code
CEEP	Centre of Enterprises with Public Participation and Enterprises of General Economic Interest
CEPI	European Coordination of Independent Producers
CFI	Court of First Instance
CFK	Stichting Contractspelersfonds KNVB
CFO	Comité français d'organisation de la Coupe du monde de football
CFSP	Common Positions in the Field of Foreign and Security Policy
CIETT	International Confederation of Private Employment Agencies
CONI	Comitato Olimpico Nazionale Italiano
COSEM	Committee on Olympic Games and Human Rights (Netherlands)
CPA	Cyclistes Professionnels Associés
CPSU	Communist Party of the Soviet Union
CSCE	Helsinki process of détente
DFB	German Football Association
DFL	Deutsche Fussball Liga GmbH
DRC	Dispute Resolution Chamber
DTCs	Data Transmission Centres
EASE	European Association of Sport Employers
EBU	European Broadcasting Union
ECA	European Club Association
ECHR	European Court of Human Rights

ECHR	European Convention on the Protection of Human Rights and Fundamental Freedoms
ECJ	European Court of Justice (now: Court of Justice of the EU)
EEIG	European Economic Interest Grouping
EFFAT	European Federation of Trade Unions in the Food, Agriculture and Tourism Sectors
EFFC	European Federation of professional Football Clubs
EL	European Lotteries
ELPA	The Automobile and Touring Club of Greece
EPCT	International Professional Cycling Teams
EPFL	Association of European Professional Football Leagues
ETUC	European Trade Union Confederation)
EU	European Union
EUROFEDOP	International Federation of Employees in the Public Service
FA	Football Association
FAPL	FA Premier League
FBO	Netherlands Federation of Professional Football Clubs
FIA	International Automobile Foundation
FIBA	International Basketball Federation
FIFA	Federation of International Football Associations
FIFPRO	International Federation of Professional Footballers
FINA	International Swimming Federation
GLA	German Leage Association
GlüStV	State treaty on games of chance (Germany)
HCC	Host state Contract
ICAS	International Council for Arbitration in Sport
ICCPR	International Covenant on Civil and Political Rights
IFs	International Federations
INEA	Institute for European Affairs
INGO	International Non-Governmental Organization
IOC	International Olympic Committee
IPC	International Paralympic Committee
KNBB	Royal Dutch Billiards Association
KNHS	Dutch National Federation of Equestrian Sports
KNVB	Royal Dutch Football Association
LottStV	State treaty concerning lotteries (Germany)
NADO	Doping Authority Netherlands
NOCs	National Olympic committees
NSF	Dutch Sports Federation
NSF	Netherlands Sports Federation
NVoD	Near Video on demand
PPV	Pay-per view
RWLG	Law on Racing Bets and Lotteries (Germany)

StGB	Criminal Code (Germany)
TEU	Treaty on European Union
UCI	International Cycling Union
UCPF	Employers' Union of Professional Football Clubs (France)
UEFA	Union of European Football Associations
UN	United Nations
UNESCO	United Nations Educational, Scientific and Cultural Organization
UNICE	Union of Industrial Employers' Confederation of Europe
UNIRE	National Union for the Betterment of Horse Breeds (Italy)
USOC	American Olympic Committee
VVCS	General Players' Union (Netherlands)
WADA	World Anti-Doping Agency

Chapter 1
What is Sports Law? *Lex Sportiva* and *Lex Ludica*: A Reassessment of Content and Terminology

Abstract Can sports law be considered as an independent substantive area of the law, does it enjoy recognition as such, and if so, why? This is actually the primary question that requires answering, because the answer to this question is not unchallenged. The question of what sports law is can then be addressed. This contribution is structured as follows: (1) Does sports law, a sports law, sports law as an area of law exist? (2) What does sports law consist of? (3) A reassessment of content and terminology, and (4) What is the 'hard core' of sports law? In summary, it can be concluded that: (1) sports law exists, (2) according to the 'sources theory' which in fact is presented in this address, it comprises a public and a private part, (3) it is proposed to name the public part lex sportiva (sporting law) and the private part lex ludica (sportive law), and (4) the 'hard core' of sports law is chiefly 'judge-made law': of the European Court of Justice (now: Court of Justice of the EU) as the public judge—at least from a European (EU) perspective (regional), and of the Court of Arbitration for Sport as the private court (global).

Contents

This is the full text of the inaugural lecture which was delivered in summarised form upon the author's acceptance of the appointment as Professor of International and European Sports Law at the School of Law of Erasmus University Rotterdam on Friday, 10 June 2011.

R. C. R. Siekmann, *Introduction to International and European Sports Law*, ASSER International Sports Law Series, DOI: 10.1007/978-90-6704-852-1_1,
© T.M.C. Asser press, The Hague, The Netherlands, and the author 2012

1.1 Introduction

What is 'sports law'? This is a question often asked by students, academics, lawyers and lay persons. Anyone attempting to formulate an answer often searches in vain for a response that is compelling and demonstrates some modicum of understanding of what 'sports law' is. Perhaps the difficulty in articulating a response is, in part, a result of uncertainty related to what information is being sought. Is the question as to what 'sports law' is intended to focus attention on the content of the practice of 'sports law'? In other words, which substantive areas of practice fall under the rubric of 'sports law'? Or is more particularly the role of the sports lawyer intended as the principal focus? In this regard, perhaps what is sought is information concerning the services provided by a lawyer in this field. Finally, perhaps the inquirer seeks an answer to a more fundamental consideration: does such a thing as 'sports law' exist?[1]

In other words, can sports law be considered as an independent substantive area of the law, does it enjoy recognition as such, and if so, why? This is actually the primary question that requires answering, because the answer to this question is not unchallenged. The question of what sports law is can then be addressed. This address is structured as follows: (1) Does sports law, a sports law, sports law as an area of law exist? (2) What does sports law consist of? (3) a reassessment of content and terminology, and (4) what is the 'hard core' of sports law? The reassessment includes my own vision of the subject matter and issues that go to make up sports law, partly in the light of a presentation of existing, previous positions and views in this regard.

[1] Cf., Davis 2001, p. 211.

1.2 Does Such a Thing as 'Sports Law' Exist?

Beloff says that the question of whether a 'lex sportiva'—which he apparently uses literally in the sense of 'sports law' here[2]—exists is a persistently recurring theme. Whether a cohesive set of rules exists or whether sports law is nothing more than a mosaic arbitrarily constructed from a diversity of generally accepted and separate areas of law—the law of obligations, torts, intellectual property, administrative law—is the subject of continuing debate. The issue is not purely academic, a qualification which cynics are inclined to use for an issue of no practical importance. Proponents of the first argument (sports law does exist) supposedly do so partly out of a wish to enhance the status of the subject,[3] which does not necessarily mean that advocates of the latter argument (sports law does not exist) can be said to be motivated in any way by a wish to belittle that status. Nonetheless, those who advocate the existence of 'sports law' clearly choose Latin terminology in order to lend the subject a semblance of classical antiquity, sometimes using the alternative term 'lex ludica',[4] even though this is a rather unfortunate choice since it might come across as faintly ludicrous if incorrectly translated ('playful law'). The question of whether 'sports law' exists is not of enormous importance, but nor is unimportant according to Beloff.[5] Mitten and Opie remark that the academic study of the law regulating sport is relatively new. In effect, they say, there is no consensus amongst scholars and academics who regularly examine the rapidly growing body of rules and case law that governs the sports industry as to whether 'sports law' is an independent area of the law or merely the application of general legislation, which would better be labelled as 'sport and the law.' The debate revolves around the question of whether the area displays the unique and coherent characteristics of a separate collection of rules or whether principles from more established legal disciplines merely appear to be finding particular or special application.[6] Davis has outlined a possible assessment framework for answering this question in relation to the subject of 'sport and the law.' But before defining that framework, those criteria, he comments that there are, roughly speaking, three views or positions.

a. The traditional view that 'sports law' does not exist: no separately identifiable body of law exists that can be designated as sports law and the possibility that such a corpus of law will ever develop is extremely remote; according to this interpretation, 'sports law' is nothing more and nothing other than an amalgamation of elements from different substantive areas of law that are relevant in

---

[2] See also *infra* under Sect. 1.3.1.

[3] By way of *oratio pro domo*.

[4] Cf., also *infra* under Sect. 1.3.4.

[5] Beloff 2005, p. 49.

[6] Mitten and Opie 2010, pp. 3–4 and n. 6, p. 4.

the context of sport; the term 'sports law' is then incorrectly chosen since sport as an activity is governed by the legal system as a whole[7];

b. The moderate position contends that 'sports law' has the capacity to develop into an independent area of law; in 2001, when Davis' article is published, proponents of this view identify developments that would appear to point in that direction; they draw attention to the *de facto* unique character of certain issues in sport that require specialised analysis and the in some cases unique application of the law to sport; and

c. 'Sports law' is a separate area of the law; supporters of this view highlight the increase in legislation and court case law specific to sport as a sign of this. Commentators argue that those who view sports law merely as an amalgamation of various other substantive areas of the law ignore the present-day reality that very few substantive areas of the law fit into separate categories that are distinct from and independent of other substantive areas of the law; overlaps exist not only within sports law, but within other areas of law as well; the interdisciplinary nature of sports law has in any event not helped the case for establishing the existence of a separate legal discipline; the supporters of this view argue, additionally, that the unwillingness to recognise sports law as a specific body of law appears to reflect the inclination of some intellectuals not to take sport seriously. In this regard, they emphasise the tendency to marginalise the academic study of sports rather than treat it as any other form of business.

The debate on the existence of sports law as an independent field of law is not extraordinary given that questions about the legitimacy of new fields of law are not uncommon. Similar controversy accompanied the emergence of 'computer law,' for example. Such diverse areas of the law as employment law, health law and environmental law ensured similar fates until they became generally recognised as specific fields of law. The process of recognising a new area of the law is slow-moving, because it is connected with a fundamental process of change in society. Inherent in this process of transformation is the development of new behavioural patterns and forms of cooperation that seek acceptance. Whether a particular field of law ought to be recognised as such is not an exact science. The process of identifying, designating and naming areas of the law is a complicated matter and is, to a certain extent, often arbitrary; there is no official recognition procedure. It is a process whereby legal practitioners and academics determine that the law is increasingly being applied to a new area of society. According to Davis,[8] at the end of the day, the answer to the question of whether sports law is recognised as an independent area of the law may depend on the perceptions of those practising, teaching and conducting academic research into that sports law.

---

[7] The classical representative of this position is the *eminence grise* of sports law in England, Grayson 1994, p. XXXVII. A recent publication in this tradition is, for example, Donnellan 2010.

[8] Davis 2001, pp. 211–214.

1.2.1 Assessment Framework

Which factors or criteria can be applied in order to determine whether an independent legal area exists?

Davis lists no fewer than eleven in his article. While these factors are a guide, their meticulous application need not necessarily provide a definitive answer to the question of whether an independent sports law discipline exists. The factors are:

1. unique application by courts of law from other disciplines to a specific context;
2. factual peculiarities within a specific context that produce problems, requiring specialised analysis;
3. issues involving the proposed discipline's subject matter must arise in multiple, existing, common law or statutory areas;
4. within the proposed discipline, the elements of its subject matter must connect, interact or interrelate;
5. decisions within the proposed discipline conflict with decisions in other areas of the law and decisions regarding a matter within the proposed discipline impact another matter within the discipline;
6. the proposed discipline must significantly affect the nation's (or the world's) business, economy, culture or society;
7. the development of interventionist legislation to regulate specific relationships;
8. publication of legal casebooks that focus on the proposed discipline;
9. development of law journals and other publications specifically devoted to publishing writings that fall within the parameters of the proposed field;
10. acceptance of the proposed field by law schools; and:
11. recognition by legal associations, such as bar associations, of the proposed field as a separately identifiable substantive area of the law.

Davis himself has not applied this assessment framework explicitly and systematically to sport. If we nonetheless apply the above criteria, which are not always clearly formulated, to 'sport and the law' then there is no doubt that we can conclude in 2011 that an independent area of the law exists that is fully deserving of the name 'sports law.'

The above listed factors particularly concern the internal cohesion within the area concerned and its own, special, independent character which distinguishes the area from the legal environment. This is probably most systematically expressed in the term 'sport specificity' that has been developed in the context of European law. This term indicates the extent to which the European Court of Justice in particular has recognised exceptions to regular law, because in some cases the rules of organised sport cannot be dispensed without this rendering it impossible to complete sports competitions in a correct and proper fashion.[9] A now classic

[9] The concept of the 'specificity of sport' has also become established beyond European Sports Law (see *infra* under Sect. 1.3.6) on a worldwide scale, for example in the FIFA player's status and transfer regulations, the rules of the FIFA Dispute Resolution Chamber (DRC) and pertinent

example, in consequence of the Lehtonen case,[10] is the recognition of only two periods during a competitive season within which professional footballers can move from one club to another (in the summer, after the end of the season, and during the so-called winter break).[11] As such, this rule is contrary to the freedom of movement of workers in the European Union, but without this rule there would be a risk of falsification of competition because, for example, a club that is in danger of relegation could suddenly and at the last moment be bolstered by an injection of funds by external backers which are not available to their competitors at that time. This would compromise the existence of a fair and even competition for all participants. It is clear that the particular characteristics of sports organisations deserve special attention, which can lead to exceptions if these exceptions are unavoidable.[12] Factors 1 and 2 are consequently met. Conflicts (see factor 5) are not always settled in favour of the sports rule, however. A good example is the 6 + 5 rule adopted by FIFA. The rule implies that only five foreign players may be selected per team in any match; the other players must be domestic players. This rule discriminates on the basis of nationality and can therefore not be applied within the European Union. Such a rule is not indispensable in order to guarantee a strong national team, for example. Talented young or experienced domestic players can also improve abroad. The Dutch national team is a good example of a team comprising many international players who ply their trade in the best foreign leagues, thereby strongly benefiting the standard of the national team. The special nature of sport is also expressed through the application of factor 7. There are many countries in the world with a general, national Sports Act. Such countries are generally considered as belonging to the group of interventionists. The so-called Football Act (*Voetbalwet*) aimed at combating unwanted behaviour by supporters and other acts of vandalism is an example of special regulatory provisions in the Netherlands. The international community similarly makes its voice heard: anti-doping conventions have been accepted by the Council of Europe and UNESCO, for example.

There is also broad compliance with the other factors, which are partly of a practical rather than substantive legal nature, such as the publication of legal casebooks, specialised journals, academic teaching and research, as well as the

(Footnote 9 continued)
CAS jurisprudence (cf., the Webster, Matuzalem and De Sanctis transfer 'buy-out' awards of CAS).

[10] Case C-176/96.

[11] So-called transfer windows.

[12] Apart from that, in this author's opinion, the old-fashioned tradition of one transfer window (between two full competitions at the start of the football season) would be sufficient and fair, since it prevents the composition of teams being changed during the winter break which unduly distorts the initial balance of strength between clubs during competition.

existence of specialised associations, at many places around the world (see factors 8–11, inclusive).[13]

There is also sufficient institutional connection or interrelationship in organised sport (cf., factor 4). Around the world organised sport is structured pyramidically, with the universal organisations for each sport, such as FIFA for football and the IOC for Olympic sports, at the top. There is a 'world court' for sport, the Court of Arbitration for Sport (CAS) which is located in Switzerland, and a World Anti-Doping Agency (WADA), in which the international community is also officially a stakeholder. Which leaves factor 3, the second part of factors 5 and 6. Matters that are sport-related occur in many different fields of law. Sports law has an inter-disciplinary character, and according to this factor that would argue in favour of the existence of an independent field of law rather than against it (factor 3). It is evident that internal decisions of sports organisations sometimes impact on another matter within the field of law of which the rules of organised sport form an inextricable part. If, for example, FIFA were to repeal its agents' rules, that would automatically have repercussions for the rules relating to player transfers as a whole (factor 5). Finally, it goes without saying nowadays that sport, and hence sports law, are of considerable economic, cultural and social importance at a national as well as international level. In England, professional football is labelled an 'industry,' reflecting the fact that football has become a marketable product and a business sector in its own right. Thanks to commercialisation and the sale of TV rights, huge sums of money now pass hands in professional sport.[14] Events such as the Olympic Games and the Football World Cup are watched by billions of people around the world (factor 6).

In summary, there is sufficient phenomenological and legal inter-relationship and external distinctness to designate 'sports law' an independent substantive area of the law.

---

[13] Mitten and Opie 2010, p. 3 and note 3, comment that in spite of the fact that almost all areas of the law—individually and in combination—regulate competition (including broad and important areas such as competition law, the law of obligations, intellectual property law and employment law), relatively few academics teach sports law or are scholars of sports law. According to the Association of American Law Schools (AALS) Directory of Law Teachers 2009–2010, there are only 120 professors teaching sports law, while more than 340 are specialised in competition law, 1800 in constitutional law and 360 in employment law. These three fields of law are the main areas of public law regulating sport in the United States. So, there is scope for a greater focus on sport on these fields of law. See the website of the ASSER International Sports Law Centre (www.sportslaw.nl. under 'The Centre') for a global listing of International and National Sports Law Associations, Sports Law Centres and Sports Law Journals.

[14] Real Madrid, for example, tops the world ranking list of clubs in terms of annual turnover for 2010 with more than EUR 438 million. The total turnover of all professional clubs exceeded 4 billion euros for the first time last year (according to data from accountancy firm Deloitte, as published in NRC Handelsblad on 11 February 2011).

1.3 What Is 'Sports Law'?

That such a thing as 'sports law' exists in 2011 would therefore appear to be a wholly justifiable position to take, at least when one adheres to the assessment framework provided by Davis. The following question may now be asked: what is sports law, what are the elements of sports law, what can it be deemed to cover?

Firstly, however, an observation, in particular regarding the nature of sports law. Beloff says that a distinction can be made between 'horizontal law'—a body of rules which applies across the full range of relevant human activity—and 'vertical law,' which is a body of rules driven by a single human activity. Torts or competition law fall into the first category. Sports law, like aviation law and banking law, falls substantially into the latter.[15]

Focused literature research then reveals that the following distinctions are explicitly made or the following terminology is explicitly used to designate sports law, or sections of it: lex sportiva, global sports law, transnational sports law, lex ludica, public international sports law ('the law of nations of sport') and European sports law. These categories are discussed successively below. It is noticeable that the term 'lex sportiva' repeatedly occurs in one meaning or another as if it were a benchmark in this regard. Incidentally, all the authors are, of course, adherents to the position that sports law does exist as an independent substantive area of the law.

1.3.1 Lex Sportiva

Nafziger comments that the arbitral decisions and opinions of the CAS in practice provide guidance in later cases, strongly influence later awards and often function as precedent. By reinforcing and helping to elaborate established rules and principles of international sports law, the accretion of CAS awards is gradually forming a source of that body of law. This source is referred to as 'lex sportiva.' He adds that the concept of a lex sportiva is normally limited to the case law of the

[15] Beloff 2005, n. 5, p. 52. For example, in the context of the topical fight against sporting fraud, in particular match fixing in relation to legal or illegal sports betting within the framework of national or international organised crime, a distinction can be made between measures that are horizontally applicable (e.g. to episodes of corruption in the private sector, independently of the different business sectors concerned) and measures that have been specifically adopted to address sporting fraud and match fixing in particular ('vertical law'); cf., Negotiated procedure EAC/25/ 2011, Study on the legal framework applicable to sporting fraud, notably match-fixing, in the EU Member States, European Commission, Directorate-General for Education and Culture, Annex 1—Terms of Reference, para 3.2, p. 4.

CAS.[16] Foster points out that the CAS itself has recognised the existence of precedent effect in accord with its own earlier arbitral awards.[17,18]

Casini says that the number of arbitral decisions made by the CAS has increased to the point that a set of principles and rules has developed relating in particular to sport: this 'judge-made law' has been given the name 'lex sportiva.' This name, which calls to mind well-known designations such as 'lex mercatoria' or 'lex electronica', has been readily adopted and its meaning has been extended over time, effectively in order to refer more generally to the transnational law produced by sports organisations.[19]

Foster comments that in 2005 the CAS was not so sure whether a concept of 'lex sportiva' exists at all. The CAS said that it was not prepared to take refuge in such uncertain concepts as that of a 'lex sportiva', as had been advocated by various authors. The exact content and the boundaries of the concept were still far too vague and uncertain to enable it to be used to determine the specific rights and obligations of sports associations towards athletes.[20] Since this comment of the CAS there had been no further references to it in the published awards of the CAS until the recent arbitration of Anderson et al v IOC,[21] which appeared to signal the acceptance that such a concept exists.[22]

Erbsen comments that the CAS has developed a fascinating body of case law that unfortunately has acquired a misleading name that obscures its nuances. An increasingly popular interpretation of the history of the CAS in the first two decades of its existence suggested that the CAS had created an entirely new body of international sports law called 'lex sportiva.' Commentators do not agree on what 'lex sportiva' means, but many share the belief that it exists. The term's inscrutability increases its allure, combining the legitimising cachet of Latin with the malleability of obscure concepts such as 'lex' and 'sport.' Erbsen goes on to say that the concept of a 'lex sportiva' cannot meaningfully describe or explain the jurisprudence of the CAS. When it was first used, the term evoked visions of an emerging, new form of sports regulation that probably helped the CAS to gain recognition and establish itself as a respected and authoritative tribunal. The term has outlived its usefulness, however. Lex sportiva has become a collective name that encompasses many

---

16 Nafziger 2004b, p. 3; also included under the title 'Lex Sportiva and CAS' in: Blackshaw et al. 2006, p. 409. See also: Nafziger 2004a, p. 48.

17 Devyatovski v IOC, 2009 A 1752.

18 Foster 2010, p. 20; paper presented during the Lex Sportiva Conference at Pelita Harapan Universitas (UPH), on 22 September 2010 in Jakarta, Indonesia, organised in collaboration with the Indonesia Lex Sportiva Instituta and with the support of the Ministry of Foreign Affairs of Indonesia, the National Olympic Committee, the T.M.C. Asser Instituut and the Indonesian football league.

19 Casini 2010, p. 3.

20 FIFA v WADA, CAS 2005/C/976 and 986.

21 CAS 2008/A/1545.

22 Foster 2010, p. 20. However, see previously also, CAS/2004/A/704, suggesting that CAS decisions constitute a 'lex sportiva' that subsequent CAS panels should consider.

different types of lawmaking and unites a diverse collection of variables under an over-simplified motto. Descriptive and normative scholarship in relation to the CAS would benefit from a more subtle interpretation of how the CAS has adapted general legal principles to the circumstances of disputes involving athletes and sports officials. According to Erbsen, the idea that the resolution of international sports disputes through arbitration is creating a 'lex sportiva' had gained increasing resonance over the previous decade. The term 'lex sportiva', which was only thought up in 1990,[23] now appears in the CAS' official descriptions of itself, in the case law of the CAS, in articles by academic specialists in sports law and academics who study general international law, in textbooks, in lectures, speeches and presentations given by sports officials and informally at academic conferences and gatherings of experts in this field. There is nonetheless considerable disagreement about the sources of law and the forms of reasoning that are encompassed by 'lex sportiva', with Erbsen referring in particular to Foster (see below) and Nafziger (see above). The increasing use of 'lex sportiva' as an amorphous euphemism for legal innovations affecting international sport causes problems, he says.[24]

1.3.2 Global Sports Law

Foster wonders whether a definable concept called 'international sports law' exists and proposes that a distinction be made between 'international sports law' and 'global sports law.' International sports law can be applied by national courts. Global sports law, on the other hand, implies a claim of immunity from national law. Foster states that some authors have used the concept of 'lex sportiva' in a superficial manner to describe what is happening with the globalisation of sports law. He argues that 'lex sportiva' should be equated to global sports law. To define 'lex sportiva' as global sports law is to express that 'lex sportiva' is a label for permanent self-regulation by international sports federations. It is a claim for non-intervention by national legal systems as well as international sports law and thus opposes the regulation of international sport by public law. Foster further explains his position that it is necessary to distinguish between the concepts of international and global sports law as follows. International law deals with the relations between states. International sports law can therefore be described as the principles of international

[23] MacLaren says that the term 'lex sportiva' was coined by the acting Secretary General of the Court of Arbitration for Sport. Matthieu Reeb, at the time of the publication of the first Digest with awards of the CAS in the period 1986–1998 (Berne, 1998), in: McLaren 2001, p. 379, footnote 11; in the introduction to the Digest of CAS Awards II 1998-2000 (The Hague/London/NewYork, 2002), Reeb writes that the Digest of CAS Awards 1986–1998 recorded the creation of a *lex sportiva* through the arbitral awards of the CAS (p. XXX). The term 'lex sportiva' is not a pure Latinism, since the adjective 'sportiva' is not Latin, the term 'lex sportiva' obviously was created by analogy with *lex mercatoria*; see generally, Kolev 2008, pp. 57 and 60–62.

[24] Erbsen 2006, pp. 441, 443–444.

public law that are applicable to sport. Global sports law, by contrast, can be provisionally defined as a transnational autonomous legal order created by the global private institutions that govern international sport. Its main characteristics are, firstly, that it is a contractual legal order and, secondly, that this legal order is not governed by national legal systems. It could therefore be described as a legal order 'without a state.' It is a *sui generis* set of principles that have developed from transnational legal norms based on the rules of international sports federations and the interpretation of those rules. This is a separate legal order that, from a global perspective, is autonomous. It implies that international sports federations cannot be regulated by national courts and governments. They can only be regulated by their own internal institutions or by external institutions which they themselves have installed or mandated for that purpose. Foster considers the fundamental distinction between international and global sports law to be crucially important. He reports that various authors have recently argued for the distinctiveness of international sports law and in doing so have described it as 'lex sportiva.' This usage confuses and merges international sports law with global sports law, contrary to his own definitions.[25]

Foster comments further that one of the claims made for the work of the CAS is that it is developing a 'lex sportiva.' The jurisprudence of the CAS is an 'international sports law,' it is argued. It involves more than the application of international law or of general legal principles to the resolution of sports disputes. A distinct jurisprudence is emerging, it is claimed: a unique set of universal legal principles that is used by the CAS in its adjudications. According to Foster, the concept 'lex sportiva' is an imprecise term covering several different concepts. It can be helpful to distinguish different uses. The 'lex sportiva' is little more than the proper interpretation and application of the regulations of sports organisations—a *lex specialis* that is applicable to the governance of international sport because its source exists in the constitutional order created by sports federations to administer sport. In a wider sense, the 'lex sportiva' can be extended to those general principles that can be derived from the diverse practice of sports federations and the rules and regulations by which they govern themselves. This is a restricted, but specific use of the concept of 'lex sportiva.' Foster says that it corresponds roughly to his own definition of a global sports law, which he equates with 'lex sportiva.' This concept has several important elements. It is essentially a transnational autonomous private legal order. This legal order is constituted by the regulatory and constitutional order established by international sports federations. It was created by and has it origin in the private global institutions that govern sport and consists of custom and practice of international sporting federations. Global sports law is a private system of governance with its own global forum, the CAS.[26]

Casini says that sport rules are genuine 'global law,' because they are spread across the entire world, they encompass both international and national levels and they directly affect private actors. Hence the global dimension of sport is, in the first

[25] Foster 2003, pp. 1–2, 8.

[26] Foster 2006, pp. 420–421.

place, normative. A 'global sports law' has emerged, which consists of the whole body of norms and standards that have been set and are implemented by sports organisations. Global sports law encompasses the rules that have been set by central sports institutions such as the IOC, the international sports federations and WADA, and by national sports associations such as national Olympic Committees and national anti-doping organisations. Global sports law, therefore, is highly heterogeneous. Casini uses the term 'lex sportiva' in the broad meaning of 'global sports law.' So the term 'global sports law' includes all the definitions that academics have so far provided to describe the principles and rules of sports organisations.[27]

1.3.3 Transnational Sports Law

Latty analyses the self-regulation of transnational sport taking the concept of 'transnational law' as the starting point: law made by private parties, without the intervention of states and across their borders, and intended to regulate activities in the community concerned. This analysis shows that the 'lex sportiva' is constructed from the legal systems of the international sports federations which are, to a certain extent, centralised by the legal order of the International Olympic Committee (IOC), assisted by the activities of the Court of Arbitration for Sport (CAS) and the World Anti-Doping Agency (WADA). The 'lex sportiva' is comparable to the 'lex mercatoria' and the canon law of the global Catholic Church. They constitute global, extra-nationally applicable rules. Latty evaluates the degree of autonomy of the 'lex sportiva.' Largely freed from national rules and only embodied in a decentralised international legal order, the 'lex sportiva' is nonetheless substantially restricted by European law.[28]

1.3.4 Lex Ludica

According to Foster, the rules of the game ('sporting law') can be distinguished as an independent set of norms and standards, separate from the concept of 'lex sportiva.' He proposes to call these principles 'lex ludica.'[29] They encompass two

---

[27] Casini 2010, pp. 2–4.

[28] Latty 2011, paper presented during the Lex Sportiva Conference at Pelita Harapan Universitas (UPH), on 22 September 2010 in Jakarta, Indonesia, organised in collaboration with the Indonesia Lex Sportiva Instituta and with the support of the Ministry of Foreign Affairs of Indonesia, the National Olympic Committee, the T.M.C. Asser Instituut and the Indonesian football league. See also: Latty 2007.

[29] In the CAS award AEK Athens and SK Slavia Praha v UEFA, 'lex ludica' is described as a set of unwritten legal principles, a sort of lex mercatoria for sports (CAS 1998/200 at para 156); see also, CAS 2009/A/1768 at para 5.2, with reference to CAS 1998/200.

types of rules that are unique because of the context of sport in which they occur and are applied. One type covers the actual rules of the game and their application, or enforcement, by referees and other match officials. The second type is what can be termed the 'sporting spirit' and covers the ethical standards that should be respected by sportsmen and women. So, the concept of 'lex ludica' includes both the official rules of the game and the principle of fair play in sport. They are principles of 'internal' sports law and governance.[30]

1.3.5 Public International Sports Law

Wax points out that public international sports law, a central component of international sports law, has so far received little attention. Defined in a positive manner, public international sports law can be considered as including all norms of international public law that are applicable to legal issues concerning sport and according to which the subjects of international public law allow themselves to be directly or indirectly governed. Defined in a negative manner, public international sports law includes all norms that are not connected with the rules and regulations of national and international sports organisations, EU sports law or national sports law. Public international sports law relates in particular to the following four areas: the struggle against apartheid and other forms of discrimination in sport, peace-keeping during the Olympic Games and preventing and combating violence in connection with sporting events (matches), the prevention of and fight against doping in sport and the question of recognising a 'right to sport' as a human right. These four areas can, in turn, be subdivided into two categories. The struggle against apartheid (against racism in general) and other forms of discrimination, the question of the recognition of a 'right to sport' as a human right as well as the prevention of and fight against doping in sport involving the actual practice of sport: in these cases, it is possible to refer to a public international sports law 'in the strict sense' of the term. Peacekeeping during the Olympic Games and preventing and combating violence in connection with sporting events (matches) by contrast do not pertain to the practice of sport as such, but are directly related to them (in a spatial sense). This category involves public international sports law 'in the broader sense.'

Public international sports law is a key component of international sports law. At a time when sport is becoming increasingly 'juridified,' public international sports law is the appropriate means of correction for which the internationalisation of sport currently has a need. On the one hand the statutes and regulations of the international sports organisations find their 'doubles partner' in public international sports law for the regulation of international sport. On the other, public international

[30] Foster 2006, p. 421.

sports law is the suitable instrument for regulating international sport in precisely these areas (and hence for achieving its goals) which depending on the nature of the issue manage to evade the powers of the sports organisations, argues Wax.[31]

1.3.6 European Sports Law

Does such a thing as European (EU) sports law exist? Weatherill says that the simple answer to this question is 'yes,' but that simple answers tend to be misleading, and that this is the case here, too. There is such a thing as EU sports law in the sense that since the entry into force of the Lisbon Treaty on 1 December 2009, sport has been explicitly recognised as an area in which the European Union has authority to intervene. However, this observation can be misleading in two quite different senses. Firstly, it ignores the fact that while December 2009 was certainly a notable milestone in the shaping of EU sports law, the relevant newly introduced Treaty provisions are in fact cautiously drafted and limited in their scope. They emphatically do not elevate the EU to the position of 'sports regulator' in Europe. So one should not get too excited about these provisions. Secondly, a focus solely on the Treaty reforms of 2009 fails to recognise that for some 35 years the EU has already exerted an influence on sports governance in Europe. Beginning with its famous judgment in Walrave and Koch in 1974, the European Court of Justice has subjected sport to the requirements of what was then Community (EC) law and is now EU law, in so far as it constitutes an economic activity. So sport was not brought within the explicit scope of the EU Treaties until December 2009, but well before that date, sport, though unmentioned by the Treaty, was required to comply with its rules in so far as it constituted an economic activity. That meant, primarily, that sporting practices were to be tested against the prohibitions in the Treaty against practices which are contrary to fair competition, which obstruct inter-State trade or which discriminate on the basis of nationality. So an EU sports law (of sorts) has developed as a result of the steady accretion of case law where sporting rules exerted an economic effect and interfered with the fulfilment of the EU's mission. The EU did not stipulate how sport should be organised, but it did rule out choices that contravened the Treaty. The core of EU sports law is therefore an established pattern with sporting practices being checked to determine whether they comply with the commercial law of the EU, and most clearly in relation to freedom of movement and competition law. When making this assessment the special characteristics of sport have always been taken into account, and since 2009 that is explicitly recognised in the Lisbon Treaty. However, EU law is

---

[31] Wax 2010, pp. 25, 28; paper presented during the Lex Sportiva Conference at Pelita Harapan Universitas (UPH), on 22 September 2010 in Jakarta, Indonesia, organised in collaboration with the Indonesia Lex Sportiva Instituta and with the support of the Ministry of Foreign Affairs of Indonesia, the National Olympic Committee, the T.M.C. Asser Instituut and the Indonesian football league. See also: Wax 2009.

anything but broad in scope. There is very little legislation at EU level that pertains directly to sport, and its 'negative' effect—the Treaty prohibitions—is primarily focused on practices which are anti-competitive or which obstruct inter-State trade. The EU has little to do with determining property rights, contract law or crime. So there is such a thing as European, or EU, sports law; it is of practical and intellectual interest, but it is quite different from and far less systematic and comprehensive than one would expect of sports law at national level.[32]

1.3.7 Summary

A further analysis of the above overview of the different views about what 'sports law' is, what forms part of it, reveals the following picture. The first thing to note is that the concept of a 'lex sportiva' evidently plays a crucial role. It is also the oldest term in the debate. However, different authors interpret it differently. Nafziger adheres to the 'classical' view that the concept of a 'lex sportiva' is restricted to the 'judge-made law' of the CAS. Erbsen, incidentally, is of the opinion that the term is an unfortunate choice. He also observes that different meanings are attached to 'lex sportiva', which does nothing to aid clarity in relation to it.

Foster has introduced the concept of a 'global sports law,' suggesting that the concept of a 'lex sportiva' be equated with it. Latty talks of a 'transnational sports law' in this connection. Both essentially understand the same thing by it, namely the rules and institutions of the international sports organisations and the accompanying jurisprudence, or case law. Their interpretation of the concept 'lex sportiva' is therefore broader than that of Nafziger since it covers more than just the jurisprudence of the CAS. In addition, Foster uses the term 'lex ludica' to refer chiefly to the rules of the game themselves.

Wax has emphasised the importance of assigning public international sports law its own place within international sports law. Finally, European (EU) sports law can be distinguished as a regional public variant (Weatherill).

1.4 A Reassessment of Content and Terminology

1.4.1 Content

It is evident from the above that the debate in literature concerning what 'sports law' is has so far taken place in a manner that is barely conducive to creating clarity. There is still no cohesive vision that systematically compares and assigns a

[32] Weatherill 2010b. See also: Weatherill 2007.

place to all possible elements and aspects. The purpose of this contribution to the debate is therefore to introduce structure in terms of content and terminology so as to engender a reassessment of them which will dispel the existing lack of clarity regarding the subject matter.

First and foremost, it may therefore be assumed that 'sports law' (or 'a' or 'the' sports law, if one wishes) does exist as a separately identifiable field, and hence substantive area of, the law. The concept 'sports law' is nevertheless made up of the elements 'sport' and 'law.' It is 'the law of sport.' The first question is therefore: what do we understand by 'sport' in this connection? This is followed by the question of what we understand by 'law' in this context.

What is 'sport'? In order to answer this question there is no need here to further examine existing (abstract) definitions of the concept of 'sport' and the choice between them. We can limit ourselves in this connection to referring functionally to one of the factors in the assessment framework of whether sports law exists, namely: that the various aspects of the subject matter in question connect, interact or interrelate (factor 4). The existence of such a connection, interaction or interrelationship is most clearly evident in the institutional structure of organised sport. Organised sport is transnational by nature. National associations for each sport are affiliated with regional, continental and international, global sports federations. This produces a pyramid, with, taking football as an example, in the Netherlands the Dutch football association, the KNVB, regionally UEFA and globally FIFA in charge. Organisationally and administratively, the sports world spans national borders. In addition to national championships, there are also European and world championships in each sport. Alongside this there exists an Olympic Movement and there are Olympic Games which unite all Olympic sports recognised as such, with the IOC at the head. Both nationally and internationally, organised sport constitutes an independent social sector. 'Sports law' therefore pertains above all to the law that applies to organised sport represented in the structure as outlined.

This can be both amateur and professional sport. It encompasses, at all levels of the pyramid, competitive sport in which championships can be contested and won. This means that recreational sports or leisure sports that are not practised competitively or in any organised sense, however important they may be from a social perspective, will not initially be studied in the context of sports law. That is not to rule out the study of this type of practice of sport, which may also include physical education at school, in advance, however. But there is little sense in conducting an academic debate about the precise definition of the concept of sport in this regard. The boundaries are fluid. There is also a grey area between what constitutes 'sport' and what is simply a 'game.' A response must naturally be formulated where an issue of law arises in relation to what constitutes a 'game' also. A person who goes out jogging on the road in an independent capacity only needs to observe the rules of the road and is not subject to any sporting rules. The essence of sport, and hence of sports law, is to be found however in the sport that is encompassed by the most suitable response to the question in factor 4 of the assessment framework.

That brings us to the question of what 'law' is in relation to 'sport.' In principle it can be stated that in the widest sense (*lato* sensu) all 'law' that pertains to 'sport,' as the latter concept is explained further above, constitutes 'sports law,' is 'sports law.' So this includes not just all the rules and regulations that have been drawn up by organised sport itself, but also all other law that has been accepted by national states and the international community in order to regulate 'sport.' This is supplemented by the combined jurisprudence of courts or other law-administering bodies of organised sport itself as well as that of 'ordinary' courts,[33] both national and international. If we label the law of sport itself as the 'private' part of sports law then it seems obvious to designate all other law as 'public.' Naturally, the private, or autonomous part, has a public base: it concerns the application of general public law, in particular in the context of the law of associations, to the specific social sector known as sport or it is law that has, at least by definition, been created in the public context. Sports organisations too cannot disengage themselves from the regular jurisdictions of which they are a part. If one were to bring together all existing law within a single framework containing the various areas of the law and then were to introduce sport into this framework, a picture (configuration) would emerge comprising a great many blank spots of varying severity. These are all those areas that are not covered by 'sports law' or where the law has not been applied to sport. The International Court of Justice and the International Criminal Court in The Hague, for example, have never yet had any involvement with sport, nor is it really conceivable that it should, although nothing should be ruled out in advance, of course.[34] Sports law therefore relates solely to a single, specific social sector.

Although the public part of sports law is of an incidental nature and the private part structural, we choose to begin with a further explanation of what can be considered as belonging to the public part because this relates to the environment of sport, how it is placed within a broader social framework, and is by definition of a higher legal order. The rules and regulations which sport has set itself are intended to legislate the sector from within and therefore constitute the private core or essence of sports law. The public part can be divided into national and international sports law. The clearest example of national sports law in a public sense is the national Sports Act which exists in some fifty countries. There are also countries that have included a provision on sports law in their Constitution.[35] This is legislation of general application that is intended to define the position of sport in society and hence to regulate the relationship between government and sport ('sport governance'). It is customary to distinguish between interventionist and non-interventionist countries.[36] The Netherlands belongs to the latter group and therefore has no provision in its Constitution, let alone a Sports Law. Within Europe it is the southern countries such as France, Portugal, Italy and Spain where

---

[33] Civil courts as well as criminal courts.

[34] Cf., as an example of a *casus belli*—in the new meaning of legal proceedings on war—an event such as the border conflict which El Salvador and Honduras waged with one another in the 1960 s following a series of football matches which escalated out of control (*casus belli* in the traditional sense) (see: Kapuściński 1978).

[35] See: Soek 2006a, pp. 28–31 and 33–35.

[36] Chaker 2004, pp. 9–11.

governments traditionally have more involvement with sport. Countries where sport is still in its infancy in terms of organisation and/or where sports law is still in the first stage of development attach great importance to having a Sports Law. Indonesia and China are random examples in this regard.[37] Apart from national, general Sports Laws there are also examples of special legislation aimed at a particular field. A well-known example is the Dutch law that specifically targets football hooliganism, also commonly referred to as the Football Act, and which has been drafted along the same lines as its English counterpart.[38] There are also special Anti-Doping Laws in Europe and elsewhere.[39] An example of national sports legislation that caused a lot of commotion at the time of the 2010 Football World Cup in South Africa is the criminalisation of participation in acts of ambush marketing (the 'Bavaria girls').

In addition to public national sports law, there also exists public international sports law. The revival of the *ekecheiria*, the longest lasting truce in history and hence international law from the earliest times (in the field of sport), has seen the United Nations engage in international peacekeeping during the Olympic Games of the modern era through a series of resolutions which since 1993 have consistently been passed with a view to preserving the 'Olympic Peace' at the forthcoming Olympic Games.[40] Between 1968 and 1993, standard resolutions against apartheid in sport were adopted by the General Assembly of the United Nations. 1977 saw the adoption in New York of the International Declaration against Apartheid in Sports, followed by a corresponding UN Convention in 1985. The UN Security Council imposed a sports boycott against South Africa due to apartheid. The global UNESCO Convention of 2005 aims to combat doping in sport. At a regional level, the Council of Europe adopted an anti-football hooliganism convention as early as 1985, followed by an anti-doping convention in 1989.[41] And the sports provision in article 165 of the Lisbon Treaty is another recent example of 'public regional sports law' which can, incidentally, be classified under European (EU) sports law.[42] At EU level also sports boycotts have

[37] See: Law Number 3 Year 2006 of the Republic of Indonesia concerning National Sports System. In China, the 1995 Sports Law is currently being reviewed, see Nafziger and Wei 1998, pp. 453–483.

[38] See: Coenen 2009, pp. 59–61 and 64–65; Pearson and James 2009, pp. 535–554.

[39] See: Koch 2007, pp. 95–158 (Part II.B: Public Law).

[40] Wax 2010, p. 26. Jacobs 1975, p. 52, says that the Games of Greek antiquity were an early example of the influence of sport on the development of international law and that these Games can therefore also be seen as one of the first steps towards the creation of true international law between ethnically related, but completely autonomous city states.

[41] For the activities of the Council of Europe in the field of sport, see Siekmann and Soek 2007. Regarding the combating of football hooliganism in the European Union, see Football Hooliganism with an EU Dimension: Towards an International Legal Framework 2004; also: Mojet and Siekmann 2009, pp. 499–533.

[42] See Siekmann and Soek 2005; see in particular regarding the 'sports article' in the Lisbon Treaty: Lisbon Treaty and EU Sports Policy 2010. See also, Weatherill 2010a, pp. 11 and 14–17. For a comparison of types of 'continental sports law' see Nafziger 2008, pp. 100–108; see also:

been imposed in the past, an example being that against Nigeria.[43] Finally, reference is made in this connection to the international Nairobi Treaty on the protection of the Olympic Symbol of the five rings (1981).

The rules and regulations which sport has set itself in a self-regulatory capacity (the private, autonomous, non-governmental part of sports law) can be divided firstly into Olympic law and the law of the national, regional and international organisations for each sport.[44] The law of the Olympic Movement (*Lex Olympica*) is laid down in the Olympic Charter and everything associated with it.[45] The law of the sports organisations can be divided into the rules of the game (in football: Laws of the Game), which are identically applicable around the world, on the one hand, and Constitutions, rules and regulations pertaining to administrative (institutional) and thematic aspects of the sport concerned, on the other. The competition regulations can also be included in this category.[46] Many rules have a transnational character, meaning that they are compulsorily applicable up to national level, or ought to be converted into a corresponding set of national rules and regulations. A good example in this regard, in the anti-doping field, is the WADA Code, which to a certain extent can also be characterised as 'semi-public' because national governments are officially involved in administering the WADA and the Code has effectively been legitimised by the UNESCO Convention against doping in sport.[47] The doping rules of the Netherlands Institute of Sports Judicial Administration (*Nederlandse Instituut Sportrechtspraak*) are an almost entirely faithful copy of the WADA Code, which must therefore be largely or fully complied with in its application. In the past each national sports association and international sports federation had its own doping rules, until, in 2004, harmonisation was achieved by means of the WADA Code.[48] Further well-known examples, in the field of football, are the rules regarding the status and transfer of professional footballers and regarding players' agents, which are about to be abolished as such.[49] At a regional level, reference can be made, for example, to the

(Footnote 42 continued)
Weatherill 2000, pp. 155 et seq.; also included in Weatherill 2007, pp. 155–176. See in general also, Siekmann and Soek 2011, pp. 41–51 and 54.

[43] See Siekmann 2008, pp. 121–124.

[44] A distinguishing feature of international sports federations (Ifs) amongst (private) international organisations is their 'normative' functions, which possibly contributes one more, minor argument to consider 'sports law' as a separate area of law.

[45] See Mestre 2009.

[46] See Siekmann and Soek 1998.

[47] See Casini 2009, pp. 421–446; See also Siekmann 2011a, b, pp. 89–96. See in general: David 2008.

[48] Siekmann et al. 1999. See also Soek 2007, pp. 159–561 (Part III: Sport Rules and Regulations).

[49] See Siekmann et al. 2007; see also Martins and Reiter 2010, pp. 7–12. Roberto Branco Martins is initiator and director of the Dutch professional football players' agents association ProAgent and general manager of the European Federation of Football Agents (EFAA).

safety and security regulations of UEFA, the European football federation, which are of particular importance in combating football hooliganism.

In sport, the role fulfilled by criminal law and 'ordinary' courts in civil disputes in regular society is assigned to disciplinary bodies and forms of arbitration at the various geographical levels for each sport.[50] In this system, the Court of Arbitration for Sport performs the general function of 'International Court for Sports,' while also acting as the appeal court in doping cases and ad hoc during Olympic Games.[51] Football has its own important international body for resolving disputes in transfer matters: FIFA's Dispute Resolution Chamber.[52]

1.4.2 Terminology

'Sports law' can therefore be considered as consisting of public and private national, regional and international (in the sense of: universal, global) sports law. Strictly speaking, the term 'lex sportiva' could be used to cover the concept of sports law in its entirety, since 'lex sportiva' means literally 'sports law' and as such is a neutral designation. The 'exotic' Latin nature of the name means it could also be deemed ideally suited to this designation, since this lends it a very clearly distinctive and exclusive character (cf., lex mercatoria). The term purportedly underlines that sports law is something distinct, a separately identifiable field, and hence substantive area of, the law. However, several objections may be raised against the use of 'lex sportiva' in this general, broad meaning. For example, that this innovation goes too far, leading as it does to further terminological confusion, and that is in no one's interest. From a purely academic perspective this may be correct: after all, every researcher is entitled to develop his own, new conceptual framework as well as what he considers to be appropriate terminology in that regard, provided he gives his reasons for doing so. In this case, however, it would not be very practical to act in this way. Firstly: sports law, or sections of it, is not taught at university level anywhere under the name 'lex sportiva.'[53] In literature, moreover, we find agreement on one thing at least, namely that 'lex sportiva', while it may not pertain exclusively to the jurisprudence of the highest judicial body in sport, the CAS (Nafziger), nonetheless in any event encompasses nothing more than the autonomous rules of organised sport itself and the associated jurisprudence (private sports law) (Foster, Latty). It is important not to disrupt a conceptual framework that has already developed and about which, as in this case,

---

[50] See Siekmann and Soek 2001. See also: Blackshaw 2009.

[51] Blackshaw et al. 2006.

[52] See de Weger 2009.

[53] Jakarta (Indonesia) is the only place to have a Lex Sportiva Instituta. It was founded several years ago by Dr Hinca Pandjaitan, a honorary member of the *Hague International Sports Law Academy* [HISLAC(a)] which was established in Djakarta in September 2010, and is the private initiative of a law firm that is not officially connected with any university.

consensus exists to a certain extent, in advance with one's own brand of reasoning. A pragmatic approach is preferable here. In the private meaning, 'lex sportiva' is 'global sports law' (Foster), or even better 'transnational sports law' (Latty), which should then not be limited in its meaning to the global, or at least the international and regional level. Lex sportiva can—to continue the Latin terminological thread—indeed be said to consist of lex sportiva internationalis (universalis), regionalis and nationalis. Thanks to the transnational, cross-border, or even supranational character, if one will, of the private part of sports law, this part of sports law constitutes *de facto* a single, continuous body of law. Anyone referring in a general sense to international sports law is implicitly also referring to its national variant. Unlike international public law, private sports law knows no boundaries. There is nothing comparable to the sovereignty of national states in the sports world. While sport may be organised along national lines, the boundaries between the associations are in effect nothing more than dotted lines (by comparison, national boundaries rather are solid lines). The clearest example of this is provided by the rules of the game for each sport. The rules of football as adopted and expounded by FIFA are the same all over the world, making it unique.

As law consists not just of legislation, but also of jurisprudence, or case law ('judge-made law'), I prefer the meaning of the use of 'lex sportiva' in the broad sense rather than the use of the term in the strict sense (CAS). Law, however, is not just formal, written law, but also practice out of which customary law may have arisen. This is addressed rarely, if at all, in the 'sports law debate,' however. But this source of law can also operate in the private sector. An interesting example of the question of whether customary law can be said to exist is provided by the rules of football. It is customary, it is seen as a moral duty (fair play), for a player possessing the ball to hit the ball out of the play if an opponent is lying injured on the ground and is unable to play on. It is then customary, the opponent has the sporting duty, not to give the ball to one of his own players from the throw-in, but to return it to the other team that had kicked the ball out of play. The party with the throw-in derives the right to throw-in the ball again from the fact that the other team had knocked the ball out of play, constituting an infringement: the ball should remain in play, otherwise it is not possible to play football. This unwritten rule may well be 'soft law' rather than customary duty and law, since the referee does not have the power to enforce this unwritten rule of fair play. Or can he claim this power by innovatively invoking the principle of 'unsporting behaviour' (formerly: ungentlemanly conduct) in disrespect for the game, which is explicitly provided for by the laws of the game (Law 12)? After all, the custom of giving the ball back is based on a gentlemen's agreement. But how then should the game be restarted? By having the throw-in taken by the other team? The laws of the game make no provision for this. By awarding a direct free kick to the other team? That is not possible, since the ball is not then validly returned into play. The player taking the throw-in could be given an official caution (yellow card), if one were to reason along these lines. Or is the offence deemed to have taken place at the moment the teammate receives the ball, so that a free kick would be possible? But who should then be shown a yellow card: the player taking the throw-in, or the player receiving the ball from the throw-in, or both? Very rarely is a throw-in taken 'mistakenly' or 'incorrectly'—even in professional football. When it does happen, it is greeted by loud disapproval from opponents and spectators alike.[54] The custom of hitting the ball out of play when an opponent is injured is under pressure nowadays, however, because it is increasingly assumed in professional football that it is the referee's duty to stop play. That is indeed true, but only in case of serious injuries. There is therefore a tendency to play on when an opponent is lying injured on the pitch. Might he just be feigning injury, for example, in order to break up the opponent's rhythm? Professional footballers do not throw the ball straight to an opposing player, anyway, but to a teammate who then kicks the ball as far as possible towards the opponent's goal or another safe area, so as not to incur any disadvantage from the custom. That teammate, of course clearly could be sanctioned by the referee for unsporting conduct in disrespect for the game.[55]

The rules, or laws, of the game are distinguished as a separately identifiable category of sports law (Foster). However, I consider 'lex ludica'—a similarly 'exotic' term, due to its evidently Latin roots—not as a type of sports law alongside 'lex sportiva', but rather as a part of it, a subspecies. The direct interrelationship is best illustrated by the example of the footballer who is ordered to leave the field of play after being given a red card by the referee and who can subsequently be given a one or two match ban as a disciplinary measure. That rules of the game which are not as such assessed by any 'ordinary' court are most autonomous in practice may be a particular feature of those rules, but that does not justify them being considered as an entirely independent category, or even being excluded from sports law. On the contrary, without the Laws of the Game sports would be non-existent and, as a consequence the same would apply to sports law! So, from this perspective lex ludica in fact might be considered as the hard core of sports law.

In my opinion, 'sports law' in the broader sense consists of more than 'lex sportiva' and the subspecies 'lex ludica.' It should also be seen as encompassing the public part (national, regional and international). There is no generally accepted, specific terminology in use for this part and its sub-parts. The German term *Sportvölkerrecht* (Wax) is so far the only suggestion, but when translated into

---

[54] A famous example of the ball not being returned to the other team occurred on 13 February 1999 during the FA Cup tie between Arsenal and Sheffield United, when Nwankwo Kanu, making his debut for Arsenal, mistakenly took a ball from a teammate that was intended for the opponent and crossed it for Marc Overmars to score the winning goal. Arsenal manager Arsène Wenger subsequently offered to have the match re-played. This happened, and Arsenal won again 2-1.

[55] The in-depth study of the Laws of the Game of Association Football in a historical and comparative (in particular, team sports) perspective will be undertaken by this author in the coming years. Especially, the Laws on the off-side rule and offences ('fouls and misconduct') are of critical importance, the latter for the benefit of their further improved application also to be examined from the perspective of generally recognised principles of criminal law (cf., the concepts of carelessness, recklessness and excessive force already having been introduced in Law 12). See, in this context, Rous and Ford 1974.

the lingua franca of international sport, English, it is rendered quite unusable in a terminological sense: 'public international sports law,' 'the law of nations of sport'? And we shouldn't forget the national variant also ('public national sports law' or 'national public sports law'?). On the other hand, 'European sports law' (Weatherill) has become a standard term. We know that this does not refer to the private regional variant of 'lex sportiva.'

In order nonetheless to produce a comprehensive nomenclature for the entire field of 'sports law,' one might wish finally to consider the following solution, as an attempt to unravel the terminological knot. Admittedly, it is a theoretical, purely academic solution that runs contrary to what is generally understood by the terms 'lex sportiva' (the laws of sport) and 'lex ludica' (the rules, or laws, of the game). 'Lex sportiva' would then stand for public sports law (the 'law' that governments set on sport), which can be divided into 'lex sportiva nationalis' and 'lex sportiva internationalis' [or 'regionalis', such as European (EU) sports law], and 'lex ludica' which would then designate sporting rules and the rules, or laws, of the game (the 'law' that sport sets for itself), which might also be divided into 'lex ludica nationalis', 'internationalis' (or 'regionalis'), with the Laws of the Game belonging qualitate qua to the 'lex ludica internationalis.' This solution would be based on the idea that we only have two 'termini technici' available to us in sports law: 'lex sportiva' and 'lex ludica' (with additionally 'Lex Olympica', of course, as the designation for the law relating to an international series of competitive events). The advantage of using the neologisms 'lex sportiva' and 'lex ludica' in this sense would also be that they are commonly used international technical terms which, as Latinisms, do not require translation into various national languages. As such, they are even more suitable than the umbrella label 'sports law,' which is derived from the lingua franca of sport, English. From this perspective, 'lex sportiva' might be distinguished in English with 'sporting law' and 'lex ludica' with 'sportive law' ('game-law') so that the triplet *sports law/sporting law/sportive law* would arise, in which case the oral pronunciation of each of these terms in practice must be very clear, of course! Finally: why use the term 'lex sportiva' for the public part and the term 'lex ludica' for the private part? Could they not just as easily be used differently, namely the other way round? The reason is that, in terms of their literal meanings, 'lex ludica' is closer to sport as a game (and that is, after all, the basis of sport as it is practised, see: the 'hard core' constituted by the rules, or laws, of the game) and 'lex sportiva' as a more general, more neutral term is, as it were, by definition further distanced from this designation and lends itself more readily to association with 'government.'

The sharp 'bright line' definition and designation of an area of the law could, incidentally, also be added as an additional (X) factor to Davis' assessment framework (no. 12). If this X factor is then applied to the present area, 'sports law,' then the outcome is not entirely positive, as is evident from the above.

1.5 The Hard Core of Sports Law

In Davis' assessment framework, which I took as my reference point in order to determine whether such a thing as 'sports law' exists, to which the answer was 'yes,' it is evidently factors 1, 2, 5 and 7 (unique application of law from other disciplines to sport; specific, and from a legal viewpoint problematical, context of sport; conflictual nature of the rules of sport with other areas of the law; interventionist legislation for sport, which would also therefore include conventions by way of international legislation) that chiefly determine the response to this question. They can be considered as the 'hard core' of the assessment framework. These are all factors or criteria that determine the distinctive nature of an area of law relative to the legal environment of other areas of the law. They are therefore not only relevant for determining whether sport and law make up 'sports law,' in other words whether sports law exists, but it can also be argued that they determine where the 'hard core' of the content of sports law might be found (*stricto* sensu). The core of why sports law exists, sports law is *sui generis*, also constitutes the core of what sports law is, what makes it special. Of course, all sports law—as described in Sect. 1.4.1 and furnished with its own terminology in Sect. 1.4.2—is by definition special, since it pertains to all law that is related to sport. But that should not be a reason in itself to practice sports law as an intellectually interesting, academic discipline. I am not therefore concerned here with this sports law 'in the broader sense.' What interests me is the dynamism that occurs when sporting rules are tested against the general norms of regular society, and what the outcome then is or could/should be. How do the rules by which the subculture of organised sport regulates itself fit into the legal framework of the rest of society? From the perspective that has been outlined, the emphasis is therefore placed on the study of 'judge-made law.' As, globally, the Court of Arbitration for Sport (CAS) is both the ultimate and the key body in this regard, it is understandable that Nafziger is keen to use the term 'lex sportiva' solely for the jurisprudence of the CAS.

Sporting rules are applied and interpreted by the CAS—also including in the light of regular general public legislation and regulations. The disputableness of some CAS awards, however can be illustrated by the following example. According to the disciplinary law of UEFA, the European football governing body, clubs are responsible for the conduct of their supporters. In the 'football hooliganism' case of Feyenoord Rotterdam versus UEFA,[56] the CAS confirmed this rule, even in those cases where the club is not to blame for the misconduct of its fans. UEFA's rule and the arbitral award of the CAS, which confirms the rule, are clearly incompatible with the fundamental principle under the rule of law and of criminal procedure of 'no punishment without guilt.' In his Rotterdam doctoral thesis on sports law,[57] Soek successfully defended the position that

[56] CAS 2007/A/1217.

[57] Soek 2006b.

disciplinary procedural law in relation to doping offences must be considered as pseudo-criminal law and the *praesumptio innocentiae* set forth in Article 6 of the European Convention on Human Rights is applicable to doping-related disciplinary law and that consequently the application of the principle of 'strict liability,' with its presumption of 'automatic' (risk) liability, is contrary to this.[58] In this case, the CAS upholds a sporting rule in spite of all the objections raised (the club had done everything possible and was simply not reasonably able to prevent this misconduct; the so-called supporters were not members of the club, or even of the official supporters club and, moreover, the European match at which they caused a disturbance took place abroad, in France). It is, however, uncertain whether this sporting rule would stand the test of criticism before a public court.

The CAS produces 'judge-made law' of private origin and thereby contributes to the development and refinement of sports law. The CAS is usually regarded as a sufficiently independent body, although in actual fact it is closely affiliated with international organised sport, and the IOC in particular. As far as I am aware, incidentally, the jurisprudence of the CAS has not yet resulted in the 'exportation' of specific legal doctrine or principles to other sectors and areas of the law in order to enrich them.

European sports law is largely based on the 'judge-made law' of the European Court of Justice. The jurisprudence of the European Court of Justice stretches from the 'landmark cases' Walrave via Bosman and Meca-Medina[59] to the most recent Bernard (Olympique Lyonnais) case regarding compensation for clubs providing training to players in professional football.[60] This has led to the development of a body of case law based on the underlying principle of respect for the autonomy of the sports associations and their rules, provided that these rules and decisions are sustainable in the light of the particular characteristics of the sport, and hence granting exceptions to EU law is justifiable and proportional.[61] The question of so-called 'sport specificity' was also addressed in the Bernard case. The European Court of Justice accepted in principle, in this regard, that compensation for providing training to talented young footballers is necessary in order to keep the profession going, although such a mechanism actually conflicts with the freedom of movement of workers to change employer. Weatherill[62] questions the judgment. The prospect of

---

[58] For a detailed elaboration of this issue in relation to the Feyenoord/UEFA case, see Mojet and Siekmann 2009, pp. 530–531.

[59] Case C-36/74, Case C-176/96 and Case C-519/04, respectively.

[60] Case C-325/08.

[61] See Parrish and Miettinen 2008. In the jurisprudence of the European Court of Justice regarding 'sports betting' [nine cases from Zenatti (1999) to Carmen Media (2010)] it is not 'sport specificity' (rules and regulations of sports organisations), but rather national lottery legislation and policy that is tested against EU law. The subject of sports betting as part of European Sports Law (ESL) is sports-related, but not 'sports-rule' related and as such it looks like to belong to the marginal topics of ESL. See also Siekmann 2011a, b, pp. 97–99, 102–117 and 120–121, and also in Anderson et al. 2011.

[62] Weatherill 2010c, pp. 3–6.

receiving compensation for providing training might equally well encourage universities or supermarkets to recruit new talent and to train young employees. Why is football any different, and ought this really to be allowable in this sector?

The European Court of Justice does not always endorse the existing sporting rules and decisions. It sets out the limits of what is permissible and what is not permissible. The clearest example of a rejection of sporting rules was, of course, the well-known Bosman case which led to the abolition of the transfer system and the nationality clauses in professional football in Europe. This ruling caused nothing short of a revolution in professional football since it meant that footballers were henceforth free to move on after the expiry of their contract without their 'new' club being entitled to any fee from their 'former' club and regardless of their nationality in so far as they moved as an EU citizen within the EU. Many open questions have been clarified by the jurisprudence of the European Court of Justice, due to a sporting rule being held up to the light. The European Commission also has made a contribution in this regard in its decision-making, particularly with regard to the collective selling of TV rights in relation to competition law. Nevertheless, numerous questions remain open as to whether a particular sporting rule is indeed compatible with EU law. A recent example may serve to illustrate this. In recent years, the European Commission has received a raft of complaints from individual sportsmen and women about discrimination on the basis of nationality when competing in individual events in another EU Member State. The question of whether one may take part in national championships in other EU countries is, of course, highly explosive in this context. Is the scope of the ban on discrimination so wide that it also allows one to 'hack into' sporting events that were traditionally reserved for subjects, 'nationals' of the country in question? It is a question that has disturbed the peace of mind of the sporting world, although there are countries (Scandinavia) where this is already possible in specific sports disciplines. Anyone required to answer these types of question finds themselves also having to respond to the preliminary, non-legal demand for the facts. A sports lawyer must know a lot about how sport is structured, how it works, including in practice. Although he need not have smelled for himself the proverbial odour of the locker room that is nonetheless considered an advantage also when applying for a job within the sector. Aspects that are evidently relevant in this case are, for example, the question of the relationship between the national championships in question and qualification for European and World Championships and the Olympic Games. This is important since in order to be allowed to compete at this level, the sportsman or woman must hold a national passport of the country he or she is representing. If a sportsman from another country then blocks his or her progress during the national championships that also grant direct international qualification in the particular sport in question, this would constitute a falsification of competition. This can occur if a fellow countryman has not met a better foreign competitor and he thereby wins the national championships, for example. Swimming is a non-contact sport, so there will not be any problems there. You swim to register your own time in your own lane. Or might there be psychological (warfare) problems as in any sporting match? Judo and fencing, however, are non-timed 'combat sports' in which participants eliminate each other in a series of knock-out rounds. If you find yourself in the half of the draw with the better foreign competitor then you will not reach the final. Tennis and badminton are also examples of sports, although of a non-contact character, with eliminating or knock-out rounds, as is boxing, of course. The conclusion must be that it is easier to justify a ban on participation in 'qualifying' national championships by non-national competitors in such sports, thereby possibly enabling an exception to be made to EU law.[63]

1.6 Conclusion

In summary, it can be concluded that: (1) *sports law* exists, (2) according to the 'sources theory' which in fact is presented in this address, it comprises a public and a private part, (3) it is proposed to name the public part 'lex sportiva' (*sporting law*) and the private part 'lex ludica' (*sportive law*), and (4) the 'hard core' of sports law is chiefly 'judge-made law': of the European Court of Justice (now: Court of Justice of the EU) as the public judge—at least from a European (EU) perspective, or court (regional), and of the Court of Arbitration for Sport as the private court (global).

Additionally, and from a different perspective, it can be argued that the Laws of the Game (the term is here used in a generic sense) are in fact the 'hard' core of sports law. They then are surrounded by the regulations of the sport governing bodies at the national, regional, and global levels. Together they form the lex ludica (sportive law). In this circular model, the lex ludica is surrounded by the lex sportiva at the various levels.

Ipse dixi.

1.6.1 Postscript

> But I forget myself and run beyond my bounds. Though yet, if I shall seem to have spoken anything more boldly or impertinently than I ought, be pleased to consider that not only Folly but a woman said it; remembering in the meantime that Greek proverb, "Sometimes a fool may speak a word in season," unless perhaps you expect an epilogue, but give me leave to tell you you are mistaken if you think I remember anything of what I have said, having foolishly bolted out such a hodgepodge of words. 'Tis an old proverb, "I hate one that remembers what's done over the cup." This is a new one of my own making: I hate a man that remembers what he hears. Wherefore farewell, clap your hands, live and drink lustily, my most excellent disciples of Folly.
>
> Erasmus of Rotterdam,
> *The Praise of Folly*, 1509;
> translated by John Wilson, 1668

[63] See: Study on the equal treatment of non-nationals in individual sports competitions, Commissioned by the European Commission to the T.M.C. Asser Instituut and Edge Hill and Leiden Universities, December 2010. See for the Study's Introduction, Analysis, Conclusion and Recommendations, and Executive Summary, The International Sports Law Journal (ISLJ) 2011/1-2, pp. 152–172.

1.7 Annex

1.7.1 An Etymology of the Termini Technici Lex Sportiva *and* Lex Ludica*: Where Do They Come From?*

In 2001, MacLaren wrote that the term 'lex sportiva' was coined by the acting Secretary General of the Court of Arbitration for Sport, Matthieu Reeb, at the time of the publication of the first Digest of CAS decisions stretching over the period from 1986 to 1998.[64] Other than in the Introduction to Digest I which is silent on the matter,[65] in the introduction to the Digest of CAS Awards II 1998–2000, Reeb writes that the Digest of CAS Awards 1986–1998 recorded the creation of a *lex sportiva* through the arbitral awards of the CAS.[66] The neologism 'lex sportiva' is not a pure Latinism, since the adjective 'sportiva' is not Latin, the term 'lex sportiva' obviously was created by analogy with the medieval *lex mercatoria* (merchant law).[67] Apart from that, Prof. Klaus Vieweg of the University of Erlangen-Nuremberg (Germany) and Vice-President of the International Association of Sports Law (IASL), informed me as follows: 'Indeed, the history of the term "Lex sportiva" is somewhat obscure. Looking at my sports law files I found that the first person to use the term "Lex sportive" probably was the first president of the IASL, Michael Stathopoulos [please, see p. 23 of the Proceedings of the 5th IASL Congress on "Sport & European Community Law" in Nafplio (Greece) which took place on 10–12 July 1997]. Matthieu Reeb was one of the speakers at the congress and he possibly picked up the term "Lex Sportiva" from the speech of our colleague Stathopoulos.'

In 2005, Beloff argued that the proponents of the proposition that there is such a coherent entity as sports law, clearly adopt the Latin phraseology to endow the subject with a spurious antiquity—sometimes using the alternative term *lex ludica*—'although that carries with it in mistranslation unhappy overtones of ludicrousness.'[68] [In mistranslation? As we shall see below 'ludicus' in fact is a neologism which was meant by its author to be cognate with 'ludus' so it would not mean 'playful,' but 'sporting' or 'sportive.']

In 2006, the T.M.C. Asser Institute and T.M.C. Asser Press published the book *The Court of Arbitration for Sport 1984–2004*,[69] including ken Foster's contribution on '*Lex Sportiva* and *Lex Ludica*: the Court of Arbitration for Sport's Jurisprudence.'[70] Foster says that a further set of principles that can be distinguished,

64 McLaren 2001, p. 379, footnote 11.

65 Reeb 1998.

66 Berne 2002, at p. XX.

67 See generally, Kolev 2008, pp. 57 and 60–62.

68 Beloff 2005, at p. 49.

69 Edited by Ian S. Blackshaw, Robert C.R. Siekmann and Janwillem Soek.

70 pp. 420–440.

and separated from the concept of 'lex sportiva,' are what can be termed the *sporting law* (italics added; RS), or rules of the game: 'I propose to call these principles "lex ludica."'[71]

Now I wondered what the origin of this term is. By whom was the term *lex ludica* invented and when (cf., *lex sportiva* and Reeb)? In my further research, it turned out that Foster did not have a precedent or source when inventing it. He was trying to follow up a suggestion that he had made in a previous article where he had distinguished various types of international sports regulation from the 'internal' law of sport. There he distinguished the technical rules of sport from the 'ethical spirit of sport.' In the chapter for the CAS Book he used the term 'lex ludica' and then employed it to cover both the formal rules of a sport and the equitable spirit of the sport.[72]

'Ludus' in classical Latin meant *inter alia* 'game,' but if one looks in the Latin dictionaries, one will not find the adjective 'ludicus,' which must be derived from the substantive 'ludus' (in Medieval Latin it neither existed.) I asked Prof. Joan Booth, Latin Language and Literature, Department of Classics, Institute of Cultural Disciplines, Faculty of Humanities, Leiden University, The Netherlands, for confirmation whether the words 'ludicus' already existed in classical Latin as an adjective derived from 'ludus.' She replied as follows: 'The short answer is "no." The classical Latin adjectival form cognate with *ludus* is *ludicer, -cra, -crum* (the masculine form *ludicer* is in fact not attested), but it does not mean what you would like it to mean. It means "sportive" in the sense of "jesting," "fun." See the entry in *The Oxford Latin Dictionary*.' So, in the standard dictionary of classical Latin, The Oxford Latin Dictionary, the word 'ludicus' is missing. Also a quick online scan in the 'Library of Latin Texts' which does not only contain classical texts, but also a number of medieval ones, the word cannnot be found. Johann Ramminger's online-database 'Neulateinische Wortliste' [Neo-Latin Vocabulary] does not list the word. Of course the term lex ludicra (with an 'r') would have been possible as to form, but not as to content (meaning). so, in fact the term lex ludica is a neologism of modern times, like lex sportiva!

Now there is a famous substantial paragraph on what sports law is, in the CAS award of 20 August 1999 in AEK Athens and SK Slavia Prague v. UEFA,[73] which reads as follows:

> 'The Panel is of the opinion that all sporting institutions, and in particular all international federations, must abide by general principles of law. Due to the transnational nature of sporting competitions, the effects of the conduct and deeds of international federations are felt in a sporting community throughout various countries. Therefore, the substantive and procedural rules to be respected by international federations cannot be reduced only to its own statutes and regulations and to the laws of the country where the federation is incorporated or of the country where its headquarters are. Sports law has developed and

[71] At p. 421.

[72] Foster 2003, at p. 4.

[73] CAS 98/200, para 156. Explicit reference to the lex ludica in this CAS award is made in CAS 29009/A/1768, Hansen v. FEI, which by the way was presided by Beloff.

> consolidated along the years, particularly through the arbitral settlement of disputes, a set of unwritten legal principles – a sort of *lex mercatoria* for sports or, so to speak, a *lex ludica* - to which national and international sports federations must conform, regardless of the presence of such principles within their own statutes and regulations or within any applicable national law, provided that they do not conflict with any national "public policy" (*ordre public*) provision applicable to a given case. Certainly, general principles of law drawn from a comparative or common denominator reading of various domestic legal systems and, in particular, the prohibition of arbitrary or unreasonable rules and measures can be deemed to be part of such *lex ludica* ...'

In particular, the use of the words '*so to speak*, a lex ludica' in the CAS award would point into the direction of the verdict's *auctores intellectuals,* who were the Panel's Italian President Prof. Masssimo Coccia (Rome) and his German co-arbitrators Dr Christoph Vedder, who is now Professor of Public Law, European Law, Public International Law and Sports Law at the University of Augsburg, and Dr Dirk-Reiner Martens (Munich). In my further research it finally turned out that Prof. Massimo Coccia in this, from an EU competition law perspective crucial, so-called ENIC case concerning multiple ownership of professional football clubs[74] in fact invented the term *lex ludica.*

To put it simply, while he was writing the award he realized that the expression 'lex sportiva' did not make any linguistic sense, given that 'sportiva' is an Italian word (not Latin) coming from the English word 'sport' coming from the French original 'desport.' So he tried to substitute *lex sportiva* with something more accurate from a Latin point of view. *Ludi* (singular *ludus*) were the 'Games' which were held in ancient Rome on various occasions and, besides the *ludi* with gladiators (a minority of them and mostly in the imperial age), there were *ludi* with equestrian competitions, wrestling competitions, human races and the like. For example the *Ludi magni* (also known as *Ludi capitolini*) were held every year since 389 BC around mid-October and included competitions of physical strength, runs, equestrian races, musical and poetry contests. So he thought that *lex ludica* could be more accurate but he used it exactly as a synonymous of *lex sportiva*, not meaning something else (while he saw in the literature an attempt to identify different notions).

However, at the time he did not do any Latin research; he was too busy finishing the award (which was already very complex in itself) and he simply relied on his classical studies in the high school (in the Italian *Liceo Classico* many hours are devoted to Latin and ancient Greek and he excelled in those subjects). In any event, the attempt to have a new term used failed and in his subsequent awards and scholarly writings. He also started using the expression 'lex sportive.' When something has gained widespread use there is no point in contesting it. It is much more interesting discussing on *what actually is or is not*, rather than on how to call it. However, I think that para 156 of the CAS award remains of fundamental importance for all students of sports law. It may still be qualified as an essential (re)assessment of content and terminology regarding sports law, in a nutshell.

---

[74] See, Commission decision of 25 June 2002 in Case 37806, ENIC/UEFA.

My conclusion is that the term 'lex ludica' was invented by two different scholars, the first in Italy and the other in England, who—not knowing about each other's deed—at different times coined the same term.

References

Anderson P, Blackshaw I, Siekmann R, Soek J (eds) (2011) Sports betting: law and policy. T.M.C. Asser Press, The Hague (due to appear in October 2011)

Beloff MJ (2005) Is there a *lex sportiva*? Sweet and Maxwell's International Sports Law Review (ISLR) 5(3):49–67

Blackshaw IS (2009) Sport, mediation and arbitration. T.M.C. Asser, The Hague

Blackshaw IS, Siekmann RCR, Soek J (eds) (2006) The court of arbitration for sport 1984–2004. T.M.C. Asser, The Hague

Casini L (2009) Global hybrid public-private bodies: the World Anti-Doping Agency (WADA). In: International Organizations Law Review 6:421–466

Casini L (2010) The Making of a *Lex Sportiva*: the court of arbitration for sport *Der Ernährer*. Draft paper for the Max Planck Institute International Conference on 'Beyond Dispute: International Judicial Institutions as Law-Makers', Heidelberg, June 14–15. (The most recent version appeared as IILJ International Law and Justice Working Paper 2010/5 under the title 'The Making of a *Lex Sportiva*: The Court of Arbitration for Sport 'The Provider'', see: http://www.iilj.org/publications/2010-5.Casini.asp; the final version appeared under the title 'The Making of a *Lex Sportiva* by the Court of Arbitration for Sport' in German Law Journal (GLJ) 2011 vol 12 number 05, pp 1317–1340)

Chaker A-N (2004) Good governance in sport—a European survey. Council of Europe Publishing, Strasbourg

Coenen PTM (2009) At last, a football law in the Netherlands? Int Sports Law J 3–4:59–65

David P (2008) A guide to the world anti-doping code—a fight for the spirit of sport. Cambridge University Press, Cambridge

Davis T (2001) What is sports law? In: Marquette sports law review, vol 11, pp 211–244 (Spring 2001)

De Weger F (2009) The jurisprudence of the FIFA dispute resolution chamber. T.M.C. Asser Press, The Hague

Donnellan L (2010) Sport and the law: a concise guide. Blackhall Publishing, Dublin

Erbsen A (2006) The substance and illusion of *lex sportiva*. In: Blackshaw IS, Siekmann RCR, Soek J (eds) The court of arbitration for sport 1984–2004. T.M.C. Asser Press, The Hague

Football Hooliganism with an EU Dimension: Towards an International Legal Framework (2004) Final report AGIS programme 2003. T.M.C. Asser Instituut, The Hague

Foster K (2003) Is there a global sports law? In: Entertainment and Sports Law Journal, vol 2, number 1, pp 1–18 (Spring 2003)

Foster K (2006) *Lex sportiva* and *lex ludica*: the court of arbitration for sport's jurisprudence. In: Blackshaw IS, Siekmann RCR, Soek J (eds) The court of arbitration for sport 1984–2004. T.M.C. Asser Press, The Hague

Foster K (2010) Lex Sportiva: transnational law in action. Int Sports Law J (ISLJ) 3–4:20–25

Grayson E (1994) Sport and the Law, 2nd edn. Butterworths, London

Jacobs FG (1975) Tourism, sports and other forms of leisure from the point of view of international law. General report on the twenty-fourth A.A.A. congress, Nicosia, 22–27 May 1972, Annuaire de l'A.A.A./Yearbook of the A.A.A. 1972/73, vol 42/43, La Haye/The Hague

Kapuściński R (1978) The Soccer War (Wojna futbolowa) Warsaw: Czytelnik

Koch H-G (2007) In: Vieweg K, Siekmann R (eds) Legal comparison and the harmonisation of doping rules—pilot study for the European Commission, Beiträge zum Sportrecht Band 27. Duncker & Humblot, Berlin

Kolev B (2008) *Lex Sportiva* and *lex mercatoria*. Int Sports Law J 1–2:57–62
Latty F (2007) La *Lex sportiva*—Recherche sur le droit transnational, Études de Droit International, vol 3. Brill, Leiden-Boston
Latty F (2011) Transnational Sports Law. Int Sports Law J (ISLJ) 1-2:34–38
Lisbon Treaty and EU Sports Policy (2010) Study for the European Parliament, commissioned to the T.M.C. Asser Instituut and Edge Hill University and Loughborough Universities, September
Martins RB, Reiter G (2010) Players' agents: past, present ...future? Int Sports Law J 1–2:7–12
McLaren RH (2001) The court of arbitration for sport: an independent arena for the world's sports disputes. Valparaiso Univ Law Rev 35(2):379–405
Mestre AM (2009) The law of the olympic games. T.M.C. Asser Press, The Hague
Mitten MJ, Opie H (2010) "Sports Law": implications for the development of international, comparative, and national law and global dispute resolution, Marquette University Law School Legal Studies Research Paper Series, Research Paper No. 10–31, June 2010
Mojet H, Siekmann R (2009) Legal aspects of combating transnational football hooliganism in Europe. In: Gardiner S, Parrish R, Siekmann RCR (eds) EU, sport, law and policy. T.M.C. Asser Press, The Hague
Nafziger JAR (2004a) International sports law. Transnational Publishers, New York
Nafziger JAR (2004b) Lex sportiva. Int Sports Law J 1–2:3–8 (Also included under the title 'Lex Sportiva and CAS' in Blackshaw et al. (2006))
Nafziger JAR (2008) A comparison of the European and North American models of sports organisation. Int Sports Law J 3–4:100–108
Nafziger JAR, Wei L (1998) China's sports law. Am J Comp Law 46(3):453
Parrish R, Miettinen S (2008) The sporting exception in European Union law. T.M.C. Asser Press, The Hague
Pearson G, James M (2009) The legality and effectiveness of using football banning orders in the fight against racism and violence at sports events. In: Gardiner S, Parrish R, Siekmann RCR (eds) EU, sport, law and policy: regulation, re-regulation and representation. T.M.C. Asser Press, The Hague
Reeb M (1998) Recueil des sentences du TAS/Digest of CAS Awards 1986–1998. Staempfli Editions SA, Berne
Sir Rous S, Ford D (1974) A history of the laws of association football. F.I.F.A., Zurich
Siekmann RCR (2008) The sports boycott of Nigeria: sports, politics and human rights. Int Sports Law J 1–2:121–124
Siekmann RCR (2011a) Anti-doping law in sport: the hybrid character of WADA and the human rights of athletes in doping cases (proportionality principle). Int Sports Law J 1–2:89–96
Siekmann RCR (2011b) Sports betting in the jurisprudence of the European Court of justice: a study into the application of the *Stare Decisis* principle, or: the application of the 'reversal method' of content analysis and the essence of the ECJ case law on sports betting. Int Sports Law J 1–2
Siekmann RCR, Soek J (2001) Arbitral and disciplinary rules of international sports organisations. T.M.C.Asser Press, The Hague
Siekmann RCR, Soek J (2011) Towards a typology of (international) comparative sports law (research). Int Sports Law J 1–2:41–51
Siekmann RCR, Soek J (eds) (2005) The European Union and sport: legal and policy documents. T.M.C. Asser Press, The Hague
Siekmann RCR, Soek J (eds) (2007) The council of Europe and sport: basic documents. T.M.C. Asser Press, The Hague
Siekmann RCR, Soek J (eds) (1998) Basic documents of international sports organisations. T.M.C.Asser Press, The Hague
Siekmann RCR, Parrish R, Martins RB, Soek J (eds) (2007) Players' agents worldwide: legal aspects. T.M.C.Asser Press, The Hague
Siekmann RCR, Soek J, Bellani A (eds) (1999) Doping rules of international sport organisations. T.M.C.Asser Press, The Hague

Soek J (2006a) Sport in national sports laws and constitutions: definition, ratio legis and objectives. Int Sports Law J 3–4:28–35

Soek J (2006b) The strict liability principle and the human rights of athletes in doping cases. T.M.C.Asser Press, The Hague

Soek J (2007) In: Vieweg K, Siekmann R (eds) Legal comparison and the harmonisation of doping rules—pilot study for the European Commission, Beiträge zum Sportrecht Band 27. Duncker & Humblot, Berlin

Wax A (2009) Internationales Sportrecht—Unter besonderer Berücksichtigung des Sportvölkerrechts, Tübinger Schriften zum internationalen und europäischen Recht Band 90. Duncker & Humblot, Berlin

Wax A (2010) Public international sports law—a 'forgotten' discipline? Int Sports Law J 3–4:25–28

Weatherill S (2000) Resisting the pressures of 'Americanization': the influence of European community law on the 'European sport model'. In: Greenfield S, Osborn G (eds) Law and sport in contemporary society. Frank Cass, London

Weatherill S (2007) European sports law: collected papers. T.M.C. Asser Press, The Hague

Weatherill S (2010a) Fairness, opennes and the specific nature of sport: does the Lisbon Treaty change EU sports law? Int Sports Law J 3–4:11–17

Weatherill S (2010b) Is there such a thing as European sports law? Global Sports Law and Taxation Reports (GSLTR) 2010/1; also in: The International Sports Law Journal (ISLJ) (2011)

Weatherill S (2010c) The *olivier bernard* case: how, if at all, to fix compensation for training young players? Int Sports Law J 1–2

Chapter 2
Towards a Typology of (International) Comparative Sports Law (Research)

Abstract This contribution presents the international comparative research that was undertaken by the ASSER international Sports Law Centre in The Hague in the previous decade, in most cases in cooperation with other national and in particular international sports law centres and individual researchers at those centres or connected with universities. The ASSER experience is used here to apply and test in practice to sports law research a set of distinctions which are proposed in general comparative law literature, such as internal and external comparative law; national and international comparative law; comparative law in the stricter and wider sense; horizontal and vertical comparative law; and macro and micro comparative law.

Contents

R. C. R. Siekmann, *Introduction to International and European Sports Law*, ASSER International Sports Law Series, DOI: 10.1007/978-90-6704-852-1_2,
© T.M.C. ASSER PRESS, The Hague, The Netherlands, and the author 2012

2.1 Introduction

Sports law is an independent field of law: it complies with the requirements that can be set for the existence of fields of law.[1] Sports law consists of a private and a public segment. The private segment is formed by the rules of organised sport. Organised sport is built up of national organisations for each sport, which are members of regional (continental) and global federations. This segment is a hierarchical pyramid with global federations such as the world football association FIFA at the top, with UEFA as the regional organisation for Europe. There is also the Olympic Games, under the auspices of the International Olympic Committee, which heads the national Olympic Committees and with which global federations cooperate.

The rules of organised sport are largely of a transnational character. For each sport there is in fact a single legal order in which the national and international levels are highly integrated. The rules of football, for example, are the same worldwide and there are uniform regulations for transfers of professional footballers from one club to another.

The private segment of sports law, also known as *lex sportiva*, forms the core of the legal field. There is also a public segment that bears far more of an incidental character in terms of regulations. This consists primarily of national legislation and a number of regional and universal treaties that relate particularly to sport. Naturally, sport is in general subject to the national and international public legal systems. In the European Union, for example, the jurisprudence of the European Court of Justice has led to the development of what could be described as European sports law.[2]

Writing from an international private law perspective, Kokkini already stated in 1988 that if one reviews the comparative law publications of recent decades, it is easy to see that, with the exception of the recognition that comparative law is not a branch of objective law, such as family law or maritime law, and that it can be helpful in achieving many objectives, there is as yet no generally accepted theory about comparative law. Those engaged in comparative law appear to be very enthusiastic about distinctions. Almost everyone active in the field feels obliged to introduce at least one new distinction, which, needless to say, reduces the chances of reaching a consensus about the theoretical principles of comparative law—and this is not even taking the confusion caused by the use of the same terms to mean different things into account. A few examples of such distinctions are:

a. internal and external comparative law (comparing legal systems of countries with the same or a different social system);
b. national and international comparative law (bilateral, between two national legal systems, or multilateral up to and including universal);

---

[1] Davis 2001, pp. 211–346. See also: Siekmann 2011.

[2] Weatherill 2011, pp. 38–41.

c. comparative law in the stricter and wider sense (the study of normative rules as such or also including the reasoning of law and the wider environment of the rules);
d. horizontal and vertical comparative law (comparing legal systems that are equivalent by law, i.e., sovereign legal communities, or comparing rules of a 'lower' and 'higher' order, such as national and supranational rules, for example); and:
e. macro and micro comparative law (comparing legal systems or groups of legal systems in their entireties or comparing specific parts of different legal systems).[3]

The above-mentioned distinctions (hereafter: 'Kokkini-criteria') in principle can also be relevant in the context of (international) comparative sports law research ('international' is used here in the ordinary meaning according to which comparative sports law per definition is 'international'; international sports law in fact is a pleonasm; cf., 'national' = bilateral according to 'Kokkini-criterion' a); bilateral means international, between two states (!)). The character of each of these criteria may be described as follows:

a. internal/external: socio-political;
b. national/international: geographical;
c. *strict/lato* sensu: literal v sociological/teleological (spirit of the law) legal interpretation;
d. horizontal/vertical: hierarchic; and
e. macro/micro: scope of the legal comparison. Of course, the follow-up of a–e might be changed in a more logical order: geographical/socio-political/hierarchic/interpretative/scope (this order is used in this article below).

As already stated, one of the few points on which there is consensus among authors concerns the recognition that comparative law can be helpful in achieving many objectives. An overabundance of literature has been published about these objectives, as authors seek to outdo each other in maximising ideals and expectations in relation to comparative law. According to Kokkini, efforts have been made to place the different objectives of comparative law into two broad categories: theoretical and practical.[4]

It is remarkable that a criterion regarding the purpose(s), the *ratio* of legal comparison is missing amongst the 'Kokkini-criteria' themselves. Of course, there may be a purely academic/scientific or theoretical purpose. However, legal comparison is a scientific research method for practical purposes too, like unification or harmonization of the law (international perspective), or the national perspective of

---

[3] Kokkini-Iatridou et al. 1988, pp. 3–5. See also, generally on comparative law: Zweigert and Kötz 1988.

[4] Kokkini-Iatridou et al. 1988, pp. 26–27.

improvement of the law also in the light of 'best practices,' 'lessons learned' from elsewhere, from abroad. So, an additional criterion as to purpose has to be formulated: (f) theoretical/practical.

From the perspective of contributing to the developing of a theory of legal comparison, regarding sports law in principle the following options of types of legal comparison would exist: (1) the comparison between national sporting rules and regulations (per sport and theme) ('private part'); (2) the comparison between international sporting rules and regulations (per theme) ('private part'); (3) the comparison between national legislation (per theme) ('public part'); (4) the combined comparison between (1) and (2) on the one hand and (3) on the other. Additionally, for example the globally valid Laws of the Game (association football) might be scrutinized for improvement by comparing them with those of other, in particular comparable team sports (why, for example, not introducing the temporary ban from the playing field which is known from ice hockey, etc.?) The striking aspect of international) comparative sports law is of course the role played by what is called here the private segment or part, that is the NGO or transnational law of sporting organisations. So, in the context of (international) comparative sports law research, a criterion must be added to the 'Kokkini-criteria': (g) private/public (or public/private if as a starting-point is taken that the public part is of a hierarchically higher legal order and not the circumstance that the private part is the hard core/inner circle of sports law). Combined, private/public legal comparison could be also a special example of horizontal/vertical comparative research. The same would apply to the combined thematic comparison between international (INGO) and national (NGO) sporting rules and regulations [for example, of course only in case the international rules and regulations are not to be 'copied' at the local level for reasons of hierarchy (cf., for example the WADA Code)]. As to the internal/external 'Kokkini-criterion' it should be noted that countries may have similar social systems at large, but different sporting systems [cf., interventionist and non-interventionist national sports models in the European Union (and beyond), see below]; the opposite is less imaginable, but might also be true.

In this article, I will present the international comparative research that was undertaken by the ASSER international Sports Law Centre in the previous decade, in most cases in cooperation with other national and in particular international sports law centres and individual researchers at those centres or connected with universities. The ASSER experience is used here to apply and test the 'Kokkini-criteria plus' in practice. To the survey will be added an example of the legal comparison between *continental* sports systems, the European and North American ones (re: the 'Americanization' debate in Europe). This can be considered macro legal comparison at the private, NGO (transnational) level, since it concerns jurisdictions, that is sporting jurisdictions, at large.

In chronological order the following research projects were undertaken and reported on:

- Klaus Vieweg and Robert Siekmann (eds), Legal Comparison and the Harmonisation of Doping Rules; Pilot Study for the European Commission, *Beiträge zum Sportrecht Band 27*, Berlin 2007 [EU commissioned study 2001][5];
- Promoting the Social Dialogue in European Professional Football (Candidate EU Member States), November 2004 [EU-commissioned study; see also: Robert C.R. Siekmann in ISLJ 2004/3-4 pp. 31–33];
- Football Hooliganism with an EU Dimension: Towards an International Legal Framework, November 2004 [EU-commissioned study];
- Janwillem Soek, *Sport in National Sport Acts and Constitutions: Definitions, Ratio Legis and Objectives*, The International Sports Law Journal (ISLJ) 2006/3-4 pp. 28–31 and 33–35 [Netherlands Ministry of Sport commissioned study];
- Robert Siekmann, *Study into the Possible Participation of EPFL and G-14 in a Social Dialogue in the European Professional Football Sector,* ISLJ 2006/3-4 [G-14 European Football Clubs Grouping commissioned study];
- Health and Safety in the Sport Sector, May 2009 [EU-commissioned study];
- Study into the Identification of Themes and Issues which can be Dealt with in a Social Dialogue in the European Professional Football Sector, May 2008 [EU-commissioned study];
- Study into the Identification of Themes and Issues which can be Dealt with in the European Professional Cycling Sector, October 200 [EU-commissioned study];
- The Role of Member States in the Organizing and Functioning of Professional Sport Activities, November 2009 [EU-commissioned study]; see also: Robert Siekmann and Janwillem Soek, *Models of Sport Governance in the European Union: The Relationship between State and Sport Authorities*, ISLJ 2010/3-4 pp. 93–95 and 98–102[6];
- The Implementation of the WADA Code in the European Union, August 2010 [commissioned by the Belgian EU Presidency];
- Study on the Equal Treatment of Non-Nationals in Individual Sports Competitions, December 2010 [EU-commissioned study];
- European Social Dialogue in Professional Basketball (forthcoming) [EU-commissioned].

And the following books consisting of thematic country-per-country studies of a comparative European/worldwide nature were published in the ASSER international Sports Law Series:

---

[5] See also: *Bestrijding van doping in de sport: een internationale terreinverkenning in publiekrechtelijk perspectief* [The fight against doping in sport: an international survey from a public law perspective], October 2001 [Netherlands Ministry of Justice commissioned study].

[6] This article will also be published in the Research Handbook on International Sports Law (Nafziger and Ross 2011, 112–130).

- I.S. Blackshaw and R.C.R. Siekmann (eds), Sports Image Rights in Europe, The Hague 2005 (second edition, forthcoming 2011);
- R.C.R. Siekmann, R. Parrish, R. Branco Martins and J.W. Soek (eds), Players' Agents Worldwide: Legal Aspects, The Hague 2008;
- I.S. Blackshaw, S. Cornelius and R.C.R. Siekmann (eds), TV Rights and Sport: Legal Aspects, The Hague 2009;
- P. Anderson, I.S. Blackshaw, R.C.R. Siekmann and J.W. Soek (eds), Sports Betting: Law And Policy (forthcoming);
- R. Siekmann and J.W. Soek (eds), National Models of Sport Governance in the European Union (forthcoming 2011).

These books were preceded by the following documentary volumes (books) of a comparative nature:

- Robert C.R. Siekmann and Janwillem Soek (eds), Basic Documents of International Sports Organisations, The Hague/Boston/London 1998;
- Robert C.R. Siekmann, Janwillem Soek and Andrea Bellani (eds), Doping Rules of International Sports Organisations, The Hague 1999;
- Robert C.R. Siekmann and Janwillem Soek (eds), Arbitral and Disciplinary Rules of International Sports Organisations, The Hague 2001.

The studies and reports will be presented hereafter according to the criteria of belonging to the public, private or private/public parts of sports law. In each case, at the end a typology according to the 'Kokkini-criteria' plus the two additional ones (theoretical/practical (purpose), and private/public (sports law) will be given. This in fact will be a typology along the lines of the 'orientation' of research. It should be noted that the results/findings of the research are not delivered here, being irrelevant in this context. Neither a typology of the methodology used in the operational/implementation phase of research will be given (cf., desk research and use of the the internet regarding literature and documentation, distribution of a questionnaire amongst stakeholders like sport and other pertinent ministries, national and international sport governing bodies and organisations, etc.). The test of the studies and reports against the 'Kokkini-criteria plus' focuses on the starting-point of the research, since the criteria deal with the issue of the point of departure of research. It is possible that the private and public segments of sports law are equally represented at the start, but that as a result of research it turns out that most information available is of a private character, or the opposite conclusion might apply. For example, before the WADA Code was adopted in 2004, all national and international sport governing bodies (per sport) had their own doping regulations, whereas only a restricted number of countries in the world had a public law on anti-doping in sport. In the opposite case, health and safety matters in sport are mainly governed by public law.

2.2 Studies and Reports: A Survey

2.2.1 *Public Studies and Reports*

2.2.1.1 National Framework Legislation on Sport: National Sports Acts and Sport Governance (2006) (hereafter: 'Sports Acts')

The study concerned a subject in the public segment of sports law, namely the phenomenon of national laws of general purport concerning sport, i.e., framework legislation that governs the relationship between public authorities and organised sport in a country. Many countries in the world have a national Sports Act, based on provisions of their Constitutions or otherwise (there are also countries that only have a Constitutional provision). Furthermore, some countries that do not have such legislation are considering whether they should introduce it. In December 2001, in the Netherlands Parliament a motion concerning the advisability of enacting national sports legislation was tabled. As a result of this, the State secretary for Sport requested the sports law section of the Faculty of Law of the Free University of Amsterdam to deliver an advisory opinion on this matter. The general question needed answering whether sports legislation at national level would be appropriate. In the Free University's opinion of September 2003 it was concluded that there was no reason to enact national legislation specifically concerning sport. The State Secretary for sport followed this conclusion. Some years later, however, it became apparent that the Netherlands government was still struggling with the question of sports legislation which covered different aspects (funding, football hooliganism, doping, etc.). The starting point was not that a Sports Act had to be prepared, but that a solid and careful study had to be undertaken into the usefulness and need for a 'foundation' for the sports policy of the Dutch government. From that perspective, the T.M.C. Asser Institute in November 2005 was asked by the Ministry of Sport to examine by means of a 'quick scan' which countries in the European Union had enacted a Sports Act. In these Acts, the definition of the term 'sport' had to be examined in addition to the factors which had motivated the various legislators to enact such laws.

With regard to the distinction between countries with and without national sports legislation, the following should be noted in the context of sport governance in Europe. In 2004 André-Noël Chaker published a study on 'Good governance in Sport—A European survey' which was commissioned by the Council of Europe. The Council of Europe was the first international organization established in Europe after the Second World War. With 46 Member States, the Council of Europe currently represents the image of a 'wider Europe.' Its main objective is to strengthen democracy, human rights and the rule of law. The Council of Europe was the first international intergovernmental organization to take initiatives, to establish legal instruments, and to offer an institutional framework for the development of sport at European level.[7] The study covers the sport-related legislation and governance regulations of twenty European countries. The aim of this study was to measure and assess sport governance in each of the participating countries. For the purposes of this study the term 'sport governance' had been given a specific meaning. Sport governance is the creation of effective networks of sport-related state agencies, sports non-governmental organisations and processes that operate jointly and independently under specific legislation, policies and private regulations to promote ethical, democratic, efficient and accountable sports activities. The legislative framework of the countries under review was analyzed according to whether they have references to sport in their constitutions and whether they have a specific law on sport at national level. There are two distinctive approaches to sports legislation in Europe. Countries have adopted an 'interventionist' or a 'non-interventionist' sports legislation model. An interventionist sports-legislation model is one that contains specific legislation on the structure and mandate of a significant part of the national sports movement, generally speaking including a general national Sports Act. All other sports-legislation models are deemed to be non-interventionist.[8]

It is a distinguishing feature of law that in time, after a shorter or longer period, it is amended, replaced or repealed. A new government will have different ideas, possibly as a result of altered social conditions. This is no different in the field of sport. Attention to national regulation of sports activities and the role of public authorities in this has increased considerably in many parts of the world, particularly in the last decade. In the People's Republic of China, interest in sports law developed in the run-up to the Olympic Games in Beijing (2008) and various universities now offer sports law courses and conduct fundamental research. China has a national Sports Act of 29 August 1995. At the end of 2010, an international scientific conference was held in Beijing on the reform of the national Sports Act.

Ideally, countries wishing to introduce a national Sports Act, reform the existing Act or introduce a completely new Act should have a review in which all possible substantive options are shown for each topic and sub-theme. That model would then be based on an inventory of all existing national Sports Acts in the world. Such an inventory could offer public authorities optimal choices. Comparative research should reveal the differences and similarities between Sports Acts, not only in purely textual terms (in terms of the letter of the law), but also in the light of the background, the reasons (*ratio legis*) for the Act as a whole (see the preamble) and its operative provisions (see the explanatory government memoranda etc.).

The purpose of this type of study is to create the systematic review outlined above, which may provide building blocks (components) and their variants for national framework legislation on sport. Such research has never before been conducted on a global scale with such a substantive scope. The Asser Institute did

[7] See: Siekmann and Soek 2007, at p. XIX.

[8] Chaker 2004.

broaden its aforementioned 'pilot study' for the Ministry of Sport on its own initiative beyond the European Union to include 50 countries, but the theme was limited and did not extend to background information such as official notes etc. Furthermore, the study is no longer up to date.

For an even better understanding of the significance of the national Sports Acts, a broader political perspective of these Acts needs to be defined. What is the national sports policy of the relevant countries? Is there an integrated government vision of the role and function of sport in society and what are the ideas of organised sport itself regarding that role and function? After all, national laws are only a legal instrument to give shape to such policy. The study of national Sports Acts in this broader light could lead to a typology of different types of national sport governance models in the world.

N.B. The typology of the legal comparison in this Study according to the 'Kokkini-criteria plus' is as follows: international/external/horizontal/lato sensu/micro/practical/public.

2.2.1.2 The Role of EU Member States in the Organizing and Functioning of Professional Sport Activities (2009) (Hereafter: 'Sport Governance')

In December 2009, the European Commission (Employment, social affairs and equal opportunities DG) commissioned the T.M.C. Asser Instituut (ASSER International Sports Law Centre) to undertake a study on 'The Role of Member States in the Organising and Functioning of Professional Sport Activities.' The background of the Study is as follows.

Article 39 of the European Community Treaty (EC Treaty) establishes the free movement of workers in what became the European Union. It prohibits all discrimination on the basis of nationality. The European Court of Justice has confirmed that professional and semi-professional sportsmen are workers within the meaning of this Article and consequently, Community law applies to them.[9] This implies the application of equal treatment and the elimination of any direct or indirect discrimination on the basis of nationality. The Court particularly stated that Article 39 EC Treaty not only applies to the action of public authorities but also extends to rules of any other nature aimed at regulating gainful employment in a collective manner and that obstacles to freedom of movement for persons could not result from the exercise of their legal autonomy by associations or organizations not governed by public law.[10]

In light of recent developments in the field of sport, however, certain international sport authorities have advocated the adoption of rules that might be contrary to Community law and in particular to the free movement-of-workers principle.

---

[9] Case 13/76 Donà, ECR 1976, p. 1333 and Case C-415/93 Bosman, ECR 1995, I-4921.

[10] Case C-415/93 Bosman, ECR 1995, I-4921.

National sport authorities, being members of the international sports authorities, should also apply the rules adopted at the international level. Therefore, the implementation at the national level of such rules would be contrary to EC law.

For example, the European Commission has published an independent study on the 'home-grown players' rule' adopted by the European football governing body. This rule requires clubs participating in the European-wide club competitions—Champions League and UEFA Cup (as from the 2009/2010 season: Europa League)—to have a minimum number of 'home grown players' in their squads. Home grown players are defined by UEFA as players who, regardless of their nationality or age, have been trained by their club or by another club in the same national association for at least three years between the age of 15 and 21. Compared with the '6+5' rule adopted by the world football governing body FIFA, which is incompatible with EU law, the Commission considers that UEFA has opted for an approach which seems to comply with the principle of free movement while promoting the training of young European players.[11] The '6+5' rule provides that at the beginning of each match, each club must field at least six players who are eligible to play for the national team of the country of the club. The European Commission, as guardian of the EC Treaty and within the framework of its competences, can initiate infringement proceedings before the European Court of Justice (ECJ) against Member States that have breached Community law. According to the case-law, an infringement procedure can be initiated against a Member State if government authorities of that Member State are at the origin of the infringement.[12] As to the actions of private entities, the ECJ has indicated that Member States might be responsible for breach of EC law by private entities, recognized as having legal personality, whose activities are directly or indirectly under State control. Possible criteria that are mentioned in this context are, in particular the appointment of the members of the entity's management committee by state authorities, and the granting of public subsidies which cover the greater part of its expenses.[13]

Therefore, the fundamental element authorizing the Commission to initiate an infringement procedure against a Member State is the existence of behaviour breaching Community law that can be attributed to the State. The same reasoning applies also in the field of professional sports activities, where in order for the services of the Commission to launch the infringement procedure, behaviour—breaching Community law attributed to the State must be present. Consequently, it is essential to determine whether and to what extent, Member States participate directly or indirectly in the organisation of professional sports activities.

Community law on the free movement of workers and in particular Article 39 of the EC Treaty being directly applicable in the Member States' legal orders, means that every EU citizen who considers that his/her rights have been violated

---

[11] Cf., IP/08/807 of 28 May 2008.

[12] Case C-95/97 Région wallone v. Commission, ECR 1997, I-1787.

[13] Case C-249/81 Commission v. Ireland, ECR 1982, 4005.

might go and seek a redress in front of the national administrative authorities and jurisdictions. If the application of EU law is at stake, national courts may request a preliminary ruling from the European Court of Justice, which is entitled to give rulings about the compatibility of sporting rules with the EU legal order. In the White Paper on Sport, adopted in 2007,[14] the Commission reaffirmed its acceptance of limited and proportionate restrictions (in line with EU Treaty provisions on free movement and European Court of Justice's rulings) to the principle of free movement in particular as regards:

- The right to select national athletes for national team competitions;
- The need to limit the number of participants in a competition; and
- The setting of deadlines for transfers of players in team sports.

In order to improve knowledge of the functioning of sport regulations across the EU and to outline the general trends in Europe, analysis of national sport legislation is required in order to determine whether and to what extent, Member States participate directly or indirectly in the organization of professional sport activities, with a view of clarifying the different levels of responsibility. This country-by-country analysis is to cover:

a. Organization of professional sport activities: the way in which professional sport activities are organized with particular focus on whether the organisation is:
   - part of general organization of sport activities or whether there are separate special rules regulating professional sport activities;
   - underpinned by general law, framework law or specific rules governing sectoral sport activities;
   - at the level of the state, or has devolved to, for example, the regional/local level.

b. Organization and functioning of sport authorities: the way in which sport authorities are organized and function, with particular focus on whether the sport authorities
   - are private actors or whether they act or operate under the auspices of the State;
   - have State participation in any of their responsibilities for the organization of professional sport activities (for example, nomination of members of governing bodies, financing, and adoption of regulations governing professional sport competitions).

c. Discrimination: whether there are direct or indirect discriminatory rules and/or practices with regard to Community citizens. The following fields of professional sport activities must be covered: football, basketball, volleyball, handball, rugby and ice-hockey (as to both men and women championships, and in both first and second divisions).

[14] COM (2007) 391 final, pp. 14–15.

The final purpose of the study was to determine, on the basis of the information gathered and the research undertaken, to what extent the organising and functioning of professional sport activities might be attributed to the State in the European Union.

N.B. the typology according to the 'Kokkini-criteria plus' is as follows: international/external/horizontal/stricto sensu/macro/practical/public.

2.2.2 *Private Studies and Reports*

2.2.2.1 Study into the Possible Participation of EPFL and G-14 in a Social Dialogue in the European Professional Football Sector (2006) (Hereafter: 'SD EPFL/G-14')

The purpose of this study was to investigate whether EPFL and G-14, as European employers' organizations may participate in a possible Social Dialogue with FIFPro under the EC Treaty in the professional football sector. An additional question to be answered was which themes might be relevant to be put on the agenda of a European Social Dialogue in particular from the perspective of G-14.

One precondition is of course that the objects, the mandate (and the tasks) of EPFL and G-14 must (implicitly or explicitly) allow them to deal with 'industrial relations' including a Social Dialogue. It was examined whether this is the case on the basis of the Statutes of both organizations, as presumably the status of employers' (interest) organization is a *conditio sine qua non* for admittance to a Social Dialogue. In this context, it was also important with regard to EPFL whether 'industrial relations' and Social Dialogue were part of the objectives of the national Leagues (at the time EPFL had 15 members). The national Leagues could only have mandated EPFL to deal with these aspects at European level if they themselves were expressly or otherwise empowered under their Statutes to do so. In view of the question concerning the (in)dependence of EPFL and G-14 in relation to UEFA and FIFA as well as of the Leagues in relation to the FAs the objectives of UEFA and FIFA had also to be taken into account.

The social partner organizations must be able to function freely, without outside intervention. This may be considered as an implicit condition for meaningful participation in a Social Dialogue in a free, democratic community of States and in its individual Member States. In the football world the clubs are affiliated to their national FA which is represented in the international federations UEFA and FIFA. This is termed a 'pyramid model' with FIFA at the top, UEFA at the European regional intermediate level and the FAs at the bottom. Football is administered according to this model. The model consists of levels of administration which transcend the clubs. The question therefore was whether EPFL and G-14 as clubs' organizations for the purposes of a Social Dialogue can operate sufficiently independently from the governing bodies. With regard to EPFL not only the relationship to the Leagues/members which must have commissioned EPFL to deal with 'industrial relations' including a Social Dialogue is important, but also the way the Leagues were affiliated to the FAs at the national level.

Apart from that, employers' and employees' organizations and EPFL and G-14 alike had to fulfil certain (explicit) criteria which were developed by the European Commission. In this context, the question could be asked which lessons were to be learned from previous practice regarding the application of the criteria in other industrial sectors, for it could be presumed that the (manner of) application of the criteria in principle also determines their precise meaning and importance. What was the 'case law,' what useful precedent exists?

There is another EU perspective which is even broader than that of the criteria and which deserved to be examined here. What did it mean for the possibility of participation of EPFL and G-14 in a Social Dialogue that 'the specific characteristics of sport' should be taken into account in the European context (Treaty of Nice)? Finally, the question of which themes might be particularly relevant for G-14 in a Social Dialogue was examined.

N.B. The typology according to the 'Kokkini-criteria plus' is as follows: international/external/horizontal/stricto sensu/micro/practical/private.

2.2.2.2 The Identification of Themes and Issues Which Can Be Dealt with in a Social Dialogue in European Professional Football (2008) (Hereafter: 'SD Football Agenda')

The White Paper on Sport states that in the light of a growing number of challenges to sport governance, social dialogue at European level can contribute to addressing common concerns of employers and athletes, including agreements on employment relations and working conditions in the sector in accordance with EC Treaty provisions. The Commission encourages and welcomes all efforts leading to the establishment of European Social Dialogue Committees in the sport sector.

In previous years several initiatives were undertaken by FIFPro, EFFC and the Asser Institute in the form of EU subsidized studies, seminars and conferences in order to promote Social Dialogue in the European professional football sector and make potential social partner organizations aware of the instrument of Social Dialogue for settling issues through negotiations between management and labour by way of a European collective bargaining agreement for their mutual benefit. Additionally, in the so-called Louvain Report conclusions were presented on the representativeness of the parties concerned. The Asser Institute undertook a separate study into the position of G-14 regarding participation in a Social Dialogue at the European level.

In November 2006, at the concluding stage of the campaign, the outcome of a FIFPro conference in Brussels with all stakeholders, including the international football governing bodies UEFA and FIFA present, was that consensus in principle exists about the usefulness of initiating the process to establish an official Social Dialogue Committee under the EC Treaty. FIFPro and EPFL were prepared to take the lead.

The purpose of this study was to identify the 'content' of a Social Dialogue in the European professional football sector, once a pertinent Committee would have been officially established under EU auspices, that is possible themes and issues which are suitable to be considered and discussed in a Social Dialogue, the formal framework for setting an agenda of topics being Article 136 et seq. of the EC Treaty.

The envisaged study was a follow-up to the previous studies that were undertaken to promote Social Dialogue in the European professional football sector in accordance with Articles 138 and 139 of the EC Treaty. In those studies, *inter alia*, social partner organisations at the national level in EU member states and candidate countries were identified and it was investigated whether a Social Dialogue existed at that level between management and labour. The first phase of operations was concluded. The second phase was the establishment of a Social Dialogue. This study was expected to facilitate Social Dialogue in the European professional football sector by anticipating the third phase in which an agenda for the Social Dialogue had to be set.

This study would help social partner organizations and other stakeholders at international and national level to become aware of the possible options regarding themes and issues which can be dealt with between management and labour in a Social Dialogue at the European level. The study was expected to facilitate the start of negotiations once the official Social Dialogue Committee would be established in the European professional football sector. It would offer social partner organizations a helpful instrument for determining their thematic framework. A similar effect was mutatis mutandis to be expected with regard to Social Dialogue in professional football at the national level of EU member states and candidate countries.

Regarding the executing of this study, the following remarks should be made:

An essential aspect to be researched in this context was to what extent the agenda and the way of dealing with themes and issues is determined by the fact that the broader framework of a Social Dialogue in European professional football in fact includes pertinent rules and regulations of the international football governing bodies UEFA and FIFA.

The practice in other industrial sectors having an official Social Dialogue Committee in operation, was studied in order to identify themes and issues which mutatis mutandis could be usefully introduced also in a Social Dialogue in European professional football ('best practices'/'lessons learned').

N.B. The typology according to the 'Kokkini-criteria plus' is as follows: international/external/horizontal/stricto sensu/micro/practical/private.

2.2.2.3 Study into the Identification of Themes and Issues Which Can Be Dealt with in Social Dialogue in European Professional Cycling (2009) (Hereafter: 'SD Cycling Agenda')

The White Paper on Sport states that in the light of a growing number of challenges to sport governance, social dialogue at European level can contribute to addressing common concerns of employers and athletes, including agreements on employment relations and working conditions in the sector in accordance with EC Treaty provisions. The Commission encourages and welcomes all efforts leading to the establishment of European Social Dialogue Committees in the sport sector.

In October 2007 Association Internationale des Groupes Cyclistes Professionnels (AIGCP), International Professional Cycling Teams (IPCT) and Cyclistes Professionnels Associés (CPA) announced that they had jointly requested the European Commission to establish a Social Dialogue Committee in the professional cycling sector in Europe. AIGCP, IPCT and CPA stated that they are convinced that this Social Dialogue, under the umbrella of the European Commission, will be a good tool to renew and modernize professional cycling and its governance.

The purpose of this study was to identify the 'content' of a Social Dialogue in the European professional cycling sector, once a pertinent Committee would have been officially established under EU auspices, that is possible themes and issues which are suitable to be considered and discussed in a Social Dialogue, the formal framework for setting an agenda of topics being Article 136 et seq. of the EC Treaty.

This study would help social partner organizations and other stakeholders at international and national level to become aware of the possible options regarding themes and issues which can be dealt with between management and labour in a Social Dialogue at the European level. The study was expected to facilitate the start of negotiations once the official Social Dialogue Committee will be established in the European professional cycling sector. It would offer social partner organizations a helpful instrument for determining their thematic framework. A similar effect was *mutatis mutandis* to be expected with regard to Social Dialogue in professional cycling at the national level of EU member states and candidate countries.

Regarding the executing of this study, the following remarks should be made:

An essential aspect to be researched in this context is to what extent the agenda and the way of dealing with themes and issues is determined by the fact that the broader framework of a Social Dialogue in European professional cycling in fact includes pertinent rules and regulations of the international cycling governing body UCI.

The practice in other industrial sectors having an official Social Dialogue Committee in operation, was studied in order to identify themes and issues which *mutatis mutandis* could be usefully introduced also in a Social Dialogue in European professional cycling ('best practices'/'lessons learned').

In December 2008, a 'riders' meeting' was organized in Barcelona in cooperation with CPA to discuss the theme under consideration with representatives of their national member associations and individual professional cyclists.

In May/July 2009, regional workshops were planned to take place in Madrid, Berlin, Brussels, Paris and Rome for discussion of the theme under consideration with stakeholders.

N.B. The typology according to the 'Kokkini-criteria plus' is as follows: international/external/horizontal/stricto sensu/micro/practical/private.

2.2.2.4 The Equal Treatment of Non-Nationals in Individual Sports Competitions in the EU Member States (2010) (Hereafter: 'Non-Nationals')

This Study was commissioned by the European Commission to an international research group which was headed by the TMC Asser Institute and further consisted of Edge Hill University, United Kingdom and Leiden University, The Netherlands. On behalf of the research team, the Study's findings were presented by Professor Stefaan van den Bogaert, Leiden University, at the European Sport Forum in Budapest (Hungary) on 21–22 February 2011.

In its 2007 White Paper on Sport, the Commission indicated its intention to launch a study to analyze access to individual competitions for non-nationals. In the 2008 Biarritz Declaration, the European ministers called on the Commission to provide clearer legal guidelines on the application of EU law to sport organizations concerning the highest priority problems they face, thereby paying due attention to the specific characteristics of sport and noting the concerns and difficulties encountered by international, European and national sport organizations in governing their sport. This study will enable the Commission to answer the EU sport ministers' call.

The Court of Justice of the European Union expressly determined in the case of *Ruckdeschel* that the general principle of equality is one of the fundamental principles of EU law. This principle requires that similar situations shall not be treated differently unless differentiation is objectively justified. With this statement, the Court of Justice has instituted a superior rule of law with general application. The fundamental principle of equal treatment finds specific expression, in particular, in the general prohibition of any discrimination on grounds of nationality, as laid down in Article 18 TFEU and further specified in Articles 45, 49 and 56 TFEU.

The prohibition of discrimination on grounds of nationality has already been applied on several occasions to the sports sector. It is now established case law that sport falls under the scope of application of the Treaty in so far as it constitutes an economic activity. The Court of Justice made this particular statement in *Walrave and Koch*, the first ever Court ruling on a sports issue, a case which turned around nationality discrimination in cycling. The Court displayed sensitivity towards the specificity of sport, which was later officially recognized in the Nice Declaration on Sport, ruling that the prohibition of nationality discrimination does not preclude rules or practices excluding foreign players from participation in certain matches for reasons which are not of an economic nature and are thus of purely sporting interest.

The Court has consistently reaffirmed this restriction on the scope of EU law in subsequent case law (e.g. *Donà, Bosman, Deliège*), adding that such rules of 'purely sporting interest' must remain limited to their proper objectives. This has for a long time offered matches between national teams shelter from the application of the Treaty free movement and competition rules. In its recent *Meca-Medina* ruling, the Court of Justice refined this approach in a competition law context, in practice dismantling the concept of rules of purely sporting interest but replacing the idea with a new test. The Court held that for the purposes of the application of the competition law rules to a particular case, account must firstly be taken of the overall context in which the decision was taken or produces its effects and, more specifically, of its objectives; subsequently, it has then to be considered whether the consequential effects restrictive of competition are inherent in the pursuit of those objectives and are proportionate to them. These findings can be transposed to the free movement context. It constitutes a new standard by which the Court of Justice of the European Union will in the future evaluate sports rules and practices.

The Court has also dealt with nationality discrimination at club level in sport. So far, it has always firmly branded these discriminatory measures as incompatible with EU law. In the wake of the judgments in *Donà* and *Bosman* there appears to be limited room for sporting federations to treat domestic players more favourably than foreign players who are protected by EU law. The decisions in *Kolpak* and *Simutenkov* have made it clear that third-country nationals who are legally residing in a host Member State and can also often rely upon a directly effective equal treatment provisions contained in international agreements concluded between the EU and the third-country from which they originate. In these cases, the Court categorically held that the justificatory arguments relating to the maintenance of a traditional link between a club and its country or the creation of a sufficient pool of players for the national team were not such as to preserve the contested nationality clauses.

However, by the same token, the Court also acknowledged that the aims of maintaining a balance between clubs by preserving a certain degree of equality and uncertainty as to results and of encouraging the recruitment and training of young players must be accepted as legitimate. The Court has thus not completely shut the door to all nationality clauses but has left it to the self-regulatory autonomy of the sporting associations to elaborate rules or practices at club level that are compatible with the requirements of EU law. The European Football Association UEFA has made use of this opportunity to introduce the so-called '4+4' or 'home-grown' rule, which requires clubs to include in their teams a minimum number of domestically trained players. The CJEU has not yet pronounced on this rule, which has already received support from the European Commission and the European

Parliament. Conversely, both European institutions appeared reluctant towards the proposal of World Football Association FIFA to gradually introduce the '6+5' rule, requiring football teams to start official matches with minimum six players eligible to play for the national team of the club. This was generally regarded as unjustifiable discrimination. Nevertheless, in the 2008 Biarritz Declaration of the sports ministers of the European Union, the ministers clearly expressed their interest in further discussion on the initiatives of international federations to encourage the teams of professional clubs to develop the presence of athletes capable of qualifying for national teams, in order to strengthen the regional and national roots of professional clubs, albeit in compliance with EU law. Despite extensive jurisprudence and countless discussions at political level, the issue of nationality clauses even in team sports has thus not yet been settled.

Until now, the situation with regard to equal treatment of non-nationals in individual sporting disciplines has been the subject of much less debate and legal scrutiny. Traditionally, individual sports have been organized on a national basis with one sports federation organizing its respective sport within its territory. This has endowed sport with a distinctly national character. The development of an internal market supported by free movement and citizenship rights has the potential to call into question this traditional feature of the so-called 'European model of sport.' This is generating debate amongst some Member States and sports organizations who are concerned for the purity of national competitions should EU non-discrimination law apply to their constitutional arrangements. For example, for cultural reasons it has been suggested that the conferment of 'national champion' titles should be reserved for nationals of the Member State within which the competition takes place. There is also concern at the prospect of some athletes being able to take part in the national championships of more than one country. Eligibility rules for international competitions and championships that are based on the representation of states (legal nationality), are logically a (co)determining factor for the nationality of sportspersons in competitions at the national level that are qualifiers for these international competitions.

Rules designed to maintain the purity of national competitions can lead to the adoption of discriminatory measures. For example, with effect from March 2008 the Belgian Swimming Federation adopted new rules excluding non-nationals from participating in national swimming championships in Belgium. The report provides a comprehensive list of such measures and the sports in which these restrictions present themselves. Some sports raise specific issues in this respect For example, the participation of non-nationals in the national championships of sports with direct elimination, such as tennis or fencing, may exert a more significant impact on the outcome of the competition than in other sports. Furthermore, the report specifies the level at which the discriminatory provisions are adopted. In determining whether the discriminatory measures involve access to sports, the conditions relating to the actual practice of sports, the determination of national records, the award of medals or titles, or any other aspect of the sport, the report investigates the objectives pursued by these measures and the consequences on each sport of removing the restrictions. In doing so, the report comprehensively enquires into the ongoing debate within the sports movement concerning the definition of the 'specificity of sport' and its application in EU law to both the economic and non-economic aspects of sport. This allows for the presentation of a typological analysis of the discriminatory measures identified.

This typology against which the directly or indirectly discriminatory measures identified is measured is essentially the same as in the context of discriminatory measures at club level and primarily consists of the Treaty rules on freedom of movement. Furthermore, the Treaty provisions on Union citizenship, which is destined to be the fundamental status of nationals of the EU Member States (*Grzelczyk*) is duly regarded in this respect.

According to settled case-law, EU citizens lawfully resident in the territory of a host Member State who find themselves in the same situation as home State nationals can rely on Article 18 TFEU to receive the same treatment in law irrespective of their nationality in all situations which fall within the scope *ratione materiae* of EU law. Those situations include those involving the exercise of the fundamental freedoms guaranteed by the Treaty and those involving the exercise of the right to move and reside within the territory of the Member States, as conferred by Article 21 TFEU. In addition, where and whenever necessary, also instruments of EU secondary legislation such as, in particular, Directive 2004/38 on the rights of citizens and their family members to move and reside in the EU and Regulation 1612/68 are taken into consideration. Essentially, all discriminatory rules are grouped in four different categories: firstly rules of purely sporting interest; secondly, rules which are inherent in the organization of the sport and necessary to pursue the objectives outlined and which therefore do not constitute a restriction of EU law; thirdly, those rules which are discriminatory but capable of justification and proportionate; and finally those rules which are discriminatory and cannot be justified and must therefore be dismissed.

Additionally, the report undertakes an assessment of the likely impact of the Lisbon Treaty which establishes sport as a competence of the EU. Article 165(1) TFEU provides that 'The Union shall contribute to the promotion of European sporting issues, while taking account of the specific nature of sport, its structures based on voluntary activity and its social and educational function.' Article 165(2) adds that Union actions shall be aimed at 'developing the European dimension in sport, by promoting fairness and openness in sporting competitions and cooperation between bodies responsible for sports, and by protecting the physical and moral integrity of sportsmen and sportswomen, especially the youngest sportsmen and sportswomen.' The likely impact of these provisions on the jurisprudence of the Court is considered. In particular, the report will consider whether these provisions constitute the legal basis for eliminating the discrimination in question or a means of insulating such measures.

First, in the Study a full evaluation of the situation per country is provided concerning the provisions in sports (competition) regulations that are discriminatory based on nationality in the sports disciplines selected, and relating to access and all other aspects of individual sports competitions. The level at which the discriminatory provisions identified are adopted (national, regional or local sports federations) is specified and it is indicated whether they are imposed at lower levels of this pyramid-shaped hierarchy. Information regarding any regulatory provisions that are discriminatory on grounds of nationality established under public administrative decision is provided.

Second, a typology analysis of the discriminatory measures identified is given. It is indicated whether the discriminatory measures involve access to sports (participation in competitions), conditions relating to the actual practice of sports, the award of medals and titles, etc. The various criteria that hamper access to competitions either directly or indirectly, are listed. A detailed list of the various objectives identified as underlying the establishment of discriminatory measures is presented. Particular attention is given to the selection of national champions, determining national records, the award of titles and medals to nationals, avoiding the award of national titles to athletes in different Member States, etc.

For the purposes of this Study the term 'non-nationals' was defined as follows:

> citizens, their family members, and workers from other EU Member States, as well as citizens of States which have signed agreements with the EU that contain non-discrimination clauses, and who are legally employed in the territory of the Member States (third country nationals).

The term 'individual sports competitions' was defined as follows:

> national competitions involving individual sportspersons, regarding sports disciplines practiced in a professional or amateur capacity within the European Union.

The individual ('non-team') sports disciplines that are covered in the Study, are the Olympic sports disciplines concerned (Winter and Summer Olympics). There are 26 Olympic sports which are whether individual disciplines themselves or to which individual disciplines belong: triathlon, modern pentathlon, tennis, table tennis, badminton, rowing, canoe/kayak, athletics, aquatics, archery, boxing, judo, shooting, weightlifting, wrestling, taekwondo, equestrian, gymnastics, skating, luge, biathlon, bobsleigh, cycling, skiing, fencing and sailing (see: www.olympic.org/en/content/Sports/).

Partly in the light of the findings of this study, the European Commission intends to 'issue guidance on how to reconcile the Treaty provisions on nationality with the organisation of competitions in individual sports on a national basis.'[15]

> N.B. The typology according to the 'Kokkini-criteria plus' is as follows: international/external/horizontal/lato sensu (cf., 'objectives underlying the establishment of discriminatory measures')/micro/practical/private (the public segment concerns a priori illegal discriminatory regulatory provisions, since they are established under public administrative decision; so they were not part of the legal comparison exercise).

[15] Communication from the Commission to the European Parliament, the Council, the European Economic and Social Committee and the Committee of the Regions, *Developing the European Dimension in Sport*, COM(2011) 12 final, Brussels, 18.1.2011, p. 13.

2.2.3 *Private/Public Studies and Reports*

2.2.3.1 Legal Comparison and the Harmonization of Doping Rules (2001) (Hereafter: 'Doping Harmonization')

In 2000, an international research group consisting of sports law experts from the University of Erlangen-Nuremberg (Germany), the T.M.C. Asser Institute for International Law, The Hague (The Netherlands), the Max Planck Institute for Foreign and International Criminal Law, Freiburg i.B. (Germany), and the Anglia Polytechnic University, Chelmsford (United Kingdom), was asked by the European Commission to undertake a research study on 'Legal Comparison and the Harmonisation of Doping Rules' within the framework of the 'Pilot Project for Campaigns to Combat Doping in Sport in Europe.'

The final report of the research study was presented on 7 November 2001 and was discussed at an international conference in Brussels, which was organized by the T.M.C. Asser Institute with the support of the Flemish Ministry for Sports during the Belgian EU Presidency. The conference was attended by representatives of international sports federations, as well as sports ministries and national sports organisations from the EU Member States.

The European Commission commissioned the study during the initial stages of the drafting of a World Anti-Doping Code. In the years following the publication of the study, work on the World Anti-Doping Code continued and was finally completed with the adoption of the 'WADA Code' in 2003. The study may be considered to have contributed significantly to the completion of this work, as it provided the drafters of the Code with an important tool, giving them an overview of the doping rules and regulations of national and international sports organizations, including a comparative analysis, as well as a survey and analysis of the relevant public law legislation available. Since the study may be considered to form part of the travaux preparatoires underlying the WADA Code, which in the meantime has entered into force and is being applied in practice, the undersigned consider it necessary that the study reflecting the legal situation in 2001 be published as a book. This publication in particular wishes to promote a better understanding of the background of the harmonization of doping rules and regulations, the results of which may be found in the WADA Code a milestone in the campaign to combat doping in sports.

The Study contains a public law part and a part concerning sports rules and regulations on anti-doping. Both parts are presented in a comparative, thematic form. The first part consists of a comparative legal analysis of anti-doping activities, in particular with regard to combating doping by means of criminal law in the 15 EU Member States at the time. In the sports rules and regulations part, the results of the study of the pertinent national instruments in the EU Member States for the then 35 Olympic international sports—together with the regulations of the International Olympic Committee (IOC), the International Paralympic Committee (IPC) and the Olympic international sports federations—were delivered. Aspects such as the following are considered in this part: definition of doping (description of the doping offence), the purpose of the ban on doping (arguments against the use of doping), system of sanctions, etc.[16]

N.B. The typology according to the 'Kokkini-criteria plus' is as follows: international/external (public level: the EU is to a certain extent a supranational body, but cf., interventionist v non-interventionist national sport models in the EU)/horizontal (on both levels: public and private)/stricto sensu/micro (one issue: doping)/practical (cf., the drafting of a WADA Code)/private and public.

2.2.3.2 Promoting Social Dialogue in European Professional Football (Candidate EU Member States) (2004) [Hereafter: 'SD Football (Candidates)']

In November 2004 the Final Report on the above-mentioned project was presented by the ASSER International Sports Law Centre to the European Commission. Part of the project was a comparative legal 'pilot' study on the basis of country studies regarding the above-mentioned subject. In addition to the 'pilot' study, in the first half of 2004 regional seminars were organized in Nicosia (Cyprus and Malta), Vilnius (Estonia, Latvia and Lithuania), Ljubljana (Hungary and Slovenia), Warsaw (Poland), Prague (Czech Republic and Slovakia), and Bucharest (for the 2007 candidate Member States Bulgaria and Romania).

In this report, three key questions which are relevant in a Social Dialogue context have been examined:

1. What is the legal basis for the relationship between a player and the club (comprising aspects concerning the regulation of sport in the country concerned, termination of contracts, compensation for training and education)?
2. What has the candidate country (now EU Member State plus Bulgaria and Romania) already done to implement Council Directive 1990/70/EC of 28 June 1999 concerning the framework agreement on fixed-term work concluded by European Trade Union Confederation (ETUC), Union of Industrial Employers' Confederation of Europe (UNICE) and Centre of Enterprises with Public Participation and Enterprises of General Economic Interest (CEEP)?
3. The possibilities for entering into a social dialogue in professional football.

The project was intended to inform about and thereby promote the concept of the Social Dialogue and of collective bargaining at the sectoral level of the professional football industry in the EU candidate countries (now Member states plus Bulgaria and Romania). The aim was to contribute to facilitating the start of consultations of management and labour at national and Community level and, in pursuance thereof, the establishment of relevant contractual relations by the exchange of information and experience on a European basis, in particular

[16] Cf., also Soek 2006.

regarding employment contracts and collective bargaining agreements. In addition, the current EU legal developments concerning labour and sports was presented, followed by a comparison with the relevant law in the candidate countries. Differences between the EU and national law were indicated and solutions for avoiding conflicts were provided. Besides promoting the Social Dialogue in the professional football sector in the candidate countries the objective of the project was also to identify the national law that is not in conformity with EU law and to propose solutions to remove any conflict.

It was expected that the project will be helpful to pave the way for starting the Social Dialogue in professional football in the EU candidate countries at national and European level by creating awareness amongst organizations involved of the possibilities the Dialogue offers for establishing effective industrial relations and, in particular, by creating common ground amongst management and labour for the purpose of future negotiations.

This project regarding the candidate countries was carried out in cooperation with the European Federation of professional Football Clubs (EFFC). It in fact is an addendum to the similar project that was undertaken by the EFFC with regard to the 15 'old' Member States in 2003–2004. In the Final Report on that project proposals are made to the European Commission for the reasoning it could adopt when dealing with a joint request from organizations who whish to establish a Social Dialogue Committee in European professional football. These proposals in principle are also fully applicable to the 10 'new' Member States, being now part of the family of EU nations.

N.B. The typology according to the 'Kokkini-criteria plus' is as follows: international/external/horizontal/stricto sensu/micro/practical/private and public.

2.2.3.3 Football Hooliganism with an EU Dimension: Towards an International Legal Framework (2004) (Hereafter: 'Football Hooliganism')

Under the terms of Article 29 of the Treaty, the European Union's objective shall be to provide citizens with a high level of safety within an area of freedom, security and justice by developing common action among the Member States in the field of police cooperation. Due to the various international and European competitions involving both national and club teams and the resultant travelling of large numbers of supporters together with the associated social and often violent disorder, football has a highly visible profile. This international dimension has made it necessary to approach security in connection with football matches in a way that extends beyond national borders. Within the EU framework, the focus is mainly on the coordination of police measures (cf., Council recommendation on guidelines for preventing and restraining disorder connected with football matches, 22 April 1996; Council Resolution on preventing and restraining football hooliganism through the exchange of experience, exclusion from stadiums and media policy, 9 June 1997; Council Resolution concerning a handbook with international recommendations for international police cooperation and measures to prevent and control violence and disturbances in connection with football matches with an international dimension, in which at least one Member State is involved, 6 December 2001 (previously, 21 June 1999); Council Decision concerning security in connection with football matches with an international dimension, 25 April 2002).

Apart from the existence of the Council of Europe's Convention on spectator violence and misbehaviour at sports events and in particular at football matches, of 19 August 1985, an international legal framework is still lacking and fundamental legal differences between Member States make it difficult to envisage the generalized application of restrictions on attendance at matches in other Member States by persons convicted of football-related offences.

Because of the lack of an international legal framework and the fundamental legal differences between Member States, tackling transnational football hooliganism in the EU is mainly based on 'adhocracy,' i.e., specific cooperation agreements and policy arrangements between individual Member States in connection with individual international competitions and matches. This results in the conflation of an 'instant coordinated approach' with a 'permanently coordinated basis.'

The purpose of the study is to determine what the fundamental legal differences between Member States (and candidate countries/Member States since 1 May 2004) exactly are and to evaluate what the precise consequences are of the absence of an international legal framework. On the basis of the results of this research, recommendations will be made for the development of a common and consistent international legal framework.

The following information was collected and analysed for the purposes of this Study:

- international legislation (treaties, decisions of intergovernmental organizations, etc.);
- an additional aspect was the *transnational* law and policy situation of the country (cf., possible bilateral treaties, agreements, or ad hoc arrangements etc. with neighbouring countries to control the cross-border movement of groups and persons concerned).
- all the laws, regulations and administrative provisions constituting the legal framework of the EU Member States and candidate countries and all the corresponding implementing measures applicable in the event of football hooliganism as well as the official documents (Memoranda, Notes to Parliament etc.) that form the basis for the Government's general policy in this field within the framework of general criminal and administrative law.
- decisions of national and international courts and tribunals;
- the academic literature in respect of the relevant legislation and court decisions;
- rules and regulations of national football associations and UEFA/FIFA as well as official policy documents regarding 'football hooliganism.'

N.B. The typology according to the 'Kokkini-criteria plus' reads as follows: international/external/horizontal/stricto sensu/micro/practical/private and public.

2.2.3.4 Health and Safety in the Sport Sector (2009) (Hereafter: 'Health and Safety')

In September 2008, in the framework of the project 'Moving forward towards European social dialogue in the sport sector: Content and Contact' (CC-project), EURO-MEI together with its managing partner EASE and its strategic partner the EOC EU Office (formerly EU Sport Office), commissioned the T.M.C. Asser Institute for international law, The Hague, The Netherlands, to undertake a comparative research study on health and safety in the sport sector. As the sport sector is in full development on all levels, not much European research exists so far on this topic. The project was undertaken in order to extend the knowledge on health and safety in the sport sector and thereby to help professionalize the sector. The research was financed by the European Commission through the above-mentioned project.

EASE and EURO-MEI are willing to be proactive to defend the specificities of the sector through European social dialogue. To prepare their social dialogue, EASE and EURO-MEI agreed to start with soft issues: issues on which a consensus is easily reached. Health and safety is one of them. The specificities of sport related to health and safety have not been taken into account yet at the different levels of the sector. The sport workers (players but also trainers and coaches) in many European countries are facing a lack of regulation specific to sports regarding health and safety issues. On the basis of the study and the results of the Conference on health and safety in the sport sector that was held in Lisbon on 1 and 2 April 2009 EASE and EURO-MEI would like to find similarities and opportunities for harmonization and to define best practices in health and safety in the sport sector. Once the European social dialogue in the sport sector will be effective, autonomous agreements and process-oriented texts (such as joint declarations) between the European social partners on those issues could provide a kind of harmonization that could help many countries to address the health, safety and well-being of workers in the sport sector.

The below comparative survey on health and safety in the sport sector is descriptive and includes a general listing of health and safety issues in a broad sense in the sport sector as well as a listing of measures taken to prevent risks and injuries and promote workers' (players', trainers', coaches') health (best practices, innovative actions) on the basis of the research undertaken. It covers relevant information on the present 27 EU Member States.

N.B. The typology according to the 'Kokkini-criteria' is as follows: international/external/horizontal/stricto sensu/micro/practical/private and public.

2.2.3.5 The Implementation of the WADA Code in the European Union (2010) (Hereafter: 'WADA Code')

The fight against doping has become an increasingly important theme on the EU agenda.

On this subject, the White Paper on Sport published by the European Commission on 11 July 2007 stated the following:

> The EU would benefit from a more coordinated approach in the fight against doping, in particular by defining common positions in relation to the Council of Europe, WADA and UNESCO, and through the exchange of information and good practices between Governments, national anti-doping organisations and laboratories. Proper implementation of the UNESCO Convention against Doping in Sport by the Member States is particularly important in this context.
>
> The Commission will play a facilitating role, for example by supporting a network of national anti-doping organisations of Member States.

In the past few years, activities in this field have essentially concentrated on the Code of the World Anti-Doping Agency (WADA) which is the subject of the Copenhagen Declaration and the UNESCO Convention against Doping in Sport. Naturally, the work of the informal European working party, the 'EU Working Group on Anti-Doping,' actively contributes to this.

Despite the increased interest in this subject, in practice the central objective of the Code, i.e., to ensure harmonized, coordinated and effective anti-doping programmes at both an international and national level with regard to the detection, deterrence and prevention of doping, is still far from being realized for a variety of reasons. The necessity for a European framework for cooperation in the fight against doping, on the basis of the Code, therefore requires further study.

An initial requirement for the achievement of strict agreements on a EU level is that reliable information is available about the state of affairs in each Member State.

With a view to the Belgian Presidency of the European Union in the second half of 2010, the Flemish Minister for Sport, Philippe Muyters, asked the T.M.C. Asser Institute of International Law in The Hague to carry out a thorough study of the application of the Code within the European Union and to catalogue its findings.

The study's inventory was undertaken on the basis of information collected from the relevant government departments and/or agencies with primary authority in the area of sport in each Member State and the National Anti-Doping Organisations (NADOs) in the European Union. As far as Belgium is concerned, a distinction was made between the four different authorities authorized to fight doping, namely: the Flemish Community, the French Community, the German-speaking Community and the Joint Community Commission.

> N.B. The typology according to the 'Kokkini-criteria plus' is as follows: international/external/horizontal/stricto sensu/micro/practical (the implementation of the WADA Code)/private and public.

2.2.3.6 Comparative Continental Sports Law: An 'Americanization' of European sports Law?

In the years shortly before the beginning of this century, in sporting and sports law circles in Europe a discussion started concerning the 'Americanization' of European (EU) professional sport. The sports models of North America and Europe were compared.[17] Some of the European sports model's features appeared to be under threat, as part of a trend which may be labelled 'Americanization' in recognition of the lurking desire to eliminate traditional rules of the game (such as promotion and relegation) which may inhibit wealth maximization on a North-American scale. Weatherill's contribution to the debate proceeded from the assumption that it was realistic to suppose that European sport, particularly football, would become ever more lucrative in the next few years in the wake of the media revolution, perhaps eventually to the extent that it would compare financially with the dominant sports in North America, but that there are aspects of the American model that will prove unpalatable in Europe.[18]

Nafziger observes that comparative legal commentary on the organisational structure of sports, particularly of professional sports, is substantial and growing.

---

[17] On 9 March 2000, an Asser Round Table Session entitled *The americanisation of sports law—the American and European sports models compared* was organized at the office of law firm CMS Derks Star Busmann Hanotiau in Utrecht and in co-operation with the Sports Law Centre of Anglia Polytechnic University and *Sportzaken* magazine/The International Sports Law Journal (ISLJ). Participants in the LLM/MA Sports Law Course of Anglia Polytechnic University, which was hosted by the T.M.C. Asser Institute in The Hague from 8 to 11 March, attended the Session. Speakers were Dr. Simon Gardiner, Sports Law Centre, Anglia Polytechnic University, Chelmsford, United Kingdom, Aaron Wise, Siller Wilk LLP, New York, United States of America, Dr. Martin Schimke, Wessing and Berenberg-Gossler Attorneys, Hamburg, Germany, James Gray, Pierski, Fitzpatrick and Gray, Milwaukee, United States of America, and Prof. Dr. Paul de Knop, Free University, Brussels, and University of Tilburg, The Netherlands. Mr Eric Vilé, CMS Derks, chaired the Session. The Session was sponsored by the FBO, the Dutch Federation of Professional Football Organisations. Simon Gardiner's and Paul de Knop's contributions were published in The International Sports Law Journal, No. 2, 2000, pp. 17–20. The official programme explained the Round Table's topic as follows: 'In recent years, especially in the post-Bosman period, professional sport in Europe appears to have been increasingly influenced by what are regarded as characteristics of the traditional North American model of sport. The growing commercialisation in European professional football, in particular, makes it relevant to thoroughly consider the usefulness and adaptability of legal and institutional instruments that are available in the United States where the major leagues of American football, baseball, basketball and ice hockey have for decennia now been "big business." This Round Table Session examines themes such as the appropriateness of closed leagues and the role of commissioners, the system of sports franchises, the relocation of clubs, anti-trust law and the collective selling of broadcasting rights, the phenomenon of club owners, cross-ownership, sponsoring, licensing and merchandising, the farm system, collective bargaining agreements and players' unions, the regulation of the sports agent, the application of salary caps, salary arbitration and free agents, the draft system, and questions of intellectual property rights. In addition, specific developments that are taking place in the "sports industry" of the United States and Europe at the time of the Round Table Session are evaluated.'

[18] Weatherill 2000, pp. 155 et seq., and: Weatherill 2007, pp. 175 and 155.

One of the main themes in Europe has been the relationship between a rather pristine European Sports Model, as it has been called, and the growing commercialization of sport. This theme has been expressed variously in analyzing the regulatory power of the European Union over sporting activity and in contrasting the European Sports Model with a so-called North American Sports Model. Both models are largely policy constructs, and the North American Model may simply that which the European Model is not. Even so, the models help each of us see our own sports culture as others see it. Although the European Sports Model has been the subject of many writings, in-depth comparisons between it and the North American Model are infrequent. Comparing the models highlights core values, sharpens analysis, and yields new insights. A few preliminary observations may be useful in defining the models. First, they are just that: models, that is general representations of reality rather than precise descriptions of organisational structures. Second, a functional analysis and evaluation of the European Sports Model inevitably must take account of the legal constraints, particularly European Union law.[19]

In the context of the debate of an 'Americanization'or even 'McDonaldization' of European sports, it is Halgreen's belief that the European sports culture is unique and worth protecting, with its extraordinary mix of amateur and professional, commercial and non-commercial interests alongside each other, serving a very important role in European societies. However, in a time of increased internationalization and globalization, it was his realistic assertion that it will not be possible simply to 'dismiss' the American Model of Sport purely for political, ideological or protectionist reasons. This is because European sport *is* part of a global sports economy, and many professional European sports, faced with the tough and unfamiliar challenges of a commercialized sports environment, have already demonstrated a strong tendency to combine the European and American sports systems in one form or another.[20]

The 'Americanization' debate which from to time comes back to the stage in Europe, is an example of international comparative legal and organizational comparison between continents and not individual countries. It concerns non-governmental sports law, the law of the 'autonomous' private sports organizations which as such is of a transnational character, not public legislation regarding sports. Of course, European sports law which sets the limits to the sporting law is the law of a supranational intergovernmental organisation of states, whereas the North American Model comprises two completely sovereign states, Canada and the United States of America which set the limits to sport by national legislative instruments.

N.B. A study on the 'Americanization' issue would start from the following 'Kokkini-criteria' qualifications: international (or: national = bilateral?; two sports systems on both sides of the Atlantic ocean, including on the one hand Canada and the United States of

---

19 Nafziger 2008, p. 100.

20 Halgreen 2004, pp. 16-17.

America, and on the other the public international organisation EU with now 27 Member States); external (!); horizontal; stricto or *lato sensu*; macro (!); theoretical or practical (practical: when the North American Football League (NFL; American rugby) established a branch in Europe, it could have been useful to first have available a study on the state of affairs in European (EU) sport in an organisational and legal sense); and private (cf., public: EU law, i.e., the jurisprudence of the European Court of Justice has adjusted the European sports model to some extent in the past decade by opening it up, as it were into a more liberal, 'American' direction; however, at the opposite, in North American pro sports there do exist closed leagues with salary caps, drafts, etc. for promoting a level playing field).

2.3 Summary and Conclusion

The European Union regularly commissions legal comparative research in areas of sports law. Such research serves to provide a picture of which private and possibly, public sport rules exist in areas of sports law in the Member States. The surveys are intended to provide information that can be used by the European Union for relevant policy development. According to the new sport provision in the Lisbon Treaty, Article 165, any harmonization of the laws and regulations of the Member States by the European Union is excluded. Of course this type of studies and reports still could theoretically (scientifically, academically) be used for unification/harmonization purposes. Used outside the EU framework the 'Doping harmonization' study is a clear example of a harmonization report; the 'WADA Code' study—by monitoring of the implementation of the Code—in fact also fulfills this purpose. On the other hand, there are possible studies and reports which are meant to be used by an individual country by way of 'best practices'/'lessons learned' from abroad. The 'Sports Acts' study is a study of this 'national' type.[21] The national/international (=bilateral/multilateral) 'Kokkini-criterion' is now here finally deleted as having turned out to be meaningless at least in the context of (international) comparative sports law; bilateral also means international and why not trilateral etc. research if and when a country looks for inspiration abroad to revise its Sports Act or other relevant legal instruments?! Instead of this distinction, it is a much better option to use this criterion in the sense of 'best practices' (national) v unification/harmonization research. So, now we have three new criteria: practical/theoretical, national/international (in a new meaning) and private/

[21] Several years ago, the Asser Institute was requested by the Singapore Sports Council who referred to the "Sports Acts" study (2006) for the Netherlands government, to present a research proposal for the purpose of the revision of the Sport Council Act (1973). Particularly, because of the Singaporese ambition to create in the country a podium for the staging of international sporting mega events the question was whether the adoption of a new Sport Act could be drafted and how. The Asser Institute then proposed a worldwide study along the lines of what is described as follow-up research in the paragraph on the "Sports Acts" pilot study, *supra* Sect. 2.2.1.1.

Table 2.1 Typology of the Asser research studies and reports according to the 'Kokkini-criteria' plusminus (or: minusplus) (in chronological order)

Studies and reports	Internal/ external	Horizontal/ vertical	Stricto/ *lato sensu*	Micro/ macro	Practical/ theoretical	National/ international	Private/ public
Doping harmonisation	External	Horizontal	Stricto sensu	Micro	Practical	International	Private/public
SD football (candidates)	External	Horizontal	Stricto sensu	Micro	Practical	International	Private/public
Football hooliganism	External	Horizontal	Stricto sensu	Micro	Practical	International	Private/public
Sports acts	External	Horizontal	*Lato sensu*	Micro	Practical	*National*	Public
SD EPFL/G14	External	Horizontal	Strict sensu	Micro	Practical	International	Private
SD football agenda	External	Horizontal	Stricto sensu	Micro	Practical	International	Private
Health and safety	External	Horizontal	Stricto sensu	Micro	Practical	International	Private/public
SD cycling agenda	External	Horizontal	Stricto sensu	Micro	Practical	International	Private
Sport governance	External	Horizontal	Stricto sensu	*Macro*	Practical	International	Public
WADA code	External	Horizontal	Stricto sensu	Micro	Practical	International	Private/public
Non-nationals	External	Horizontal	*Lato sensu*	Micro	Practical	International	Private

public added to the 'Kokkini-criteria' (plus) whereas one criterion: national/international (in the old meaning) has disappeared (minus) (Table 2.1).

N.B. The 'Americanization' debate is an example of continental comparative sports law (Europe/North America). Its typology is emphatically 'external' and 'macro.'

Sports law is two- or double-layered: there are private and a public segments—the (I)NGO part of the law on the one hand (sporting rules and regulations) and legislation as well as treaties on the other hand. The specific institutional characteristics of organized sport are 'juridified' by and in its own, private rules and regulations. In the context of comparative law research, this crucial feature of sports (law) may be characterized as an example of 'sport specificity.' So, the double stratification of sport and thereby sports law is the major, core aspect of (international) comparative sports law. Minor specific characteristics are a result of adapting the initial 'Kokkini-criteria' to organized sport and sports law. 'External' means in the sporting context for example research into interventionist *versus* non-interventionist states, not only in Europe but also worldwide. 'Macro' means In the sporting context comparative research into sport governance at large regarding national and/or international sport governing bodies (cf., the comparison between legal systems or jurisdictions of national states under the law of nations). Like in the inter-state context, this may also apply to comparative research regarding several crucially differing types of sports governance (see, the 'Americanization' debate). If sport governance is macro, Sports Acts research is relatively micro. Generally speaking, sport governance in the private segment concerns internal sport governance ('intra sport'), whereas Sports Acts concern the relationship between state and national organised sport which may be characterised as external sport governance ('intra state'). So, there are two (interrelated) types of sport governance.

References

Chaker A-N (2004) Good governance in sport—a European survey. Council of Europe Publishing, Strasbourg

Davis T (2001) What is sports law? Marquette Sports Law Rev 11:211–244

Halgreen L (2004) European sports law: a comparative analysis of the European and American models of sport. Thomson, Copenhagen

Kokkini-Iatridou D et al (1988) Een inleiding tot het rechtsvergelijkend onderzoek (An Introduction to Comparative Legal Research). Kluwer, Deventer

Nafziger JAR (2008) A comparison of the European and North American models of sports organisation. Int Sports Law J 3–4:100–108

Nafziger JAR, Ross SF (eds) (2011) Research handbook on international sports law. Cheltenham: Edward Elgar

Siekmann R (2011) What is sports law? Lex Sportiva and Lex Ludica: a Reassessment of content and terminology. Int Sports Law J 3–4:3–13 (forthcoming; inaugural lecture of 10 June 2011 at the newly established special chair for International and European Sports Law of Erasmus University Rotterdam, The Netherlands)

Siekmann RCR, Soek J (eds) (2007) The council of Europe and sport: basic documents. T.M.C. Asser Press, The Hague
Soek J (2006) The strict liability principle and the human rights of athletes in doping cases. T.M.C. Asser Press, The Hague (PhD, Erasmus University Rotterdam)
Weatherill S (2000) Resisting the pressures of 'Americanization': the influence of European community law on the 'European sport model'. In: Greenfield S, Osborn G (eds) Law and sport in contemporary society. Frank Cass, London [reproduced in: Willamette J Int Law Disput Resolut 37 (2002)]
Weatherill S (2007) European sports law: collected papers. T.M.C. Asser Press, The Hague
Weatherill S (2011) Is there such a thing as EU sports law? Int Sports Law J 1–2:38–41
Zweigert K, Kötz H (1988) Introduction to comparative law, 3rd edn. Clarendon Press, Oxford

Chapter 3
The Specificity of Sport: Sporting Exceptions in EU Law

Abstract The classical and still and ever current central (legal) question in the debate on the position of sport in the European Union is whether sport is 'special,' whether it deserves specific treatment under European Law and to what extent and why. In other words should sport be exempted from the EC Treaty? It is the discussion on what is called in the jargon the 'specificity of sport' and the 'sporting exception.'[1] In this article the general framework which the EU institutions developed regarding the specificity of sport, is dealt with. What are in fact the basics in this respect? Which sporting exceptions concerned have been accepted and which not and why? What is the result of a comparison of exceptions and justifications, what is the overall picture of the sport specificity practical application by the Commission as the EU day-to-day executive organ and the European Court of Justice as the EU supreme judicial organ? The cases and issues will be categorised according to whether they concern internal market freedoms (movement of workers and provision of services) or EU competition law in sport organisational matters.

Contents

This article is an updated and expanded version of Siekmann (2008), pp. 37–49.

[1] See in particular Parrish and Miettinen (2008).

R. C. R. Siekmann, *Introduction to International and European Sports Law*,
ASSER International Sports Law Series, DOI: 10.1007/978-90-6704-852-1_3,

© T.M.C. ASSER PRESS, The Hague, The Netherlands, and the author 2012

3.1 Introduction

Not everybody knows that the European Union has a fairly extensive record in the field of sport. In 2005 the ASSER International Sports Law Centre published a book containing some 900 pages of selected legal and policy documents (resolutions of the European Parliament, decisions of the European Commission, memoranda, jurisprudence of the European Court of Justice, etc.) and another 900 pages were put on the Centre's website.[2] The EU has dealt with a wide range of subjects since the so-called Walrave case in 1974. The Book provides a detailed insight into what could be called the *acquis communautaire sportive* ('EU Sport Acquis') for the present and future (candidate) Member States. Apart from texts of a general policy character, specific subjects concern Boycott, Broadcasting, Community Aid and Sport Funding, Competition, Customs, Diplomas, Discrimination, Doping, Education and Youth, Freedom to provide services and of movement of workers, Olympic Games, State Aid, Tax, Tobacco Advertising, Trade Marks, Vandalism and Violence.[3]

The classical and still and ever current central (legal) question in the debate on the position of sport in the European Union is whether sport is 'special,' whether it deserves specific treatment under European Law and to what extent and why. In other words should sport be exempted from the EC Treaty? It is the discussion on what is called in the jargon the 'specificity of sport' and the 'sporting exception.'[4] In this article I will deal with the general framework which the EU institutions

[2] Siekmann and Soek (2005).

[3] The White Paper on Sport pays attention to additional marginal, 'soft law' themes—also from a sports law perspective—like volunteering, social inclusion and integration, prevention of and fight against racism and violence, the environmental dimension of sport, supporters.

[4] See in particular, Parrish and Miettinen (2008).

developed regarding the specificity of sport. What are in fact the basics in this respect? I will deal with the following items:

1. The initial position of sport in the European (EC and EU) Treaties,
2. The 1997 Declaration on Sport in the Treaty of Amsterdam,
3. The Helsinki Report on Sport and the 2000 Declaration on Sport in the Treaty of Nice,
4. *Close reading* the references—general and specific—to the Declarations on Sport (Amsterdam, Nice) regarding the 'specificity of sport,' in the jurisprudence of the European Court of Justice and the decision-making practice of the Commission,[5]
5. The 2007 White Paper on Sport,
6. The specificity of sport in the White Paper,
7. 'Sport' in the Constitutional Treaty (Constitution for Europe) and the Reform (Lisbon) Treaty, and
8. Specificity of sport in the 2011 'White Paper-plus.'
9. An overview of the practice of application regarding the 'sport specificity' concept in the European Commission's decision-making and the European Court of Justice's jurisprudence before and after the Lisbon Treaty, in which an explicit 'sport provision' (Article 165 TFEU) is incorporated (for the first time in the history of the EC/EU basic treaties), is added.

Which sporting exceptions concerned have been accepted and which not and why (cf., the *ratio*, objective justifications for the sporting measures and their proportionality)? How the test of proportionality precisely is executed by the ECJ and the Commission is not separately scrutinised in this article. Generally speaking, it may be observed that if and when a sporting measure is justified, but not proportional, the additional question is whether and if yes, which alternative, proportional measure(s) would be available. Pending cases will not be dealt with and nor will possible, potential issues be discussed. What is the result of a comparison of exceptions and justifications, what is the overall picture of the sport specificity practical application by the Commission as the EU day-to-day executive organ and the European Court of Justice as the EU supreme judicial organ? The cases and issues will be categorised according to whether they concern

[5] Cf., 'Close reading' describes, in literary criticism, the careful, sustained interpretation of a brief passage of text. Such a reading places great emphasis on the particular over the general, paying close attention to individual words, syntax, and the order in which sentences and ideas unfold as they are read. It is now a fundamental method of modern criticism. Close reading is sometimes called *explication de texte*, which is the name for the similar tradition of textual interpretation in French literary study. In the present, legal research context, 'close reading' for example would imply an answer to the question whether the words 'specificity of sport' are explicitly used in the decision-making practice the European Commission and the case-law of the Court.

internal market freedoms (movement of workers and provision of services) or EU competition law in sport organisational matters.

3.2 Sport not in European Treaties

In the European Treaties up to the Constitutional and Reform (Lisbon) Treaties there was not any general legal basis, no competence for the Communities/ European Union to deal with sport, as it was the case for culture. So, there was no section on sport nor are there any provisions on sport in the Treaties. This at the same time implied that sport was not exempted from the Treaties. Since the Walrave case[6] it is clear that as far as sport is an economic activity European Law in principle is applicable to it. This is steady European jurisprudence. In their decisions the Commission and European Court of Justice have considered to what extent this is the case. Two of the basic freedoms of the Communities/EU are essential in this respect: the freedom of movement for workers and fair competition. I will not go further into that here.

3.3 Treaty of Amsterdam: 1997 Declaration on Sport

The Treaty of Amsterdam amended the Treaty on the European Union and the Treaties Establishing the European Communities. The Declaration on Sport is annexed to the Treaty of Amsterdam. It emphasises the social significance of sport, in particular its role in forging identity and bringing people together. The EU institutions are therefore called on to listen to sports associations when important questions affecting sport are at issue. In this connection special consideration should be given to the particular characteristics of amateur sport, the Declaration states. In 1998 the European Commission published a staff working paper entitled 'The Development and Prospects for Community Action in the Field of Sport.' In this document the educational, health, social, cultural and recreational functions of sport are recognised. It is also stressed however that sport fulfils an important economic role in Europe and that a general exemption of sport from European Law could not be allowed. The Amsterdam Declaration on Sport had no legal force; it clearly was a general policy statement. We will see hereafter how this kind of documents (see below also on the Nice Declaration) were made use of, were taken into account in particular in the decision-making of the European Commission and the jurisprudence of the European Court of Justice.

---

[6] ECJ, Case No. C-36/74 [1974] ECR 1405.

3.4 Treaty of Nice: 2000 Declaration on Sport

In Nice the Declaration on 'the specific characteristics of sport and its social function in Europe, of which account should be taken in implementing common policies' was adopted. This Declaration which is annexed to the Presidency Conclusions of the Nice European Council Meeting, was based on the so-called Helsinki Report on Sport (1999), which was a Report from the European Commission to the European Council (of Heads of State and Government) 'with a view to safeguarding current sports structures and maintaining the social function of sport within the Community framework.'[7]

In the Introduction of the Helsinki Report on Sport it is said that the report gives pointers for reconciling the economic dimension of sport with its popular, educational, social and cultural dimensions. In section 4 of the Report on 'Clarifying the legal environment of sport' it is suggested that sport must be able to assimilate the new commercial framework in which it must develop, without at the same time losing its identity and autonomy, which underpin the functions it performs in the social, cultural, health and educational areas. The Report continues by stating that while the EC Treaty contains no specific provisions on sport, the Community must nevertheless ensure that the initiatives taken by the national State authorities or sporting organisations comply with Community law, including competition law, and respect in particular the principles of the internal market (freedom of movement for workers, freedom of establishment and freedom to provide services, etc.). In this respect, accompanying, coordination or interpretation measures at Community level might prove to be useful. They would be designed to strengthen the legal certainty of sporting activities and their social function at Community level. However, as Community powers currently stand, there can be no question of large-scale intervention or support programmes or even of the implementation of a Community sports policy. If it is advisable, as wished by the European Council and the European Parliament, to preserve the social function of sport, and therefore the current structures of the organisation of sport in Europe, there is a need for a new approach to questions of sport both at European level and in the Member States, in compliance with the Treaty, especially with the principle of subsidiarity, and the autonomy of sporting organisations, the Report continues. The Report proposes the acceptance of a new approach which involves preserving the traditional values of sport, while at the same time assimilating a changing economic and legal environment. In terms of the economic activity that it generates, the sporting sector is subject to the rules of the EC Treaty, like the other sectors of the economy. The application of the Treaty's competition rules to the sporting sector must take account of the specific characteristics of sport, especially the interdependence between sporting activity and the economic activity that it generates, the principle of equal opportunities and the uncertainty of the results. The Report continues by stating that with a view to an improved definition of the legal environment, it is possible to give examples, without

[7] COM(1999) 644.

prejudice to the conclusions that the Commission could draw from the in-depth analysis of each case, of practices of sports organisations. Three types of practices are distinguished in the Report:

1. Practices which do not come under the competition rules,
2. Practices that are, in principle, prohibited by the competition rules, and
3. Practices likely to be exempted from the competition rules.

In the Report's Conclusion it is observed that the system of promotion and relegation is one of the characteristics of European sport. In 1998 the Commission's DG Education and Culture under which sport comes, had published a consultation document regarding 'The European Model of Sport' in which the organisation and structure of sport in Europe is described. Basically the structure resembles a pyramid with a hierarchy, it was said. The clubs form the foundation of this pyramid. Regional federations form the next level, the clubs are usually members of these organisations. National federations, one for each discipline, represent the next level. They represent their branch in the European or international federations. They form the top of the pyramid. In the Nice Declaration on Sport it is said that sporting organisations and the Member States have a primary responsibility in the conduct of sporting affairs. Even though not having any direct powers in this area, the Community must, in its action under the various Treaty provisions, take account of the social, educational and cultural functions inherent in sport and making it special, in order that the code of ethics and the solidarity essential to the preservation of its social role may be respected and nurtured. The European Council also stresses its support for the independence of sports organisations and the right to organise themselves through appropriate associative structures. It recognises that, with due regard for national and Community legislation and on the basis of a democratic and transparent method of operation, it is the task of sporting organisations to organise and promote their particular sports, particularly as regards the specifically sporting rules applicable and the make-up of national teams, in the way which they think best reflects their objectives. It is noted in the Nice Declaration on Sport that sports federations have a central role in ensuring the essential solidarity between the various levels of sporting practice, from recreational to top-level sport. While taking account of developments in the world of sport, federations must continue to be the key feature of a form of organisation providing a guarantee of sporting cohesion and participatory democracy, the Declaration says.

3.4.1 Comment

The conclusion must be that it is essential for the Community to take account of the specific characteristics of sport. The Amsterdam Declaration refers to the 'social significance of sport,' especially 'particular characteristics of amateur sport.' The Helsinki Report in its entitlement refers to 'safeguarding current sports structures and maintaining the social function of sport within the Community framework' and then stresses *inter alia* 'the *specific* characteristics of sport, especially the interdependence between sporting activity and the economic activity that it generates, the principle of equal opportunities and the uncertainty of the results.' And the Nice Declaration in its entitlement refers to 'the *specific* characteristics of sport and its social function in Europe' (italics added, RS). This starting-point implies that in principle exemptions from Community law are possible. Apart from that, the rules and regulations of sports organisations without which a sport cannot exist or which are necessary for the organisation of sport or competitions may be completely beyond competition law. The rules which are inherent to sport are first and foremost the so-called 'rules of the game' (*lex ludica*). Their purpose is not to distort competition, according to the above-mentioned DG X consultation document of 1998. In the Helsinki Report on Sport it is emphasised that the basic freedoms guaranteed by the EC Treaty, generally speaking do not conflict with the rules, regulations and measures taken by sports organisations, provided that these are objectively justified, non-discriminatory, necessary and proportionate.

3.5 The Declarations on Sport (Amsterdam, Nice) in the Jurisprudence of the European Court of Justice and Commission Decision-Making

Both Declarations on Sport (Amsterdam, Nice) are important policy statements by the Heads of State and Government of the EC/EU Member States (European Council), which however do not have a legally binding character (*soft law*). The question then is whether these texts which underline the specificity of sport in general terms, were used in concrete cases by the EC/EU when European law was applied to sport and how they were used. In other words, was account taken of these documents in the decisions of the Commission and the European Court of Justice? It is clear that general/specific references to the Declarations would add to their official status and relevance in a legal perspective.

In the Deliège case,[8] the Court states that it is to be remembered at the outset that, having regard to the objectives of the Community, sport is subject to Community law only in so far as it constitutes an economic activity within the meaning of Article 2 EC (with the Court's explicit reference to the Walrave and Bosman cases). In the Bosman case—the Court continues to argue—it had also recognised that sporting activities are of considerable social importance in the Community. That case-law—it is said—is also supported by the Declaration on Sport (Amsterdam), which emphasises the social significance of sport and calls on the bodies of the European Union to give special consideration to the particular characteristics of amateur sport. In particular, that Declaration is consistent with the above-mentioned case-law (Walrave, Bosman) in so far as it relates to situations in which sport constitutes an

[8] ECJ, Case No. C-51/96, [2000] ECR I-2549 paras 41–42.

economic activity. This formula is literally repeated in the Lehtonen case[9] and Meca-Medina case (2004, First Instance).[10] It is additionally stated in Meca-Medina that the Court's considerations on the nature of the IOC anti-doping rules are *echoed*(!) in the Community support plan to combat doping in sport (1999), according to which 'doping symbolises the contrast between sport and the values it has traditionally stood for,' in the Commission's working paper entitled 'Development of and prospects for Community action in sport,' which states that 'sport plays a morally elevating role in society' through 'the values associated with fair play, solidarity, fair competition and team spirit' which it brings, and in the Helsinki Report on Sport, according to which 'the rules inherent to sport are, first and foremost, the "rules of the game" and "the aim of these rules is not to distort competition."'

It is interesting to observe that the Amsterdam and Nice Sport Declarations are used by the Court for the support of argument. It is even said that the Declaration of Amsterdam is consistent with case-law in so far as it relates to situations in which sport constitutes an economic activity. So, the basis for the argument already was laid down by the Court itself previously in Walrave and Bosman the ECJ decisions which are pre-Amsterdam and -Nice. In the Court's reasoning it looks like the Declarations 'codified' the case-law and for that reason could be referred to by the Court again. The Court was not influenced by the Declarations, but the Declarations were 'dictated' by the Court's case-law.

The explicit reference to the Amsterdam Declaration on Sport and the Helsinki Report on Sport (cf., the Nice Declaration on Sport) however is not repeated in the appeal decision by the Court in Meca-Medina.[11] My possible explanation for this is that the appeal decision in Meca-Medina in fact rejected the traditional, extensive concept of the 'sporting exception' which excluded so-called *purely* sporting rules like the Laws of The Game (*lex ludica*) and others from being tested against EU law, in advance. If this analysis would be correct, the references to the Sport Declarations in the Court's previous sports jurisprudence are now part of history, outdated. Apart from that and however, the Amsterdam and Nice Declarations in fact now have been substituted by the 'sport provision' in the Lisbon Treaty (see below in Sect. 3.8) which mentions 'the specific nature of sport' to be taken account of by the EU when contributing to the development of the European dimension in sport. For the first time, reference to Article 165 TFEU is made in the Bernard (Olympique Lyonnais) case where it is said (in para 40) that account must be taken of the *specific* characteristics of sport in general, and football in particular, and of their social and educational function; the relevance of those factors is also corroborated by them being mentioned in the second subpara of Article 165(1) TFEU. In the 'White Paper plus,' it is said that in the Bernard case, in particular the Court mentioned two elements included in the Treaty as being constitutive of the EU's action in the field of sport: the social and educational function of sport as

[9] ECJ, Case No. C-176/96 [2000] ECR I-2681 paras 32–33.

[10] CFI, case No. T-313/02 [2004] ECR II-3291 paras 37–38.

[11] ECJ, Case No. C-519/04 P, OJ C 224/8, 2006.

well as its specific nature. These two aspects are interlinked, the social and educational values of sport being among the characteristics which make sport special and set it apart from other sectors of the economy.[12]

In Commission practice, explicit reference was made to the Nice Declaration in UEFA Champions League.[13] The Commission fully endorsed the *specificity of sport* (sic!), as expressed for example in the declaration of the European Council in Nice in December 2000. On that occasion the Council encouraged the mutualisation of part of the revenue from the sales of TV rights, at the appropriate levels, as beneficial to the principle of solidarity between all levels and areas of sport. The Commission understood that it is desirable to maintain a certain balance among the football clubs playing in a league because it creates better and more exciting football matches, which could be reflected in/translate into better media rights. The same applied to the education of new players, as the players are a fundamental element of the whole venture. The Commission recognised that a cross-subsidisation of funds from richer to poorer may help achieve this. The Commission was therefore in favour of the financial solidarity principle, which was also endorsed by the European Council declaration on sport in Nice in December 2000. So, financial solidarity is one more specific characteristic to be added to the list.

Some other, particular characteristics were mentioned above under Sect. 3.5.1 Comment, such as: current sport structures, the position of amateur sport, the principle of equal opportunities and uncertainty of results (balanced competition). We will see below in Sect. 3.10 what will be the findings in this context on the basis of the practical application of the sport specificity principle in EU practice.

3.6 The 2007 White Paper on Sport[14]

On 11 July 2007 the European Commission adopted the White Paper on Sport which is its first comprehensive strategic initiative in the field of sport. On average, the Commission adopts only two or three white papers per year, and the fact that

---

[12] Commission Staff Working Document 'Sport and free movement', Accompanying document to the Communication from the Commission to the European Parliament, the Council, the European Economic and Social Committee and the Committee of the Regions 'Developing the European Dimension in Sport', Brussels, 18.1.2011, SEC(2011) 66/2, p. 6.

[13] Case 27398 Joint selling of the commercial rights of the UEFA Champions league, OJ 2003 L 291/25. Paras 131 and 165.

[14] A *green paper* released by the European Commission is a discussion document intended to stimulate debate and launch a process of consultation, at European level, on a particular topic. A green paper usually presents a range of ideas and is meant to invite interested individuals or organisations to contribute views and information. It may be followed by a *white paper*, an official set of proposals that is used as a vehicle for their development into law. In preparing the White Paper on Sport (COM(2007) 391 final) the Commission had held numerous consultations with sport stakeholders on issues of common interest as well as an on-line consultation. Cf., also, Weatherill (2008), pp. 3–8.

the communication on sport got this status is therefore an acknowledgement of the comprehensive nature, longer-term value and political weight of the document. The White Paper has to be seen in the overall context in which sport has been addressed at EU level. It is the culmination of a long process: the Amsterdam Declaration of 1997, the Nice Declaration of 2000, and then the agreement of the Intergovernmental Conference in 2004 to include sport in the Treaty (see hereafter in connection with the Constitutional and Reform (Lisbon) Treaties), coupled with the positive results of the European Year of Education through Sport 2004, all reflect the European framework that already existed for sport. This framework put the accent on the special characteristics of sport, and in particular its social and educational values.

The White Paper has focus on three domains: the societal role of sport, the economic importance of sport, and the organisation of sport. The Commission was well aware that some actors, especially those representing professional sports, expected it to go further in terms of regulatory measures and seeking exemptions for the sport sector from the application of EU law. It is important to point out that the White Paper respects the principle of subsidiarity, the autonomy of sport organisations and the current EU legal framework. When developing the concept of specificity of sport, the Commission could not go beyond the limits of existing EU competences. The White Paper takes full account of this European context for sport: the initiative does not weaken the application of EU law to sport, but it provides further clarity on the application of EU legal provisions in this sector. A comprehensive initiative on sport appeared to be appropriate at this particular point in time for several reasons. In general, the political landscape was favourable to the launch of a broad EU initiative on sport. Several processes took place during the last year in parallel with the preparation of the White Paper, such as notably the debate on governance in European football, which resulted in the Independent European Sport Review ('Arnaut Report')[15] and the European Parliament's reports and resolution on the future of professional football in Europe and on the role of sport in education. The White Paper was driven by high expectations from sport

[15] A publication of May 2006 by MR José Louis Arnaut, former Portuguese Foreign Minister, at the initiative of the UK Sports Minister and financed by UEFA. See also—in reply to the 'Arnaut Report'—the 'Wathelet Report': *Sport Governance and EU Legal Order: Present and Future*, by Prof. Melchior Wathelet, Universities of Louvain-la-Neuve and Liège (Belgium) and a former Member of the European Court of Justice, in: The Intyernational Sports Law Journal (ISLJ) 2007/3–4, pp. 3–9 and 10–11. The Wathelet Report was amongst others supported by Professor Stephen Weatherill, Jacques Delors Professor of European Community Law, University of Oxford, United Kingdom; Professor Roger Blanpain, Universities of Leuven, Belgium and Tilburg (The Netherlands), and co-founder and first President of FIFPro; Professor Klaus Vieweg, Director of the German and International Sports Law Research Unit, University of Erlangen-Nuremberg, Germany; and Dr Richard Parrish, Director of the Centre for Sports Law Research, Edge Hill University, United Kingdom. The report was distributed also in its original French language version throughout Europe by means of a press-release of the ASSER International Sports law Centre (T.M.C. Asser Instituut, The Hague, The Netherlands; see: www.sportslaw.nl/NEWS).

stakeholders, who wished to see their concerns addressed in EU policy making, including the need to better promote sport and to achieve more legal certainty. Social and economic developments in and outside the field of sport have brought about new challenges for sport, some of which need European responses. The White Paper proposes a mix of instruments to address the role of sport in Europe, such as studies and surveys, platforms and networks, enhanced cooperation dialogue structures, recommendations, and mobilisation of EU programmes. It should be stressed that the emphasis is on 'soft' measures, not on regulatory or legislative action, for which there is no specific EU competence.

The chapter of the White Paper on the organisation of sport addresses a number of aspects of the governance of sport and of the *specificity of sport*. First, it should be noted that the word 'specificity' as such does not appear in earlier official EU texts. In the Helsinki report of 1999 reference was to the need to 'take account of the specific characteristics' of sport, within the Nice Declaration of 2000 reference was made to how the Community must take account of the functions which make sport 'special.' The White Paper devotes a section to the issue of specificity, thus shedding light on the Commission's position regarding this concept. Regarding the repeated requests by stakeholders for more legal 'certainty,' it should be stressed that the White Paper text provides more legal clarity for European sport within the limits of the EU's current competencies. For the first time ever the Commission takes stock of the European Court's case law and Commission decisions in the area of sport. However, in the current absence of a specific legal competence for sport, a case-by-case approach remains the basis for the Commission's control of the implementation of EU law in the sport sector, in line with the current Treaty provisions, and taking full account of the Nice Declaration—the Commission stated.

At its meeting in June 2007, the European Council gave a mandate to the Intergovernmental Conference which lead to the signature of the Lisbon Treaty in December 2007. The Commission welcomed the fact that the mandate set out that the provisions on sport agreed in the 2004 Intergovernmental Conference (regarding the 'Constitution for Europe') would be inserted into the new Treaty. These provisions on sport, giving the Union 'soft.' supporting competences in this area, were inserted into the text of the then Article 149 of the EC Treaty, which also dealt with education, youth and vocational training (see below). It was the intention of the Member States to ratify the Reform (Lisbon) Treaty by mid 2009. This meant that it seemed likely that additional important developments would occur at EU level in the area of sport in the next few years. Ratification of the Reform (Lisbon) Treaty would give the EU the possibility to define a sport policy, to incorporate sport into the work of the Council of Ministers, and to create an EU Sport Programme.[16] The White Paper should thus be seen as an instrument to pave the way for the implementation of a possible future Treaty provision on sport. The White Paper would remain the basis for the Commission's involvement in the

[16] The Lisbon Treaty (TEU and TFEU) went into force on 1 December 2009.

sport sector until after the entry into force of the Reform (Lisbon) Treaty—the Commission stated in 2007.

3.7 The Specificity of Sport in the White Paper

Over the years, the EU has produced some colourful jargon to describe various concepts and operating principles, such as the principle of 'subsidiarity,' whereby matters so far as possible are dealt with not at the Community level, but at the Member States' level. The term 'specificity of sport' has entered into common parlance in practice to refer to the special characteristics of sport recognised in the Nice Declaration on Sport (2000). In a separate para the White Paper contains for the first time some guidance—but not an exhaustive one—on the meaning of the 'specificity of sport,' based on the case law of the European Court of Justice and the decisions of the European Commission in previous cases. Before setting out this guidance, it should be noted that the para clearly states in its first sentence that 'Sport activity is subject to the application of EU Law.' Particularly, in so far as it constitutes an economic activity (cf., competition law and internal market provisions). According to the White Paper, the specificity of European sport can be approached through 'two prisms':

- The specificity of sporting activities and of sporting rules, such as separate competitions for men and women, limitations on the number of participants in competitions, or the need to ensure uncertainty concerning outcomes and to preserve a competitive balance between clubs taking part in the same competition;
- The specificity of the sport structure, including notably the autonomy and diversity of sport organisations, a pyramid structure of competitions from grassroots to elite level and organised solidarity mechanisms between the different levels and operators, the organisation of sport on a national basis, and the principle of a single federation per sport.

The White Paper points out that the specificity of sport has been recognised and taken into account in various decisions of the European Court of Justice and the European Commission over the years. In Bosman for example, the European Court of Justice stated that: 'In view of the considerable social importance of sporting activities and in particular football in the Community, the aims of maintaining a balance between clubs by preserving a certain degree of equality and uncertainty as to results and of encouraging the recruitment and training of young players must be accepted as legitimate.' And the White Paper adds that, in line with the established case law, the specificity of sport will continue to be so recognised, but it cannot be construed so as to justify a general exemption of sport from the application of EU law. The White Paper then goes on to give some examples of organisational sporting rules that are not likely to offend EU competition law, provided that their anticompetitive effects, if any, are inherent and proportionate to the legitimate objectives pursued (see in more detail below in Sect. 3.9 on the 'Practical application of the "sport specificity" concept in Commission practice and ECJ jurisprudence'): 'rules of the game' (rules fixing the length of matches or the number of players on the field); rules concerning the selection criteria for sports competitions; rules on 'at home' and 'away from home' matches; rules preventing multiple ownership in club competitions; rules concerning the composition of national teams; rules against doping; and rules concerning transfer periods.

The White Paper adds that, in determining whether a certain sporting rule is compatible with EU Competition Law, an assessment can only be made on a case-by-case basis, as confirmed by the European Court of Justice in the Meca-Medina case. In that case, the Court dismissed the notion of 'purely sporting rules' as irrelevant for the question of the applicability of EU competition rules to the sport sector. The Court recognised that the specificity of sport must be taken into account in the sense that the restrictive effects of competition inherent in the organisation and proper conduct of competitive sport are not in breach of the EU competition rules, where these effects are proportionate to the legitimate genuine sporting interest pursued. In other words, the proportionality test requires that each case is assessed on its own merits according to its own particular features or characteristics. Thus, it is not possible to formulate general guidelines on the application of EU Competition Law to the sports sector.

3.8 Sport in the Constitutional and Reform (Lisbon) Treaties

What exactly did the provisions on sport in the Constitution for Europe entail? In the first place it must be established that the pertinent Article 282 was part of Part III of this Treaty concerning Internal Policies and Action, more especially, Chapter V of Part III, concerning 'Areas where the Union may take coordinating, complementary or supporting action'; in other words, it shall have competence to carry out such type of actions in relation to the actions of the Member States. In this context, Article 282 was part of section 4 concerning 'Education, Youth, Sport and Vocational Training.' Article 282 was therefore 'soft law' by nature and this was reflected by its paragraph 4 which determined that 'in order to contribute to the achievement of the objectives referred to in this Article (a) European laws or framework laws shall establish incentive actions, excluding any harmonization of the laws and regulations of the Member States' and '(b) The Council, on a proposal from the Commission, shall adopt recommendations.' Although therefore regulations (European laws) and directives (framework laws) could be adopted in the field op sport, this could only be the case for the purpose of establishing 'incentive actions' and moreover with the exclusion of the harmonisation of national legislation. It must further be remarked that, as appeared from paragraph 3 of Article 282, the EU and the Member States should foster cooperation with third countries (non-Member States) and the competent international organisations in the field of sport, especially the Council of Europe.

Apart from and next to the legal instruments available, what were the objectives of the EU in the field of sport according to the Constitutional Treaty? Para 1, second sentence, of Article 282 indicated that 'the Union shall contribute to the promotion of European sporting issues, while taking account of its specific nature, its structures based on voluntary activity and its social and educational function.' Para 2 added that 'the Union action shall be aimed at ... (g) developing the European dimension in sport, by promoting fairness and openness in sporting competitions and cooperation between bodies responsible for sport, and by protecting the physical and moral integrity of sportsmen and sportswomen, especially young sportsmen and sportswomen.'

The sport provisions in Article III-282 'codified' in fact the philosophy and phraseology of the Sport Declarations of Nice and Amsterdam, referring to the social and educational functions of sport and taking account of its specific nature. Promoting 'fairness' and 'openness' in sporting competitions as such is a newly introduced element in this context. Are 'fairness' and 'openness' new principles of EU sports law and what precisely is meant by them? In fact there is not available any substantial preparatory work (*travaux préparatoires*) from negotiating Lisbon regarding the 'sport provision.'[17] In the EP-commissioned Study on *Lisbon Treaty and EU Sports Policy* (September 2010),[18] the possible impact of the words 'fairness' and 'openness' in relation to a number of ongoing issues in European sport is discussed: collective sale of sports rights; local training of players (FIFA 6+5 and UEFA home grown players rules); status and transfer of players; anti-doping rules; player release rule (national team sports); licensing, financial fair play and salary capping; players' agents; sports betting; multiple club ownership; participation of EU non-nationals in individual national championships; the rights of third-country nationals; national territorial tying; selection criteria; composition of national teams; the protection of sports associations from competition. According to the White Paper, with reference to the Helsinki Report on Sport and the Nice Declaration, one of the basic elements of the so-called European Sports Model is 'a system of open competitions based on the principle of promotion/relegation.'

In Article 149 of the Reform Treaty (Title XI: Education, vocational training, youth and sport' and Article 165 of the Lisbon Treaty (TFEU)) the foregoing is repeated again:

[17] See Weatherill (2010), pp. 11 and pp. 14–17.

[18] The Study was executed by the T.M.C. Asser Instituut, The Hague, The Netherlands, and Edge Hill and Loughborough Universities, UK.

'The Union shall contribute to the promotion of European sporting issues, while taking account of the specific nature of sport, its structures based on voluntary activity and its social and educational function.' (Para 1)

'Community action shall be aimed at: developing the European dimension in sport, by promoting fairness and openness in sporting competitions and cooperation between bodies responsible for sports, and by protecting the physical and moral integrity of sportsmen and sportswomen, especially the youngest sportsmen and sportswomen.' (Para 2)

'The Community and the Member States shall foster cooperation with third countries and the competent international organisations in the field of education and sport, in particular the Council of Europe': (Para 3)

3.9 Sport Specificity in the 2011 'White Paper Plus'

The so-called White Paper-plus contains the following statement on the 'specificity of sport':

'The specific nature of sport, a legal concept established by the Court of Justice of the European Union which has already been taken into account by the EU institutions in various circumstances and which was addressed in detail in the White Paper on Sport and the accompanying Staff Working Document, is now recognised by Article 165 TFEU. It encompasses all the characteristics that make sport special, such as for instance the interdependence between competing adversaries or the pyramid structure of open competitions. The concept of the specific nature of sport is taken into account when assessing whether sporting rules comply with the requirements of EU law (fundamental rights, free movement, prohibition of discrimination, competition, etc.).

Sporting rules normally concern the organisation and proper conduct of competitive sport. They are under the responsibility of sport organisations and must be compatible with EU law. In order to assess the compatibility of sporting rules with EU law, the Commission considers the legitimacy of the objectives pursued by the rules, whether any restrictive effects of those rules are inherent in the pursuit of the objectives and whether they are proportionate to them.

Legitimate objectives pursued by sport organisations may relate, for example, to the fairness of sporting competitions, the uncertainty of results, the protection of athletes' health, the promotion of the recruitment and training of young athletes, financial stability of sport clubs/teams or a uniform and consistent exercise of a given sport (the "rules of the game").' (italics added; RS)[19]

[19] Communication from the Commission to the European Parliament, the Council, the European Economic and Social Committee and the Committee of the Regions "Developing the European Dimension in Sport", Brussels 18.1.2011, COM(2011) 12 final, pp. 10–11.

3.10 The Practical Application of the 'Sport Specificity' Concept in Commission Practice and ECJ Jurisprudence

3.10.1 The Application of Internal Market Freedoms (Movement and Services) to Sport[20]

The European Court of Justice has taken a number of important decisions in this area:

In *Walrave & Koch*[21] and *Donà v Mantero*,[22] the European Court of Justice (ECJ) stated clearly that regulations based on nationality which limit the mobility of sportsmen are not in conformity with the principle of free movement of workers.

In its *Walrave*, *Donà* and *Bosman*[23] rulings, the ECJ recognised an exception to the principle of free movement of sportsmen for reasons which are not of an economic nature. The ECJ has since the early 1970 s acknowledged that rules which restrict the nationality of players in national teams are to be considered as 'pure sporting' rules and thus do not fall under (then) Articles 39 and 49 EC. In *Walrave* the ECJ stated that the rule of the International Cycling Union (Union Cycliste Internationale, UCI) requiring that the pacemaker must be of the same nationality as the stayer in 'world cycling championships behind motorcycles' was in compliance with EC law.

In its *Bosman* ruling the ECJ stated: 'Having regard to the objectives of the Community, sport is subject to Community law in so far as it constitutes an economic activity within the meaning of Article 2 of the Treaty, as in the case of the activities of professional or semi-professional footballers, where they are in gainful employment or provide a remunerated service.' In its interpretation of the principle of free movement for sportsmen, the Court formulated two types of prohibition. Firstly, the Court prohibited all discrimination based on nationality and declared nationality quotas in sport clubs not in conformity with Article 39. Secondly, in order to ensure the full effectiveness of the principle of free movement of sportsmen (after the expiry of a contract) the Court also condemned obstacles to free movement. One consequence was the end of allowances for a transfer at the end of a contract.

The transfer system of players is an example of the specificity of sport. While no comparable phenomenon exists in other economic areas, transfers of players between clubs play an important role in the functioning of team sports, and, in particular, professional team sports. Transfer rules aim to protect the integrity of sporting competition and to avoid problems such as money laundering, but they must be in compliance with EU law. In its Bosman ruling, the Court of Justice

---

[20] See Accompanying document to the White Paper on Sport, pp. 43–44, 47–48.

[21] Case 36/74 of 12 December 1974.

[22] Case 13/76 of 14 July 1976.

[23] Case C-415/93 of 15 December 1995.

unequivocally stated that 'nationals of a Member State have, in particular, the right, which they derive directly from the Treaty, to leave their country of origin, to enter the territory of another Member State and reside there in order to pursue an economic activity. Provisions which preclude or deter a national of a Member State from leaving his country of origin in order to exercise his right to free movement therefore constitute an obstacle to that freedom, even if they apply without regard to the nationality of the workers concerned.' Restrictive transfer rules may also constitute an infringement of EU competition law. The Bosman ruling stated that professional football is an economic activity and therefore subject to EU law.

The judgement of the Court in the Bernard case,[24] is of particular interest as it is the first ruling covering a sport-related case adopted after the entry into force of the Lisbon Treaty. The ruling provides further insight into the Court's interpretation of the issue of free movement of professional sportspeople. The focus of the ruling concerns limitations to the rules on free movement of workers laid down in Article 45 TFEU, arising from training compensation schemes. The *Olympique Lyonnais* ruling confirms most of the elements and the legal reasoning developed by the Court in the Bosman ruling, at a distance of 15 years.

According to the Court, Article 45 TFEU does not rule out schemes which, in order to attain the objective of encouraging the recruitment and training of young players, guarantees compensation to the club which provided the training if, at the end of the training period, a young player signs a professional contract with a club in another Member State, on condition that the scheme is suitable to ensure the attainment of that objective and does not go beyond what is necessary to attain it. In the Bernard ruling, the Court confirmed an important point raised in the Bosman ruling, namely that the recruitment and training of young players is to be considered a legitimate objective of general interest. The Court also provided additional guidance for assessing whether training compensation schemes can be considered as suitable to attain this objective: according to the Court, such schemes must be related to the actual cost of training. This was not the case of the scheme discussed in the main proceedings, since it linked the payment to potential damages suffered by the clubs and was thus unrelated to the actual training costs. The Court offered another important element in order to assess whether training compensation schemes are inherent and proportionate to their legitimate objective: when carrying out this assessment, account should be taken of the costs borne by the clubs in training both future professional players and those who will never play professionally. The Court affirmed hereby the principle that training costs may be calculated on the basis of the so-called 'player factor,' i.e. the number of players that need to be trained in order to produce a professional player.

According to the Court, Article 45 TFEU does not rule out schemes which, in order to attain the objective of encouraging the recruitment and training of young players, guarantees compensation to the club which provided the training if, at the

[24] *Olympique Lyonnais*, case C-325/08, delivered on 16 March 2010.

end of the training period, a young player signs a professional contract with a club in another Member State, on condition that the scheme is suitable to ensure the attainment of that objective and does not go beyond what is necessary to attain it. In the *Bernard* ruling, the Court confirmed an important point raised in the *Bosman* ruling, namely that the recruitment and training of young players is to be considered a legitimate objective of general interest. The Court also provided additional guidance for assessing whether training compensation schemes can be considered as suitable to attain this objective: according to the Court, such schemes must be related to the actual cost of training. This was not the case of the scheme discussed in the main proceedings, since it linked the payment to potential damages suffered by the clubs and was thus unrelated to the actual training costs. The Court offered another important element in order to assess whether training compensation schemes are inherent and proportionate to their legitimate objective: when carrying out this assessment, account should be taken of the costs borne by the clubs in training both future professional players and those who will never play professionally. The Court affirmed hereby the principle that training costs may be calculated on the basis of the so-called 'player factor,' i.e. the number of players that need to be trained in order to produce a professional player.

When considering the autonomy of a federation to organise its competitions, two particular cases are relevant. In its *Deliège*[25] ruling, the Court stressed that selection criteria in judo based on a limit to the number of national participants in an international competition does not constitute a restriction on the freedom to provide services, as such a limitation may ensure certain important characteristics of sporting competitions and pursues a sporting interest only.

Furthermore, in 2000 in its *Lehtonen*[26] ruling, the Court considered that the setting of deadlines for transfers of players may meet the objective of ensuring the equity of sporting competitions (transfers late in the season may upset the competitive balance and damage the regularity of the competition). In order to be justified, rules of this type defined by sporting organisations may not go beyond what is necessary to achieve the legitimate aim pursued. In this case the proper functioning of the championship as a whole was 'inherent' to the sports organisation and the 'transfer window' which prevented basketball players from joining another club during the season could be linked to the integrity of the competition. The Lehtonen case implied that certain restrictions on labour mobility may be justified in order to ensure certain important characteristics of sporting competition such as transfer windows.

Limited and proportionate restrictions to the principle of free movement, in line with Treaty provisions and ECJ rulings, can thus be accepted as regards:

- The right to select national athletes for national team competitions (Walrave);
- The acceptability of training compensation schemes for young players (Bernard);

[25] Case C-51/96 and C-191/97 of 11 April 2000.

[26] Case C-117/96 of 13 April 2004.

– The need to limit the number of participants in a competition (Deliège);
– The setting of deadlines for transfers of players in team sports (Lehtonen).

3.10.2 The Application of EU Competition Law to the Organisation of Sport[27]

3.10.2.1 ECJ Case Law

3.10.2.1.1 Anti-Doping Rules (*Meca Medina*)

The economic importance of sport has grown dramatically in recent years and continues to grow. As a result, the Commission has had to deal with an increasing number of cases in the area of antitrust related to the sport sector and has resolved these cases either formally through decisions or informally.

The material provisions of the EC Treaty are [*now: Articles 101 and 102 TFEU, RS*]

- Article 81 which forbids agreements between undertakings and decisions by associations of undertakings that prevent, restrict or distort competition in the common market, subject to some narrowly defined exceptions; and
- Article 82 which prohibits the abuse by one or more undertakings of a dominant position within the common market.

It has long been established by the case-law of the Community Courts and the decisional practice of the Commission that economic activities in the context of sport fall within the scope of EC law, including EC competition rules and internal market freedoms. This has recently been confirmed specifically with regard to the anti-trust rules, Articles 81 and 82 of the EC Treaty, by the *Meca Medina* ruling of the European Court of Justice (ECJ).[28] This judgment is of paramount importance for the application of EC competition law to the sport sector since this is the first time the ECJ has ever pronounced on the application of Articles 81 and 82 to organisational sporting rules. In prior judgments the cases were decided solely on the basis of other provisions of the EC Treaty, most notably those on the freedom of movement for workers and the freedom to provide services. The very existence of an authoritative interpretation of the anti-trust provisions of the Treaty in the context of organisational sporting rules by the ECJ represents a significant contribution to legal certainty in this area.

The Community Courts and the Commission have consistently taken into consideration the particular characteristics of sport setting it apart from other

---

27 See: Commission Staff Working Document "The EU and sport: background and context", Accompanying document to the White Paper on Sport, Brussels, 11.7.2007, SEC(2007) 935, pp. 35–37, 38–40, 49 and 55.

28 Case T-313/02, ECR 2004 II-3291, and Case C-519/04, ECR 2006 I-6991.

economic activities that are frequently referred to as the 'specificity of sport.' Although no such legal concept has been developed or formally recognised by the Community Courts, it has become apparent that the following distinctive features may be of relevance when assessing the compliance of organisational sporting rules with Community law:

Sport events are a product of the contest between a number of clubs/teams or at least two athletes. This *interdependence between competing adversaries* is a feature specific to sport and one which distinguishes it from other industry or service sectors.

If sport events are to be of interest to the spectator, they must involve *uncertainty as to the result.* There must therefore be a certain degree of equality in competitions. This sets the sport sector apart from other industry or service sectors, where competition between firms serves the purpose of eliminating inefficient firms from the market. Sport teams, clubs and athletes have a direct interest not only in there being other teams, clubs and athletes, but also in their economic viability as competitors.

The organisational level of sport in Europe is characterised by a monopolistic *pyramid structure.* Traditionally, there is a single national sport association per sport and Member State, which operates under the umbrella of a single European association and a single worldwide association. The pyramid structure results from the fact that the organisation of national championships and the selection of national athletes and national teams for international competitions often require the existence of one umbrella federation. The Community Courts and the Commission have both recognised the importance of the freedom of internal organisation of sport associations.

Sport fulfils important *educational, public health, social, cultural and recreational functions.* The preservation of some of these essential social and cultural benefits of sport which contribute to stimulating production and economic development is supported through arrangements which provide for a redistribution of financial resources from professional to amateur levels of sport (principle of solidarity).

Controversial discussions in the past have never called into question the recognition of these unique characteristics of sport. Rather, they centered on the question of the precise impact of the specificity of sport on the application of EC competition law. It was argued by some that so-called 'purely sporting rules' automatically fall outside the scope of EC anti-trust rules and cannot, by definition, be in breach of those provisions.

The ECJ has unequivocally rejected this approach in *Meca Medina* and held that the qualification of a rule as 'purely sporting' is not sufficient to remove the athlete or the sport association adopting the rule in question from the scope of EC competition rules. The Court insisted, on the contrary, that whenever the sporting activity in question constitutes an economic activity and thus falls within the scope of the EC Treaty, the conditions for engaging in it then are subject to obligations resulting from the various provisions of the Treaty including the competition rules. The Court spelled out the need to determine, on a case-by-case basis and irrespective of the nature of the rule, whether the specific requirements of Articles 81 EC or 82 EC are met. It further clarified that the anti-doping rules at issue were capable of producing adverse effects on competition because of a potentially unwarranted exclusion of athletes from sporting events.

In the light of *Meca-Medina*, it appears that a considerable number of organisational sporting rules, namely all those that determine the conditions for professional athletes, teams or clubs to engage in sporting activity as an economic activity, are subject to scrutiny under the anti-trust provisions of the Treaty.

The landmark *Meca Medina* ruling has therefore substantially enhanced legal certainty by clearly pronouncing that there exists no such thing as a category of 'purely sporting rules' that would be excluded straightaway from the scope of EC competition law.

This is not to say, however, that the ECJ has decided not to take into account the specific features of sport referred to above when assessing the compatibility of organisational sporting rules with EC competition law. Rather, it has ruled that this cannot be done by way of declaring certain categories of rules a priori exempt from the application of the competition rules of the Treaty. In other words, the recognition of the specificity of sport cannot entail the categorical inapplicability of the EC competition provisions to organisational sporting rules but it has to be included as an element of legal significance within the context of analysing the conformity of such rules with EC competition law.

The second aspect of the *Meca Medina* ruling contributing to increased legal certainty, apart from clarifying under which conditions EC competition law is applicable to sporting rules, is the establishment of a methodological framework for the examination of the compatibility of sporting rules with Articles 81 EC and 82 EC [*now: Articles 101 and 102 TFEU; RS*]

The ECJ spelled out that not every sporting rule that is based on an agreement of undertakings or on a decision of an association of undertakings which implies a restriction of the freedom of action is prohibited by Article 81(1). In assessing the compatibility with this provision account must be taken of the *overall context* in which the rule was adopted or the decision was taken or produces its effects, and more specifically, of its *objectives*; and whether the restrictive effects are *inherent* in the pursuit of the objectives; and are *proportionate* to them.

In applying those principles to the case at hand, the ECJ found that the objective of the challenged anti-doping rules was to ensure fair sport competitions with equal chances for all athletes as well as the protection of athletes' health, the integrity and objectivity of competitive sport and ethical values in sport. The restrictions caused by the anti-doping rules, in particular as a result of the penalties, were considered by the ECJ to be 'inherent in the organisation and proper conduct of competitive sport.' The ECJ also carried out a proportionality test examining, with a positive result, whether the rules were limited to what is necessary as regards (i) the threshold for the banned substance in question and (ii) the severity of the penalties.

This demonstrates that the instruments of EC competition law provide sufficient flexibility in order to duly take into account the specificity of sport and illustrates how the distinctive features of sport play an essential role in analysing the admissibility of organisational sporting rules under EC competition law. Where these features form the basis of a legitimate sporting objective, a rule pursuing that objective is not in breach of EC competition law provided that restrictions contained in the rule are inherent in the pursuit of that objective and are proportionate to it. It needs to be underscored that the *Meca Medina* ruling excludes the possibility of a pre-determined list of sporting rules that are in compliance with or in breach of EC competition law. Apart from the refusal by the ECJ to recognise purely sporting rules as automatically falling outside the scope of the Treaty competition rules or automatically compliant with them it is the requirement of a proportionality test that prevents any general categorisation. That test implies the need to take account of the individual features of each case. Even for the same kind of rule (e.g., licensing rules for sport clubs) conditions may and do vary greatly from sport to sport and from Member State to Member State (e.g., depending on the national legal obligations relating to financial management and transparency there may or may not be a need to include licensing requirements of a particular type in the statutes of a sport association). In many if not most cases there are many conceivable shapes and forms of any particular type of rule. This, as well as the interrelation with other rules, the assessment of which is often indispensable to judge the proportionality of a certain regulation as a whole, renders it virtually impossible to comment on the compatibility of certain types of rules with EC competition law in general terms.

Nevertheless, the body of existing case law of Community Courts, relating to the application of Treaty provisions other than the competition rules, as well as the decision-making practice of the Commission concerning Articles 81 EC and 82 EC can assist in identifying the types of rules that may normally be considered not to infringe EC competition rules. These decisions will have to be reviewed in the light of the *Meca Medina* judgment but they remain relevant inasmuch as they identify objectives that may be recognized as legitimate within the context of carrying out the examination outlined above—while bearing in mind the proviso that a specific assessment based on the circumstances of each individual case involving, most notably, a proportionality test, is indispensable and that therefore one can only express varying degrees of likelihood of compliance with EC competition law.

3.10.2.1.2 Players' Agents (*Piau* Case)

As regards the compatibility of federations' rules with EU competition law, even if the restrictions they impose on these sport-related professions are not likely to be considered inherent in the pursuit of a legitimate sporting objective, they may nevertheless be justified under Article 81(3) or Article 82 EC (now: Articles 101 and 102 TFEU). The aim of a football agent is to introduce a player for a fee to a club or clubs to each other with a view of employment. In the Piau case the Court of First Instance considered that this activity clearly does not pursue a purely sporting interest. The CFI questioned the legitimacy of FIFA's right to regulate the profession of football agents—which would normally be the prerogative of public authorities—, a profession which is not specific to sport and which is of unequivocally economic nature. However, the CFI acknowledged that the players' agent profession needs to be supervised by some entity. It has recognised as legitimate the objective for raising professional standards for players' agents by introducing a qualitative (as opposed to quantitative) selection in the quasi total absence of any national laws or self-regulation in that respect.[29]

The Piau case does *not* represent a sporting exception as is explicitly stated in the CFI ruling (para 105): '... the applicant's argument that the 'specific nature of sport' may not relied on to justify a derogation from the rules on competition must be rejected as irrelevant. The [Commission's] contested decision is not based on such an exception and envisages the exercise of the occupation of players' agent as an economic activity, without claiming that it should be accepted as falling within the scope of the specific nature of sport, which in fact it does not.'

According to the Accompanying Document to the White Paper[30] the *Piau* case concerned a sporting rule adopted in relation to an activity ancillary to sport (football agents) and not relating to the sporting activity itself (football). It may be questioned whether this distinction is reasonable from the perspective of (international) sports law taken as a coherent, comprehensive legal branch of law (cf., the very existence of FIFA Players' Agents Rules; who would and could deny that the agents are members of the football family?!).[31] So, the Piau case in fact was the first time the ECJ has ever pronounced on the application of articles 81 and 82 EC (now: Articles 101 and 102 TFEU) to organisational sporting rules.

3.10.2.2 Commission Decision-Making Practice

3.10.2.2.1 Sports Media Rights

The Commission has taken decisions in three cases involving the joint selling of rights to broadcast games played by football clubs on the basis of Article 81 EC, namely *UEFA Champions League*,[32] *German Bundesliga*[33] and *FA premier League*.[34] The Commission's consistent policy has been that joint selling constitutes a horizontal restriction of competition under Article 81(1) EC. At the same time, the Commission also acknowledges that joint selling creates certain efficiencies and may, under certain circumstances, fulfil the conditions of Article 81(3) EC and therefore not constitute a violation of Article 81 EC. The Commission remedied the negative effects of joint selling by requiring, e.g., the selling of rights in several individual rights packages following an open and transparent tendering process. Moreover, the duration of rights contracts should not exceed three years and unsold rights would fall back for individual exploitation by the clubs. The abovementioned

---

[29] CFI and upheld in appeal by the ECJ: Cases T-193/02 and C-171/05P, ECR 2005 II-209 and ECR 2006 I-37 respectively. See also, Martins (2009).

[30] At p. 35, n. 99.

[31] Siekmann (2011).

[32] Case 37398, OJ 2003 L 291/25.

[33] Case 37214, OJ 2005 L 134/46.

[34] Case 38173, OJ 2008 C 7/18.

decisions had the effect of opening up media rights markets to broadcasters and new media service providers by making several different rights packages available while safeguarding the social and cultural aspects of football. This prevented the concentration of all available rights in the hands of a single media operator and ensured that a maximum amount of rights was made available to sports fans. The question if and under which conditions joint selling can be justified on the basis of Article 81(3) has to be examined in the light of the specific circumstances of each individual case.

The Declaration of the Nice European Council of 7–9 December 2000 on the specific characteristics of sport and its social function in Europe mentions (point 15) that the sale of television broadcasting rights is one of the greatest sources of income today for certain sports. The European Council stated that moves to encourage the mutualisation of part of the revenue from such sales, at the appropriate levels, would be beneficial to the principle of solidarity between all levels and areas of sport. The joint selling of media rights for sporting competitions may facilitate the redistribution of revenues based on the principle of mutual support and based on the principle that these revenues should be redistributed to all those involved in sport: amateurs, volunteers, young people in training centres, sports teachers etc. However, it is important to note that a system of joint selling does not automatically lead to an equitable redistribution of the revenues. It is the primary responsibility of the national league associations, sport associations and clubs concerned to agree on a form of redistribution that is in line with the principle of solidarity expressed in the Declaration of Nice European Council. It should be noted that financial solidarity can also be achieved on the basis of individual selling of sports media rights, provided that it is accompanied by a robust solidarity mechanism.

3.10.2.2.2 'At Home and Away from Home' Rule (*Mouscron* Case)

The French city of Lille had lodged a complaint against UEFA under Article 82 EC as regards a rule for UEFA competitions to the effect that each club must play its home match at its own ground. The Belgian football club Excelsior Mouscron had thus been refused to switch its home match in the 1997/98 UEFA Cup against FC Metz from Mouscron to Lille. The Commission rejected the complaint as it considered the 'home and away from home' rule as well as the exceptions contained therein to constitute a sporting rule that did not fall within the scope of Articles 81 and 82 EC. The Commission found that the organisation of football on a national territorial basis was not called into question by Community law. The Commission considered the rule indispensable for the organisation of national and international competitions in view of ensuring equality of chances between clubs. The Commission also found that the rule did not go beyond what was necessary. The Commission noted that the exceptions had to be applied in an objective and non-discriminatory manner in order to escape Articles 81 and 82 EC. The Commission considered that Lille was active in the market for the renting of stadiums. The Commission also considered whether

UEFA was dominant in the market for organising European club competitions in football although the question was left open.[35]

3.10.2.2.3 Multiple Ownership of Sport Clubs/Teams (*ENIC* Case)

ENIC, a company that owned stakes in six professional football clubs in various Member States had lodged a complaint against a rule adopted by UEFA in 1998, which stated that no two clubs or more participating in a UEFA club competition may be directly or indirectly controlled by the same entity or managed by the same person. The Commission rejected the complaint concluding that there was no restriction of Article 81(1) EC because the objective of the rule was not to distort competition, but to guarantee the integrity of the competitions organised by UEFA. It concluded that the rule 'aims to ensure the uncertainty of the outcome and to guarantee that the consumer has the perception that the games played represent honest sporting competitions.' The Commission also found that the rule did not go beyond what was necessary to ensure its legitimate aim: i.e., to protect the uncertainty of the results in the interest of the public.[36]

3.10.2.2.4 Ticketing

In *1998 Football World Cup*[37] the European Commission stated that ensuring effective safety at football matches is essential and may, in particular circumstances, justify the implementation of special ticket sales arrangements by tournament organisers. Nevertheless, in order to determine whether and, if so to what extent, security considerations may justify ticketing arrangements which would otherwise be deemed to infringe Community law (Article 82 EC Treaty), each set of arrangements must be considered on their individual merits in the light of an objective assessment what is necessary to achieve reasonable security objectives such as the segregation of rival groups of supporters by way of ticket allocation distributed by UEFA member associations among their own supporters and related to seats located at opposite ends of the stadium, non-transferability of tickets, etc. In *1998 Football World Cup* no explicit reference was made to the concept of sport specificity.

---

[35] Case 36851; IP/99/965 of 9 December 1999.

[36] Case 37806 of 25 June 2002.

[37] Case 36888, OJ 2000 L 5/55.

3.10.2.2.5 Access to Major Sporting Events on Television

The 'Television without Frontiers' Directive'[38] recognised the specificity of sport[39] in the media context and its importance for (television) viewers. In Article 3a (now, Article 14 of the Audiovisual Media Services Directive)[40] it provided for a possibility for the Member States to take measures to ensure in respect of events regarded as being of major importance to society (sport events being one of the foremost examples), that a significant part of the public is not deprived of the possibility of following such events on free television. The national lists, once notified to the Commission, are verified for their compatibility with Community law and published in the Official Journal. The new Article 3j (in the final version: 15) of the Audiovisual Media Services Directive enhances access of viewers to events of high interest for society (including sport events): broadcasters exercising exclusive rights to such events have to grant other broadcasters the right to use extracts for the purpose of short news reports (based on the right to information of European citizens).

3.10.2.2.6 Summary: Sporting Exceptions

On the basis of a close-reading of the full texts of the relevant Court case-law and Commission decision-making practice, the sporting exceptions and their justification(s) may be summarised as follows:

discrimination of EU non-nationals in national representative teams/justification: the formation of national teams is a question of purely sporting interest only (see: the particular nature and context of international representative matches) and as such has nothing to do with economic activity (Walrave para 8/operative part 2 ('dictum'); Donà para 14/operative part 1; Bosman 123);

training compensation schemes for young players ('joueurs espoirs')/justification: in view of the considerable social importance of sporting activities and in particular football in the European Union, the objective of encouraging the recruitment and training of young players must be accepted as legitimate; the prospect of receiving training fees is likely to encourage football clubs to seek new talent and train young players (Bernard/Olympique Lyonnais para 39 with reference to Bosman para 106; and Bernard para 41/see also the 'dictum' of the Bernard case);

limitation of the number of participants in a competition (other than national teams)/justification: such a limitation is inherent in the organisation of an international high-level sports event, which necessarily involves certain selection rules or

---

[38] Council Directive No. 89/552/EEC of 3 October 1989.

[39] N.B. The term is explicitly used by the Commission in this context in the Accompanying Document to the White Paper on Sport, at p. 53, para 4.8. Media.

[40] Council Directive No. 2010/13/EU, OJ No. L 95 of 15 April 2010, and OJ L 263 of 6 October 2010 (corrigendum). See also, the recent Judgments of the General Court of Justice of the EU of 17 February 2011 in UEFA v European Commission concerning the inclusion of World Cup matches in the national lists of Belgium and the United Kingdom (Cases T-55/08, 68/08 and 385/07).

criteria being adopted; the adoption of one system for selecting participants rather than another must be based on a large number of considerations unconnected with the personal situation of any athlete, such as the nature. The organisation and the financing of the sport concerned (Deliège paras 64–65 and 68/'dictum');

transfer deadlines in team sports/justification: the objective of ensuring the regularity of sporting competitions; late transfers might be liable to change substantially the sporting strength of one or other team in the course of the championship, thus calling into question the comparability of results between the teams taking part in that championship, and consequently the proper functioning of the championship as a whole (Lehtonen paras 53–54);

anti-doping rules/justification: the general objective of the rules is to combat doping in order for competitive sport to be conducted fairly and it includes the need to safeguard equal chances for athletes, athletes' health, the integrity and objectivity of competitive sport and ethical values in sport; a restriction of competition is inherent in the organisation and proper conduct of competitive sport and its very purpose is to ensure healthy rivalry between athletes;

supervision of the players' agents profession/'sport specificity' is not applicable (no sporting exception). (Piau para 105 CFI);

sports media rights/justification: the mutualisation of part of the revenue from the sales of TV rights, at the appropriate levels, is beneficial to the principle of solidarity between all levels and areas of sport.

'at home and away from home' rule/justification: this rule must be assessed within the context of the national geographical organisation of football in Europe; the rule which stipulates that every club must play its home match at its own ground and not in its opponent's country, is needed to ensure equality between clubs (Mouscron);

no multiple ownership of sport clubs/justification: the main purpose of the rule is to protect the integrity of the competition and to avoid conflicts of interests that may arise from the fact that more than one club controlled by the same owner or managed by the same person play in the same competition; it aims to ensure the uncertainty of the outcome and to guarantee that the consumer has the perception that the games played represent honest sporting competition between the participants, as consumers may suspect that teams with a common owner will not genuinely compete; without the rule, the proper functioning of the market where the clubs develop their economic activities would be under threat, since the public's perception that the underlying sporting competition is fair and honest is an essential precondition to keep its interest and marketability; if sporting competitions were not credible and consumers did not have the perception that the games played represent honest sporting competition between the participants, the competitions would be devaluated with the inevitable consequence over time of lower consumer confidence, interest and marketability; without a solid sporting foundation, clubs would be less capable of extracting value from ancillary activities and investment in clubs would lose value.[41] (paras 28, 32 ENIC);

*ticketing arrangements/*justification: spectators' safety and security at football matches;

free access to sporting events of major importance to society on television/ justification: right of information of European citizens.

3.11 Summary and Conclusion

The classical and still current central (legal) question in the debate on the position of sport in the European Union is whether sport is 'special,' whether it deserves specific treatment under European Law and to what extent and why. In other words, should sport be exempted from the EC Treaty? The 'specificity of sport' is the legal concept (and method or instrument of appreciation or assessment) that is applied by the European Commission and the European Court of Justice to tackle this question on a case-by-case basis, in order to determine whether the sporting rules and regulations concerned are acceptable in EU law. Do they have justifiable objectives? Next to that, the proportionality test requires that each case is assessed on its own merits according to its own particular features or characteristics. The concept of 'sport specificity' may be distinguished in sport specificity *lato* sensu and sport specificity *stricto* sensu. Sport specificity *lato* sensu concerns the external, societal context of sport, the 'extra-sportive' role and function of sport, in particular professional sport, as a policy instrument in the society at large. Sport specificity *stricto* sensu applies to how sport is regulated and organised. It is the internal, purely sporting side of the coin. *Lato* sensu, the importance of the social (cultural, recreational, health) and educational functions of sport was stressed in the Court's case-law and basic documents like the Amsterdam and Nice Declarations and is codified in the 'sport article' 165 of the Lisbon Treaty. Sport is said to play a morally elevating role in society through its traditional values of fair play, solidarity, fair competition and team spirit. Additionally, the Audiovisual Media Services Directive recognises the specificity of sport with regard to securing free television access to sporting events of major importance (Olympic Games, Football World Cup and European Championship, etc. and major national events like, for example, Wimbledon and the Tour de France) to society. This in fact is a sporting exception which may be implemented by Member States on the basis of the Directive. It in fact is a recognition of the 'breaking news' value and societal relevance of major sporting events which give them an exceptional status. However, in this case the sport industry is not unique, 'special' in comparison with

[41] Should two clubs under joint control or ownership meet at a certain stage of the competition, the public's perception of the authenticity of the result would be jeopardised; in the present case, for example, ENIC's business interests in the field of the provision of betting services could be seen by some as an obstacle to the development of fair competition on the pitch (para 35 ENIC).

other industrial sectors. *Stricto* sensu, the organisation of sport on a national basis, the principle of a single federation per sport, the pyramid structure of open competitions, separate competitions for men and women, voluntariness, the position of amateur sport, the interdependence between competing adversaries, the principle of equal opportunities and uncertainty of results (competitive balance), financial solidarity (especially, professional football), national teams of '(EU-) nationals,' compensation schemes for young players (football), limitation of the number of participants in a competition (other than national teams), transfer deadlines in team sports, anti-doping rules, 'at home and away from home' rule (football), no multiple ownership in sport clubs, ticketing arrangements for safety reasons, are particular characteristics of sport(s) itself—at least from an EU law perspective. The most specific, most purely sporting rules are the Laws of the Game for each individual sport (*lex ludica*). The Laws of the Game are in fact the very core of sports law and apply worldwide. By their very nature they are not contrary to EU competition law if EU competition law would apply, since the 'playing field' is 'level' for competitors, in individual and team sports, in every aspect. In football the playing field is symmetrical, divided into two completely equal halves, the duration of a game is divided into two equal halves of each 45 minutes, opposing teams change sides (halves) after lemon time, competitions are based on a system of home and away matches for all teams equally.

The applicability of the concept of sport specificity was explicitly not accepted by the ECJ in the Piau case (players' agents) and of course in Bosman and Donà either (transfer system, nationality clauses in professional club football). There is a number of other issues regarding which the sport specificity option was not even considered in principle, because that would have been totally out of order. Of course, these cases are still part of (European) sports law, but in a more marginal position one might say. This case-law (or Commission practice) is not about testing sporting rules against EU law, but about determining whether (category 1) EU law is also applicable to a particular sporting issue, or (category 2) whether particular sports-related national legislation or decision-making is in conformity with EU law, or (category 3) whether particular sporting rules or practices of a completely non-sport specific character are acceptable under EU law. These cases and issues are really 'off the field of play'! Examples are: (category 1) equal treatment clauses for non-EU nationals in agreements with third countries (Kolpak, Simutenkov, Kahveci)[42]; (category 2) ECJ rulings with regard to gambling and/or betting services; (category 3) FIA case[43]: in this case the Commission dealt with a conflict of interest situation arising from the fact that a sport association was not only the regulator but also the commercial exploiter of a sport. FIA rules prohibited drivers and race teams that held a FIA licence from participating in non-

[42] Cases C-438/00, C-265/03, and C-152/08.

[43] Press releases IP/99/434 of 30 June 1999, and IP/01/1523 of 30 October 2001.

FIA authorised events. Circuit owners were prohibited from using the circuits for races which could compete with Formula One. Another similar case is MOTOE.[44] MOTOE is a non-profit-making association governed by private law, whose object is the organisation of motorcycling competitions in Greece. MOTOE's activities consisted not only in taking part in administrative decisions authorising the organisation of motorcycling events, but also in organising such events itself and in entering, in that connection, into sponsorship, advertising and insurance contracts.

References

Martins RB (2009) The *Laurent Piau* case of the ECJ on the status of players' agents. In: Gardiner S, Parrish R, Siekmann RCR (eds) EU, sport, law and policy—regulation, re-regulation and representation. The Hague, pp 247–258, and previously published in 1–2, Int Sports Law J (2007):43–51

Parrish R, Miettinen S (2008) The sporting exception in European Union law. The Hague

Siekmann RCR (2008) Is sport 'Special' in EU law and policy? In: Blanpain R (ed) The future of sports law in the European Union—beyond the EU reform treaty and the white paper. Alphen aan den Rijn

Siekmann RCR (2011) What is sports law? Lex Sportiva and Lex Ludica: a Reassessment of content and terminology. Int Sports Law J 3–4:3–13

Siekmann R, Soek J (eds) (2005) The European Union and Sport: legal and policy documents. The Hague

Weatherill S (2008) The white paper on sport as an exercise in 'Better Regulation'. Int Sports Law J 1–2:3–8

Weatherill S (2010) Fairness, openness and the specific nature of sport: Does the Lisbon Treaty change EU sports law? Int Sports Law J 3–4:11–17

[44] Case C-49/07.

Chapter 4
EU Competition Law and Professional Sport: The Collective Selling of TV Rights in Europe and the Dutch Equestrian Case: How The *Meca Medina* 'Test' for Organisational Sporting Rules is Applied

Abstract In this chapter, first the Meca Medina 'test' for organisational sporting rules under the EU competition law provisions will be presented as this methodological approach is described in the White Paper on Sport Secondly, amongst the few by and large settled competition law issues—like the UEFA 'at home and away from home' rule (on the basis of the national territoriality principle), the ban on multiple ownership of sport clubs/teams participating in the same UEFA competition, and the assessment of ticketing arrangements for sport events—the major, typical one is that of the collective selling of broadcasting rights which will be dealt with in detail. Thirdly and finally, by way of a concrete, random example from the T.M.C. Asser Institute's sports law advisory services it will be demonstrated how the 'test' was executed in the 'Dutch Equestrian Case.'

Contents

R. C. R. Siekmann, *Introduction to International and European Sports Law*,
ASSER International Sports Law Series, DOI: 10.1007/978-90-6704-852-1_4,
© T.M.C. ASSER PRESS, The Hague, The Netherlands, and the author 2012

4.1 Introduction

With regard to the question of the application of Articles 101 and 102 TFEU (formerly, Articles 81 and 82 EC Treaty) to professional sport, a whole range of topics can be identified as being of interest in this context. In an EP-commissioned report on 'Professional Sport in the Internal Market,'[1] several unresolved competition law issues that might require further adjudication by the EU, were mentioned; many of these outstanding legal issues related to the European and global 'umbrella' governing bodies FIFA and/or UEFA's regulation of professional football: the possible formation of new leagues (so-called break-away leagues), club licensing, the mandatory player release rule for international representative matches, state aid to professional football clubs, the possible introduction of salary caps, etc.

In this chapter, first the *Meca Medina* 'test' for organisational sporting rules under the EU competition law provisions will be presented as this methodological approach is described in the White Paper on Sport.[2] Secondly, amongst the few by and large settled competition law issues—like the UEFA 'at home and away from home' rule (on the basis of the national territoriality principle), the ban on multiple ownership of sport clubs/teams participating in the same UEFA competition, and the assessment of ticketing arrangements for sport events—the major, typical one is that of the collective selling of broadcasting rights which will be dealt with in detail. Thirdly and finally, by way of a concrete, random example from the T.M.C. Asser Institute's sports law advisory services it will be demonstrated how the 'test' was executed in the 'Dutch Equestrian Case.'[3]

[1] Project No IP/A/IMCO/ST/2005-004, Commissioned by the Committee on the Internal Market and Consumer Protection of the European Parliament on the initiative of Toine Manders (MEP, September 2005, T.M.C. Asser Instituut, The Hague, The Netherlands, in cooperation with Edge Hill College, United Kingdom and Sport2B, The Netherlands).

[2] SEC(2007) 935, at pp. 64–69.

[3] 'Discussion on the Application of European Union Competition Law to the Procedures for the Assignment of Category I, Category II and International Competitions in the Netherlands—KNHS', commissioned by the T.M.C. Asser Instituut to Prof. Dr. Richard Parrish, Director of the Centre for Sports Law Research, Edge Hill University, United Kingdom, May 2010.

4.2 Testing Organisational Sporting Rules Under EU Competition Law

4.2.1 General Principles

4.2.1.1 The *Meca Medina* Judgments[4]

The ECJ (now: Court of Justice of the EU), *Meca Medina* judgment is the first judgment in which the Community Courts applied Articles 81 and 82 EC (now: Articles 101 and 102 TFEU) to a sporting rule adopted by a sports association relating to a sporting activity (swimming). The Commission had already applied Articles 81 and 82 EC in individual cases concerning sporting activities, and the ECJ's ruling broadly confirmed the Commission's approach adopted in these cases. Sport cases previously decided by the Community Courts had concerned the application of the EC Treaty provisions on the economic freedoms, such as free movement of persons or services. The ECJ's judgment in *Meca Medina* provides valuable guidance as regards the methodological approach towards assessing a sporting rule under Articles 81 and 82 EC.

The case concerned a complaint by two professional long distance swimmers who challenged the compatibility with Articles 81 and 82 EC of the anti-doping rules adopted by the International Olympic Committee (IOC) and implemented by the swimming governing body Fédération Internationale de Natation Amateur (FINA). Both the CFI and the ECJ reiterated that sport is subject to Community law only insofar as sport constitutes an economic activity. Both Courts found no violation of Article 81 or 82 EC, thus confirming the decision of the Commission.

Unlike the CFI, the ECJ explicitly held that the qualification of a rule as 'purely sporting' was not sufficient to remove the athlete or the sports association adopting the rule in question from the scope of Articles 81 and 82 EC. Having rejected the relevance of the simple reference to 'purely sporting rules,' the ECJ went on to describe the methodological approach that has to be applied to decide whether a given conduct falls within Articles 81 and/or 82.

It first found that the specific requirements of Articles 81 and 82 EC must be examined irrespective of the nature of the rule, in particular it must be determined 'whether the rules which govern that [sport] activity emanate from an undertaking, whether the latter restricts competition or abuses its dominant position, and whether that restriction or that abuse affects trade between Member States.'

The ECJ concluded, however, that the anti-doping rules in question did not infringe Article 81(1) EC despite the fact that the penalties under the anti-doping rules were capable of producing restrictive effects on competition as they could lead to the exclusion of athletes from sport events. The ECJ reached this

[4] Case T-313/02 (ECR 2004 II-329) and Case C-519/04 P (ECR 2006 I-699)

conclusion on the basis of the principles set up in the *Wouters* judgment.[5] In this respect, the ECJ reiterated that account must be taken of (i) the *overall context* in which the rules were taken or produce their effects and of their *objectives* and (ii) whether the restrictive effects are *inherent* in the pursuit of the objectives and (iii) are *proportionate* to them. The ECJ found that the objective of the anti-doping rules was to ensure fair sport competitions with equal chances for all athletes as well as the protection of athletes' health, the integrity and objectivity of competitive sport and ethical values in sport. The limitations of action imposed on the athletes by the anti-doping rules were considered by the ECJ to be 'inherent in the organisation and proper conduct of competitive sport.' The ECJ also examined whether the rules were limited to what is necessary as regards (i) the threshold for the banned substance in question and (ii) the severity of the penalties (in respect of which the ECJ also noted that the athletes had not argued that the penalties imposed were excessive). The ECJ found that the rules were proportionate in both cases. The appeal was therefore rejected.

4.2.1.2 The 'Test' for Organisational Sporting Rules Under Articles 81 and 82 EC

In line with the ECJ's *Meca Medina* judgment, the Commission follows the *methodological approach* described below in order to assess whether a rule adopted by a sports association relating to the organisation of sport infringes Articles 81 and/or 82 EC.

Step 1. Is the sports association that adopted the rule to be considered an 'undertaking' or an 'association of undertakings'?

a. The sports association is an 'undertaking' to the extent it carries out an 'economic activity' itself (e.g., the selling of broadcasting rights).
b. The sports association is an 'association of undertakings' if its members carry out an economic activity. In this respect, the question will become relevant to what extent the sport in which the members (usually clubs/teams or athletes) are active can be considered an economic activity and to what extent the members exercise economic activity. In the absence of 'economic activity,' Articles 81 and 82 EC do not apply.

Step 2. Does the rule in question *restrict competition* within the meaning of Article 81(1) EC or constitute an *abuse* of a dominant position under Article 82 EC?

This will depend, in application of the principles established in the *Wouters* judgment, on the following factors:

[5] *Wouters* is a non-sporting case; Case C-309/99 (ECR 2002 I-1577), paras 97 and 110. The CFI had explicitly rejected the application of *Wouters* in its judgment at para 65. Cf., Weatherill 2006; also in: Weatherill 2007.

a. the *overall* context in which the rule was adopted or produces its effects and its *objectives*;
b. whether the restrictions caused by the rule are *inherent* in the pursuit of the objectives;
and
c. whether the rule is *proportionate* in light of the objectives pursued.

Step 3. Is *trade between Member States* affected?
Step 4. Does the rule fulfill the conditions of *Article 81(3) EC*?

4.2.1.3 Undertakings and Association of Undertakings

Article 81 EC applies to 'undertakings' and 'associations of undertakings,' while Article 82 EC applies to 'undertakings.' The ECJ has defined the term 'undertaking' broadly to include 'every entity engaged in an economic activity, regardless of the legal status of the entity and the way in which it is financed.' Economic activity is any activity consisting of 'offering goods or services on the market.' Economic activity may take place at various levels in the sport sector, including by individual athletes, sport clubs and sports associations.

Individual athletes. The ECJ found that a high-level judoka participating in an international competition was exercising an economic activity—even if she was not remunerated by the organiser—due to the fact that such services are normally remunerated and that the participation in the event generates economic activity (e.g., the sale of tickets, transmission by broadcasters, sponsoring agreements). In the same judgment (*Deliege*) the ECJ also stated that the amateur status of athletes does not necessarily remove them from the scope of economic activities. While independent athletes thus constitute undertakings, In *Bosman* Advocate General Lenz considered that football players employed by a football club do not constitute undertakings. However, even if athletes are employed by a sport club, they may be considered undertakings insofar as they carry out economic activities independent thereof, e.g., by entering into sponsoring agreements.

Sport clubs/teams. It is settled case law that sport clubs/teams are undertakings within the meaning of Article 81 and 82 EC to the extent they carry out economic activities. Sport clubs/teams carry out economic activity, e.g., by selling tickets to the sport events, selling broadcasting rights or concluding sponsoring or advertising agreements.

National sports associations may be both undertakings under Articles 81 and 82 EC and associations of undertakings under Article 81 EC. Sports associations are undertakings where they themselves carry out economic activity, e.g., by commercially exploiting a sport event. Sports associations are associations of undertakings under Article 81 EC to the extent they constitute groupings of sport clubs/teams or athletes for which the practice of sport constitutes an economic activity. In *Piau* the CFI also held that the fact that a national association gathers both amateur and professional clubs/teams is of no importance as far as the classification as an association of undertakings is concerned. Article 82 EC does not include the concept of 'association of undertakings.' However, the CFI has found that even where a sports association is not itself active on a given market, it may be considered an undertaking under Article 82 EC to the extent the association is the emanation of its members which are active on the market.

International sports associations (such as the IOC, UEFA or FIFA) which have as their members national sports associations, are undertakings to the extent they themselves carry out activities of economic nature such as the conclusion of advertising contracts, the commercial exploitation of sport events or the conclusion of contracts relating to broadcasting rights. International sports associations not carrying out economic activities themselves may be associations of undertakings and may sometimes be also referred to as 'associations of associations of undertakings' under Article 81 EC. They also constitute undertakings under Article 82 EC to the extent they group members which in turn constitute undertakings.

4.2.1.4 Restrictions Under Articles 81(1) and 82 EC

National and/or international sports associations' also including European associations, are normally the bodies that adopt sporting rules, which sport clubs/teams and athletes need to adhere to. Sporting rules adopted by national or international sports associations may constitute agreements or decisions by undertakings or associations of undertakings within the meaning of *Article 81(1) EC*. Rules drawn up unilaterally by sporting associations consisting of undertakings will usually constitute decisions by an association of undertakings. Such sporting rules, like any other decisions or agreements, are prohibited if they have as their object or effect the restriction or distortion of competition within the common market and affect trade between Member States. Rules adopted by international sport associations will normally affect trade between Member States. However, in view of the fact that rules of national sport associations usually concern a sport in the whole territory of a given Member State and in light of today's high level of internationalisation of professional sport, rules adopted by national sport associations may often affect trade between Member States.

Article 82 EC prohibits any abuse by one or more undertakings of a dominant position within the common market or in a substantial part of it in so far as it may affect trade between Member States. For the purposes of applying this provision, the relevant market must be determined. As mentioned earlier, sports associations usually have practical monopolies in a given sport and may thus normally be considered dominant in the market of the organisation of sport events under Article 82 EC. Even where a sporting association is not active on a given market, it may be considered to hold a dominant position if it operates on that market through its members (e.g., sport clubs/teams). Sport clubs/teams (and athletes) may also hold a collective dominant position under Article 82 EC to the extent that they present themselves as a 'collective entity vis à vis their competitors, their trading partners and consumers' as a result of the implementation of rules adopted by a national or international sports association.

4.2.1.5 Sporting Rules Pursuing Legitimate Objectives Whose Effects are Inherent and Proportionate to Their Objectives

The ECJ has explicitly acknowledged in *Meca Medina* that even in cases where a sporting rule restricts the freedom of action of the athletes it may not breach Articles 81 and 82 EC to the extent the rule in question pursues a legitimate objective and its restrictive effects are inherent in the pursuit of that objective and are proportionate to it. The test adopted by the ECJ for sporting rules under Article 81 EC differs from the test under Article 39 and 49 EC (now: Articles 45 and 56 TFEU regarding free movement of persons/workers and of services respectively) where the ECJ examines whether the sporting rule is of 'purely sporting interest' (in which case the Articles 39 and 49 EC do not apply) or is based on 'reasons of an economic nature' in which case Article 39 and 49 EC apply.

Legitimate objectives of sporting rules will normally relate to the 'organisation and proper conduct of competitive sport' and may include, e.g., the ensuring of fair sport competitions with equal chances for all athletes, the ensuring of uncertainty of results, the protection of the athletes' health, the protection of the safety of spectators, the encouragement of training of young athletes, the ensuring of financial stability of sport clubs/teams or the ensuring of a uniform and consistent exercise of a given sport (the 'rules of the game'). The specificity of sport, i.e. the distinctive features setting sport apart from other economic activities, such as the interdependence between competing adversaries, will be taken into consideration when assessing the existence of a legitimate objective.

The restrictions caused by a sporting rule must be *inherent* in the pursuit of its objective. The ECJ found, e.g., that the penalties contained in the anti-doping rules in *Meca Medina* were inherent for the proper conduct of competitive sport and the healthy rivalry of athletes. Likewise, the prohibition on the ownership of two or several sport clubs/teams competing against each other was found by the Commission to be inherent for ensuring the uncertainty of results. Rules inherent in the organisation and proper conduct of competitive sport also include the 'rules of the game,' i.e., rules which determine the number of players, their function, duration of the competition/game etc. Obvious examples of rules of the game include the rule that a football team must have eleven players or a rule that regulates the dimensions of the goals. To the extent that rules of the game do not relate to economic activity, they would fall outside the scope of application of EC competition law.

The sporting rule must also be *proportionate* in relation to its objective in order for it not to infringe Articles 81(1) and 82 EC and must be applied in a transparent, objective and non-discriminatory manner. In *Meca Medina* the ECJ considered whether the limit for the presence of the banned substance in question in the athlete's body was disproportionate (i.e., too low) and concluded that the rules did not go beyond what was necessary to ensure the proper conduct of competitive sport. Consequently, the proportionality of each sporting rule will have to be assessed on a case-by-case basis while taking into account the relevant facts and circumstances.

4.2.1.6 Justification Under Article 81(3)

Where a restriction under Article 81(1) EC is found, such restriction may be justified under Article 81(3). Article 81(3) EC provides that the prohibition contained in Article 81(1) EC may be declared inapplicable in case of agreements which contribute to improving the production or distribution of goods or to promoting technical or economic progress, while allowing consumers a fair share of the resulting benefits, and which do not impose restrictions which are not indispensable to the attainment of these objectives and do not afford such undertakings the possibility of eliminating competition in respect of a substantial part of the products concerned. Such a justification is most likely to apply *where* a *rule is not inherent in the organisation or proper conduct of sport* so as to justify the application of *Wouters* but *where the beneficial effects of a rule outweigh its restrictive effects*.

4.2.1.7 Conclusions

The above considerations demonstrate that the application of Articles 81 and 82 EC provides *sufficient flexibility* to take account of the specificity of sport and does not impede sporting rules that pursue a legitimate objective (such as the organisation and proper conduct of sport), are indispensable (inherent) to achieve the objective and proportionate in light of the objective pursued. At the same time, the ECJ's *Meca Medina* judgment strongly confirms that it is not possible to predetermine an exhaustive list of sporting rules which breach Article 81 and/or 82 EC (or of those which do not) as has been suggested on various occasions. The areas covered by sporting rules are much too wide and too diverse as to possibly categorise them. Instead, it is necessary to examine the specific requirements of Articles 81 and 82 EC in each individual case. It is therefore only possible to clarify on a case-by-case basis which rules do not breach Articles 81 and 82 EC. The increasing body of case law at EU and national level will, however, assist in identifying the types of rules that may normally be considered not to infringe Articles 81 and 82 EC. A general exemption of sporting rules or of activities of sports associations is therefore neither possible nor warranted.

4.3 The Collective Selling of Sports Media Rights[6]

4.3.1 Introduction

For many media operators sports media rights are crucial and constitute 'vital input.' The European Commission found as early as 1991 that 'sport is ... particularly attractive to ... commercial operators whether as part of general entertainment channels or specialist channels. Audience ratings can be very high for certain events, and are also popular with commercial sponsors.' [In later decisions the Commission stated, e.g., that movies and sports are 'key sales drivers' for pay-TV operators. In view of the economic significance of broadcasting rights, the application of competition rules is of fundamental importance in this sector. For example, the broadcasting rights for the 2006 World Cup were sold by FIFA for around €1 billion to TV operators worldwide. The UK broadcasting rights for the three seasons of English Premiership football as of season 2007/2008 were sold by the English Football Association for around €2.5 billion (totalling €4.1 billion for the broadcasting rights on a worldwide basis).

Other than in the area of regulatory aspects of sport, the exercise of economic activity is generally not a debated issue in the field of sports media rights. All broadcasting organisations, including public television broadcasting organisations, are undertakings within the meaning of Articles 81 and 82 EC. The activities of acquiring and sublicensing television rights and the sale of advertising slots all constitute examples of activities of an economic nature covered by Articles 81 and 82 EC.

Competition relating to the sale and acquisition of sports media rights has three important features. Firstly, the *rapid evolution* of the media sector including new technological developments necessitates that market definitions are kept under constant review.

Secondly, the *supply and demand structure* as regards sports media rights is characterised by few powerful players at each level of the supply chain, which are competing for scarce and highly valuable sport rights: At the top of the value chain, in the *upstream markets*, initial rights owners (usually sports associations or clubs) sell rights of sport events to sports rights intermediaries, such as sports rights agencies or the European Broadcasting Union (EBU) or directly to retail operators. The intermediaries, which often acquire the initial media rights to a certain event in a product and geographical bundle, subsequently re-sell the rights to retail operators. The *downstream transmission markets* constitute the final stage of the value chain, covering the provision of sports media services to consumers by retail operators (e.g., broadcasting companies, internet service providers, mobile operators).

Thirdly, sports media rights are most attractive when broadcast live because once the outcome of an event is known the value of the right declines together with viewer interest.

[6] Cf., White Paper on Sport, pp. 78 et seq.; cf., in general, Blackshaw et al. 2009.

It is also important to note that the 'Television without frontiers' Directive in Article 3a sets out conditions allowing events which are considered to be of major importance for society, including sport events, to be broadcast freely to the public.[7] Each Member State may therefore draw up a list of events which have to be broadcast in unencoded form, even if exclusive rights have been purchased by pay-TV channels.

4.3.2 Market Definitions

Market definitions are particularly complex in the fast changing world of media rights. In the media sector, products and services are not always (or no longer) clearly separable and are, also due to technological or economic 'convergence,' often marketed in a bundle.

In previous Commission decisions, *upstream product markets* for the acquisition of sports media rights have been identified for certain audiovisual content. This was done on the basis of specific criteria, such as brand image, the ability to attract a particular audience, the configuration of that audience and advertising/sponsoring revenues. With regard to sport events, the Commission identified separate markets for the rights to broadcast sport events for the first time in 1996. Subsequently, the Commission has defined narrower markets, e.g., for (i) the broadcasting rights for certain major sport events (the Commission considered that there was a strong likelihood that distinct markets existed for the acquisition of broadcasting rights for some major sporting events such as the Olympic Games; and it confirmed that regular major sport events, i.e., sport events that take place throughout the year or throughout a significant time period each year such as Formula One and Moto Grand Prix races are not in the same market as major irregular sport events (e.g., Olympic Games) which take place for a few weeks every 4 years), (ii) the broadcasting (and new media) rights for football events played regularly throughout every year where national (non-representative/club) teams participate (national leagues and cups, the UEFA Champions league and the UEFA Cup (now: Europa League)), and (iii) the broadcasting rights for football events that do not take place regularly where national (representative) teams participate (e.g., the Football World Cup or the European Football Championship).

---

[7] Directive 97/36/EC of 30 June 1997 amending Council Directive 89/552/EEC on the coordination of certain provisions laid down by law, regulation or administrative action in Member States concerning the pursuit of television broadcasting activities, OJ 1997 L 202/6; now: Article 14 of the Audiovisual Media Services Council Directive, No. 2010/13/EU, OJ no. L 95 of 15 April 2010, and OJ L 263 of 6 October 2010 (corrigendum). The new Article 15 of the Audiovisual Media Services Directive enhances access of viewers to events of high interest for society (including sport events): broadcasters exercising exclusive rights to such events have to grant other broadcasters the right to use extracts for the purpose of short news reports (based on the right to information of European citizens).

The main *downstream product markets* that have been identified in past cases are: Pay TV (regardless of a further possible distinction, within Pay-TV, between Video on demand (VoD), Near Video on demand (NVoD) and Pay-per view (PPV)), free TV, and content services delivered via the Internet and mobile devices. With regard to TV markets, taking technological developments and a limited degree of substitutability into consideration, the Commission has repeatedly held that separate markets exist for pay TV and free TV. This conclusion has been based on the different trading relationships involved, the different conditions of competition, the price of the services, and the characteristics of the two types of television. With regard to new media, the Commission found in its decision-making practice separate downstream markets for on-demand sport content services delivered via wireless mobile devices or via the Internet.

With regard to the *geographic markets* the Commission has held thus far that the *downstream markets* are of a national character or at least confined to linguistic regions. The geographical borders of the *upstream markets* also tend to be national not only for national events (e.g., rights for national football leagues) but also for international sport events since such rights are normally also sold on a national basis. This is due to the national character of distribution as a result of national regulatory regimes, language barriers and cultural factors.

Considering the technological developments, market definitions may evolve in the future, warranting careful and continued market research on the accuracy of the market definition for each case situation.

4.3.3 Competition Concerns Resulting from the Behaviour of Sellers

4.3.3.1 Decision Making Practice

The Commission's decision making practice is limited thus far to cases relating to the joint selling of exclusive rights under Article 81 EC. No decisions have been adopted with regard to the behaviour of a single seller (e.g., sport associations or sports rights agencies) under Article 82 EC. It is important to note that the decisions and the remedies adopted in these decisions do not constitute an exhaustive list of remedies for future cases but they merely represent possible options to deal with competition issues arising in this area. The Commission may decide to adopt additional or different remedies in future cases.

4.3.3.1.1 Introduction

In the upstream market Article 81(1) EC applies to *joint selling agreements* leading to competition restrictions, like foreclosure and output limitation, that would unlikely have occurred in the absence of the agreements. Joint selling describes, for example, the situation where sport clubs entrust the selling of their media rights to their sports association which then sells the rights collectively on their behalf. A joint selling arrangement is a *horizontal* agreement which prevents the individual clubs each having a relatively small market share from individually competing in the sale of sports media rights. One price is applied to all rights collectively which constitutes price-fixing. In addition, the number of rights available in the upstream acquisition markets is often reduced which may create barriers to entry on downstream broadcasting markets and may lead to access foreclosure in these markets.

The Commission has recognised that joint selling may create *efficiencies* and accepted joint selling arrangements under Article 81(3) EC. A joint selling arrangement has the potential of improving the media product and its distribution to the advantage of football clubs, broadcasters and viewers. The Commission in its decisions has in particular identified three types of benefits:

- The creation of a *single point of sale* provides efficiencies by reducing transaction costs for football clubs and media operators
- *Branding* of the output creates efficiencies as it helps the media products getting a wider recognition and hence distribution
- The *creation of a league product*: This is a product that is focused on the competition as a whole rather than the individual football clubs participating in the competition. This is attractive to many viewers

In order to ensure that the positive effects of joint selling outweigh the negative effects on competition, the Commission has sought in past decisions to remedy the competition concerns resulting from the collective sale of exclusive sports media rights by attaching conditions to a declaration of exemption or making commitments binding on undertakings. The accepted solution in each case depended on the facts of the individual case including the degree of market power and the restrictive practices found.

A preliminary question that is of relevance for the assessment of joint selling concerns *the ownership of the rights*. In the UEFA Champions League decision, the Commission considered that the rights for the matches were not solely owned by UEFA, since the latter could at best be considered as a co-owner of those rights together with the football clubs for individual matches; the Commission also stated that the question of ownership is to be determined by national law. The question of the ownership is important because in cases where the rights are solely owned, e.g., by the football association, issues may arise under Article 82 EC rather than under Article 81 EC as the sale of rights would be carried out by a single seller and not jointly.

4.3.3.1.2 Decisions Adopted by the Commission

The Commission has decided on three major cases involving joint selling of rights to broadcast games played by football clubs on the basis of Article 81 EC, namely UEFA Champions League (UEFA CL), German Bundesliga (DFB) and FA

Premier League (FAPL).[8] In these cases the collectively sold exclusive sports rights risked to restrict output and to foreclose access for operators on the downstream broadcasting markets. In order to remedy the output restrictions and foreclosure effects caused by collective selling in UEFA CL, DFB and FAPL the Commission developed a number of (non-exhaustive) remedies, see below under Sect. 4.3.3.2, and established the conditions under which it considered that joint selling, in the specific circumstances of each respective case, would be permissible under Article 81 EC.

UEFA CL. In the UEFA CL decision the Commission for the first time accepted joint selling of football media rights and laid out the principles for a pro-competitive rights structure. The original arrangements provided for the sale of UEFA Champions League free and pay-TV rights on an exclusive basis in a single bundle to a single broadcaster per territory for several years in a row. Buyers had only one source of supply and a single large broadcaster per territory would acquire all free and pay-TV rights, to the exclusion of all others, resulting in a number of rights being left unexploited and output restrictions. Following Commission intervention, UEFA amended its joint selling arrangements. The available rights were unbundled into several packages (in total 14) enabling more than one broadcaster to acquire rights to the UEFA Champions League. The packages were sold on the basis of an objective and non-discriminatory tender procedure. Although UEFA had the exclusive right to sell the packages of live rights, individual clubs could sell certain live rights (package 4) relating to their matches, in case UEFA would fail to sell.

Certain restrictions remained however. Indeed, the exclusive sale of live rights by UEFA still prevented individual clubs from competing in the sale of those rights, a single price was fixed, broadcasters only had one point of supply in respect of most live rights and the exploitation of deferred rights was subject to limitations.

On the other hand, the Commission considered that joint selling also led to a number of positive effects and the Commission concluded that the amended joint selling agreement met the conditions for a justification under Article 81(3) EC.

The joint selling *improved the distribution of rights* to the UEFA Champions League through the creation of a quality branded product, exploited exclusively by UEFA and independent of the interests of individual clubs. The single point of sale enabled the acquisition of coverage for the whole UEFA Champions League season, allowing programming to be planned in advance. The only alternative to ensure coverage of the entire league would have been to acquire rights from many individual clubs. However, due to the knock-out nature of the UEFA Champions League this meant that a broadcaster could not know in advance which clubs would make it through to the end. Such an exercise was uneconomic especially as the value of individual club rights would plummet if that club was eliminated. The single point of sale therefore ensured full coverage and reduced the broadcasters' financial risk. Distribution was further improved by ensuring that certain live rights could be sold

[8] Case 37398, OJ 2003 L 291/25; Case 37214, OJ 2005 L 134/46; and Case 38173, OJ C 7.

by individual clubs where UEFA had been unable to sell the rights within one week after the draw for the first round for the UEFA Champions League.

Consumers benefited directly from the improved distribution of rights and increased coverage created by the joint selling. In addition, the efficiencies created by the single point of sale allowed broadcasters to invest more in improving production and transmission. Access to deferred and archived content was also made more readily accessible.

The Commission considered that the restrictions on competition were *indispensable* to the creation of a UEFA Champions League branded product sold via a single point of sale and the related benefits. UEFA had a legitimate interest in creating a Champions League focused product separate from the interests of individual clubs, as it benefited UEFA, the clubs and the supporters/viewers of the Champions League. The exclusive joint selling of live rights, without parallel sales through individual clubs was also indispensable to ensuring the quality and attractiveness of the UEFA Champions League product to broadcasters.

The joint selling arrangements were *not likely to eliminate competition* in respect of a substantial part of the football rights market because substitutable rights to other football events taking place regularly throughout the year were available (e.g., national football league rights). In addition, both UEFA and individual clubs sold a number of categories of UEFA Champions League rights in parallel ensuring multiple sources of supply for interested buyers.

DFB and FAPL. In the sales process of the German and English top national football leagues, the Bundesliga and the FAPL respectively, similar competition concerns arose as those found in UEFA CL These were cases of principally national character that had been opened by the Commission prior to modernisation. In the case of DFB, it is also noteworthy that the German Act against Restraints on Competition contained an exception for the joint selling of sports media rights between 1999 and 2005. Following modernisation, it is less likely—but not excluded—that the Commission would intervene in this type of cases. Following modernisation, it is less likely—but not excluded—that the Commission would intervene in this type of cases. In order to address these concerns, in both cases commitments were made to amend the original joint selling arrangements by the respective leagues on behalf of their individual club members. The commitments offered by both the Deutscher Liga-Fußballverband (the German Leage Association (GLA), the rights-holder for the Bundesliga matches) and the FAPL (the rights holder for the Premiership matches) were made legally binding under Article 9(1) of Regulation 1/2003. The commitments from both the GLA and the FAPL included the unbundling of rights into separate rights packages for TV broadcasting and mobile platforms, the possibility for individual clubs to exploit certain unsold rights and rights unused by the initial purchaser, as well as the exploitation of deferred rights and rights for the new internet broadcasting (the internet broadcasting rights were sold as a separate package in DFB but not in FAPL) and telephony broadcasting markets. Rights were to be disposed of using a public tender procedure and exclusive rights contracts were not to exceed three football seasons.

In addition, as regards the FAPL, the open and competitive bidding process for the rights packages was made subject to scrutiny by an independent Monitoring Trustee. Furthermore, no single purchaser was allowed to acquire all the live rights packages, as first applied from the sale of rights to the 2007/2008 season (no single buyer rule). This commitment was negotiated by the Commission in order to end the monopoly of British Sky Broadcasting Group plc ('BSkyB') over the rights to the FAPL in the United Kingdom. Following the acquisition in May 2006 of two of the six FAPL live rights packages by Setanta, an Irish pay-TV sports channel, BSkyB ceased to be the exclusive holder of live Premier League matches.

4.3.3.2 Remedies Applied in Previous Cases to Address Competition Concerns

The Commission's practice highlights a number of possible approaches which, separately or in combination, have been used in order to address competition concerns resulting from joint selling arrangements concerning exclusive sports media rights under Article 81 EC. The list of remedies below is *not exhaustive or binding* for future cases and different or new remedies may be adopted depending on the specific circumstances of a given case.

4.3.3.2.1 Tendering

In order to reduce the risk of *foreclosure* effects in the downstream markets in UEFA CL, DFB and FAPL the Commission required the collective sellers on the upstream market to organise a competitive bidding process under non-discriminatory and transparent terms ('non-discriminatory and transparent *tendering*'). This approach gives all potential buyers an opportunity to compete for the rights.

4.3.3.2.2 Limitation of the Duration of Exclusive Vertical Contracts

The Commission acknowledges the need for a certain degree of exclusivity to protect the value of sports media rights, in particular live rights. The risk of long-term market *foreclosure* has been addressed in UEFA CL, DFB and FAPL by requiring the collective selling entity to limit the *duration* of the exclusive rights offered in vertical contracts to no more than three football seasons ('sun setting'). In a particular decision, the commitments offered went even further; the notifying party undertook to buy football rights for no longer than two seasons at the time and only for satellite distribution. Longer contract duration would risk creating a situation where a successful buyer would be able to establish a dominant position on the downstream market reducing the scope for effective ex ante competition in the context of future bidding rounds.

4.3.3.2.3 Limitation of the Scope of Exclusive Vertical Contracts

In UEFA CL, DFB and FAPL the Commission sought to limit the risk of market *foreclosure* resulting from a single buyer acquiring all the valuable rights—by obliging the collective selling entity to unbundle the media rights in separate packages, thereby limiting the scope of the exclusivity. More specifically the Commission required:

- *A reasonable amount of different packages*: The creation of two or more independently valid live packages was required. The reason for this was that as live rights are often sold to one media operator, the creation of various packages would enable more than one media operator to acquire the rights.
- *Meaningful packages*: The large size of packages may create foreclosure concerns and the Commission has, e.g., in FAPL, requested the sale of several meaningful packages to enable also less powerful operators with less financial means to bid for the packages that suited their needs. At the same time, a package may not be 'meaningful' (independently valid) if it is much smaller than other packages. The objective is to allow the respective purchasers of the package(s) to compete effectively on the downstream market.
- *Earmarked packages* for special markets/platforms: Due to the strong asymmetric value of rights for different distribution platforms, access to sports media rights may be foreclosed to downstream market operators in certain evolving markets or platforms (for example 3G networks or internet markets). By providing for specific packages for certain distribution platforms ('earmarking') in UEFA CL, DFB and FAPL mobile operators and internet service providers were enabled to acquire rights. In the Bundesliga decision, three separate packages for live rights were earmarked for (i) TV (pay-TV and free-TV), (ii) internet and (iii) mobile phones. In the Premier League decision, only two separate packages for live rights were earmarked for (i) audio-visual rights on a 'technology neutral basis' (including pay-TV, free-TV and internet) and (ii) audio-visual mobile rights. This was due to the increasing convergence of the TV and internet platforms (e.g., as a result of IPTV). The question as to which type of markets or platforms should be earmarked (e.g., to protect or encourage their development) will depend in particular on the market conditions in the country/countries in question.
- *No conditional bidding*: In FAPL, an obligation was imposed on the seller to accept only stand-alone unconditional bids for each individual package. The rights would be sold to the highest standalone bidder. Such unconditional selling is aimed at preventing a powerful buyer interested in acquiring the most valuable package(s) from offering a bonus on condition that all the valuable rights are sold to it, thus inciting initial rights owners not to sell at least some packages to competitors in the same market or operators in neighbouring markets.

4.3.3.2.4 Fall-Back Option, Use Obligation, Parallel Exploitation

In order to limit the risk of output restrictions caused by the collective sale of exclusive rights, the Commission required in UEFA CL, DFB and FAPL that there should be *no unused rights*. Rights that are not sold by the collective entity within a certain time period fell back to the individual clubs for parallel exploitation ('*no hoarding*'). In addition, the Commission ensured market availability of less valuable rights such as deferred highlights and new media rights by imposing the *parallel exploitation* of these rights by individual clubs and UEFA in UEFA CL.

4.3.3.2.5 No Single Buyer Obligation

In order to prevent that all packages of valuable live rights were sold to the dominant pay-TV operator in the United Kingdom, BSkyB, the Commission considered it necessary to impose a *no single buyer* obligation on the collective selling entity in the FAPL decision. Over a number of years prior to the FAPL decision BSkyB had acquired all the valuable live-TV packages that were made available on the market by the joint seller. Additional remedies were therefore deemed necessary to prevent downstream foreclosure and to ensure access also of other market players. Importantly, in the absence of such remedies there was a risk that competition would remain eliminated well beyond the duration of any on-going contract as due to the long-term presence of the dominant buyer competition was ineffective. It is noteworthy that these considerations were of relevance only in FAPL whereas due to the structure of the markets the issue did not arise in the UEFA CL and DFB cases. In UEFA CL there was no need to examine the individual national market situations. In DFB there was also no need at that time to look into the vertical effects, considering the value of the different packages and the distribution of market players (also taking into account the bankruptcy of Kirch which had previously acquired the Bundesliga rights).

It should be noted in this context that in the DFB decision the Commission reserved the possibility of opening a separate investigation at the downstream level in case several packages with exclusive exploitation rights would be acquired by a single purchaser ('vertical reserve'). The *ex ante* risk that one single buyer would acquire all the packages in a non-discriminatory tender procedure was rather small, as due to the bankruptcy of the company Kirch no powerful pay-TV operator was present in the German downstream market. Such an investigation would thus target the dominant buyer rather than the seller. However, it would not be excluded to act also against the joint seller as the emergence on the market of a dominant buyer would likely constitute a material new fact within the meaning of Article 9(2) of Regulation 1/2003 justifying the re-opening of the procedure.

4.3.3.2.6 Trustee

The Commission in FAPL also required that the tender procedure was overseen by a *trustee* that reported back to the Commission to ensure and guarantee that the tender procedure was undertaken in a fair, reasonable and non-discriminatory manner.

4.3.4 Conclusion

The remedies described above are examples of remedies that have been used to date to address competition concerns arising in the area of sports media rights. However, it is important to note that there is no 'standard' or 'one-size-fits-all' approach that applies to cases involving sports media rights. The Commission will have to carefully assess each individual case in order to determine, where necessary, the appropriate remedy or remedies, taking into account the specific facts and circumstances, in particular also considering the technological developments of the relevant markets.

4.4 The Dutch Equestrian Case[9]

4.4.1 The Contested Procedure

(1) For the purpose of determining the calendar for category I competitions and international competitions, the rules of the Dutch National Federation of Equestrian Sports (KNHS) state that 'both for competition participants and competition organisers it is important to aim to determine a competition calendar which from a sporting point of view and a commercial point of view coincides as much as possible with the wishes of all parties involved.' For this reason, in the year preceding a certain calendar year, a planning procedure is followed 'in order to be able on time to determine a balanced competition calendar for that calendar year.'

(2) Rule 1.2 states that when deciding on applications for international competitions in the Netherlands (1) Per date and per discipline only one application for the organisation of a category I competition can be approved on the condition that no Dutch championship is being organised on that date for the age category concerned in the discipline concerned (2) If there are several applications for the organisation of an international competition in the same discipline the following

[9] Naming by analogy of the so-called *Swiss Equestrian Case*, Gundel v The International Equestrian Federation (FEI), decided by the Swiss Federal Supreme Court on15 March 1993, concerning the legal status of CAS awards.

becomes relevant (2(a)) a competition application for an international competition at level 4* or 5* is always given priority over an application for an international competition at level 1*, 2* or 3* (2(b)) the KNHS argues in favour of the competition application for which it is true that the requested date is the traditional annual date on which an international competition is organised in the discipline concerned (2(c)) it will be attempted by mutual agreement to select another date for the organisation which does not traditionally and annually organise a competition in the discipline concerned. In this, the possibilities for an alternative competition programme are also considered (3) If, in the case of bottlenecks concerning the above, competition organisers reach agreement on an alternative solution it is possible in consultation with the to depart from the starting points given. (4) If, in the case of bottlenecks concerning the above, competition organisers are unable to reach agreement on an alternative solution, the Calendar Commission will issue a binding decision.

4.4.2 The EU Competition Law Provisions

(1) Article 101 Treaty on the Functioning of the European Union (TFEU) (ex 81 TEC) provides that: 101(1) The following shall be prohibited as incompatible with the internal market: all agreements between undertakings, decisions by associations of undertakings and concerted practices which may affect trade between Member States and which have as their object or effect the prevention, restriction or distortion of competition within the internal market, and in particular those which: (a) directly or indirectly fix purchase or selling prices or any other trading conditions; (b) limit or control production, markets, technical development, or investment; (c) share markets or sources of supply; (d) apply dissimilar conditions to equivalent transactions with other trading parties, thereby placing them at a competitive disadvantage; (e) make the conclusion of contracts subject to acceptance by the other parties of supplementary obligations which, by their nature or according to commercial usage, have no connection with the subject of such contracts.

(2) Article 101 (2) provides that: Any agreements or decisions prohibited pursuant to this Article shall be automatically void and 101(3) states that: The provisions of para 1 may, however, be declared inapplicable in the case of: any agreement or category of agreements between undertakings, any decision or category of decisions by associations of undertakings, any concerted practice or category of concerted practices, which contributes to improving the production or distribution of goods or to promoting technical or economic progress, while allowing consumers a fair share of the resulting benefit, and which does not: (a) impose on the undertakings concerned restrictions which are not indispensable to the attainment of these objectives; (b) afford such undertakings the possibility of eliminating competition in respect of a substantial part of the products in question.

(3) Article 102 (ex 81 TEC) provides that: Any abuse by one or more undertakings of a dominant position within the internal market or in a substantial part of it shall be prohibited as incompatible with the internal market in so far as it may affect trade between Member States. Such abuse may, in particular, consist in: (a) directly or indirectly imposing unfair purchase or selling prices or other unfair trading conditions; (b) limiting production, markets or technical development to the prejudice of consumers; (c) applying dissimilar conditions to equivalent transactions with other trading parties, thereby placing them at a competitive disadvantage; (d) making the conclusion of contracts subject to acceptance by the other parties of supplementary obligations which, by their nature or according to commercial usage, have no connection with the subject of such contracts.

4.4.3 First Consideration: Is the Sports Association that Adopted the Rule Considered an Undertaking or an Association of Undertakings?

(1) According to the Court of Justice, 'the concept of an undertaking encompasses every entity in an economic activity, regardless of the legal status of the entity and the way it is financed.'[10] Economic activity is any activity consisting of 'offering goods or services on the market.'[11]

(2) It is now well established in EU law that sports bodies, including clubs, teams, national associations and international federations are undertakings within the meaning of Article 101 and 102 TFEU to the extent they carry out economic activity. In *Walrave*, the Court of Justice held that 'having regard to the objectives of the Community, the practice of sport is subject to Community law only in so far as it constitutes an economic activity within the meaning of Article 2 of the Treaty.'[12]

(3) In the White Paper on Sport the Commission states that sports associations are undertakings where they themselves carry out economic activity, for example through the commercial exploitation of the sport.[13] It added that sports associations are associations of undertakings under Article 101 TFEU where they constitute groupings of sport clubs/teams or athletes for which the practice of sport constitutes an economic activity.

---

[10] Case 41/90 *Höfner v Macroton* ECR 1991, I-1979, para 21.

[11] Case 118/85 *Commission v Italy* ECR 1987 2599, para 7.

[12] Case 36/74 *Walrave and Koch v Association Union Cycliste Internationale* [1974] ECR 1405 para 4. Hereafter referred to as *Walrave*.

[13] Commission of the European Communities, Commission staff working document. The EU and Sport: Background and Context, SEC(2007) 935, pp. 66–67

(4) In *Piau*, the Court of First Instance (CFI) held that the fact that a national association gathers both amateur and professional clubs/teams is of no importance as far as the classification as an association of undertakings is concerned.[14]

(5) The concept of an 'association of undertakings' is not to be found in Article 102 TFEU which deals with abuses of dominant market positions. However, the CFI has found that even where a sports association is not itself active on a given market, it may be considered an undertaking under Article 102 TFEU to the extent the association is the emanation of its members which are active on the market.[15]

(6) In the case of *MOTOE*, the European Court first had to establish whether a not-for-profit association (The Automobile and Touring Club of Greece—'ELPA') with statutory powers to authorise applications for the organisation of motorcycling competitions in Greece was an undertaking. In scrutinising the functions of ELPA, the Court found that ELPA organises motorcycling events in Greece and enters into sponsorship, advertising and insurance contracts designed to exploit those events commercially. Therefore, those activities constitute a source of income for ELPA.[16] This was sufficient to satisfy the economic activity test.

(7) The contested rule described in Sect. 4.4.1 above (the authorisation rule) is a rule of a national association, the KNHS. National associations perform both regulatory and commercial functions and in practice it is often difficult to separate the two. If it can be shown that the functions of the KNHS are no more than purely regulatory in nature, then the body will not be considered an undertaking subject to the application of EU competition law. The question of whether EU competition law can be raised in this case therefore becomes irrelevant.

(8) It is clear that the contested rule provides the KNHS with the authority to decide which event to authorise in cases where requests have been made to stage more than one event which are to be organised on more or less the same date. The decision to approve or reject a request will therefore entail economic consequences for the applicants, who are assumed to be private companies seeking to make a profit from the organisation of equestrian events.

(9) However, the mere fact that economic effects flow from the exercise of its regulatory function may not, in itself, be sufficient to establish it as an undertaking. For example, in *Wouters* the Court found that the Bar of the Netherlands could not be considered an undertaking despite economic effects flowing from the exercise of its regulatory functions.[17]

(10) Whether the KNHS is to be considered an undertaking will require scrutiny of its functions. For example, is it engaged in the economic exploitation of the sport such as entering into sponsorship, advertising and insurance contracts? From

---

[14] Case T-193/02, *Laurent Piau v Commission of the European Communities* [2005] ECR II-209, para 70. Hereafter referred to as *Piau*.

[15] *Piau*, paras 112 & 116.

[16] Case 49/07 *Motoe v Ellinko Dimosio*, [2008] ECR I-4863, para 23, hereafter referred to as *Motoe*.

[17] Case 309/99 *Wouters and others v Algemene Raad van de Nederlandse Orde van Advocaten*, [2002] ECR I-1577, hereafter referred to as *Wouters*

the KNHS website, it appears that the national association has entered into a sponsorship agreement with Rabobank and this is due to continue to 2012. It would appear that this is a source of income for the KNHS.

(11) Given this, and the connection between sponsorship and event organisation over which the KNHS plays a central role, it would be reasonable to assume that for the purposes of EU law, the KNHS is an undertaking carrying out economic activity.

4.4.4 Second Consideration: Does the Contested Rule Restrict Competition Within the Meaning of Article 101 TFEU or Constitute an Abuse of a Dominant Position Under Article 102 TFEU?

(1) Rules adopted by sports bodies, such as national associations, may constitute agreements or decisions by undertakings or associations of undertakings within the meaning of Article 101 TFEU. These rules are prohibited if they have as their *object* or *effect* the restriction or distortion of competition within the common market and affect trade between Member States.

(2) It is common for sports governing bodies to adopt authorisation rules. It is conceivable that a governing body might employ such rules to exclude competitors from organising rival competitions in an attempt to preserve their regulatory and commercial authority. In such circumstances, the *object* of the contested rule may indeed be to distort competition. In *Formula One*, the European Commission considered that the Fédération Internationale de l'Automobile (FIA) had used such authorisation rules to block the organisation of races which competed with the events organised or promoted by the FIA.[18]

(3) Authorisation rules may serve the legitimate aim of ensuring the proper functioning of sporting competition in so far as they promote the efficient and effective scheduling of events. The argument is as follows: competition participants and spectators benefit from a schedule of events so that clashes can be avoided and competition organisers benefit commercially from an effective competition calendar.

(4) It stands to reason that a sufficient number of participants are required to make an event viable and competition between events being staged on the same day may call into question that viability.

(5) It might also be raised that it falls within the expert judgment of a governing body to determine what constitutes a balanced and viable schedule/timetable. In this regard, it might be claimed that only a governing body is in a position to

[18] COMP 35.163, Notice published at OJ 2001 C169/5. See also Commission press release, 30 October 2001, IP/01/1523, 'Commission closes its investigation into Formula One and other four-wheel motor sports'.

balance the competing interests of stakeholders. In *Deliège* the Court of Justice acknowledged that 'it naturally falls to the bodies concerned, such as organisers of tournaments, sports federations or professional athletes' associations, to lay down appropriate rules and to make their selections in accordance with them. [68] In that connection, it must be conceded that the delegation of such a task to the national federations, which normally have the necessary knowledge and experience, is the arrangement adopted in most sporting disciplines, which is based in principle on the existence of a federation in each country.'[19]

(6) If the above arguments in support of authorisation rules are to be accepted, the *object* of the rule is not to distort competition.

(7) However, the mere fact that authorisation rules may not have as there *object* a restriction of competition is not sufficient to remove it from the EU competition law prohibitions. It is also necessary to assess whether the *effect* of the rule is restrictive and if so, whether this effect is inherent in the pursuit of the objectives being pursued.

(8) In *Wouters* the Court of Justice stated that in determining whether an agreement amounts to a restriction, 'account must first of all be taken of the overall context in which the decision of the association of undertakings was taken or produces its effects. More particularly, account must be taken of its objectives ... it has then to be considered whether the consequential effects restrictive of competition are inherent in the pursuit of those objectives.'[20]

(9) This methodological framework has been employed in the sports related competition law cases of *ENIC*[21] and *Meca-Medina*.[22] In the sporting context, the *Wouters* approach is now likely to be favoured by the Commission and the Court over the previous method, often referred to as the 'sporting exception.' Prior to *Meca-Medina* it is conceivable that authorisation rules would be defended by those imposing such rules on the grounds cited in the *Walrave* judgment, para 8. Referring to nationality discrimination in national team sports, the Court of Justice held that the prohibition on nationality discrimination 'does not affect the composition of sport teams, in particular national teams, the formation of which is a question of *purely sporting interest* and as such has nothing to do with economic activity.'[23]

(10) The purely sporting defence was expunged in *Meca-Medina* in which the Court held that 'it is apparent that the mere fact that a rule is purely sporting in nature does not have the effect of removing from the scope of the Treaty the person

---

[19] Joined Cases 51/96 and 191/97 *Deliège v. Ligue francophone de Judo et disciplines Associeés Asb* [2000] ECR I-2549, paras 67–68.

[20] *Wouters*, points 97 and 110.

[21] Case COMP/37 806: *ENIC/UEFA*, hereafter referred to as *ENIC*. See also Commission Press Release IP/02/942, 27 June 2002, 'Commission closes investigation into UEFA rule on multiple ownership of football clubs.'

[22] Case 519/04 P *David Meca-Medina and Igor Majcen* v *Commission* [2006] ECR I-6991, hereafter referred to as *Meca-Medina*.

[23] *Walrave* para 8.

engaging in the activity governed by that rule or the body which has laid it down.'[24]

(11) The correct assessment on whether authorisation rules amount to a restriction is the *Wouters* method. In this sense, the question to pose is whether the consequential effects of the contested rule are inherent in the pursuit of the stated objectives.

(12) The contested rule states that 'per date and per discipline only one application for the organisation of a category I competition can be approved on the condition that no Dutch championship is being organised on that date for the age category concerned in the discipline concerned.' The justification for this rule appears to be that 'both for competition participants and competition organisers it is important to aim to determine a competition calendar which from a sporting point of view and a commercial point of view coincides as much as possible with the wishes of all parties involved.'

(13) The legitimate objectives of sporting rules will generally relate to the 'organisation and proper conduct of competitive sport.'[25] In this connection, the Commission and the Court of Justice have been willing to apply EU law in such a way that pays respect to certain specificities of sport, such as the need to promote competitive balance, the need to encourage the education and training of young players and the need to preserve the integrity of sporting competition.

(14) The KNHS will attempt to connect the authorisation rule with the legitimate objective of ensuring the proper functioning of the sport. In other words there needs to be some system for organising the sporting calendar so as to avoid conflicts. In many sports this argument would be accepted as participants cannot be in two places at once and competition may undermine the economic viability of the events. If this is to be accepted, then it becomes more likely that the consequential effects of the contested rule will be considered inherent in the pursuit of the stated objectives and the rule will then, subject to proportionality control, fall outside the scope of the Treaty.

(15) These arguments are strengthened further if one considers the counterfactual argument. In other words, could sport operate in the absence of authorisation rules? Whilst arguments between two event organisers may be finely balanced and it may be possible to argue for the staging of both events without negative consequences, what of a scenario in which multiple event organisers wished to stage an event on the same day(s)? In such circumstances it would appear reasonable that a governing body would wish to adopt some procedure for authorising events so as to avoid potentially damaging conflicts.

(16) The counter argument is that the restrictive effects cannot be considered to be inherent in the pursuit of the stated objectives. It would need to be shown that the staging of more than one competition per date and per discipline is not

---

[24] *Meca-Medina* para 27.

[25] *Meca-Medina* paras 45 and 46.

damaging to the sport. This could be established, for example, by demonstrating that there are a sufficient number of riders able to participate in both events.

(17) Further, if it could be established that similar events take place in other member states close by, such as Belgium, without apparent damaging consequences, the argument could be undermined further.

(18) But even if these facts could be established, they do not necessarily undermine the *principle* of authorisation rules, just the fitness for purpose of specific regimes such as the one adopted by the KNHS. This is discussed further below.

4.4.4.1 Proportionality

(19) Not only must a sporting rule pursue a legitimate objective, it must also be proportionate in relation to that objective in order for it not to infringe Articles 101 and 102 TFEU. It must also be applied in a transparent, objective and non-discriminatory manner.

(20) If the objective of the rule is accepted (that it ensures the timely construction of a balanced calendar which benefits the relevant stakeholders), then the focus shifts onto whether the authorisation rule in question goes beyond what is necessary to achieve the stated objective. In other words, how else could the objective be achieved?

(21) Para 2 of the contested rule states that if there are several applications for the organisation of an international competition in the same discipline the following becomes relevant: (a) a competition application for an international competition at level 4* or 5* is always given priority over an application for an international competition at level 1*, 2* or 3* (b) the KNHS argues in favour of the competition application for which it is true that the requested date is the traditional annual date on which an international competition is organised in the discipline concerned (c) it will be attempted by mutual agreement to select another date for the organisation which does not traditionally and annually organise a competition in the discipline concerned. In this, the possibilities for an alternative competition programme are also considered.

(22) First, it will need to be considered whether events compete in the same market. Do these events attract the same riders for instance? Therefore, is it always reasonable to give priority to higher ranked events even though they may not compete in the same market as lower ranked events?

(23) Second, to what extent does the recognition of historic rights unfairly obstruct entry into the market for new competition organisers? Presumably, existing event organisers have already laid claim to the most commercially valuable dates in the calendar. The recognition of such historic rights appears to preclude access to the market for new market entrants, or those event organisers wishing to change dates. This rule has the potential to be anti-competitive and discriminatory as it is reasonable to assume that historic rights are more likely than not to be held by Dutch event organisers than non-Dutch organisers. Given that events are organised in other Member States of the EU, it is reasonable to assume that non-Dutch event organisers who are active in other national markets are unable to penetrate the Dutch market. Less restrictive and discriminatory means of achieving the objective could be considered, such as an open and transparent tendering process.

(24) Finally, one needs to consider wider questions of how decisions (such as the contested rule) are arrived at within the sport and whether changes in prevailing governance standards could mitigate against the emergence of such disputes.

(25) In this connection, the Commission argued in the White Paper on Sport that governance issues in sport should fall within a territory of autonomy and that most challenges can be addressed through self-regulation which must however be 'respectful of good governance principles.'[26]

(26) This built on an earlier intervention made by the Member States during the Nice Treaty deliberations in 2000 in which the European Council stressed 'its support for the independence of sports organisations and their right to organise themselves through appropriate associative structures. It recognises that, with due regard for national and Community legislation and on the basis of a *democratic* and *transparent* method of operation, it is the task of sporting organisations to organise and promote their particular sports, particularly as regards the specifically sporting rules applicable … in the way which they think best reflects their objectives.'

(27) In this light, it needs to be considered whether the current approach adopted by the KHNS to setting the events calendar pays sufficient attention to these principles. For example, given that the rule is designed to protect the interest of stakeholders, what is level of consultation with participants and event organisers? Do they have a voice within existing decision making structures?

(28) Finally, para 4 of the contested rule states that if 'in the case of bottlenecks concerning the above, competition organisers are unable to reach agreement on an alternative solution, the Calendar Commission will issue a binding decision.' It is not clear from this statement whether this affords the parties a right of a hearing and an appeal. In *Motoe*, a case also involving authorisation rules in sport, the Court of Justice held that there needs to be a means of appealing a negative decision.[27]

4.4.4.2 Application of Article 102 TFEU

(29) Article 102 TFEU prohibits any abuse by an undertaking of a dominant position within the common market or in a substantial part of it in so far as it may

---

[26] Commission of the European Communities (2007), 'White Paper on Sport', COM(2007) 391 final, s.4.

[27] *Motoe*, para 53.

affect trade between Member States. For this provision of the Treaty to apply, an analysis of the relevant market must be undertaken.

(30) In sport it is common for sports governing bodies to hold practical monopolies. Many sports operate an organisational structure in which a single entity assumes control of the sport at global level, an affiliated body assumes responsibility for the sport at regional (European) level and another affiliated body regulates the sport at national level.

(31) The Court has made clear that the concept of a 'dominant position' under Article 102 TFEU concerns a position of economic strength held by an undertaking, which enables it to prevent effective competition from being maintained on the relevant market by giving it the power to behave to an appreciable extent independently of its competitors, its customers and, ultimately, consumers.[28]

(32) The KNHS is in one such position of economic strength as it has the power to authorise the organisation of events on the Dutch territory, a power which effectively regulates the access of undertakings to that relevant market.

(33) However, Article 102 TFEU only prohibits the *abuse* of a dominant position, it does not prohibit market power *per se*. In determining whether the conduct of the undertaking amounts to an abuse, one needs to consider that the KNHS commercially exploits equestrian events in the Netherlands through, for example, entering into sponsorship contracts.

(34) It also needs to be established whether the KNHS is itself active in the market for the organisation of equestrian events in the Netherlands.

(35) Given one or both of these situations detailed in (33) and (34), there is a strong case for the Court's *MOTOE* reasoning to be applied. In this case, ELPA both organised and commercially exploited motorcycling events in Greece whilst simultaneously acting as the authorising body for applications for the staging of new events. This, the Court found, was a conflict of interest as it gave ELPA an advantage over competitors which could lead to market foreclosure.[29]

(36) The two cases display further similarities given that the KNHS decision (it would appear) cannot be appealed, as was also the case in *MOTOE*. Commenting on this issue, the Court in *MOTOE* found that 'such a rule, which gives a legal person such as ELPA the power to give consent to applications for authorisation to organise motorcycling events without that power being made subject by that rule to restrictions, obligations and review, could lead the legal person entrusted with giving that consent to distort competition by favouring events which it organises or those in whose organisation it participates.'[30]

(37) The conclusion drawn by the Court in *MOTOE* was that 'a legal person whose activities consist not only in taking part in administrative decisions authorising the organisation of motorcycling events, but also in organising such events itself and in entering, in that connection, into sponsorship, advertising and

---

[28] *Motoe* para 37.

[29] *Motoe* para 51.

[30] *Motoe* para 52.

insurance contracts, falls within the scope of Articles 82 EC and 86 EC. Those articles preclude a national rule which confers on a legal person, which organises motorcycling events and enters, in that connection, into sponsorship, advertising and insurance contracts, the power to give consent to applications for authorisation to organise such competitions, without that power being made subject to restrictions, obligations and review.'[31]

(38) The *MOTOE* judgment represents a softening of the Commission's approach adopted in *Formula One*. In this case, the Commission objected to the rules of the FIA which had a number of consequences on the market for the organisation of motor racing competitions. In particular, the FIA was accused of abusing a dominant position in breach of Article 102 TFEU by using its regulatory monopoly to maintain its commercial strength. In 2001, the Commission adopted a Notice under Article 19(3) of Regulation 17/62, signalling its satisfaction with undertakings made by the FIA to the effect of making internal structural changes which were designed to separate the FIA's regulatory function from its commercial exploitation of Formula One, thus reducing restrictions on competitors.

(39) In light of the above, it is reasonable to assume that if a conflict of interest is identified in the functions of the KNHS, rather than requiring a pure separation between the commercial and regulatory functions of the KNHS, the Commission and Court of Justice would wish to see improvements made in the governance standards applicable in that sport. For example, new authorisation rules should be transparent, objectively justified, non-discriminatory and consistently applied and could be negotiated with relevant stakeholders with decisions subject to a hearing and independent appeal. In these circumstances, it would be difficult to identify an 'abuse' of power by the governing body as safeguards in the system counter potentially self-interested decision making.

4.4.5 Third Consideration: Is Trade Between Member States Affected?

(1) Articles 101 and 102 TFEU only apply to the acts of undertakings within the European Union that have an effect on trade between Member States. The anti-competitive effects must also be appreciable.

(2) In the White Paper on Sport the Commission concluded that rules adopted by *international* sport associations will normally affect trade between Member States. However, in view of the fact that rules of *national* sport associations usually concern a sport in the whole territory of a given Member State and in light of today's high level of internationalisation of professional sport, rules adopted by national sport associations may often affect trade between Member States.[32]

---

[31] *Motoe* para 53.

[32] Commission of the European Communities, Commission staff working document. The EU and Sport: Background and Context, SEC (2007) 935, footnote 178.

(3) In *MOTOE*, the Court held that the assessment of whether the effect on trade between Member States is appreciable must take account of the conduct of the dominant undertaking in question, in so far as Article 101 TFEU precludes all conduct which is capable of affecting freedom of trade in a manner which might harm the attainment of the objectives of a single market between the Member States, in particular by sealing off domestic markets or by affecting the structure of competition within the single market.[33]

(4) It continued by stating that the fact that the conduct of an undertaking in a dominant position relates only to the marketing of products in a single Member State is not sufficient to preclude the possibility that trade between Member States might be affected. Such conduct may have the effect of reinforcing the partitioning of markets on a national basis, thereby holding up the economic interpenetration which the Treaty is designed to bring about.[34]

(5) In light of the dominant position held by the KNHS in the national market and given that its authorisation rules have the potential to partition the European market along national lines, it seems that the effect on trade requirement is met.

(6) That said, some authority on the partitioning of national markets does exist. In *Mouscron*, the French communauté urbaine de Lille had lodged a complaint against UEFA under Article 82 EC (now 102 TFEU) challenging UEFA's rule that for clubs competing in UEFA competitions each club must play its home match at its own ground. The Belgian football club Excelsior Mouscron had requested a one off switch to Lille in France and had been refused on these grounds. The Commission rejected the complaint as it considered the 'home and away from home' rule did not fall within the scope of Articles 81 and 82 EC (now 101 and 102 TFEU). The Commission found that the organisation of football on a national territorial basis was *not called into question by Community law*. The Commission considered the rule indispensable for the organisation of national and international competitions in view of ensuring equality of chances between clubs. The Commission also found that the rule did not go beyond what was necessary.[35]

4.4.6 Fourth Consideration: Does the Rule Fulfil the Conditions of Article 101(3) TFEU?

(1) If the contested rule is found to amount to a restriction under Article 101(1) TFEU, such a restriction may be justified under Article 101(3). Article 101(3) provides that the prohibition contained in Article 101(1) may be declared inapplicable in case of agreements which contribute to improving the production or

---

[33] *Motoe* para 41.

[34] *Motoe* para 42.

[35] Commission decision of 9 December 1999, Case 36851, *C.U. de Lille/UEFA (Mouscron)*, decision not published; also see Commission press release IP/99/965 of 9 December 1999.

distribution of goods or to promoting technical or economic progress, while allowing consumers a fair share of the resulting benefits, and which do not impose restrictions which are not indispensable to the attainment of these objectives and do not afford such undertakings the possibility of eliminating competition in respect of a substantial part of the products concerned.

(2) An argument can be presented that authorisation rules do contribute to improving the production or distribution of goods or to promoting technical or economic progress, while allowing consumers a fair share of the resulting benefits. The arguments for this assertion are presented above.

(3) That said, the potential for the KNHS to perform a dual (regulatory and commercial) role which may lead to conflicts of interest undermines this proposition. Therefore it becomes necessary to assess whether the beneficial effects of the rule outweigh its restrictive effects.

4.4.7 The Relevance of Article 165 TFEU

(1) Title XII (Article 165) of the TFEU provides that 'The Union shall contribute to the promotion of European sporting issues, while taking account of the specific nature of sport, its structures based on voluntary activity and its social and educational function.' Under this provision, Union action is to be aimed at 'developing the European dimension in sport, by promoting fairness and openness in sporting competitions and cooperation between bodies responsible for sports, and by protecting the physical and moral integrity of sportsmen and sportswomen, especially the youngest sportsmen and sportswomen.' The competence allows the Union to adopt incentive measures in the field of sport but it specifically excludes the harmonisation of national laws.

(2) Article 165 does not contain a horizontal clause *requiring* the EU institutions to take account of the 'specific nature of sport' in the application of other Treaty competencies such as free movement and competition law. Therefore, Article 165 does not amount to an invitation for sports bodies to adopt restrictive practices within their respective sports. Therefore, Article 165 does not offer the contested rule in question immunity from the EU competition law prohibitions.

(3) Nevertheless, Article 165 is relevant to the current discussion. In *Bernard*, the first post-TFEU sports case of the Court of Justice, Article 165 was cited to corroborate the Court's view that the specific characteristics of sport allows football clubs to seek compensation for the training of their young players where those players wish to sign their first professional contract with a club in another Member State.[36]

(4) In this connection, it is conceivable that reference to the promotion of *fairness and openness in sporting competitions* contained within Article 165(2)

[36] Case 325/08, *Olympic Lyonnais v Bernard & Newcastle United*, judgment of 16 March 2010.

will be raised to both defend and attack authorisation rules in sport, such as the one contained in the KNHS rules. The governing body will defend the rule on the grounds of *fairness*, in so far as the rule grants the governing body the role of balancing the interests of all stakeholders. Opponents of the rule will argue the rule fails to promote *openness* in sporting competition by restricting access to competitions. They are also likely to argue that the rule fails to satisfy the *fairness* principle in circumstances where the staging of two or more events on the same day(s) can take place without obvious negative consequences in terms of sporting and commercial considerations.

(5) Also contained in Article 165(2) is reference to developing *cooperation between bodies responsible for sports*. In the White Paper on Sport, the Commission argued that governance issues in sport should fall within a territory of autonomy and that most challenges can be addressed through self-regulation which must however be 'respectful of good governance principles.'[37] Article 165 could therefore be raised by an aggrieved party who feels that a decision of a governing body has caused them to suffer a detriment without them having sufficient opportunity to have an input into the decision making process.

4.4.8 Conclusions

(1) National sports associations are to be considered undertakings carrying out economic activity. As such, they are subject to EU competition law.

(2) As a *general* statement it is safe to conclude that authorisation rules adopted by sports bodies are compatible with EU law. A governing body, who holds specialist expert knowledge of their sport, should not be dislodged as the central body to decide on such matters. Authorisation rules pursue a legitimate objective and the consequential restrictive effects of such rules have the strong potential to be considered inherent in the pursuit of the stated objectives. In other words, authorisation rules have the potential to be fit for the purpose of achieving the objective of ensuring the proper functioning of sport, from both a sporting and commercial perspective.

(3) However, *individual* authorisation rules require scrutiny to ensure compliance with EU law. There may be specific conditions in which inherency arguments cannot be supported. For example, an inherency argument cannot be supported if it can be demonstrated that the staging of two or more events on the same day(s) does not undermine legitimate sporting or commercial considerations. This calculation must be made on an evidenced based case-by-case basis.

(4) Rules considered inherent in the pursuit of legitimate objectives must remain proportionate. The recognition of historic rights potentially gives rise to

[37] Commission of the European Communities (2007), 'White Paper on Sport', COM(2007) 391 final, s.4.

anti-competitive and discriminatory concerns and it would appear that less restrictive means of achieving the stated objectives might be considered. In this connection, special consideration should be given to the question of whether changes in prevailing governance standards in sport could minimise the most restrictive elements of authorisation rules. The apparent failure to offer an appeal against a negative decision appears out of step with current Court jurisprudence and should be corrected.

(5) The KNHS would appear to hold a dominant position in the market for the organisation of equestrian events in the Netherlands. The potential for a finding of 'abuse' is heightened if the KNHS acts in such a way as to reveal a conflict of interest between its commercial exploitation of the sport and its authorisation function. Amendments in governance structures and standards could minimise the scope for a finding of 'abuse.'

(6) It would appear that the effect on trade requirement is satisfied.

(7) If the contested rule is found to amount to a restriction under Article 101(1) TFEU, the restriction may be capable of qualifying for an exemption under Article 101(3).

(8) Article 165 TFEU is relevant to the current discussion but does not exempt authorisation rules from the scope of EU competition law. The question of *fairness and openness* in sporting competitions could be raised to defend and attack authorisation rules but the weight attached to such arguments remain secondary to the normal application of the principles contained in Articles 101 and 102 TFEU.

(9) The above analysis does not preclude an action being brought in national law.

4.5 Summary and Conclusion

It has long been established by the case-law of the Community Courts and the decisional practice of the Commission that economic activities in the context of sport fall within the scope of EC law, including EC competition rules and internal market freedoms. This has been confirmed specifically with regard to the anti-trust rules, Articles 81 and 82 of the EC Treaty (now: Articles 101 and 102 TFEU), by the 2007 *Meca Medina* ruling of the European Court of Justice (ECJ). This judgment is of paramount importance for the application of EC competition law to the sport sector since this is the first time the ECJ has ever pronounced on the application of Articles 81 and 82 to organisational sporting rules. In prior judgments the cases were decided solely on the basis of other provisions of the EC Treaty, most notably those on the freedom of movement for workers and the freedom to provide services. The very existence of an authoritative interpretation of the anti-trust provisions of the Treaty in the context of organisational sporting rules by the ECJ represents a significant contribution to legal certainty in this area. The Meca Medina methodological framework, the 'test' of applying EC/EU anti-trust law to organisational sporting rules for the examination of their compatibility of course also includes criteria relating to the specificity of sport.

However, in this chapter the focus is on the economic, the products-and-markets aspects of the matter. The Dutch Equestrian Case provides a random example of how the Meca Medina 'test' criteria are systematically applied in practice in a concrete case. The major issue of the collective selling of sports media rights clearly shows how the Commission's approach to the relevant product markets is. Of course, the preliminary question to be answered is: who is or are the owner(s) of the media rights, in other words the matches? The clubs—the home team always having the rights, since it is played at its venue, or are the rights distributed amongst the home and away teams, because they jointly 'make,' produce the match, they have the 'intellectual property rights' (N.B. football players 'think with their feet'; so, for some a football match also is a work of art)[38]; or, a third option, are the rights in the hands of the competition organiser (national FA or League, UEFA or FIFA) who will then distribute the revenues amongst the clubs concerned on an equal basis or according to a particular performance or alternative ratio (cf., sport-specific financial solidarity mechanisms and the concept of balanced competition)? The legal situation concerning ownership of media rights is different in various Member States. As to product markets, The Commission—no decision has been taken by the Court as yet on the matter—considers that upstream and downstream markets are relevant to an assessment of the effects of joint selling arrangements. At the upstream markets initial rights owners (usually sports associations and clubs) sell rights of sport events to sports rights intermediaries, such as sports rights agencies or the organisation of national broadcasting organisations EBU (European Broadcasting Union), or directly to public or private retail operators. The downstream markets cover the final provision of sports media services to consumers by retail operators (broadcasting companies, internet service providers, mobile operators). The products may be supplied by the retail operators by free-TV, pay-TV and pay-per view, video, etc. Nationally listed major sporting events must be relayed on free TV to secure their open access for the society at large. Apart from highlights and short reporting, the products are 'sport-specific' as far as they correspond to particular matches and competition structures. Major (mega) sporting events such as the Olympic Games (Summer and Winter), the Football World Cup and European Football Championship (the final rounds to be distinguished from the qualifying stages), are clearly individual products. These are major 'irregular' sport events unlike sport events that take place throughout the year or throughout a significant time period each year such as the Formula One races. Friendly or pre-season practice matches in professional football are even more 'incidental.' In Europe, 'regular' club competitions at the calendar are the highly branded UEFA

[38] Cf., clubs must have different owners when playing in the same competition, cf. the CAS award of 20 August 1999 in AEK Athens and Slavia Prague v. UEFA (CAS 98/200) (*ENIC* case) on this issue.

Champions League and the Europa League (former UEFA Cup) competitions, and the national club football leagues such as those in the 'Big Five' professional football countries: that is the English Premier League, the German Bundesliga, the Serie A in Italy, the Primera Division in Spain and Ligue 1 in France. There is a difference between competitions of a 'knock out' (elimination) type and of a 'at home and away' type, also at the national professional football level. At the European level, both Leagues start with knock out qualifiers (home and away matches), continue in a groups phase and end up with knock out matches in the final stages of competition. Remedies to address competition concerns such as tendering, limited duration of contracts, packaging, are essential instruments in order to avoid anti-competitive instances of the collective selling of TV rights.

References

Blackshaw I, Cornelius S, Siekmann R (eds) (2009) TV rights and sport: legal aspects. T.M.C. Asser Instituut/T.M.C. Asser Press, The Hague

Weatherill S (2006) Anti-doping revisited—the demise of the rule of 'purely sporting interest'? In: ECL Rev., pp 645 et seq.

Weatherill S (2007) European Sports Law—collected papers. The Hague, pp 335–353

Chapter 5
Sports Betting in the Jurisprudence of the European Court of Justice: A Study into the Application of the *Stare Decisis* Principle, or: The Application of the 'Reversal Method' of Content Analysis and The Essence of the ECJ Case Law on Sports Betting

Abstract To determine the evolution of the jurisprudence of the European Court of Justice (ECJ) on 'sports betting' is a complex task. In this contribution, an innovative method of research the purpose of which is to facilitate that effort considerably, is presented. The method starts from the fact that the ECJ jurisprudence is based on the stare decisis principle which is expressly applied by the Court when it makes references to the sources used, that is its previous decisions and the relevant paragraphs therein. The traditional method of academic analysis shows how the jurisprudence evolved from the first 'sports betting' case up to and including the at the time of his writing most recent one. According to the alternative method it is preferred to reverse the chronological order of study, starting from the most recent case and going back to the first one. This operational method is similar to the approach taken by the Court when drafting a new decision. The new method is supposed to be a more objective, neutral, non-arbitrary and non-impressionist combination of close reading and feed-back; it might be called the 'reversal' or 'retrospective' method. This method allows us to determine which paragraphs in previous decisions are most important (or relatively important). In this contribution, the 'reversal' method is systematically and consistently tested in practice. What is the essence of the jurisprudence of the ECJ on sports betting, on the basis of the application of this method?

This contribution is an elaborated version of a paper that was presented by this author at the 6th international seminar on Sports Law and Taxation organised by NOLOT, Amsterdam, 4 December 2009. Since that time, the ECJ produced new jurisprudence on sports betting such as the Ladbrokes, Sporting Exchange ('Betfair'), Otto Sjöberg and Anders Gerdin v. Swedish State, and Carmen Media rulings. The information on the new case-law was added and incorporated in this contribution.

R. C. R. Siekmann, *Introduction to International and European Sports Law*, ASSER International Sports Law Series, DOI: 10.1007/978-90-6704-852-1_5,

© T.M.C. Asser press, The Hague, The Netherlands, and the author 2012

Contents

5.1 Introduction

Kaburakis' Article on 'ECJ Jurisprudence and Recent Developments in EU Sports Betting'[1] so far is the only substantial one on the matter.[2] From the Article it becomes clear that to determine the evolution of the jurisprudence of the European Court of Justice (ECJ) on 'sports betting' is a complex task. In this contribution I am presenting an innovative, although time-consuming method of research the purpose of which is to facilitate that effort considerably. The method starts from the fact that the

[1] In: Gardiner et al. (2009). A partly adaptation of this Article will appear in print under the title: "European Union Law, Gambling, and Sport Betting. European Court of Justice Jurisprudence, Member States Case Law, and Policy", in: Anderson et al. (2011). A general work of reference on EU law and gambling/betting is: Littler and Fijnaut (2007).

[2] A short overview on 'Sports Betting and European Law is presented by Marios Papaloukas in: Papaloukas (2010).

ECJ jurisprudence is based on the *stare decisis* principle which is expressly applied by the Court when it makes references to the sources used, that is its previous decisions and the relevant paragraphs therein (this of couse does not exclude the possibility that phrasings in previous decisions are used literally later on without an express reference to the paragraphs concerned). Kaburakis in fact uses the traditional method of analysis by showing how the jurisprudence evolved from the first 'sports betting' case up to and including the at the time of his writing most recent one. According to the alternative method it is preferred to reverse the chronological order of study, starting from the most recent case and going back to the first one. This operational method is similar to the approach taken by the Court when drafting a new decision. The new method is supposed to be a more objective, neutral, non-arbitrary and non-impressionist combination of close reading and feed-back; it might be called the 'reversal' or 'retrospective' method. This method allows us to determine which paragraphs in previous decisions are most important (or relatively important). It is possible that express references to these paragraphs occur more than once in their successors. So, when we closely read the text of later decisions, they may give us feed-back about the relative importance of their predecessors. If there is no reference to a 'sports betting' case at all, it must logically be concluded that this is a (very) minor case and in any case not a landmark one. Of course, in this perspective the relative importance of the one most recent decision cannot be determined, since there are not any succeeding references made to it yet. It is not only possible to determine what the relative importance of paragraphs in preceding 'sports betting' decisions is, but also to determine what the influence of previous non-'sports betting' decisions, of a gambling type or not has been (see below for definitions of the concepts of 'gambling' and 'sports betting'). Finally, it should be observed that in principle in non-betting/gambling and non-sports betting cases express reference may be made to sports betting/gambling cases. This would illustrate the influence of 'sports betting' jurisprudence the other way round.

Of course, in using the 'reversal' method of analysis, one should also take into account if and to what extent the factual backgrounds of the cases differ from each other, and whether possibly the applicable law has changed in the meantime (the latter is not the case from a EU perspective, because EU '(sports) betting' law Is ECJ case law). Of course, other aspects are a changing membership of the Court as well as Court members changing their views over time, whether or not under the impact of changing views on 'sports betting' in the society at large, in particular regarding state monopolies and the position of state-run operators. In this respect, the Advocate-General's Opinions may be of major importance, and it is to be seen whether express reference is made to them in the ECJ's decisions and rulings.

In this contribution, the 'reversal' method will be systematically and consistently tested in practice. While using the method it will be refined in applying it, if necessary. 'Rules' for the use of the method will be developed in the process of its application. By using this method, it should be possible to determine the essentials of the case-law, its core content. Of course, it cannot be excluded that paragraphs that do not refer to previous ones in fact are of similar of even more importance than those. The latter of course is part of the test. I will present the 'reversal' method in the process of its application, step-by-step—in order to verify its applicability with regard to the 'sports betting' jurisprudence of the ECJ. So, this contribution has two purposes regarding questions to be answered: will the 'reversal' method work and how will it work? What is the essence of the jurisprudence of the ECJ on sports betting, on the basis of the application of this method? An additional question of course would be whether and how the 'reversal' method reasonably may be compared with the results of the traditional method in order to know whether the outcome is qualitatively better. If the ECJ has applied the *stare decisis* principle consistently, one would say that the essence of its jurisprudence logically should come to the surface by using the 'reversal' method of analysis.

5.1.1 Definition of 'Sports Betting'

Before being in a position to apply the 'reversal' method to the case law of the ECJ on 'sports betting,' it must be determined which decisions of the ECJ belong to the case-law. For that purpose, we need a definition which circumscribes 'sports betting.' In his Article, Kaburakis gives no definition of 'sports betting.' With reference to previous jurisprudence, he states: '[...] one would anticipate a similar ECJ analysis in a *per se sport betting case* (italics added, RS); indeed it did not take long after *Läärä* for such a case to come before the court.'[3] He continues: 'The factual background of *Zenatti* is [...] revisited by the ECJ in the ensuing *Gambelli* and *Placanica* cases, which set the tone for modern legal handling of EU sport betting policies.'[4]

In the Services Directive[5] it is stated in Article 2(h) that 'gambling activities [...] involve wagering a stake with pecuniary value in games of chance [...].'[6]

In the EL Code of Conduct for Sports Betting[7] 'gambling' is identified as 'all types of games, including lotteries and betting transactions, involving wagering a stake with monetary value in games in which participants may win in full or in part, a monetary prize based, totally or partially, on chance or uncertainty of an outcome.' According to the EL Code, '*sports betting*' includes 'all sports betting-based games (i.e. fixed and running odds, totalisator/toto games, live betting, other games and football pools offered by sports betting operators, etc.).' In this context, sports is defined as 'all physical human activities with specific rules, shared by a great number of participants, and involving competition amongst the different participants. Olympic sports, sports having as one's purpose to become Olympic

---

[3] Kaburakis (2009), p. 560.

[4] *Idem.*

[5] Directive 2006/123/EC of the European Parliament and of the Council of 12 December 2006 on services in the internal market, O.J. 2006 L 76/36.

[6] Similarly, Article 1(5)(d) of the E-commerce Directive, Directive 2000/31/EC of 8 June 2000, O.J. 2000 L.17/1.

[7] EL = European Lotteries, which is the non-profit-making association representing the state-licensed lotteries and toto companies In Europe.

sports and minor spors may be included in sports.' So, the EL Code in fact has no definition of what sports betting is.

In *Zenatti* (para 18) the phrase reading '[...] bets on sporting events, even if they cannot be regarded as games of pure chance [...]' is found. So, generally speaking it may be concluded that 'sports betting' are particularly games of, to a certain extent calculated chance, that are connected with a competitive sporting event ('[...] betting on sporting events is not a game of chance, but of informed prediction of the result'; '[...] an [...] in my view usual [...] distinction may be made between lotteries and betting on sporting events on the ground that the latter involves an element of skill absent from the former [...],' cf., Opinion of Advocate-General Fennelli re Zenatti, paras 14 and 23 respectively; 'Sports bets are not dependent on chance in the same way as lotteries. A bettor's chances of winning may also be affected by his skill and, above all, his knowledge. There is therefore some debate among legal commentators as to whether betting is to be classified as a game of skill or a game of chance. The fact that the events involved are largely dependent on chance, particularly in the case of bets placed on entire blocks of games, would suggest that it is a game of chance.' Cf., Opinion of Advocate-General Alber re Gambelli, para 71). 'Sports betting' (or spelled as 'sport betting,' see Kaburakis) is not pure gambling. Apart from such 'impressionist' considerations, 'sports betting' purely is sport-related betting.

This contribution will commence with describing and comparing the factual backgrounds, the 'facts' of the sport-related betting decisions and rulings of the ECJ which cover a period of now twenty years. It will be examined whether the societal context changed and the views on sports betting evolved in the course of time. Then, the 'law,' the case-law will be analysed by using the 'reversal' method and finally presenting the results of this analysis. It is supposed that the outcome will learn us about what is the essence of the ECJ jurisprudence on 'sports betting.' Of course, the most recent ECJ ruling itself cannot be scrutinised by the 'reversal' method, since by definition references to that ruling are non-existent. So, whether new aspects are to be added to the *stare decisis*, the doctrine of the ECJ. on the basis of that ruling is to determined in future.

5.2 Legal and Factual Context of the Case-Law

5.2.1 Zenatti (1999)[8]

In Italy, under Article 88 of Royal Decree No 773 of 18 June 1931 approving the consolidated version of the laws on public order (GURI No 146 of 26 June 1931),

[8] Cf., Case C-67/98, Judgment of the Court of 21 October 1999, paras 3–7 of the preliminary ruling, ECR (1999) I-07289.

'[n]o licence shall be granted for the taking of bets, with the exception of bets on races, regattas, ball games and other similar contests where the taking of bets is essential for the proper conduct of the competitive event.'

Bets could be placed on the outcome of sporting events taking place under the supervision of the Comitato Olimpico Nazionale Italiano (National Olympic Committee, 'CONI') or on the results of horse races organised though the Unione Nazionale Incremento Razze Equine (National Union for the Betterment of Horse Breeds, 'UNIRE'). The use of the funds collected in the form of bets and allocated to those two bodies was regulated and must in particular serve to promote sporting activities through investments in sports facilities, especially in the poorest regions and in peripheral areas of large cities, and support equine sports and the breeding of horses. Under various legislative provisions adopted between 1995 and 1997, arrangements for and the taking of bets reserved to CONI and UNIRE might be entrusted, following tendering procedures and on condition of payment of the prescribed fees, to persons or bodies offering appropriate safeguards.

Article 718 of the Italian Penal Code made it a criminal offence to conduct or organise games of chance and Article 4 of Law No 401 of 13 December 1989 (GURI No 401 of 18 December 1989) prohibited the unlawful participation in the organisation of games or betting reserved to the State or to organisations holding a State concession. Moreover, unauthorised gaming and betting were covered by Article 1933 of the Civil Code, according to which no action lies for the recovery of a gaming or betting debt. Nor, except in the event of fraud, could any sum paid voluntarily be reclaimed.

Since 29 March 1997, Mr Zenatti had acted as an intermediary in Italy for the London company SSP Overseas Betting Ltd ('SSP'), a licensed bookmaker. Mr Zenatti runned an information exchange for the Italian customers of SSP in relation to bets on foreign sports events. He sent to London by fax or Internet forms which have been filled in by customers, together with bank transfer forms, and received faxes from SSP for transmission to the same customers.

By decision of 16 April 1997 the Questore di Verona ordered Mr Zenatti to cease his activity on the ground that it was not one that could be licensed under Article 88 of the Royal Decree, since that provision allowed betting to be licensed only where it is essential for the proper conduct of competitive events.

Mr Zenatti initiated proceedings for judicial review of that decision before the Tribunale Amministrativo Regionale (Regional Administrative Court), Veneto and applied for an interim order suspending its enforcement. On 9 July 1997 the Tribunale Amministrativo Regionale granted an interim order to that effect.

The Questore di Verona appealed to the Consiglio di Stato for that order to be set aside.

The Consignilio di Stato considered that the decision to be given called for an interpretation of the Treaty provisions on the freedom to provide services.

5.2.2 Gambelli (2003)[9]

Under Article 88 of the Regio Decreto No 773, Testo Unico delle Leggi di Pubblica Sicurezza (Royal Decree No 773 approving a single text of the laws on public security), of 18 June 1931 (GURI No 146 of 26 June 1931), no licence was to be granted for the taking of bets, with the exception of bets on races, regatta, ball games or similar contests where the taking of the bets was essential for the proper conduct of the competitive event.

Under Legge Finanziaria No 388 (Finance Law No 388) of 23 December 2000 (ordinary supplement to the GURI of 29 December 2000), authorisation to organise betting was granted exclusively to licence holders or to those entitled to do so by a ministry or other entity to which the law reserves the right to organise or carry on betting. Bets could relate to the outcome of sporting events taking place under the supervision of the CONI, or its subsidiary organisations, or to the results of horse races organised through the UNIRE.

Articles 4, 4a and 4b of Law No 401 of 13 December 1989 on gaming, clandestine betting and ensuring the proper conduct of sporting contests (GURI No 294 of 18 December 1989 as amended by Law No 388/00, Article 37(5) of which inserted Articles 4a and 4b into Law No 401/89, provided as follows:

> 'Unlawful participation in the organisation of games or bets
> Article 4
>
> 1. Any person who unlawfully participates in the organisation of lotteries, betting or pools reserved by law to the State or to entities operating under licence from the State shall be liable to a term of imprisonment of 6 months to 3 years. Any person who organises betting or pools in respect of sporting events run by CONI, by organisations under the authority of CONI or by UNIRE shall be liable to the same penalty. Any person who unlawfully participates in the public organisation of betting on other contests between people or animals, as well as on games of skill, shall be liable to a term of imprisonment of 3 months to 1 year and a minimum fine of ITL 1 000 000.
> 2. Any person who advertises competitions, games or betting organised in the manner described in para 1 without being an accomplice to an offence defined therein shall be liable to a term of imprisonment of up to 3 months and a fine of between ITL 100 000 and ITL 1 000 000.
> 3. Any person who participates in competitions, games or betting organised in the manner described in para 1 without being an accomplice to an offence defined therein shall be liable to a term of imprisonment of up to 3 months or a fine of between ITL 100,000 and ITL 1,000,000.
> [...]
>
> Article 4a
> The penalties laid down in this Article shall be applicable to any person who without the concession, authorisation or licence required by Article 88 of [the Royal Decree] carries out activities in Italy for the purpose of accepting or collecting, or, in any case,

[9] Cf., Case C-243/01, Judgment of the Court of 6 November 2003, paras 7–15 of the preliminary ruling, ECT (2003) I-13031.

assisting in the acceptance or collection in any way whatsoever, including by telephone or by data transfer, of bets of any kind placed by any person in Italy or abroad.

Article 4b

[...] the penalties provided for by this Article shall be applicable to any person who carries out the collection or registration of lottery tickets, pools or bets by telephone or data transfer without being authorised to use those means to effect such collection or registration.'

The Public Prosecutor and the investigating judge at the Tribunale di Fermo (Italy) established the existence of a widespread and complex organisation of Italian agencies linked by the internet to the English bookmaker Stanley International Betting Ltd ('Stanley'), established in Liverpool (United Kingdom), and to which Gambelli and others, the defendants in the main proceedings, belong. They were accused of having collaborated in Italy with a bookmaker abroad in the activity of collecting bets which is normally reserved by law to the State, thus infringing Law No 401/89.

Such activity, which is considered to be incompatible with the monopoly on sporting bets enjoyed by the CONI and which constitutes an offence under Article 4 of Law No 401/89, is performed as follows: the bettor notifies the person in charge of the Italian agency of the events on which he wishes to bet and how much he intends to bet; the agency sends the application for acceptance to the bookmaker by internet, indicating the national football games in question and the bet; the bookmaker confirms acceptance of the bet in real time by internet; the confirmation is transmitted by the Italian agency to the bettor and the bettor pays the sum due to the agency, which sum is then transferred to the bookmaker into a foreign account specially designated for this purpose.

Stanley was an English capital company registered in the United Kingdom which carries on business as a bookmaker under a licence granted pursuant to the Betting, Gaming and Lotteries Act by the City of Liverpool. It was authorised to carry on its activity in the United Kingdom and abroad. It organised and managed bets under a UK licence, identifying the events, setting the stakes and assuming the economic risk. Stanley paid the winnings and the various duties payable in the United Kingdom, as well as taxes on salaries and so on. It was subject to rigorous controls in relation to the legality of its activities, which were carried out by a private audit company and by the Inland Revenue and Customs and Excise.

Stanley offered an extensive range of fixed sports bets on national, European and world sporting events. Individuals could participate from their own home, using various methods such as the internet, fax or telephone, in the betting organised and marketed by it.

Stanley's presence as an undertaking in Italy was consolidated by commercial agreements with Italian operators or intermediaries relating to the creation of data transmission centres. Those centres made electronic means of communication available to users, collect and register the intentions to bet and forward them to Stanley.

Gambelli and others were registered at the Camera di Commercio (Chamber of Commerce) as proprietors of undertakings which run data transfer centres and had received due authorisation from the Ministero delle Poste e delle Comunicazioni (Minister for Post and Communications) to transmit data.

The judge in charge of the preliminary investigations at the Tribunale di Fermo made an order for provisional sequestration and the defendants were also subjected to personal checks and to searches of their agencies, homes and vehicles. Mr Garrisi, who is on the Board of Stanley, was taken into police custody.

Gambelli and others brought an action for review before the Tribunale di Ascoli Piceno against the orders for sequestration relating to the data transmission centres of which they are the proprietors.

The Tribunale di Ascoli Piceno decided to stay proceedings and to refer the question to the European Court of Justice for a preliminary ruling.

5.2.3 *Placanica (2007)*[10]

The references for a preliminary ruling had been made in the course of criminal proceedings against Mr Placanica, Mr Palazzese and Mr Sorricchio for failure to comply with the Italian legislation governing the collection of bets. The legal and factual context of these references is similar to the situations that gave rise to the judgments in Case C–67/98 Zenatti [1999] ECR I–7289 and Case C–243/01 Gambelli and Others [2003] ECR I–13031.

Italian legislation essentially provided that participation in the organising of games of chance, including the collection of bets, is subject to possession of a licence and a police authorisation. Any infringement of that legislation carried criminal penalties of up to three years' imprisonment.

Until 2002 the awarding of licences for the organising of bets on sporting events was managed by the CONI and the UNIRE, which had the authority to organise bets relating to sporting events organised or conducted under their supervision. That resulted from Legislative Decree No 496 of 14 April 1948 (GURI No 118 of 14 April 1948), read in conjunction with Article 3(229) of Law No 549 of 28 December 1995 (GURI No 302 of 29 December 1995, Ordinary Supplement) and Article 3(78) of Law No 662 of 23 December 1996 (GURI No 303 of 28 December 1996, Ordinary Supplement).

Specific rules for the award of licences were laid down, in the case of CONI, by Decree No 174 of the Ministry of Economic Affairs and Finance of 2 June 1998 (GURI No 129 of 5 June 1998) and, in the case of UNIRE, by Decree No 169 of the President of the Republic of 8 April 1998 (GURI No 125 of 1 June 1998).

Decree No 174/98 provided that the award of licences by CONI was to be made by means of calls for tender. When awarding the licences, CONI had, in particular, to make sure that the share ownership of the licence holders was transparent and

[10] Cf., Joined cases C-338/04, C-359/04 and C-360/04, Judgment of the Court of 6 March 2007, paras 2–14 and 18–31 of the preliminary ruling, ECR (2007) I-1891.

that the outlets for collecting and taking bets were rationally distributed across the national territory.

In order to ensure transparency of share ownership, Article 2(6) of Decree No 174/98 provided that where the licence holder took the form of a company, shares carrying voting rights had to be issued in the name of natural persons, general partnerships or limited partnerships, and could not be transferred by simple endorsement.

Similar provision was made with regard to the award of licences by UNIRE.

In 2002, following a number of legislative initiatives, the competences of CONI and UNIRE with respect to bets on sporting events were transferred to the independent authority for the administration of State monopolies, acting under the supervision of the Ministry of Economic Affairs and Finance.

Pursuant to an amendment introduced at that time by Article 22(11) of Law No 289 of 27 December 2002 (GURI No 305 of 31 December 2002, Ordinary Supplement) all companies—without any limitation as to their form—may now take part in tender procedures for the award of licences.

Police authorisation could be granted only to those who held a licence or authorisation granted by a Ministry or other body to which the law reserved the right to organise or manage betting. Those conditions were laid down in Article 88 of Royal Decree No 773, approving a single text of the laws on public security (Regio Decreto No 773, Testo unico delle leggi di pubblica sicurezza), of 18 June 1931 (GURI No 146 of 26 June 1931), as amended by Article 37(4) of Law No 388 of 23 December 2000 (GURI No 302 of 29 December 2000, Ordinary Supplement).

Furthermore, by virtue of Article 11 of the Royal Decree, read in conjunction with Article 14 thereof, a police authorisation could not be issued to a person who had had certain penalties imposed on him or who had been convicted of certain offences, in particular offences reflecting a lack of probity or good conduct, and infringements of the betting and gaming legislation.

Once authorisation had been granted, the holder must, pursuant to Article 16 of the Royal Decree, permit law enforcement officials access at any time to the premises where the authorised activity was pursued.

Article 4 of Law No 401 of 13 December 1989 on gaming, clandestine betting and ensuring the proper conduct of sporting contests (GURI No 294 of 18 December 1989) as amended by Article 37(5) of Law No 388) provided in respect of criminal penalties for malpractice in the organising of games of chance:

1. Any person who unlawfully participates in the organising of lotteries, betting or pools reserved by law to the State or to entities operating under licence from the State shall be liable to a term of imprisonment of 6 months to 3 years. Any person who organises betting or pools in respect of sporting events run by CONI, or by organisations under the authority of CONI, or by UNIRE shall be liable to the same penalty. Any person who unlawfully participates in the public organising of betting on other contests between people or animals, or on games of skill, shall be liable to a term of imprisonment of 3 months to 1 year and a minimum fine of ITL 1 000 000. [...]

2. Any person who advertises competitions, games or betting organised in the manner described in para 1, albeit without being an accomplice to an offence defined therein, shall be liable to a term of imprisonment of up to 3 months and a fine of between ITL 100 000 and ITL 1 000 000.
3. Any person who participates in competitions, games or betting organised in the manner described in para 1, albeit without being an accomplice to an offence defined therein, shall be liable to a term of imprisonment of up to 3 months or a fine of between ITL 100 000 and ITL 1 000 000.

   [...]

4a. The penalties laid down in this Article shall be applicable to any person who, without the concession, authorisation or licence required by Article 88 of [the Royal Decree], carries out activities in Italy for the purposes of accepting or collecting, or, in any case, of assisting the acceptance or in any way whatsoever the collection, including by telephone or by data transfer, of bets of any kind accepted by any person in Italy or abroad.

   [...]'

According to the documents before the Court, CONI—acting in accordance with the Italian legislation—launched a call for tenders on 11 December 1998 for the award of 1,000 licences for sports betting operations, that being the number of licences considered on the basis of a specific assessment to be sufficient for the whole of the national territory. At the same time, a call for tenders in respect of 671 new licences for the taking of bets on competitive horse events was organised by the Ministry of Economic Affairs and Finance in agreement with the Ministry of Agricultural and Forestry Policy, and 329 existing licences were automatically renewed.

The application of the provisions concerning the transparency of share ownership that were in force at the time of those calls for tender had primarily the effect of excluding the participation of operators in the form of companies whose shares were quoted on the regulated markets, since in their case the precise identification of individual shareholders was not possible on an ongoing basis. Following those calls for tender, a number of licences—valid for six years and renewable for a further six years—were awarded in 1999.

Stanley International Betting Ltd is a company incorporated under English law and a member of the group Stanley Leisure plc, a company incorporated under English law and quoted on the London (United Kingdom) stock exchange. Both companies have their head office in Liverpool (United Kingdom). Stanley Leisure operates in the betting and gaming sector and is the fourth biggest bookmaker and the largest casino operator in the United Kingdom.

Stanley is one of Stanley Leisure's operational conduits outside the United Kingdom. It is duly authorised to operate as a bookmaker in the United Kingdom by virtue of a licence issued by the City of Liverpool. It is subject to controls by the British authorities in the interests of public order and safety; to internal controls over the lawfulness of its activities; to controls carried out by a private audit company; and to controls carried out by the Inland Revenue and the United Kingdom customs authorities.

In the hope of obtaining licences for at least 100 betting outlets in Italy, Stanley investigated the possibility of taking part in the tendering procedures, but realised that it could not meet the conditions concerning the transparency of share ownership because it formed part of a group quoted on the regulated markets. Accordingly, it did not participate in the tendering procedure and holds no licence for betting operations.

Stanley operated in Italy through more than 200 agencies, commonly called ‘data transmission centres’ (DTCs). The DTCs supply their services in premises open to the public in which a data transmission link is placed at the disposal of bettors so that they can access the server of Stanley’s host computer in the United Kingdom. In that way, bettors are able—electronically—to forward sports bets proposals to Stanley (chosen from lists of events, and the odds on them, supplied by Stanley), to receive notice that their proposals have been accepted, to pay their stakes and, where appropriate, to receive their winnings.

The DTCs are run by independent operators who have contractual links to Stanley. Mr Placanica, Mr Palazzese and Mr Sorricchio, the defendants in the main proceedings, are all DTC operators linked to Stanley.

According to the case-file forwarded by the Tribunale (District Court) di Teramo (Italy), Mr Palazzese and Mr Sorricchio applied, before commencing their activities, to Atri Police Headquarters for police authorisation in accordance with Article 88 of the Royal Decree. Those applications met with no response.

Accusing Mr Placanica of the offence set out in Article 4(4a) of Law No 401/89 in that, as a DTC operator for Stanley, Mr Placanica had pursued the organised activity of collecting bets without the required police authorisation, the Public Prosecutor brought criminal proceedings against him before the Tribunale di Larino (Italy).

That court expressed misgivings as to the soundness of the conclusion reached by the Corte suprema di cassazione in Gesualdi, with regard to the compatibility of Article 4(4a) of Law No 401/89 with Community law. The Tribunale di Larino was uncertain whether the public order objectives invoked by the Corte suprema di cassazione justified the restrictions at issue.

Accordingly, the Tribunale di Larino decided to stay proceedings and to refer the uestion to the European Court of Justice for a preliminary ruling.

The Atri police authorities charged Mr Palazzese and Mr Sorricchio with pursuing, without a licence or a police authorisation, an organised activity with a view to facilitating the collection of bets, and placed their premises and equipment under preventive seizure on the basis of Article 4(4a) of Law No 401/89. Upon confirmation of the seizure measures by the Public Prosecutor, Mr Palazzese and Mr Sorricchio each brought an action challenging those measures before the Tribunale di Teramo.

In the view of that court, the restrictions imposed on companies quoted on the regulated markets, which prevented them in 1999 from taking part in the last tender procedure for the award of licences for the operation of betting activities, are incompatible with the principles of Community law because they discriminate against operators who are not Italian. In consequence—like the Tribunale di Larino—the Tribunale di Teramo has doubts as to whether the judgment in Gesualdi is sound.

The Tribunale di Teramo decided to stay proceedings and to refer the following question to the Court for a preliminary ruling.

5.2.4 *Commission v Italy (2007)*[11]

In Italy, horse-race betting and gaming operations were originally run exclusively by the UNIRE, which had the option of operating the services of collecting and taking bets directly or delegating them to third parties. The UNIRE entrusted the operation of those services to bookmakers.

Law No 662 of 23 December 1996 (ordinary supplement to the GURI No 303, of 28 December 1996) subsequently assigned responsibility for the organisation and management of horse-race betting and gaming to the Ministry of Finance and the Ministry of Agriculture, Food and Forestry Resources, which were authorised either to operate the activity directly or through public bodies, companies or bookmakers appointed by them. Para 78 of Article 3 of Law No 662 states that there is to be a reorganisation, by way of regulation, of the organisational, functional, fiscal and penal aspects of horse-race betting and gaming, as well as the sharing out of revenue from such betting.

In implementation of Article 3 of Law No 662, the Italian Government adopted Presidential Decree No 169 of 8 April 1998 (GURI No 125 of 1 June 1998), which provided in Article 2 that the Ministry of Finance, in agreement with the Ministry of Agricultural and Forestry Policy, was to award licences for horse-race betting operations to natural persons or companies fulfilling the relevant conditions by means of calls for tender organised in accordance with Community rules. As a transitional measure, Article 25 of Decree No 169/1998 provided for an extension of the period of validity of the licences granted by UNIRE until 31 December 1998, or, if it proved impossible to organise calls for tender by that date, the end of 1999.

A Ministerial Decree of 7 April 1999 (GURI No 86 of 14 April 1999) subsequently approved the plan to reinforce the network of outlets collecting and taking bets on horse-races with a view to increasing the number of betting shops across the whole of Italy from 329 to 1000. Whereas 671 new licences were put out to tender, the directive of the Ministry of Finance of 9 December 1999 provided for the renewal of UNIRE's 329 'old licences.' In implementation of that directive, the decision of the Ministry of Finance of 21 December 1999 (GURI No 300 of 23 December 1999) renewed the said licences for a period of six years starting 1 January 2000.

Decree-Law No 452 of 28 December 2001 (GURI No 301 of 29 December 2001), converted after amendment into Law No 16 of 27 February 2002 (GURI No 49 of 27 February 2002), subsequently provided that the 'old licences' were to be reallocated in accordance with Decree No 169/1998, that is, by way of a Community call for tenders, and that they would remain valid until that reallocation had been finalised.

Finally, Decree-Law No 147 of 24 June 2003 extending time-limits and emergency provisions in budgetary matters (GURI No 145 of 25 June 2003), now

[11] Cf., Case C-260/04, judgment of the Court of 13 September 2007, paras 2–10 of the preliminary ruling, ECR (2007) I-7083.

Law No 200 of 1 August 2003 (GURI No 178 of 2 August 2003), provides in Article 8(1) that the financial status of each licence holder has to be assessed in order to resolve the problem of 'the guaranteed minimum,' a levy which every licence holder had to pay to UNIRE irrespective of the actual amount of revenue generated during the year, which had proven to be excessive and had led to an economic crisis in the horse-race betting sector. In implementation of that law, the special commissioner appointed by UNIRE adopted decision No 107/2003 of 14 October 2003, which extended the period of validity of the licences that had already been granted until the deadline for the last payment, set for 30 October 2011, and, in any event, until the date on which the new licences are allocated by means of a call for tenders, in order to take the necessary steps to calculate the amounts to be paid by the licence holders.

Following a complaint lodged by a private operator in the horse-race betting sector, on 24 July 2001 the Commission sent the Italian authorities a letter of formal notice pursuant to Article 226 EC, drawing their attention to the incompatibility of the Italian system of granting licences for horse-race betting operations, and, in particular, the renewal by the contested decision of the 329 old licences granted by UNIRE without a competitive tendering procedure, with the general principle of transparency and the requirement of publication resulting from Articles 43 and 49 EC. In response, the Italian Government announced, by letters dated 30 November 2001 and 15 January 2002, respectively, the bill for and the adoption of Law No 16 of 27 February 2002.

Since the Commission was not satisfied with the implementation of the provisions of that law, it issued a reasoned opinion on 16 October 2002 in which it asked the Italian Republic to adopt the necessary measures to comply with the reasoned opinion within two months of its receipt. By letter of 10 December 2002, the Italian Government responded that it had to conduct a detailed assessment of the financial status of existing licence holders before issuing calls for tenders.

Since it received no further information concerning the completion of that assessment and the launching of a call for tenders for the purposes of reallocating the licences at issue, the Commission decided to bring the present action.

5.2.5 Liga Portuguesa de Futebol Profissional (2009) (hereafter: Liga Portuguesa)[12]

In Portugal games of chance are, in principle, prohibited. However, the State has reserved the right to authorise, in accordance with the system which it deems most appropriate, the operation of one or more games directly, through a State body or a body controlled directly by the State, or to grant the right to operate such games to

[12] Cf., Case C-42/07, Judgment of the Court of 8 September 2009, paras 3–28 of the preliminary ruling, ECR (2009) I-7633.

private entities, whether profit-making or not, by calls for tender conducted in accordance with the Code of Administrative Procedure.

Games of chance in the form of lotteries, lotto games and sports betting are known in Portugal as games of a social nature ('jogos sociais') and the operation of such games is systematically entrusted to Santa Casa.

Each type of game of chance organised by Santa Casa is instituted separately by a decree-law and the entire organisation and operation of the various games offered by it, including the amount of stakes, the system for awarding prizes, the frequency of draws, the specific percentage of each prize, methods of collecting stakes, the method of selecting authorised distributors, and the methods and periods for payment of prizes, are covered by government regulation.

The first type of game in question was the national lottery (Lotaria Nacional), which was established by a royal edict of 18 November 1783, and a concession was awarded to Santa Casa, the concession being renewed regularly thereafter. Today that lottery consists in the monthly drawing of numbers by lot.

Following a number of legislative developments, Santa Casa acquired the right to organise other games of chance based on the drawing of numbers by lot or on sporting events. This led to the introduction of two games involving betting on football matches called 'Totobola' and 'Totogolo,' respectively enabling participants to bet on the result (win, draw or loss) and the number of goals scored by the teams. There are also two lotto games, namely Totoloto, in which six numbers are chosen from a total of 49, and EuroMillions, a type of European lotto. Players of Totobola or Totoloto may also take part in a game called 'Joker,' which consists in the drawing of a single number by lot. Lastly, there is also the Lotaria Instantânea, an instant game with a scratch card, commonly called 'raspadinha.'

In 2003 the legal framework governing lotteries, lotto games and sports betting was adapted in order to take account of technical developments enabling games to be offered by electronic means, in particular the internet. Those measures feature in Decree-Law No 282/2003 of 8 November 2003 (*Diário da República* I, series A, No 259, 8 November 2003). They seek essentially, first, to license Santa Casa to distribute its products by electronic means and, secondly, to extend Santa Casa's exclusive right of operation to include games offered by electronic means, in particular the internet, thereby prohibiting all other operators from using those means.

Article 2 of Decree-Law No 282/2003 confers on Santa Casa, through its Departamento de Jogos (Gaming Department), exclusive rights for the operation by electronic means of the games in question and for any other game the operation of which may be entrusted to Santa Casa, and states that that system covers all of the national territory, and includes, in particular, the internet.

Under Article 11(1) of Decree-Law No 282/2003 the following are classed as administrative offences:

(a) the promotion, organisation or operation by electronic means of games [the operation of which has been entrusted to Santa Casa], in contravention of the exclusive rights granted by Article 2 [of the present Decree-Law], and also the issue, distribution or sale of virtual tickets and the advertisement of the related draws, whether they take place within national territory or not;
(b) the promotion, organisation or operation by electronic means of lotteries or other draws similar to those of the Lotaria Nacional or the Lotaria Instantânea, in contravention of the exclusive rights granted by Article 2, and also the issue, distribution or sale of virtual tickets and the advertisement of the related draws, whether they take place within national territory or not; […].

Article 12(1) of Decree-Law No 282/2003 sets the maximum and minimum fines for the administrative offences laid down in, *inter alia*, Article 11(1)(a) and (b) of that Decree-Law. For legal persons, the fine is to be not less than EUR 2 000 or more than three times the total amount deemed to have been collected from organising the game in question, provided that the triple figure is greater than EUR 2 000 but does not exceed a maximum of EUR 44 890.

The activities of Santa Casa were, at the material time, regulated by Decree-Law No 322/91 of 26 August 1991 adopting the statutes of Santa Casa da Misericórdia de Lisboa (*Diário da República* I, series A, No 195, 26 August 1991), as amended by Decree-Law No 469/99 of 6 November 1999 (*Diário da República* I, series A, No 259, 6 November 1999) ('Decree-Law No 322/91').

The preamble to Decree-Law No 322/91 emphasises the importance of the various aspects of Santa Casa—historical, social, cultural and economic—and concludes that the Government must pay 'specific and continuous attention in order to prevent negligence and failures […] while nevertheless granting [Santa Casa] the broadest possible autonomy in the management and operation of games of a social nature.'

Under Article 1(1) of its statutes, Santa Casa is a 'legal person in the public administrative interest.' The administrative organs of Santa Casa consist, by virtue of Article 12(1) of its statutes, of a director and a board of management. Pursuant to Article 13 of those statutes, the director is appointed by decree of the Prime Minister, the other members of Santa Casa's board of management being appointed by decree of the members of the Government under whose supervision Santa Casa falls.

Under Article 20(1) of its statutes, Santa Casa has been given specific tasks in the areas of protection of the family, mothers and children, help for unprotected minors at risk, assistance for old people, social situations of serious deprivation, and primary and specialised health care.

The earnings generated by the operation of games of chance are allocated between Santa Casa and other public-interest institutions or institutions involved in social projects. Those other public-interest institutions include associations of voluntary fire crews, private social solidarity institutions, establishments for the safety and rehabilitation of handicapped persons, and the cultural development fund.

The operation of games of chance falls within the responsibilities of the Gaming Department of Santa Casa. That department is governed by regulations adopted, as in the case of Santa Casa's statutes, by Decree-Law No 322/91, and it has its own administrative and control organs.

In accordance with Article 5 of the regulations governing the Gaming Department, the administrative organ of that department consists of the director of Santa Casa, who is the ex officio chairman, and two deputy directors appointed by joint decree of the Minister for Employment and Solidarity and the Minister for Health. Pursuant to Articles 8, 12 and 16 of the regulations of the Gaming Department, the majority of the members of the committees in charge of games, draws and complaints are representatives of the public authorities, that is to say, the General Tax Inspectorate and the District Government in Lisbon. Accordingly, the chairman of the complaints committee, who has a casting vote, is a judge appointed by decree of the Minister for Justice. Two of the three members of that committee are appointed by decree of the chief tax inspector and decree of the chief administrative officer (prefect) of the District of Lisbon respectively, while the third member of the committee is appointed by the director of Santa Casa.

The Gaming Department has the powers of an administrative authority to open, institute and prosecute proceedings concerning offences involving the illegal operation of games of chance in relation to which Santa Casa has the exclusive rights, and to investigate such offences. Decree-Law No 282/2003 confers upon the directors of the Gaming Department, *inter alia*, the necessary administrative powers to impose fines as provided for under Article 12(1) of that Decree-Law.

Bwin is an on-line gambling undertaking which has its registered office in Gibraltar. It offers games of chance on an internet site.

Bwin has no establishment in Portugal. Its servers for the on-line service are in Gibraltar and Austria. All bets are placed directly by the consumer on Bwin's internet site or by some other means of direct communication. Stakes on that site are paid by credit card in particular, but also by other means of electronic payment. The value of any winnings is credited to the gambling account opened for the gambler by Bwin. The gambler may use that money in order to gamble or ask for it to be transferred to his bank account.

Bwin offers a wide range of on-line games of chance covering sports betting, casino games, such as roulette and poker, and games based on drawing numbers by lot which are similar to the Totoloto operated by Santa Casa.

Betting is on the results of football matches and other sporting events. The different games offered include bets on the result (win, draw or loss) of football matches in the Portuguese championship equivalent to the Totobola and Totogolo games operated exclusively by Santa Casa. Bwin also offers on-line betting in real time, in which the odds are variable and change as the sporting event in question unfolds. Information such as the match score, the time elapsed, yellow and red cards given, and so on, are displayed in real time on the Bwin internet site, thus enabling gamblers to place bets interactively as the sporting event unfolds.

The Liga is a private-law legal person with the structure of a non-profit-making association, made up of all the clubs taking part in football competitions at professional level in Portugal. It organises, *inter alia*, the football competition corresponding to the national First Division and is responsible for the commercial operation of that competition.

A sponsorship agreement, concluded by the Liga and Bwin on 18 August 2005 for four playing seasons starting in 2005/2006, made Bwin the main institutional sponsor of the First Football Division in Portugal. Under the terms of that agreement, the First Division, previously known as the 'Super Liga,' changed its name first to the Liga betandwin.com, and then subsequently to the Bwin Liga. In addition, the Bwin logos were displayed on the sports kit worn by the players and affixed around the stadiums of the First Division clubs. The Liga's internet site also included references and a link allowing access to Bwin's internet site, making it possible for consumers in Portugal and other States to use the gambling services thus offered to them.

Subsequently, in exercising the powers conferred on them by Decree-Law No 282/2003, the directors of the Gaming Department of Santa Casa adopted decisions imposing fines of EUR 75000 and EUR 74500 respectively on the Liga and Bwin in respect of the administrative offences referred to in Article 11(1)(a) and (b) of that Decree-Law. Those sums represent the aggregated amounts of two fines imposed on each of the Liga and Bwin for promoting, organising and operating, via the internet, games of a social nature reserved to Santa Casa or such similar games, and also for advertising such gambling.

The Liga and Bwin brought actions before the national court for annulment of those decisions, invoking, *inter alia*, the relevant Community rules and case-law.

The Tribunal de Pequena Instânza Criminal do Porto (Local Criminal Court, Oporto) (Portugal) decided to stay the proceedings and to refer the question to the European Court of justice for a preliminary ruling.

5.2.6 *Sporting Exchange Ltd ('Betfair') (2010)*[13]

Article 1 of the Law on games of chance (Wet op de kansspelen; 'the Wok') provides:

> Subject to the provisions of Title Va of this Law, the following are prohibited:
>
> (a) providing an opportunity to compete for prizes if the winners are designated by means of any calculation of probability over which the participants are generally unable to exercise a dominant influence, unless a licence therefor has been granted pursuant to this Law;
>
> (b) promoting participation either in an opportunity as referred to under (a), provided without a licence pursuant to this Law, or in a similar opportunity, provided outside the Kingdom of the Netherlands in Europe, or to maintain a stock of materials intended to publicise or disseminate knowledge of such opportunities; [...]

[13] Cf., Case C-203/08, Judgment of the Court of 3 June 2010, paras 3–19.

Article 16(1) of the Wok is worded as follows:

> The Minister for Justice and the Minister for Welfare, Public Health and Culture may grant to one legal person with full legal capacity a licence, for a period to be determined by them, to organise sports-related prize competitions in the interests of bodies operating for public benefit, particularly in the area of sport and physical education, culture, social welfare and public health.

Article 23 of the Wok states:

1. A licence to organise a totalisator may be granted only in accordance with the provisions of this Title.
2. "Totalisator" shall mean any opportunity provided to bet on the outcome of trotting or other horse races, on the understanding that the total stake, apart from any deduction permitted by or by virtue of the law, will be distributed among those who have bet on the winner or on one of the prize winners.

According to Article 24 of the Wok, the Minister for Agriculture and Fisheries and the Minister for Justice may grant to one legal person with full legal capacity a licence to organise a totalisator for a period to be determined by them.

Article 25 of the Wok provides:

1. The Ministers referred to in Article 24 shall impose certain conditions on a licence to organise a totalisator.
2. Those conditions relate, inter alia, to:
   a. the number of trotting and other horse races;
   b. the maximum stake per person;
   c. the percentage retained before distribution among the winners and the particular use of that percentage;
   d. the supervision of the application of the Law by the authorities;
   e. the obligation to prevent or take measures to prevent, so far as possible, unauthorised betting or the use of intermediaries at venues where trotting or other horse races take place.
3. The conditions may be amended or supplemented.

Under Article 26 of the Wok:

> A licence granted in accordance with Article 24 may be withdrawn before its expiry by the Ministers referred to in that Article in the event of a breach of the conditions imposed pursuant to Article 25.

Article 27 of the Wok prohibits the offer or provision to the public of an intermediary service in the placing of bets with the operator of a totalisator.

Netherlands legislation in relation to games of chance is based on a system of exclusive licences under which (i) the organisation or promotion of games of chance is prohibited unless an administrative licence for that purpose has been issued, and (ii) only one licence is granted by the national authorities in respect of each of the games of chance authorised.

Furthermore, there is no possibility at all of offering games of chance interactively via the internet in the Netherlands.

The Stichting de Nationale Sporttotalisator ('De Lotto'), which is a non-profit-making foundation governed by private law, has held the licence for the organisation of sports-related prize competitions, the lottery and numbers games since 1961. The licence for the organisation of a totalisator on the outcome of horse races was granted to a limited company, Scientific Games Racing BV ('SGR'), which is a subsidiary of Scientific Games Corporation Inc., a company established in the United States.

According to De Lotto's constitution, its objects are the collection of funds by means of the organisation of games of chance and the distribution of those funds among institutions working in the public interest, particularly in the fields of sport, physical education, general welfare, public health and culture. De Lotto is managed by a five-member commission whose chairman is appointed by the Minister. The other members are designated by the Stichting Aanwending Loterijgelden Nederland (Foundation for the Use of Lottery Funds) and by the Nederlands Olympisch Comité/Nederlandse Sport Federatie (Netherlands Olympic Committee/Netherlands Sports Federation).

Betfair operates within the gaming sector. Its services are provided solely via the internet and by telephone. From the United Kingdom, it provides the recipients of its services with a platform for betting on sporting events and horse races, known as a 'betting exchange,' on the basis of British and Maltese licences. Betfair has no office or sales outlet in the Netherlands.

As Betfair wished actively to offer its services on the Netherlands market, it requested the Minister to determine whether it required a licence in order to carry on such activities. It also applied to the Minister for a licence to organise sports-related prize competitions and a totalisator on the outcome of horse races, whether or not via the internet. By decision of 29 April 2004, the Minister refused those requests.

The objection lodged in respect of that decision was dismissed by the Minister on 9 August 2004. In particular, the Minister took the view that the Wok provides for a closed system of licences which does not allow for the possibility of licences being granted to provide opportunities for participating in games of chance via the internet. As Betfair could not obtain a licence for its current internet activities under the Wok, it was prohibited from offering those services to recipients established in the Netherlands.

Betfair also lodged two objections to the Minister's decisions of 10 December 2004 and 21 June 2005 concerning the renewal of licences granted to De Lotto and to SGR, respectively.

Those objections were dismissed by decisions of the Minister dated 17 March and 4 November 2005, respectively.

By judgment of 8 December 2006, the Rechtbank's-Gravenhage (District Court, The Hague) declared Betfair's appeals against the dismissal decisions referred to above to be unfounded. Betfair subsequently appealed against that judgment to the Raad van State (Council of State).

5.2.7 Ladbrokes (2010)[14]

Article 1 of the Law on games of chance (Wet op de kansspelen; 'the Wok') provides:

Subject to the provisions of Title Va of this Law, the following are prohibited:

(a) providing an opportunity to compete for prizes if the winners are designated by means of any calculation of probability over which the participants are generally unable to exercise a dominant influence, unless a licence therefor has been granted pursuant to this Law;
(b) promoting participation either in an opportunity as referred to under (a), provided without a licence pursuant to this Law, or in a similar opportunity, provided outside the Kingdom of the Netherlands in Europe, or to maintain a stock of materials intended to publicise or disseminate knowledge of such opportunities; [...]

Article 16 of the Wok is worded as follows:

1. The Minister for Justice and the Minister for Welfare, Public Health and Culture may grant to one legal person with full legal capacity a licence, for a period to be determined by them, to organise sports-related prize competitions in the interests of bodies operating for public benefit, particularly in the area of sport and physical education, culture, social welfare and public health.
2. The proceeds from prize competitions [...] shall be applied in respect of the interests which the legal person intends to serve by organising and operating sports-related prize competitions.
3. At least 47.5% of total proceeds from games of chance organised pursuant to this Title and to Title IVa, to be calculated on the basis of a calendar year, shall be allocated to the distribution of prizes. [...]

Article 21 of the Wok states:

1. The Ministers referred to in Article 16 shall lay down rules concerning licences for the organisation of sports-related prize competitions.
2. Those rules relate, inter alia, to:

   a. the number of competitions to be organised;
   b. the method of determining results and the prize scheme;
   c. the management and covering of organisational costs;
   d. the allocation of revenue from competitions organised;
   e. the constitution and regulations of the legal person;
   f. monitoring of compliance with the legislation by the authorities;
   g. delivery and publication of the report to be drawn up annually by the legal person concerning its activities and financial results.

Netherlands legislation in relation to games of chance is based on a system of exclusive licences under which (i) the organisation or promotion of games of

---

[14] Cf., Case C-258/08, Judgment of the Court of 3 June 2010, paras 3–13 of the preliminary ruling.

chance is prohibited unless an administrative licence for that purpose has been issued, and (ii) only one licence is granted by the national authorities in respect of each of the games of chance authorised.

Furthermore, there is no possibility at all of offering games of chance interactively via the internet in the Netherlands.

De Lotto is a non-profit-making foundation governed by private law which holds a licence for the organisation of sports-related prize competitions, the lottery and numbers games. Its objects, according to its constitution, are the collection of funds by means of the organisation of games of chance and the distribution of those funds among institutions working in the public interest, particularly in the fields of sport, physical education, general welfare, public health and culture.

The Ladbrokes companies are engaged in the organisation of sports-related prize competitions and are particularly well known for their bookmaking business. They offer a number of mainly sports-related games of chance on their internet site. They also offer the possibility of participating via a freephone number in the betting activities which they organise. The companies do not physically carry on any activity in the Netherlands.

De Lotto alleged that the Ladbrokes companies were, via the internet, offering games of chance to persons residing in the Netherlands for which they did not have the requisite licence under the Wok, and made an application for interim relief to the Rechtbank Arnhem (District Court, Arnhem) for the Ladbrokes companies to be required to put an end to that activity.

By judgment of 27 January 2003, the Rechtbank judge hearing the application for interim relief allowed the application and ordered the Ladbrokes companies to take steps to block access to their internet site for persons residing in the Netherlands and to make it impossible for such persons to participate in telephone betting. Those measures were confirmed by the judgments of the Gerechtshof te Arnhem (Regional Court of Appeal, Arnhem) and the Hoge Raad der Nederlanden (Supreme Court) of 2 September 2003 and 18 February 2005, respectively.

On 21 February 2003, De Lotto also issued proceedings against the Ladbrokes companies in a substantive action before the Rechtbank Arnhem. In its application, De Lotto sought confirmation of the coercive measures imposed on those companies by the judge who had heard the application for interim relief. By decision of 31 August 2005, the Rechtbank allowed De Lotto's application and ordered the Ladbrokes companies, on pain of imposition of a periodic penalty, to maintain the measures blocking access to games of chance via the internet or by telephone for persons residing in the Netherlands. That decision was upheld by the judgment of the Gerechtshof te Arnhem of 17 October 2006; the Ladbrokes companies therefore appealed in cassation to the referring court.

The Hoge Raad der Nederlanden took the view that an interpretation of European Union law was required to enable it to determine the dispute before it, and decided to stay the proceedings and to refer the questions to the European Court of justice for a preliminary ruling.

5.2.8 *Otto Sjöberg and Anders Gerdin v. Swedish State (2010) (hereafter: Sjöberg/Gerdin)*[15]

The Lotterilag governs all categories of gambling offered to the public in Sweden.

The objectives of Swedish gaming policy were summarised as follows in the *travaux préparatoires* for the Lotterilag:

> The main purpose underlying the gaming policy is [...] to have in future a healthy and safe gaming market in which social protection interests and the demand for gaming are provided for in controlled forms. Profits from gaming should be protected and always reserved for objectives which are in the public interest or socially beneficial, that is, the activities of associations, equestrian sports and the State. As has been the case hitherto, the focus should be on prioritising social protection considerations whilst offering a variety of gaming options and taking heed of the risk of fraud and unlawful gaming.

The Swedish legislation on gambling seeks to:

- counter criminal activity;
- counter negative social and economic effects;
- safeguard consumer protection interests, and
- apply the profits from lotteries to objectives which are in the public interest or socially beneficial.

Para 9 of the Lotterilag provides that a licence is, as a general rule, required to organise gambling in Sweden.

Under para 15 of the Lotterilag, a licence may be issued to a Swedish legal person which is a non-profit-making association and which under its statutes has as its main purpose the advancement of socially beneficial objectives in Sweden and carries on activities which serve mainly the advancement of that objective. Under para 45 of the Lotterilag, the Swedish Government may also grant a special licence to organise gambling in cases other than those provided for in that law.

In accordance with a fundamental principle of the Swedish legislation on gambling, which provides that the profits from the operation of gambling should be reserved for socially beneficial objectives or those which are in the public interest, the Swedish gambling market is shared between, on the one hand, non-profit-making associations whose purpose is the advancement of socially beneficial objectives in Sweden which have been granted licences under para 15 of the Lotterilag, and, on the other, two operators which are either State owned or mainly State controlled, namely, the State owned gaming company Svenska Spel AB and Trav och Galopp AB, which is jointly owned by the State and the equestrian sports organisations, those companies holding special licences under para 45 of the Lotterilag.

Under para 48 of the Lotterilag, a public authority, namely the Lotteriinspektion, is the central body responsible for monitoring compliance with the Lotterilag.

---

[15] Cf., Joined Cases C-447/08 and C-448/08, Judgment of the Court of 8 July 2010, paras 3–25 and 27 of the preliminary ruling.

On the basis of that law, the Lotteriinspektion is authorised to draw up the regulations relating to the monitoring and internal rules necessary for the various games. It exercises supervision over Svenska Spel AB's activity and carries out inspections and regular checks.

Under Article 52 of the Lotterilag, the Lotteriinspektion can issue the directions and prohibitions necessary for compliance with the provisions of that law and decide on the rules and conditions adopted on the basis of it. Such a direction or prohibition may be accompanied by an administrative penal

Under para 14 of Chap. 16 of the Criminal Code (Brottsbalken, 'the Brottsbalk'), the organisation without a licence of gambling in Sweden constitutes an offence of unlawful gaming. This is punishable with a fine or imprisonment of up to two years. If the infringement is deemed serious, it is punishable, as an offence of unlawful gaming set out in para 14a of Chap. 16, with imprisonment for between six months and four years.

In addition, under para 54(1) of the Lotterilag, anyone who, intentionally or through gross recklessness, organises unlawful gambling or unlawfully owns certain types of slot machines is liable to a fine or a prison sentence of up to six months.

The provisions of the Brottsbalk relating to the offence of unlawful gaming cover specifically described criminal offences. Criminal offences which are less serious and which, for this reason, do not fall within para 14 thereof, fall within the scope of para 54(1) of the Lotterilag. Under Article 57(1) of the Lotterilag, that latter provision does not apply where the criminal offence is subject to a penalty provided for by the Brottsbalk.

Since the Lotterilag applies only in Sweden, the prohibition on organising a lottery without a licence does not apply to gambling operated abroad. Nor does that prohibition apply to gambling offered on the internet from another State to Swedish consumers and the same law does not prohibit Swedish consumers from participating in gambling organised abroad. Similarly, a licence granted under that law confers on its holder a right to offer gambling services only within the territorial scope of the Lotterilag, that is to say, within Sweden.

Under para 38(1)(1) of the Lotterilag, it is prohibited, in commercial operations or otherwise to promote, without a special licence and for the purpose of profit, participation in unlicensed gambling, organised within Sweden or abroad.

Under para 38(2), a derogation from the prohibition referred to in para 38(1) may be granted as regards gambling which is organised on the basis of international cooperation with Swedish participation by a foreign operator authorised to organise gambling, under the rules applicable in the State where he is established, and to cooperate on an international level.

Para 54(2) of the Lotterilag provides that a fine or a maximum of six months' imprisonment may be imposed on persons who, in commercial operations or otherwise for the purpose of profit, illegally promote participation in gambling organised abroad, if the promotion specifically relates to consumers resident in Sweden.

Under para (4)(1) of Chap. 23 of the Brottsbalk, it is not only the perpetrator of certain criminal acts who is liable for them, but also the person who promotes them by aiding or abetting them. Furthermore, under para (4)(2), even a person who is not regarded as the co-perpetrator of the offence is held responsible if he has encouraged a third party to commit it, if he has provoked it or if he has aided its perpetrator in any other way.

At the material time, Mr Sjöberg was the editor-in-chief and the publisher of the Expressen newspaper. In that capacity, he had sole responsibility for the publication by that newspaper, between November 2003 and August 2004, of advertisements for gambling organised abroad by the companies Expekt, Unibet, Ladbrokes and Centrebet.

Mr Gerdin, for his part, was, at the material time, the editor-in-chief and publisher of the Aftonbladet newspaper. In that capacity, he had sole responsibility for the publication by that newspaper, between November 2003 and June 2004, of advertisements for gambling organised abroad by those companies.

Expekt, Unibet, Ladbrokes and Centrebet are private operators established in Member States other than the Kingdom of Sweden who offer internet gambling, in particular to persons resident in Sweden. These games include, among others, sports betting and poker.

The Åklagaren (Public Prosecutor's Office) subsequently took proceedings against Mr Sjöberg and Mr Gerdin for infringement of para 54(2) of the Loterrilagen, for having promoted, unlawfully and for profit, the participation of Swedish residents in gambling organised abroad.

On 21 June and 6 September 2005, Mr Sjöberg and Mr Gerdin were each ordered by the Stockholms tingsrätt (District Court, Stockholm) to pay a criminal penalty of SEK 50000 in respect of infringement of the Lotterilag.

Mr Sjöberg and Mr Gerdin both appealed against the judgment concerning them before the Svea hovrätt (Court of Appeal, Svea). That court however refused to allow the admissibility of the appeal brought against those two judgments.

The parties concerned appealed against those decisions of the Svea hovrätt before the Högsta domstolen (Supreme Court) and that latter court, on 5 February 2008, issued a decision declaring that the appeals before the Svea hovrätt were admissible, thereby referring the two cases back to it.

The Svea Hovrätt decided to stay the proceedings and to refer to the European Court of Justice the questions for a preliminary ruling.

5.2.9 *Carmen Media (2010)*[16]

Para 284 of the Criminal Code (Strafgesetzbuch; 'the StGB') provides:

> (1) Whosoever without the authorisation of a public authority publicly organises or operates a game of chance or makes equipment for it available shall be liable to imprisonment of not more than two years or a fine.
> [...]

[16] Cf., Case C-46/08, Judgment of the Court of 8 September 2010, paras 3–25 and 38.

(3) Whosoever in cases under subpara 1 above acts
on a commercial basis
[...]
shall be liable to imprisonment of between three months and five years
[...].

Apart from bets concerning official horse races, which fall primarily under the Law on Racing Bets and Lotteries (Rennwett- und Lotteriegesetz; 'the RWLG'), and the installation and use of gambling machines in establishments other than casinos (gaming arcades, cafes, hotels, restaurants and other accommodation), which fall primarily within the Trade and Industry Code (Gewerbeordnung) and the Regulation on Gambling Machines (Verordnung über Spielgeräte und andere Spiele mit Gewinnmöglichkeit), determination of the conditions under which authorisations within the meaning of para 284(1) of the StGB may be issued for games of chance has taken place at the level of the various *Länder*.

Para 1(1) of the RWLG provides:

> An association wishing to operate a mutual betting undertaking on horse races or other public horse competitions must first obtain the authorisation of the competent authorities in accordance with the law of the *Land*.

Para 2(1) of the RWLG provides:

> Any person wishing, on a commercial basis, to conclude bets on public horse competitions or serve as intermediary for such bets (Bookmaker) must first obtain the authorisation of the competent authorities in accordance with the law of the *Land*.

By the State treaty concerning lotteries in Germany (Staatsvertrag zum Lotteriewesen in Deutschland; 'the LottStV'), which entered into force on 1 July 2004, the *Länder* created a uniform framework for the organisation, operation and commercial placing of gambling, apart from casinos.

In a judgment of 28 March 2006, the Bundesverfassungsgericht (Federal Constitutional Court) held, concerning the legislation transposing the LottStV in the *Land* of Bavaria, that the public monopoly on bets on sporting competitions existing in that *Land* infringed para 12(1) of the Basic Law, guaranteeing freedom of occupation. That court held in particular that, by excluding private operators from the activity of organising bets, without at the same time providing a regulatory framework capable of ensuring, in form and in substance, both in law and in fact, effective pursuit of the aims of reducing the passion for gambling and combating addiction to it, that monopoly had a disproportionately adverse effect on the freedom of occupation thus guaranteed.

The State treaty on games of chance (Glücksspielstaatsvertrag; 'the GlüStV'), concluded between the *Länder* and which entered into force on 1 January 2008, establishes a new uniform framework for the organisation, operation and intermediation of games of chance aiming to satisfy the requirements laid down by the Bundesverfassungsgericht in the said judgment of 28 March 2006.

The explanatory report on the draft of the GlüStV ('the explanatory report') shows that the main aim of the latter is the prevention and combating of addiction to games of chance. According to the explanatory report, a study dating from April 2006, carried out, at the request of the Commission of the European Communities, by the Swiss Institute of Comparative Law and concerning the market for games of chance in the European Union, clearly showed the effectiveness which may result, in that perspective, from legislation and a strict channelling of the activities concerned.

As regards the specific area of bets on sporting competitions, the explanatory report indicated that whilst, for the great majority of persons placing bets, such bets might be only for relaxation and entertainment, it was very possible, on the evidence contained in the available scientific studies and expert reports, that, if the supply of those bets were significantly increased, the potential for dependency likely to be generated by them would be significant. It was thus necessary to adopt measures for preventing such dependency by imposing limits on the organisation, marketing and operation of such games of chance. The channelling and limitation of the market for those games by the GlüStV was to be obtained, in particular, by maintaining the existing monopoly on the organisation of bets on sporting competitions and on lotteries with particular risk potential.

According to para 1 of the GlüStV, the objectives of the latter are as follows:

1. to prevent dependency on games of chance and on bets, and to create the conditions for effectively combating dependency,
2. to limit the supply of games of chance and to channel the gaming instinct of the population in an organised and supervised manner, preventing in particular a drift towards unauthorised games of chance,
3. to ensure the protection of minors and players,
4. to ensure the smooth operation of games of chance and the protection of players against fraudulent manoeuvres, and to prevent criminality connected with and arising from games of chance.

Para 2 of the GlüStV states that, with regard to casinos, only paras 1, 3 to 8, 20 and 23 apply.

Para 4 of the GlüStV states:

(1) The organisation or intermediation of public games of chance may take place only with the authorisation of the competent authority of the *Land* concerned. All organisation or intermediation of such games is prohibited without such authorisation (unlawful games of chance).
(2) Such authorisation shall be refused where the organisation or intermediation of the game of chance is contrary to the objectives of para 1. Authorisation shall not be issued for the intermediation of games of chance unlawful according to the present State treaty. There is no established right to the obtaining of an authorisation.
[...]
(4) The organisation and intermediation of public games of chance on the internet are prohibited.

Para 10 of the GlüStV provides:

(1) In order to attain the objectives set out in para 1, the *Länder* are under a statutory obligation to ensure a sufficient supply of games of chance. They shall be assisted by a technical committee composed of experts specialised in combating dependency on games of chance.
(2) In accordance with the law, the *Länder* may undertake that task either by themselves or through the intermediary of legal persons under public law or private law companies in which legal persons under public law hold a direct or indirect controlling shareholding.
[...]
(5) Persons other than those referred to in subpara 2 shall be authorised to organise only lotteries and games in accordance with the provisions of the third section.

The third section of the GlüStV concerns lotteries with a low risk of danger, which may be authorised under highly restrictive conditions and exclusively for organisers pursuing public interest or charitable aims.

Para 25(6) of the GlüStV states:

The *Länder* may, for a maximum period of one year after the entry into force of the State treaty, in derogation from para 4(4), permit the organisation and intermediation of lotteries on the internet where there is no reason to refuse them pursuant to para 4(2) and where the following conditions are met:

- exclusion of minors or prohibited players guaranteed by identification and authentication measures, in compliance with the directives of the Commission for the protection of minors as a closed group of media users;
- limitation of stakes, as fixed in the authorisation, to EUR 1 000 per month, and guarantee that credit is prohibited;
- prohibition of particular incitements to dependency by rapid draws and of the possibility of participating interactively with publication of results in real time; as regards lotteries, limitation to two winning draws per week;
- localisation by use of the most modern methods, in order to ensure that only persons within the scope of the authorisation may participate;
- establishment and operation of a programme of social measures adapted to the specific conditions of the internet, the effectiveness of which is to be assessed scientifically.

According to the explanatory report, the transitional provision contained in para 25(6) of the GlüStV aims to provide equitable relief for two operators of commercial games who operate almost entirely on the internet and respectively employ 140 and 151 persons, by giving them sufficient time to bring their activity into conformity with the distribution channels authorised by the GlüStV.

The GlüStV was transposed by the Land Schleswig–Holstein by the law implementing the State treaty on games of chance in Germany (Gesetz zur Ausführung des Staatsvertrages zum Glücksspielwesen in Deutschland) of 13 December 2007 (GVOBl. 2007, p. 524; 'the GlüStV AG').

Para 4 of the GlüStV AG provides:

(1) In order to achieve the objectives set out in para 1 of the GlüStV, the Land Schleswig–Holstein shall concern itself with supervision of games of chance, the guarantee of a sufficient provision of games of chance, and scientific research in order to avoid and prevent the dangers of dependency connected with games of chance.

(2) In accordance with para 10(1) of the GlüStV, the Land Schleswig–Holstein shall fulfil that function through the intermediary of NordwestLotto Schleswig–Holstein GmbH & Co. KG. (NordwestLotto Schleswig–Holstein), the shares of which are held, directly or indirectly, in whole or in part, by the Land. [...]
(3) NordwestLotto Schleswig–Holstein may organise lottery draws, scratch cards and sporting bets, as well as lotteries and additional games in the matter. [...].

Para 5(1) of the GlüStV AG provides:

Authorisation under para 4(1) of the GlüStV for games of chance which are not lotteries having a low potential for danger (para 6) presupposes:

1. the absence of grounds for refusal set out in para 4(2), first and second sentences, of the GlüStV,
2. compliance with:
   (a) the requirements concerning the protection of minors in accordance with para 4(3) of the GlüStV,
   (b) the internet prohibition contained in para 4(4) of the GlüStV,
   (c) the restrictions on advertising contained in para 5 of the GlüStV,
   (d) the requirements concerning the programme of social measures contained in para 6 of the GlüStV, and
   (e) the requirements on explanations concerning the risks of dependency in accordance with para 7 of the GlüStV,
3. the reliability of the organiser or the intermediary, who must, in particular, ensure that the organisation and intermediation are carried out in a regular manner and easily verifiable by players and the competent authorities,
4. the participation, in accordance with para 9(5) of the GlüStV, of the technical committee in the introduction of new games of chance, of new distribution channels or in considerable enlargement of existing distribution channels and a guarantee that a report on the social repercussions of the new or enlarged supply of games of chance has been drafted,
5. a guarantee that the organisers, within the meaning of para 10(2) of the GlüStV, participate in the concerted system for prohibiting certain players in accordance with paras 8 and 23 of the GlüStV,
6. a guarantee that players prohibited from gambling in accordance with the first sentence of para 21(3) and the first sentence of para 22(2) of the GlüStV are excluded, and
7. compliance by intermediaries in commercial gambling with para 19 of the GlüStV.

If the conditions in the first sentence are met, authorisation should be given. Para 9 of the GlüStV AG provides:

By derogation from para 4(4) of the GlüStV, in the case of lotteries, organisation and intermediation on the internet may be authorised until 31 December 2008 if compliance with the conditions set out in para 25(6) of the GlüStV is guaranteed. [...]

Carmen Media is established in Gibraltar, where it obtained a licence authorising it to market bets on sporting competitions. For tax reasons, however, that licence is limited to the marketing of bets abroad ('offshore bookmaking').

In February 2006, wishing to offer such bets via the internet in Germany, Carmen Media applied to the Land Schleswig–Holstein for a declaration that that activity was lawful, having regard to the licence which Carmen Media holds in Gibraltar. In the alternative, it applied for the issuing of an authorisation for its activity, or, failing that, for tolerance of that activity until the establishment of an authorisation procedure for private offerors of bets which complies with Community law.

Those applications having been rejected on 29 May 2006, Carmen Media brought an action on 30 June 2006 before the Schleswig–Holsteinisches Verwaltungsgericht (Schleswig–Holstein Administrative Court).

The Schleswig–Holsteinisches Verwaltungsgericht decided to stay the proceedings before it and to refer the questions to the European Court of Justice for a preliminary ruling.

5.2.10 Summary of the Legal and Factual Context of the Case-Law

The factual background of *Zenatti* was revisited by the ECJ in the ensuing Gambelli and Placanica cases, which set the tone for modern legal handling of EU sports betting policies. *Zenatti* concerned the prohibition imposed on the defendant from acting as an intermediary in Italy for a company established in the United Kingdom specializing in the taking of bets on sporting events.

Gambelli involved a similar background to *Zenatti*. The defendants were accused of having unlawfully organised clandestine bets and of being the proprietors of centres carrying on the activity of collecting and transmitting betting data, which constituted an offence of fraud against the State.

The European Court of Justice was given a third opportunity to assume a definite stance on such matters of restrictive practices and national policies on sports betting in violation of the provisions of the EC Treaty, in *Placanica*. Once again, like in *Gambelli* Stanley and its agents in Italy were involved (in all three 'Italian' cases, including *Zenatti* UK-based sports betting enterprises were involved; so, in fact these were 'UK/Italian' cases); the latter (in *Placanica*) were three defendants who were prosecuted by the Italian State for running the 'data transmission' sites one found in *Zenatti* and *Gambelli*. Until 2002, the method of licensing sport betting operators was reserved by and for the state-affiliated and licensed organisations CONI (Italian National Olympic Committee) and UNIRE (horse-racing) respectively. In 2002, the competences of the CONI and UNIRE with respect to bets on sporting events were transferred to the independent authority for the administration of State monopolies, acting under the supervision of the Ministry of Economic Affairs and Finance. Other than the subjective difficulty in obtaining such a license from Italian authorities, the Italian Penal Code criminalised such sport betting activities, as foreign sport betting operators would not be allowed to run their business without a license. It is expressly stated in *Placanica* that the legal and factual context of this case is similar to the situations that gave rise to the judgements in *Zenatti* and *Gambelli*.

The judgment in *Commission v Italy* (all other sports betting cases mentioned here are preliminary rulings of the ECJ) concerned a complaint lodged by a private operator, Italy had failed to fulfil its obligations under the EC Treaty by renewing 329 licences for horse-race betting operations without inviting any competing bids.

The case of *Liga Portuguesa de Futebol Profissional* concerned fines imposed on the plaintiffs on the ground that they had infringed the Portuguese legislation governing the provision of certain games of chance via the internet. It is a case of modern times, that is a case of so-called 'remote gambling'—without intermediaries like in *Zenatti*, *Gambelli* and *Placanica*. Bets are placed directly by the consumer on the internet or by some other means of direct communication. In 2003 the legal framework in Portugal governing *inter alia* sports betting had been adapted in order to take account of technical developments enabling games to be offered by electronic means, in particular the internet.

The conclusion is that the factual context of *Zenatti*, *Gambelli* and *Placanica* is similar, and *Liga Portuguesa de Futebol Profissional* is a case of 'remote gambling,' whereas *Commission v Italy* is essentially different from these cases.

Since the Liga Portuguesa case, four new rulings were delivered by the European Court of Justice in 2010 only, in chronological order: Ladbrokes and Sporting Exchange ('Betfair') on the same day (3 June 2010), Sjöberg/Gerdin, and Carmen Media. The first four cases were Ïtalian ones (Zenatti, Gambelli, Placanica and Commission v. Italy), followed by a Portuguese one; after these Southern European cases the focus now has shifted to Northern Europe: Betfair and Ladbrokes are Dutch cases, Sjöberg/Gerdin is a Swedish one, and Carmen Media a German one.

In the Ladbrokes and Betfair cases UK-based sports betting enterprises were involved. The case concerned the possible unlawful conduct of Ladbrokes on the Netherlands market for games of chance, and the rejection of Betfair's applications for a licence to organise games of chance in the Netherlands. it is observed that Netherlands legislation in relation to games of chance is based on a system of exclusive licences, and there is no possibility at all of offering games of chance interactively via the internet in the Netherlands. De Lotto holds the licence for the organisation of sports-related prize competitions and others.

In Sweden (Sjöberg/Gerdin case), under the Criminal Code the organisation without a licence of gambling constitutes an unlawful act. Under the Lotteries Act it is prohibited to promote, without a special licence and for the purpose of profit, participation in unlicensed gambling, organised within Sweden or abroad. Expekt, Unibet, Ladbrokes and Centrebet are private operators established in Member States other than Sweden who offer internet gambling, in particular to persons resident in Sweden. These games include, among others, sports betting. The Swedish newspaper publishers Sjöberg and Gerdin promoted the participation of Swedish residents in gambling organised abroad.

The Carmen Media case concerned the refusal of a request by Carmen Media for acknowledgement of the right to offer bets on sporting competitions via the internet in the Land Schleswig–Holstein. Carmen Media is established in Gibraltar, where it obtained a licence authorising it to market bets on sporting competitions abroad ('offshore bookmaking').

The Ladbrokes, Betfair, Sjöberg/Gerdin and Carmen Media cases like Liga Portuguesa are all remote gambling cases.

5.3 The Case-Law Presented According to the 'Reversal' Method

5.3.1 Carmen Media

40 In that regard, it should be noted that activities which consist in allowing users to participate, for remuneration, in a game of chance constitute 'services' for the purposes of Article 49 EC (see, to that effect, Case C-275/92 *Schindler* [1994] ECR I-1039, para 25, and Case C-67/98 *Zenatti* [1999] ECR I-7289, para 24).

41 Therefore, as consistent case-law shows, such services fall within the scope of Article 49 EC where the provider is established in a Member State other than the one in which the service is offered (see, to that effect, *Zenatti*, paras 24 and 25). That is particularly so in the case of services which the provider offers via the internet to potential recipients established in other Member States and which he provides without moving from the Member State in which he is established (see, to that effect, *Gambelli and Others*, paras 53 and 54).

44 Such a finding is, moreover, without prejudice to the ability of any Member State whose territory is covered by an offer of bets emanating, via the internet, from such an operator, to require the latter to comply with restrictions laid down by its legislation in that area, provided those restrictions comply with the requirements of European Union law ('EU law'), particularly that they be non-discriminatory and proportionate (Joined Cases C-338/04, C-359/04 and C-360/04 *Placanica and Others* [2007] ECR I-1891, paras 48 and 49).

45 In that regard, it should be noted that, with regard to the justifications which may be accepted where internal measures restrict the freedom to provide services, the Court has held several times that the objectives pursued by national legislation in the area of gambling and bets, considered as a whole, usually concern the protection of the recipients of the services in question, and of consumers more generally, and the protection of public order. It has also held that such objectives are amongst the overriding reasons in the public interest capable of justifying obstacles to the freedom to provide services (see to that effect, in particular, *Schindler*, para 58; *Läärä and Others*, para 33; *Zenatti*, para 31; Case C-6/01 *Anomar and Others* [2003] ECR I-8621, para 73; and *Placanica and Others*, para 46).

46 The case-law of the Court of Justice thus shows that it is for each Member State to assess whether, in the context of the legitimate aims which it pursues,

it is necessary wholly or partially to prohibit activities of that nature, or only to restrict them and to lay down more or less strict supervisory rules for that purpose, the necessity and the proportionality of the measures thus adopted having only to be assessed having regard to the objectives pursued and the level of protection sought to be ensured by the national authorities concerned (see to that effect, in particular, *Läärä and Others*, paras 35 and 36; *Zenatti*, paras 33 and 34; and Case C-42/07 *Liga Portuguesa de Futebol Profissional and Bwin International* [2009] ECR I-7633, para 58).

55 As a preliminary observation, it should be noted that, in para 67 of the judgment in *Gambelli and Others*, after stating that restrictions on gaming activities might be justified by imperative requirements in the public interest, such as consumer protection and the prevention of both fraud and incitement to squander money on gambling, the Court held that that applied only in so far as such restrictions, based on such grounds and on the need to preserve public order, were suitable for achieving those objectives, inasmuch as they must serve to limit betting activities in a consistent and systematic manner.

60 The Court has also held that, in the matter of games of chance, it is in principle necessary to examine separately for each of the restrictions imposed by the national legislation whether, in particular, it is suitable for achieving the objective or objectives invoked by the Member State concerned and whether it does not go beyond what is necessary in order to achieve those objectives (*Placanica and Others*, para 49).

65 The Court has, similarly, held that it is for the national courts to ensure, having regard in particular to the actual rules for applying the restrictive legislation concerned, that the latter genuinely meets the concern to reduce opportunities for gambling and to limit activities in that area in a consistent and systematic manner (see to that effect, in particular, *Zenatti*, paras 36 and 37, and *Placanica and Others*, paras 52 and 53).

66 As the Court has already held in those various respects, in *Gambelli and Others*, paras 7, 8 and 69, in so far as the authorities of a Member State incite and encourage consumers to participate in lotteries, games of chance or betting to the financial benefit of the public purse, the authorities of that State cannot invoke public order concerns relating to the need to reduce opportunities for gambling in order to justify restrictive measures, even if, as in that case, the latter relate exclusively to betting activities.

85 However, the margin of discretion which the Member States thus enjoy in restricting gambling does not exonerate them from ensuring that the measures they impose satisfy the conditions laid down in the case-law of the Court, particularly as regards their proportionality (see, in particular, *Liga Portuguesa de Futebol Profissional and Bwin International*, para 59 and case-law cited).

86 According to consistent case-law, where a system of authorisation pursuing legitimate objectives recognised by the case-law is established in a Member State, such a system cannot render legitimate discretionary conduct on the part of the national authorities which is liable to negate the effectiveness of provisions of EU law, in particular those relating to a fundamental freedom such

as that at issue in the main proceedings (see, in particular, Case C-203/08 *Sporting Exchange* [2010] ECR I-0000, para 49).

87 Also, if a prior administrative authorisation scheme is to be justified, even though it derogates from a fundamental freedom, it must be based on objective, non-discriminatory criteria known in advance, in such a way as to circumscribe the exercise of the authorities' discretion so that it is not used arbitrarily. Furthermore, any person affected by a restrictive measure based on such a derogation must have an effective judicial remedy available to them (see *Sporting Exchange*, para 50 and case-law cited).

101 The Court has already had occasion to emphasise the particularities concerned with the offering of games of chance on the internet (see *Liga Portuguesa de Futebol Profissional and Bwin International*, para 72).

102 It has thus observed in particular that, because of the lack of direct contact between consumer and operator, games of chance accessible via the internet involve different and more substantial risks of fraud by operators against consumers compared with the traditional markets for such games (*Liga Portuguesa de Futebol Profissional and Bwin International*, para 70).

5.3.2 Sjöberg/Gerdin

32 It must be recalled at the outset that Article 49 EC requires the abolition of all restrictions on the freedom to provide services, even if those restrictions apply without distinction to national providers of services and to those from other Member States, when they are liable to prohibit, impede or render less advantageous the activities of a service provider established in another Member State where it lawfully provides similar services. Moreover, the freedom to provide services covers both providers and recipients of services (Case C-42/07 *Liga Portuguesa de Futebol Profissional and Bwin International* [2009] ECR I-0000, para 51 and the case-law cited).

36 Article 46(1) EC, applicable in this field by reason of Article 55 EC, allows restrictions justified on grounds of public policy, public security or public health. In addition, a certain number of overriding reasons in the general interest have been recognised by case-law, such as the objectives of consumer protection and the prevention of both fraud and incitement to squander money on gambling, as well as the general need to preserve public order (see Joined Cases C-338/04, C-359/04 and C-360/04 *Placanica and Others* [2007] ECR I-1891, para 46 and *Liga Portuguesa de Futebol Profissional and Bwin International*, para 56).

37 In that context, it must be observed that the legislation on gambling is one of the areas in which there are significant moral, religious and cultural differences between the Member States. In the absence of Community harmonisation in the field, it is for each Member State to determine in those areas, in accordance

with its own scale of values, what is required to protect the interests in question (*Liga Portuguesa de Futebol Profissional and Bwin International*, para 57).

38 The mere fact that a Member State has opted for a system of protection which differs from that adopted by another Member State cannot affect the assessment of the need for, and proportionality of, the provisions enacted to that end. Those provisions must be assessed solely by reference to the objectives pursued by the competent authorities of the Member State concerned and the level of protection which they seek to ensure (*Liga Portuguesa de Futebol Profissional and Bwin International*, para 58).

39 The Member States are therefore free to set the objectives of their policy on gambling and, where appropriate, to define in detail the level of protection sought. However, the restrictive measures that they impose must satisfy the conditions laid down in the case-law of the Court as regards their proportionality (*Liga Portuguesa de Futebol Profissional and Bwin International*, para 59).

40 It is thus necessary to examine in particular whether, in the cases in the main action, the restriction on advertising imposed by the Lotterilag in respect of gambling organised in Member States other than the Kingdom of Sweden, by private operators for the purpose of profit, is suitable for achieving the legitimate objective or objectives invoked by that Member State, and whether it does not go beyond what is necessary in order to achieve those objectives. National legislation is moreover appropriate for ensuring attainment of the objective pursued only if it genuinely reflects a concern to attain it in a consistent and systematic manner. In any event, those restrictions must be applied without discrimination (*Liga Portuguesa de Futebol Profissional and Bwin International*, paras 60 and 61).

49 Although in principle criminal legislation is a matter for which the Member States are responsible, the Court has consistently held that European Union law sets certain limits to their power, and such legislation may not restrict the fundamental freedoms guaranteed by European Union law (*Placanica and Others*, para 68).

50 It follows moreover from the case-law of the Court that restrictive measures imposed by the Member States on account of the pursuit of objectives in the public interest must be applied without discrimination (*Placanica and Others*, para 49, and *Liga Portuguesa de Futebol Profissional and Bwin International*, para 60).

54 In that context, it must be recalled that the cooperation between the national courts and the Court of Justice established by Article 267 TFEU is based on a clear division of responsibilities. In proceedings brought on the basis of that Article, the interpretation of provisions of national law is a matter for the courts of the Member States, not for the Court of Justice (see, to that effect, *Placanica and Others*, para 36, and *Liga Portuguesa de Futebol Profissional and Bwin International*, para 37).

5.3.3 Ladbrokes

15 Article 49 EC requires the abolition of all restrictions on the freedom to provide services, even if those restrictions apply without distinction to national providers of services and to those from other Member States, when they are liable to prohibit, impede or render less advantageous the activities of a service provider established in another Member State where it lawfully provides similar services. The freedom to provide services is for the benefit of both providers and recipients of services (Case C-42/07 *Liga Portuguesa de Futebol Profissional and Bwin International* [2009] ECR I-0000, para 51 and the case-law cited).

16 It is common ground that the legislation of a Member State under which exclusive rights to organise and promote games of chance are conferred on a single operator, and which prohibits any other operator, including an operator established in another Member State, from offering via the internet services within the scope of that regime in the territory of the first Member State, constitutes a restriction on the freedom to provide services enshrined in Article 49 EC (*Liga Portuguesa de Futebol Profissional and Bwin International*, para 52, and Case C-203/08 *Sporting Exchange* [2010] ECR I-0000, para 24).

17 However, it is necessary to assess whether such a restriction may be allowed as a derogation expressly provided for by Articles 45 EC and 46 EC, applicable in this area by virtue of Article 55 EC, or justified, in accordance with the case-law of the Court, by overriding reasons in the public interest (see, to that effect, *Liga Portuguesa de Futebol Profissional and Bwin International*, para 55).

18 Article 46(1) EC allows restrictions justified on grounds of public policy, public security or public health. A certain number of overriding reasons in the public interest which may also justify such restrictions have been recognised by the case-law of the Court, including, in particular, the objectives of consumer protection and the prevention of both fraud and incitement to squander money on gambling, as well as the general need to preserve public order (*Liga Portuguesa de Futebol Profissional and Bwin International*, para 56).

19 In that context, moral, religious or cultural factors, as well as the morally and financially harmful consequences for the individual and for society associated with betting and gaming, may serve to justify a margin of discretion for the national authorities, sufficient to enable them to determine what is required in order to ensure consumer protection and the preservation of public order (*Gambelli and Others*, para 63, and *Placanica and Others*, para 47).

20 The Member States are free to set the objectives of their policy on betting and gambling according to their own scale of values and, where appropriate, to define in detail the level of protection sought. The restrictive measures that they impose must, however, satisfy the conditions laid down in the case-law of the Court, in particular as regards their proportionality (see, to that effect, *Placanica and Others*, para 48, and *Liga Portuguesa de Futebol Profissional and Bwin International*, para 59).

21 Specifically, restrictions based on the reasons referred to in para 18 of the present judgment must be suitable for achieving those objectives, inasmuch as they must serve to limit betting activities in a consistent and systematic manner (see, to that effect, *Gambelli and Others*, para 67).

22 According to the case-law of the Court, it is for the national courts to determine whether Member States' legislation actually serves the objectives which might justify it and whether the restrictions it imposes do not appear disproportionate in the light of those objectives (*Gambelli and Others*, para 75, and *Placanica and Others*, para 58).

25 As the Court has already held, it is possible that a policy of controlled expansion in the betting and gaming sector may be entirely consistent with the objective of drawing players away from clandestine betting and gaming—and, as such, activities which are prohibited—to activities which are authorised and regulated. In order to achieve that objective, authorised operators must represent a reliable, but at the same time attractive, alternative to a prohibited activity. This may as such necessitate the offer of an extensive range of games, advertising on a certain scale and the use of new distribution techniques (*Placanica and Others*, para 55).

26 While it is true that the grounds of the judgment in *Placanica and Others* refer solely to the objective of crime prevention in the betting and gaming sector, whereas, in the present case, the Netherlands legislation is also designed to curb gambling addiction, the fact remains that those two objectives must be considered together, since they relate both to consumer protection and to the preservation of public order (see, to that effect, Case C-275/92 *Schindler* [1994] ECR I-1039, para 58; Case C-124/97 *Läärä and Others* [1999] ECR I-6067, para 33; and Case C-67/98 *Zenatti* [1999] ECR I-7289, para 31).

52 That question falls within the same legal framework as the first question referred in the case giving rise to the judgment in *Sporting Exchange* and is identical to it.

54 In that regard, it should be noted that the internet gaming industry has not been the subject of harmonisation within the European Union. A Member State is therefore entitled to take the view that the mere fact that an operator such as the Ladbrokes companies lawfully offers services in that sector via the internet in another Member State, in which it is established and where it is in principle already subject to statutory conditions and controls on the part of the competent authorities in that State, is not a sufficient assurance that national consumers will be protected against the risks of fraud and crime, in the light of the difficulties liable to be encountered in such a context by the authorities of the Member State of establishment in assessing the professional qualities and integrity of operators (see, to that effect, *Liga Portuguesa de Futebol Profissional and Bwin International*, para 69).

55 In addition, because of the lack of direct contact between consumer and operator, games of chance accessible via the internet involve different and more substantial risks of fraud by operators against consumers compared with the traditional markets for such games (*Liga Portuguesa de Futebol Profissional and Bwin International*, para 70).

57 It follows from this that, in the light of the specific features associated with the provision of games of chance via the internet, the restriction at issue in the main proceedings may be regarded as justified by the objective of combating fraud and crime (see, to that effect, *Liga Portuguesa de Futebol Profissional and Bwin International*, para 72).

5.3.4 Sporting Exchange ('Betfair')

23 Article 49 EC requires the abolition of all restrictions on the freedom to provide services, even if those restrictions apply without distinction to national providers of services and to those from other Member States, when they are liable to prohibit, impede or render less advantageous the activities of a service provider established in another Member State where it lawfully provides similar services. The freedom to provide services is for the benefit of both providers and recipients of services (Case C-42/07 *Liga Portuguesa de Futebol Profissional and Bwin International* [2009] ECR I-0000, para 51 and the case-law cited).

24 It is common ground that legislation of a Member State such as the legislation at issue in the main proceedings constitutes a restriction on the freedom to provide services enshrined in Article 49 EC (see, to that effect, *Liga Portuguesa de Futebol Profissional and Bwin International*, para 52, and Case C-258/08 *Ladbrokes Betting & Gaming and Ladbrokes International* [2010] ECR I-0000, para 16).

25 However, it is necessary to assess whether such a restriction may be allowed as a derogation expressly provided for by Articles 45 EC and 46 EC, applicable in this area by virtue of Article 55 EC, or justified, in accordance with the case-law of the Court, by overriding reasons in the public interest (see, to that effect, *Liga Portuguesa de Futebol Profissional and Bwin International*, para 55).

26 Article 46(1) EC allows restrictions justified on grounds of public policy, public security or public health. A certain number of overriding reasons in the public interest which may also justify such restrictions have been recognised by the case-law of the Court, including, in particular, the objectives of consumer protection and the prevention of both fraud and incitement to squander money on gambling, as well as the general need to preserve public order (*Liga Portuguesa de Futebol Profissional and Bwin International*, para 56).

27 In that context, moral, religious or cultural factors, as well as the morally and financially harmful consequences for the individual and for society associated with betting and gaming, may serve to justify a margin of discretion for the national authorities, sufficient to enable them to determine what is required in order to ensure consumer protection and the preservation of public order (Case C-243/01 *Gambelli and Others* [2003] ECR I-13031, para 63, and Joined Cases C-338/04, C-359/04 and C-360/04 *Placanica and Others* [2007] ECR I-1891, para 47).

28 The Member States are free to set the objectives of their policy on betting and gambling according to their own scale of values and, where appropriate, to define in detail the level of protection sought. The restrictive measures that they impose must, however, satisfy the conditions laid down in the case-law of the Court, in particular as regards their proportionality (see, to that effect, *Placanica and Others*, para 48, and *Liga Portuguesa de Futebol Profissional and Bwin International*, para 59).

29 According to the case-law of the Court, it is for the national courts to determine whether Member States' legislation actually serves the objectives which might justify it and whether the restrictions it imposes do not appear disproportionate in the light of those objectives (*Gambelli and Others*, para 75, and *Placanica and Others*, para 58).

33 It should be noted in that regard that the internet gaming industry has not been the subject of harmonisation within the European Union. A Member State is therefore entitled to take the view that the mere fact that an operator such as Betfair lawfully offers services in that sector via the internet in another Member State, in which it is established and where it is in principle already subject to statutory conditions and controls on the part of the competent authorities in that State, cannot be regarded as amounting to a sufficient assurance that national consumers will be protected against the risks of fraud and crime, in the light of the difficulties liable to be encountered in such a context by the authorities of the Member State of establishment in assessing the professional qualities and integrity of operators (see, to that effect, *Liga Portuguesa de Futebol Profissional and Bwin International*, para 69).

34 In addition, because of the lack of direct contact between consumer and operator, games of chance accessible via the internet involve different and more substantial risks of fraud by operators against consumers compared with the traditional markets for such games (*Liga Portuguesa de Futebol Profissional and Bwin International*, para 70).

36 It follows that, in the light of the specific features associated with the provision of games of chance via the internet, the restriction at issue in the main proceedings may be regarded as justified by the objective of combating fraud and crime (*Liga Portuguesa de Futebol Profissional and Bwin International*, para 72).

49 Nevertheless, such a system cannot render legitimate discretionary conduct on the part of the national authorities which is liable to negate the effectiveness of provisions of European Union law, in particular those relating to a fundamental freedom such as the freedom to provide services.

50 It has consistently been held that if a prior administrative authorisation scheme is to be justified, even though it derogates from a fundamental freedom, it must be based on objective, non-discriminatory criteria known in advance, in such a way as to circumscribe the exercise of the authorities' discretion so that it is not used arbitrarily (Case C-389/05 *Commission* v *France* [2008] ECR I-5397, para 94, and Case C-169/07 *Hartlauer* [2009] ECR I-1721, para 64). Furthermore, any person affected by a restrictive measure based on such a

derogation must have a judicial remedy available to them (see, to that effect, Case C-205/99 *Analir and Others* [2001] ECR I-1271, para 38).

59 In any event, the restrictions on the fundamental freedom enshrined in Article 49 EC which arise specifically from the procedures for the grant of a licence to a single operator or for the renewal thereof, such as those at issue in the main proceedings, may be regarded as being justified if the Member State concerned decides to grant a licence to, or renew the licence of, a public operator whose management is subject to direct State supervision or a private operator whose activities are subject to strict control by the public authorities (see, to that effect, Case C–124/97 *Läärä and Others* [1999] ECR I–6067, paras 40 and 42, and *Liga Portuguesa de Futebol Profissional and Bwin International*, paras 66 and 67).

5.3.5 Liga Portuguesa de Futebol Profissional

37 In that connection, it should be noted that the cooperative arrangements established by Article 234 EC are based on a clear division of responsibilities between the national courts and the Court of Justice. In proceedings brought on the basis of that Article, the interpretation of provisions of national law is a matter for the courts of the Member States, not for the Court of Justice, and the Court has no jurisdiction to rule on the compatibility of national rules with Community law. On the other hand, the Court does have jurisdiction to provide the national court with all the guidance as to the interpretation of Community law necessary to enable that court to rule on the compatibility of those national rules with Community law (Joined Cases C-338/04, C-359/04 and C-360/04 *Placanica and Others* [2007] ECR I-1891, para 36).

51 Article 49 EC requires the abolition of all restrictions on the freedom to provide services, even if those restrictions apply without distinction to national providers of services and to those from other Member States, when they are liable to prohibit, impede or render less advantageous the activities of a service provider established in another Member State where it lawfully provides similar services (see, to that effect, Case C-76/90 *Säger* [1991] ECR I-4221, para 12, and Case C-58/98 *Corsten* [2000] ECR I-7919, para 33). Moreover, the freedom to provide services is for the benefit of both providers and recipients of services (see, to that effect, Joined Cases 286/82 and 26/83 *Luisi and Carbone* [1984] ECR 377, para 16).

52 It is accepted that the legislation of a Member State which prohibits providers such as Bwin, established in other Member States, from offering via the internet services in the territory of that first Member State constitutes a restriction on the freedom to provide services enshrined in Article 49 EC (see, to that effect, Case C-243/01 *Gambelli and Others* [2003] ECR I-13031, para 54).

55 It is necessary to consider to what extent the restriction at issue in the main proceedings may be allowed as a derogation expressly provided for by Articles 45 EC and 46 EC, applicable in this area by virtue of Article 55 EC, or justified, in accordance with the case-law of the Court, by overriding reasons in the public interest.

56 Article 46(1) EC allows restrictions justified on grounds of public policy, public security or public health. In addition, a certain number of overriding reasons in the public interest have been recognised by case-law, such as the objectives of consumer protection and the prevention of both fraud and incitement to squander money on gambling, as well as the general need to preserve public order (see, to that effect, *Placanica and Others*, para 46 and case-law cited).

57 In that context, as most of the Member States which submitted observations to the Court have noted, the legislation on games of chance is one of the areas in which there are significant moral, religious and cultural differences between the Member States. In the absence of Community harmonisation in the field, it is for each Member State to determine in those areas, in accordance with its own scale of values, what is required in order to ensure that the interests in question are protected (see, inter alia, Case 34/79 *Henn and Darby* [1979] ECR 3795, para 15; Case C-275/92 *Schindler* [1994] ECR I-1039, para 32; Case C-268/99 *Jany and Others* [2001] ECR I-8615, paras 56 and 60, and *Placanica and Others*, para 47).

58 The mere fact that a Member State has opted for a system of protection which differs from that adopted by another Member State cannot affect the assessment of the need for, and proportionality of, the provisions enacted to that end. Those provisions must be assessed solely by reference to the objectives pursued by the competent authorities of the Member State concerned and the degree of protection which they seek to ensure (Case C-124/97 *Läärä and Others* [1999] ECR I-6067, para 36, and Case C-67/98 *Zenatti* [1999] ECR I-7289, para 34).

59 The Member States are therefore free to set the objectives of their policy on betting and gambling and, where appropriate, to define in detail the level of protection sought. However, the restrictive measures that they impose must satisfy the conditions laid down in the case-law of the Court as regards their proportionality (*Placanica and Others*, para 48).

60 In the present case, it is thus necessary to examine in particular whether the restriction of the provision of games of chance via the internet, imposed by the national legislation at issue in the main proceedings, is suitable for achieving the objective or objectives invoked by the Member State concerned, and whether it does not go beyond what is necessary in order to achieve those objectives. In any event, those restrictions must be applied without discrimination (see, to that effect, *Placanica and Others*, para 49).

61 In that context, it must be recalled that national legislation is appropriate for ensuring attainment of the objective pursued only if it genuinely reflects a

concern to attain it in a consistent and systematic manner (Case C-169/07 *Hartlauer* [2009] ECR I-0000, para 55).

64 The Court has also recognised that limited authorisation of games on an exclusive basis has the advantage of confining the operation of gambling within controlled channels and of preventing the risk of fraud or crime in the context of such operation (see *Läärä and Others*, para 37, and *Zenatti*, para 35).

66 In that regard, it is apparent from the national legal framework, set out in paras 12 to 19 of the present judgment, that the organisation and functioning of Santa Casa are governed by considerations and requirements relating to the pursuit of objectives in the public interest. The Gaming Department of Santa Casa has been given the powers of an administrative authority to open, institute and prosecute proceedings involving offences of illegal operation of games of chance in relation to which Santa Casa has the exclusive rights.

67 In that connection, it must be acknowledged that the grant of exclusive rights to operate games of chance via the internet to a single operator, such as Santa Casa, which is subject to strict control by the public authorities, may, in circumstances such as those in the main proceedings, confine the operation of gambling within controlled channels and be regarded as appropriate for the purpose of protecting consumers against fraud on the part of operators.

69 In that regard, it should be noted that the sector involving games of chance offered via the internet has not been the subject of Community harmonisation. A Member State is therefore entitled to take the view that the mere fact that an operator such as Bwin lawfully offers services in that sector via the internet in another Member State, in which it is established and where it is in principle already subject to statutory conditions and controls on the part of the competent authorities in that State, cannot be regarded as amounting to a sufficient assurance that national consumers will be protected against the risks of fraud and crime, in the light of the difficulties liable to be encountered in such a context by the authorities of the Member State of establishment in assessing the professional qualities and integrity of operators.

70 In addition, because of the lack of direct contact between consumer and operator, games of chance accessible via the internet involve different and more substantial risks of fraud by operators against consumers compared with the traditional markets for such games.

72 It follows that, in the light of the specific features associated with the provision of games of chance via the internet, the restriction at issue in the main proceedings may be regarded as justified by the objective of combating fraud and crime.

5.3.6 Commission v Italy

20 As the Commission rightly observed, the Italian Government has not denied, either during the pre-litigation procedure or in the course of these proceedings, that the award of licences for horse-race betting operations in Italy constitutes a public

service concession. That classification was accepted by the Court in Placanica and Others (C-338/04, C-359/04 and C-360/04 [2007] ECR I-0000), in which it interprets Articles 43 and 49 EC in relation to the same national legislation.

26 In those circumstances, it is necessary to consider whether the renewal may be recognised as an exceptional measure, as expressly provided for in Articles 45 EC and 46 EC, or justified, in accordance with the case-law of the Court, for reasons of overriding general interest (see, to that effect, Case C-243/01 Gambelli and Others [2003] ECR I-13031, para 60, and Placanica and Others, cited above, para 45).

27 On that point, a certain number of reasons of overriding general interest have been recognised by the case-law, such as the objectives of consumer protection and the prevention of both fraud and incitement to squander on gaming, as well as the general need to preserve public order (Placanica and Others, cited above, para 46).

28 Although the Member States are free to set the objectives of their policy on betting and gaming and, where appropriate, to define in detail the level of protection sought, the restrictive measures that they impose must nevertheless satisfy the conditions laid down in the case-law of the Court as regards their proportionality (Placanica and Others, cited above, para 48).

29 It should therefore be examined whether the renewal of the licences without inviting any competing bids is suitable for achieving the objective pursued by the Italian Republic and does not go beyond what is necessary in order to achieve that objective. In any case, the renewal must be applied without discrimination (see, to that effect, Gambelli and Others, paras 64 and 65, and Placanica and Others, paras 49).

5.3.7 *Placanica*

2 The references have been made in the course of criminal proceedings against Mr Placanica, Mr Palazzese and Mr Sorricchio for failure to comply with the Italian legislation governing the collection of bets. The legal and factual context of these references is similar to the situations that gave rise to the judgments in Case C-67/98 Zenatti [1999] ECR I-7289 and Case C-243/01 Gambelli and Others [2003] ECR I-13031.

36 Admittedly, as regards the division of responsibilities under the cooperative arrangements established by Article 234 EC, the interpretation of provisions of national law is a matter for the national courts, not for the Court of Justice, and the Court has no jurisdiction, in proceedings brought on the basis of that Article, to rule on the compatibility of national rules with Community law. On the other hand, the Court does have jurisdiction to provide the national court with all the guidance as to the interpretation of Community law necessary to enable that court to rule on the compatibility of those national rules

with Community law (see, in particular, Case C-55/94 Gebhard [1995] ECR I-4165, para 19, and Wilson, paras 34 and 35).

42 The Court has already ruled that, in so far as the national legislation at issue in the main proceedings prohibits—on pain of criminal penalties—the pursuit of activities in the betting and gaming sector without a licence or police authorisation issued by the State, it constitutes a restriction on the freedom of establishment and the freedom to provide services (see Gambelli and Others, para 59 and the operative part).

43 In the first place, the restrictions imposed on intermediaries such as the defendants in the main proceedings constitute obstacles to the freedom of establishment of companies established in another Member State, such as Stanley, which pursue the activity of collecting bets in other Member States through an organisation of agencies such as the DTCs operated by the defendants in the main proceedings (see Gambelli and Others, para 46).

44 Secondly, the prohibition imposed on intermediaries such as the defendants in the main proceedings, under which they are forbidden to facilitate the provision of betting services in relation to sporting events organised by a supplier, such as Stanley, established in a Member State other than that in which the intermediaries pursue their activity, constitutes a restriction on the right of that supplier freely to provide services, even if the intermediaries are established in the same Member State as the recipients of the services (see Gambelli and Others, para 58).

45 In those circumstances, it is necessary to consider whether the restrictions at issue in the main proceedings may be recognised as exceptional measures, as expressly provided for in Articles 45 EC and 46 EC, or justified, in accordance with the case-law of the Court, for reasons of overriding general interest (see Gambelli and Others, para 60).

46 On that point, a certain number of reasons of overriding general interest have been recognised by the case-law, such as the objectives of consumer protection and the prevention of both fraud and incitement to squander on gaming, as well as the general need to preserve public order (see, to that effect, Case C-275/92 Schindler [1994] ECR I-1039, paras 57 to 60; Case C-124/97 Läärä and Others [1999] ECR I-6067, paras 32 and 33; Zenatti, paras 30 and 31; and Gambelli and Others, para 67).

47 In that context, moral, religious or cultural factors, as well as the morally and financially harmful consequences for the individual and for society associated with betting and gaming, may serve to justify a margin of discretion for the national authorities, sufficient to enable them to determine what is required in order to ensure consumer protection and the preservation of public order (Gambelli and Others, para 63).

48 However, although the Member States are free to set the objectives of their policy on betting and gaming and, where appropriate, to define in detail the level of protection sought, the restrictive measures that they impose must nevertheless satisfy the conditions laid down in the case-law of the Court as regards their proportionality.

49 The restrictive measures imposed by the national legislation should therefore be examined in turn in order to determine in each case in particular whether the measure is suitable for achieving the objective or objectives invoked by the Member State concerned and whether it does not go beyond what is necessary in order to achieve those objectives. In any case, those restrictions must be applied without discrimination (see to that effect Gebhard, para 37, as well as Gambelli and Others, paras 64 and 65, and Case C-42/02 Lindman [2003] ECR I-13519, para 25).

52 As regards the objectives capable of justifying those obstacles, a distinction must be drawn in this context between, on the one hand, the objective of reducing gambling opportunities and, on the other hand—in so far as games of chance are permitted—the objective of combating criminality by making the operators active in the sector subject to control and channelling the activities of betting and gaming into the systems thus controlled.

53 With regard to the first type of objective, it is clear from the case-law that although restrictions on the number of operators are in principle capable of being justified, those restrictions must in any event reflect a concern to bring about a genuine diminution of gambling opportunities and to limit activities in that sector in a consistent and systematic manner (see, to that effect, Zenatti, paras 35 and 36, and Gambelli and Others, paras 62 and 67).

55 Indeed it is the second type of objective, namely that of preventing the use of betting and gaming activities for criminal or fraudulent purposes by channelling them into controllable systems, that is identified, both by the Corte suprema di cassazione and by the Italian Government in its observations before the Court, as the true goal of the Italian legislation at issue in the main proceedings. Viewed from that perspective, it is possible that a policy of controlled expansion in the betting and gaming sector may be entirely consistent with the objective of drawing players away from clandestine betting and gaming—and, as such, activities which are prohibited—to activities which are authorised and regulated. As the Belgian and French Governments, in particular, have pointed out, in order to achieve that objective, authorised operators must represent a reliable, but at the same time attractive, alternative to a prohibited activity. This may as such necessitate the offer of an extensive range of games, advertising on a certain scale and the use of new distribution techniques.

58 It will be for the referring courts to determine whether, in limiting the number of operators active in the betting and gaming sector, the national legislation genuinely contributes to the objective invoked by the Italian Government, namely, that of preventing the exploitation of activities in that sector for criminal or fraudulent purposes. By the same token, it will be for the referring courts to ascertain whether those restrictions satisfy the conditions laid down by the case-law of the Court as regards their proportionality.

61 The Court has already ruled that, even if the exclusion from tender procedures is applied without distinction to all companies quoted on the regulated markets which could be interested in those licences—regardless of whether they are established in Italy or in another Member State—in so far as the lack of foreign

operators among the licensees is attributable to the fact that the Italian rules governing invitations to tender make it impossible in practice for companies quoted on the regulated markets of other Member States to obtain licences, those rules constitute prima facie a restriction on the freedom of establishment (see Gambelli and Others, para 48).

68 Although in principle criminal legislation is a matter for which the Member States are responsible, the Court has consistently held that Community law sets certain limits to their power, and such legislation may not restrict the fundamental freedoms guaranteed by Community law (see Case C-348/96 Calfa [1999] ECR I-11, para 17).

5.3.8 Gambelli

46 Where a company established in a Member State (such as Stanley) pursues the activity of collecting bets through the intermediary of an organisation of agencies established in another Member State (such as the defendants in the main proceedings), any restrictions on the activities of those agencies constitute obstacles to the freedom of establishment.

48 In so far as the lack of foreign operators among licensees in the betting sector on sporting events in Italy is attributable to the fact that the Italian rules governing invitations to tender make it impossible in practice for capital companies quoted on the regulated markets of other Member States to obtain licences, those rules constitute prima facie a restriction on the freedom of establishment, even if that restriction is applicable to all capital companies which might be interested in such licences alike, regardless of whether they are established in Italy or in another Member State.

53 The Court has also held that, on a proper construction, Article 49 EC covers services which the provider offers by telephone to potential recipients established in other Member states and provides without moving from the Member State in which he is established (Case C-384/93 Alpine Investments [1995] ECR I-1141, para 22).

54 Transposing that interpretation to the issue in the main proceedings, it follows that Article 49 EC relates to the services which a provider such as Stanley established in a Member State, in this case the United Kingdom, offers via the internet—and so without moving—to recipients in another Member State, in this case Italy, with the result that any restriction of those activities constitutes a restriction on the freedom of such a provider to provide services.

58 The same applies to a prohibition, also enforced by criminal penalties, for intermediaries such as the defendants in the main proceedings on facilitating the provision of betting services on sporting events organised by a supplier such as Stanley, established in a Member State other than that in which the intermediaries pursue their activity, since the prohibition constitutes a restriction on the right of the bookmaker freely to provide services, even if the intermediaries are established in the same Member State as the recipients of the services.

59 It must therefore be held that national rules such as the Italian legislation on betting, in particular Article 4 of Law No 401/89, constitute a restriction on the freedom of establishment and on the freedom to provide services.

60 In those circumstances it is necessary to consider whether such restrictions are acceptable as exceptional measures expressly provided for in Articles 45 and 46 EC, or justified, in accordance with the case-law of the Court, for reasons of overriding general interest.

62 As stated in para 36 of the judgment in Zenatti, the restrictions must in any event reflect a concern to bring about a genuine diminution of gambling opportunities, and the financing of social activities through a levy on the proceeds of authorised games must constitute only an incidental beneficial consequence and not the real justification for the restrictive policy adopted.

63 On the other hand, as the governments which submitted observations and the Commission pointed out, the Court stated in Schindler, Läärä and Zenatti that moral, religious and cultural factors, and the morally and financially harmful consequences for the individual and society associated with gaming and betting, could serve to justify the existence on the part of the national authorities of a margin of appreciation sufficient to enable them to determine what consumer protection and the preservation of public order require.

64 In any event, in order to be justified the restrictions on freedom of establishment and on freedom to provide services must satisfy the conditions laid down in the case-law of the Court (see, inter alia, Case C-19/92 Kraus [1993] ECR I-1663, para 32, and Case C-55/94 Gebhard [1995] ECR I-4165, para 37).

65 According to those decisions, the restrictions must be justified by imperative requirements in the general interest, be suitable for achieving the objective which they pursue and not go beyond what is necessary in order to attain it. They must in any event be applied without discrimination.

67 First of all, whilst in Schindler, Läärä and Zenatti the Court accepted that restrictions on gaming activities may be justified by imperative requirements in the general interest, such as consumer protection and the prevention of both fraud and incitement to squander on gaming, restrictions based on such grounds and on the need to preserve public order must also be suitable for achieving those objectives, inasmuch as they must serve to limit betting activities in a consistent and systematic manner.

68 In that regard the national court, referring to the preparatory papers on Law No 388/00, has pointed out that the Italian State is pursuing a policy of substantially expanding betting and gaming at national level with a view to obtaining funds, while also protecting CONI licensees.

69 In so far as the authorities of a Member State incite and encourage consumers to participate in lotteries, games of chance and betting to the financial benefit of the public purse, the authorities of that State cannot invoke public order concerns relating to the need to reduce opportunities for betting in order to justify measures such as those at issue in the main proceedings.

75 It is for the national court to determine whether the national legislation, taking account of the detailed rules for its application, actually serves the aims which

might justify it, and whether the restrictions it imposes are disproportionate in the light of those aims.

5.3.9 *Zenatti*

24 As the Court held in Schindler, the Treaty provisions on the freedom to provide services apply, in the context of running lotteries, to an activity which enables people to participate in gambling in return for remuneration. Such an activity therefore falls within the scope of Article 59 of the EC Treaty (now, after amendment, Article 49 EC) if at least one of the providers is established in a Member State other than that in which the service is offered.

25 In this case, the services at issue are provided by the organizer of the betting and his agents by enabling those placing bets to participate in a game of chance which holds out prospects of winnings. Those services are normally provided for remuneration consisting in payment of the stake and they are cross-frontier in character.

30 According to the information given in the order for reference and the observations of the Italian Government, the legislation at issue in the main proceedings pursues objectives similar to those pursued by the United Kingdom legislation on lotteries, as identified by the Court in Schindler. The Italian legislation seeks to prevent such gaming from being a source of private profit, to avoid risks of crime and fraud and the damaging individual and social consequences of the incitement to spend which it represents and to allow it only to the extent to which it may be socially useful as being conducive to the proper conduct of competitive sports.

31 As the Court acknowledged in para 58 of Schindler, those objectives must be considered together. They concern the protection of the recipients of the service and, more generally, of consumers as well as the maintenance of order in society and have already been held to rank among those objectives which may be regarded as constituting overriding reasons relating to the public interest (see Joined Cases 110/78 and 111/78 Ministère Public v Van Wesemael [1979] ECR 35, para 28, Case 220/83 Commission v France [1986] ECR 3663, para 20, and Case 15/78 Société Générale Alsacienne de Banque v Koestler [1978] ECR 1971, para 5). Moreover, as held in para 29 of this judgment, measures based on such reasons must be suitable for securing attainment of the objectives pursued and not go beyond what is necessary to attain them.

33 However, determination of the scope of the protection which a Member State intends providing in its territory in relation to lotteries and other forms of gambling falls within the margin of appreciation which the Court, in para 61 of Schindler, recognized as being enjoyed by the national authorities. It is for those authorities to consider whether, in the context of the aim pursued, it is necessary to prohibit activities of that kind, totally or partially, or only to restrict them and to lay down more or less rigorous procedures for controlling them.

34 In those circumstances, the mere fact that a Member State has chosen a system of protection different from that adopted by another Member State cannot

affect the appraisal as to the need for and proportionality of the provisions adopted. They must be assessed solely in the light of the objectives pursued by the national authorities of the Member State concerned and of the level of protection which they seek to ensure.

35 As the Court pointed out in para 37 of its judgment of 21 September 1999 in Case C-124/97 Läärä and Others [1999] ECR I-0000 in relation to slot machines, the fact that the games in issue are not totally prohibited is not enough to show that the national legislation is not in reality intended to achieve the public-interest objectives at which it is purportedly aimed, which must be considered as a whole. Limited authorisation of gambling on the basis of special or exclusive rights granted or assigned to certain bodies, which has the advantage of confining the desire to gamble and the exploitation of gambling within controlled channels, of preventing the risk of fraud or crime in the context of such exploitation, and of using the resulting profits for public-interest purposes, likewise falls within the ambit of those objectives.

36 However, as the Advocate General observes in para 32 of his Opinion, such a limitation is acceptable only if, from the outset, it reflects a concern to bring about a genuine diminution in gambling opportunities and if the financing of social activities through a levy on the proceeds of authorised games constitutes only an incidental beneficial consequence and not the real justification for the restrictive policy adopted. As the Court observed in para 60 of Schindler, even if it is not irrelevant that lotteries and other types of gambling may contribute significantly to the financing of benevolent or public-interest activities, that motive cannot in itself be regarded as an objective justification for restrictions on the freedom to provide services.

37 It is for the national court to verify whether, having regard to the specific rules for governing its application, the national legislation is genuinely directed to realising the objectives which are capable of justifying it and whether the restrictions which it imposes do not appear disproportionate in the light of those objectives.

5.3.10 Analysis of the Case-Law

The paras in *Carmen Media* which explicitly refer to previous rulings are:

- 40, 41, 44, 45, 46, 55, 60, 65, 66, 85, 86, 87, 101, and 102 (14 in total, making 26 references to previous rulings).
- Carmen Media being the most recent case of all, not any reference is made to this ruling.

The paras in *Sjöberg/Gerdin* which explicitly refer to previous rulings are:

- 32, 36, 37, 38, 39, 40, 49, 50, and 54 (9 in total, making 13 references to previous rulings).
- There are no paragraphs in Sjöberg/Gerdin to which reference is made in a later ruling, that is Carmen Media. Table 5.1

The paragraphs in *Ladbrokes* which explicitly refer to previous rulings are:

- 15, 16, 17, 18, 19, 20, 21, 22, 25, 26, 52, 54, 55, and 57 (14 in total, making 19 references to previous rulings).
- There is one paragraph in Ladbrokes to which reference is made in another ruling:
- 16 (in Sporting Exchange 24).

The paragraphs in *Sporting Exchange* (*'Betfair'*) which explicitly refer to previous rulings are:

- 23, 24, 25, 26, 27, 28, 29, 33, 34, 36, and 59 (11 in total, making 15 references to previous rulings).
- The paragraphs in Sporting Exchange to which reference is made in a later ruling are:
- 24 (in Ladbrokes 16), 49 (in Carmen Media 86), and 50 (in Carmen Media 87).
- A general reference (without a specific paragraph or paragraphs mentioned) to Sporting Exchange is made in Ladbrokes 52 (N.B. Ladbrokes and Sporting Exchange are of the same date, 3 June 2010, and refer to each other, see also above). The total number of references to Sporting Exchange is: 4.

The paragraphs in *Liga Portuguesa* which explicitly refer to previous rulings are:

- 37, 52, 56, 57, 58, 59, 60, and 64 (8 in total, making 10 references to previous rulings).

The paragraphs in *Liga Portuguesa* to which reference is made in later rulings are:

- 37 (in Sjöberg/Gerdin 54), 51 (in Sporting Exchange 23, in Ladbrokes 15, in Sjöberg/Gerdin 32), 52 (in Sporting Exchange 24, in Ladbrokes 16), 55 (in Sporting Exchange 25, in Ladbrokes 17), 56 (in Sporting Exchange 26, in Ladbrokes 18, in Sjöberg/Gerdin 36), 57 (in Sjöberg/Gerdin 37), 58 (in Sjöberg/Gerdin 38, in Carmen Media 46), 59 (in Sporting Exchange 28, in Ladbrokes 20, in Sjöberg/Gerdin 39, in Carmen Media 85), 60 (in Sjöberg/Gerdin 40, Sjöberg/Gerdin 50), 61 (in Sjöberg/Gerdin 40), 66 (Sporting Exchange 59), 67 (Sporting Exchange 59), 69 (in Sporting Exchange 33, in Ladbrokes 54), 70 (in Sporting Exchange 34, in Ladbrokes 55, in Carmen Media 102), and 72 (in Sporting Exchange 36, in Ladbrokes 57, in Carmen Media 101). The total number of references to Liga Portuguesa is: 31.

The paragraphs in *Commission v Italy* which explicitly refer to previous rulings are:

- 20, 26, 27, 28, and 29 (5 in total, making 8 references to previous rulings).
- There are no paragraphs in Commission v Italy to which reference is made in any later ruling.

The paragraphs in *Placanica* which explicitly refer to previous rulings are:

- 2, 42, 43, 44, 45, 46, 47,49, 53, and 61 (10 in total, making 18 references to previous rulings).

The paragraphs in *Placanica* to which reference is made in later rulings are:

- 36 (in Liga Portuguesa 37, in Sjöberg/Gerdin 54), 45 (in Commission v Italy 26), 46 (in Commission v Italy 27, in Liga Portuguesa 56, in Sjöberg/Gerdin 36, in Carmen Media 45), 47 (in Liga Portuguesa 57, in Sporting Exchange 27, in Ladbrokes 19), 48 (in Commission v Italy 28, in Liga Portuguesa 59, in Sporting Exchange 28, in Ladbrokes 20, in Carmen Media 44), 49 (in Commission v Italy 29, in Liga Portuguesa 60, in Sjöberg/Gerdin 50, in Carmen Media 44, in Carmen Media 60), 52 (in Carmen Media 65), 53 (in Carmen Media 65), 55 (in Ladbrokes 25), 58 (in Sporting Exchange 29, in Ladbrokes 22), and 68 (Sjöberg/Gerdin 49).
- A general reference to Placanica is made in Commission v Italy 20 and Ladbrokes 26.
- The total number of references to Placanica is: 28.

There is one paragraph in *Gambelli* which explicitly refers to a previous ruling: 67 (one reference).

The paragraphs in Gambelli to which reference is made in later rulings are:

- 46 (in Placanica 43), 48 (in Placanica 61), 53 (in Carmen Media 41), 54 (in Liga Portuguesa 52, in Carmen Media 41), 58 (in Placanica 44), 59 (in Placanica 42), 60 (in Placanica 45, Commission v Italy 26), 62 (in Placanica 53), 63 (in Placanica 47, in Ladbrokes 19, in Sporting Exchange 27), 64 (in Placanica 49, in Commission v Italy 29), 65 (in Placanica 49, in Commission v Italy 29), 67 (in Placanica 46, in Placanica 53, in Ladbrokes 21, in Carmen Media 55, in Carmen Media 66), 68 (in Carmen Media 66), 69 (in Carmen Media 66), and 75 (in Ladbrokes 22, in Sporting Exchange 29).
- A general reference to Gambelli is made in Placanica 2.
- A reference to 'the operative part' of Gambelli is found in Placanica 42.
- A reference to 'case-law cited' in Placanica 46 (including Gambelli 67) is made in Liga Portuguesa 56.
- The total number of references to Gambelli is: 29.

Zenatti being the first ruling of all, there are no paragraphs in Zenatti which explicitly refer to previous rulings.

The paragraphs in Zenatti to which reference is made in later rulings are:

- 24 (in Carmen Media 40, in Carmen Media 41), 25 (in Carmen Media 41), 30 (in Placanica 46), 31 (in Placanica 46, in Ladbrokes 26, in Carmen Media 45), 33 (in Carmen Media 46), 34 (in Liga Portuguesa 58, in Carmen Media 46), 35 (in Placanica 53, in Liga Portuguesa 64), 36 (in Gambelli 62, in Placanica 53, in Carmen Media 65),and 37 (in Carmen Media 65).
- General references to Zenatti are made in Gambelli 63, Gambelli 67, and Placanica 2.
- A reference to 'case-law cited' in Placanica 46 (including Zenatti 30 and Zenatti 31) is made in Liga Portuguesa 56.
- Total number of references to Zenatti: 20.

Table 5.1 Analysis of the case-law

	Zenatti	Gambelli	Placanica	Comm./ It.	Liga Port.	Sport. Exch.	Ladbrokes	Sjöberg	Carmen M.
	(0)	(3)	(18)	(8)	(11)	(15)	(19)	(13)	(26)
Zenatti (20)	x	3	5	0	3	0	1	0	8
Gambelli (29)		x	13	3	2	2	3	0	6
Placanica (28)			x	5	5	3	5	4	6
Comm./It. (0)				x	0	0	0	0	0
Liga Port. (31)					x	10	8	9	4
Sport. Exch. (4)						x	2	0	2
Ladbrokes (1)						1	x	0	0
Sjöberg (0)								x	0
Carmen M.									x
	[20]	[32]	[46]	[8]	[42]	[19]	[20]	[13]	[26]

N.B. The rulings at the horizontal line are the referring ones, the rulings at the vertical line are referred to. The number of times that a reference is made is indicated. The 'Indirect' references from Liga Portuguesa 56 to 'case-law cited' in Placanica 46—that is Zenatti 30–31 and Gambelli 67—have been counted twice. The totals are indicated between brackets on the left side after the (abbreviated) names of the rulings. The totals of references made per ruling are indicated between brackets under the (abbreviated) names of the rulings at the horizontal line. The totals of the vertical and horizontal lines per ruling are indicated underneath the Table between square brackets. Each reference has two aspects: a stare decisis creating, generating one ('active reference,' see also horizontal total numbers) and a stare decisis receiving one ('passive reference,' see vertical total numbers). Stare decisis works both ways: because of the relevance of argument in the previous ruling it is referred back to, but this 'recognition' materialises only if an (explicit) back-reference is made.

It is striking that Commission v Italy (which is not a preliminary ruling like all others) is in an isolated position in relation to the other cases. Not any reference is made to this 'old' case. Liga Portuguesa is the ruling most referred to, although it succeeded to four previous rulings, and was followed by only four new ones.

However, it looks like a central position is a good position also with regard to contributing to *stare decisis* (in a 'passive' manner). Zenatti, Gambelli and Placanica 'score less,' although the difference with Liga Portuguesa is not so impressive as with the newest four, of the year 2010. On the other hand, the 'active' role of Liga Portuguesa is restricted. Placanica and the new rulings of, in particular, Ladbrokes and Carmen Media have a much higher score. Apart from 'content' (see below), the total ('passive' and 'active' references) of Placanica provides the number one position: 46 (Liga Portuguesa (42) is in second position, Gambelli (32) in third, and Carmen Media (26 'active' references!) in fourth). What are the average scores? On the one ultimate end, Zenatti, being the first ruling, could not refer to any previous case, and on the other ultimate end. Carmen Media, being the most recent ruling, could not be referred to. And the opposite is also true. Zenatti could be referred to in 8 rulings; so, the average currently is: 20/8 = 2,5. The other averages as to 'passive' references are as follows: Gambelli: 29/7 = appr. 4; Placanica: 28/6 = appr. 4,5; Commission v Italy: 0/5 = 0; Liga Portuguesa: 31/4 = appr. 7,7; Sporting Exchange: 4/3 = 1,3,; Ladbrokes and Sjöberg score less than 1. It is clear that Liga Portuguesa is by far most prominent, followed by Placanica and Gambelli. The averages as to 'active' references are: Gambelli: 3/1 = 3, Placanica: 18/2 = 9, Commission v Italy: 8/3 = appr. 3, Liga Portuguesa: 11/4 = appr. 3, Sporting Exchange: 15/5 = 3, Ladbrokes: 19/6 = appr. 3, Sjöberg: 13/7 = appr. 2, and Carmen Media: 26/8 = appr. 3. So, Placanica is by very far most prominent, The conclusion is that Placanica and Liga Portuguesa are the most prominent rulings of all in several respects.

Now, the 'content' of the paragraphs which have been referred to more than once will be focused on:

- six times: Gambelli 67; five times: Placanica 48 and 49; four times: Zenatti 31, Placanica 46, and Liga Portuguesa 59; three times: Zenatti 36; Gambelli 63,
- Placanica 47, and Liga Portuguesa 51, 56, 70, and 72; twice: Zenatti 24, 30, 34, and 35; Gambelli 54, 60, 64, 65, and 75; Placanica: 36 and 58; Liga Portuguesa:
- 52, 55, 58, 60, and 69; once: Zenatti 25, 30, 33, and 37 (and three general references); Gambelli 46, 48, 53, 58, 59, 62, 68, and 69 (and a general reference, a reference to its operative paragraph and a reference to 'case-law cited'), Placanica 45, 52, 53, 55, and 68 (and two general references); Liga Portuguesa: 37, 57, 61, 66, and 67; Sporting Exchange 24, 49, and 50; Ladbrokes 16.

The paragraphs referred to five and four times read in full as follows:

First of all, whilst in Schindler, Läärä and Zenatti the Court accepted that restrictions on gaming activities may be justified by imperative requirements in the general interest, such as consumer protection and the prevention of both fraud and incitement to squander on gaming, restrictions based on such grounds and on the need to preserve public order must also be suitable for achieving those objectives, inasmuch as they must serve to limit betting activities in a consistent and systematic manner. (*Gambelli 67*)

However, although the Member States are free to set the objectives of their policy on betting and gaming and, where appropriate, to define in detail the level of protection sought, the restrictive measures that they impose must nevertheless satisfy the conditions laid down in the case-law of the Court as regards their proportionality. (*Placanica 48*)

The restrictive measures imposed by the national legislation should therefore be examined in turn in order to determine in each case in particular whether the measure is suitable for achieving the objective or objectives invoked by the Member State concerned and whether it does not go beyond what is necessary in order to achieve those objectives. In any case, those restrictions must be applied without discrimination (see to that effect Gebhard, para 37, as well as Gambelli and Others, paras 64 and 65, and Case C-42/02 Lindman [2003] ECR I-13519, para 25). (*Placanica 49*)

As the Court acknowledged in para 58 of Schindler, those objectives must be considered together. They concern the protection of the recipients of the service and, more generally, of consumers as well as the maintenance of order in society and have already been held to rank among those objectives which may be regarded as constituting overriding reasons relating to the public interest (see Joined Cases 110/78 and 111/78 Ministère Public v Van Wesemael [1979] ECR 35, para 28, Case 220/83 Commission v France [1986] ECR 3663, para 20, and Case 15/78 Société Générale Alsacienne de Banque v Koestler [1978] ECR 1971, para 5). Moreover, as held in para 29 of this judgment, measures based on such reasons must be suitable for securing attainment of the objectives pursued and not go beyond what is necessary to attain them. (*Zenatti 31*)

On that point, a certain number of reasons of overriding general interest have been recognised by the case-law, such as the objectives of consumer protection and the prevention of both fraud and incitement to squander on gaming, as well as the general need to preserve public order (see, to that effect, Case C-275/92 Schindler [1994] ECR I-1039, paras 57 to 60; Case C-124/97 Läärä and Others [1999] ECR I-6067, paras 32 and 33; Zenatti, paras 30 and 31; and Gambelli and Others, para 67). (*Placanica 46*).

The Member States are therefore free to set the objectives of their policy on betting and gambling and, where appropriate, to define in detail the level of protection sought. However, the restrictive measures that they impose must satisfy the conditions laid down in the case-law of the Court as regards their proportionality (*Placanica and Others*, para 48). (*Liga Portuguesa 59*).

The above cited paragraph may be generalised and summarised as follows (cross-references to immediately preceding, 'scoring'and 'non-scoring' paragraphs of course have been taken into account contextually).

Member States are free to set the objectives of their policy on betting and gambling and, where appropriate, to define in detail the level of protection sought. However, the restrictive measures that they impose must satisfy the conditions laid down in the case-law of the Court as regards their proportionality. (N.B. Since *Placanica 48* and *Liga Portuguesa 59* are identical (Liga Portuguesa referring to Placanica), the number of references in fact amounts to 9 for this reference.) Restrictions on gaming activities must be justified by imperative requirements (overriding reasons; *Zenatti 31*) in the general interest, such as consumer protection (protection of the recipients of the service, *Zenatti 31*) and the prevention of both fraud and incitement to squander on gaming; restrictions based on such grounds and on the need to preserve public order must also be suitable for achieving those objectives, inasmuch as they must serve to limit betting activities in a consistent and systematic manner. (*Gambelli 67*) Those objectives must be considered together. (*Zenatti 31*) The measures must not go beyond what is necessary in order to achieve those objectives. In any case, those restrictions must be applied without discrimination. (*Placanica 49*) Moral, religious and cultural factors, and the morally and financially harmful consequences for the individual and society associated with gaming and betting, could serve to justify the existence on the part of the national authorities of a margin of appreciation sufficient to enable them to determine what consumer protection and the preservation of public order require. (see below).

The paragraphs referred to three times read in full as follows:

However, as the Advocate General observes in para 32 of his Opinion, such a limitation is acceptable only if, from the outset, it reflects a concern to bring about a genuine diminution in gambling opportunities and if the financing of social activities through a levy on the proceeds of authorised games constitutes only an incidental beneficial consequence and not the real justification for the restrictive policy adopted. As the Court observed in para 60 of Schindler, even if it is not irrelevant that lotteries and other types of gambling may contribute significantly to the financing of benevolent or public-interest activities, that motive cannot in itself be regarded as an objective justification for restrictions on the freedom to provide services. (*Zenatti 36*).

On the other hand, as the governments which submitted observations and the Commission pointed out, the Court stated in Schindler, Läärä and Zenatti that moral, religious and cultural factors, and the morally and financially harmful consequences for the individual and society associated with gaming and betting, could serve to justify the existence on the part of the national authorities of a margin of appreciation sufficient to enable them to determine what consumer protection and the preservation of public order require. (*Gambelli 63*).

In that context, moral, religious or cultural factors, as well as the morally and financially harmful consequences for the individual and for society associated with betting and gaming, may serve to justify a margin of discretion for the national authorities, sufficient to enable them to determine what is required in order to ensure consumer protection and the preservation of public order (Gambelli and Others, para 63). (*Placanica 47*).

Article 49 EC requires the abolition of all restrictions on the freedom to provide services, even if those restrictions apply without distinction to national providers of services and to those from other Member States, when they are liable to prohibit, impede or render less advantageous the activities of a service provider established in another Member State where it lawfully provides similar services (see, to that effect, Case C-76/90 *Säger* [1991] ECR I-4221, para 12, and Case C-58/98 *Corsten* [2000] ECR i-7919, para 33). Moreover, the freedom to provide services is for the benefit of both providers and recipients of services (see, to that effect, Joined Cases 286/82 and 26/83 *Luisi and Carbone* [1984] ECR 377, para 16). (*Liga Portuguesa 51*).

Article 46(1) EC allows restrictions justified on grounds of public policy, public security or public health. In addition, a certain number of overriding reasons in the public interest have been recognised by case-law, such as the objectives of consumer protection and the prevention of both fraud and incitement to squander money on gambling, as well as the general need to preserve public order (see, to that effect, *Placanica and Others*, para 46 and case-law cited). (*Liga Portuguesa 56*).

In addition, because of the lack of direct contact between consumer and operator, games of chance accessible via the internet involve different and more substantial risks of fraud by operators against consumers compared with the traditional markets for such games. (*Liga Portuguesa 70*).

It follows that, in the light of the specific features associated with the provision of games of chance via the internet, the restriction at issue in the main proceedings may be regarded as justified by the objective of combating fraud and crime. (*Liga Portuguesa 72*).

N.B. Since the paragraphs of *Gambelli 63* and *Placanica 47* are identical (Planacia referring to Gambelli), the number of references in fact amounts to 6 for this reference. So, its essence is (to be) added to the above summary: moral, religious and cultural factors, and the morally and financially harmful consequences for the individual and society associated with gaming and betting, could serve to justify the existence on the part of the national authorities of a margin of appreciation sufficient to enable them to determine what consumer protection and the preservation of public order require.

5.4 Sports Betting and the Concept of 'Sports Law'

Is 'sports betting' part of sports law, international and European sports law, respectively, or is 'sports betting' just an example of 'sport and the law'?[17] Of course it is a part of sports law, if we take the broader concept of sports law as the standard of evaluation: everywhere that sport and law meet, we may speak of 'sports law.' But does sports betting also belong to the hard core of the concept, where sports rules and regulations, the specific 'sporting law,' is tested against regular public, societal law—to find out whether there is a conflict of law or not? It does not seem like that, since rules and regulations of sports governing bodies do not exist, at least not in the context of ECJ jurisprudence. In ECJ jurisprudence 'sports betting' in principle is not treated differently from other forms of gambling which may be illustrated by the fact that in sports betting cases explicit reference is made to non-sports betting cases like *Schindler* and *Läärä* by way of *stare decisis.* Whereas in landmark cases of European Sports Law like *Walrave*, *Bosman,* and

[17] See, for a discussion whether sports law exists, whether there is a sports law, and what it is, what it consists of, the author's inaugural lecture as professor of International and European Sports Law at the School of Law of Erasmus University Rotterdam, 10 June 2010; see for the English-language version, Siekmann (2011).

Meca-Medina, sporting measures and practices were tested, the ECJ jurisprudence on sports betting is not of a similar character; it is marginal. What is tested against EU law, is national public legislation on lotteries, including sport lotteries. So, Member States' law is the 'intermediary' between the ECJ and organised sport. Sports betting, like, for example football hooliganism belongs to the world at large around sport, it is away from the playing field, off the pitch, and generally speaking not directly related to what happens on the field of play. In ECJ jurisprudence on sports betting there are only a few observations which show to some extent the specificity of sport in this context, for example it is said that an objective of national legislation may be to allow sports betting only to the extent to which it may be socially useful as being conducive to the proper conduct of competitive sports (Zenatti, 30) Here sports betting is linked with the promotion of sporting activities through investments in sports facilities, especially in the poorest regions and in peripheral areas of large cities (Zenatti, 4). Sports betting has a role in the broader context of sports funding at the amateur and recreational grass-roots level. Or: '[...] the possibility cannot be ruled out that an operator which sponsors some of the sporting competitions on which it accepts bets and some of the teams taking part in those competitions may be in a position to influence their outcome directly or indirectly, and thus increase its profits.' (*Liga Portuguesa 71*).[18] Here sports betting clearly is connected to the threat of fraud and corruption in sport. In the White Paper on Sport it is said that, since in some Member States parts of the profits generated by lotteries may be allocated to public interest goals, including sport, questions were raised if 'the specificity of sporting needs' may allow for restrictions on the free movement of gambling services in order not to decrease the level of these profits.[19]

5.5 Conclusion

The 'reversal or retrospective method' of content analysis introduced in this contribution (see above in 5.1 Introduction for the detailed explanation of its meaning and way of application) in fact is kind of a statistical method of research

[18] Cf., also in this context, the CAS award of 20 August 1999 in AEK Athens and Slavia Prague v. UEFA (CAS 98/200), para 35 (*ENIC* case): 'The ratio of the rule [the UEFA ban on the multiple ownership of clubs/teams competing in the same competition; RS] is manifest: if two or more clubs participating in the same contest are under control of or managed by one single entity, there is cause for concern that in a given situation the existence of opposing interests which underlies any sport competition will not be apparent. For instance, should two clubs under joint control or ownership meet at a certain stage of the competition, the public's perception of the authenticity of the result would be jeopardised. In the present case, for example ENIC's business interests in the field of the provision of betting services could be seen by some as an obstacle to the development of fair competition on the pitch.'

[19] Commission Staff Working Document—The EU and Sport: Background and Content, Accompanying document to the White Paper on Sport (2007), p. 109.

applied to law. By its application. legal science moves to a certain extent into the direction of becoming exact science.

Sports betting is not defined in the jurisprudence of the European Court of Justice. Generally speaking, it may be defined as sports-related betting.

The essence of the ECJ jurisprudence on sports betting may be summarized as follows on the basis of the application of the 'reversal method' of content analysis:

> Member States are free to set the objectives of their policy on betting and gambling and, where appropriate, to define in detail the level of protection sought. However, the restrictive measures that they impose must satisfy the conditions laid down in the case-law of the Court as regards their proportionality. Restrictions on gaming activities must be justified by imperative requirements or overriding reasons in the general interest, such as consumer protection and the prevention of both fraud and incitement to squander on gaming; restrictions based on such grounds and on the need to preserve public order must also be suitable for achieving those objectives, inasmuch as they must serve to limit betting activities in a consistent and systematic manner. Those objectives must be considered together. The measures must not go beyond what is necessary in order to achieve those objectives. In any case, those restrictions must be applied without discrimination. Moral, religious and cultural factors, and the morally and financially harmful consequences for the individual and society associated with gaming and betting, could serve to justify the existence on the part of the national authorities of a margin of appreciation sufficient to enable them to determine what consumer protection and the preservation of public order require.

In a specific context, in the White Paper on Sport[20] the following general observation is made by the European Commission with regard to sports betting: 'There has been no judgment of the European Court of Justice so far which would explicitly refer to the question of funding of sporting activities as a general interest objective that would justify restrictions on the fundamental freedoms of the Internal Market. However, sport has been mentioned as one of many good causes which are financed with revenues from the organisation of gambling services (such as lotteries, betting services, etc.). In many Member States there are special rules regarding the provision of such services, including provisions that reserve such services to particular operators. The Court has made it clear that even though the financing of good causes, such as social works, charitable works, sport or culture can be supported in a significant way by the profits obtained from lotteries or other forms of gambling activity, this does not undermine the economic nature of these services, and as such does not automatically exclude them from the application of Community law. Moreover, even if it is not irrelevant that lotteries and other types of gambling may contribute significantly to the financing of benevolent or public-interest activities, that motive cannot in itself be regarded as an objective justification for restrictions on the freedom to provide services. In fact, it can constitute only an incidental beneficial consequence and not the justification for the adoption or continuation of restrictive policies.'

The ECJ jurisprudence on sports betting is part of 'sports law,' in particular international (EU) sports law, although it does not belong to its hard core from a

---

[20] Accompanying document, at p. 105.

doctrinal point of view, the specificity of sport not playing any systematic role in relation to this subject of sports law. The ECJ has tested and will continue testing national legislation and policy on sports betting against EU law; in this context it does not test any rules and regulations of sports organisations whether they might be acceptable under EU law (such rules and regulations are non-existent in this context). The subject of sports betting is a matter of 'sport relatedness' rather than 'sport rules-relatedness.'

References

Anderson P, Blackshaw I, Siekmann R, Soek J (eds) (2011) Sports betting: law and policy. T.M.C Asser Press, The Hague

Gardiner S, Parrish R, Siekmann RCR (2009) EU, sport, law and policy: regulation, re-regulation and representation. T.M.C Asser Press, The Hague, pp 555–580

Kaburakis A (2009) ECJ jurisprudence and recent developments in EU sports betting. In: Gardiner S, Parrish R, Siekmann RCR (eds) EU, sport, law and policy: regulation, re-regulation and representation. T.M.C. Asser Press, The Hague, pp 555–580

Littler A, Fijnaut C (eds) (2007) The regulation of gambling—European and national perspectives. Leiden/Boston

Papaloukas M (2010) Sports betting and European law. In: The International Sports Law Journal (ISLJ) 1–2:86–88

Siekmann RCR (2011) What is sports law? Lex Sportiva and Lex Ludica: a Reassessment of content and terminology. In: The International Sports Law Journal (ISLJ) 3–4:3–13

Chapter 6
History/Football Politics/Social Dialogue in Sport: Study into the Possible Participation of EPFL and G-14 in a Social Dialogue in the European Professional Football Sector

Abstract In the light of a growing number of challenges to sport governance, social dialogue at European level can contribute to addressing common concerns of employers and athletes, including agreements on employment relations and working conditions in the sector in accordance with TFEU (formerly, EC Treaty) provisions. In line with the principle of autonomy, the social partners can choose if and when to address a joint request to set up a sectoral social dialogue committee to the Commission. It will examine any request according to the conditions laid out. Taking into account the specificity of the sport structure, social partner organizations could identify relevant third bodies that they want to invite to take part in their social dialogue as observers. It should be kept in mind that a European social dialogue is, above all, a bi-partite dialogue between social partners.

Contents

R. C. R. Siekmann, *Introduction to International and European Sports Law*,
ASSER International Sports Law Series, DOI: 10.1007/978-90-6704-852-1_6,
© T.M.C. ASSER PRESS, The Hague, The Netherlands, and the author 2012

6.1 Preface

6.1.1 Social Dialogue in Sport

In the light of a growing number of challenges to sport governance, social dialogue at European level can contribute to addressing common concerns of employers and athletes, including agreements on employment relations and working conditions in the sector in accordance with TFEU (formerly, EC Treaty) provisions. The Commission has been supporting projects for the consolidation of social dialogue in the sport sector in general as well as in the football sector. These projects have created a basis for social dialogue at European level and the consolidation of European-level organizations. A Sectoral Social Dialogue Committee can be established by the Commission on the basis of a joint request by social partners. The Commission considers that a European social dialogue in the sport sector or in its sub-sectors (e.g. football) is an instrument which would allow social partners to contribute to the shaping of employment relations and working conditions in an active and participative way. In this area, such a social dialogue could also lead to the establishment of commonly agreed codes of conduct or charters, which could address issues related to training, working conditions or the protection of young people.

European social dialogue is a unique and indispensable component of the European social model. It refers to the discussions, consultations, negotiations and joint actions undertaken by the social partner organizations representing the two sides of industry (management and labour). It is a useful means by which the social partners assist in the definition of European employment and social standards, and play an important role in the governance of the Union.

Article 154 TFEU (formerly, Article 138 EC Treaty) gives the Commission the role to promote social dialogue, gives recognition to social dialogue at European level and obliges the Commission to consult the European social partners before submitting proposals in the social policy field. Article 139 (now: Article 155

TFEU) offers the possibility to negotiate agreements that can be implemented either in accordance with the procedures and practices specific to management and labour in the Member States, or by Council decisions for areas that are listed in Article 153 TFEU (formerly, Article 137 EC Treaty).

Through its decision of 20 May 1998,[1] the Commission established sectoral social dialogue committees at European level. The sectoral social dialogue committees are established with due regard for the autonomy of the social partners. The social partner organizations must apply jointly to the European Commission in order to take part in social dialogue at European level. The European organizations representing employers and workers must, when submitting this application, meet a number of criteria:

- Relate to specific sectors or categories, and be organised at European level;
- Consist of organizations which are themselves an integral and recognized part of Member States' social partner structures, and have the capacity to negotiate agreements, and which are representative of several Member States;
- Have adequate structures to ensure their effective participation in the work of the committees.

In July 2007 when the White Paper on Sport was published[2] 34 sectoral social dialogue committees were recognised by the Commission, but at the time there was neither a committee for sport nor for a part of the sport sector. The roots of the sport movement in non-profit organizations and in volunteering had slowed down the emergence of social partners in the sport sector in most Member States. Increasing professionalization has, however, led to the emergence of social dialogue and collective bargaining in a number of Member States.

On the occasion of the agreement between UEFA and FIFA with the Commissioners in charge of competition, sport and social affairs concerning the revised FIFA rules relating to the international transfers of football players in 2001, the Commissioners invited FIFA and UEFA to encourage clubs to start or pursue social dialogue with the representative bodies of football players. They stressed that social dialogue could be an effective method to discuss and come to common solutions on important matters concerning employment and the social situation in the sector. Furthermore, they offered the Commission's assistance to social dialogue at European level.

Ever since, the Commission has been supporting projects for the consolidation of social dialogue in the sport sector globally as well as specifically in the football sector. These projects have created a momentum for social dialogue at European level and the consolidation of European-level organizations. They have also improved the understanding and awareness of the opportunities that social dialogue offers.

---

[1] 98/500/EC.

[2] White Paper on Sport, on Social Dialogue at p. 19 and at pp. 59–62 of the Accompanying document to the White Paper.

In the sport sector, they have helped in setting up the European Association of Sport Employers (EASE) that identified suitable national employers' organizations in the sector, in co-operation with UNI-Europa, which represents employees in the services sector in several existing European Social Dialogue Committees. In the football sector, the international professional football players' trade union, FIFPro, has run several projects with the objective of setting up a European social dialogue in the football sector. The EPFL (Association of European Professional Football Leagues) has been given the mandate to consider social dialogue issues at European level and where appropriate act as a social partner.

Articles 154 and 155 TFEU give recognition to the dialogue between management and labour at Community level. In the sport sector, federations play traditionally a specific role in the organization of sport. Given that they are the guardians of the sporting rules and that their statutes often mention that they represent the interests of both employees and employers, it is essential to identify genuine social partner organizations that have the mandate to represent one side of industry only and negotiate on its behalf.

In many Member States, social partner organizations in the sport sector are fragmented and display a low level of organization. EU enlargement to countries with relatively weak industrial relations structures has reinforced the challenge.[3] In several Member States, however, social partner organizations are well established and many athletes' organizations belong to a service or cross-industry trade union. Hence, it is important to offer continued and targeted support for the consolidation of representative European social partners.

The sports sector is very diverse. Some disciplines have their own industrial relations. Moreover, important differences can be noted between grassroots and elite-level sport, professional and amateur sport, and team and individual sport. The football sector, specifically, has often taken the lead in initiatives on social dialogue in Europe.

In the light of a growing number of challenges to sport governance, social dialogue at European level can create an added value:

- A European social dialogue gives the opportunity to address issues of employment relations and the social situation in the sector as well as to negotiate agreements in accordance with EU and national law and with the autonomy that is a characteristic of both social dialogue and of European sport.
- A European sectoral social dialogue committee can be a forum of exchange and mutual learning that initiates its own activities and commissions analyses and research in the sector.
- The Commission consults the European social partners on matters pertaining to employment and social affairs and they can make sure that their views are heard by agreeing joint declarations and joint statements.

---

[3] Cf., the T.M.C. Asser Institute's EU-commissioned study: Promoting the Social Dialogue in European Professional Football (Candidate EU Member States), November 2004; see also: Siekmann 2004, pp. 31–33.

- Some parts of the sport labour market are very integrated at the European, if not the international, level. A European social dialogue gives the opportunity to address matters of common interest to all national employers' and athletes' organizations. This is complementary to national social dialogue.
- At a stage when social partner organizations and social dialogue at national level are not consolidated in all Member States, a European social dialogue can provide an incentive to engage also in a social dialogue at national level.

The Commission encourages and welcomes all efforts with the objective of establishing European Social Dialogue Committees in the sport sector. It continues to give support to both sides of industry and it continues its open dialogue with all sport organizations on this issue.

In line with the principle of autonomy, the social partners can choose if and when to address a joint request to set up a sectoral social dialogue committee to the Commission. It will examine any request according to the conditions laid out above. Taking into account the specificity of the sport structure, social partner organizations could identify relevant third bodies that they want to invite to take part in their social dialogue as observers. It should be kept in mind that a European social dialogue is, above all, a bi-partite dialogue between social partners.

It is difficult to predetermine the form social dialogue in the sport sector should take. The Commission will examine any request to set up a sectoral social dialogue committee in a pragmatic manner.

6.1.2 History: Football Politics (Asser G-14/EPFL Participation Study)

The G-14[4] was founded in September 2000 as an independent official European Economic Interest Grouping (EEIG) under EC law by 14 leading European professional football clubs to provide a unified voice (the official slogan of the G-14 was: "The Voice of the Clubs") in negotiations with the European worldwide football governing bodies UEFA and FIFA. New members could join by invitation only. In August 2002, four more clubs joined, taking the membership to 18, but the organization retained its original name. The clubs came from the top divisions of the professional then "Big Five" football countries (England, France, Germany,

[4] "G-..." means "Group of ..."; cf., G-7, a group of seven industrialized nations of the world formed in 1976 when Canada joined the Group of Six (United States of America, France, Germany, Italy, Japan, United Kingdom). In 1997, the Group added Russia, thus becoming the G-8. The G-20 is a group of Finance Ministers and Central Bank Governors from 20 major economies in the world (19 countries plus the EU).

Italy, and Spain) plus the Netherlands and Portugal.[5] They had won around 250 national premier league titles between them. G-14 members had won the European Cup/Championship League 41 times out of 51 seasons. As the leading clubs in European football, their power on the world stage was best demonstrated during the 2006 FIFA World Cup held in Germany, where they provided 22% of participating players. This supported their assertion that national associations should pay players' wages whilst on international duty and provide compensation in the case of injuries. In April 2004, G-14 initiated a preliminary investigation into FIFA by the Swiss Competition Commission, when they complained of FIFA's requiring their players to be available for FIFA international competitions without compensating the clubs. FIFA president Sepp Blatter refused to negotiate with the G-14 on the matter. In September 2005, the G-14 clubs decide to take FIFA to court over paying players for international (association team) matches after the Belgian club Charleroi lost Abdelmajid Oulmers for eight months when he was injured playing for Morocco. Prior to the 2006 World Cup, the G-14 members demanded a "fair percentage" of receipts from tournaments, such as the World Cup. To compensate for the clubs releasing players to compete in these tournaments. Generally speaking, too many decisions with direct and substantial commercial implications were taken by the football governing bodies who disallowed input from the clubs who were immediately affected by those decisions.[6]

Against this background, in 2006 the T.M.C. Asser Institute was commissioned by G-14 to undertake a Study into their possible participation (and, in comparison, that of EPFL) in a future Social Dialogue in the European professional football sector. The Study is a practical example of testing whether and if yes, on what conditions potential stakeholder organizations may be allowed to take part in a European Social Dialogue Committee envisaged. The findings of the Study were as follows.[7]

6.2 Chapter 1: Introduction

The purpose of this study is to investigate whether EPFL and G-14, as European employers' organizations may participate in a possible Social Dialogue with FIFPro under the EC Treaty in the professional football sector. An additional question to be answered is which themes might be relevant to be put on the agenda of a European Social Dialogue in particular from the perspective of G-14.

---

[5] Barcelona, Real Madrid, Liverpool, Manchester United, Juventus, Milan, Internazionale, Marseille, Paris Saint-Germain, Bayern Munich, Borussia Dortmund, Ajax, PSV, Porto, Arsenal, Lyon, Bayer Leverkusen, and Valencia.

[6] See, Weatherill 2007, at p. 271.

[7] Previously published, under this paper's main title in The International Sports Law Journal (ISLJ) 2006/3–4 pp. 69–71 and 74–85.

One precondition is of course that the objects, the mandate (and the tasks) of EPFL and G-14 must (implicitly or explicitly) allow them to deal with "industrial relations" including a Social Dialogue. We will examine whether this is the case on the basis of the Statutes of both organizations, as presumably the status of employers' (interest) organization is a conditio sine qua non for admittance to a Social Dialogue. This point will be dealt with in Sect. 6.3 "Mandate, Tasks and Purposes." In this context, it is also important with regard to EPFL whether "industrial relations" and Social Dialogue are part of the objectives of the national Leagues (EPFL now has 15 members). The national Leagues can only have mandated EPFL to deal with these aspects at European level if they themselves are expressly or otherwise empowered under their Statutes to do so. In view of the question concerning the (in)dependence of EPFL and G-14 in relation to UEFA and FIFA as well as of the Leagues in relation to the FAs (see below in Sect. 6.4 "(In)dependence") the objectives of UEFA and FIFA must also be taken into account.

The social partner organizations must be able to function freely, without outside intervention. This may be considered as an implicit condition for meaningful participation in a Social Dialogue in a free, democratic community of States and in its individual Member States. In the football world the clubs are affiliated to their national FA which is represented in the international federations UEFA and FIFA. This is termed a "pyramid model" with FIFA at the top, UEFA at the European regional intermediate level and the FAs at the bottom. Football is administered according to this model. The model consists of levels of administration which transcend the clubs. The question therefore is whether EPFL and G-14 as clubs' organizations for the purposes of a Social Dialogue can operate sufficiently independently from the governing bodies. This point will be investigated in detail in Sect. 6.4 "(In)dependence." With regard to EPFL not only the relationship to the Leagues/members which must have commissioned EPFL to deal with "industrial relations" including a Social Dialogue is important, but also the way the Leagues are affiliated to the FAs at the national level.

Apart from that, employers' and employees' organizations and EPFL and G-14 alike have to fulfil certain (explicit) criteria which have been developed by the European Commission. This aspect shall be dealt with in Sect. 6.5 "EU Admissibility Criteria". In this context, the question may be asked which lessons can be learned from previous practice regarding the application of the criteria in other industrial sectors, for it may be presumed that the (manner of) application of the criteria in principle also determines their precise meaning and importance. What is the "case law," what useful precedent exists? (Sect. 6.6 "Representation in the Context of Present Social Dialogue Committees").

There is another EU perspective which is even broader than that of the criteria and which deserves to be examined here. What does it mean for the possibility of participation of EPFL and G-14 in a Social Dialogue that "the specific characteristics of sport" should be taken into account in the European context (Treaty of Nice)? This question will be dealt with in Sect. 6.7 "Specificity of Sport".

In Sect. 6.8 "Agenda of Topics" the question of which themes might be particularly relevant for G-14 in a Social Dialogue is examined.

Finally, Sect. 6.9 "Summary, Conclusions and Recommendations" contains a summary of the conclusions of this study into the possible participation of EPFL and G-14 in a Social Dialogue in the European professional football sector.

6.3 Chapter 2: Mandate, Tasks and Purposes

EPFL

The relevant objectives of the Association of European Union Premier Professional Leagues, the predecessor of the current EPFL (Association of European Professional Football Leagues), were as follows: to participate in and appoint representatives to UEFA's Professional Football Committee and to work with UEFA for the good of professional association football in Europe; and to foster friendly relations between the Association and the players' unions operating within the territory of member Leagues (Article 2 of the Accord of the Association).

The tasks and purposes of the current EPFL are formulated as follows. Each member has agreed with the other members to form a non-profit association to create and/or increase cooperation amongst themselves in order to develop their own activities and to act jointly whilst promoting professional football in accordance with the respective statutes and regulations of the UEFA and FIFA (Preamble of the Constitution of the Association of European Professional Football Leagues). The Association will have the following two objectives: (a) To fulfil and comply with the Memorandum of Understanding signed between the Leagues and UEFA on 6 June 2005 and 1 July 2005 (respectively) and approved by FIFA in Marrakech on 10 September 2005. The Leagues and the EPFL have the duty to notify to FIFA and UEFA any activity which may have an impact on the Memorandum of Understanding. (b) To administer all rights and duties arising from the abovementioned Memorandum of Understanding. In this respect, the Association will inter alia have the following purposes: to be the voice of professional football Leagues in Europe on all matters of common interest; to achieve full recognition by FIFA and UEFA; to participate in and appoint representatives to the UEFA Professional Football Committee and/or such other UEFA committees as may from time to time be agreed; to foster friendly relations between the Association and organizations representing players operating within the territory of member and associate member Leagues; to consider Social Dialogue issues at a European level and where appropriate act as a social partner (Article 1.3 of the EPFL Constitution).

Article 3 of the Memorandum of Understanding between UEFA and EPFL dealing with Objectives of Cooperation inter alia states that to protect and promote the common values and concerns (see Article 2) the parties agree as follows: to create and develop, in conjunction with player representatives, a tripartite European football dialogue between the EPFL, UEFA and player representatives, so as to ensure that the specificity of football is always included when discussing labour-related matters and, if appropriate, to reach agreements in this forum in accordance with the tripartite agreement dated 27 January 2004 whilst also recognizing UEFA's presence as a third party in any social dialogue in Europe in order that UEFA fulfils the roles of, inter alia: guardian of sporting rules and values; representative of those territories where clubs and players are not represented by the EPFL/player representatives involved in such a dialogue; and guarantor of the essential solidarity between the various levels of football practice, from recreational to top-level football.

As to the objectives of UEFA and FIFA, the first objective of UEFA is to deal with all questions relating to European football (Article 2 of the UEFA Statutes). Among the objectives of FIFA are to improve the game of football constantly and promote it globally and to control every type of Association Football (Article 2 of the FIFA Statutes).

The following conclusion may be drawn from this. As "the voice of the Leagues" EPFL seemingly wishes to manifest itself as the better alternative for G-14, "the voice of the clubs." EPFL desires to be the representative in all matters of common interest of which a European Social Dialogue is clearly one. EPFL is thus duly authorized by its members, the national Leagues, to participate in a European Social Dialogue, irrespective of whether this is an EU Dialogue or an informal non-EU Dialogue. The first objective of EPFL is to fulfil and comply with the Memorandum of Understanding with UEFA, according to which EPFL shall recognize "UEFA's presence in any social dialogue in Europe."

Austria

The purpose of the Austrian League (*Österreichische Fusball-Bundesliga*) is to promote Austrian elite football, to deal with all questions concerning elite football, to promote the sportive and economic interests of the clubs in particular, and to regulate the working conditions of the clubs' employees, in particular also by concluding collective bargaining agreements (Article 1 of the League Statutes).

The purpose of the Austrian Football Association (FA) is to promote, supervise and regulate association football in Austria, to represent association football at home and abroad and to maintain relations with FIFA and UEFA, while observing the Statutes, Regulations and decisions of FIFA and UEFA (Article 2 of the FA Statutes). We may therefore conclude that the Austrian League is expressly authorized to participate in "industrial relations," including the conclusion of collective labour agreements.

Belgium

The purpose of the Belgian League (*Ligue Professionelle de Football/Liga Beroepsvoetbal*) is the promotion and development of professional football in Belgium (Article 3 of the League Statutes). From Article 3 it also follows that the League represents the clubs as employers of the professional football players in Belgium, both nationally and internationally. The Belgian FA has attributed to the League the full and sole competence to represent professional football in Belgium (Article 39 of the League Statutes; see also Sect. 6.4 "(In)dependence" below under "Belgium").

The purpose of the Belgian FA is to handle the administrative and sportive organization of association football (Article I/3 of the FA Statutes).

The Belgian League is thus expressly an employers' organization and as such is mandated to participate in "industrial relations."

Denmark

The objectives of the Association of Danish League Clubs (*Divisionforeningen*) are to promote football through the Danish Football League and to arrange permanent cooperation between the members for the benefit of the members and Danish football (Article 2 of the League Statutes). Article 18 of the League Statutes deals with cooperation with the players' union.

The aim of the Danish Football Association is to promote and develop Danish football both nationally and internationally (Article 2 of the FA Statutes).

The Danish League is expressly authorized to participate in "industrial relations."

England

The objectives of the English League (Football Association Premier League Limited) amongst others are to organize and manage under the jurisdiction of the Football Association a League of association football clubs ("the Premier League"), and generally to adhere to and comply with the applicable rules and regulations of the Football Association (Article 3 of the League Memorandum of Association).

One objective of the English FA is to promote the game of Association Football in every way in which the Association shall think proper (Article 3 of the FA Memorandum of Association).

According to the Chaidron Report,[8] the English FA is the overall regulatory authority of the game, whereas the Premier and Football Leagues handle employment issues for the clubs.

The conclusion therefore is that no provision has been made concerning "industrial relations" in the English League Statutes, or in the Memorandum, or in the Articles of Association.

Finland

The objectives of the Finnish League (*Jalkapalloliiga RY*/Football League Association) are to organize annually the top national football League, in which every member club is represented by one team, and to establish solid cooperation among the member clubs and act as an impartial common body between the member clubs. The Association's main objective is to actively raise the level of Finnish football (Article 2 of the League Statutes).

The purpose of the Finnish FA as the national governing body in football is to direct, manage and guide the development of football in Finland (Article 2 of the

[8] Study on the Representativeness of the Social Partner Organisations in the Professional Football Players Sector (EU-25—Bulgaria, Romania and Turkey), Research Project conducted on behalf of the Employment and Social Affairs DG of the European Commission, Université Catholique de Louvain, Institut des Sciences du Travail, February 2006.

FA Statutes). The Association shall realize its purpose by acting as the governing body directing, representing and managing football activities in Finland and abroad thereby following the rules, instructions and regulations of the international federations to which the FA is affiliated (Article 3(1) of the FA Statutes).

The conclusion is that the Finnish League Statutes do not refer to "industrial relations."

France

The object of the French League (*Ligue de Football Professionnel*) is to guarantee the practise and administration of professional football in accordance with the Statutes and Regulations of the FA and with the provisions of the agreement concluded between the FA and the League.

The League is authorized to take all decisions regarding the organization and development of professional football. More specifically, the League is authorized to organize, administer and regulate professional football including the first and second League divisions (Articles 5 and 6 of the League Statutes).

The objectives of the French FA among others are to organize, develop and supervise the training in and practise of football in France, to develop and maintain relations with the League and to maintain all necessary relations with the other member FAs of FIFA (Article 1 of the FA Statutes).

The Preamble of the Statutes of the French Employers' Union of Professional Football Clubs [*Union Patronale des Clubs Professionnels de Football* (*UCPF*)] states that the Union is a professional trade union (*syndicat*) in accordance with the provisions of the Labour Act. The purpose of the UCPF is to protect the general and specific interests of the football clubs in Leagues 1 and 2 and in the (National) Third Division, especially in relation to the different authorities in charge of professional football, namely the FA and the League (Article 4 of the UCPF Statutes).

In order to realize this purpose, the UCPF may notably take every action to protect professional footballers' interests against all *syndicats* representing the management of professional clubs and may accede to and/or cooperate with any employers' organization, either national or international (Article 5 of the UCPF Statutes).

According to the Chaidron Report, the UCPF protects and promotes the interests of professional clubs (also as employers) vis-à-vis the various bodies that control professional football. The sole mission of the UCPF is to represent professional clubs, particularly in the field of Social Dialogue.

The French League Statutes make no provision for "industrial relations." In France, UCPF is the professional football employers' organization and as such is expressly authorized to participate in "industrial relations."

Germany

The purpose and task of the German League (*Ligaverband*) is to administer and operate the competitions of the first and second *Bundesliga* which are delegated by the FA to the League (Preamble and Article 4 of the League Statutes). Another purpose and task is to promote the sportive and economic interests of all its members together towards governing bodies and other third parties (Article 4 of the League Statutes). For the performance of its tasks and the implementation of its purposes the League has established the *Deutsche Fussball Liga GmbH* (DFL) (Article 4 of the League Statutes).

The main task of the German FA is to be responsible for the practise of association football. The FA has full responsibility for the unity of German football (Preamble of the DFB Statutes). The purposes and tasks of the FA are in particular to promote association football and its development, to represent German football at home and abroad and to organize the first and second *Bundesliga* (Article 4 of the FA Statutes).

The conclusion is that the German League Statutes do not contain any provisions that explicitly refer to "industrial relations." However, "industrial relations," both nationally and internationally, could be considered to come within the scope of the provision stating that the League promotes the sportive and economic interests of all its members together (by authorizing EPFL on the European level).

Greece

The Greek FA's aims are to organize, propagate, administer, supervise and generally promote association football on Greek territory, to organize championships on a national level and assign organizational duties to the Greek Association of Professional Football Clubs (Article 2 of the FA Statutes).

NB: The Greek League in its present form (Hellenic Football League) is to be dissolved shortly and replaced by a completely new Super League.

Conclusion: not applicable.

Ireland

The objectives for which the Irish League (*Eircom League*) has been established are amongst others to be a governing body for all member clubs and to represent and further the interests of the League, member clubs and the game of association football, to organize an annual League competition for member clubs, to regulate the activities of the League, to cooperate with or assist the FA in any way which the League shall think proper and to enter into or adopt any agreement with such bodies, and to cooperate with FIFA and UEFA (Article 4 of the League Statutes).

The main objectives of the Irish FA are to promote, foster and develop the game of Association Football. In furtherance exclusively of the foregoing main objective, the FA shall among others have the following subsidiary objectives: to cooperate with FIFA and UEFA in all matters relating to the game of football or the rules and regulations affecting the same (Article 3 of the FA Memorandum of Association).

No reference is thus made to "industrial relations" in the Irish League Statutes.

Italy

Article 1 of the Italian League Statutes amongst other things provides that the League (*Lega Nazionale Professionisti/Lega Calcio*) represents the clubs in the conclusion of employment contracts and the drafting of standard contracts and in their relations with third parties.

The Leagues also represents the associated clubs in the conclusion of employment contracts and the drafting of the relevant standard contract (Article 7 of the FA Statutes).

The Italian FA is a recognized private association with legal status. Its objective is to promote and regulate the game of football and related aspects (Article 1 of the FA Statutes).

The conclusion is therefore that the Italian League does deal with employment issues.

Portugal

The main purposes of the Portuguese League (*Liga Portuguesa de Futebol Profissional*) are among others to exercise its authority as an autonomous FA body in accordance with the Sports Act; to promote and protect the common interests of its members and to manage matters inherent to the organization and the practise of professional football and its competitions; and to organize and regulate competitions of a professional nature which take place under the auspices of the FA (Article 5 of the League Statutes). In order to pursue the common interests and to fulfil its social objective, the League also acts in among others the following capacities: as a representative of all members together towards all entities with which they have a common interest, to act in pursuit and defence of these interests, especially towards the Professional Footballers' Union, the National Association of Football Coaches, and other professional associations that include persons employed by the clubs, and to be the authority to negotiate and conclude agreements and contracts that are binding on the member clubs, i.e. collective labour agreements (Article 6 of the League Statutes).

The main objective of the Portuguese FA is to promote, organize, regulate and monitor the training and practice of association football (Article 2 of the FA Statutes).

According to the Chaidron Report, the League was originally only an employers' organization, but when the applicable Law came into force it additionally acquired the role of autonomous body of the FA and assumed responsibility for the organization and management of professional competitions.

The Portuguese League Statutes therefore do refer to "industrial relations."

Scotland

The objectives for which the Scottish Premier League Limited has been established are amongst others to organize and manage and commercially exploit, under the jurisdiction of the Scottish FA, a League of association football clubs; to cooperate with the FA in all matters relating to the operations of the League and to cooperate where appropriate with the FIFA and UEFA, and to take such steps as are necessary to observe and comply with the FA's articles of association (Article 3 of the League Memorandum of Association).

The Scottish FA's objectives are inter alia to promote, foster, and develop the game of Association football (Article 3 of the FA Memorandum of Association).

No mention is made of "industrial relations" in the Scottish League Statutes, or in the Memorandum, or in the Articles of Association.

Spain

The objective of the Spanish League (*Liga Nacional de Futbol Profesional*) is inter alia to organize and promote official nationwide professional football competitions (Article 2 of the League Statutes). The League shall further act as it deems necessary to pursue its corporate purpose. Pursuant to the Sports Act and its enabling regulations, the task and responsibility of the League is to organize official nationwide professional football competitions, in coordination with the FA and in accordance with the criteria established by the Higher Council for Sports to guarantee compliance with national and international commitments. This coordination shall be implemented by means of agreements between the parties, the contents of which shall, to all intents and purposes, form part of the corporate purpose of the League. Agreements or arrangements entered into with the Higher Council for Sports and the Association of Spanish Footballers shall also form part of the corporate purpose of the League (Article 3 of the League Statutes).

The Spanish FA is responsible for the governance, administration, management, organization and regulation of association football (Article 4 of the FA Statutes).

The conclusion is that the Spanish League is an employers' organization.

Sweden

The Swedish Football Association has as its objective the promotion and administration of the sport of football in Sweden (Article 1 of the FA Statutes).

According to the Chaidron Report, the League (*Foreningen Svensk Elitfotboll*) is charged with administering professional clubs, organizing the professional clubs' League championship, and representing its members in a range of settings, including collective bargaining.

The Swedish League is therefore an employers' organization.

The Netherlands

The main purpose of the Dutch League (*Eredivisie NV*) is to promote the quality of football in the Netherlands, amongst other things by participating in and administering the *Eredivisie CV* (Article 3 of the League Statutes).

The purpose of the Netherlands Federation of Professional Football Clubs (FBO) is to promote the interests of professional football clubs in the Netherlands. The FBO tries to achieve this purpose by inter alia representing the clubs' interests in the field of labour relations and by concluding collective labour agreements with employees who are employed by its members. As such the FBO represents its members as parties to these agreements on the employer side (Article 2 of the FBO Statutes).

The main purpose of the Dutch FA is to promote and support the promotion of association football (Article 4 of the FA Statutes).

There are no provisions in the Dutch League Statutes concerning "industrial relations." In the Netherlands, FBO is the professional football employers' organization that is explicitly authorized to participate in "industrial relations." The ECV is a member of EPFL.

G-14

Every G-14 founding member is a principal European professional football club. With the other members these have agreed to form a European Economic Interest Grouping (EEIG) subject to Council Regulation (EEC) No. 2137/85 of 25 July 1985 so as to initiate or increase mutual cooperation for the purpose of developing own activities and to act jointly in the promotion of professional football (Preamble of the G-14 Foundation Agreement).

The G-14 amongst others has the following objectives: to promote the cooperation, amicable relations and unity between the member clubs; to promote and improve the professional football competition in all its aspects and safeguard the general interests of the member clubs; to promote the interests of the member clubs and to consider the collective affairs that are important for these clubs; to promote cooperation and relations between G-14 on the one hand and the FIFA, the UEFA, and other sports institutions or professional football clubs on the other; to negotiate the format, administration and operation of the club competitions with the FIFA, the UEFA and other sports institutions (Article I.3. of the G-14 Foundation Agreement).

According to the Preamble of Council Regulation No. 2137/85, a harmonious development of economic activities and a continuous and balanced expansion throughout the Community depend on the establishment and smooth functioning of a common market offering conditions analogous to those of a national market. To bring about this single market and to increase its unity, a legal framework which facilitates the adaptation of their activities to the common conditions of the Community should be created for natural persons, companies, firms and other legal bodies in particular. To that end it is necessary that those natural persons, companies, firms and other legal bodies should be able to cooperate effectively across frontiers. Cooperation of this nature can encounter legal, fiscal or psychological difficulties. The creation of an appropriate Community legal instrument in the form of a European Economic Interest Grouping would contribute to the achievement of the abovementioned objectives and therefore proves necessary. Article 3 of the Regulation provides that the purpose of a grouping shall be to facilitate or develop the economic activities of its members and to improve or increase the results of those activities.

Of the 10 Principles of G-14, no. 9 states that Social Dialogue is critical: issues between players as employees and clubs as employers must be discussed and resolved within the context of the European Social Dialogue.

The conclusion therefore is that the G-14 is a European Economic Interest Grouping for the promotion of professional football. In its Statutes no reference is made to "industrial relations."

In respect of Social Dialogue, G-14 due to its nature is first interested in *international* football issues and secondly in the *harmonization* of specific national issues from an international perspective.

6.3.1 Summary Concerning the Question of Mandate

According to its Statutes, the EPFL is explicitly authorized by its members, the national Leagues, to participate in a European Social Dialogue. At the national level, some Leagues in their Statutes are expressly described as employers' organizations, while others are expressly authorized to participate in "industrial relations." Under the Austrian, French and Dutch League Statutes, the conclusion of collective labour agreements is referred to as an instrument of Social Dialogue. In addition to the Leagues in France and the Netherland, there are separate employers' organizations for the purpose of "industrial relations." In all cases where no reference is made to a League either as an employers' organization or as having the power to participate in "industrial relations," this does not mean that the League is barred from acting as such, which can also be manifest in practice. The broad, all-encompassing official purposes of the respective national FAs do not contradict this conclusion either. Of course, the same is true for the purposes of UEFA and FIFA in their capacity of "umbrella" organizations to the FAs and—through them—the Leagues, and besides that in their direct relations with EPFL. It may not be concluded that the national Leagues have illegally empowered EPFL to participate in "industrial relations"/Social Dialogue.

In the G-14 Statutes no reference is made to "industrial relations."

6.4 Chapter 3: (In)dependence

EPFL

As to the EPFL's predecessor, in a Memorandum of Understanding (1998) concluded between certain of the founding member Leagues on the one hand and UEFA on the other the parties recorded the essential terms of their cooperation and involvement relating to European professional football. As part of this cooperation and involvement UEFA agreed to establish a permanent Professional Football Committee (Preamble of the Association Accord). The Association's representatives on the Committee shall reflect a balance between the major Leagues (England, France, Germany, Italy and Spain) and the remaining Leagues (Article 5(3) of the Association Accord).

According to the Preamble and Paras 1–2 and 6–8 of the Memorandum of Understanding, it complies with the wish of UEFA, as the parent body of European football, to take care of the specific matters of concern to the Leagues and professional football and, within the framework of the UEFA Statutes, to devote time and attention to these needs. It complies with the common wish of the Leagues and UEFA to enter into a Memorandum of Understanding, for the purpose of establishing future cooperation. The essential terms of this cooperation and involvement are inter alia recorded as follows: UEFA, within the framework of its Statutes, shall support the Leagues in their specific issues and problems related to professional football. UEFA agrees to establish a permanent Professional Football Committee. The aim and duty of this Committee shall inter alia be friendly cooperation between the Leagues and UEFA within the framework of the UEFA Statutes. The discussions shall be conducted with the guarantee of full transparency to the UEFA Member Associations. All activities shall be undertaken in a democratic manner, and in a spirit of mutual trust. Its aim shall further be to promote and safeguard the interests of Professional Football Leagues within Europe with regard to their specific problems and to advise UEFA's Executive Committee on problems relating to Professional Football. Amongst the competences of the Committee are entering into talks with players' unions and contacting the European Union bodies after consultation with UEFA.

In September 2005 the FIFA Executive Committee ratified the Memorandum agreed between the European Professional Football League (EPFL) and UEFA, as well as the constitutional terms of the EPFL as an association under Swiss law in accordance with the provisions negotiated with UEFA, which are as follows.

Each of the member Leagues is one of Europe's principal premier professional football Leagues and is duly authorized and mandated by the relevant competent bodies to enter into this Constitution (Preamble of the Constitution of the Association of European Professional Football Leagues). Associate membership of the Association shall be open to all major non-premier professional football Leagues. The individual members and associate members shall have the following obligations: to fully comply with the Statutes, Regulations and Decisions of FIFA, UEFA and EPFL as well as the Memorandum of Understanding and ensure that these are also respected by its own members and affiliates, where necessary (Articles 2.3, 3.2 and 3.4 of the EPFL Constitution).

According to the Preamble of the Memorandum of Understanding between UEFA and EPFL all members of EPFL must be officially recognized by their respective UEFA member association and represent their member clubs as well as being entrusted with certain tasks, obligations and/or powers as delegated by the FA in question and/or national legislation such as, but not necessarily limited to, the organization of the top division national championship and the commercialization of rights. All members of EPFL recognize their subordination to their respective FAs, fully respecting them and implementing their Statutes, Regulations and Decisions where applicable. All members of EPFL shall also respect the Statutes, Regulations and Decisions of FIFA and UEFA where applicable.

According to Article 1 of the Statutes of UEFA, "League" is defined as a combination of clubs within the territory of a member association and which is subordinate to and under the authority of that member association. Under the FIFA Statutes the League is considered an organization that is subordinate to an association. Article 18 of the FIFA Statutes provides that Leagues or any other groups of clubs affiliated to a member of FIFA shall be subordinate to and recognized by that member. The member's statutes shall define the scope of authority and the rights and duties of these groups. The statutes and regulations of these groups shall be approved by the member. Every member shall ensure that its affiliated clubs can take all decisions on any matters regarding membership independently of any external body. This obligation applies regardless of an affiliated club's corporate structure.

The EPFL in its original form was restricted to *EU* Premier Leagues, while now it is expressly described as a *European* organization. Of course, "European" might simply refer to "EU" and it is true that the former 12 and present 15 members of EPFL all originate in ("old") EU Member States. However, this change of name could also be interpreted as better reflecting EPFL's close ties with UEFA as a pan-European organization, and as a loosening of its ties with the EU.

Obviously, through the Memorandum of Understanding with UEFA and under its Constitution, EPFL and its members (the national Leagues) and the members of the FAs (the clubs) are closely linked to UEFA and FIFA, and not only as far as EPFL's objectives are concerned. The close tie between EPFL and UEFA also becomes apparent through EPFL's permanent membership of UEFA's Professional Football Committee. According to the UEFA and FIFA Statutes, recognized Leagues are subordinate to the respective FAs.

The conclusion is that EPFL is mandated to participate in a European Social Dialogue.

However, generally speaking it cannot operate independently from football's national and international governing bodies. It has even officially recognized "UEFA's presence as a third party in any Social Dialogue in Europe."

Austria

The Austrian League is a member of the Austrian FA (Article 1 of the League Statutes and Article 4 of the FA Statutes).

Membership of the League obliges the clubs to recognize the Statutes and decisions of the League, of the FA, of UEFA and of FIFA (Article 4 of the League Statutes).

The FA is a member of FIFA and UEFA. This membership obliges the FA and the League to recognize the FIFA and UEFA Statutes (Article 2 of the FA Statutes). The members of the FA are obliged to observe the Statutes and Decisions of the FA (Article 7 of the FA Statutes).

According to the Chaidron Report the League was set up as a voluntary, legally independent organization of the professional clubs and at the same time as a member of the FA.

Decisions on professional football are delegated to the League. This means that the organization of the First and the Second Division falls within the purview of the League, which is an affiliate of the FA. The *Bundesliga* represents the employers' side of professional football. There is no Social Dialogue in Austria.

The Austrian League is therefore a member of both the Austrian FA and of EPFL.

Belgium

The Belgian League counts as its members the professional clubs playing in the First Division of the national championship. The League's members have authorized it to represent them as the association of clubs/employers of professional football players in Belgium, both within the framework of national and international bodies (Article 3 of the League Statutes). Article 39 states that by approving these Statutes, the Belgian FA confers upon the League the capacity of sole representative of professional football in Belgium to the exclusion of any other association.

As a member of FIFA the Belgian FA is recognized by all foreign FAs as the only association representing association football in Belgium (Article I/4 of the FA Statutes).

The Belgian League is thus closely linked to the Belgian FA and is a member of EPFL.

Denmark

The League (Association of Danish League Clubs) is a member of the Danish Football Association. As a member of the FA, the Association and its members are at all times subject to the applicable statutes and regulations that apply to the FA (Articles 1 and 3 of the League Statutes).

According to the Chaidron Report, the Association is a mixed association. Apart from being a special interest organization of the clubs, the Association is also an employers' organization, and this means that, in this particular role, the social partner is the players' union instead of the FA. As a member of the FA, the Association is obliged to comply with the rules of the FA, UEFA and FIFA. As an employers' organization however the Association is obliged to follow another set of rules when it comes to negotiating employment and working conditions for Danish players, namely the rules on collective bargaining in Denmark.

The Danish League is a member of the Danish FA and of EPFL.

England

The English League (The FA Premier League Limited) shall adhere to and comply with the FA Rules (Article 78 of the League Statutes).

The English League is a member of EPFL.

Finland

In the Finnish League Statutes no provision is made regarding the institutional relationship between the League and the Football Association.

Article 28 of the Finnish FA Statutes provides that a group formed by FA member clubs may only take part in football activities with the permission of and subordinate to the FA. The rules and regulations of such a group must be submitted to the FA for approval.

According to the Chaidron Report, as a member of FIFA, the FA has responsibility for all activities connected with football in Finland. Indeed, League One and all other Leagues or competitions are managed by the FA. However, for the top League (*Veikkausliiga* (League One)) there is one exception in that its management is partly delegated to an independent association.

The League represents professional clubs playing in the *Veikkausliiga*.

All professional clubs are members of the FA. The League is not a member of the FA. The League is fully recognized by the FA. It is an independent organization, not a subdivision of the FA.

Social Dialogue does not take place in Finnish football.

The Finnish League is thus not a member of the Finnish FA, but, as "a group formed by FA member clubs," it is subordinate to the FA. The League is a member of EPFL.

France

Professional football as defined by the French FA in its Statutes and Regulations and according to its Decisions is delegated to the League on the conditions indicated in the Agreement between the FA and the League. The League has administrative, financial and sportive autonomy in accordance with the Statutes and Regulations of the FA. The League organises, administers and regulates the First and Second Division (Articles 1 and 2 of the Agreement between the FA and the League). The League consists of clubs that participate in the First and Second Division, established in conformity with the Law (Article 7 of the League Statutes).

According to the Chaidron Report, at European level the League has not given EPFL a mandate in legal terms in negotiations at European level. The League is only a member of EPFL, but does believe that the EPFL could emerge as a legitimate actor in a European Social Dialogue.

It can be concluded that according to the Agreement with the French FA, the French League has autonomy in organizing the First and Second Divisions. The League is a member of EPFL.

Germany

The German League is the organization representing the clubs playing in the first and second *Bundesliga* (Preamble and Article 1 of the League Statutes). The League is a member of the German FA. On the basis of this membership the League must function in accordance with the Statutes and Regulations of the FA and with the basic agreement with the FA. These documents are directly binding upon the League and its members (Article 3 of the League Statutes).

The FA is a member of FIFA and UEFA. Based on its FIFA membership, the FA must comply with FIFA and UEFA provisions, which implies that these are also binding upon the League and its members. The League may also become a member of other organizations, provided that this does not affect the rights of FIFA, UEFA and FA (Article 3 of the League Statutes and Article 3 of the FA Statutes).

The *Deutsche Fussball Liga GmbH* (DFL) is in charge of the operational affairs of the League (*Ligaverband*). Within the scope of the FA Statutes, the basic agreement between the FA and the League and the Statutes of the League, the DFL is authorized to take all and any action serving the purpose of the DFL (Preamble and Article 2 of the DFL Statutes).

According to the Chaidron Report, the *Ligaverband* was founded to give professional clubs greater autonomy (independence) within the FA. The *Ligaverband/*

DFL is not an employers' organization and therefore does not take part in collective bargaining. There is no official Social Dialogue in German football.

The German League is a member of the German FA. It is explicitly allowed to become a member of other organizations. The League is a member of EPFL.

Greece

According to its Statutes the Greek League is a member of the Greek FA. The League accepts unreservedly the Statutes, Regulations and Decisions of the FA. The position of the League in relation to the FA is also dealt with in the Sports Act.

The FA is the sole and exclusively competent highest authority representing Greek football. It is a member of FIFA and UEFA. Amongst other things, the FA is obliged to accept FIFA's and UEFA's statutes, regulations, directives and decisions, and to ensure that these are also accepted by all parties involved in Greek football (Article 1 of the FA Statutes).

According to the Chaidron Report, the FA has delegated to the League the right to organize the professional football championships. The League is responsible for the organization of the professional competitions, i.e. Divisions 1, 2 and 3.

There is no Social Dialogue (formal or informal) in Greek football.

At European level, the League as a member of EPFL has delegated to EPFL its power of negotiation (in the field of employment).

The Greek League is a member of EPFL.

Ireland

The amalgamation of member clubs shall be known as the FAI National League and shall trade as the *Eircom League* (Article 1 of the League Statutes).
According to the Chaidron Report, the *Eircom League* is not a legal entity in itself, even though the FA and the League are two independent organizations. The League recognizes that they are subservient to the FA as the FA is the national association. There are no specific formal structures, such as joint committees, devoted to Social Dialogue in football.

The Irish League is a member of EPFL.

Italy

The Italian League is a private association of all clubs affiliated to the Italian FA that take part in the A and B Series championships. As an association of clubs affiliated to the FA, the League also performs the functions assigned to it by the FA Statutes and Regulations. For the realization of its objectives it enjoys organizational and administrative autonomy and, acting as a representative for the associated clubs, performs all the related duties and powers arising, save for those which, in accordance with the law, FA Statutes or Regulations, fall to the FA (Article 1 of the League Statutes).

The FA carries out its functions in accordance with the resolutions and guidelines of FIFA, UEFA, the IOC and CONI (Article 2 of the FA Statutes).

The Italian League has organizational autonomy in relation to the Italian FA. It is a member of EPFL.

Portugal

The Portuguese League is an association under private law which is governed by its Statutes, by the Regulations that are issued in accordance with the Statutes and by applicable law (Article 1 of the League Statutes). In the pursuit of its purposes, the League, in its capacity of an autonomous organ of the Portuguese FA, has exclusive authority in among others the following fields: the organization and regulation of competitions of a professional nature and, by means of a Protocol with the FA, the definition of the applicable regime with regard to sportive, financial and property relations between the League and the FA. In order to pursue the common interests and to fulfil its social objective, the League as we have seen above also acts in among others the following capacities: as a representative of all members together towards all entities with which they have a common interest, to act in pursuit and defence of these interests, especially towards the Professional Footballers' Union, the National Association of Football Coaches, and other professional associations that include persons employed by the clubs, and to be the authority to negotiate and conclude agreements and contracts that are binding on the member clubs, i.e. collective labour agreements (Article 6 of the League Statutes).

The Portuguese FA is governed by its Statutes and by the rules to which it is bound through its affiliation to FIFA and UEFA (Article 1 of the FA Statutes). With regard to competitions of a professional nature, the League is responsible for exercising the FA's authority where organization and management are concerned. The applicable regime with regard to sportive, financial and property relations between the League and the FA is defined by means of a protocol between the League and the FA (Articles 53 and 54 of the FA Statutes).

According to the Chaidron Report, under the law and the FA Statutes, the organization, regulation, management and administration of professional football in Portugal comes exclusively under the authority of the Portuguese Professional Football League. The League is a member of the FA. A protocol between the FA and the League establishes the criteria and regulations for interaction between the two organizations. The League is a legal person distinct from the FA. Under the law the FA has public powers for self-regulation by delegation from the State. The FA has no way of intervening in the autonomy of the League to regulate professional football competitions, as this is how the arrangements are set out in the law. There is Social Dialogue in the football sector, with the League representing the employers. At European level the League has delegated to EPFL its power of negotiation as an employer for the European Social Dialogue.

The Portuguese League is a member of the Portuguese FA. The relationship of (functional autonomy) between the League and the FA is also secured by public law. The League is a member of EPFL.

Scotland

According to Article 97 of the Scottish League Statutes, nothing in these Articles shall relieve any member of the League from its obligations as a full member club of the FA to comply with the applicable articles of association of the FA. Each member shall procure that the League observes and complies with all relevant articles of association of the FA applicable to it.

Article 5 of the Scottish FA Statutes provides that all members shall be subject to and shall comply with the Articles of Association and with any regulations or decisions promulgated by the FA or by FIFA or UEFA.

The Scottish League is a member of EPFL.

Spain

The Spanish League is a sports association under private law which, in accordance with the Sports Act, has as its exclusive and compulsory members all clubs participating in official nationwide professional football competitions, and is legally entrusted with organizing these competitions, in cooperation with the Spanish FA. The League has its own legal status and full capacity to act in pursuit of its aims, and is independent from the FA, of which it forms part, with regard to its own internal organization and operation (Article 1 of the League Statutes).

The Spanish FA is a private association, albeit of public utility, which is governed by the Sports Act. The FA is affiliated to FIFA and UEFA, whose Statutes it accepts and undertakes to observe.

The FA is amongst others composed of the League (Articles 1 and 2 of the FA Statutes). The League is a private sports association composed exclusively and compulsorily of First and Second Division clubs, insofar as they participate in official professional competitions at national level. It has distinct legal personality and with regard to its internal organization and functioning enjoys autonomy towards the FA, of which it forms parts. The League shall organize its own competitions in coordination with the FA (Article 16 of the FA Statutes).

According to the Chaidron Report, the clubs delegate the negotiation of collective agreements with players' representatives to the League.

The conclusion is that the Spanish League is affiliated to the Spanish FA, but autonomous in its operations. It is a member of EPFL.

Sweden

The Swedish Leagues are administered by the Swedish Football Association (Chap. 10, Article 1 of the League Statutes).

According to the Chaidron Report the Leagues (*Allsvenskan, Superettan* and the First Division) enjoy administrative, financial and sportive autonomy in accordance with the statutes and regulations of the FA. The Leagues are affiliated to the FA. They are in charge of organizing League championship matches and, under FA control, supervise the professional clubs. In Sweden, the FA is not separate from the Leagues and hence no specific regulations exist concerning the relationship between the two or regulations on the purpose of the Leagues. There is a Social Dialogue in Swedish football. At European level the League has delegated its competence (i.e. its power to negotiate) in the field of employment relations to the EPFL.

The Swedish League is part of the Swedish FA and a member of EPFL.

The Netherlands
The Dutch League is an organ of the professional football section of the FA (Article 2 of the FA Professional Football Regulations).

FBO is a member of the Dutch national general cross-industry employers' organization *VNO-NCW*.

According to the Chaidron Report, FBO is an independent organization.

Every three years there is a formal Social Dialogue in the sense that a collective labour agreement is negotiated and concluded with FBO.

The Dutch League is an organ of the Dutch FA. The League is also a member of EPFL. A representative of FBO is a member of the League delegation to EPFL (Article 2.6.1 of the EPFL Constitution: A member League may also authorize any other person as it sees fit to act as the representative of the member League).

G-14
The conclusion must be that there is no formal relationship between G-14 and UEFA or FIFA other than that the members of G-14 are on the one hand also members of their national FAs and, on the other hand, of the national Leagues and in that capacity are indirectly associated with UEFA, FIFA on the one hand and EPFL on the other. In this respect and within the framework of the "pyramid model," G-14 may under private association law be considered through its member clubs to be a part of and subordinate to the FAs, the Leagues, UEFA, FIFA and EPFL. However, within the framework of its official purposes G-14 and its members are fully independent from a legal perspective, as (European) public law prevails over private (association) law and G-14 has formally been established as a European Economic Interest Grouping.

6.4.1 Summary on (In)dependence

The EPFL is directly and very closely linked to UEFA and FIFA. It cannot operate independently in a European Social Dialogue. At the national level, the same is true for the EPFL member Leagues in their relationship with the respective national FAs, as most Leagues are separate legal entities. Leagues are generally either members of the FA, are subordinate to the FA, or are affiliated with the FA. Where Leagues have organizational and administrative autonomy towards the FA, this autonomy is functional for the purpose of fulfilling the tasks that are assigned to them by the FAs. Of some EPFL member Leagues (i.e. in France, Greece, Italy, Portugal and Spain) their position and authority (status) and relationship with the FA is even regulated and secured under public law (Sports Act).

In terms of (in)dependence, compared with EPFL G-14 is at the other end of the spectrum.

The G-14 is an independent organization which is multinational (transnational) in that it—as opposed to EPFL—does not represent a national level at the international level. In that respect, it does not correspond to the pyramid model, as it lies outside and beyond the boundaries of this model.

6.5 Chapter 4: EU Admissibility Criteria

At sectoral level, the Social Dialogue underwent an important development in 1998, when the Commission decided on the establishment of sectoral Dialogue committees promoting the Dialogue between the social partners in the sectors at European level (COM (1998) 322 final of 20 May 1998, Communication from the Commission "Adapting and promoting the Social Dialogue at Community level"). The document laid down precise provisions concerning the establishment, representativeness and operation of new sectoral committees, intended as central bodies for consultation, joint initiatives and negotiation. The sectoral Social Dialogue committees are established with due regard for the autonomy of the social partners. The social partner organizations must apply jointly to the European Commission in order to take part in a Social Dialogue at European level. The European organizations representing employers and workers must, when submitting this application, meet a number of criteria (Article 1 of the Commission Decision of 20 May 1998 (98/500/EC) on the establishment of Sectoral Dialogue Committees promoting the Dialogue between the social partner at European level, OJ L 225, 12.8.1998, p. 27), i.e. they must:

- be cross-industry, or relate to specific sectors or categories and be organized at European level;
- consist of organizations which are themselves an integral and recognized part of Member States' social partner structures and with the capacity to negotiate agreements, and which are representative of all Member States, as far as possible;
- have adequate structures to ensure the effective participation in the consultation process.

For the purpose of setting up sectoral Dialogue committees, the European Commission asks organizations representing employers and workers wishing to establish such a committee to complete a questionnaire and attach it to their joint request. Apart from the EU criteria and other possible considerations regarding admissibility to a Social Dialogue, this would mean that EPFL and G-14 would be dependent on the willingness of FIFPro and vice versa for participation in a Social Dialogue. The tripartite agreement of 27 January 2004 between UEFA, EPFL and FIFPro implies mutual recognition.

EPFL and G-14 are both organizations relating to the specific sector of professional football and they are organized at European level. The member Leagues of EPFL belong to Europe's principal premier professional football Leagues. G-14 is an Economic Interest Grouping under EU law. For these reasons, they can both be considered to fulfil the first requirement.

As to the second criterion, the following is to be observed. EPFL consists of organizations which in many, but not all cases are an integral and recognized part of the Member States' social partner structures. Among the purposes of most national Leagues is to participate as an employers' organization in industrial relations; in some cases the capacity to negotiate collective labour agreements is even explicitly mentioned and in most cases there is an official Social Dialogue in the national professional football sector in which social partners recognize each other officially. Some 80% of the national Leagues belonging to the EPFL are recognized as representatives of the clubs in the clubs' capacity of employers of the players. In 11 EPFL countries collective labour agreements exist. In the Netherlands the independent employers' organization FBO, representatives of which are recognized as official representatives of the League within the EPFL framework, is a member of the national general cross-industry employers' organization. As to the sub-criterion of representativeness in all Member States, the EPFL is represented in 14 of the "old" EU Member States (in Luxembourg there is no professional football sector and Scotland is represented individually). The new EU member countries are invited to join the EPFL with full membership status, but separate professional football League organizations do not yet exist in most "new" EU Member States. In October 2004 the EPFL represented 458 professional clubs. On the whole, the EPFL represented 100% of the top Division clubs of the 15 Members of the EU belonging to the EPFL, 67% of the Second Division clubs of these Members, 61% of the top Division clubs of the 25 countries of the enlarged European Union, 33% of the top Division clubs of the 52 UEFA countries, 52% of the top and Second Division clubs of the 31 European countries where a professional football League currently exists, 93% of the European club competition winners, and 95% of the European top Division championships turnover. It may therefore be concluded that under the present circumstances the EPFL is "as far as possible" represented in the current 25 EU Member States.

G-14 has 18 elite clubs from the "Big Five" professional football countries (England, France, Germany, Italy and Spain) plus top clubs from Portugal and the Netherlands as its members. G-14 members are regular participants in the final rounds of the European Champions League and were frequent winners of European club competitions. In financial terms it presently covers 35% of the turnover in the EU professional football market. It is obvious that G-14 does not consist of organizations which are part of national social partner structures. Whether G-14 can be considered as being "representative of all Member States, as far as possible," also depends on the interpretation of the nature (configuration) of the professional football market in Europe. In this interpretation and context, the fact that G-14 as such is not linked to national social partner structures (with the capacity to negotiate agreements) could be said to be irrelevant.

The pyramid structure in football is traditionally made up of national associations, which represent the clubs at the regional and global (universal), international level. As a consequence, there are national professional football markets (national championships) and at the regional level there is a European market which in the past consisted of several Cup competitions, namely a competition for national champions (I), one for national cup winners (II) and one for runners-up (III). These were pure knock-out competitions. In the champions and cup winners Cups—the oldest and most prestigious competitions—each UEFA member was represented by one club. The introduction of the Champions League was the result of the changing economic and financial circumstances in European professional football. The risk of being eliminated in the early stages of the European Cups was no longer acceptable for the principal clubs. Therefore a competition model element was added by introducing group stages, which guaranteed a considerably larger number of matches to the elite clubs. The permanent coefficient ranking for UEFA members was introduced on the basis of the previous results of the clubs per country in Europe. This resulted in the arrangement that three or four clubs from the "Big Five" football countries can directly qualify for the final rounds of the Champions League, whereas a few single positions are attributed to a B category of countries and the clubs of all other UEFA countries have to qualify through preliminary rounds. The other two European Cups were combined into one, i.e. the UEFA Cup, which was still a knock-out tournament (to which a preliminary group stage was added in 2002). Besides the national football markets, two international markets—the Champions League and the UEFA Cup—can nowadays be distinguished at the European level. This situation is reflected by the existence of the G-14 as a European Economic Interest Grouping representing elite clubs the majority of which regularly, if not continuously, participate in the Champions League (in total they have won 41 Championship League Cups and former European Champion Clubs' Cups out of 51; the G-14 represents the clubs with the most significant "on the pitch" records in European club competitions), as well as by the existence of the European Club Forum that is for the main part made up of regular UEFA Cup participants (also including the G-14 members). The European Club Forum is composed of 102 members, plus clubs with sporting merit, representing a corresponding number of European top-division clubs. The number of clubs per country is established on the basis of the ranking position of the member associations. In principle the clubs are selected according to their individual coefficient ranking. No lower-Division clubs are admitted. As a mark of recognition of their sporting merit, those clubs which have won at least five UEFA club competition trophies are granted a regular seat in the Forum. The Forum was set up in 2002 as the body to reinforce dialogue between UEFA and Europe's major clubs. The European Club Forum has the status of an UEFA Expert Panel. The Forum is also represented in the UEFA Club Competitions Committee. Generally speaking, whereas the European elite clubs could be qualified as "multinationals," the clubs at the UEFA Cup level and below could be described as "small and medium-sized enterprises" (SME).

In this context it should be observed that in Spain the so-called G-12—a grouping of now seventeen major clubs of the League—as an economic interest grouping in fact fulfils a function at the national level which is similar to that of G-14 at the European level.

We may conclude that the second criterion (member organizations should be part of Member States' social partner structures and be representative of all Member

States, as far as possible) is to be considered irrelevant in the context of the Champions League if this League, in terms of Social Dialogue, is regarded as a "subsector" of the (European) professional football sector at the European level which in fact it is. It is actually difficult to imagine how an organization that seeks to protect the interests of a certain category of clubs like G-14 in the context of Social Dialogue could be organized differently, that is in accordance with the above-mentioned closely interconnected (the second depending on the first) subcriteria. A number of 15 out of 18 G-14 clubs represent the "Big Five" Leagues: England: 3, France: 3, Germany: 3, Italy: 3, Spain: 3. Regular or even continuous Champions League participants are well represented in G-14 so that reasonably G-14 may be considered as a legitimate social partner (on the employers' side) in a Social Dialogue.

As to the question whether the European organizations have the capacity to negotiate agreements, it should be observed that the EPFL may be considered to have adequate structures to ensure the effective participation in a European Social Dialogue in the professional football sector. One of the official tasks and purposes of the EPFL is to consider Social Dialogue issues at a European level and where appropriate act as a social partner.

G-14 is not (yet) explicitly empowered under its Statutes to fulfil a similar function.

6.6 Chapter 5: Representation in the Context of Present Social Dialogue Committees

Before embarking on an analysis of the facts in other relevant sectors, a general observation concerning the "representativeness test" should be made. It would have been helpful to this research if information on the methods employed by the European Commission in determining the representativeness of social partner organizations were publicly available. However, the only information currently available is the text of the criteria, with no information having been published concerning the procedure and points of view related to the granting of EU social partner status.

The composition of Social Dialogue Committees in other industrial sectors may bring some clarity with regard to the exact meaning of the criteria defined by the European Commission in the abovementioned Decision of 20 May 1998. Which precedents are relevant for the establishment of a Social Dialogue Committee in professional football? At this moment there are 32 Social Dialogue Committees in operation. In order to give a comprehensive overview the sectors most relevant for the football industry will be analyzed.

The most common structure for a Social Dialogue Committee should ideally be the "two-partner" model: there are two industrial organizations which have recognized each other as the other party in a Social Dialogue. Examples of sectors where this is the case are Telecommunications (UNI-Europa on the workers' side and EUROFEDOP on the employers' side); Commerce (UNI-Europa on the workers' side and EuroCommerce on the employers' side) and Agriculture (EFFAT on the workers' side and GEOPA/COPA on the employers' side).

However, the vast majority of Social Dialogue Committees have several (more than one) representative organizations acting on the two sides of the industry. We will take a closer look at the representatives on the side of the employers in the sectors of Civil Aviation, Temporary Work, and Audiovisual and Chemical Industries.

In the Civil Aviation sector the employers are represented by the Association of European Airlines (AEA), the European Regions Airline Association (ERA), the International Air Carrier Association (IACA) and the Civil Air Navigation Services Organisation (CANSO). These organizations represent the majority of employers in the Civil Aviation sector at large. A relevant aspect is the increasing role of low-cost carriers and independent ground handlers. Due to the expansion of the budget flights market these companies face a greater need for the representation of their interests in the Civil Aviation sector. The representative organizations of these undertakings may request to be recognized as social partners in the near future.

The Temporary Work sector has only one representative on the employers' side, but the method of representation is of interest for this research. The employers are gathered in the European Organization of the International Confederation of Private Employment Agencies (CIETT). CIETT represents the national federations in the 25 EU Member States, Norway, Romania and Switzerland. Besides having the national federations (groupings of undertakings) as a member, the CIETT has six corporate members, namely the largest employment agencies in Europe: Adecco, Kelly Services, Manpower, Randstad, Vedior and USG. The interests of these large undertakings are different from the interests of the smaller private employment agencies.

A factor in relation to the representativeness issue in the Temporary Work sector is that the six corporate members are juxtaposed to the national federations that are members of the CIETT. Thus, the individual corporate members have decided that their interests on the EU "umbrella" level are not ideally represented by the CIETT as a whole and that individual membership safeguards the position of these large undertakings in a better way on the European level. Their membership of a general representative organization, which is a social partner on the national level, thus does not imply membership of the overall international organization due to a difference in interests on the EU level. The national federations and undertakings are both direct members of the CIETT.

In the Audiovisual sector the employers are represented by multiple organizations: the European Union of Broadcasters (EBU), the European Coordination of Independent Producers (CEPI), the Association of Commercial Television (ACT), the Association of European Radios (AER) and the International Federation of Film Producers Association (FIAPF).

We would like to illustrate the positions of the EBU and the ACT. The EBU is the largest professional association of national broadcasters in the world. The Union has 74 active members in 54 countries of Europe, North Africa and the Middle East. The EBU negotiates broadcasting rights for major sports events and operates Eurovision and Euroradio. EBU represents the interests of their members vis-à-vis the EU institutions and in the Social Dialogue.

The ACT represents the interests of commercial broadcasters at the EU institutions. The ACT's 25 member companies are active in twenty-one European countries and encompass several business models, from free-to-air television broadcasters to multimedia groups and digital TV platform operators. Cumulatively, these companies offer many hundreds of television channels and are the leading source of information and entertainment to millions of European citizens.

Although there is an overall organization for national broadcasters, the interests of commercial broadcasters are of a different character to such an extent that they considered the creation of a separate representative social partner organization necessary. For this reason the 25 members established the ACT.

The Chemical Industry provides another point of view in relation to representation issues. In the Chemical Industry the employers are represented vis-à-vis the workers by means of the European Chemical Employers' Group (ECEG). In this sector another actor also participates in the Social Dialogue, namely the European Chemical Industry Council (CEFIC). The CEFIC has federation members which are national federations of chemical industry undertakings and individual corporate members (cf. the corporate membership of the private employment agencies in the CIETT). The CEFIC does not have a formal social partner structure, but having been recognized by the social partners the CEFIC plays an important role in the Social Dialogue on the EU level.

This last aspect is clearly illustrated in the joint declaration of the social partners in the Chemical Industry at the time of the establishment of a formal Social Dialogue:

> The Social Partner Dialogue between ECEG and EMCEF (workers) will not be limited to social affairs subjects, but will—whenever appropriate together with the European Chemical Industry Council (CEFIC) and with close involvement of other relevant institutions and associations of the industry—focus as well on business issues, general economic conditions, environmental and other questions. Such a broader approach, which takes into account all conditions and frameworks under which the companies of the sector operate in Europe can bring a real added value to these companies, their employees and the European economy as a whole.

Since its establishment and the incorporation of CEFIC the Social Dialogue Committee has been quite active. CEFIC is a co-party to various joint declarations and has been incorporated in the Bi-annual Working Programme of the Social Dialogue Committee.

It has become clear that, although not having a formal social partner structure, the CEFIC forms an integral part of the Social Dialogue Committee due to its nature and due to the variety of issues that may form the content of a Social Dialogue on the EU level.

The accumulation of the abovementioned facts leads to the following assumptions in relation to the possible participation of the G-14 in a Professional Football Social Dialogue Committee.

- Whenever the industry changes and new interests come to the surface new organizations can be allowed to take part in the Social Dialogue (cf. the low-budget carriers in the Civil Aviation Industry).
- It appears that the European Commission takes a rather flexible approach to the application of the criteria for representativeness of social partner organizations. This is illustrated by the allowed individual membership of the six major employment agencies in the Temporary Work sector. In fact, the six major agencies have "double representation" in the Social Dialogue on EU level, as for example Vedior is not only a member of and represented by the *Algemene Bond Uitzendondernemingen* (ABU), but on EU level is also an individual member of the CIETT. This fact does not stand in the way of the simultaneous membership of ABU and Vedior of CIETT.
- As long as the relevant interests are apparent and the EU geographical area is more or less covered, organizations taking part in a Social Dialogue can consist of a limited number of undertakings. The ACT in the Audiovisual sector has a relatively small number of members, but their interests require specific representation on the EU level, especially when taking into account the existence of other "giant" organizations in the same sector such as EBU.
- There are various methods of participation in the Social Dialogue. The ACT for example is a direct member of the Social Dialogue Committee in the Audiovisual sector, while the CEFIC in the Chemical Industry is included by the social partners now that some issues cannot be discussed without the participation of the CEFIC as a stakeholder.

As regards the position of G-14 in the professional football sector, the European Commission should take a flexible approach in allowing G-14 to play a role in the Social Dialogue. An argument against participation by G-14 could be that this would lead to "double representation," now that the G-14 members are also direct members of the respective national Leagues and, as such, indirect members of EPFL. However, this situation is comparable to that of the CIETT which can therefore serve as a precedent.

From the situation in the other sectors it emerges that a very important aspect is the existence of relevant interests. These interests would legitimize the creation of special representation.

The relevance of "non-social" issues could also be an (additional) legitimization for participation in a Social Dialogue. This situation is illustrated by the circumstances in the Audiovisual and the Chemical Industry, corresponding with what has been outlined above concerning the existence of "multinationals" and SMEs in the professional football industries (see Sect. 6.5 "EU Admissibility Criteria"), i.e. that different interests require different representation. G-14's interests are different from those of an SME group of undertakings (cf. also the Agenda of topics listed in Sect. 6.8 "Agenda of Topics").

It has also become clear that different forms of membership exist, namely either direct membership (cf. ACT) or membership through inclusion (cf. CEFIC). The actual form of membership needs to be decided upon by the European Commission, after a formal request by the social partners.

An important aspect, which is of key importance to recognition as a social partner, is the recognition of the (specific) nature of the organization by other social partners. In professional football, G-14 should be formally recognized by the other pertinent organizations FIFPRO and EPFL.

This is supported by the fact that for example in November 2005 the President of FIFPRO after a meeting with G-14 declared: "We have had a constructive conversation today with G-14 members on a number of common issues. It now makes sense to put in place a detailed framework for further discussions and to agree on a process for taking our conversation forward. We think this should be done under the umbrella of the European Social Dialogue."

Thus, in this (informal) statement the existence of common interests is stressed as well as the position of G-14 as a "logical" partner in future social negotiations.

6.7 Chapter 6: Specificity of Sport

In addition to the EU admissibility criteria discussed in Sect. 6.5 "EU Admissibility Criteria" and Sect. 6.6 "Representation in the Context of Present Social Dialogue Committees", another aspect which might support the positioning of G-14 as a Social Dialogue partner should be dealt with here. This aspect concerns the general acceptability or recognition of G-14 as an official partner in European football which logically also affects G-14's possible participation in the Social Dialogue. In his article "Is the Pyramid Compatible with EC Law?" (*The International Sports Law Journal* (ISLJ) 2005/3–4 pp. 3 et seq.), Stephen Weatherill, who is Jacques Delors Professor of EC Law at Oxford University, United Kingdom, points out that the Declaration which is attached to the Treaty of Nice as Annex IV on the specific characteristics of sport and its social function in Europe, of which account should be taken in implementing common policies, includes a consideration on the *role of sports federations*: "The European Council stresses its support for the independence of sports organizations and their right to organize themselves through appropriate associative structures. It recognizes that, with due regard for national and Community legislation and on the basis of a democratic and transparent method of operation, it is the task of sporting organizations to organize and promote their particular sports, particularly as regards the specifically sporting rules applicable and the make-up of national teams, in the way which they think best reflects their objectives. It notes that sports federations have a central role in ensuring the essential solidarity between the various levels of sporting practice, from recreational to top-level sport … While taking account of developments in the world of sport, federations must continue to be the key feature of a form of organization providing a guarantee of sporting cohesion and participatory democracy."

As the European Court of Justice has made clear in *Deliège* and *Lehtonen* this material may be aptly cited in the exploration of the nature and scope of the relevant EC rules (in casu quo, concerning the FIFA mandatory player release system for national team matches), as Weatherill observes. This Declaration (and the previous Declaration of Sport attached to the Treaty of Amsterdam) asserts the *conditional* recognition of the virtues of governing bodies, and the regulatory discretion which they are allowed. In particular, sports federations are expected to operate "on the basis of a democratic and transparent method of operation" and they "must continue to be the key feature of a form of organization providing a guarantee of sporting cohesion and participatory democracy." Insistence on the virtues of participation chimes in with the broader agenda mapped out by the Commission in its 2001 White Paper on European Governance. It is perfectly possible to take these broad recommendations of good, transparent and participatory governance and to deploy them in a concrete legal setting. In that vein, Weatherill would argue that the absence of such necessary levels of participation is a powerful reason for arguing that practices imposed on football clubs fall within the sphere of application of EC law, for it is not necessary for the federations to maintain such an exclusion of input from directly affected interests. The European Commission's 1999 Helsinki Report on Sport similarly expresses the view that "... the basic freedoms guaranteed by the Treaty do not generally conflict with the regulatory measures of sports organizations, provided that these measures are objectively justified, non-discriminatory, necessary and proportional," Weatherill continues.

Moreover, were the Treaty establishing a Constitution for Europe, signed in October 2004, to enter into force (which is admittedly currently improbable) Article III—282(1)g would provide that "Union action shall be aimed at developing the European dimension in sport, by promoting fairness and openness in sporting competitions and cooperation between bodies responsible for sports, and by protecting the physical and moral integrity of sportsmen and sportswomen, especially young sportsmen and sportswomen." This lends yet more weight to the argument that the absence of such "cooperation between bodies responsible for sports" would warrant the conclusion that a process of rule making which excludes the (directly affected) clubs is inconsistent with EC law.

The arguments advanced by Weatherill would seem to apply equally to the positioning of a key stakeholder like G-14 with regard to its envisaged participation in a Social Dialogue, not in the least because the FIFA mandatory player release system could very well be part of the agenda for discussions with FIFPro, as especially elite (and other) players' interests (see also the match calendar issue) are involved (see Sect. 6.8 "Agenda of Topics").

Finally, in this context and more directly, one might argue that an organization like G-14 is now a factual and integral part of European professional football and is therefore in its own right an aspect of "the specific characteristics of sport of which account should be taken in implementing common policies" (cf. the Nice Declaration), such as promoting Social Dialogue in the European professional football sector. The same of course applies to EPFL.

6.8 Chapter 7: Agenda of Topics

The themes to be discussed in a Social Dialogue depend on the nature of the employers' and employees' organizations involved in the Social Dialogue. Some general themes would concern all organizations on both sides, but others would obviously be more specific to certain organizations only. EPFL, for example, is a generally representative organization whose territorial scope is restricted to Europe. G-14, on the other hand, is an organization which represents the interests of elite clubs in Europe, but is aiming to expand to include elite clubs in South America. This would put G-14 on a level with the international players' union FIFPro, which again is a general organization similar to EPFL. G-14's immediate partner at European or even global level should by nature be an organization representing the interests of elite players in Europe or worldwide. However such an organization does not (yet) exist. A comparable organization is ProProf in the Netherlands. This organization was established some years ago as an alternative for the general players' union VVCS to represent the specific interests of elite players. Elite players prefer to invest the capital they have earned rather than put it (partially) into a general players' pension fund. They therefore need to be advised differently from the average professional football player in the Netherlands. The Executive Board of ProProf consists of representatives of agents of leading Dutch players. In the Netherlands, there is thus an independent national Social Dialogue of a general nature between FBO (besides the two League organizations (ECV and CED for the Second Division) and the FA) and VVCS in which ProProf is also involved. Things will be organized differently in the future, however, with FBO/ECV as a member of EPFL on one side and VVCS, as a member of FIFPro, and ProProf on the other. A Social Dialogue with EPFL and G-14 on one side and FIFPro on the other at the European level would be just the opposite. In both situations, special interests (see ProProf and G-14) would be represented in a general framework. In the Netherlands a recent initiative by several leading players' agents (cf. the previous ProProf initiative) has been to establish a national players' agents organization, named ProAgent (see also below under "Players' agents"). ProAgent is aiming for the creation of a European organization in the near future which would (also) be entitled to represent the players' interests at European level, in addition to FIFPro.

Returning more specifically to the themes which could be discussed in a Social Dialogue, G-14 would obviously join sides with EPFL where their views on general themes coincide. Naturally, the opposite might occur with regard to other issues. It might also be the case that G-14 and FIFPro have similar interests with regard to UEFA and/or FIFA (e.g. the related themes of player release and international match calendars).

The formal framework of the European Social Dialogue is laid down in Articles 136 et seq. of the EC Treaty. In principle, agreements between social partners may address any topic. The social partners are therefore not bound to deal only with social subjects. The topics mentioned in the EC Treaty include:

- Working conditions
- Information and consultation of the employees
- Integration of those excluded from the labour market
- Equality of men and women with regard to labour market opportunities and treatment at work
- Social security and protection of the employees
- Protection of employees on terminating the employment contract
- Representation and collective defence of the collective interests of the employees and employers, including employee participation
- Employment conditions for subjects of third countries who are legally resident in a Community territory
- Financial contributions for enhancing employment and creating jobs.

Below, I will give a list (in alphabetical order) of (topical) themes which could be of specific interest to G-14. In each case the background of the theme is described (why is it an issue?) and it is explained why the theme would be suitable for inclusion in a Social Dialogue. The appropriate heading(s) in the EC Treaty (see above) is/are also given, i.e.: the "home-grown" rule (freedom of movement/ freedom of employment), the player release system (working conditions), image rights (protection of employees after terminating the employment contract), salary capping (control of player wages), pension funds (social security and the protection of employees), investment (player) funds (freedom of movement/freedom of employment), non-EU nationals/work permits (freedom of movement), the international match calendar (working conditions), artificial turf (working conditions), the pyramid structure (European Sports Model), and players' agents. The last two issues are of a general and fundamental nature touching on the very structure of professional football in Europe (i.e. representation and collective protection of the collective interests of employees and employers by means of a Social Dialogue), but some interests can also be said to be specific to G-14. The following issues could also be considered suitable for inclusion in a Social Dialogue, although they are not currently specific to G-14 as such: transfer rules, TV rights, player unemployment, change of nationality/naturalizations (representative teams), licensing, state aid, the Service Directive, doping, football hooliganism, corporate social responsibility (CSR), good governance in sport, multiple ownership of clubs, etc.

Of course, when social partners meet in a Social Dialogue, it would be useful if all issues of concern to the European professional football sector were discussed, even if they are not "social" as such. The opportunity of all parties involved meeting should be used to maximum advantage. In particular, in a Social Dialogue all developments occurring in "Brussels" and affecting professional football should be considered.

6.8.1 Artificial Turf

6.8.1.1 Introduction

In September 2005, FIFPro approached G-14 to form a united front against artificial turf. FIFPro is opposed to the introduction of artificial turf in professional football. Out of the 18 G-14 members, 17 (not including Ajax Amsterdam) turned out to be fierce opponents of this new development. A FIFPro/G-14 coalition on this issue will face the FAs and UEFA/FIFA in opposition. The main question is whether artificial turf is detrimental to the quality of play and whether players will be more vulnerable to injuries as a result. In both respects, clubs and players have common interests. However, we should remember that the quality of artificial turf continues to improve. Of course, there is no argument against the view that real football should only be played on natural grass.

6.8.1.2 Suitable for Social Dialogue

The quality of play is in the interest of both clubs and players, as is the reduction of injury risks. Here there is clearly a common interest to be protected against football's governing bodies. Although this may not seem to be a theme which is of specific interest to G-14, the history of the issue shows that it could become one, given FIFPro's request to G-14 to create a united front to oppose artificial turf.

6.8.2 "Home-grown" Players Rule

6.8.2.1 Introduction

UEFA will impose specific quotas on clubs for the inclusion of locally trained players between the age of 15 and 21 in Champions League and UEFA Cup matches. The rationale behind these quotas is that they would enhance the training and development of young talent. From next season, at least four "home-grown" players must be included in teams for European club games—at least two trained by a club's own academy and a further two trained by other clubs within the same association. By the 2008/2009 season, the minimum number of "home-grown" players required should have been increased to eight.

6.8.2.2 Suitable for Social Dialogue

The new rule would seem to restrict the freedom of movement of young players as it implies "indirect" or "hidden" discrimination. Such discrimination would be based on different criteria than nationality, i.e. training in the club and/or national association, but would indirectly result in the discrimination of foreigners. Most of the "home-grown" players would be nationals and not foreigners, making it more difficult for foreign players to move to a country where they had not been trained and educated. The "home-grown" players rule could potentially restrict cross-border labour mobility. This raises the question of the compatibility of the "home-grown" players rule with European Law (Article 39 of the EC Treaty: freedom of movement for workers). An issue like this which concerns the freedom of movement/employment of players from the perspectives of both employers' and employees' organizations could be included in the Social Dialogue. The rule concerns European level (Champions League, UEFA Cup) football and would appear to directly affect G-14 interests. It is clear that the "home-grown players" rule is in the interest of the national FAs. The underlying idea is that the national teams would be strengthened if enough youngsters were given the opportunity to play in the premier League of their own country. This explains why UEFA introduced this rule, which is particularly important for the "Big Five" in Europe. For a country like the Netherlands, the rule is less applicable to the national team as the best players play abroad in the premier Leagues of the "Big Five." On the other hand, this rule is not directly in the interest of the (elite) clubs, as they need the best home-grown and foreign players. There is therefore a conflict of interest between clubs and associations in this respect. G-14 and FIFPro would seem to be united against UEFA/FIFA and FAs on this issue because the absolute freedom of movement/employment of any player, local or foreign, is also in the interest of FIFPro.

6.8.3 Image Rights

6.8.3.1 Introduction

Given the huge media interest in football, the advent of new technology and the "Hollywood" status of players, the financial exploitation of image rights has become increasingly important in professional football. Players entering into a fixed-term employment contract with a club already have to sign a separate contract regarding their image rights. This contract gives the club the right to profit from the player's image rights. Image rights contracts apply to a longer period than the employment contract. When the player reaches the end of his employment contract, the former club can request that the new club buys out the image rights contract. Naturally the new club is keen to exploit the player's image.

6.8.3.2 Suitable for Social Dialogue

Due to the tendency to financially exploit the image of elite players it is likely to be in the interest of G-14 clubs that the "transfer" of image rights from one club to the other is regulated in general terms in the Social Dialogue. Players would need the same legal certainty.

6.8.4 International Match Calendar

6.8.4.1 Introduction

The interests of clubs, in particular elite clubs and national football associations as well as UEFA and FIFA, are increasingly contradictory as far as the international match calendar is concerned. The main reason is the rising number of international matches. In Europe, after the fall of the Soviet Union, UEFA acquired many more member countries. The qualification groups for the European Championship and World Cup subsequently became larger. The Confederations Cup (national teams) is a new FIFA tournament and the World Cup for club teams became a tournament instead of a single match between the champions of Europe and South Africa in Tokyo as before. On the other hand, the winner of the UEFA Champions League currently has to play thirteen matches up to and including the final. The (elite) clubs needed more guaranteed matches to secure their income. Although the second groups round of the Champions League was abolished some years ago, a one group round was recently introduced in the UEFA Cup competition. More matches mean more TV and sponsoring income for FAs as well as for FIFA and UEFA, particularly during the final rounds of the European National Teams Cup and the World Cup. The number of finalists has also considerably increased, meaning more matches. Too many national team matches prevent (elite) clubs from playing enough international friendly games and tournaments abroad, which would usually be held during the closed season. However every two years, the summer calendar is full of national team football. Furthermore, the FIFA match calendar now includes international friendly and practice matches throughout the year. Then there is another problem for European (elite) clubs. The final round of the Africa Cup takes place during the League season in Europe and, according to the FIFA rules, clubs are obliged to allow their foreign players to play for their country (including preparation). Generally speaking, every national team match means that the clubs' international players (nationals and foreigners) are not at the disposal of the club during their preparation. As a result, the elite clubs are often unable to implement a regular training programme at the club. On the other hand, playing for the national team greatly increases the quality and value of a player.

The result of playing too many matches is the potential mental and physical overburdening of the players. This naturally affects the quality of play.

6.8.4.2 Suitable for Social Dialogue

Such stress is not in the interest of the clubs or the players. There is common ground here for G-14 and FIFPro to propose solutions. Moreover, the clubs' financial and commercial interests are directly at stake. Sometimes their players return injured from international matches. The players are their working capital in which they have invested large sums of money under (the operation of) the current transfer rules. They cannot play enough friendly games and tournaments and they therefore merchandize their teams internationally. The match calendar issue brings up the broader issue regarding the validity and conditions of the compulsory FIFA player release system as it now stands. From the point of view of labour (industrial) relations, an overly heavy match calendar resulting in the overburdening of players must be modified in accordance with the international rights of employees. These state that the number of working hours per day, etc. must not be disproportionate and that the tasks assigned must be physically and mentally acceptable (labour/rest balance). It is therefore in the interest of clubs and players that the players are protected against overburdening.

The current challenge facing G-14 with regard to the player release system seems to be securing the modification of the match calendar. Objectively, there are various options to achieve this: the introduction of two or more levels of competition for UEFA and FIFA qualifying matches (preliminary rounds or even an A and B group, etc. with promotion and relegation), fewer dates reserved for friendly matches on the national team calendar, the abolition of the Confederations Cup and World Cup for teams in their present form, fewer matches during the final rounds of the European Cup and World Cup, and reduction of the number of teams and therefore matches in national Premier League competitions. As the players are "in the ownership" of the clubs, it seems logical that the clubs' commercial interests would prevail. After all, which came first: the club or the nation?

6.8.5 Investment (Player) Funds

6.8.5.1 Introduction

The current trend for clubs to use investment funds to maximize the budget for the acquisition of players is in principle a threat to the freedom of movement of players as well as the freedom of employment of players. The extra budget is created by attracting external investors and involving them in the acquisition of players. The external investors receive a return on investment which is created when a player moves from one club to another. The external investors obtain the federative rights to the player. This means that they receive their money back, including a profit, when the player is registered for his new club at the national FA. The highest return on investment for the investors is naturally obtained when a player is transferred at the moment that he is worth the most.

6.8.5.2 Suitable for Social Dialogue

In order to avoid infringing Article 39 of the EC Treaty with regard to the free movement of workers, it must be guaranteed that the external investors gathered in the fund do not have a decisive vote in the movement of the player. An infringement of the free movement of workers can easily occur through clauses in a contract or by means of actual practice. The free movement of players must be safeguarded and the authority of the investors' funds over the players controlled by the clubs. Investment funds are financially the most attractive in relation to young elite players, and young and other elite players usually play for elite clubs. There is therefore a clear common interest between G-14 and FIFPro here.

6.8.6 Non-EU Nationals

6.8.6.1 Introduction

Germany recently abolished the rule whereby only a limited number of non-EU players were allowed to play in professional football. The 36 clubs in the first and second *Bundesliga* are now allowed to have an unlimited number of non-EU nationals under contract. This was decided by the German professional League (DFL). This amendment implies that elite clubs like Bayern Munich, Schalke 04 and Werder Bremen, which have the financial means to invest in the transfer of foreign players from Africa and South-America, can now strengthen their position on the players' market from an international/European perspective. On the other hand, under the new UEFA "home-grown" players rule, the clubs will be obliged to include at least four such youngsters in their squad. In addition the German FA (DFB) requires a restriction in the number of players per team. This would give local players more chance to play.

6.8.6.2 Suitable for Social Dialogue

The German example shows that the unrestricted admission of non-EU players is in the interest of the elite clubs. However, if FAs apply different national rules in this respect, they will jeopardize the international/European competitive status quo. And that is currently the case.

Moreover, besides having different sporting rules, national legislation also differs from country to country regarding work permits. Therefore from the perspective of G-14, EU harmonization with the highest degree of openness towards non-EU nationals could be the solution to the problem. However, it is possible that, on behalf of its EU member players' unions, FIFPro would not support unrestrictedness as it would prefer to protect the labour market for EU nationals first and foremost. It is in the interest of the FAs and thus UEFA/FIFA to oppose openness, as openness would weaken the quality of national representative teams, especially in the EU's major footballing nations. FAs (and national governments!) could strengthen the national team by getting better foreign players naturalized under accelerated public nationality law procedures. However this way of operating is increasingly being opposed by restricting the availability of a new "sport nationality" to foreigners under the sporting rules of the IFs and national sports-governing bodies.

6.8.7 Pension Funds

6.8.7.1 Introduction

A so-called bridging pension may allow the player to deposit a percentage of his salary into a fund during his active career. This arrangement enables the professional football player to save money for later on in life, after his professional career. At the end of his career he financially bridges the years up to his pension by means of payments from the fund. These payments will then fall under a favourable tax rate. The CFK (*Contractspelersfonds KNVB*) is just such a fund in the Netherlands. However a European fund would have to guarantee that fund deposits are made by the player's own choice and not by obligation (indirectly) imposed on him by the FA.

6.8.7.2 Suitable for Social Dialogue

The specific interest of G-14 is not to oppose the introduction of a European fund if the issue were tabled by FIFPro for example, but to create guarantees during negotiations that participation in the fund is voluntary for the players. A pension fund is not always the best solution for elite players, a case which was illustrated by the founding of ProProf in the Netherlands as a reaction to CFK. The issue of pension funds is a good example of the monitoring role which could be exercised by G-14 by being a partner in the Social Dialogue regarding new developments in European professional football.

6.8.8 Players' Agents

6.8.8.1 Introduction

Players' agents, FIFA and others not working for the official national players' unions, have a permanent commercial interest in concluding as many "transfers" of players as possible because of the commission they receive from each transfer. This often results in unrest within players' groups and clubs, also beyond the official transfer periods. During transfer windows, there is currently a continuing "circulation" of players per professional footballing nation, in Europe and the world at large. Proportionally, too much money that is "in the game" goes to agents to the detriment of clubs and players alike.

6.8.8.2 Suitable for Social Dialogue

In the Netherlands, an initiative was recently introduced to try and organize the agents. This initiative involved the FBO (the clubs' organization for both Leagues which is still independent from the Premier League organization ECV, but which appears set to become integrated into ECV and First Division (cf. Championship in UK) CED), ECV, CED and the FA. The Dutch FA is enthusiastic about this initiative. One could imagine the establishment of a European or even a global players' agents' organization which could participate in regular tripartite dialogue with employers' and employees' organizations. Certain issues could be settled in the Social Dialogue, but would require the consent of the agents if the settlement were to work in practice, for example "salary capping." The agents would then have to operate within the financial boundaries determined in the Social Dialogue. In the Social Dialogue, FIFPro could support the mutual salary capping agreement approved by the G-14 members. Besides the above considerations, which are still largely academic due to the lack of a working international players' agents representative organization (the IAFA (International Association of Football Agents) is a dead body), the position of players' agents with regard to their important financial involvement in European professional football could and should be considered as an agenda item for the Social Dialogue. The quality and effectiveness of the FIFA Player Agents rules is one of the specific issues to be studied in this context.

6.8.9 Player Release System

6.8.9.1 Introduction

Under the FIFA rules, clubs are obliged to allow their players to play for the national team.

This is naturally an honour for the player, but he still might not voluntarily accept such an invitation. It could be argued that by playing for the national team, the value of players increases, which is undoubtedly a positive thing for the club. The value of players who participate in the European Championship and the World Cup increases even more. However, the pertinent FIFA rule which is confirmed at national level in the FA Statutes of each country dates back to "amateur" times. The clubs have to pay insurance for their players even when they are preparing and playing in the national team squad. If players return to their clubs injured from international matches, the club's strength is weakened in its home competition and European matches due to the absence of such key players. The clubs receive no compensation from their FA, UEFA or FIFA for having fulfilled the mandatory player release rule for international matches. The extra international matches for the national team imply an added physical and mental burden for the players concerned. Moreover, from the point of view of fair competition law, it is quite unique that firms are required to put their employees on loan to another firm for a certain period of time which then makes money out of the activities of those employees during those periods! In particular, the presence of elite players from elite clubs in the final rounds of European (and other regional) and World Cup championships allows the FAs, UEFA and FIFA to earn vast sums from broadcasting rights, sponsorships, gates, etc. The money spent by TV companies on international matches and the sponsoring they obtain may not be re-invested in the clubs' game!

6.8.9.2 Suitable for Social Dialogue

This player release issue is an international/European issue which is initially relevant to elite clubs like the G-14 members. This is illustrated by the club cases G-14 is supporting/directly involved in versus FIFA. However, whatever the court decides, whether it be favourable or a compromise, due to the threat of overburdening players it is also in the interest of FIFPro that the player release rule is amended for the benefit of the clubs. The rule should be amended in the direction of evenhandedness between football-governing bodies and the clubs. This issue is the perfect illustration of the fact that the clubs, elite or otherwise, should be able to independently negotiate with UEFA and FIFA on the basis of having been officially recognized by those bodies as partners.

6.8.10 Pyramid Structure

6.8.10.1 Introduction

The current prevailing pyramid structure (European Sports Model) dates from "amateur" times, as the protection of the vital interests of the clubs, particularly the professional elite clubs, is not an integral part of the system. The reason for this state of affairs is that the clubs are indirectly represented by the FAs in UEFA and FIFA. In a purely formal sense, the clubs are considered to have tacitly agreed to all UEFA and FIFA decisions which affect them. In a way, UEFA and FIFA operate as the "government of the State of Football." According to the "one club, one vote" and "one association, one vote" democratic principle of decision making, a small minority of clubs like G-14, although they financially represent 35% of the professional football market in Europe, has to accept the decisions taken by the greater majority of clubs and FAs. In a regular industry in a democratic society, commercial firms are independent of each other and do not depend on the public authorities either. In professional football in Europe, the opposite is the case. The least that could be done to alter this would be to introduce official participatory democracy for the clubs in the decisions of FAs, UEFA and FIFA in all questions which directly or indirectly affect them.

6.8.10.2 Suitable for Social Dialogue

G-14 needs to participate with FIFPro in the Social Dialogue to protect its vital interests in relation to players' interests. A second step is for the present structure of professional football in Europe to be placed on the Social Dialogue agenda from a much broader perspective. A workable option might be to let UEFA and FIFA govern amateur football, the "grass roots" of the game, as well as representative football. The same would naturally apply to the national FAs. Professional club football (the Leagues) would acquire an independent position, although remaining contractually linked for certain practical purposes and (impartial) services (national teams, referees, disciplinary law, etc.) to the present governing bodies.

6.8.11 Salary Capping

6.8.11.1 Introduction

Players' salaries constitute the clubs' greatest expenditure. Increasing competition keeps pushing up salaries. Increases are sometimes so excessive that clubs spend more on salaries than they receive in revenues. The imminent problems are obvious: salaries rise, revenues drop, clubs go bankrupt or (in the smaller Leagues) there will be an even greater exodus of top players. A salary cap is in place for a number of sports in the United States, where it is also part of a collective labour agreement. A salary cap comes in two forms: hard or soft. A hard cap links the salary to a percentage which the employer may maximally spend on salaries. A soft cap also links the money to a percentage which the employer may maximally spend on salaries, but in this case the percentage is linked to the revenues which the club generates in a given season. With a soft cap the salary limit can be subject to deviation under some circumstances. A soft cap is more relevant to football. In practice a salary cap creates financial stability in the sector. It must be noted that a salary cap can only be introduced successfully if this is done across the entire EU—in other words if it is transnational. The use of salary caps in professional football has been suggested as a solution to the problem of clubs spending unsustainable levels of player wages in order to compete at the highest level. Salary caps are by definition restrictive. Depending on the form they take they restrict the amount clubs can spend on wages, thus restricting the supply and demand for players. Capping is therefore likely to be considered an issue for EU competition law. Careful consideration should be given to the overall context in which the decision to employ a salary cap was taken. An environment of economic crisis in professional football would make salary caps more likely to survive legal challenge. In this environment, salary caps may be justified on the grounds that they maintain the economic viability of teams competing in the League and that they preserve the competitive balance between clubs. Some commentators have argued that the softer the cap the harder the law should intervene. If the objective of the cap is to safeguard competitive balance, then a hard cap should be preferred as this imposes a flat ceiling on the spending of all clubs. A soft cap, which links spending to revenue, disproportionately affects the ability of small clubs to improve their position. This places them at a competitive disadvantage and at risk of closure. Competition law, which is designed to promote competition, could not sanction a system which curtails competition to this level. The fact that a hard cap is more restrictive and less appealing to the larger undertakings and high earners is not relevant under this analysis. As long as players have the right of free movement to seek alternative employment, a hard cap should not amount to a breach of competition law. To achieve maximum legal certainty in this field, the international players' union (FIFPro) must give its consent to such a move although high-earning players are less likely to consent to a hard cap. Consent could be provided through a collective labour agreement with the employers (clubs).

6.8.11.2 Suitable for Social Dialogue

In the light of the above, capping does not seem to be suitable for discussion in the Social Dialogue with FIFPro in general. The general introduction of capping in European professional football is not in the interest of G-14. If EPFL introduced it into the Social Dialogue with G-14 and FIFPro or if FIFPro itself wished to place it on the agenda, G-14 should use its monitoring role in the Social Dialogue and block discussion at least as far as G-14 clubs are concerned. Besides, a cap would considerably restrict the room for manoeuvre of players' agents to increase salaries and thus their own commission. And, very specifically, the members of G-14 themselves have internally agreed on a "hard" cap by way of a gentlemen's agreement: a maximum of 70% of the budget should go to player salaries. An alternative for capping is licensing for the purpose of maintaining the economic viability of clubs (cf. the newly introduced UEFA licensing system). Of course, salary capping could be part of a licensing system.

6.9 Chapter 8: Summary, Conclusions and Recommendations

It is recommended that the G-14 explicitly incorporate participation in a European Social Dialogue in its Statutes as one of the official purposes (cf. EPFL).

If we compare the role of FAs as the central governing bodies in the pyramid structure (European Sports Model) with that of the government of a country in a democratic society, it is difficult to imagine how a conflict of interests could be avoided between governing bodies and (statutorily, contractually and/or factually non-independent) social partner organizations representing the clubs as employers in a Social Dialogue. A similar conclusion would in principle apply to the issue of (in)dependence at the European level. EPFL is "very" representative, but not independent. Functional, factual independence with regard to "industrial relations"/Social Dialogue at the European level in relation to UEFA and FIFA and also of their members in relation to the national FAs should be explicitly incorporated in the EPFL Statutes at the least. Apart from that, the recognition of UEFA's presence as a third party in *any* Social Dialogue in Europe—even if it is neutral to both social partners' interests—has to be deleted from the Memorandum of Understanding between UEFA and EPFL to which explicit reference is made in the EPFL Constitution, since a Social Dialogue in EU terms never has a tripartite character.

G-14 is an organization (EEIG) officially recognized under EU law, possessing—under the present circumstances of the pyramid model in professional football—a maximum degree of independence of its members in relation to UEFA, FIFA and the FAs. However, other than is the case for the first criterion (representativeness in as many EU Member States as possible), the G-14 does not fulfil the second EU criterion, since its members/clubs as such are not part of the national social partner structures. However, it could be argued that this is not relevant if the Champions League is considered as a "sub-sector" of the European professional football sector (see also under Sect. 6.7). If this view is taken G-14 would be a legitimate social partner on the employers' side in a Social Dialogue.

There are a number of precedents in other sectors of industry as to participation of specific organizations as (additional) partners in the pertinent Social Dialogue Committees (cf. the direct representation by (groupings of) individual undertakings/companies in the Temporary Work and Audiovisual Sectors; the incorporation of a "non-social" representative organization in the Chemical Sector) that would allow for the argument that G-14 could be admitted to a Social Dialogue in the professional football sector, on the condition of course that partner organizations would recognize G-14's involvement.

Because of the requirement of participatory democracy in sports federations (governing bodies) under European law, it may very well be argued that G-14 in order to be able to protect its interests should be entitled to participate in a Social Dialogue. Moreover, notwithstanding the fact that it is not officially recognized by the football-governing bodies, the very existence of G-14 has become a aspect of the "specific characteristics of sport" of which account should also be taken in promoting Social Dialogue in the professional football sector.

The phenomenon of organized competition is a *conditio sine qua non* for sport and as such it is a "specific characteristic of sport" by which professional football (again) differs from the average industrial sector. The Champions League could be qualified as a "subsector" of the European professional football sector. The specificity of the Champions League as a separate competition—with its own financial-economic characteristics—could be used as yet another argument for not automatically applying the EU admissibility criteria for the purposes of a Social Dialogue in this case.

The following themes have been identified as being of special interest for G-14 in a Social Dialogue: artificial turf, the "home-grown" players rule, image rights, the international match calendar, investment (player) funds, non-EU nationals, the pension fund, players' agents, the player release system, the pyramid structure, and salary capping.

6.9.1 Informal Social Dialogue

Finally and apart from the above, it is suggested that the European Commission could take steps to introduce an informal Social Dialogue which would continue until all aspects concerning participation have been clarified. This has in fact been done before in other sectors and could prove perfect for paving the way for a comprehensive Social Dialogue and negotiation result.[9] All parties in the European football sector would have to be represented in the temporary Committee and given the opportunity to express their views and ideas and receive feedback from the European Commission and Social Dialogue experts. The participants in Committee meetings should all be parties who are stakeholders in football, i.e. UEFA, FIFPro, the Sport Unit of the European Commission's Directorate-General for Education and Culture, the Directorate-General for Employment and Social Affairs, the Directorate-General for Competition, the G-14, the EPFL including other Leagues and an organization representing national initiatives like the G-12 (Spain) and G-5 (Belgium).

6.10 Postscript: New Developments in Football Governance

In January 2008 a Memorandum of Understanding was signed between the newly-formed European Club Association (ECA) and UEFA.[10] The ECA comprised 103 clubs drawn from all of UEFA's 53 member associations and is described by UEFA as "an independent autonomous body representing the European clubs." Membership of the ECA was based on a national association allocation depending on association ranking positions.[11] UEFA considered the ECA as "the sole body representing the interests of clubs at European level." The establishment of the ECA formed part of a package of measures designed to resolve the dispute between the G14 and UEFA/FIFA over mandatory player release rules and the fixing of the international match calendar. FIFA rules (Annex 1 to FIFA Regulations for the Status and Transfer of Players, July 2005) provided for the

[9] Franssen 2002, p. 57, para 3.2.7.

[10] UEFA Media Release 2008a.

[11] Association ranking position (number of clubs): 1–3 (5), 4–6 (4), 7–15 (3), 16–26 (2), and 27–53 (1); the precise number of clubs from each member association to be established every two years at the end of the UEFA season.

mandatory release of players for national association representative matches. The FIFA regulations did not provide for clubs who are required to release a player to receive financial compensation. The Association calling up a player was expected to bear the costs of travel actually incurred by the player as a result of the call-up. The club for which the player concerned was registered was responsible for his insurance cover against illness and accident during the entire period of his release. This cover must also extend to any injuries sustained by the player during the international match for which he was released. Clubs refusing to comply with the mandatory release clause could be subject to a points or game forfeiture.

A challenge to these provisions was due to be heard before the European Court of Justice.[12] The referring court in the case asked the ECJ to consider whether

> the obligations on clubs and football players having employment contracts with those clubs imposed by the provisions of FIFA's statutes and regulations providing for the obligatory release of players to national federations without compensation and the unilateral and binding determination of the coordinated international match calendar constitute unlawful restrictions of competition or abuses of a dominant position or obstacles to the exercise of the fundamental freedoms conferred by the EC Treaty and are they therefore contrary to Articles 81 and 82 of the Treaty or to any other provision of Community law, particularly Articles 39 and 49 of the Treaty?

A party to the action was G14, the economic interest grouping comprising 18 of the leading European clubs. The G14 explained that professional clubs had no direct representation on the bodies that make the rules and, not surprisingly, these regulations favour federations over clubs. The Charleroi/Oulmers case was an example of how a lack of representation could lead to rules which favour one party over another. G14 believed that these rules, which were imposed on all clubs without their consent, are unfair, undemocratic and must change.

Meeting at FIFA headquarters in Zurich in January 2008, representatives of ECA, UEFA and clubs agreed on the intention to regulate their future relationship with a number of actions including the establishment of the ECA, the dissolution of G14, the withdrawal of the Charleroi ECJ case and the payment of financial contributions for player participation in European Championships and World cups.[13]

---

[12] Case C-243/06, Charleroi/Oulmers, 07 C 212, 2 September 2006.

[13] UEFA Media Release 2008b, p. 1. As part of the Memorandum of Understanding it was agreed to distribute every four years an amount from the UEFA European Football Championship to national associations for them to pass on to their clubs who have contributed to the successful staging of a UEFA EURO™. The target distribution amount for UEFA EURO 2008™ is €43.5 million and for UEFA EURO 2012™ €55 million (providing financial results are substantially similar to those of UEFA EURO 2008™). The payments shall be made on a "per day per player" basis. The distribution amount for UEFA EURO 2008™ of €43.5 million is divided by the total number of days which gives a "per player per day" amount of approximately €4,000. For UEFA EURO 2012™ this is expected to be approximately €5,000. As well as the direct financial benefits from UEFA EURO™ for the clubs, the Memorandum of Understanding also ensures that UEFA is set to schedule qualifying matches for the UEFA EURO™, whenever possible, in maximum groups of six.

FIFA President Joseph Blatter explained that the agreement took care of the legitimate aspirations and requests of clubs to access the decision-making levels of international football. Initially the ECA Board was composed of 11 members, plus four representatives appointed by the Executive Board to the UEFA Professional Football Strategy Council. The Professional Football Strategy Council was established in June 2007 and included amongst its membership representatives of the EPFL, representatives of the European Club Forum whose members represent the interests of the clubs participating in the UEFA competitions, and representatives of FIFPro (Division Europe) who represented professional players in Europe. UEFA described the Council as a body to identify solutions to improve collaboration between the various stakeholders of European football; dealing with problems pertaining to the social dialogue in European professional football matters.

These developments in football governance demonstrated that stakeholder dialogue and representation were becoming established governance standards within the football sector. This has been the product of efforts by the EU institutions to encourage dialogue, pressure exerted through the courts by clubs seeking greater representation, and a willingness by UEFA to adapt existing governance structures to accommodate the views of stakeholders. In this connection, the establishment of n official Sectoral Social Dialogue Committee for professional football in July 2008 became operational in European professional football, in which EPFL and FIFPro participated as partner organisations and ECA was active as an additional component to EPFL.

Social dialogue is a cornerstone of the European social model and gives employers, athletes and sport workers the opportunity to shape labour relations in the sport sector through an autonomous dialogue in the general EU legislative and institutional framework. The work in the European social dialogue committee which was launched in the sector of professional football in 2008, has progressed towards the establishment of minimal contractual requirements for football players. In addition, several potential European social partner organisations have expressed their interest in creating a social dialogue committee for the whole sport and active leisure sector. The Commission encourages this development and invites social partners to further consolidate representativeness at EU level. It will propose a test phase to facilitate the introduction of such dialogue.

6.10.1 Specificity of Sport

What is the relationship of the instrument of Social Dialogue to sports law, which position it occupies in sports law? At the outset, it should be stated that Social Dialogue in sport as such belongs to the (regional) branch of European Sports Law. European Sports Law now is a matter of applying—in the case of SD optionally—general, regular EU law to sport(s) under the "umbrella" of the in 2009 newly introduced "general sport provision," Article 165 TFEU. According to this provision, the "specific nature of sport" must be taken account of by the European Union while developing the European dimension in sport.

There may be distinguished several aspects of the relevance of the so-called "sport specificity" concept in this context. First, their autonomy is characteristic of both Social Dialogue and of European sport. In particular when negotiating (collective bargaining) agreements, the parties concerned—management (employers/clubs) on the one hand and labour (employees/sportspersons) on the other—materially may come to "sport specific" solutions for the issues at stake (of course in accordance with EU and national law). It is important to note that (collective bargaining) agreements in a Social Dialogue Committee in the matters which are explicitly mentioned in Article 153, para 1 sub (a)–(k) TFEU (from "the improvement in particular of the working environment to protect workers' health and safety" up to and including "the modernisation of social protection systems without prejudice to the social security and social protection of workers") may be given—at the joint request of the signatory parties—generally mandatory force in the sport sector concerned by EU Council decision on the basis of Article 155, para 2 TFEU. Second, taking into account the institutional specificity of the sport structure (according to Article 165 TFEU, the "structures of sport" must be considered also by the EU while contributing to the promotion of European sporting issues), social partner organisations might think fit for relevant third parties like European sport governing bodies to take part in their bi-partite Social Dialogue, with observer status. Thirdly and finally, what does it mean for the possibility of potential social partner organisations themselves (cf, G-14 and EPFL) to participate in a Social Dialogue in the sport sector concerned, that the specificity of sport (and its structures) should be taken account of?

References

Franssen E (2002) Legal aspects of the European social dialogue. Social Europe Series, Intersentia:Antwerp

Siekmann RCR (2004) Promoting the social dialogue in professional football in the New Eu Member States. In: The International Sports Law Journal 3–4:31–33

UEFA Media Release (2008a) New era in football begins with the formation of the European Club Association, 21/01/08, No.007

UEFA Media Release (2008b) Victory for football as a whole, 15/01/2008, No.4

Weatherill S (2007) Is the Pyramid Compatible with EC Law? In: Weatherill S, European Sports Law—Collected Papers, The Hague; previously published in The International Sports Law Journal (2005) 3–4, pp. 3 et seq

Chapter 7
Sport and Nationality: "Accelerated" Naturalisation for National Representative Purposes and Discrimination Issues in Individual and Team Competitions Under EU Law

Abstract Sport and nationality is a complex issue with diverse manifestations. The first main question which will be dealt in this paper is how so-called national teams that represent a country in international ("inter-state") competition (Olympic Games, world and regional championships, and other representative sporting events) are composed—on the basis of the legal nationality of their members, or on the basis of a special "sporting nationality" according to which additional or other criteria are applicable whether a sportsperson is allowed to participate in the national team. The same question arises with regard to individual athletes who represent a country in international competition. This question will be discussed in particular in the context of the problems that have been created by what may be called accelerated (quick) naturalisation ("passport shopping"). The second main question is how "sporting nationality" is regulated outside the scope of national representation, that is at the level of national club team and individual competition. May sportspersons from abroad participate in the club competitions in other countries of which they do not possess the legal nationality, in particular under EU law? In this paper we will discuss topical discrimination issues: the discrimination of non-team sportspersons in individual national championships; and: the discrimination of professional football players: the FIFA 6+5 and UEFA home grown players rules.

Contents

R. C. R. Siekmann, *Introduction to International and European Sports Law*, ASSER International Sports Law Series, DOI: 10.1007/978-90-6704-852-1_7,

© T.M.C. ASSER PRESS, The Hague, The Netherlands, and the author 2012

7.1 Introduction

Nationality is both in international and national law an important connecting factor for the attribution of rights and duties to individual persons and States. Under international law States have for example the right to grant diplomatic protection to persons who possess their nationality. Under national law the obligation to fulfil military service and the rights to become a member of parliament or to have high political functions are frequently linked to the possession of the nationality of the country concerned. However, there is no standard list of rights and duties which normally are linked to the nationality of a State under national and international law. National States are in principle autonomous in their decision which rights and duties will be connected to the possession of nationality, whereas under international law the consequences of the possession of a nationality are also a subject of discussion. Nationality can be defined as "the legal bond between a person and a State." This definition is, *inter alia*, given in Article 2(a) of the European Convention on Nationality (1997). Article 2(a) immediately adds the words "and does not indicate the person's ethnic origin." In other words, nationality is a legal concept and not a sociological or ethnical concept. The nationality of a country in this legal sense is acquired or lost on the basis of a nationality statute. A person possesses a nationality if he or she possesses this nationality by virtue of the general nationality statute or other relevant legislation, rules of implementation, case law and legal practice.[1]

Sport and nationality (or: nationality in sport) is a complex issue with diverse manifestations. The first main question which will be dealt in this article is how so-called national teams that represent a country in international ("inter-state") competition (Olympic Games, world and regional championships, and other representative sporting events) are composed—on the basis of the legal nationality of their members, or on the basis of a special "sporting nationality" according to which additional or other criteria are applicable whether a sportsperson is allowed to participate in the national team. The same question arises with regard to individual athletes who represent a country in international competition. Are there nationality statutes etc., which also have specific "sporting nationality" provisions

[1] De Groot 2006, p. 3.

(provisions for representative sporting purposes)? Or does the determination of "sporting nationality" completely belong to the jurisdiction of organised sport, in which case the international sports federations in principle still could refer to the general legal nationality ("passport nationality") of teams and sportspersons, or could have their own different rules and regulations to provide for the eligibility of sportspersons for international competition.

The first question will be discussed in particular in the context of the problems that have been created by what may be called *accelerated* (quick) naturalisation. Changes in nationality were becoming increasingly frequent in sports, for a number of reasons stemming in particular from certain countries' desire to assert themselves on the international scene, and/or the athletes' desire to benefit from the best possible material conditions. The rules for obtaining nationality vary considerably from one country to another, which has created sometimes appalling inequality of treatment from one athlete to another. International sports authorities have been overwhelmed by this once marginal phenomenon which had suddenly become a major issue in a number of sports. They have reacted "case by case" to attend to the most urgent cases first, while trying to maintain some level of sportsmanlike fairness. However, the time had come to find comprehensive, uniform solutions that would be valid for the long term.[2] In The Netherlands the *Kalou* case (2006) is the landmark case on this issue.[3]

The second main question is how "sporting nationality" is regulated outside the scope of national representation, that is at the level of national club team and individual competition. May sportspersons from abroad participate in the club competitions in other countries of which they do not possess the legal nationality?

Discrimination on grounds of nationality is prohibited under EU law, which establishes the right for any citizen of the Union to move and reside freely in the territory of the Member States. EU law also aims to abolish any discrimination based on nationality between workers of the Member States as regards employment, remuneration and other conditions of work and employment. Equal treatment also concerns citizens of States which have signed agreements with the EU that contain non-discrimination clauses, and who are legally employed in the territory of the Member States ("non-EU nationals").

The composition of national representative teams is inherent in the organisation of competitions opposing national teams. Rules concerning the composition of

---

[2] The theme of "accelerated" or quick naturalisation of sportspersons for national representative purposes was the core issue at the Scientific Conference on Nationality in Sports, see note 1 *supra*. The importance of this Conference was amply illustrated by the participation in the concluding panel of IOC President Jacques Rogge, high representatives of four international sports federations (i.e. basketball, ice-hockey, skating and skiing) and of the 800 m world record holder Wilson Kipketer.

[3] On 4 April 2006 the sixth Asser International Sports Law Lecture on *Nationaliteit en Sport: publiekrecht v sportrecht* [Nationality and Sport: Public Law v Sports Law] was organised with reference to the Kalou case. Speakers were, amongst others, Prof.Dr Gerard-René de Groot, Professor of comparative law and private international law, University of Maastricht, The Netherlands, and Mr Jelle Kroes, Everaert Immigration Lawyers, Amsterdam.

national teams, in particular rules that exclude non-national sportspersons, whether EU or non-EU nationals, from national teams, have been considered as rules that do not infringe EU law free movement provisions.

In this article we will also discuss topical discrimination issues in particular under EU law:

- the discrimination of *sportspersons* ("EU non-nationals") in individual national championships;
- the discrimination of *professional football players* ("EU non-nationals"): 6+5 and home grown players rules.

7.2 The "Accelerated" Naturalisation for National Representation Issue

When international law refers to nationality, this reference has to be understood as a reference to the general legal nationality of a State acquired on the basis of a ground for acquisition provided by the statute on nationality of the State concerned. This is for example the case where Article 15 of the Universal Declaration of Human Rights states that everyone has the right to a nationality and that no one shall be arbitrarily deprived of his nationality nor denied the right to change his nationality. Next to this general legal nationality which indicates the formal legal bond between a person and a State, States or International Organisations may—for special purposes—introduce a so-called "functional nationality" or "autonomous nationality." If for certain purposes a functional nationality is introduced, the grounds for acquisition and loss of this specific nationality have to be defined in detail. In De Groot's opinion, the question had to be answered whether the development of a functional, autonomous sporting nationality was desirable. In principle, a negative answer to this question was advisable. The regulations of the grounds for acquisition and loss of a functional nationality is a very complicated task, if one does not want to use simply the place of birth as the only ground for acquisition of the functional nationality without any ground for loss of the functional nationality in question. Even the fiction that one is deemed to have the nationality of the country where one has ordinary residence needs considerable further elaboration, because of the fact that the definition of residence differs from country to country. However, De Groot continues, there was an attractive alternative for the development of a functional nationality, which would come quite close to a separate *sporting nationality*, but was in fact not an independent notion, and which did not require to regulate the grounds for acquisition and loss in detail. One might for the determination whether a person qualifies to represent a certain country in international sporting competitions use as a basic requirement the possession of the general legal nationality of the State concerned, but add—insofar as it was desirable—additional requirements which would guarantee that the nationality is the manifestation of a genuine link between the sportsperson and the State concerned. The essential question then was of course which additional requirement(s) should be added and in which cases these additional requirement(s) should be fulfilled. The reason to add—in certain cases—(an) additional requirement(s) next to the condition of the possession of the nationality of the country concerned, before a person qualifies to represent a country in international sporting competition, was in order to ensure that a real, *genuine link* exists between the sportsperson concerned and the country he or she wishes to represent. However, one had to realise that the general legal nationality normally is already a manifestation of such a genuine link. With other words: normally the general legal nationality was only attributed, if a genuine link existed between the sportsperson concerned and the State in question. De Groot observes that in the international community of states an enormous variety of grounds for acquisition and grounds for loss of nationality exists. An indirect consequence of this fact for sports was an unequal competition for States which respect to excellent sporting (wo)men and shocking inequalities between athletes. There were also equalities caused by the different attitudes of States in respect of quick naturalisation. De Groot was of the opinion that in all cases where a genuine link was lacking, an additional residence requirement would be reasonable. The next question was of course how long the additional residence requirement should be. He submitted that the required period of habitual residence should be shorter than the lowest residence requirement for regular naturalisation, which was three years. It was therefore—in his opinion—attractive to require a habitual residence of two years of continuous residence immediately before naturalisation. If at the moment of naturalisation this condition was not fulfilled, the naturalised sportsperson would only be eligible to represent his new country, after he would have resided two years in the country (the residence period directly before the naturalisation and after the naturalisation were to be added up). A period of two years should not be required, if the naturalised sportsperson had in the past a continuous and uninterrupted residence of five years in the country concerned. Such an uninterrupted period of residence in the past guaranteed the existence of a genuine link between the sportsperson and the country of the newly acquired nationality. Under such circumstances there was no need any more to require an uninterrupted habitual residence of two years before and/or after the moment of naturalisation. This additional rule of five years residence was realistic in view of the fact that young athletes frequently received part of their sporting education and made part of their sporting career in another country than the one where they grew up. The introduction of an additional residence requirement would prevent that sportspersons qualified to represent a country in international competition without having a genuine link with the country concerned.[4]

[4] De Groot 2006, pp. 3–4, 8. The expression "genuine link" refers implicitly to the Nottebohm decision of the International Court of Justice, where the words "genuine connection" are used explicitly [ICJ Reports 1955, 4 (23)].

7.2.1 Comment

At the time of the Lausanne Conference on Nationality in Sports the issue of "accelerated" (or quick) naturalisation was highly topical and over the past few years had only become more important. The core of the problem was the extreme diversity of the legislation concerning the acquisition of "regular" nationality in the world community of states. The conditions and required residency periods for naturalisation differ greatly per country. In one country, a candidate national must have resided in that country's territory for at least three years in order to be eligible for naturalisation, while in another country this may be five years, and in yet another country ten years. States have further established quite diverse additional requirements as to the necessary degree of the candidate's local societal integration. On the other hand, however, the legislation in some countries permits that a foreigner is naturalised almost instantly for reasons of general, national interest. Traditionally, the sports community in principle followed the "regular" public law rules concerning nationality. However, already in the past considerable obstacles were put into place by, for example, the international basketball federation FIBA to prevent accelerated naturalisation, or rather, to avoid its consequences by applying residency requirements in respect of the receiving country. A well-known example was the FIFA rule that once a player had played for a particular country in a officially binding, non-friendly international match (European Championship, World Championship: qualifiers and tournament matches) that player can never play for another country again, regardless of possible naturalisation or even the possession of dual nationality. Another measure was the "waiting period": during, for example, two years following his/her naturalisation, the athlete may not qualify for his/her new country. The general starting point is the doctrine of the genuine link between a person and a country as developed by the International Court of Justice at The Hague in one of its classic public international law judgment, the Nottebohm case. In this way, what has become known as a "sporting nationality" has developed in addition to "regular" nationality, whereby the sporting nationality is decisive for the question of whether the athlete may represent a particular country in international matches, championships and competitions such as the Olympic Games and the Football World Championship. In sporting terms, like for example in club football the genuine link doctrine is a matter of the sportsperson's national identity and the local society having the possibility of identification with him or her from the perspective of (inter)national representation.

The world of organised sport found itself forced to tighten the rules further. Rules concerning the "sporting nationality" were in fact as divergent between the various international sports federations as they are between the different national public laws concerning "regular" nationality. Top sport nowadays equals commerce and is a matter of national prestige. This gave rise to national sports federations and national public authorities doing a one-two in association football terms.[5] If, for example, a wealthy country was able to naturalise one of the world's top long distance runners from a poorer country by just giving him a passport, that country would suddenly have won a place on the map. And if the foreign athlete was the No. 4 of his country and in fact the No. 4 also of the world, because the first three of his country had won gold, silver and bronze at the last Olympics and World Championship, he or she also for purely sporting reasons would have an excellent argument to move abroad, Individual sports such as athletics were perfectly suited for this type of "coup." However, in team sports, situations like these could not be ruled out either! Moreover, the long distance runner would also see his/her financial situation and his or her family conditions improve considerably as compared to if he/she had continued to run for his/her country of origin. This also indicated the conflict of interests between the possibilities for further development of the top athlete, who after all had to make a living from his/her sport, i.e. the interests of the "market" on the one hand, and the way in which sport is organised worldwide, namely based on territorial nationality, that is state borders, on the other hand. This had resulted in the "commercialisation of the passport." Naturalisation was the perfect tool for this type of "muscle drain" at the level of national sports representation (cf. "brain drain" in connection with scientists).

Of course organised sport had to defend itself against the phenomenon of accelerated naturalisation. In order to create a level playing field, it made sense to harmonise or unify the rules concerning sporting nationality and to seek a common denominator with refinements where necessary per type of sport (either individual or a team sport) and branch of sport, etc. Here clearly was a task for the international sports law community. This did however require a prior investigation into all the underlying facts and circumstances. For example, one could not blame an individual athlete who was one of the world's top runners for trying to seek domicile elsewhere when only three athletes per country may be delegated to the Olympics and he/she was outrun in the national qualifiers by three fellow countrymen simply because his/her country belonged to the world's top in long distance running. Every athlete after all seeks to attain the highest possible level. It is therefore recommended that these rigid rules for participation are made more flexible by issuing additional "wild cards" based on the world ranking or some other effective system. So, no "wild cards" to admit the less best, the sub-optimal athletes to the Olympics on order to have as many countries as possible represented, but rather not excluding beforehand those who in fact belong also to the top elite in a particular (individual or team) sport (notwithstanding the Olympic value of "participating [as opposed to winning] comes first," since winners wish to

[5] The "one-two" is an explosive combination that consists of two passes between two players. The first pass is a pass in the length or width of the playing field and the second pass is a first-time return pass; the player who has played the first ball will run into the "depth" of the field (that is, in the direction of the opposing team's goal) and will receive the ball behind his opponent's back. A well-done "one-two" creates confusion in the opposing team's defence and is an effective instrument against a tight defence, in particular when the first passer comes from far at full speed (see: Siekmann 1978, p. 42, see also: Siekmann 1980, pp. 61–62).

participate also themselves: citius, altius, fortius (Olympic motto, Pierre de Coubertin, 1894!).

De Groot had proposed a residence/waiting period of two years which is shorter than the minimum in the international community of states (three years). Why? He does not provide us with any explicit reasoning for his proposal. Probably, the period should be shorter because sport may be considered a "subculture" of society? However, from the sport's perspective, that might be a reason just to intensify what is in fact a disciplinary sanction. The criterium of "residence" also might or even must be translated more concretely for the sporting context, such as permanent club membership, regular participation in the national championship and international non-representative and club competitions and matches.

In the residence/waiting period a sportsperson should not only be a formal resident of the country concerned and live in fact elsewhere for most of the time—otherwise than staying abroad for the participation in sporting events (like tennis players do much more than the average athlete).

The naturalisation issue in fact consists of two phenomena which might be solved at the same time from a sporting perspective: a. quick naturalisation (the inequality of length between residence periods according to the regular nationality legislation), b. special, accelerated naturalisation for sporting purposes (see for example the Kalou case). Any residence period chosen by an international federation would at the same time also solve the problem of countries the regular residence of which under public law is relatively or even extremely long. It would mean that in such cases a sportsperson might acquire the sporting nationality of the country concerned earlier than his general legal one. The issue of statelessness on one hand and multiple (double etc.) nationality and its consequences for sporting representative purposes might also be solved in this perspective, residence being the decisive criterion again. De Groot makes the additional statement that these persons should be eligible as representatives of their country of residence as a consequence of the Geneva Convention relating to the status of refugees (1951), respectively of the New York Convention relating to the status of stateless persons (1954).[6]

Why not systematically link (a) the residence/waiting period for regular naturalisation with (b) the additional residence/waiting period to get "sporting" nationality, for example: (a) 4 years plus (b) 0 year; (a) 3 years plus (b) 1 year; (a) 2 years plus (b) 2 years; (a) 1 year plus (b) 3 years; (a) 0 years plus (b) 4 years? Or, alternatively, a system of "transfer windows" might be introduced, which would mean that a sportsperson would qualify for representing a new country only if he or she would have acquired the new nationality in any case before the start of a new Olympiad or before the beginning of a new campaign of qualifying matches for the final tournament (Football World Cup), in both cases a period of four years (etc.)?

[6] De Groot 2006, p. 4.

The Olympic Movement (IOC) has an omni-sport character but the only events are Olympic Games (global, Winter/Summer; continental/regional, such as for example the Asian Games), whereas the international federations like the world football governing body FIFA are single sport organisations (regional and World Championships).

Rules 41-45 of the Olympic Charter concern the eligibility code for participation in the Olympic Games. The Bye-law to Rule 42 on the nationality of competitors reads in full as follows: "2. A competitor who has represented one country in the Olympic Games, in continental or regional games or in world or regional championships recognised by the relevant IF [International Federation], and who has changed his nationality or acquired a new nationality, may participate in the Olympic Games to represent his new country provided that at least three years have passed since the competitor last represented his former country. The period may be reduced or even cancelled, with the agreement of the NOCs and IF concerned, by the IOC Executive Board, which takes into account the circumstances of each case." The Bye-law reads in full as follows with regard to the issue of double/multiple nationality: "1. A competitor who is a national of two or more countries at the same time may represent either one of them, as he may elect. However, after having represented one country in the Olympic Games, in continental or regional games or in world or regional championships recognised by the relevant IF, he may not represent another country unless he meets the conditions set forth in para 2 below [see *supra*] that apply to persons who have changed their nationality or acquired a new nationality."

The articles in the Regulations Governing the Application of the Statutes of FIFA read in full as follows regarding nationality issues:

VII. Eligibility to Play for Representative Teams

15 Principle

1. Any person holding a permanent nationality that is not dependent on residence in a certain country is eligible to play for the representative teams of the Association of that country.
2. With the exception of the conditions specified in Article 18 below, any Player who has already participated in a match (either in full or in part) in an official competition of any category or any type of football for one Association may not play an international match for a representative team of another Association.

16 Nationality entitling players to represent more than one Association

1. A Player who, under the terms of Article 15, is eligible to represent more than one Association on account of his nationality, may play in an international match for one of these Associations only if, in addition to having the relevant nationality, he fulfils at least one of the following conditions:
   (a) He was born on the territory of the relevant Association;
   (b) His biological mother or biological father was born on the territory of the relevant Association;
   (c) His grandmother or grandfather was born on the territory of the relevant Association;

(d) He has lived continuously on the territory of the relevant Association for at least two years.

[...]

17 Acquisition of a new nationality

Any Player who refers to Article 15 para 1 to assume a new nationality and who has not played international football in accordance with Article 15 para 2 shall be eligible to play for the new representative team only if he fulfils one of the following conditions:

(a) He was born on the territory of the relevant Association;
(b) His biological mother or biological father was born on the territory of the relevant Association;
(c) His grandmother or grandfather was born on the territory of the relevant Association;
(d) He has lived continuously for at least five years after reaching the age of 18 on the territory of the relevant Association.

18 Change of Association

1. If a Player has more than one nationality, or if a Player acquires a new nationality, or if a Player is eligible to play for several representative teams due to nationality, he may, only once, request to change the Association for which he is eligible to play international matches to the Association of another country of which he holds nationality, subject to the following conditions:
(a) He has not played a match (either in full or in part) in an official competition at "A" international level for his current Association, and at the time of his first full or partial appearance in an international match in an official competition for his current Association, he already had the nationality of the representative team for which he wishes to play.
(b) He is not permitted to play for his new Association in any competition in which he has already played for his previous Association.
2. If a Player who has been fielded by his Association in an international match in accordance with Article 15 para 2 permanently loses the nationality of that country without his consent or against his will due to a decision by a government authority, he may request permission to play for another Association whose nationality he already has or has acquired.

[...]

According to the Olympic Charter the "waiting" period is not dependent on residence; the applicable criterion is a purely sporting one (last representation of his/her former country), whereas according to the FIFA Statutes the "waiting" period is a real residential one (two years in case of multiple nationality; five years in case of naturalisation).

7.2.2 Kalou Case

In 2005, in The Netherlands the gifted Ivory Coast footballer Salomon Kalou who then was a striker for the Rotterdam professional football club Feyenoord applied for accelerated naturalisation with a view to the upcoming Football World

Championship in Germany in 2006. Amongst others, Johan Cruyff, national coach Marco van Basten and the Minister for Sports supported his application which was, however, rejected by the Minister for Aliens Policy and Integration. Kalou subsequently started proceedings against the State of the Netherlands before the administrative courts, on which occasion Van Basten promised Salomon Kalou a place in the line-up for the 2006 World Cup for which the Dutch team had meanwhile qualified. In The Netherlands the situation was such that based on the Netherlands Nationality Act (Article 10) the directions for application of this Act include special rules which also apply for top athletes. According to this so-called *topsporters regeling* [elite sportspersons' regulations] the making of an exception is justified when it turned out that accelerated naturalisation would serve "a Dutch cultural interest" which also included a Dutch sporting interest which could happen in case of representing The Netherlands by participating in international sporting tournaments and matches. There was also a detailed Circular from the Ministry of Health, Welfare and Sports, of 9 April 1999, to the national sports organisations concerning this matter. In these guidelines the (minimum) sporting performance level for being eligible for accelerated naturalisation was determined. Preferably, the sportsperson concerned should also be role model for young athletes or for fair play campaigns and the like. He or she must add "surplus (excess) value" to a specific sport or sport in general. During the proceedings, the expert witness in nationality law Professor De Groot (Maastricht University) indicated the manifest applicability of the top athletes regulations which permit accelerated naturalisation by derogation from the standard requirements. The court ordered the Minister to re-evaluate her decision and improve the reasoning underlying it, following which the Minister appealed to the Council of State as the highest administrative law judicial instance. The outcome there was identical. The Minister did not, however, amend her position.

Comment

The *Kalou* case is a clear example of the application of exceptional public legislation for the purposes of "sporting" naturalisation. Apart from that, it should be observed that never before had a national team coach of the Dutch Football Association (KNVB) attempted opportunistically to reinforce the national team by means of accelerated naturalisation. This author is a principled opponent of such practices, in casu, by receiving Dutch nationality, Salomon Kalou would have also acquired a direct ticket to play, as an EU national, without any impediment in the English Premier League, which obviously was his particular aim at the time—the Premier League being the most prestigious and best paying football competition in the world.[7] Moreover, Kalou by opting to play for the Ivory Coast might still have performed at the 2006 World Championship in Germany, and even appear together with his older brother Bonaventure Kalou, who was an ex-Feyenoord player and at

[7] Cf., for example the Worlds Series in the United States of America as the top of the world competition in professional baseball.

the time playing for Paris Saint-Germain in France. In addition, fate had ironically ruled that The Netherlands and the Ivory Coast were to be in the same group during the pool stage of the World Championship and would therefore have to play each other! From the perspective of the spirit of sport (fair play) as an ethical consideration, another consideration is that Salomon Kalou missed out on the entire qualification process for the World Championship and that his participation would be at the expense of another player who possibly did contribute to some degree to the Dutch team's qualification for the 2006 World Cup.

7.3 Sport and Discrimination in EU Law

7.3.1 The Discrimination of Sportspersons ("EU Non-Nationals") in Individual National Championships

In November 2008, the present author was informed about the following concrete case which fits in this context. The European swimming association LEN was confronted by the following case. The Belgian national swimming association made it impossible by way of its Statutes that a Dutch swimmer (with Dutch nationality) living in Belgium would participate in the Belgian national championship. There turned out to be in Europe different regulations: in Scandinavian countries there were much more possibilities. A Swedish swimmer might participate in the Finnish national championship and become champion of Finland. In The Netherlands a foreigner might participate in the national championship, but could not swim a Dutch record. The question was what the legal position under EU law is.

Some Member States and sports organisations have signalled to the European Commission their preoccupations with the situation of competitions involving individual sportspersons and leading to the conferment of National Championship titles. On cultural grounds, they were of the opinion that the conferment of such titles should be reserved for nationals of the Member State within which the competition takes place. A more technical concern was linked to the fact that in some cases, results in a national championship serve as a basis for the qualification of nationals to international competitions or for the composition of national teams. The legality of residence clauses also would need to be examined, as some sports organisations were concerned that some sportspersons could take part in different national championships.[8] In the White Paper on Sport, the European Commission stated that membership of sports clubs and participation in competitions were relevant factors to promote the integration of residents into the society of the host country. As regards access to individual competitions for non-nationals, the Commission intended to launch a study to analyse all aspects of this complex

[8] Accompanying Document to the White Paper on Sport, p. 45.

issue.[9] In 2009 the Commission launched a study to assess the implications of the Treaty provisions on non-discrimination on grounds of nationality in individual sports. The study was finalised in December 2010.[10]

The Commission will issue guidance on how to reconcile the Treaty provisions on nationality with the organisation of competitions in individual sports on a national basis.[11]

The Study's Executive Summary reads as follows:

> "Non-discrimination is a general principle of EU law. One of the best known rules derived from this principle is the EU prohibition against nationality discrimination. The rule against discrimination on the basis of nationality is reflected in Treaty articles which prohibit nationality discrimination in all situations which fall within the scope of the EU Treaties. These rights are also granted to non-nationals who are protected by EU law. EU law currently grants freedom of movement rights of equal treatment to EU citizens but also to certain third country nationals such as non-EU family members of EU citizens and third country nationals who derive rights from international agreements between the EU and their non-EU member state. Equal treatment requires the abolition of both direct discrimination and rules which, whilst not framed in terms of nationality, in fact lead to unequal treatment.
>
> Thus, nationality should not, as a matter of EU law, be a valid way to distinguish between domestic citizens and non-nationals. Yet sports within Europe generally remain organised on the basis of nationality. Under the 'European model of sport', national sports governing bodies are responsible for the organisation of sport within the national territory. As a consequence, sport is often inherently based on nationality. This creates tensions between the requirement to treat all EU citizens without regard to their nationality, and the pre-existing structures based on nationality and national territories by which many European sports are organised.
>
> Even where rules are not expressly based on nationality, they may be prohibited under EU law. Restrictions to freedom of movement are considered discriminatory where nationals and non-nationals are governed by identical rules but where these indirectly favour nationals over non-nationals. For example, since residency requirements are more likely to be satisfied by nationals than by non-nationals, the Court has held that these are indirectly discriminatory, and therefore unlawful, unless justified and proportionate. Furthermore, EU law requires not only equal treatment of non-nationals but in fact prohibits all unjustified rules which hinder or render less attractive the exercise of free movement rights. Thus, when sports rules restrict the freedom of movement of non-nationals, they must be justified.
>
> The Court of Justice of the European Union has in its case law sought to strike a balance between protecting EU citizens' rights to free movement and non-discrimination, and the specific characteristics of sport and the autonomy of sports governing bodies to organise

---

[9] White Paper on Sport, Brussels 2007, COM(2007) 391 final, pp. 14 and 16.

[10] Study on the Equal Treatment of Non-Nationals in Individual Sports Competitions, Report committed by the European Commission, T.M.C. Asser Instituut, Edge Hill University and Leiden University, The Hague, December 2010. The Study's findings were presented by Prof. Stefaan van den Boogaert, Europa Institute, Faculty of Law, University of Leiden, The Netherlands, at the EU Sport Forum in Budapest, Hungary, on 21–22 February 2011. He is the author of Boogaert 2005.

[11] "Developing the European Dimension in Sport", Communication from the Commission to the European Parliament, the Council, the European Economic and Social Committee and the Committee of the Regions, COM(2011) 12 final, Brussels 2011, p. 13.

sporting competitions. It has accepted that nationality rules in national team sports are matters of 'purely sporting interest' which have 'nothing to do with economic activity' and are therefore outside the scope of EU law. It has in later cases considered that some rules are 'inherent to the organisation and proper functioning of sport' and therefore do not in law constitute restrictions of EU free movement rights even where the situation is otherwise within the scope of the EU treaty. Where the Court has found that a sporting practice has restricted freedom of movement rights, it has carefully considered the justifications put forward to examine whether such rules are both justified and proportionate. In so doing the Court of Justice has accepted a number of sports-specific justifications such as the need to educate and train young players and the need to ensure the regularity of competitions. It may even be argued that the Court might accept justifications for nationality rules in sport which would not be acceptable in the context of other activities, thereby recognising that the specific characteristics of sport require specific treatment within EU law.

Despite such guidance from the Court of Justice, it has maintained that neither sporting activities nor nationality discrimination in sport can be categorically excluded from the scope of EU law. Although the Lisbon Treaty has conferred a supporting, coordinating and supplementing competence to the EU in the field of sport, its references to 'openness and fairness' as guiding principles suggest that no significant exemption will be forthcoming solely on the basis of Article 165 of the Treaty on the Functioning of the European Union. In its recent case law, the Court has confirmed that issues regarding the compatibility of sporting practices with EU law must be resolved on a case by case basis. Although sports governing may wish that the EU institutions should provide legally certain guidance as to whether various such practices are considered acceptable, it is difficult to extrapolate firm guidance applicable to all sporting practices from the body of cases which has thus far been decided. When guidance issued in the past has been contrary to EU law, the mere fact that it has been issued by an EU institution has not protected sporting practices from being declared unlawful by the Court of Justice of the European Union.

Although the full legal framework applicable to sport has not yet been definitively settled, a presumption now exists that the general EU law rules apply to sport just as to any other activity within the scope of EU law unless a limited exemption can be identified. Within the general framework, it is clear that non-nationals are entitled to equal treatment and that restrictions to their freedom of movement between Member States must be justified and proportionate. According to settled case law, free movement rights include rights to equal treatment and unrestricted access to leisure activities such as sport even where the sport is not organised on a professional basis. Since citizens and their family members enjoy equal treatment in Member States other than their state of origin, they also enjoy as a matter of EU law equal access to both amateur and professional sport regardless of whether the citizen is also enjoying rights as a worker or a provider of services. Thus, non-nationals protected by EU law have a legal right to access sport in Member States other than their state of nationality. Even if the Court's exemption for nationality rules in national team sports were to be extended to individual sports by analogy, such rules would need to be carefully reasoned and limited to their proper function in order to escape censure. Other methods of analysis also require a proportionate justification in order to ensure that restrictions to non-nationals' free movement rights escape censure under EU law.

This study examines restrictions to the access of non-nationals to individual sporting competitions in the EU Member States. Its national experts have compiled data on the rules in all Member States as regards twenty-six Olympic sports in which competitors are individuals rather than teams. These include the triathlon, modern pentathlon, tennis, table tennis, badminton, rowing, canoe/kayak, athletics, aquatics, archery, boxing, judo, shooting, weightlifting, wrestling, taekwondo, equestrian sports, gymnastics, skating, luge, biathlon, bobsleigh, cycling, skiing, fencing and sailing. The data includes both rules that distinguish on the basis of nationality and rules which, whilst based on criteria other than nationality, hinder or make less attractive the freedom of movement of non-nationals.

Any rules which hinder or make less attractive the exercise of non-nationals' freedom of movement rights must be justified under EU law. This study therefore also seeks to comprehensively list the justifications put forward by sports governing bodies for those rules. However, although national experts have requested information on both the rules themselves and any justifications for those rules, relatively few justifications were put forward to explain restrictive sports rules. This raises the inference that the many substantially unjustified restrictions to the access of non-nationals to sporting competitions are unlawful under EU law. There are also instances of justifications which are difficult to accept in the context of the established legal framework and which therefore as a matter of law seem unlikely to survive a legal challenge. For example, it is not settled law that access to domestic competitions can be restricted on the basis of nationality solely because the competition is organised by the national governing body.

An examination of the rules of specific sports organisations by country also demonstrates that a single sport can be subject to very different rules across the EU Member States. This suggests that some national rules are more restrictive than necessary. In some cases, the difference arises because even some Olympic sports have no national governing bodies in certain Member States. Although this study was limited to the twenty-six identified individual Olympic sports, a further investigation beyond Olympic sports may reveal a significant additional number of these situations. In cases where sports did have domestic governing bodies in all EU Member States, the national rules governing access to sports were also not always uniform. Even where such sports had European-level governing bodies, their rules often left domestic governing bodies with significant margins of discretion regarding the access of non-nationals to domestic competitions. The diversity of rules regarding access may suggest that some of those rules are more restrictive than is necessary. For example, if one governing body does not require a long period of prior residence, it may be more difficult for another governing body within the same sport to demonstrate that its longer residence requirement is proportionate and thus acceptable under EU law.

After identifying the rules governing access of non-nationals to individual competitions in the selected sports, the study then maps rules and those justifications which have been offered against the general framework of EU free movement rules in an effort to determine whether the rules could, if challenged, be declared lawful by the Court of Justice of the European Union. Four categories of sporting rules emerge from this analysis. The first category of rules which do not fall within the scope of the Treaties and are thus not subject to EU law includes 'purely sporting' rules. The second category involves rules that do not in law constitute restrictions to free movement such as those rules which are inherent to the organisation and proper functioning of sport'. The third category involves rules which, whilst constituting restrictions, may be justified and proportionate. Finally, the study observes that some rules cannot be considered justified or proportionate and would therefore be unlikely to survive a legal challenge in their current form.

'Purely sporting' rules are outside the scope of EU law. EU law does 'not prevent the adoption of rules or of a practice excluding foreign players from participation in certain matches for reasons which are not of an economic nature, which relate to the particular nature and context of such matches and are thus of sporting interest only'. However, such rules must be 'limited to their proper objective'. It may be difficult to demonstrate that the exclusion of all non-nationals from all sporting competitions constitutes a 'purely sporting' rule. Furthermore, since the Court has clarified that 'the mere fact that a rule is purely sporting in nature does not have the effect of removing from the scope of the Treaty the person engaging in the activity governed by that rule or the body which has laid it down', the exclusion of a specific restriction does not imply the exclusion of all restrictions within that sport. The most likely candidates as 'purely sporting' rules may include rules regarding the distribution of national representative honours and nationality rules in national team sports. It may even be argued that the distribution of medals has so marginal an economic dimension that it could fall within this category of rules.

Some sporting rules do not in law constitute restrictions to freedom of movement. Since they are not restrictions, they may not always need detailed justification. Some rules have been considered inherent in the organisation and proper functioning of sport by the Court of Justice. These could include rules limiting the number of participants in a judo tournament. Other hindrances to free movement may be so 'uncertain and indirect' that they are not in law considered restrictions and therefore do not require justification. In some cases, the Court has distinguished between non-discriminatory rules which hinder access and must be justified, and non-discriminatory rules which affect issues other than access and which therefore do not require justification. Any rule which as a matter of EU law does not require justification is likely to offer a wide margin of appreciation to sports governing bodies.

However, rules which constitute restrictions to freedom of movement must be justified and proportionate. These include all rules restricting access to sporting competitions as well as any rules involving the unequal treatment of non-nationals. Several sport-specific justifications, such as the need to ensure the regularity of competitions and the need to educate and train young players, have in principle been accepted by the Court of Justice. However, it remains doubtful whether directly discriminatory rules can be justified other than by reference to Treaty grounds of public policy, public security and public health. In such cases, it may be difficult to find a justification which the Court will be prepared to accept. Furthermore, all restrictions must be proportionate: they must be suitable for achieving the lawful aims but also the least restrictive measures which will achieve those aims. Thus, rules established by national bodies which are more restrictive than the rules of other national bodies within the same sport may be difficult to justify since the existence of less restrictive measures in other domestic systems implies that less restrictive measures can achieve those aims.

The final category of rules identified by the study includes those restrictions which are not justified and proportionate and therefore breach EU law. Prominent past examples of these include the 3+2 rule, which restricted the access of non-nationals to professional football and was declared unlawful in the Bosman case. Even if the Court could be argued to offer a wide margin of appreciation to sporting rules in some cases, there is also a body of modern case law that demonstrates careful examination of the proportionality of such rules. The onus will be on governing bodies to demonstrate the justifications and proportionality of restrictions. In the absence such evidence, which in the context of this study was often not forthcoming despite direct requests addressed to sports governing bodies, restrictions on the access of non-nationals will be contrary to EU law.

It is clear that the principles of fairness and openness which are reinforced by Article 165 of the Lisbon Treaty have not yet been uniformly implemented by sports governing bodies within the European Union. There are many sports where the access of non-nationals is restricted by reference to nationality even in cases where no element of national representation can be identified. In some sports, access even at an amateur level is restricted by rules such as residence requirements that restrict the equal access of non-nationals. Organising bodies have not always clearly articulated the reasons for restricting the access of non-nationals, and where reasons have been articulated, they are not always in compliance with EU law. The diversity of practices also suggests that some practices within the same sport are more restrictive than others, and that the more restrictive practices may not be proportionate and are therefore not justified under EU law.

There are several ways to ensure the greater compliance of sporting rules with EU law. It may be that many sports bodies lack the expertise and specialist knowledge required in order to ensure that their practices comply with EU law and in particular that non-nationals are able to access sport where appropriate. In such cases, sports bodies, Member State administrations and non-nationals themselves would mutually benefit from the exchange of good practices and from training specifically targeted at ensuring awareness of and compliance with EU law. However, where national associations fail to make adjustments required by EU law and where Member States fail to protect the rights of non-nationals to access sports, it may be necessary for the Commission to consider more direct approaches such as infringement proceedings. Infringement proceedings and domestic legal challenges which result in preliminary references to the Court of Justice of the European Union would also offer opportunities to clarify the legal framework in those areas where sports governing bodies are legitimately concerned about a lack of legal certainty. Whilst the Court of Justice remains committed to a case-by-case analysis, a greater body of case law would provide a greater degree of certainty, in particular, where the Commission has already investigated practices and raised doubts about their restrictive effects, it may be necessary for the Court of Justice be given an opportunity to directly consider such issues. The resulting legal certainty will assist sports governing bodies to develop practices that both protect the specific features of sport whilst complying with the rights of non-nationals under EU law."

The Study's recommendations are summarised as follows:

"On the basis of the EU Treaty provisions on citizenship, non-discrimination on grounds of nationality and freedom of movement, the relevant secondary legislation and the case law of the Court of Justice of the EU in this respect, the following suggestions are made:

1. As far as access of foreign athletes to national competitions is concerned, it is recommended as a rule under EU law to encourage and allow the participation of foreign athletes (EU citizens and also third-country nationals to the extent that they may benefit from EU rights) as much as possible, while taking into account the constraints imposed by the organization of a specific sporting event and respecting the need to ensure the training of young players and the regularity of the competition.
2. *As far as participation of foreign athletes in national championships is concerned, it is in general recommended under EU law that these athletes be allowed to compete in the national championship of a given sporting discipline, provided that they do not exert a direct and substantial influence on the outcome of the competition. In sports which involve direct eliminations, it is accepted in principle that foreigners may be excluded from participation in the national championship, as they exert too direct and substantial an influence on the outcome of the tournament.*
3. As far as the award of national titles is concerned, under EU law winning the national title may remain the exclusive prerogative of nationals of a given country. This can be classified as a rule which comes under the scope of the EU Treaty, but does not form a restriction to freedom of movement as it is inherent to the organisation and proper functioning of national titles and proportionate and therefore does not violate EU law.
4. As far as the award of medals in championships and the setting of national records is concerned, this is likely to be a matter of purely sporting interest which does not come under the scope of application of the EU Treaty.
5. The European Commission is invited to enter into a constructive dialogue with national federations who still apply unacceptable discriminatory measures on grounds of nationality, so as to have these measures removed. If necessary, the Commission may have to undertake enforcement action so as to preserve the equal treatment rights of athletes."

Comment

As far as the participation by EU non-nationals in individual national championships is concerned, it should be observed that, where results in a national championship—or other national qualifier—serve (or co-serve) as a basis for the qualification of nationals to international competitions or for the composition of national teams (the national championship—or other national qualifier—being a "qualifier" for the participation in Olympic Games, continental (regional) and World Championships), direct eliminations sports could and even should lose their "open" character (direct eliminations sports—contact/combat sports and also others, non-contact sports—are characterised by a knock-out competition structure; the Olympic sport disciplines of this type are the following: badminton, boxing, fencing, judo, table tennis, taekwondo, tennis, and wrestling). Such a rule would prevent the threat of distortion of "pure" sporting competition. However, for example, in the marathon discipline, individual sport without direct eliminations, it is possible and acceptable to organise parallel competitions at once—as an international qualifier for nationals as well as an "open" national championship for all participants, nationals and non-nationals.

7.3.2 *The Discrimination of Professional Football Players ("EU Non-Nationals")*[12]

7.3.2.1 FIFA 6+5 Rule[13]

Until the mid-1990s, nationality clauses (nationality quotas) were an established part of the top-class sport system in Europe. Both top national associations as well as their respective central organisations regularly stipulated that each club could only sign or let a certain number of sports-people of foreign nationality play. Since the 1960s, in the course of setting up national professional leagues, numerous European football associations created regulations one after another that limited the possibility of signing players with foreign nationality. However, as early as 1976 the European Court of Justice cast doubt on the admissibility of completely excluding foreign players from league matches in the Donà ruling.[14] For this reason, the national regulatory frameworks of the associations either placed numerical limits on the number of foreign footballers that could be employed by clubs, or else there was a maximum number of foreign players permitted to take part in matches. For example, the regulations of the German Football Association (DFB) placed such limitations on the first and second divisions of the German league. Accordingly, a first or second division club was only granted the licence

---

[12] In The Hague, On 5 June 2008 the ASSER international Sports Law Centre organised a seminar on "6+5 and home-grown players rule: solutions for the protection of club identity and the quality of national representative teams?" The speakers were: Dr. Ruben Conzelmann, the author of Conzelmann 2008, and Dr. Stefaan van den Bogaert, (then) Senior Lecturer in EU Law, Faculty of Law, University of Maastricht, The Netherlands.

[13] Cf., Prokopets 2009

[14] Case 13/74 Donà (1976) ECR 1333, para 14.

required to participate in competition if it had a minimum of 12 licensed players under contract. Of these twelve, a maximum of three foreigners was permitted. However, members of other EU states and other foreign players who had been entitled to play for a German club continuously for the past five years (of which at least three had to have been as a junior player) did not count as foreigners; these players were known as so-called "football Germans." According to these German regulations, a number of statutes of other national sports associations recognised a concept of nationality in terms of sports law, so that clubs could in theory sign on players from other EU states without limit. However, this was also limited by the so-called "3+2 rule," which stipulated that a maximum of two players from other EU member states or so-called "football Germans" could be used concurrently with three foreigners. In 1991, The European football governing body UEFA had adopted this "3+2 rule" permitting each national association to limit to three the number of foreign players whom a club was allowed to field in any first division match in their national championships, plus two players who had played in the country of the relevant national association for an uninterrupted period of five years, including three years as a junior (the junior requirement in fact being of a "home grown" type, see below).

In the 1995 Bosman ruling,[15] the European Court of Justice declared that such nationality clauses within association rules in professional league football—in contrast to national teams—were contrary to Community law because they breached the fundamental freedoms of the EC treaty, especially freedom of movement for workers (Article 48 EC Treaty). Starting from the 1996/1997 season, a number of national football associations (DFB, Premier League, Primera Division, Serie A, Ligue 1) decided on this basis to implement the new framework decided on by the European Court of Justice for nationality clauses. With immediate effect, nationals of the 52 member associations of UEFA could be signed on and fielded without restriction of number. The limitations of the "3+2 rule" were therefore largely lifted by all European national football associations. For non-EU players restrictions on the part of the football associations continue to exist widely.[16] The Bosman ruling not only prohibited domestic football leagues in EU member states, but also UEFA, from imposing quotas on foreign players to the extent that they discriminated against nationals of EU states. Also, UEFA had a rule that prohibited teams in its club competitions from naming more than three "foreign" players in their match day squads.

It is clear that since the Bosman ruling the number of foreigners within European football leagues has risen significantly, and this has had problematical consequences, in particular, for the competition situation among clubs and the promotion of local junior players. It has also led to the call for a renewed minimum quota ("6+5 rule") for the deployment of native players for league games.

[15] Case C-415/93 [1995] ECR I-4921.

[16] Cf., Martins 2004, also in: Gardiner et al. 2009.

The FIFA Congress, at is meeting in Sydney (Australia) on 29 and 30 May 2008, decided to fully support the objectives of the 6+5 rule as laid down at the Congress and voted in favour of a resolution on 6+5. The 6+5 rule provides that at the beginning of each match, each club must field at least six players eligible to play for the national team of the country of the club. There is no restriction, however, on the number of non-eligible players under contract with the club, nor on substitutes to avoid non-sportive constraints on the coaches (potentially 3+8 at the end of the match). The objective of this rule is to restore the national identity of football clubs who have increasingly resorted to fielding foreign players in their squad. It is also intended to reduce the increasing gap between the big and small football clubs. The foundations of football are harmony and balance between national team football and club football. The clubs' loss of national identity is endangering the former and has led to increasing inequality among the latter, thereby widening the financial and sporting gap between the two, reducing the competitiveness of club competitions and increasing the predictability of their results. The objective of the 6+5 rule is safeguarding (1) the education and training of young players, (2) training clubs, and (3) the values of effort and motivation in football, particularly for young players, is a fundamental element of protecting national teams and restoring sporting and financial balance to club football. The universal development of football over the last century would not continue if there were increasing inequalities between continents, countries and protagonists in football. The declared aims of the 6+5 rule are:

- to guarantee equality in sporting and financial terms between clubs;
- the promotion of junior players;
- to improve the quality of national teams, and
- to strengthen the regional and national identification of clubs and a corresponding link with the public.

The objective was to have an incremental implementation starting at the beginning of the 2010–2011 season to give clubs time to adjust their teams over a period of several years: 4+7 for 2010–2011, 5+6 for 2011–2012, and 6+5 for 2012–2013.

According to the 6+5 rule, a football club must begin a game with at least six players entitled to play for the national team of the country where the club concerned is located. This means that a maximum of five players may be used at the beginning of the match who are not entitled to play for the national team of the league association concerned. The decisive criterion in applying the 6+5 rule is thus entitlement to play in the relevant national team. This is determined in Articles 15 et seq. of the implementation rules of the FIFA statutes (eligibility to play for representative teams; see above). The nationality of players is thus not always the decisive criterion for deciding whether a player is entitled to play in a national team. On the contrary, in cases of later change of nationality or the acquisition of a new nationality by a national player, this will not generally imply a right to play for the other national team. According to the INEA (Institute for European Affairs)'s Expert Opinion regarding the Compatibility of the '6+5 Rule' with European Community Law (24 October 2008),[17] this aspect of the mechanism of the 6+5 rule, which is clearly different from a nationality clause, should be particularly emphasised. The idea of the "foreign footballer" or the "native footballer" in the meaning of the 6+5 rule is consequently not the same as the concept of a foreigner for purposes of nationality. Besides this difference in approach of the 6+5 rule compared to foreigner clauses, a further key characteristic of the concept calls for emphasis: the limitation of the 6+5 rule only applies to the use of the players, not the composition of the squad. This means that there are no restrictions;—on the number of players not entitled to play whom a club can sign on, nor—for substitutions during the match, meaning that in the course of a game the balance could change to 3+8, the UNTEA's Expert Opinion argues.

The 6+5 rule has on numerous occasions been described as illegal by the European Union. On 28 November 2008, following the informal Sports Ministers' meeting in Biarritz (France) Commissioners Jan Figel' and Vladimit Špidla stated that their position was clear: FIFA's 6+5 rule is based on direct discrimination on the grounds of nationality, and is thus against one of the fundamental principles of EU law.

There is as yet no binding agreement as to how the 6+5 rule will actually be formulated. FIFA expressly favours a flexible rule allowing for exceptions and transitional periods for individual member associations. This makes it clear that so far, there has not been a fixed proposal, rather, there is currently still a concept in principle for discussion.

Comment

The FIFA 6+5 rule for club competition implies a linkage to the FIFA eligibility rules for national representative teams that partially deviate from public nationality (naturalisation) law. One of the consequences thereof is that a player possessing the passport of an EU Member State is not allowed to participate in club competition, if at the same time he is not eligible to represent that country internationally at a representative level. This would come down to the discrimination of local nationals ("self-discrimination"). Under the 6+5 rule EU non-nationals remain discriminated, since there are no players possessing a foreign passport may play for whatever national representative team. The 6+5 rule, being linked to the FIFA eligibility rules, does not even take into account the fact that a foreign player may have played for years in another EU country, which fact was even taken into account under the "classic" nationality clauses (quotas) like the 3+2 rule. The 6+5 rule makes the building up of the status of a "football German" etc. on the basis of "genuine link" impossible. Generally speaking, the 6+5 rule is a post-Bosman variable of the pre-Bosman 3+2 rule. It is true that the conditions of the 3+2) rule were stricter than the 6+5 rule (3+2 amounts to five foreigners and 6+5 also means five foreigners, however the "2" of the 3+2 rule needed to prove their "genuine (sporting) link" with the country in question.

[17] At p. 27.

7.3.3 UEFA Home Grown Players' Rule

One of the biggest challenges facing European football is that, since the European Court of Justice's Bosman ruling of 1995 and the rapid growth of television revenue, the richest clubs have been able to stockpile (or "hoard") the best players, making it easier for them to dominate both national and European competitions.

At the same time, clubs have fewer incentives to train their own players or give a genuine chance to young players from their region. This trend is exacerbated by the increasingly unreliable financial compensation for training young players who leave early, and the ability of many European clubs to "poach" young players from the age of 16 from across the European Union.

UEFA's rule aims to encourage the local training of young players, and increase the openness and fairness of European competitions. It also aims to counter the trend for hoarding players, and to try to re-establish a "local" identity at clubs.

The UEFA Executive Committee adopted the *locally trained* or *home grown* players' rule on 2 February 2005 and they received the support of the national associations at the governing body's Congress in Tallinn on 21 April 2005.

From 2008/09, clubs in the UEFA Champions League and UEFA Europa League required a minimum of eight home grown players in a squad limited to 25. These rules are also in force in several national leagues across Europe.

UEFA introduced the rule in three phases:

Season 2006/07: minimum of four home grown players in 25-man squad

Season 2007/08: minimum of six home grown players in 25-man squad

Season 2008/09: minimum of eight home grown players in 25-man squad

Clubs have no obligation to put a certain number of home grown players on the field of play, or on the match sheet. They are entirely free in their team and match day squad selection.

UEFA defines locally-trained or home grown players as those who, regardless of their nationality, have been trained by their club or by another club in the same national association for at least three years between the age of 15 and 21. Up to half of the locally-trained players must be from the club itself ("club-trained"), with the others being either from the club itself or from other clubs in the same association ("association-trained").

In May 2008, the European Commission published an independent study on the "home-grown players" rule adopted by UEFA.[18] It stated that this rule requires clubs participating in the Champions League and the UEFA Cup to have a minimum number of "home-grown players" in their squads. Compared with the "6+5" plan proposed by FIFA, which is incompatible with EU law, the Commission considers that UEFA has opted for an approach which seems to comply with the principle of free movement of workers while promoting the

---

[18] Study on training of young sportsmen/women in Europe/Home-grown players rule, April 2008; see Part II regarding, in particular the home grown players'rule (ineum Consulting/Taj Société d'Avocats).

training of young European players. The Commission also notes that the measures are designed to support the promotion and protection of quality training for young footballers in the EU. This study had been announced in the White Paper on Sport in July 2007.

Vladimir Špidla, Member of the European Commission responsible for employment, social affairs and equal opportunities, declared that "Compared with the intentions announced by FIFA to impose the so-called '6+5' rule, which is directly discriminatory and therefore incompatible with EU law, the 'home-grown players' rule proposed by UEFA seems to me to be proportionate and to comply with the principle of free movement of workers."

Ján Figel, European Commissioner in charge of education, training, culture and youth, stated that "Measures which require the top European clubs to preserve quality training structures seem to me to be necessary. The UEFA rules thus avoid the risk of professional football clubs abandoning training structures."

According to Action 9 of the Pierre de Coubertin Action Plan, part of the White Paper on Sport, "Rules requiring that teams include a certain quota of 'home-grown players' could be accepted as being compatible with the Treaty provisions on free movement of persons if they do not lead to any direct discrimination based on nationality and if possible indirect discrimination effects resulting from them can be justified as being proportionate to a legitimate objective pursued, such as enhancing and protecting the training and development of talented young players." This approach received the support of the European Parliament in its Resolution on the White Paper on Sport.

"Home-grown players" are defined by UEFA as players who, regardless of their nationality or age, have been trained by their club or by another club in the national association for at least three years between the age of 15 and 21. The UEFA rule does not contain any nationality conditions. It also applies in the same way to all players and all clubs participating in competitions organised by UEFA.

Although it was difficult at the moment to state with any certainty that the "home-grown players" rule will lead to indirect discrimination on the basis of nationality, the potential risk of this cannot be discounted, as young players attending a training centre at a club in a Member State tend to be from that Member State rather than from other EU countries.

Nevertheless, the objectives underlying UEFA's "home-grown players" rule, namely promoting training for young players and consolidating the balance of competitions, seemed to be legitimate objectives of general interest, as they are inherent to sporting activity.

Since the rules adopted by UEFA would be implemented gradually in successive stages (to include four "home-grown players" out of 25 for the 2006/07 season and eight out of 25 as from the 2008/09 season), their practical effects would not be totally clear for a number of years.

Therefore, in order to be able to assess the implications of the UEFA rule in terms of the principle of free movement of workers, the Commission would closely monitor its implementation and undertake a further analysis of its consequences by 2012.[19]

In the so-called follow-up "White paper plus" of 18 January 2011, the European Commission stated that *indirect discrimination* occurs when rules apply criteria of differentiation other than nationality but lead, in fact, to the same results as direct discrimination. In this case, only rules that are necessary, proportionate to the achievement of legitimate objectives, and do not discriminate directly on the basis of nationality, may be compatible with Article 45 TFEU. For instance, rules such as UEFA's "home-grown players" which aim to encourage the recruitment and training of young players and ensure the balance of competitions, can be compatible with EU free movement provisions (i) in so far as they are able to achieve efficiently those legitimate objectives, (ii) if there are no other measures available which can be less discriminating and (iii) if the rules in question do not go beyond what is necessary to the attainment of their objectives. The Commission would nevertheless monitor the application of these rules closely on a case by case basis in order to verify that the criteria are met.

On 28 May 2008 the Commission had published an independent study carried out on its behalf to examine the effects of UEFA's rules setting a minimum number of "home-grown players" for clubs participating in its football competitions. On the basis of the results of the study, the Commissioners responsible for free movement of workers and for sport considered that the approach followed by UEFA in adopting these rules complied prima facie with the principle of free movement of workers while promoting the training of young European athletes.

"Home-grown players" are defined by UEFA as players who, regardless of their nationality or age, have been trained by their club or by another club in the same national association for at least three years between the age of 15 and 21. The UEFA rule does not contain any conditions based on nationality. It applies in the same way to all players and all clubs participating in competitions organised by UEFA. Its aim is to encourage clubs to establish efficient training centres with a view to ensuring the creation and maintenance of high-level talent pools of future professional players.

The objectives underlying UEFA's home-grown players rules, namely promoting the recruitment and training of young players and ensuring the balance of competitions, can be considered legitimate objectives of general interest. The provisions of the rules appear to be inherent in and proportionate to the achievement of such objectives. However, since the rules risk having indirect discriminatory effects and since their implementation has been gradual over several years, the Commission would carry out further analysis on the rules in 2012.

It should be noted that UEFA's home-grown players rules have not been examined from the angle of EU competition law. Similar schemes aimed at

---

[19] See, Press release IP/08/807 of 28 May 2008.

establishing quotas of locally trained players for clubs participating in team sports competitions had been brought to the attention of the Commission since the adoption of UEFA's rules. Each scheme needed to be examined taking into account the specific provisions of the scheme itself, the characteristic of the sport discipline concerned and the general context in which the scheme is proposed.

Rules leading to direct discrimination on grounds of nationality are not compatible with EU law. The same is true for rules based on criteria directly linked to nationality. For example, rules establishing quotas of players in clubs based on eligibility to play for the national team of the country where the club is located, when the main criterion for such eligibility is nationality, are not compatible with EU law.[20]

7.4 Summary and Conclusion

Nationality law in sport (or sport(s) nationality law) consists of a public and private part. The public part concerns specific exceptions of accelerated or quick naturalisation for sporting reasons in the "national interest." The private rules of the international sports organisations (eligibility rules for the participation in Olympic Games and world/regional international championships) in general refer to and apply public nationality legislation. However, in order to counter accelerated naturalisation, those rules have also created a level playing field for all by introducing a residence or waiting period of a purely sporting (IOC) or a non-sporting (for example, FIFA) character which in fact amounts to a specific "sporting nationality" deviating from the public/passport nationality rules. If the waiting period is based on the last representation of the former country (IOC) as a starting point, the public international law doctrine of a "genuine link" in nationality matters in fact is reflected in sports law, i.e. the existence of a genuine connection between the sportsperson concerned and his or her local club and/or national association.

Discrimination on grounds of nationality is prohibited under EU law. Sporting rules concerning the composition of national representative teams, in particular rules that exclude non-national sportspersons, whether EU or non-nationals, from national team, have been considered as rules that do not infringe EU law free movement provisions. A (still or forever theoretical) alternative model for the composition of national representative teams could be that such teams would represent the national football associations not on the basis of the players possessing local ("passport") nationality, but on the basis of a selection of the players that participate and have participated—for a minimum period of time to be

---

[20] Commission Staff Working Document "Sport and Free Movement", Accompanying document to the Communication from the Commission to the European Parliament, the Council, the European Economic and Social Committee and the Committee of the Regions "Developing the European Dimension in Sport", SEC(2011) 66/2.

determined—in the national championship competitions. This would result in what could be called "national FA teams" of a non-discriminatory character. Again, such an alternative could be considered as an example of "genuine link" of a purely sporting character.

As far as participation of foreign athletes ("EU non-nationals") is concerned it is in general recommended under EU law that these athletes be allowed to compete in the national championship of a given sporting discipline, provided that they do not exert a direct and substantial influence on the outcome of the individual competition. In sports which involve direct eliminations (knock-out completion structure), it is accepted in principle that foreigners may be excluded from participation in the national championship, as they exert too direct and substantial an influence on the outcome of the tournament. This of course is not the case with regard to non-direct elimination sports of a timing (for example, swimming) or jury type (for example, gymnastics) character. In addition, it should be observed that, where results in a national championship serve (or co-serve) as a basis for the qualification to international representative competitions or for the composition of national teams, direct eliminations sports could and even should lose their "open" character.

In the Bosman ruling the European Court of Justice prohibited any discrimination based on nationality and declared nationality quotas in sports clubs ("nationality clauses") not in conformity with the principles of free movement for sportsmen. The FIFA 6+5 rule for club competition is of a pre-Bosman type. It implies a linkage to the FIFA eligibility rules for national representative teams that partially deviate from public nationality (naturalisation) law. Since the FIFA eligibility rule is not of a "genuine sporting link" character in sporting terms, the 6+5 rule is either. The 6+5 rule implicitly refers to the EU law discrimination exception for the composition of national representative teams and seemingly embodies the intention to expand the working of that exception also into the realm of club football. However, sporting rules establishing quotas of players in clubs based on eligibility to play for the national team of the country where the club is located, when the main criterion for such eligibility is nationality, are not compatible with EU law.

Finally, the UEFA locally trained or home grown players' rule is of a purely sporting "genuine link" character, since it is based on the location (whereabouts) of the education and training of young football players. The rule is accepted by the European Commission for the time being and will be re-evaluated in 2012. The rule may be and already is easily circumvented by contracting talented players from abroad sufficiently early in order that they be trained for at least three years between the age of 15 and 21 by the club and in the country concerned.

From the perspective of the EU law and policy concept of "sport specificity" the following observations can be made. The exception recommended for the participation of EU non-nationals in national championships abroad in direct eliminations (knock-out competition) sports, is a very clear example of sport specificity. Without the acceptance of such an exception, it would be impossible to fairly organise national championships that are at the same time "qualifiers" for international representative championships (Olympic Games, world and regional championships). The justifications (education and training of young players, protection of national teams, sporting and financial balance in club competitions) brought forward by FIFA for introducing the 6+5 rule, are not sufficient grounds for setting aside the non-discrimination and free movement principles of EU law, whereas the home grown players rule which is based on similar considerations (training of young players and promotion of balanced competition), but—other than the 6+5 rule—is in itself of a genuine, purely sporting link character, is for the time being an acceptable form of "indirect discrimination" in the European Commission's view. In this context, it is relevant to note that the argument of the education and training of young players was accepted by the European Court of Justice in their jurisprudence (Bosman and Olympique Lyonnais/Bernard cases) in relation to the justification of the training compensation system in professional football (which is in fact an exception to the abolition of the transfer system).

For "non-EU nationals" restrictions on the part of the football associations continue to exist widely. Once admitted under national immigration laws and the pertinent competition regulations of those football associations, players from third countries must enjoy equal treatment if and when they are citizens of States which have signed agreements with the EU that contain non-discrimination clauses, and who are legally employed in the territory of the Member State concerned. Rules that limit the opportunities of professional sportsmen from such third countries to take part in certain matches (as part of their professional activity), in comparison with sportspersons who are EU citizens, involve discrimination and run counter to the equal treatment clauses in the agreements. This means that players who are nationals of a country which has concluded such an agreement with the EU cannot be excluded on the basis of their nationality from a team sent out on the field. Such clauses do not, however, amount to the conferral of a right of free movement within the EU. Because of the considerable differences between EU Member States' immigration laws and the competition regulations of the national football associations as to the admittance of "non-EU nationals," there is not a situation of "level playing field" (fair competition) between them regarding the recruitment of third country players.

References

Conzelmann R (2008) Modelle für eine Förderung der inländerischen Nachwuchssportler zur Stärkung der Nationalmannschaften. Beiträge zum Sportrecht Band 30. Duncker & Humblot, Berlin (see also, Models for the promotion of home grown players for the protection of national representative teams, 2008, Int Sports Law J 3–4:26–30)

de Groot G-R (2006) Sporting nationality: remarks on the relationship between the general legal nationality of a person and his 'sporting nationality'. Int Sports Law J 1–2:3–9

Gardiner S, Parrish R, Siekmann RCR (eds) (2009) EU, sport, law and policy—regulation, re-regulation and representation. T.M.C. Asser Press, The Hague, pp 227–246

Martins RB (2004) The Kolpak case: Bosman times ten? Football fears the arrival of Bosman, Bosmanovic and Osman. Int Sports Law J 1–2:26–37

Prokopets M (2009) Limits on foreign professional players competing in the Russian federation: problems and prospects. Int Sports Law J 3–4:33–37

Siekmann R (1978) Voetbalwoordenboek [football dictionary], with a foreword by Jan Mulder. Het Spectrum, Utrecht, p 42

Siekmann R (1980) Moderne voetbaltheorie [modern football theory]. Het Spectrum, Utrecht, pp 61–62

van den Bogaert S (2005) Practical regulation of the mobility of sportsmen in the EU post *Bosman*. European Monographs, vol 48. Kluwer Law International, The Hague

Chapter 8
International Professional Football Law: Webster, Matuzalem and De Sanctis—The CAS Transfer 'Buy-Out' Rulings

Abstract The subject of international professional football law consists of a broad range of (in particular, European) subtopics such as nationality issues, Social Dialogue in the European professional football sector, the collective selling of TV rights from an EU competition law perspective, legal aspects of combating transnational football hooliganism in Europe, the matter of sports betting-related sporting fraud, etc. This chapter focuses on a crucial aspect of the issue of players' contracts and transfer issues (the other topic of the diptych being dealt with in Bosman, which will be treated in this chapter from a global (FIFA and DRC/CAS) perspective. The 'hard core' of professional football law may be situated in the player/club relationship (contracts/transfers) to which the players' agent issue is attached. The other central relationship in professional football is that of clubs and association/league (f.e. *re* the TV rights collective selling issue). The sequence of paragraphs in this chapter is as follows: (1) a short introduction to the FIFA Dispute Resolution Chamber (DRC) and the Court of Arbitration for Sport (CAS); (2) The FIFA Regulations on the Status and Transfer of Players ('contractual stability'); (3) 'valid contract (compensation) cases': (a) Webster case; (b) Matuzalem Case; and (c) De Sanctis.

Contents

R. C. R. Siekmann, *Introduction to International and European Sports Law*,
ASSER International Sports Law Series, DOI: 10.1007/978-90-6704-852-1_8,

© T.M.C. ASSER PRESS, The Hague, The Netherlands, and the author 2012

8.1 Introduction

The subject of international professional football law consists of a broad range of (in particular, European) subtopics such as nationality issues, one of which is dealt with in *Bosman* (discrimination, non-equal treatment of EU nationals, see also the issue of the FIFA 6+5 and UEFA home grown players rules in the EU law context), Social Dialogue in the European professional football sector, the collective selling of TV rights from an EU competition law perspective, legal aspects of combating transnational football hooliganism in Europe (UEFA/Council of Europe context), the matter of sports betting-related sporting fraud, etc. This chapter focuses on a crucial aspect of the issue of players' contracts and transfer issues (the other topic of the diptych being dealt with in *Bosman*,[1] which will be treated in this chapter from a global (FIFA and DRC/CAS) perspective. The 'hard core' of professional football law may be situated in the player/club relationship (contracts/transfers; cf. Bosman I/freedom of movement for workers) to which the players' agent issue is attached.[2] The other central relationship in professional football is that of clubs and association/league (f.e. *re* the TV rights collective selling issue). The sequence of paragraphs in this chapter is as follows: (1) a short introduction to the FIFA Dispute Resolution Chamber (DRC) and the Court of Arbitration for Sport (CAS); (2) The FIFA Regulations on the Status and Transfer of Players ('contractual stability'); (3) 'valid contract (compensation) cases': (a) Webster case; (b) Matuzalem Case; and (c) De Sanctis.

---

[1] The famous *Bosman* ruling of the ECJ might be characterised as the 'the mother of all sports law verdicts' (cf., in Dutch football literature, the 1974 World Cup 1–2 loss versus Germany is usually characterised as the 'mother of all defeats'; cf., Willemsen 1994. Jean-Louis Dupont was the advocate of Bosman in the ECJ case; see: "A Law Unto Himself: The Lawyer Who Changed the Face of Football", in: Bent et al. 2000, pp. 9–22; also in: The International Sports Law Journal (ISLJ) 2007/3–4 pp. 94–97 ('History'); see also, Jean-Louis Dupont in the Foreword to 'European Sports Law: Collected Papers', The Hague 2007 (p. V) by Professor Stephen Weatherill, University of Oxford, United Kingdom: 'We have one important thing in common: we are both, in our respective ways, humble pioneers in this evolving field of law. He is a distinguished academic and I am an enthusiast practitioner. As such, we are, in a sense, in a symbiotic relationship. In practicing before the European Court of Justice as a sports lawyer, I am always pleased to draw on his insights and ideas in testing my arguments; and he, of course, draws on the actual decisions of the Court itself, to provide a coherent and critical legal analysis of how sport is being regulated at the European level and a European sports law policy is emerging ...'), and its follow-up, *Olympique Lyonnais/Bernard*.

[2] See Siekmann et al. 2007; see also Martins and Reiter 2010, pp. 7–12. Roberto Branco Martins is director of the Dutch players' agents association *ProAgent* and general secretary of the European Federation of Football Agents (*EFAA*).

8.2 DRC and CAS

In 2001 the football world governing body FIFA established a Dispute Resolution Chamber (DRC). The DRC has since then developed into a major and influential resolution body, with an impressive and ever increasing caseload. The DRC is FIFA's deciding body that provides arbitration and dispute resolution on the basis of equal representation of players and clubs and an independent chairman. The DRC adjudicates on a regular basis in the presence of a varying composition of members. In total, the DRC includes 10 player representatives and 10 club representatives whereas decisions are regularly passed in a composition of 5 (2 player representatives, 2 club representatives, 1 chairman). The relevant decisions are published on FIFA.com. DRC proceedings are free of charge. The DRC is competent for employment-related disputes between clubs and players that have an international dimension as well as for disputes between clubs related to Training Compensation and Solidarity Mechanism. In the application and adjudication of law, the DRC shall apply the FIFA Statutes and regulations whilst taking into account all relevant arrangements, laws and/or collective bargaining agreements that exist at national level, as well as *the specificity of sport* (italics added; RS). So, it is remarkable that the central concept of EU sports law ('sport specificity')—next to the ostensible subspecies of openness and fairness (see Article 165 TFEU)[3]—has been transferred to general, international (global, universal, worldwide) sports (football) law. In the Memorandum of Understanding of 11 October 2007 between the European football governing body UEFA and the global players' union FIFPro, the parties more specifically and explicitly recognised, next to the subspecies of 'the specificity of the career of a professional footballer,' 'the specificity of sport,' etc.[4]

The Court of Arbitration for Sport (CAS; French: *Tribunal Arbitral du Sport* or *TAS*) is an international arbitration body set up to settle disputes related to sport. Its headquarters are in Lausanne and its courts are located in New York, Sydney and Lausanne, Switzerland. Temporary courts are built in current Olympic Host Cities. The body was originally conceived by International Olympic Committee (IOC) President Juan Antonio Samaranch, who foresaw the need for a specialised body to resolve sporting disputes outside the normal court system, to deal with disputes arising during the Olympics. His aim was for CAS to become the supreme court of world sport. It was established as part of the IOC in 1984. The draft Statute of the CAS was elaborated, amongst others, by the late Judge Kéba Mbaye, a member of the International Court of Justice in The Hague. Ten years later, a case decided by

---

[3] Cf., Weatherill 2010, pp. 11 and 14–17.

[4] For more details please consult the Regulations for the Status and Transfer of Players as well as the Rules Governing the Procedures of the Players' Status Committee and the Dispute Resolution Chamber. See also in particular, Weger 2008a, pp. 1–43. DRC Database (www.drcdatabase.com) which is seated in Amsterdam, gives access to all published decisions of the DRC (as from 2002); all decisions are summarised, analysed, sorted, ranked and where necessary commented upon.

the CAS was appealed to the Federal Supreme Court of Switzerland, challenging CAS impartiality. The Swiss court ruled that the CAS was a true court of arbitration, but drew attention to the numerous links which existed between the CAS and the IOC. In response, the CAS underwent reforms to make itself more independent of the IOC, organisationally and financially. The biggest change resulting from this reform was the creation of an 'International Council of Arbitration for Sport' (ICAS) to look after the running and financing of the CAS, thereby taking the place of the IOC. Generally speaking, a dispute may be submitted to the CAS only if there is an arbitration agreement between the parties which specifies recourse to the CAS. Currently, all Olympic International Federations but one, and many National Olympic Committees, have recognised the jurisdiction of the CAS and included in their statutes an arbitration clause referring disputes to it. Through compliance with the 2009 World Anti-Doping Code all Olympic International Federations have recognised the jurisdiction of CAS for anti-doping rule violations. Its arbitrators are all high level jurists and it is generally held in high regard in the international sports community. As of 2004, the majority of recent cases considered by the CAS dealt with transfer disputes within professional football (soccer) or with doping. The disputes to which a federation, association or other sports-related body is part are a matter for arbitration in the sense of the CAS Code (Statutes of the Bodies Working for the Settlement of Sports-Related Disputes), only insofar as the statutes or regulations of the said sports-related bodies or a specific agreement so provide.[5] Under an agreement between FIFA and ICAS, the jurisdiction of the newly foreseen Arbitration Tribunal for Football (*TAF*), to which decisions of the Dispute Resolution Chamber were to be appealed, would be exercised by the CAS. FIFA has recognised the CAS since December 2002 to resolve disputes between FIFA, members, confederations, leagues, clubs, players, officials and licensed match agents and players' agents (FIFA Statutes, Art. 59 paragraph 1; now: Art. 62 paragraph 1). From then on, the CAS was ready to act as an appeal committee for decisions taken by the DRC. Article 61 paragraph 1 (now: Article 63 paragraph 1) of the FIFA Statutes explicitly stated that decisions of the DRC could be appealed against before the CAS. CAS shall primarily apply the various regulations of FIFA and, additionally, Swiss law. Generally speaking, the *stare decisis* principle is not included in the CAS Code.

8.3 FIFA Transfer Rules: Contractual Stability

Bosman did not address the wider and more serious issue of the legality of the payment of transfer fees for players who are still under valid contract. Following the *Bosman* case, transfer fees in football had continued to spiral, peaking at the

[5] See on CAS in general, Blackshaw et al. 2006. See in particular, regarding CAS case-law on football and doping: Wild 2011 and David 2008.

€75 m paid by Real Madrid to Juventus Turin for Zinedine Zidane in 2001. However, the demanding of such a fee by the selling club has the potential to severely restrict freedom of movement between EU states for players. In 1998, the Commission issued a statement of objections concerning FIFA's *international* transfer rules for contracted players ('Regulations for the Status and Transfer of Players'). Following negotiations between the Commission and FIFA, the latter committed itself to modify its transfer rules on the basis of certain principles. In 2002, the Commission therefore decided to close its investigations.[6]

The main principles agreed upon during the discussions with FIFA and UEFA in 2002 were:

- measures to support the training of players, *e.g.* through training compensation for young players (under the age of 23) and a solidarity mechanism in order to redistribute a significant proportion of income to professional and amateur clubs involved in the training of a player;
- establishing a transfer period per season;
- specification of contractual arrangements between players and clubs, *e.g.* regulating duration of contracts (a minimum duration of 1 year and a maximum duration of 5 years) and specifying when breaches of contracts are possible (including sanctions); and
- ensuring that arbitration is voluntary and does not prevent recourse to national courts in case of disputes.

The principles read in full as follows[7]:

- players aged under 23, a system of training compensation should be in place to encourage and reward the training effort of clubs, in particular small clubs;
- creation of solidarity mechanisms that would redistribute a significant proportion of income to clubs involved in the training and education of a player, including amateur clubs;
- international transfer of players aged under 18 to be allowed subject to agreed conditions; the football authorities will establish and enforce a code of conduct to guarantee the sporting, training and academic education to be provided;
- creation of one transfer period per season, and a further limited mid-season window, with a limit of one transfer per player per season;
- minimum and maximum duration of contracts of respectively 1 and 5 years;
- contracts to be protected for a period of 3 years up to 28; 2 years thereafter;
- the system of sanctions to be introduced should preserve the regularity and proper functioning of sporting competition so that unilateral breaches of contract are only possible at the end of a season;
- financial compensation can be paid if a contract is breached unilaterally whether by the player or the club;

6 See Commission press release IP/02/824 of 5 June 2002.

7 See also previously, IP/01/314 of 05/03/2001.

- proportionate sporting sanctions to be applied to players, clubs or agents in the case of unilateral breaches of contract without just cause, in the protected period;
- creation of an effective, quick and objective arbitration body with members chosen in equal numbers by players and clubs and with an independent chairman;
- arbitration is voluntary and does not prevent recourse to national courts.

The FIFA transfer regulations read as follows regarding 'Maintenance of contractual stability between professionals and clubs' (Articles 13–18):

'13 **Respect of contract**
A contract between a professional and a club may only be terminated upon expiry of the term of the contract or by mutual agreement.

14 **Terminating a contract with just cause**
A contract may be terminated by either party without consequences of any kind (either payment of compensation or imposition of sporting sanctions) where there is just cause.

15 **Terminating a contract with sporting just cause**
An established professional who has, in the course of the season, appeared in fewer than ten per cent of the official matches in which his club has been involved may terminate his contract prematurely on the ground of sporting just cause. Due consideration shall be given to the player's circumstances in the appraisal of such cases. The existence of sporting just cause shall be established on a case-by-case basis. In such a case, sporting sanctions shall not be imposed, though compensation may be payable. A professional may only terminate his contract on this basis in the 15 days following the last official match of the season of the club with which he is registered.

16 **Restriction on terminating a contract during the season**
A contract cannot be unilaterally terminated during the course of a season.

17 **Consequences of terminating a contract without just cause**
The following provisions apply if a contract is terminated without just cause:

1. In all cases, the party in breach shall pay compensation. Subject to the provisions of article 20 and Annexe 4 in relation to training compensation, and unless otherwise provided for in the contract, compensation for the breach shall be calculated with due consideration for the law of the country concerned, the specificity of sport, and any other objective criteria. These criteria shall include, in particular, the remuneration and other benefits due to the player under the existing contract and/or the new contract, the time remaining on the existing contract up to a maximum of 5 years, the fees and expenses paid or incurred by the former club (amortised over the term of the contract) and whether the contractual breach falls within a protected period.
2. Entitlement to compensation cannot be assigned to a third party. If a professional is required to pay compensation, the professional and his new club shall be jointly and severally liable for its payment. The amount may be stipulated in the contract or agreed between the parties.
3. In addition to the obligation to pay compensation, sporting sanctions shall also be imposed on any player found to be in breach of contract during the protected period. This sanction shall be a four-month restriction on playing in official matches. In the case of aggravating circumstances, the restriction shall last six months. These sporting sanctions shall take effect immediately once the player has been notified of the relevant decision. The sporting sanctions shall remain suspended in

the period between the last official match of the season and the first official match of the next season, in both cases including national cups and international championships for clubs. This suspension of the sporting sanctions shall, however, not be applicable if the player is an established member of the representative team of the association he is eligible to represent, and the association concerned is participating in the final competition of an international tournament in the period between the last match and the first match of the next season. Unilateral breach without just cause or sporting just cause after the protected period shall not result in sporting sanctions. Disciplinary measures may, however, be imposed outside the protected period for failure to give notice of termination within 15 days of the last official match of the season (including national cups) of the club with which the player is registered. The protected period starts again when, while renewing the contract, the duration of the previous contract is extended.

4. In addition to the obligation to pay compensation, sporting sanctions shall be imposed on any club found to be in breach of contract or found to be inducing a breach of contract during the protected period. It shall be presumed, unless established to the contrary, that any club signing a professional who has terminated his contract without just cause has induced that professional to commit a breach. The club shall be banned from registering any new players, either nationally or internationally, for two registration periods.
5. Any person subject to the FIFA Statutes and regulations (club officials, players' agents, players, etc.) who acts in a manner designed to induce a breach of contract between a professional and a club in order to facilitate the transfer of the player shall be sanctioned.

18 **Special provisions relating to contracts between professionals and clubs**

1. If an agent is involved in the negotiation of a contract, he shall be named in that contract.
2. The minimum length of a contract shall be from its effective date until the end of the season, while the maximum length of a contract shall be 5 years. Contracts of any other length shall only be permitted if consistent with national laws. Players under the age of 18 may not sign a professional contract for a term longer than 3 years. Any clause referring to a longer period shall not be recognised.
3. A club intending to conclude a contract with a professional must inform the player's current club in writing before entering into negotiations with him. A professional shall only be free to conclude a contract with another club if his contract with his present club has expired or is due to expire within six months. Any breach of this provision shall be subject to appropriate sanctions.
4. The validity of a contract may not be made subject to a successful medical examination and/or the grant of a work permit.
5. If a professional enters into more than one contract covering the same period, the provisions set forth in Chapter IV shall apply.'

The definition of the term 'protected period' reads as follows in the FIFA transfer regulations: 'a period of three entire seasons or 3 years, whichever comes first, following the entry into force of a contract, where such contract is concluded prior to the 28th birthday of the professional, or two entire seasons or 2 years, whichever comes first, following the entry into force of a contract, where such contract is concluded after the 28th birthday of the professional.'

8.3.1 Comment[8]

The system of transfers was abolished following the Bosman case but was replaced by another transfer system. Clubs started signing players for longer contracts, not to ensure the players would see out their term of contract but to guarantee that the transfer fee in relation to ongoing contracts would be as high as possible. The players cooperated with this because they were paid much higher salaries if they signed a long term contract. Or rather, their agents demanded hefty salaries in exchange for the willingness to sign long term contracts. The old system of transfers may have been undermined where expiring contracts were concerned but clubs and players were free to determine the duration of the contracts. In addition, players could still get out of a contract when a club appeared that was willing to pay them much more, which also represented an opportunity for them to play at a higher level. In other words they had their cake and ate it too, while on the other hand they also ensured their club would get a lot of money in the form of a transfer fee. So the club also profited from this new unofficial but factual transfer system. Everyone was better off: not only the players and the clubs but also the players' agents who also benefitted from lots of transfers. There was much more money involved in professional football, in short, there was much more 'trade.' It was no longer a question of 'trade in players' because players had acquired full contractual freedom as opposed to the past. Due to the fact that after to the Bosman case quotas could no longer be imposed on the numbers of EC foreign players per club, there were more players available on the national market than previously. Player and agent power was therefore substantially strengthened while the position of the clubs was relatively weaker, but that had already been the direct consequence of the Bosman ruling. Trainers had a hard time during the transfer period: you could never be sure of the team: discontented players could leave just like that. It was virtually impossible to build a team over the longer term, which did nothing for the level of the game.

This was the reality behind the official façade of the contracts. Everyone, in other words all the parties directly involved, had an interest in maintaining this new post Bosman 'transfer code.' No real chance therefore that a new Jean Marc Bosman would throw a spanner in the works. The great advantage of the new 'unwritten law' was that it was legal on the outside, whereas the old pre Bosman transfer system had been legally untenable. The new system developed in practice. If a club wanted to force a player to stick to his contract whatever the cost in spite of what has been outlined above, that club was of course literally fully entitled to do so because *pacta sund servanda*, a *contract is a contract*, (contracts should be complied with in good faith). However in doing so the club would be breaking the modern transfer code, after all, the expectation of the player was that the club would stick to the code; hadn't the player voluntarily cooperated in creating the long term contract? He would not have entered into a contract with such a long

[8] See, the Introduction by this author to Hendrickx 2002, pp. 1 et seq.

duration had he known that the club would officially make him keep to that contract. The club violated the gentleman's agreement by which the player would help the club earn a lot of money, because it would not be possible to keep him anyway if another club was to make him a much bigger offer. In the meantime, although the player might have earned much more under a long term contract (in addition to the duration of the contract, obviously the amount of the player's salary also played an important role in determining the transfer fee), which was a second condition subject to which the player agreed, if the player had signed a contract for a shorter term he might have earned less but would have been out of contract sooner and able to demand a much higher down payment from his new club. When entering into or renewing the contract the club was aware that this could serve a purpose other than the official objective of contracting the player for the long term. The new transfer code, just like the former system, could only operate effectively if it was respected by all the parties involved. This does not mean to say that the new code was desirable. Surely there is nothing strange about players only signing contracts they truly intended to adhere to on the one hand, and clubs being willing to allow them to adhere to the contracts on the other hand, exceptional circumstances excluded. The new code however was the result of the shift in the power position in paid football between players/agents and clubs in the aftermath of the Bosman case. It was not formal contract law but the new code that represented the reality. Formal contract law was merely the means (long term contracts) to allow the new code to be effective.

It is common knowledge that the European Commission was gradually losing patience with the increasingly astronomical amounts paid in transfer fees. Where the Bosman ruling had eliminated the hopeless situation of 'expiring contracts,' a new monster had shown its ugly head in the form of 'ongoing contracts' that seemed to have undermined the consequences of the Bosman ruling through the extra long duration of the contracts. Thus the Commission started negotiations with the FIFA and the UEFA to revise the transfer rules with a view to bringing an end to this situation. As we know, the Commission and both international football associations reached an agreement last year as a follow-up to the Bosman ruling. The question as to the actual status of these agreements is an interesting one. This is not a formal legal agreement; let there be no misunderstanding about that. It is more of a gentleman's arrangement in the sense that the football world now knows the margins within which it must always abide by European law. It is an agreement under which neither the Commission nor the UEFA/FIFA have any legal obligations. It is rather a set of political guidelines as to how the football associations should act. Of course hard European law still prevails. In last instance: anyone wishing to know what is allowed and what is not can appeal to the European court, the Court of Justice in Luxembourg. Obviously the Commission cannot interfere with the hard core of European law by making a unilateral compromise with the football world! Parties applying the new FIFA transfer rules correctly will not face the Commission's opposition on grounds of their acting contrary to European law. In the meantime the new transfer rules are caught between the devil of European law and the deep blue sea of national employment law. When players are granted more freedom of movement based on the national employment law of the member states, which is explicitly respected in the agreements between the Commission and associations, naturally no objections arise ('most favourable treatment'): by definition more freedom of movement also means more competition between the clubs on the market for players. Contrary to this it has already been suggested that a second Jean Marc Bosman could show up to undermine the new transfer rules with an appeal to national employment law! Should national employment law grant less freedom (this is, however, unlikely), the European Commission's interpretation of the EC Treaty on this issue shall of course prevail as a minimum and it is in principle always possible to have this interpretation tested by the European Court. The Bosman ruling was based on the freedom of movement rules set out in the EC Treaty; the rules governing competition are explicitly not taken into account. The new FIFA rules are however apparently a reflection of both types of law. For example, for young players a training allowance is now payable. This seems to reflect the ruling in the Bosman case that adequate and proportional means to protect the training of young players are justified to maintain the competitive balance in the competition (in addition to the allocation of TV funds etc.). The training allowance for young players, the maintaining of contractual stability in the world of football (for example by setting minimum contract durations) and the limiting of the transfer periods, major issues in the new FIFA rules, all seem to be intended to promote the competitive balance in the competition. Apparently from the perspective of competition law the Commission saw no reason to object to shifting a little towards limiting the consequences of the Bosman ruling. On the other hand the very long term contracts (post Bosman), which were believed to restrict competition, are also abolished as a result of the maximums set in the FIFA transfer rules. The new transfer rules (right of association) are caught in an area fraught with tension between the requirements imposed under European law and the principles of national employment law.

8.4 'Valid Contract (Compensation) Cases'

8.4.1 Webster *Case*[9]

On 30 January 2008, the Court of Arbitration for Sport (CAS) rendered its judgment in what is commonly referred to as the 'Webster case'.[10] This case revolves

[9] In The Hague, on 21 April 2008, an international sports law seminar was organised on 'Webster, DRC and CAS: A New *Bosman*?' Speakers: Prof. Frank Hendrickx, Universities of Leuven and Tilburg, Frans de Weger, De Vos Law Firm, Amsterdam, and Steven Jellinghaus, De Voort Hermes De Bont Law Firm, Tilburg; Chairman: Dr Stefaan van den Bogaert, University of Maastricht.

[10] CAS 2007/A/1298 & 1299 & 1300.

around the question of the amount of the compensation that the player Webster must pay to his former club, Heart of Midlothian F.C. (hereinafter 'Hearts') for breaching his contract with that Scottish club prematurely and unilaterally after the expiry of the protected period. In an extensively argued decision, Hearts had claimed compensation for unjustified breach of contract by Webster under the provisions of Article 17 of the FIFA transfer regulations and the DRC awarded them the sum of £625,000 on 4 April, 2007. The parties appealed to CAS. CAS reached the conclusion that Webster must pay the residual value of the contract (between Webster and Hearts) as compensation. The judgment stated that in the course of the session, the parties reached agreement on the amount of that residual value: £150,000. Principally, CAS considered that Article 17 of the FIFA Regulations for the Status and Transfer of Players (hereinafter the 'FIFA Regulations'), under which Webster breached his contract, is not an exception to the main rule that contracts may not be unilaterally terminated, and therefore cannot be seen as a provision allowing a club or a player to unilaterally terminate a contract, without grounds, whether during or after the protected period. Termination of a contract under Article 17 can be seen as wrongful breach of contract, and as such Webster must pay compensation to Hearts. On the issue of the determination of the amount of the compensation for breach of contract, CAS considers that priority must be given to the provisions in that area in the contract in question. If the contract has no provisions in that area (which was the case with Webster's contract), the amount of the compensation must be determined based on the criteria in Article 17 of the FIFA Regulations, which refer to the law of the country in question, the specificity of the sport and other criteria, with the most important factors being the player's remaining salary under the existing contract, the transfer sum that the player's old club may have to pay (spread out over the entire term of the contract) and whether the breach of contract was within or after the protected period. CAS considers that which of these aspects must be considered in the specific case in the determination of the amount of the compensation to be paid depends on the circumstances of the breach (during or after the protected period, breach by club or by player). CAS is of the opinion that the protection that clubs enjoy during the protected period (severe penalties on breach by the players) entitles the players to some degree of protection after the protected period. In CAS's view, if the compensation for breach to be paid after the protected period were to be punitive in nature or result in a financial benefit to the club, this would be a violation of that protection. The compensation for breach after the protected period must be the same for both players and clubs, and must be set on the basis of criteria that lead to this equality of compensation. With this in mind, CAS considers that the determination of the amount of the compensation to be paid by Webster cannot be based on any hypothetical value of the player on the transfer market (club's loss of profit), nor can it take into account the player's transfer value, for the reason that either one would enrich the club and express a punitive measure against the player. In its judgment CAS determines that independently of such considerations there is no economic, moral or legal justification for a club to demand the market value of the player as loss of profit. Finally, CAS considers that the value of the contract between Webster and his new club (Wigan Athletic) is irrelevant to the determination of the amount of the compensation to be paid, being that the only relevant factor is the value of the contract breached by Webster. CAS concludes by determining that the compensation to be paid by Webster to Hearts must be the remaining value of Webster's contract with Hearts. If a club prematurely terminates a temporary contract with a player, it must generally pay that player the remaining salary under that contract, and so in view of the consideration that after the protected period the compensation upon breach must be the same for both club and player, this rule must be applied in the event of termination by a player.

8.4.1.1 The Ratio Decidendi of the Award

The interpretation and application of Article 17 of the FIFA transfer regulations to the present case are set out in the section on 'Merits of the Appeals' under de subheading 'Level of Compensation Owed by Hearts' (paragraphs 60–89) of the CAS award, which, in view of their importance, are reproduced *in extenso* as follows:

60. Having dealt with the foregoing preliminary points, the Panel shall now analyse the factors to be taken into consideration according to the wording of article 17 of the FIFA Status Regulations when determining the level of compensation. Article 17 par. 1 refers to three categories of factor, which the Panel shall examine in turn: the law of the country concerned, the specificity of sport and any other objective criteria (followed by a list of examples).
61. With respect to the *law of the country concerned* and as indicated earlier, the Panel considers that it is Scottish law but that the Panel has the discretion to decide whether or not any provisions of Scottish law should be applied in determining the level of compensation.
62. The Panel finds there are several reasons not to apply the rules of Scottish law invoked by Hearts.
63. One reason is that Hearts is relying on general rules and principles of Scottish law on damages for breach of contract, i.e. on provisions of Scottish law that are neither specific to the termination of employment contracts nor to sport or football, while article 17 of the FIFA Status Regulations was adopted precisely with the goal of finding in particular special solutions for the determination of compensation payable by football players and clubs who unilaterally terminate their contracts without cause. In other words, it is important to bear in mind that it is because employment contracts for football players are atypical, i.e. require that the particularities of the football labour market and the organization of the sport be accounted for, that article 17 was adopted. At the same time, footballers' contracts remain more akin to employment contracts (and are generally characterized as such under national laws), than to some form of commercial contract to which general rules on damage are applicable.
64. The Panel therefore sees no reason to renounce application of the specific solutions and criteria laid down in article 17 of the FIFA Status Regulations in favour of general rules on contract damages. On the contrary, the fact that several of the applicable choice-of-law rules (article 60 par. 2 of the FIFA Statutes and art. R58 of the CAS Code) underline the primary application of the regulations chosen by the parties, that article 17 par. 1 itself refers to the specificity of sport and that it is in the interest of football that solutions to compensation be based on uniform criteria rather than on

provisions of national law that may vary considerably from country to country, are all factors that reinforce the Panel's opinion that in this case it is not appropriate to apply the general principles of Scottish law on damages for breach of contract invoked by Hearts.

65. Consequently, in determining the level of compensation, the Panel will not rely on Scottish law.
66. With respect to the "*specificity of sport*," article 17 par. 1 of the FIFA Status Regulations stipulates that it shall be taken into consideration, without however providing any indication as to the content of such concept.
67. In light of the history of article 17, the Panel finds that the specificity of sport is a reference to the goal of finding particular solutions for the football world which enable those applying the provision to strike a reasonable balance between the needs of contractual stability, on the one hand, and the needs of free movement of players, on the other hand, i.e. to find solutions that foster the good of football by reconciling in a fair manner the various and sometimes contradictory interests of clubs and players.
68. Therefore the Panel shall bear that balance in mind when proceeding to an examination of the other criteria for compensation listed in article 17.
69. With regard to the *other criteria* for determining compensation, article 17 par. 1 leaves a substantial degree of discretion to the deciding authority to account for the circumstances of the case, since after stipulating that compensation may be calculated on the basis of *"any other objective criteria,"* it provides that *"These criteria shall include, in particular, the remuneration and other benefits due to the player under the existing contract and/or the new contract, the time remaining on the existing contract up to a maximum of five years, the fees and expenses paid or incurred by the Former Club (amortised over the term of the contract) and whether the breach falls within a Protected Period."*
70. In that relation is it noteworthy that independently from the specificities of a given case, the criteria listed in article 17 need to cope with a number of categories of cases, notably those where unilateral termination occurs inside the protected period as distinct from those where it occurs outside such period and those cases where unilateral termination is by the Player as distinct from those where termination is by the Club. It is therefore logical that article par. 1 includes a broad range of criteria, many of which cannot in good sense be combined, and some of which may be appropriate to apply to one category of case and inappropriate to apply in another.
71. Furthermore, in seeking to balance appropriately the interests of clubs and players for the good of the game, it is necessary to bear in mind that because article 17 of the FIFA Status Regulations applies to the unilateral termination of contracts both by players and by clubs, the system of compensation provided by article 17 must be interpreted and applied in a manner which avoids favouring clubs over players or vice versa.
72. In the foregoing context, the Panel finds it appropriate to consider that the clubs particular need for contract stability is specifically and adequately addressed by means of the Protected Period and the provisions designed to enforce it, which comprise the basic period of protection as defined in paragraph 7 of the "Definitions" contained in the FIFA Status Regulations, the automatic renewal of that period upon the contract being extended (article 17 par. 3, last sentence) and the relatively severe sanctions that can be imposed in case of disrespect for the Protected Period (article 17 par. 3); such stability being further enhanced for clubs and players alike by article 16 of the FIFA Status Regulations, which entirely prohibits unilateral termination during the course of a Season.
73. The clubs' special interest having been recognized and protected in such regulatory manner, the Panel finds that, beyond the Protected Period and subject to the parties' contractual stipulations, compensation for unilateral termination without cause should not be punitive or lead to enrichment and should be calculated on the basis of criteria

that tend to ensure clubs and players are put on equal footing in terms of the compensation they can claim or are required to pay. In addition, it is in the interest of the football world that the criteria applicable in a given type of situation and therefore the method of calculation of the compensation be as predictable as possible.

74. Accordingly, the Panel deems that in the present case the alleged estimated value of the Player on the transfer market, upon which Heart's is basing its main claim (GBP 4 million), by alternatively claiming such amount as lost profit or as the replacement value of the Player, cannot come into consideration when determining compensation on the basis of article 17 par. 1 of the FIFA Status Regulations because any such form of compensation was clearly not agreed upon contractually and to impose it by regulation would simultaneously cause the Club to be enriched and be punitive vis à vis the Player.
75. Indeed, in this case the Player was initially purchased by the Club for an amount of GBP 75'000 whereas it is today claiming a market value of GBP 4 million. This means that independently from the question of amortization of the initial purchase amount, that the Panel shall deal with below, the Club is claiming to be entitled to a profit of at least GBP 3.9 million on the sole premise that it trained and educated the Player.
76. In any event, subject to it being validly agreed by an enforceable contract, the Panel finds there is no economic, moral or legal justification for a club to be able to claim the market value of a player as lost profit.
77. From an economic perspective there in no reason to believe that a player's value on the market owes more to training by a club than to a player's own efforts, discipline and natural talent. An empirical study might even demonstrate the contrary, i.e. that a talented and hardworking player tends to fare well, stand out and succeed independently from the exact type of training he receives, whereas an untalented and/or lazy player will be less successful no matter what the environment. Also market value could stem in part from charisma and personal marketing. In any case, it is clear that a club cannot simply assume it is the only source of success of a player and thus claim his entire market value, particularly without bringing any proof (which would be very difficult) of its paramount role in the player's success leading to his market value. In this case, Hearts have underlined the Player's success and alleged his market value but have brought no evidence that the Club entirely or even predominantly generated the alleged market value in question through its training and education.
78. In addition from an economic and moral point of view, it would be difficult to assume a club could be deemed the source of appreciation in market value of a player while never be deemed responsible for the depreciation in value. Consequently, if the approach relied on by Hearts were followed, players should be entitled to claim for example that they are owed compensation for their alleged decrease in market value caused by such matters as being kept on the bench for too long or having an incompetent trainer, etc. Obviously, such a system would be unworkable and would not serve the good of the football.
79. From a regulatory standpoint, to allow clubs to claim the market value of players as lost profit under article 17 of the FIFA Status Regulations would not make sense and would amount to double counting, since, as mentioned earlier, article 20 and annex already provide for a system of compensation to clubs for the training and education of players, and it is not by chance that such compensation is not based on the player's market value but on demonstrable investment made and costs incurred by the club.
80. Moreover, since a club's possible entitlement to the transfer or market value of players is entirely absent from the criteria of compensation listed in article 17 par. 1 and there is no reference to any such form of compensation in favour of Hearts in the Player's employment contract, to apply such criteria and thereby imply it into the contract would contradict both the principle of fairness and the principle of certainty.

81. Finally, because of the potentially high amounts of compensation involved, giving clubs a regulatory right to the market value of players and allowing lost profits to be claimed in such manner would in effect bring the system partially back to the pre-Bosman days when players' freedom of movement was unduly hindered by transfer fees and their careers and well-being could be seriously affected by them becoming pawns in the hands of their clubs and a vector through which clubs could reap considerable benefits without sharing the profit or taking corresponding risks. In view of the text and the history of article 17 par. 1 of the FIFA Status Regulations, allowing any form of compensation that could have such an effect would clearly be anachronistic and legally unsound.
82. For the above reasons, the Panel finds that Hearts is not entitled to claim any part of the Player's alleged market value as lost profit or on any other ground and that as a result its corresponding claim for GBP 4 million must be rejected.
83. Neither can Hearts claim the right to reimbursement of any portion of the fee of GBP 75'000 initially paid by it to purchase the Player from his former club, since according to the criteria laid down in article 17 par. 1 in this respect, which the Panel finds reasonable, that fee must be deemed amortised over the term of the contract, and in this case the Player remained with the club for a longer period in total than the initially agreed fixed term of 4 years.
84. In addition, the Panel is not convinced that beyond the Protected Period it is admissible for a club to reclaim a portion of the engagement fee as compensation for unilateral termination unless such form of compensation is stipulated in the employment contract, since contractual fairness would tend to require that upon accepting his employment a player be fully aware of the financial engagements he has undertaken and the way in which they can affect his future movements. In other words, if a club expects an engagement fee to be proportionately reimbursable beyond the Protected Period—which is a matter that cannot be implied—there should be a negotiation and a meeting of the minds on the subject.
85. Among the other criteria of compensation referred to in article 17 par. 1, the Panel considers that the remuneration and benefits due to the Player under his new contract is not the most appropriate criterion on which to rely in cases involving unilateral termination by the Player beyond the Protected Period, because rather than focusing on the content of the employment contract which has been breached, it is linked to the Player's future financial situation and is potentially punitive.
86. Instead the Panel finds it more appropriate to take account of the fact that under a fixed-term employment contract of this nature both parties (club and player) have a similar interest and expectation that the term of the contract will be respected, subject to termination by mutual consent. Thus, just as the Player would be entitled in principle to the outstanding remuneration due until expiry of the term of the contract in case of unilateral termination by the club [subject it may be, to mitigation of loss], the club should be entitled to receive an equivalent amount in case of termination by the Player. This criterion also has the advantage of indirectly accounting for the value of the Player, since the level of his remuneration will normally bear some correlation to his value as a Player. Thus a Player receiving very high remuneration (and thereby being able to expect high remuneration in case of a change of club) will have a correspondingly high amount of compensation to pay even if he terminates his contract outside the Protected Period, and the earlier such termination occurs the higher will be the total amount of compensation owed.
87. For the above reasons, the Panel finds that Heart's claim of GBP 330,524 based on the difference between the value of the old and new contract must be rejected and that the most appropriate criteria of article 17 par. 1 to apply in determining the level of compensation owed to Hearts by the Player is the remuneration remaining due to the

Player under the employment contact upon its date of termination, which the parties have referred to as the residual value of the contract.

88. Consequently and because the parties have agreed that such residual value represents an amount of GBP 150'000, the Panel considers the foregoing amount to be due to Hearts as full compensation under article 17 par. 1 of the FIFA Status Regulations for the Player's termination of his contract.
89. Having determined that Hearts is entitled to such amount as fair and adequate compensation for the Player's unilateral termination of his employment contract and since the criteria listed in article 17 par. 1 are not designed to be cumulative *per se*, the Panel sees no reason to award any other amount as an additional head of damage.'

8.4.1.2 Summary[11]

The factors to be taken into consideration according to Article 17 of the FIFA transfer regulations in order to determine the level of compensation are the following: (a) the law of the country concerned, (b) the specificity of sport and (c) any other objective criteria.

Regarding the law of the country concerned, it is Scottish law, but in the Panel's opinion there were reasons not to apply that. In particular it is stressed that the particularities of the football labour market and the organisation of the sport were considered, and that—with reference to 'sport specificity'—it is in the interest of football that solutions to compensation be based on uniform criteria, i.e., Article 17 of the FIFA transfer regulations, rather than on provisions of national law that may vary considerably from country to country.

As to 'sport specificity' as such, in the Panel's view in the present case it is a reference to the purpose of finding a balance between contract stability and freedom of movement, i.e., between, clubs' and players' interests, for the good of football (cf., the FIFA motto: 'For the good of the game').

With respect to the 'other criteria' for determining compensation, the Panel finds that there is no economic, moral or legal justification for a club to be able to claim the market (transfer) value of a player as lost profit. The Panel does not directly connect market value with training by a club. A player's market value might be even depreciated by the club which is a correct analysis, I think, since in particular football performance has a lot to do with talent and personal charisma. Apart from that, playing for the national representative team might also very much help in increasing a player's market value. Moreover, clubs are already separately compensated for the training and education of players, under the FIFA transfer regulations, the Panel observes.

Using market value as an argument would bring us back into pre-Bosman times when transfer fees obstructed players' freedom of movement. In relation to

[11] Cf., Blackshaw 2008, Weger 2008b, and Soek 2008, pp. 14–15 and 18–23.

transfer fees, the Panel makes another important observation: the engagement fee that was paid by the club to purchase the player from his former club, must be deemed *amortised* over the term of the contract, and beyond the 'protected period' no reimbursement of (a portion of the) transfer fee would be acceptable at all.

Further, the remuneration under the new contract is not considered relevant by the Panel in case of unilateral termination beyond the 'protected period,' since it is linked to the player's future financial situation.

Finally, the remaining remuneration (residual contractual value) due until expiry of the contract, however, is a relevant criterion in the Panel's opinion, since it normally will have some correlation to the player's value.

8.4.2 Matuzalem *Case*

On 2 July 2007, the Brazilian player Matuzalém notified in writing FC Shakhtar Donetsk (Ukraine) of the fact that he unilaterally terminated their contractual relationship with immediate effect. On 5 July, Shakhtar replied that Matuzalém and/or his new club should pay the sum in the release clause of €25 million, or Shakhtar would start legal action. However, on 18 July, he was presented as the latest signing of Real Zaragoza (Spain). Shakhtar informed Zaragoza to request the club to pay the fee. The Matuzalém case was passed to the FIFA Dispute Resolution Chamber (DRC) on 2 November 2007, who ordered Matuzalém and Zaragoza jointly and severally liable to pay €6,800,000 to Shakhtar. On 19 March 2008, Shakhtar appealed to the Court of Arbitration for Sport (CAS) as the club thought the fee set by FIFA DRC was too low. On 20 March Matuzalém and Zaragoza also made an appeal to CAS for the compensation. On 19 May 2009, following a Shakhtar lawsuit, the CAS ordered Matuzalém to pay €11,858,934 to Shakhtar for breach of contract.[12]

8.4.2.1 The Ratio Decidendi of the Award

The interpretation and application of Article 17 of the FIFA transfer regulations to the present case are set out in Section B ('Merits') under the subheading 'III. (...) What Is The Correct Calculation of The Compensation?' of the CAS award, which, in view of their importance are reproduced *in extenso* as follows:

> **'III.2. The Rationale of art. 17 of the FIFA Regulations for the Calculation of Compensation**
>
> 76. According to art. 17 para. 1 of the FIFA Regulations, if the parties have not agreed on a specific amount in a way as described above, the compensation for a unilateral

[12] CAS 2008/A/1519 & 1520.

breach and a premature termination shall be calculated as follows :
With due consideration:

- For the *law of the country concerned*;
- Of the *specificity of sport*;
- And of *any other objective criteria, including* in particular:
- The *remuneration* and *other benefits* due to the player under the existing and/or the new contract;
- The *time remaining* on the existing contract up to a maximum of 5 years;
- The *fees and expenses* paid or incurred by the Former Club (amortised over the term of the contract); and
- Whether the contractual breach falls *within the Protected Period* as defined under the "Definitions" chapter in the FIFA Regulations.

77. The task for the body assessing the entity of the compensation due is therefore to verify and analyze as carefully as possible all the elements above and take them in due consideration.
78. An appropriate application in the present matter of art. 17 of the FIFA Regulations makes necessary for the Panel to recall the rationale of the rule, as debated also by the parties during the Hearing.
79. Art. 17 of the FIFA Regulations is part of chapter IV of the FIFA Regulations, i.e. of that part that deals with and try to foster the maintenance of contractual stability between professionals and clubs. Within the framework of the "reconstruction" of the FIFA and UEFA rules following the well-known *Bosman* decision, the concept of contractual stability was introduced to move forward and replace the former transfer fee system: accordingly, the pre-*Bosman* transfer fees due after the expiry of a contract have been replaced by compensations due for the breach or undue termination of an existing agreement.
80. Within such system of values, the provision contained in art. 17 FIFA Regulations, i.e. the financial and the disciplinary consequences due under certain conditions in the event of a breach and a unilateral, premature termination respectively, plays in view of the Panel a central role. The purpose of art. 17 is basically nothing else than to reinforce contractual stability, i.e. to strengthen the principle of *pacta sunt servanda* in the world of international football, by acting as deterrent against unilateral contractual breaches and terminations, be it breaches committed by a club or by a player.
81. This, because contractual stability is crucial for the well functioning of the international football. The principle *pacta sunt servanda* shall apply to all stakeholders, "small" and "big" clubs, unknown and top players, employees and employers, notwithstanding their importance, role or power.
82. The deterrent effect of art. 17 FIFA Regulations shall be achieved through the impending risk for a party to incur disciplinary sanctions, if some conditions are met (cf. art. 17 para. 3 to 5 FIFA Regulations), and, in any event, the risk to have to pay a compensation for the damage caused by the breach or the unjustified termination. In other words, both players and club are warned: if one does breach or terminate a contract without just cause, a financial compensation is due, and such compensation is to be calculated in accordance with all those elements of art. 17 FIFA Regulations that are applicable in the matter at stake, including all the non-exclusive criteria listed in para. 1 of said article that, based on the circumstances of the single case, the panel will consider appropriate to apply.
83. The Panel wishes to highlight that art. 17 FIFA Regulations speaks of a "compensation" (in the French version: "indemnité," in the Spanish version: "indemnización," in the German version "Entschädigung"). According to art. 28 FIFA Regulations, the English text of the rules shall be the authoritative in the event of any

discrepancy. The Panel finds comfort that the four mentioned versions are consistent and that in all languages the term used does refer to a "compensation," i.e. an amount to be paid in order to compensate the injured party for the damage suffered because of the breach or the premature termination of the contract.

84. As in almost all cases where a party is called to compensate another party for the damage caused, it is hardly possible for a party to predict in advance how big the damage and how much the compensation will be, provided no appropriate penalty clause has been negotiated and inserted in advance in the employment contract. Art. 17 FIFA Regulations, by focussing on the full compensation due to the injured party for the damage caused, makes impossible for instance for players and clubs to calculate in advance whether a transfer via unilateral and unjustified breach or an unjustified termination, respectively, would be more or less expensive than an "ordinary" transfer, with a transfer fee to be paid to the transferring club, or an ordinary termination, respectively.

85. When calculating the compensation due, the judging body will have to establish the damage suffered by the injured party, taking in consideration the circumstances of the single case, the arguments raised by the parties and the evidence produced. Of course, it is the injured party that requests compensation who bears the burden of making, as far as possible, sufficient assertions and who bears as well the burden of proof.

86. As it is the compensation for the breach or the unjustified termination of a valid contract, the judging authority shall be led by the principle of the so-called *positive interest* (or "expectation interest"), i.e. it will aim at determining an amount which shall basically put the injured party in the position that the same party would have had if the contract was performed properly, without such contractual violation to occur. This principle is not entirely equal, but is similar to the praetorian concept of *in integrum restitutio*, known in other law systems and that aims at setting the injured party to the original state it would have if no breach had occurred.

87. The fact that the judging authority when establishing the amount of compensation due has a considerable scope of discretion has been accepted both in doctrine and jurisprudence. Already for this reason, this Panel does not feel itself bound by the alleged existence of an internal "list" established, apparently—on the basis of what the parties have exposed during the hearing—by some members of the FIFA DRC in order to help the DRC to set some fix, standard amounts when compensation is due. First, it has remained undisputed among the parties that such a "list" is not part of any official FIFA rule or regulation and that it does not have any binding nature. Furthermore, should the DRC have applied in the past such "list," secretly or openly, to establish the amount of compensation in the meaning of art. 17 para. 1 of the FIFA Regulations, this would have been in deviation of the clear mandate given to the judging authority by art. 17 para. 1 FIFA Regulation itself, i.e. to establish on a case-by-case basis the prejudice suffered by a party in case of an unjustified breach or termination of contract, with due consideration of all elements of the case including all the non-exclusive criteria mentioned in art. 17 para. 1 of the FIFA Regulations.

88. The principle of the "positive interest" shall apply not only in the event of an unjustified termination or a breach by a player, but also when the party in breach is the club. Accordingly, the judging authority should not satisfy itself in assessing the damage suffered by the player by only calculating the net difference between the remuneration due under the existing contract and any a remuneration received by the player from a third party. Rather, the judging authority will have to apply the same degree of diligent and transparent review of all the objective criteria, including the specificity of the sport, as foreseen in art. 17 para. 1 FIFA Regulations.

89. To conclude, the calculation of the compensation due under art. 17 FIFA Regulations shall be diligent and there is no power for the judging authority to set the amount due in a fully arbitrary way. By asking the judging authorities, i.e. the competent FIFA

bodies and, in the event of an appeal, the CAS, to duly consider a whole series of elements, including such a wide concept like "sport specificity," and asking the judging authority to even consider "any other objective criteria," the authors of art. 17 FIFA Regulations achieved a balanced system according to which the judging body has on one side the duty to duly consider all the circumstances of the case and all the objective criteria available, and on the other side a considerable scope of discretion, so that any party should be well advised to respect an existing contract as the financial consequences of a breach or a termination without just cause would be, in their size and amount, rather unpredictable. At the end, however, the calculation made by the judging authority shall be not only just and fair, but also transparent and comprehensible.

90. Against this background, the Panel comes now to the evaluation of the damage caused by the Player and to the calculation of the compensation due by him to Shakhtar Donetsk, and so to the review of the criteria that may or may not be relevant in the present case.

III.3. The Calculation of the Compensation

3.3.1. The Remuneration Element

91. Through the unjustified termination of a player, a club like any other employer, loses the value of the services of the employee. In this case, the Panel wishes to make the following consideration to calculate such value.
92. One of the non-exclusive criteria mentioned in art. 17 para. 1 of the FIFA Regulations is the remuneration and other benefits due to a player under the existing and the new contract. While the information on the remuneration under the existing contract may provide a first indication on the value of the services of the player for that employing club, the remuneration under the new contract may provide an indication not only on the value that the new club/clubs is/are giving to the player, but possibly also on the market value of the services of the player and the motive behind the decision of the player to breach or terminate prematurely the agreement.
93. In the present matter, based on the evidence submitted, the following can be noted:
94. The yearly remuneration, including the benefits due to the Player under his agreement with Shakhtar Donetsk was at the moment of the unilateral termination of approx. EUR 1,200,000. This corresponds to the findings of the DRC, has been accepted by Shakhtar Donetsk and no evidence produced leads the Panel to other conclusions.
95. The yearly remuneration paid to the Player by Real Zaragoza for the season 2007/2008 was of approx. EUR 1,000,000 plus bonuses.
96. As mentioned above, Real Zaragoza loaned the Player to the Italian Club SS Lazio in July 2008. The remuneration of the Player under his agreement with SS Lazio was of approx. EUR 895,000 for the first, and of approx. EUR 3,220,900 for each the second and the third season, each amount plus bonuses.
97. While the Player was still in loan to SS Lazio, Real Zaragoza and the Player decided to extend their contractual relationship for one season, i.e. until the summer 2011, and agreed in a yearly retribution of approx. EUR 2,320,000, to be effective when the Player were to play again with Real Zaragoza.
98. The above shows that the Player, after leaving Shakhtar Donetsk, maintained in the football season 2007/2008 basically the same level of salary, but was able to raise his remuneration sensibly in the following seasons. To some extent, these facts can be interpreted as supporting the arguments raised by the Player that he did not leave Shakhtar Donetsk for economic reasons. This seems to the Panel to have some merit in relation with the first season, i.e. the season 2007/2008, played by the Player with Real Zaragoza and in accordance with his first contract with that club.
99. With regard to the season 2008/2009, i.e. the second season that was originally covered by the agreement of the Player with Shakhtar Donetsk, the Panel observes

that pursuant to the contract of the Player with SS Lazio, the fix remuneration for that season was of EUR 895,000. However, and even though the Player was officially only loaned to SS Lazio for a period of one season, the employment contract between the Player and SS Lazio was already concluded for three seasons, with a substantially higher fix remuneration for the second and the third season: from EUR 895,000 to EUR 3,220,900 p.a., i.e. an amount that is almost four times the one of the first reason. The Panel notes that the Player, Real Zaragoza and SS Lazio were well aware of the risks of the pending litigation against Shakhtar Donetsk. Indeed, in the loan agreement between Real Zaragoza and SS Lazio the price for the option granted to SS Lazio and giving to this club the right to making the transfer of the Player definitive was made subject to the outcome of the present CAS proceedings.

100. Taking in consideration that on one side in the second employment contract concluded by the Player and Real Zaragoza the fix remuneration for the season 2008/2009 was put at EUR 2,320,000, and that on the other side over the 3 years the average fix remuneration of the Player under the contract with SS Lazio is of EUR 2,445,600 p.a., the Panel concludes that for the purposes of the calculation of the compensation under art. 17 para. 1 FIFA Regulations, the fix yearly remuneration of the Player can be considered to have been of approx. EUR 1 mio. (plus bonuses) in the season 2007/2008, and of an average value of approx. EUR 2,445,600 (plus bonuses) in the season 2008/2009.

101. The Panel is of the view that the above-mentioned amounts show the value that third parties, including Real Zaragoza and the Player himself, gave to the services of the Player and also, through the explicit clause, to a potential breach of the new contract between the Player and Real Zaragoza. Therefore, it is appropriate to consider such figures as part of the calculation of the overall loss suffered by Shakhtar Donetsk.

102. However, the value of the services of a player is only partially reflected in the remuneration due to him, since a club has to make also certain expenditures to obtain such services. In order to calculate the full amount of the value of the services lost, one has therefore not simply take into consideration the amount of outstanding remuneration but one shall take also in account what a club would—under normal circumstances—have to spend on the (transfer) market to contract the services like the ones of the Player.

103. While the objective element of the non-amortized expenses will be handled later, the following shall be clarified: The value of the services of a player at a given point of time may be lower, higher or equal to the one when the player had started to play for a club. In the event of a breach by a player, a panel has therefore to analyze the amount necessary to acquire and keep the working force of the player. In doing so, the Panel only acknowledges economic reality in the world of football, i.e. that services provided by a player are traded and sought after on the market, are attributed an economic value and are—according to art. 17 FIFA Regulations—worth legal protection. The Panel is eager to point out that the sole object of this approach are the services provided by a player and not the human being as such.

3.3.2. The Value of the Services

104. Against such a background, when a transfer of a player is realized on the basis of a valid transfer agreement between two clubs, the amount of the transfer fee is likely to represent the value in exchange of which the transferring club was willing to waive its rights as employer and to renounce to the services of the player. When there is no transfer agreement or where a transfer agreement remains unrealized because of the breach by the player, an amount offered and originally accepted by the club will probably be also fairly close to the value of the services of that player and serve therefore as an important indication for the value of the damage caused and to be compensated. Finally, where no offer was made by a third club, a "sign

on-fee" and/or the fee that a fourth club offered to the new club to acquire the services of the player, may also be important indications for the value of the expenditures necessary to obtain the services of the player. In other words, an offer made by a third party is very likely to reflect or at least bring some additional information on the value that a third party (and possibly the market) is giving to the services of the player at stake.

105. Furthermore, the Panel notes that as mentioned above, on 17 July 2008, Real Zaragoza transferred the Player on a loan basis for one football season to SS Lazio. The loan agreement, signed by Real Zaragoza, the Player and SS Lazio contains an option clause providing the Italian club with the right to make the transfer definitive, by exercising the option before 15 May 2009 and paying a corresponding fee. This fee is set at EUR 13 mio. plus VAT, respectively at EUR 14 mio. plus VAT if SS Lazio reaches the UEFA Champions League during the 2008/2009 football season. The fee is further raised to EUR 14 mio. plus VAT and EUR 15 mio. respectively, if the present CAS proceedings ends with an award imposing the Player and Real Zaragoza to pay to Shakhtar Donetsk more than EUR 7 mio.

106. In the same loan agreement the parties have also agreed that an insurance policy against accidents of the Player must be put in place and that the coverage must be, for a case of total disablement of the Player, EUR 13 mio.

107. Against this background, the following calculation can be made: To obtain the services of the Player for a period of 3 years, SS Lazio has declared to be willing to pay an amount of between EUR 13 to 15 mio. plus an average yearly salary of EUR 2,445,600. On its side, Real Zaragoza has shown to be willing to renounce to the services of the Player on a definitive basis for such a fee of between EUR 13 to 15 mio., and to be willing to pay a yearly average fix salary of approx. EUR 1,880,000 (resulting from the salary paid in the season 2007/2008, i.e. approx. EUR 1 mio., and the one agreed for the seasons 2009/2010 and 2010/2011, i.e. approx. EUR 2,320,000 p.a.). Applying the average fee of EUR 14 mio., the yearly average costs for SS Lazio would be of approx. EUR 7,112,267 (resulting from adding the fee of EUR 14 mio. with the salaries over 3 years, i.e. approx. EUR 7,336,800, for an interim total of EUR 21,336,800 and thereafter divided by three, i.e. the number of the seasons) while those of Real Zaragoza would be approx. EUR 6,546,667 (resulting from adding the fee of EUR 14 mio. with the salaries over 3 years, i.e. EUR 5,640,000, for an interim total of EUR 19,640,000, and thereafter divided by three, i.e. the number of the seasons). In other words, these amounts can be used as an indication of the value of the services of the Player for SS Lazio and for Real Zaragoza, on a yearly basis.

108. As mentioned above, the Player had a valid contract with Shakhtar Donetsk with a remaining duration of 2 years. By applying the total costs of SS Lazio and Real Zaragoza to a period of 2 years, the value is of approx. EUR 14,224,534 and approx. EUR 13,093,334, respectively.

109. Finally, the Panel notes that the loan agreement between SS Lazio and Real Zaragoza, co-signed by the Player, foresees that in the event SS Lazio does not make use of its option right, the Player must return to Real Zaragoza. In the event of a breach of such return obligation, the Player shall pay to Real Zaragoza an indemnity of EUR 22.5 mio.

110. The loan agreement has been signed and concluded by the Player, Real Zaragoza and SS Lazio in relation with the football season 2008/2009, i.e. the last season that was originally covered by the agreement between the Player and Shakhtar Donetsk. It can therefore give an additional, objective indication on the economic value attributed to the services of the Player by two clubs and acknowledged by the Player himself. The Panel, however, is not satisfied that under the specific circumstances of this case, the fact that Real Zaragoza and the Player agreed on a penalty clause of EUR 22.5 mio.

to be paid by the Player in the event of the breach of his contract with Real Zaragoza shall be taken into due consideration when calculating the value of the services of the Player and the amount of the damage suffered by Shakhtar Donetsk. Indeed, while in other circumstances one could possibly consider the amount of such a penalty clause as a valid indicator of the value of the services of a player, in this case the Panel retains from the evidence submitted that the amount of EUR 22.5 has more a deterrent effect than an appreciation nature.

111. Finally, even though the FIFA Regulations do not mention this criterion explicitly, as in any situation where a party requests compensation for damages, the judging authority has also to consider that any injured party has the obligation to take reasonable steps to mitigate the effects and loss related to his or her damage. This well-recognized principle is confirmed by art. 44 para. 1 of the Swiss Code of Obligations which states that a judge may reduce or completely deny any liability for damages if circumstances for which the injured party bears the responsibility have aggravated the damage.

112. CAS panels have admitted this, in particular in cases where it was the club that had terminated a contract without just cause. So it was recognised that a player has to make reasonable efforts to seek other employment possibilities and, in the event he finds a new club, the damage has to be reduced for the amount the player was able to earn elsewhere.

113. The Panel agrees that an injured party has the obligation to try to mitigate the damages he/she is suffering. The Panel observes, however, that this obligation should not apply only to players when they are suffering for an unjustified termination by a club, but also to clubs that are claiming compensation for the damage caused by an unjustified termination by a player. So for instance the club will have to take reasonable measures to find a replacement to the player and cannot simply lay back and claim at a later stage that it did not have enough players for that specific role. Also, the club has to find a replacement which is from a sporting and an economical point of view reasonable.

114. Where the injured party has not or not fully complied with the duty to mitigate the damages, the judging authority will, as mentioned, consider this and possibly reduce the amount due for compensation. When deciding on such a potential reduction, the judging authority will have a wide discretionary power to decide on the appropriate amount, taking into consideration the specific circumstances of the case and the responsibilities of both the parties.

115. In the present case, upon due consideration of all the evidence submitted, the Panel is not satisfied that Shakhtar Donetsk can be reproached for having failed to take reasonable steps to mitigate the damage. This does not imply, however, that the replacement costs claimed by Shakhtar Donetsk are automatically accepted as part of the damage suffered by the club. This issue will be handled separately, below.

3.3.3. Lost Earnings: The Missed Transfer Fees

116. It is generally recognised that the loss of earnings (*lucrum cessans*) is a possible part of the damage caused through an unjustified termination of an employment agreement. In particular, in the event of an unjustified termination by a player, the issue to be answered is whether the club has suffered a loss of profits. While some of such profits may be easy to determine, for instance if, because of the termination, the club has to pay a penalty to a sponsor, some other may be more difficult to establish.

117. Specifically, the Panel is aware of the criticism raised by some authors and by some other CAS panels against the possibility of considering as a part of the damage to be compensated by a player, the claim of his former club for the opportunity to receive a transfer fee that has gone lost because of the premature termination of the employment contract. Indeed, whether losing a mere chance to achieve a transfer can

be considered as being itself damage, is debatable, but the correct handling of the issue is straightforward: the loss of a possible transfer fee can be considered a compensable damage head if the usual conditions are met, i.e. in particular if between the breach or the unjustified termination of the agreement and the lost opportunity to realize a certain profit there is the necessary logical nexus.

118. One may take into consideration for instance whether an offer made by a third party was accepted or not by the original club and/or by the player, but the transfer finally failed because of the unjustified departure of the player to another club.

119. On the other side, to avoid any over-compensation, if a club will claim—and receive—compensation for a lost transfer fee, it will hardly be in position to claim additionally also the value of the services lost for the remaining duration of the agreement: would have the club transferred the player, it would have had the transfer fee, but not the services of the player any longer.

120. Therefore, as described above, third parties' offers may be relevant within the evaluation of the amount of the damage suffered by the abandoned club in two possible ways: first, such offers can provide important information on the value of the services of the player, and a panel shall take into consideration a third party good faith offer made to the club, as an additional element to assess the value of the services of the player; second, a loss of a transfer fee may or may not be a compensable damage head, depending on whether the club is in position to prove that the conditions to claim compensation of such a loss of profits are met, including in particular the logical nexus between the termination and the claimed damage.

121. In the present matter the Panel notes that on 1 June 2007, the Italian club U.S. Città di Palermo confirmed to Shakhtar Donetsk its interest for the Player and the fact that it was willing to pay a transfer fee of USD 7 mio. Shakhtar Donetsk turned this offer down. For the above reasons the Panel is of the view that Real Zaragoza is wrong in stating that the offer made by the club U.S. Città di Palermo on 1 June 2007 cannot be taken into any consideration as Shakhtar Donetsk turned it down. Even admitting that under the present specific circumstances no direct damage was suffered by Shakhtar Donetsk because of a potential but never concretized transfer, the Panel, for the abovementioned reasons, will take such offer into due consideration as an additional element to establish the value of the services of the Player and the loss caused by the Player to Shakhtar Donetsk through the premature termination of his contract. At the same time, based on the specific circumstances of this case, the Panel is satisfied that Shakhtar Donetsk is not in position to claim the amount of USD 7 mio. as compensable loss of profits.

3.3.4. Interim Conclusion

122. Considering the total value of the services of the Player expressed by SS Lazio and Real Zaragoza, the Panel concludes that the services of the Player had, for a remaining duration of 2 years, a value of between approx. EUR 14,224,534 and approx. EUR 13,093,334, respectively. The offer submitted by US Palermo (USD 7 mio.) does not correspond to an additional amount of lost profit, and does not provide compelling reasons to revise the above calculations.

123. Further, because of the termination of the contract Shakhtar Donetsk will actually not have to pay any salary more to the Player, so that the corresponding amount corresponds much more to saved expenses than to damage. Therefore, to simply equalize the amount of salaries to be paid by the former club to the damage suffered by the same club is not what art. 17 para. 1 of the FIFA Regulations asks the judging body to do and would deprive the compensation foreseen under art. 17 of the FIFA Regulations of its meaning.

124. From the above-mentioned amounts one shall therefore deduct the salaries that Shakhtar Donetsk is no more obligated to pay to the Player for the same remaining

duration of the contract, i.e. EUR 2.4 mio. (by multiplying the yearly salary of Shakhtar Donetsk of EUR 1.2 mio. by two), so that a first interim amount corresponds to a value of between approx. EUR 11,824,534 and EUR 10,693,334.

125. Finally, for the reasons set forth above, the Panel does not retain as relevant for the calculation of the compensation to Shakhtar Donetsk the fact that Real Zaragoza and the Player agreed on an indemnity amount of EUR 22.5 mio. to be paid by the Player in the event of unjustified termination.

III.4. The Fees and Expenses Paid or Incurred by the Former Club

126. According to art. 17 FIFA Regulations the amount of fees and expenses paid or incurred by the former club, and in particular those expenses made to obtain the services of the player, is an additional objective element that must be taken in consideration. Art. 17 para. 1 requires those expenses to be amortised over the whole term of the contract. This, independently on whether the club—because of any applicable accounting rule—has amortized the expenditures in such a linear way or not.

127. In the present matter, the DRC has recognised the fee paid by Shakhtar Donetsk to the club of Brescia, i.e. EUR 8 mio. as being such a kind of expenses. The Panel agrees and shares also the calculation made in the Appealed Decision according to which such fee was to be amortised in accordance with art. 17 FIFA Regulations over a period of 5 years, i.e. the entire contract period. Therefore, the non-amortised part of the transfer fee is equal to 2/5 of EUR 8 mio, i.e. EUR 3.2 mio.

128. The DRC refused to take into consideration as expenses the amount allegedly paid by Shakhtar Donetsk as solidarity contributions. The Panel concurs, because based on the FIFA Regulations Shakhtar Donetsk had the right to deduct such payments from the transfer fee due to the club of Brescia. If it did not do so, it was because of its own decision or of the contractual arrangements it entered into with the club of Brescia, respectively.

129. Shakhtar Donetsk has further claimed that payments made to some agents had to be considered as expenses as well. In general, payments to agents can be considered as being part of the costs incurred by a club in order to obtain the services of a player.

130. However, in the present matter, the Panel shares the view of the DRC on this point and considers that Shakhtar Donetsk was not able to convince the Panel that such payments were linked to the transfer of the Player or, at least, that the final financial burden of such payments, made by a company called Medco, has been taken by Shakhtar Donetsk.

131. As no other charges, fees, expenses have been submitted, the Panel will consider, when establishing the amount of the non-amortised fees and expenses, only the amount of EUR 3.2 mio. of the non-amortised transfer fee paid originally to Brescia Calcio. However, since in the present case the Panel was able to calculate the value of the lost services of the Player at the moment of the breach and on the basis of convincing evidence, and taking into consideration that within such value of the lost services the value of the fees to acquire such services has been incorporated, there is no reason to add to such value the amount of the non-amortized fees of Shakhtar Donetsk.

132. The issues relating to the expenses incurred by Shakhtar Donetsk in connection with the hiring of new players after and because of the departure of the Player will be discussed below.

III.5. Extra Replacement Costs

133. As mentioned above, the criteria listed in art. 17 para. 1 FIFA Regulations are nonexclusive. Accordingly, a panel is called to examine whether in the concrete

dispute there are any other objective criteria to be taken into consideration when assessing the amount of compensation due under art. 17 para. 1 FIFA Regulations.

134. Among such additional objective criteria the question arises whether the expenses that a club incurs to replace a player that has left prematurely shall be considered.

135. In general, one will note that some replacement costs would arise in any event, i.e. after an ordinary expiry of an agreement same as upon a premature termination. This is the case for instance in relation with ordinary expenses for scouting services. Swiss jurisprudence in employment matters recognises for instance a claim for replacement costs where the employer had extra costs.

136. Further, in the event a club pays a transfer fee to a third party to obtain the services of a new player, the value of such fee is in principle the transfer of that new player. Therefore, in order to claim that fee, or part of it, as part of the compensation due by the player that had previously breached the contract, the club should be able to prove several factual elements. It would have for instance to prove that the new player was hired in substitution of the other player, which requires not only that the players are playing in more or less the same position on the pitch (e.g. it is hard to prove that a forward would substitute a goalkeeper or a defender), but also that the club decided to hire the new player because of the termination by the other player. The Panel is well aware that since clubs are transferring players basically during each transfer window, this second requirement will normally not be proven easily, but nevertheless it is the club that has the burden to prove such factual circumstances if it wishes to have those expenses by compensated by the "old" player. Furthermore, the club will be asked to prove that there is a link between the amount of the transfer fee paid for the new player and the premature termination by the other player. This will possibly be the case for a part of the fee if the club is able to determine that it had to raise the fee for instance in order to anticipate the transfer, because of the gap left by the other player, or if the club is entering a loan agreement on a temporary basis only for the purposes of filling the gap caused by the termination of the player.

137. In the present matter, Shakhtar Donetsk has claimed that to replace the Player it had to hire on a urgent basis the player Nery Alberto Castillo and pay a transfer fee of EUR 20 mio.

138. The Panel is aware that the player Castillo is, similarly as the Player, a midfielder. However, beside this, Shakhtar Donetsk was not able to convince the Panel that the transfer of the player Castillo and the payments made for this transfer were linked to the gap left by the Player or that the costs of hiring the player Castillo have been somehow increased by the termination of the Player.

139. Against the above background, the Panel is of the view that it is appropriate not to consider the costs caused by the transfer of the player Castillo when assessing the compensation due to Shakhtar Donetsk.

III.6. Further Expenditures

140. The Panel comes now to the analysis of whether a club would be entitled to claim that the amount invested in the training of a player must be taken into consideration when assessing the compensation under art. 17 para. 1 FIFA Regulations.

141. The FIFA Regulations have clarified indeed that training compensation in the meaning of art. 20 and Annex 4 and compensation for breach/premature termination under art. 17 of the FIFA Regulations are two different subjects and that there is no prejudicial effect of any training compensation, possibly due to the club in accordance with art. 20 and Annex 4 of the FIFA Regulations, on the compensation due under art. 17 para. 1. Indeed, art. 1 para. 2 of Annex 4 foresees that the obligation to pay training compensation "is without prejudice to any obligation to pay compensation for breach of contract."

142. However, whether or not in the event of an unjustified termination by a player a club will have a right to claim compensation on the basis of art. 17 para. 1 and para. 2 and the new club will also be obliged, if the applicable conditions are met, to pay in addition training compensation on the basis of art. 20 and Annex 4 of the FIFA Regulations, as stated by the FIFA Commentary to the same provision, is an issue that does not need to be answered here, for the following reasons.
143. In the present matter, the Panel is appreciative that Shakhtar Donetsk did not seek to "build up" fictive figures and has not submitted having made any particular investments on the training or formation of the Player that the Panel would need to take into consideration when assessing the compensation due by the Player. For these reasons, the Panel does not have to take account of any further investments in determining the level of compensation owed to Shakhtar Donetsk in application of art. 17 para. 1 FIFA Regulations.

III.7. The "Law of the Country Concerned"

144. As mentioned above, art. 17 para. 1 of the FIFA Regulations asks the judging body to take into due consideration the law of the country concerned. The purpose of this is to make sure that any outcome, which the judging body will reach, shall somehow take into consideration any special aspect of the concerned local law. The law of the country concerned is the law governing the employment relationship between the player and his former club, i.e. normally the law with which the dispute at stake has the closest connection. This will be under ordinary circumstances the law of the country of the club of which the employment contract has been breached or terminated, respectively. To apply instead of such governing law automatically Swiss law as being the law applicable "by default," would mean to possibly overlook the corrective influence that the "law of the country concerned" shall have.
145. The fact that the law of the country concerned is the one of the country of the club, of which the employment contract has been breached or terminated, is confirmed in the Commentary to the FIFA Regulations published by FIFA itself. Commenting on art. 17 para. 1 FIFA confirms that the provision is referring to the law of the country "where the club is domiciled." Further, when commenting on the scope of the Regulations, and on art. 1 para. 2 in particular, FIFA namely states in connection with national regulations that "the associations shall provide for appropriate means to protect contractual stability, which is one of the fundamental principles on which the Regulations are based. The associations are, however, free to establish in which way this obligation has to be complied with, since the various principles outlined in para. 3b) are to be considered as a strong recommendation, i.e. every association is allowed to include the principles it deems necessary and appropriate for its own football system in order to reflect the particular needs of the country concerned."
146. Therefore, the law of the country of the club of which the employment relationship is at stake has to be considered by the judging authority while it is assessing the amount of the compensation due under art. 17 par. 1 of the FIFA Regulations. Depending on the content of the relevant law, such corrective influence may be in favour of the player, and diminish the compensation due to his former club, or in favour of the club, and lead to an increase of the compensation.
147. In the present matter, after review of all the submissions made and the evidence produced by the parties, the Panel is of the opinion that neither of the parties have submitted to the Panel any compelling legal arguments according to which a national law could have an effect on the calculation of the compensation due, nor have they

specified in particular any arguments of Ukrainian (or of Swiss) law which—within the meaning of the criterion—should be taken into due consideration by the Panel.

148. For these reasons, the Panel concludes that it is not in position to take this criterion into due consideration.

III.8. Additional Objective Criteria

149. Following the requirements of art. 17 FIFA Regulations the Panel comes now to examine whether there are other objective elements to consider when determining the level of the compensation due to Shakhtar Donetsk.

150. Such elements could be for instance the damage incurred by a club, which—because of the premature termination—is not any longer in the position to fulfil some obligations towards a third party, like a sponsor or an event organiser to whom the presence of the player was contractually warranted. Of course, it would be up to the club to prove the link between the damage suffered and the breach of the contract by the player.

151. However, in the present matter, Shakhtar Donetsk did not submit that it had suffered any particular additional damage because of the premature termination of the contract by the Player, so that the Panel does not have to take account of any such additional damages when assessing the compensation to be paid to Shakhtar Donetsk under art. 17 para. 1 FIFA Regulations.

III.9. The Specificity of the Sport

3.9.1. Sport Specificity in General

152. Sport, similarly to other aspects of social life, has an own specific character and nature and plays an own, important role in our society. This rather simple consideration has found an important confirmation in December 2000 in the European Council's Declaration on the specific characteristics of sport and its social function in Europe (the "Nice Declaration"), then for instance in the Independent European Sport Review, and recently in the White Paper on Sport and the Lisbon Treaty of the European Union, which provides explicitly that the European Union "shall contribute to the promotion of European sporting issues, while taking account of the specific nature of sport, its structures based on voluntary activity and its social and educational function."

153. Similarly as for the criterion of the "law of the country concerned," the judging body has to take into due consideration the specific nature and needs of sport when assessing the circumstances of the dispute at stake, so to arrive to a solution which takes into reasonable account not only the interests of player and club but, more broadly, those of the whole football community.

154. CAS has confirmed this latter, broad approach recently:

"The Panel considers that the specificity of the sport must obviously take the independent nature of the sport, the free movement of the players (cf. CAS 2007/A/1298, 1299 & 1300, no. 131 ff.) but also the football as a market, into consideration. In the Panel's view, the specificity of the sport does not conflict with the principle of contractual stability and the right of the injured party to be compensated for all the loss and damage incurred as a consequence of the other party's breach. This rule is valid whether the breach is by a player or a club. The criterion of specificity of sport shall be used by a panel to verify that the solution reached is just and fair not only under a strict civil (or common) law point of view, but also taking into due consideration the specific nature and needs of the football world (and of parties being stakeholders in such world) and reaching therefore a decision which can be recognised as being an appropriate evaluation of the interests at stake, and does so fit in the landscape of international football.

Therefore, when weighing the specificity of the sport a panel may consider the specific nature of damages that a breach by a player of his employment contract with a club may cause. In particular, a panel may consider that in the world of football, players are the main asset of a club, both in terms of their sporting value in the service for the teams for which they play, but also from a rather economic view, like for instance in relation of their valuation in the balance sheet of a certain club, if any, their value for merchandising activities or the possible gain which can be made in the event of their transfer to another club. Taking into consideration all of the above, the asset comprised by a player is obviously an aspect which cannot be fully ignored when considering the compensation to be awarded for a breach of contract by a player (cf. CAS 2005/A/902 & 903, no. 122 ff.; more restrictive CAS 2007/A/1298, 1299 & 1300, no. 120 ff.)."

155. Based on this criterion, the judging body shall therefore assess the amount of compensation payable by a party under art. 17 para. 1 of the FIFA Regulations keeping duly in mind that the dispute is taking place in the somehow special world of sport. In other words, the judging body shall aim at reaching a solution that is legally correct, and that is also appropriate upon an analysis of the specific nature of the sporting interests at stake, the sporting circumstances and the sporting issues inherent to the single case.

156. Taking into account the specific circumstances and the course of the events, a panel may consider, as guidance, also that under Swiss law (art. 337c para. 3 and art. 337d para. 1 of the Swiss Code of Obligations), a judging authority is allowed to grant a certain "special indemnity" to the employee, in the event of an unjustified termination by the employer, and to the employer, in the event of an unjustified termination by the employee. In "ordinary" employment law the employee is normally considered the weak party, and it is therefore understandable that such "special indemnity" is potentially much higher in the event of an unjustified termination by an employer than by an employee. However, professional football is a special sector, and the Panel considers that it may be often wrong to treat the players as being the weak party *per se*. Much more, the specific circumstances of a case may lead a panel to increase the amount of the compensation, by letting itself inspire, *mutatis mutandis*, by the concept of fair and just indemnity foreseen in the art. 337c para. 3 and art. 337d para. 1 Swiss Code of Obligations, without applying the strict quantitative limits foreseen in such rules. However, it must be acknowledged that under ordinary circumstances any compensation based on the specificity of sport is limited as to its scope of application, since the concept serves only the purpose to verify the solution for compensation reached otherwise (N 154). It follows from this that the amount of damages that may be awarded on the basis of the specificity of sport is clearly subordinated in relation to the other compensable damage heads. In particular, the criteria is not meant to award additional amounts where the facts and circumstances of the case have been taken already sufficiently into account when calculating a specific damage head. Furthermore, the element of the specificity of sport may not be misused to undermine the purpose of art. 17 para. 1, i.e. to determine the amount necessary to put the injured party in the position that the same party would have had if the contract was performed properly (see N 86). In light of this the assessment of damages that are punitive in character is particularly sensitive. Finally, it follows from this that no compensation is possible for facts and circumstances that are clearly not compensable otherwise (e.g. lost chances, see N 116 et seq.).

157. Whether in the present case such an additional indemnity shall be granted to Shakhtar Donetsk, will be discussed below.

3.9.2. The Time Remaining on the Existing Contract Up To a Maximum of 5 Years

158. One of the elements that concretize the concept of sport specificity is the issue about the remaining time of the contract that has been breached or terminated, respectively.

159. Art. 17 para. 1 FIFA Regulations requires the judging body to duly consider the duration of the employment relationship that has been breached or terminated, and in particular to consider the remaining time of such relationship. The rationale is easy to understand:
It is criticisable to breach or terminate prematurely a contract. But even more criticisable is to breach an agreement, which is supposed to still have a substantial duration, as the other party had reason to believe and count on the continuation of the relationship.
160. The Panel observes that the Player terminated the agreement with Shakhtar Donetsk after three football seasons, with two more football seasons being part of the agreement.
161. The remaining time under the existing contract between Shakhtar Donetsk and the Player was therefore important, as two seasons out of five are a substantial period of time. The situation would have been different if the Player had just a few months of valid contract to serve.
162. Accordingly, the Panel will take into due consideration as an element to establish the amount of the compensation due by the Player that he terminated his agreement with Shakhtar Donetsk with two seasons still remaining under the agreement.

3.9.3. Does The Contractual Breach Fall Within the Protected Period?

163. It is debatable, if another element that concretizes the concept of sport specificity is the issue about whether the breach or the termination of the contract did take place during or outside of the so-called "Protected Period."
164. In the chapter "Definitions" of the FIFA Regulations "Protected Period" is defined as "a period of three entire Seasons or 3 years, whichever comes first, following the entry into force of a contract, if such contract was concluded prior to the 28th birthday of the Professional, or to a period of two entire Seasons or 2 years, whichever comes first, following the entry into force of a contract, if such contract was concluded after the 28th birthday of the Professional."
165. It is true that breaches and terminations within the Protected Period are considered a particular serious form of unlawful behaviour. It is for that reason that art. 17 para. 3 to 5 provide in such cases for proportionate sporting sanctions to be applied to players, clubs or agents. However, it is an open issue whether the breach within a protected period may also be taken into account when assessing the compensation due, since the same facts and circumstances would possibly be taken into account twice by the judging body to the detriment of the player. In the present matter, the Panel notes that the Player, born on 10 June 1980, was 24 years old when he concluded the contract with Shakhtar Donetsk, i.e. on 26 June 2004. Accordingly, in this case the Protected Period is a period of 3 years or of three football seasons, whichever comes first, following the entry into force of the contract.
166. It has remained undisputed among the parties that the termination of the contract with Shakhtar Donetsk has been made by the Player upon expiry of the Protected Period applicable to him.
167. Accordingly, the Panel when establishing the compensation due to Shakhtar Donetsk will consider that the unilateral, premature termination occurred outside of the Protected Period, so that the compensation due by the Player shall not be increased on the basis of this particular criterion.

3.9.4. The Status and the Behaviour of the Player

168. An additional and important element of sport specificity that must be taken into due consideration when establishing the compensation due in the event of breach or undue termination is the behaviour and the status of the parties involved, with a particular attention to the behaviour of the party that did not respect the contractual obligations in place.

169. In the Appealed Decision, the DRC has considered as a penalising element of "sport specificity" the fact that the Player by accepting an increase of his salary on 1 April 2007 and deciding shortly afterwards to leave Shakhtar Donetsk has offended the good faith of the club. Also, DRC observed that the Player left the club without indicating in advance his wish to look for other employment opportunities.
170. The Panel shares to some extent the criticism expressed by the DRC about the behaviour of the Player. The Panel is indeed not satisfied that the reasons submitted by the Player and his representative can be accepted as full justifications of the Player's behaviour.
171. The Panel wishes, however, to add the following remarks as with regard to the Player's behaviour:
172. On the one side, against the Player, the Panel notes that the Player joined Shakhtar Donetsk in summer 2004, coming from a rather small Italian club, Brescia. After two seasons with Shakhtar Donetsk the Player became during the 2006/2007 season captain of the team and was elected also best player. This speaks in favour of a successful club career. Even accepting that the Player may have not decided to leave Shakhtar Donetsk for personal gain reasons, it remains that the Player left the club just a few weeks before the start of the qualifying rounds of a competition which is obviously very important to Shakhtar Donetsk, i.e. the UEFA Champions League.
173. The Panel will take the above into due consideration as an element to establish the value of the loss caused by the Player to Shakhtar Donetsk through the premature termination of his agreement
174. On the other side, in favour of the Player, the Panel is not satisfied that the fact that the Player was playing in the central midfield of Shakhtar Donetsk does make his loss more critical, in sporting terms, than the loss of another member of the team. The Panel believes that in general it may be possible to consider whether a player in breach or terminating prematurely his contract was a player of the "core team" of the club or not. It is possible that the damage caused to a club by the breach or termination of a player that has hardly played in the precedent season and has mostly not be taken into consideration by the coach for playing matches, is of minor entity than the loss of a top player of the team. These considerations are also reflected in art. 15 of the FIFA Regulations (right to terminate a contract for sporting just cause). The player's position on the pitch, however, does hardly influence the importance of that player for the club and therefore does usually not have an impact on the damage caused and the compensation to be paid, respectively.'

8.4.2.2 Summary

In paragraphs 76–89, the Panel describes and comments on the background of Article 17 of the FIFA transfer regulations in detail.

Coming to the calculation of the compensation, the Panel then reviews the (non-exclusive) criteria in the context of the present case.

The remuneration under existing contract is first indication of the player's value; the remuneration under the new contract may provide an indication on his market value and the motive behind the decision of the player to terminate prematurely the agreement.

However, the player's value is only partially reflected in the remuneration due to him, since a club would—under normal circumstances—have to spend a fee on the (transfer) market to contract the player, whereby economic reality in the world of football is acknowledged. A 'sign on-fee' may also be a relevant indicator in this context.

A possible loan agreement whereby a player is transferred to a third party (club) can give additional, objective information on the player's economic value.

A club will have to take reasonable measures to find a replacement to the player and cannot simply lay back and claim at a later stage that it did not have enough players for that specific role. Also, the club has to find a replacement which is from a sporting and an economic point of view reasonable.

Regarding possible extra replacement costs, the club would have for instance to prove that the new player was hired in substitution of the other player, which requires that the players are playing in more or less the same position on the pitch (for example, it is hard to prove that a forward would substitute a goalkeeper or a defender).

Possible lost earnings as a result of missed third parties' offers (transfer fees) can provide important information on a player's value.

Training compensation and compensation for termination of contract are two different subjects and there is no prejudicial effect of any training compensation on compensation under Article 17 of the FIFA transfer regulations.

An additional objective element to determine compensation might be for example that a club is not any longer in the position to fulfill some obligations Towards a third party, like a sponsor or an event organiser to whom the presence of the player was contractually warranted. For example, the participation of a top player (if not injured) could be a contractual condition in relation to a friendly or practice match or tournament, which would attract a larger crowd and considerably more TV income and gate money for that event.

Dealing with 'sport specificity,' the Panel explicitly refers to EU documents/ instruments like the Nice Declaration, the White Paper on Sport and the Lisbon Treaty, and, remarkably also to the Independent European Sport Review, which has the mere status of a private report which was commissioned by the pan-European football governing body UEFA. Similarly as for the criterion of the 'law of the country concerned,' the specific nature and needs of sport have to be taken into consideration in order that the dispute is taking place in the somehow special world of sport, and that *in casu* the interests of the whole football community be respected. Professional football is a special sector, and it may be often wrong to treat the players as being the weak party *per se,* the Panel considers. In the Panel's view, one of the elements that concretise the concept of sport specificity is the issue about the remaining time of the contract. Now that the Panel itself observes that the rationale is easy to understand since it is criticisable to terminate prematurely a contract and even more a contract of still substantial duration, it is very much questionable whether this is a manifestation of 'sport specificity'! In the Panel's opinion, it is debatable whether another element that concretises the concept of sport specificity which it does, i.e., the 'protected period' issue, is relevant. Terminations within this period are considered a particular serious form of unlawful behaviour which would lead to sporting sanctions under Article 17 of the FIFA transfer regulations, but taking this into account also when determining compensation, in fact would mean that the party concerned is 'punished' twice. Finally, the Panel discusses the status and behaviour of the player as an additional and important element of sport specificity. For example, if a player is the season captain or other 'core team' player (and possibly was elected also best player additionally) and leaves the club a few weeks before the start of a very important competition like the UEFA Champions League, this might be taken into consideration. The conclusion must be that the remaining time of a contract is not 'sport specific,' that the 'protection period' yes or no issue is 'sport specific,' but not relevant, and, thirdly, that behaviour offending 'good faith' in specific circumstances might be 'sport specific' and a relevant element to be considered.

8.4.3 De Sanctis *Case*

On 8 June 2007 the player De Sanctis unilaterally terminated his contract with Udinese (Italy), by using the Webster ruling. He signed a 4-year contract with Sevilla FC (Spain), worth €1,381,578.94 a season (€1.05 million in net). Udinese submitted the case to the FIFA Dispute Resolution Chamber as Udinese and De Sanctis failed to agree the compensation. On 10 December 2009 the DRC awarded Udinese liable to receive €3,933,134 from De Sanctis, quoting Matuzalém's case as legal reference. The case was then appealed to the Court of Arbitration for Sport and on 1 March 2011 the CAS awarded Udinese a sum of € 2,250,055.[13]

8.4.3.1 The Ratio Decidendi of the Award

The interpretation and application of Article 17 of the FIFA transfer regulations to the present case are set out in Section IV.6 ('The merits') (in particular, paragraphs 60–103) of the CAS award. Which, in view of their importance are reproduced *in extenso* as follows:

> 60. The Panel notes that there have been a number of previous awards delivered by CAS panels on this very issue (Webster, Matuzalem, El-Hadary and Pyunik, to mention a few where the breach is on the part of the player). The Panel also notes both the different facts and outcomes in these awards, and the views of those panels in relation to the method of calculation, i.e. that *"each of the factors listed in Article 17 is relevant, but that any of them may be decisive on the facts of a particular case ... Article 17.1 does not require the judging authority ... to necessarily evaluate and give weight to any and all of the factors listed therein"* (paras 201 and 202 of El-Hadary); *"Article 17.1 includes a broad range of criteria ... some of which may be appropriate to apply to one category of case and inappropriate to apply in another."* (para 135 [70] of Webster); and *"the task for the body assessing the entity of the compensation*

[13] CAS 2010/A/2145, 2146 & 2147.

due is therefore to verify and analyze as carefully as possible all the elements above and take them in due consideration." (para 77 of Matuzalem).

61. The Panel also notes the "positive interest" principle that was referred to in Matuzalem and equally applied in El-Hadary, as such a panel *"will aim at determining an amount which shall basically put the injured party in the position that the same party would have had if the contract was performed properly"* (para 86 of Matuzalem).
62. As such, it is this Panel's role to consider each of the criteria within Art. 17.1 of the Regulations and indeed any other objective criteria in the light of the specific facts of this case and to determine how much weight, if any at all, to apply to each in determining the amount of compensation due in this particular case. In addition, the onus is on the parties to provide the evidence for the panel to carry out this task. The Panel notes the facts involved in the previous awards, and suspects that those in cases to follow, are and will be different from each other, but that the role of a panel remains the same, to apply all of the Art. 17.1 criteria and any other objective criteria to the specific facts and determine which are relevant and which are not and to ensure *"the calculation made … shall be not only just and fair, but also transparent and comprehensible."* (para 89 of Matuzalem) with a view to putting the injured party in the position it would have been in had no breach occurred.
(c) Is there a liquidated damages clause?
63. The Panel noted that it is to look at the Old Contract first, to see if the parties have agreed a contractual remedy for the breach of the Old Contract. Such a clause is often referred to as a penalty clause or a liquidated damages clause.
64. In this instance, there was nothing in the Old Contract, but the Panel did note that there was one in the New Contract. It is only the Old Contract that it is relevant for this question; such a clause in the New Contract may assist a judging authority if it follows Matuzalem principles in seeking to assess the value of the player's services.
65. With no such clause in the Old Contract, the Panel returns to Art. 17.1 of the Regulations for the criteria to follow.

(d) How should the *"objective criteria"* of Art. 17 of the Regulations be applied?

66. The Panel notes that Article 17.1 of the Regulations states: *"These criteria shall include, in particular, the remuneration and other benefits due to the player under the existing contract and/or the new contract, the time remaining on the existing contract up to a maximum of five years, the fees and expenses paid or incurred by the Former Club (amortised over the term of the contract) and whether the contractual breach falls within a Protected Period."* It is clear to this Panel that the list is not intended to be definitive. Indeed, if the positive interest principle is to be applied, then other objective criteria can and should be considered, such as loss of a possible transfer and replacement costs, as were considered in the Matuzalem and El-Hadary cases.
However, the Panel also notes that for compensation to be due in such instances there must be the logical nexus between the breach and loss claimed. The loss of a transfer fee was awarded in El-Hadary, where the new club and the old club had been directly negotiating a fee at the time of the breach ("*it appears to the Panel that, as a consequence of the early termination of the Player's employment contract, Al-Ahly was deprived of the opportunity to obtain a transfer fee of USD 600,000,*" para 221 of El-Hadary). The Panel also noted that within FIFA's commentary on the Regulations, such matters as whether a collective bargaining agreement is in force could be considered.
67. In the jurisprudence available and referred to by the parties in their submissions and during the hearing, the Panel notes that previous panels did not feel bound to consider the Art. 17.1 criteria in a strict order, but rather consider the most appropriate to the facts of their case first. Udinese in both its submissions and at the hearing provided the

Panel with details of the replacement costs it had incurred, it alleged, as a direct result of the Player's breach. Whilst replacement costs are not referred to in Art. 17.1 of the Regulations, these have been considered in previous CAS jurisprudence (such as Matuzalem, El-Hadary and *CAS 2009/A/1856 Club X vs. A* and *CAS 2009/A/1857 A vs. Club X*) in order to establish the "positive interest," and it thus seems a logical place to start—to see what loss the injured party has actually suffered as a result of the breach, before comparing this with the theoretical calculations a judging authority is directed to make under Art. 17.1 of the Regulations; as stated by the panel in El-Hadary (para 200) "*... Article 17.1 of the FIFA Transfer Regulations is an attempt by FIFA to give some directions on how to calculate the damage suffered.*" The Panel also notes that in these type of cases, which have different facts from others and will have been through the DRC, a panel has the benefit of hindsight or the benefit of seeing how the breach of contract has actually effected the injured party, as the CAS panel may be looking at a breach that happened many years ago. Indeed, in Matuzalem, the panel was able to derive a lot of information from that player's next contracts.

68. The Panel notes that in the event that a player waits until the last match of a season, at the end of the protected period and then hands in his notice within 15 days thereof, he avoids the sporting sanctions as set out in Art. 17.3 of the Regulations. However, it then leaves the old club in the position where it is obliged to mitigate its position, but in a short period of time. As detailed in para 111 of Matuzalem, "*... any injured party has the obligation to take reasonable steps to mitigate the effects and loss related to his or her damage. This well-recognized principle is confirmed by art. 44 para. 1 of the Swiss Code of Obligations, which states that a judge may reduce or completely deny any liability for damages if circumstances for which the injured party bears the responsibility have aggravated the damage.*"
69. Whilst there is an obligation on the old club to mitigate its position, how this is done in practice will vary from case to case. In some instances the breach is not in accordance with the notice "window" detailed in Art. 17.3 of the Regulations and the old club may find it impossible to mitigate immediately, as they are outside a transfer window; in other cases clubs may do nothing, when they could have or may seek to bring in a replacement player of greater value than the player in breach—in all instances it is the judging authorities' role to review the particular facts of the case concerned, with the benefit of being able to look back at what actually was done and how that worked out in the specific case. What is normal in football today is the shortage of time available for the injured party in which to make replacements.
70. In this case, Udinese had argued before the DRC that the breach had resulted in certain losses such as sponsorship, ticket sales and the like, but the DRC had rejected these in the Appealed Decision and the claims were not made to the CAS. However, Udinese submitted and provided evidence to support the claim that they had to bring back one of their squad who was on loan to Rimini as a replacement. That player, H., was subject to a loan agreement between Udinese and Rimini, under which Rimini could acquire his transfer for the sum of EUR 1,200,000. During the hearing, the representative of Udinese confirmed that Rimini had exercised its option prior to Udinese's receipt of the Player's Notice and this evidence has not been contradicted by the other parties. Udinese had a right to counter offer, by which it could reject Rimini's transfer, waive the sum of EUR 1,200,000 and take the player back, but that required an additional payment to Rimini of EUR 250,000, which they duly made and paid, as a result of the Player's breach.
71. Udinese also submitted that it felt H. would be too inexperienced to be the immediate direct replacement for the Player. He was 22 years old in that moment and he had never played in Serie A or in another primary European league, whereas the Player was 30 years old, the regular starting keeper in a Serie A team for many years, with

international experience. As such, they also brought in an experienced goalkeeper, C., aged 37, on a free transfer. The representative of Udinese explained at the hearing that their tactic was to have the older, experienced goalkeeper to be the initial replacement for the Player, whilst continuing to train and develop the younger one, so he could takeover during the next 3 years, the unexpired period of the Player's Old Contract. The Panel noted Udinese acted quickly to bring these players in, both before the Player had signed with Sevilla, but after the receipt of the Player's Notice. The Panel also noted the specific position of the Player—a goalkeeper. Only one is on the pitch at anytime for a club and they tend to be rotated less. Outfield players can often play in different positions and are easier to replace from a squad.

72. The Panel noted the comments of Sevilla during the hearing, stating that three other goalkeepers had left Udinese at the end of the 2006/2007 season, and, as such, queried whether these two goalkeepers were direct replacements for the Player or whether Udinese would have brought these players back/in anyway. In addition, the Panel noted the submissions of the Player that one player should not be replaced by two new ones. The representative of Udinese at the hearing confirmed their submissions that these two players, H. and C., were brought in specifically as a result of the Player's breach. On balance, the Panel feels that in this instance Udinese had acted reasonably, immediately upon receipt of the Player's Notice, and forgone the transfer fee for H., paid the counter offer fee and then committed itself to H.'s wages for the next 3 years, to fill the gap left by the Player. The Panel also accepts that Udinese had not replaced like with like and further mitigated its position by bringing in the more experienced goalkeeper as the starting replacement for the Player. Ordinarily, replacing one player with two might seem odd, but the Panel considers as reasonable the strategy of Udinese to replace the Player with both the young player, with potential eventually, and the old player, with experience immediately. Udinese therefore committed itself to the additional costs of C.'s salary. The speed in which Udinese acted and the fact that we are dealing here with a goalkeeper and not a midfield player, for example, made it easier for the injured party to make the logical nexus between these replacement costs/loss and the breach, proving that these two new players were hired in direct substitution for the Player; done as a result of the Player's termination of the Old Contract; and Udinese was able to produce copies of the agreements with Rimini, which expressly set out the sums payable to bring H. back and copies of the new players' contracts. In addition, Udinese did bring in other goalkeepers over the remainder of the Old Contract period, just as other goalkeepers went. Using the ability to look back at how things turned out, the Panel can see that Udinese's strategy here worked, as eventually H. replaced C. as first team choice and remained in that position as at the date of the hearing.

73. The Panel notes that Udinese did not directly claim the sums it paid out from the Player and Sevilla, but instead sought to use these sums as a reason for the Panel not to look to deduct any savings Udinese made, by not having to pay the Player's remuneration and benefits under the Old Contract. The Panel felt Udinese was still looking for these sums to be taken into account in the overall scheme of calculating compensation, so the Panel does not consider that taking them into account would constitute an *ultra petita* ruling; in addition, the Panel notes that under Swiss law the *ultra petita* doctrine applies only with reference to a party's motions and not to its reasoning and arguments supporting those motions. Therefore, it accepts that Udinese suffered and awards as compensation, the following replacement costs:Lost transfer fee from Rimini for H. EUR 1,200,000
Additional counter offer fee paid for H. EUR 250,000
Salary of H. (3 years) EUR 1,179,000
Salary of C. (3 years) EUR 1,881,000
Total EUR 4,510,000

74. Whilst the Panel notes Udinese has suffered some direct loss, which it has been able to quantify, the purpose of Art. 17.1 of the Regulations is to lay out some criteria by which a judging authority, be it the DRC or a CAS panel, can look to establish the total loss or damage suffered by the Player's breach. The Panel should look to see if an injured party has in fact suffered more loss than the direct losses; roughly the same; or, indeed, should the injured party have brought in a new player of greater value than the one in breach, whether in fact it should be compensated for all its replacement costs. As stated by the panel in Matuzalem (para 114) "*... the judging authority will have a wide discretionary power to decide on the appropriate amount, taking into consideration the specific circumstances of the case and the responsibilities of both the parties.*" The injured party has a well established duty to mitigate and the level to which this has been done has to be considered by the judging authority. Each case will turn on its own facts, so this Panel will now review these in light of the Art. 17.1 criteria.
75. The Panel also notes the burden of proof is with the injured party, as it requests the compensation for the Player's breach.

Loss of transfer fee

76. The Panel notes the different approaches of previous panels—on the one hand, the Webster case where that panel felt transfer fees were not a possible factor in assessing compensation; whereas, in both Matuzalem and El-Hadary, the panels felt it was possible, if the injured party could provide sufficient evidence.
77. In this case, none of the parties produced any evidence of any offers made or pending for the Player. Udinese did produce the details of three other international goalkeepers that had transferred between clubs over the previous couple of years; however, this was not taken by the Panel as evidence of any loss suffered by Udinese in relation to this Player, more background information to be used in assessing the specificity of sport criterion below.
78. As such, as no party advanced any submissions under this criterion, the Panel did not use it as part of assessing the compensation due to Udinese.

Remuneration and other benefits

79. The Panel notes that this criterion has proved the most contentious to date. The panels in Matuzalem and El-Hadary both sought to calculate the value of the services of the player looking at the amount the injured party, the old club, would have to pay to replace the player. Those panels felt there were two components, the wages of the replacement player and the cost to acquire him. They felt that the amount the new club were willing to pay the player in breach gave the best indication of what a theoretical replacement player would be paid. Those panels then had to look for evidence as to what the old club would have to pay to acquire a replacement player. In El-Hadary, the two clubs had started negotiations as to a transfer fee the new club would pay the old; in Matuzalem, the panel took the evidence from the contracts the new club entered into with a third club. In both instances the remuneration under the old contract was treated as being saved and deducted. This all contrasts with the Webster decision, in which compensation was the remuneration for the unexpired part of the old contract, not the new (as it could be "*potentially punitive*") and that panel did not look at what the old club might have to pay to acquire a replacement player and queried whether the costs of acquiring any player should be amortised beyond the protected period. The protected period being defined in the Regulations as "*a period of three entire seasons or three years, whichever comes first, following the entry into force of a contract, if such contract was concluded prior to the 28th birthday of the Professional, or to a period of two entire Seasons or two years, whichever comes first, following the entry into force of a contract, if such contract was concluded after the 28th birthday of the Professional.*"

80. In this matter, Udinese claimed that the compensation should be the remuneration under the New Contract, for the 3 years that were unexpired on the Old Contract. It felt that any savings made under the Old Contract should not be deducted, as they had been used to acquire the replacement players, H. and C. Udinese did not request the acquisition costs of a replacement player be used in addition to calculate the value of the Player's services, rather submitted that his market value should be awarded as compensation, under the specificity of sport criterion.
81. On the other hand, both Sevilla and the Player submitted that the facts of this case were closer to those in Webster and that the compensation should be limited to the net remuneration payable under the Old Contract, over the 3 year unexpired term, and disregarding other benefits, such as rent and the loyalty bonus (if not reduced further pursuant to their arguments that using the Swiss Code of Obligations any award should be limited to 8 months salary, as a maximum).
82. The Panel has determined that the applicable law in this matter is contained within the Regulations, with Swiss Law applying subsidiarily. The Panel did not believe that there was any gap or *lucuna* within the Regulations that required the Panel to utilise Art. 339c(2) of the Swiss Code of Obligations when assessing any damage under this criterion and further notes Udinese's submission that Art. 17.1 actually directs a judging authority to look at *"the time remaining on the existing contract up to a maximum of five years"* as opposed to placing any maximum limit. As such the Panel rejects the claims of Sevilla and the Player to limit the amount of compensation awarded to a maximum of 8 months salary.
83. The Panel has determined that in this specific case, there are considerable actual damages suffered as a result of the breach. The Panel further notes that it had limited evidence provided to it by the parties in order to attempt to calculate the theoretical calculation of the value of the services of the Player in order to put the injured party, Udinese, back in the position it would have been if there had been no breach by the Player.
84. If the Panel attempted to follow a Matuzalem or El-Hadary type calculation, then it would need to look at the remuneration under the New Contract, submitted as:
Annual salary EUR 331,578
Annual contract premium EUR 1,050,000
Annual total EUR 1,381,578
Three year total EUR 4,144,734
To complete the theoretical calculation, that sum would be less the savings under the Old Contract, but then the Panel would seek to assess the acquisition costs Udinese would have to pay for a replacement goalkeeper by looking at the value of the Player. Quite apart from the fact that Udinese did not actually advance the argument that the Panel should look to calculate the value of the Player's services, as would be requested under the Matuzalem approach, and that both Sevilla and the Player argued the Webster principles should be followed here instead, the Panel were not provided with clear evidence that would enable them carry out this task, in particular what would the acquisition costs of a theoretical replacement player be. During the hearing the Panel were made aware of the amount Napoli paid for the Player, 2 seasons after he left Udinese, i.e. EUR 1,500,000—if Napoli signed him for a 3 year contract, does that place his acquisition value at EUR 500,000 per season? Indeed, the Panel noted Sevilla loaned the Player out to Galatasaray for the 2008/2009 season, for a loan fee of EUR 500,000.
85. The Player at the hearing submitted that he had become a far better player after he left Udinese, so was the transfer fee paid by Napoli something that should be used to compensate Udinese? Would he have received as much remuneration and contract premium in the New Contract by Sevilla if they had paid to acquire him? Is it safe for a judging authority to use a transfer fee paid 2 years after the breach as evidence as to

the amount a replacement player might have cost Udinese at the time of the breach?—a lot can happen in football in 2 years. How much of that transfer fee was down to the Player's *"own efforts, discipline and natural talent"* or from his *"charisma and personal marketing"* (see para 142 of Webster)?; On the other hand, if Napoli paid EUR 1,500,000 for the Player when he was 2 years older, might they have paid more at the time of the breach?

86. Udinese did not produce concrete evidence of any offers for the Player, just the details from a website of some other transfers of goalkeepers over the last few years, where the Panel had no details of those players' salaries, unexpired terms, etc. There was no expert evidence provided. If this was a personal injury claim for damages, one might expect the judging authority to be provided with expert evidence, reports and statements. Here, the Panel was not put in a position by Udinese where it could safely value the services of the Player. In the absence of any concrete evidence with respect to the value of the Player, the Panel cannot apply exactly the same calculation as in Matuzalem and shall use a different calculation method to determine the appropriate compensation, the one which would be the closest to the amount that Udinese would have got or saved if there had been no breach by the Player. By using the value of the replacement costs only rather than the estimated value of the Player, the Panel does not seek to depart from the Matuzalem jurisprudence but wishes to emphasize that there is not just one and only calculation method and that each case must be assessed in the light of the elements and evidence available to each CAS panel.
87. The Panel can still use the remuneration of the Old Contract, as directed by Art. 17.1 of the Regulations when considering the issue of whether Udinese has saved the remuneration that it would have paid the Player. The Panel believes it is correct to deduct these as part of the calculation of compensation, but also to give credit for the actual replacement costs incurred. In this case, keeping the consistent approach (see for example the grossing up in the *CAS 2009/A/1856 and 1857* decision, at paras 196 and 197) of looking at the gross sums (as tax rates differ from country to country and, more basically, in any playing contract, the club's obligation is to pay the whole contract sum, and the tax liability is the player's; for convenience and usually as a result of tax legislation, the club deduct the tax at source and pay it on the player's behalf to the government), Udinese have saved the following:
The yearly salary of the Player EUR 623,000
The yearly loyalty bonus EUR 350,878
The annual rent contribution EUR 9,700
A yearly total EUR 983,578
The total for the 3 years EUR 2,950,734
The Panel determined that the loyalty bonus and the rent should be treated as remuneration, whether they were detailed in the Udinese Contract or an agreement between the same parties, supplemental to the Udinese Contract. The Panel did not agree with Sevilla's submissions that the loyalty bonus *"is effectively an appearance bonus."* If the Player had remained, yet never physically played again, say due to an injury or loss of form, that bonus would still be due. Only the squad bonuses were uncertain and required participation in matches. The Panel very much doubts whether the Player would not have made a claim for the loyalty bonus, had it been Udinese that breached the Old Contract prematurely.
So at this juncture, the Panel has determined to award Udinese as compensation for the Player's breach:
The replacement costs EUR 4,510,000
Less, the savings made EUR 2,950,734
Sub total EUR 1,559,266
Time remaining under the Old Contract

88. The Panel noted that the time remaining under the Old Contract is taken into account when looking at the period for replacement costs, i.e. 3 years of the replacement costs, less 3 years of the savings made.
89. However, the Panel also notes that the Player had concluded 2 years of his 5 years on the Udinese Contract. In certain previous cases, such as Matuzalem, this was dealt with in the specificity of sport and the Panel determined to deal with the same below.

Fees and expenses amortised

90. Udinese had argued before the DRC that the initial fees paid to Juventus Turin should have been amortised over the entire period the Player was under contract with it. In addition, it claimed the agent's fees paid in relation to the Udinese Contract should be amortised over the 5 year period of that contract on a pro rata basis, year by year. In the DRC Decision, it was decided that the fees paid to Juventus Turin had been amortised over the first 5 years of the Player's time with Udinese, but EUR 36,000 was allowed as part of the compensation for the agent's fees.
91. However, Udinese did not appeal the DRC's Decision in regard of the unamortised fees and expenses; the Player and Sevilla both submitted that there was no proof the agent was actually paid; and Udinese confirmed at the hearing that it no longer made any claim in relation to the agent's fees. As such, no party made any claim under this criterion and the Panel therefore determined it had no relevance in assessing the level of compensation due to Udinese.

In or out of the protected period

92. Whilst Udinese had argued before the DRC that the breach occurred within the protected period, this had been disputed by the Player and Sevilla, and the DRC, in the Appealed Decision, determined that the breach was outside of the protected period. As such the arguments were not advanced to the CAS. It was therefore common ground that the breach occurred outside of the protected period.
93. The Panel noted that in certain previous cases, such as Matuzalem, this was dealt with in the specificity of sport criterion and determined to deal with the same below.

(e) Law of Country concerned

94. None of the parties made any submissions on this criterion, despite Art. 17.1 of the Regulations requiring the judging body to consider the law of the country concerned. In this instance, the law would be Italian Law, as it has the closest connection to the injured party, the party in breach and the employment contract itself.
95. The Panel finds this criterion is of no relevance for the calculation of the compensation due in this matter and agrees with the El-Hadary conclusion in para 208, *"that law of the country concerned may be relevant in favour of the player or in favour of the club, or be utterly irrelevant. It is up to the party which believes that such factor could be in its favour to make sufficient assertions in this regards. If it does not, the judging authority will not take that factor into account in order to assess the amount of compensation. In no way does this mean that the judging authority failed to properly evaluate this matter."*

(f) Specificity of Sport

96. The Panel noted it *"should aim at reaching a solution that is legally correct, and that is also appropriate upon an analysis of the specific nature of the sporting interests at stake, the sporting circumstances and the sporting issues inherent to the single case."* (para 155 of Matuzalem and confirmed at para 233 of El-Hadary). The Panel agreed with the jurisprudence set out in previous cases mentioned herein that the specificity of sport is not an additional head of compensation nor a criteria allowing to decide in equity, but a correcting factor which allows the Panel to take into consideration other objective elements which are not envisaged under the other criteria of Art. 17 of the Regulations.

97. In this specific case, Udinese has suffered loss as a result of the Player's breach. Udinese has mitigated its position, in a reasonable way. It did not go out and acquire a more expensive replacement; instead it brought in an experienced, older goalkeeper on a free transfer and brought back a younger goalkeeper with prospects. However, the Panel is not convinced that these direct replacement costs have fully compensated Udinese for the loss it suffered as a result of the breach.
98. At the hearing, Udinese submitted that the market value of the Player was evidenced by the liquidated damages clause in the New Contract, a sum of EUR 15,000,000. However, Udinese also conceded that this was set at an artificially high level and that a more realistic level would be a third or half of this sum.. So should the Panel look at the value set in the New Contract, should the Player have looked to breach that, i.e. EUR 15,000,000?; or perhaps the lower of the suggestions made by Udinese, i.e. a third of that sum (as all parties agreed at the hearing that clubs tended to set the sums in a liquidated damages clause far in excess of the player's true market value—these clauses are more a deterrent than a price tag), so EUR 5,000,000 and should the Panel, as suggested by Udinese, use the specificity of sport criterion to award that sum to Udinese? To further their position, Udinese also submitted that the Panel should look at the market value/transfer fees paid for other goalkeepers in the market around that time and use the specificity of sport to award between EUR 5 m and EUR 10 m to Udinese.
99. The Panel, in addition to being unimpressed by a few pages downloaded from a sporting website as evidence to support this submission, did not find that there was any similarity between those transfers and this specific case, and also determines that the specificity of sport is a correcting factor, and not one that enables a transfer fee through the back door. The Panel noted that Udinese quoted para 156 of Matuzalem in its submission, in which that panel stated this head of compensation is limited, that it serves to correct and should not be misused, yet then Udinese request between EUR 5,000,000 and EUR 10,000,000 under this criterion.
100. In addition, the Panel did consider the parties' submission regarding the time left unexpired on the Old Contract—3 years left of a 5 year contract; the special role of the Player in the eyes of sponsors, fans and his colleagues at Udinese; the position he played on the pitch and the success he had brought to Udinese; whether it was felt there was any evidence that the Player and Sevilla had met before the Player handed his notice in (and on that point, the Panel noted the lack of evidence produced by Udinese to back up its allegations); but also the time he had given to the club; whether he was a "model professional" or not; the fact he was outside the protected period; that he felt he followed a "process" set out in Art. 17.3 of the Regulations; whether the Player felt as Udinese had not offered him a new deal, after 2 years on the 4th contract, it was a sign he was not their future or whether any renegotiation would typically have occurred a few months later; and the like. On balance, the Panel felt that a downside of Udinese's strategy to replace the Player with the older, experienced goalkeeper and with the younger goalkeeper with potential was a factor that is specific to football and sport in general, that is the effect it will have on the fans and sponsors.
101. The Panel noted that Udinese had attempted to quantify such losses before the DRC—a near impossible task. However, the Panel notes that the Player was a senior professional, with whom the club had enjoyed some of their greatest successes. The fans and sponsors of all clubs demand immediate success and results. The Panel believes that at any club, when a key player is sold or goes and time is required for a new "hero" to materialise, revenues will be affected, the injured party will suffer losses which it may not be able to prove in Euros. This, in the opinion of the Panel, is where the specificity of sport can be used and should be used.

102. The Panel notes that in the various previous cases mentioned above, only the panels in Bourgas and Matuzalem awarded any sum for the specificity of sport, where the breach is by the player. The Regulations offer no express guidance as how a judging authority should calculate compensation under this basis. However, the commentary to the Regulations states, as a footnote on the specificity of sport:
"… *Furthermore, there was also the possibility of awarding additional compensation. This additional compensation may, however, not surpass the amount of six monthly salaries* …"
In the Appealed Decision, the DRC awarded a sum of EUR 350,000, but did not offer any detail as to how they arrived at this sum. In Bourgas, the panel rounded the compensation up—having worked from the remuneration due under the old contract, but then reviewing the increased remuneration the player received at his new clubs. In Matuzalem, the CAS panel considered Swiss Law as guidance, to fill that gap or *lacuna*, in particular, Art. 337c(3) and article 337d(1) of the Swiss Code of Obligations. Further, two of the parties in their submissions referred to the Swiss Code of Obligations as being applicable in this case. The Player did in his written submissions put forward an excerpt from academic paper, suggesting Swiss Law had no place here, but the author referred to was actually a panel member in the Matuzalem case, so without the entire paper, the Panel decided to follow the jurisprudence. That panel stated "… *the specific circumstances of a case may lead a panel to increase the amount of the compensation, by letting itself inspire, mutatis mutandis, by the concept of fair and just indemnity in the … Swiss Code of Obligations.*" In that instance that panel awarded additional compensation in the form of an additional indemnity amount equal to 6 months of the salary under the new club's contract. That panel used as further support Art. 42 para 2 of the Swiss Code of Obligations, stating "*if the exact amount of damages cannot be established, the judge shall assess them in his discretion, having regard to the ordinary course of the events and the measures taken by the damaged party to limit the damages.*" The Panel in this determines to follow the specificity of sport jurisprudence detailed in Matuzalem. So, taking into account the specific facts of this matter, determines the additional compensation for Udinese shall be EUR 690,789, being 6 months remuneration under the New Contract.
103. As such, the total compensation due to Udinese is:
The replacement costs EUR 4,510,000
Less, the savings made EUR 2,950,734
EUR 1,559,266
Add, the specificity of sport EUR 690,789
Total EUR 2,250,055
Such sum being payable jointly and severally by the Player and Sevilla.'

8.4.3.2 Summary

The Panel noted that there have been a number of previous awards delivered by CAS panels on this very issue (Webster, Matuzalem and others, where the breach is on the part of the player).

With regard to 'loss of transfer fee,' the panel notes the different approaches of previous panels—on the one hand, the Webster case where that panel felt transfer fees were not a possible factor in assessing compensation, whereas, in both Matuzalem and El-Hadary, the panels felt it was possible, if the injured party could provide sufficient evidence.

With regard to 'remuneration and other benefits,' The Panel notes that this criterion has proved the most contentious to date. Matuzalem and El-Hadary contrasted with the Webster decision, in which compensation was the remuneration for the unexpired part of the old contract, not the new.

8.5 Conclusion

The Webster award (CAS) deals with the breach of contract by a player outside the protected period. During this term Webster was offered a contract extension. Because he refused, in effect Webster was banned from the first eleven (by sitting on the bench) despite his high potential and all his efforts. So in May 2006 Webster decided to terminate his contract due to end on 30 June 2007. Webster could leave for a compensation of £150,000 plus interest. The Webster Award has often been styled the new 'Bosman.' Because of the lenient compensation, clubs were afraid of future compensation barely reaching a quarter of the possible transfer sums. These fears arose through the CAS' remaining value approach in calculating compensation. However, the Matuzalem decision demonstrated that these fears did not materialise. It in fact reversed the decision in *Webster*. The Matuzalem award is also about breach of contract outside the protected period without just cause. The Panel ordered Matuzalem to pay FC Shakhtar Donetsk compensation of €11,858,934 plus interest. In calculating the compensation the Panel considered the non-amortised transfer sum and the sports-related damages. However, it did not accept the contractual buy-out clause as the basis for calculating compensation. The De Sanctis award confirmed the findings of the Matuzalem ruling in determining compensation for the termination of the contract by the player: essential factors are his transfer value and the value of his new contract. So far, *Matuzalem* in fact turned out to be *stare decisis*.

As to the relevance of the 'sport specificity' concept in professional football matters beyond the scope of EU sports law, first it is remarkable to observe that this concept was introduced explicitly in the DRC rules ('applicable material law') and the FIFA transfer regulations (Article 17). This gives the concept not only European, but also worldwide relevance, at least in this branch of sport industry and its law. Explicitly using the concept of 'sport specificity' in their regulations, it looks like as if the private football authorities defend their institutional autonomy and self-regulation against the intrusive public EU sports law that admits only sport-specific exceptions. So, 'sport specificity' would represent here two sides of the same coin. In CAS jurisprudence on Article 17 matters the reference to 'sport specificity' in fact is of minor importance. However, important is that Article 17 of the FIFA transfer regulations should 'prevail' over national law provisions that may vary considerably from country to country (Webster) and that with respect to the criterion of 'the law of the country concerned' the specific nature and needs of sport, in particular those of the special world of professional football have to be taken into consideration (Matuzalem). In this context, it is interesting to note that the CAS Panel in the so-called *ENIC case* of 20 August 1999 (AEK Athens and SK Slavia Prague v UEFA) was of the opinion that all sporting institutions, and in particular all international federations, must abide by general principles of law. Due to the transnational nature of sporting competitions, the effects of the conduct and deeds of international federations are felt in a sporting community throughout various countries. Therefore, the substantive and procedural rules to be respected by international federations cannot be reduced only to its own statutes and regulations and to the laws of the country where the federation is incorporated or of the country where its headquarters are. Sports law has developed and consolidated along the years, particularly through the arbitral settlement of disputes, a set of unwritten legal principles, to which national and international sports federations must conform, regardless of the presence of such principles within their own statutes and regulations or within any applicable national law, provided that they do not conflict with any national 'public policy' provision applicable to a given case. 'Certainly, general principles of law drawn from a comparative or common denominator reading of various domestic legal systems and, in particular, the prohibition of arbitrary or unreasonable rules and measures can be deemed to be part of such sports law,' the CAS Panel says.[14]

References

Bent I, McIlroy R, Mousley K, Walsh P (2000) *Football Confidential*. London

Blackshaw I (2008) The CAS appeal decision in the Andrew Webster case. The International Sports Law Journal (ISLJ) 1–2:14–20

Blackshaw IS, Siekmann RCR, Soek J (eds) (2006) The Court of Arbitation for Sport 1984–2004. The Hague

David P (2008) A guide to the world anti-doping code—a fight for the spirit of sport. Cambridge University Press, Cambridge

Hendrickx F (ed) (2002) *Transfers en makelaars in de sport* [Transfers and agents in sport]. Antwerpen

Martins RB, Reiter G (2010) Players' agents: past, present … future? The International Sports Law Journal (ISLJ) 1–2:7–12

Siekmann RCR, Parrish R, Martins RB, Soek J (eds) (2007) Players' agents worldwide: legal aspects. The Hague

Soek J (2008) The prize for freedom of movement. The International Sports Law Journal (ISLJ) 1–2:24–28

Weatherill S (2010) Fairness, openness and the specific nature of sport: does the Lisbon Treaty change EU Sports Law? The International Sports Law Journal (ISLJ) 3–4:11–17

Weger F de (2008a) The jurisprudence of the FIFA Dispute Resolution Chamber. The Hague

Weger F de (2008b) The Webster case: justified panic as there was after Bosman? In: The International Sports Law Journal (ISLJ) 1–2:20–23

Wild A (ed) (2011) CAS and football: landmark cases. The Hague (forthcoming)

Willemsen C (1994) De moeder aller nederlagen [The mother of all defeats]. Nederlandse Sportbibliotheek [Netherlands Sport Library] 6. Amsterdam

---

[14] CAS 98/200, para. 156.

Chapter 9
Anti-Doping Law in Sport: the Hybrid Character of WADA and the Human Rights of Athletes in Doping Cases (Proportionality Principle)

Abstract The special characteristic of "anti-doping law" from an institutional, organisational perspective is the fact that national governments and intergovernmental organisations (IGOs) directly participate in WADA and the close linkage between the UNESCO Convention and the WADA Code. This issue will be discussed in detail in the first part of this article. The hot issue of the legal aspects of the fight against doping in sport is the relationship between "anti-doping law" and the human rights of athletes in doping cases, that is the applicability of general public human rights law to doping in sport. In the second part of the article a case of this type in which in 2009 this author was personally involved as a member of the appeals committee of the Instituut Sportrechtspraak [Netherlands Institute for Sport Adjudication] will be presented. The Appeals Board's decision was finally submitted to the CAS which was and still is the first time in history with regard to a Dutch case.

Contents

R. C. R. Siekmann, *Introduction to International and European Sports Law*,
ASSER International Sports Law Series, DOI: 10.1007/978-90-6704-852-1_9,
© T.M.C. ASSER PRESS, The Hague, The Netherlands, and the author 2012

9.1 Introduction

Generally speaking, what may be termed "sports law" consists of two parts, a public and a private one. The private part is formed by the rules and regulations of organised sport. Organised sport is built up of national and international organisations for each sport. The national associations are members of regional (continental) and universal, global and worldwide federations (IFs). From an institutional point of view, this part is hierarchically structured with—in association football—universal federations such as FIFA at the top and with UEFA as the regional organisation for Europe. Besides, the Olympic Games which have an "omnisport" character, are organised under the umbrella of the IOC in cooperation with IFs regarding the technical sporting aspects. The private part of sports law is the core part of this field of law, whereas the public one is of a non-systematic, fragmented nature. This part mainly consists of national legislation and a number of agreements under public international law (treaties) which relate specifically to sport.

"Anti-Doping law" belongs to "sports law." In the past, its private part was represented by national and international anti-doping regulations. With the introduction of the WADA Code in 2003 (WADA = World Anti-Doping Agency; officially, the correct naming is WAD Code (WADC), however, the Code is popularly known as and called WADA Code) this part was uniformised in one single international legal instrument. The public part consists of a number of national Anti-Doping Acts as well as two treaties which deal with the subject under consideration, that is the Council of Europe's Anti-Doping Convention of 1989 (and its Additional Protocol) and the UNESCO International Convention against Doping in Sport of 2005. As far as disciplinary law is concerned, the (private) jurisprudence of the Court of Arbitration for Sport (CAS) plays a very significant role. The special characteristic of "anti-doping law" from an institutional, organisational perspective is the fact that national governments and intergovernmental organisations (IGOs) directly participate in WADA and the close linkage between the UNESCO Convention and the WADA Code. This issue will be discussed in detail in the first part of this article. The hot issue of the legal aspects of the fight against doping in sport is the relationship between "anti-doping law" and the human rights of athletes in doping cases, that is the applicability of general public human rights law to doping in sport. In the second part of the article a case of this type in which in 2009 this author was personally involved as a member of the appeals committee of the *Instituut Sportrechtspraak* [Netherlands Institute for Sport Adjudication] will be presented. The Appeals Board's decision was finally submitted to the CAS which was and still is the first time in history with regard to a Dutch case.

9.2 WADA: A Public–Private Body

According to Richard Pound, Member of the IOC and the first Chairman of WADA, in 2002, the seminal event that led to the creation of the World Anti-Doping Agency (WADA) was the Tour de France in 1998. During the event, the French police found doping substances in the possession of certain of the teams and proceeded to arrest not only officials, but also athletes. The sight of athletes being led away by the police, to face possible criminal charges, was most dramatic. It also delivered a "wake-up" message to all other sports; if this could happen to one of the major European sports, in its showcase event, then it could also happen to them. The prospect of sport being governed by criminal law, with the concomitant intervention of the state, was thoroughly unattractive.

The situation was compounded by remarks made by IOC President Juan Antonio Samaranch to a Spanish journalist during the same Tour de France, in which he speculated that the list of substances prohibited was too long and that, so far as he was concerned, anti-doping scrutiny should be limited solely to substances that were harmful to the athletes, regardless of their performance-enhancing capacities. This statement drew considerable media attention, much of which was to the effect that the IOC was going "soft" on drug use and that much of its previous rhetoric concerning anti-doping was nothing more than pious claptrap. This led Samaranch to call a special meeting of the IOC Executive Board in August 1998. During the course of discussions on the issue, a suggestion emerged that what was required, inter alia, was an independent anti-doping agency, that would be completely neutral in its activities and that would have a governance structure designed to ensure that no organisation or groups of organisations could control it. The model suggested at the meeting of the IOC Executive Board was that used in the resolution of sports-related disputes, pursuant to which the Court of Arbitration for Sport (CAS) is governed by the International Council for Arbitration in Sport (ICAS), an organisation made up of representatives of the IOC, the International Federations (IFs), the national Olympic committees (NOCs) and athletes. The effect of such a governance structure has been such that CAS has been recognised as an independent body by the Swiss courts.

The IOC Executive Board also decided to organise a World Conference on Doping in Sport in February 1999 in Lausanne, to which not only members of the Olympic family would be invited, but also representatives of governments and of international organisations. In preparation for the meeting, the working group charged with developing the concept of an international anti-doping agency contemplated a series of the equal blocks of members, consisting of the IOC, the IFs, NOCs, athletes, governments and a sixth group containing representatives of sponsors, sporting good manufacturers, event organisers and, possibly, the pharmaceutical industry. In the interim, the IOC Medical Code was made more generic and turned into the Olympic Movement Anti-Doping Code to become effective on January 1, 2000, so that there would be a uniform set of rules to be applied in doping matters. At a meeting in Lausanne in November 1998, the IFs agreed they would adopt such a code and the stage was set for the World Conference the following February.

Unfortunately, not only on general principles pertaining to the IOC, but also with respect to smooth functioning of the World Conference on Doping in Sport, the Salt Lake City bidding scandal erupted in December 1998 and consumed more virtually all public attention on the failings of the IOC as an organisation to ensure proper governance of its own members. The level of media attention to this issue amounted to a virtual firestorm that drew all attention away from the important substantive content of the proposed World Conference. Despite the risks involved in proceeding with the Conference, and the risk that the anti-doping agenda might be hijacked, the IOC decided, in view of the importance of anti-doping efforts, that the Conference should nevertheless proceed, which it did in early February. A good deal of the Conference was taken up by criticism of the IOC, not only in relation to anti-doping activities, but also in relation to virtually everything it did or had ever done. When the proposed model of the independent anti-doping agency was put forward in this context, the governments present declared themselves completely opposed to the suggested governance structure. They insisted that governments must have at least an equal share of the governing body of any such agency.

Then Pound continues: "Samaranch, who was chairing the Conference, considered this rejection of the governance structure a disaster and thought that the Conference was doomed to complete failure. [Readers will, I hope, forgive the use of the first person singular at this juncture, but since the next portion of the saga involved me, it seems unnecessarily convoluted to resort to a third-person narrative.] I persuaded him that this could be turned to the IOC's advantage in several respects: the governments, who had been resolutely critical of the IOC and its anti-doping efforts, would now have to make themselves part of the solution and their participation at this level could mean that the IOC would not have to assume the full costs of such an agency. Although he was pessimistic, Samaranch delegated me to meet with the government representatives, headed by the United Kingdom and Spain, and to see what might be possible. The meeting was shorter than anyone expected. I asked if the governments were insistent on a 50–50 governance mechanism for the independent agency. They were. I said that was fine with the Olympic Movement and that we welcomed such an equal partnership. The government representatives, obviously expecting bitter resistance to their position, were astonished. I said there was one condition. What was that, they inquired? That if they had 50% control of the governance body, they must assume 50% of the costs. The Olympic Movement did not need governments to tell it how to spend its money. Not unpredictably, the prospect of spending money raised certain problems with governments and they said they would need some time to see whether this might be possible. That was agreeable to the IOC, I said, provided that the timetable for reaching a decision was accelerated beyond the normal pace for reaching government decisions. The matter would have to be fast-tracked or the Olympic Movement would proceed on its own, without government involvement, because the matter of doping in sport was too important not to proceed with all possible haste. The governments were now trapped. If they refused to participate, their own rhetoric would be exposed as devoid of both content and commitment to eradicating drugs from sport."[1]

The governments agreed to a fast-track operation and during the summer of 1999, the terms of government participation and the structure of the organisation were negotiated. The resulting organisation was named the World Anti-Doping Agency, or WADA, and was established as a private foundation under Swiss law (Articles 80 et seq. of the Swiss Civil Code) in November 1999, with an equal number of representatives from the Olympic Movement and of the governments from all five continents. The initial concept was to have a Foundation Board of 32 members. The 16 from the Olympic Movement were to be four members each named by the IOC, the IFs, the NOCs and the IOC Athletes Commission and the governments were to name 16 from the various continents. This was later increased to add additional representatives on both sides (government and sport) up to 18 each, maintaining the 50–50 balance.[2] According to the Constitutive Instrument of Foundation (September 2009), the seat of WADA is in Lausanne (Switzerland) and its headquarters are in Montreal (Canada). The Foundation Board takes its decisions by an absolute majority of the votes of the members present; in the event of a tie, the chairman has the casting vote. The first members of the Foundation Board, including the first chairman, were appointed by the founder (IOC). The Foundation Board is self-organised. It elects from its members, or from personalities chosen outside of its members, a chairman and a vice-chairman. The Foundation is an equal partnership between the Olympic Movement and public authorities. To promote and preserve parity among the stakeholders, the Foundation Board will ensure that the position of chairman alternates between the Olympic Movement and public authorities, To further maintain equal partnership between the Olympic Movement and the public authorities, the vice chairman must be a personality nominated by the public authorities if the chairman is a person nominated by the Olympic Movement, and vice versa.[3] The Foundation Board delegates to an Executive Committee of twelve members, the majority chosen from amongst the Foundation Board members, the actual management and running of the Foundation, the performance of all its activities and the actual administration of its assets. The chairman and vice-chairman of the Foundation Board automatically hold the position of chairman and vice-chairman. The Executive Committee takes its decisions by an absolute majority of the votes of the members present; in the event of a tie, the chairman has the casting vote. The Executive Committee is competent to take all decisions which are not reserved by the Law or by the present statutes for the Foundation Board. The Foundation Board may propose amendments to the statutes to the supervisory authority (that is

[1] Pound 2002, pp. 53–55.

[2] The five European members of the WADA Foundation Board are designated half by the Council of Europe and half by the EU.

[3] Currently, the WADA President is John Fahey (Australia) and the Vice President is Prof. Arne Ljungqvist (Sweden), IOC Member and President of the IOC Medical Commission.

the Swiss Federal Department of the Interior). Any proposed amendment, in particular any change to the object of the Foundation, is reserved and must be approved by a two-third majority of the Foundation Board members present.

One of the most interesting legal aspects of WADA is its legal status. Created by notarial deed, pursuant to Swiss law and subject to oversight by Swiss authorities, it does not conform with the legal format that most governmental organisations prefer and with which they are comfortable. Governments are clearly more comfortable with public entities and intergovernmental organisations; they are not comfortable with private organisations and are not entirely certain how to deal with such entities. Initial expressions of preference by governments were to turn WADA into a public entity, in which governments could be members. This, of course, completely disregarded the other half of the governance structure, namely the Olympic Movement, none of the organs of which are public entities and some of which (such as athlete members) are entirely personal. At least for the time being, governments agreed to see whether it is possible to operate through a hybrid organisation.[4] The Constitutive Instrument of Foundation of WADA provides that the Agency will be entitled to prepare plans and proposals in light of its conversion, if necessary, into a different structure, possibly based on public international law.

In spite of its formally private nature, WADA carries out functions that aim to further public goals such as promoting and coordinating at the international level the fight against doping in sport in all its forms, including through in- and (unannounced) out-of-competition testing. However, WADA's most important activity (in terms of its "public" function) is its role as a global standard setter. WADA carries out significant normative functions such as updating the prohibited list of substances and the establishment of international technical standards with regard to analyses, and also produces "soft-law" in the form of recommendations and good practices. Beside these tasks, WADA carries out other relevant administrative activities, such as monitoring anti-doping tests during major sports events. The most significant outcome of WADA's activities is the World Anti-Doping Code (WADC), which was adopted in 2003 and entered into force on 1 January 2004.[5] WADA's Signatories (i.e. those entities signing the Code and agreeing to comply with it) include the IOC, NOCs, NADOs, WADA, and others. Governments instead were not asked to be signatories to the Code, but rather to accept the UNESCO Convention against Doping in Sport, which was unanimously approved by 191 governments at the UNESCO's General Conference. The Convention is currently ratified by 110 States. Article 4 concerns the relationship of the Convention to the Code provides *inter alia* that States Parties commit themselves to the principles of the Code as the basis for the measures to achieve the objectives of the Convention, which may include legislation, regulation, policies and administrative practices.

[4] See again, Pound 2002, p. 57.

[5] A second version of the Code was unanimously adopted by WADA's Foundation Board and endorsed at the Third World Conference on Doping in Sport, in Madrid, on 17 November 2007; the new Code entered into force on 1 January 2009.

However, the Code itself, reproduced for information purposes as Appendix to the Convention, is not an integral part of the Convention and does not create any binding obligations under international law for States Parties. Casini states that, although the WADA Code formally rests on an instrument of private law (as it itself clarifies: most governments cannot be parties to, or bound by, private non-governmental instruments such as the Code), it displays rather a hybrid nature, due to the role played by public authorities both in WADA's decision-making process and in the procedure for the drafting of the Code. Putting aside any concerns regarding the classification of WADA, this body offers a prime example of an *equal* institutional public–private partnership (PPP) that is unusual both at the global level and in domestic contexts. A second set of issues refers to the binding force of the WADA Code. The Code offers, in fact, a prime instance of a formally private source of norms that show to a high degree a public character, cf., in particular governments taking part both in the decision-making and Code-drafting process as well as the UNESCO Convention expressly referring to WADA and its Code. Casini concludes that the WADA Code provides a very relevant example of norms that cannot be labelled as fully private or fully public, but rather as *sources de caractère mixte*.[6] It is remarkable that the WADA Code itself provides that it be interpreted as an independent and autonomous text and not by reference to the existing law or statutes of the Signatories [cf., Olympic Movement] or governments. This would mean that the WADA Code does not belong to the public or private part of sports law; it is international sports law of a *sui generis* character. The same would apply to WADA as an institution because of its public/private nature.

9.3 The Dutch Billiard Social Drugs Case and the Principle of Proportionality

9.3.1 First Instance: Instituut Sportrechtspraak: Royal Dutch Billiards Federation (KNBB) (Complainant) v N. Zuijkerbuijk (Defendant)

On 5 April 2009, during a match in the Dutch Three-Cushion Billiards Premier League, held in Apeldoorn, the defendant was selected for an anti-doping control. The analytical report received by the Doping Authority from the anti-doping laboratory stated that analysis of the A urine sample revealed the presence of benzoylecgonine (a metabolite of cocaine). The analysis of the B urine sample confirmed the presence of this substance. On grounds of the confirmation by the analysis of the B sample of the analysis of the A sample of the defendant, the party concerned was declared to have tested positive. The presence of said substance

[6] See: Casini 2009, pp. 439–441. The French expression has been applied to sports law, that is to the WADA Code by Franck Latty (2007, p. 391).

was thus established. Cocaine appeared on the 2009 Prohibited List accompanying the Doping Regulations of the Institute for Sports Law followed by the Royal Dutch Billiards Association (KNBB) in the category "substances and methods prohibited in competition." The presence alone of a connected substance, in this case a metabolite of a substance that appeared on said list, in a urine sample of an athlete selected for an anti-doping control was deemed sufficient proof that the Doping Regulations had been violated. The party concerned did not have any valid dispensation for the use of said substance. In its decision dated 25 August 2009 the Disciplinary Committee of the Institute for Doping Law also ruled that Article 3 para 1 of the Doping Regulations had been violated. Under Article 38.1 of the Doping Regulations the Disciplinary Committee excluded the person concerned from competition for a period of 2 years. Such a sanction could be imposed in the case of a first violation under the provisions laid down in this article unless the conditions set out under a) and b) of this article were met. Cocaine is not a specified substance. The athlete had not discharged the burden of proving that he bears no (significant) level of fault or negligence and neither did he admit violating the anti-doping rule prior to this doping case. The KNBB Board had not established any aggravating circumstances. The Disciplinary Committee found that none of the conditions to reduce/extend the standard sanction period was met.

In the appeal, the defendant did not dispute the violation but he was appealing against the duration of the imposed penalty. In its decision of 26 November 2009, the appeals committee confirmed the verdict of the disciplinary committee dated 25 August 2009 that the violation was proven but reduced the ineligibility period imposed in the decision of the disciplinary committee. In the appeal, the defendant admitted using cocaine. The violation of Article 3(1) of the Doping Regulations had therefore been established. The substantive grounds for the appeal by the defendant related exclusively to the penalty, which he considered to be excessively long.

Article 38 of the Doping Regulations stipulated a period of ineligibility of 2 years for a first violation of Article 3 unless the conditions in Articles 39 (Specific substances), 40 (No fault or negligence) and/or 41 (No plausible level of fault or negligence) for the reduction of the penalty have been met. The appeals committee noted, on the basis of the 2009 Prohibited List, that cocaine was not a specific substance. The reduction of the ineligibility period on the grounds of Article 39 of the Doping Regulations was therefore inappropriate. Article 40(1) of the Doping Regulations stipulated as a condition for the non-imposition of the ineligibility period that the defendant did not know or suspect, and could not reasonably have known or suspected, even after exercising the greatest possible care, that he had used the prohibited substance. The defendant stated in his appeal form and at the hearing that he deliberately used the prohibited substance, in this case cocaine. The fact that he did not realise at that time the consequences to which this use could lead did not detract from the fact that the condition stated in Article 40(1) had not been fulfilled. There were therefore no factual grounds based on Article 40 of the Doping Regulations for the non-imposition of the eligibility period. Article 41(1) of the Doping Regulations stipulated as a condition that there should be no question of a plausible level of fault or negligence. This was the case if the athlete can demonstrate that his fault or negligence was not significant in relation to the violation of the regulations given the circumstances of the case. It had been established that the defendant deliberately used the cocaine. This excluded the possibility of the absence of any significant fault or negligence in the sense of Article 41 of the Doping Regulations.

During the hearing, the defendant argued that the penalty imposed upon him was excessive and therefore disproportional. The appeals committee considered this to be an explicit appeal to the principle of proportionality. In this case: the disproportionality of the penalty in relation to the prohibited behaviour being punished. It must therefore examine the penalty in the light of this principle.

The principle of proportionality is a fundamental principle of proper justice (or *due process*). Although it was not, in principle, an explicit statutory component of Dutch criminal or procedural law, it was generally recognised and accepted. Disciplinary law was less formal than criminal law; the principle of proportionality should therefore be applied more widely in disciplinary law than in criminal law.

Disciplinary law was a component of the provisions regulating the membership relationship. This was a relationship in private law that was subject to statutory provisions relating to associations, as set out in book 2 of the Netherlands Civil Code. The statutory standard for the argument of proportionality was found in section 8(2) of the Netherlands Civil Code.

In the opinion of the appeals committee, doping regulations to which athletes who engaged in their sports as members of an association were necessarily subject must, firstly, meet the standards that government regulations in general and their application with respect to criminal law in particular are required to meet. In addition, there were also the standards of a fair trial—in part against the background of European law—and of section 2.8(2) of the Netherlands Civil Code (see *infra*).

The WADA Code and therefore the Doping Regulations had a very strict and rigid—and by comparison with normal criminal law, a very severe—system of penalties. Certainly in cases like the present one, in which the performance-enhancing effects of the prohibited substance found were at best disputed, the implications of the application of this rigid system of penalties must therefore be examined at all times in the light of the standards that prevail in normal criminal law, including the principle of proportionality. As it will emerge below, the appeals committee knew that it was supported in this respect by the CAS and the EC Court of Justice, without it being necessary to make clear whether the CAS or the Court were guided by this principle of criminal law.

The principle of proportionality implied that the application of anti-doping regulations must not go further than is strictly necessary to effectively combat doping.[7] In his thesis, Soek summed up the principle as follows (p. 389):

---

[7] See, for example, Soek 2006, p. 381 et seq.

"The proportionality principle is widely recognized and accepted. It prohibits the taking of any measure which in view of its objective must be considered to go beyond what is appropriate and necessary. The application of the principle involves the balancing of the interests of the person or persons affected by the measure and the possibly wider social aim which it is intended to achieve. The CAS has regularly considered whether the doctrine of proportionality could be applied in reduction of a penalty. The application of fixed penalties for doping offences made it difficult to weigh the severity of the offence against the severity of the penalty. Nevertheless, as the CAS at one occasion concluded, when the circumstances of the case so allowed the appellant's sentence could properly be reduced by reference to proportionality considerations."

The CAS had applied the proportionality principle—with the reduction of fixed penalties—in a number of cases, including in particular CAS 2000/A/270, Meca-Medina and Majcen v. FINA, to which Soek referred, and later in: CAS 2006/A/1025, Puerta/v. ITF and CAS 2007/A/1252, FINA v. Mellouli and TSF.[8]

In an Advisory Opinion about the implementation of the WADA Code in the FIFA Disciplinary Code (CAS 2005/C/976 and 986, FIFA and WADA; para 139, pp. 52–53) the CAS had the following to say with particular reference to the proportionality principle (section 1.4.3):

"A long series of CAS decisions have developed the principle of proportionality in sport cases. This principle provides that the severity of a sanction must be proportionate to the offense committed. To be proportionate, the sanction must not exceed that which is reasonable required in the search of the justifiable aim. Both the Swiss Federal Supreme Court and a significant part of Swiss legal doctrine have upheld the principle of proportionality. [...] The panel is of the view that the principle of proportionality is guaranteed under the WADC; moreover, proportional sanctions facilitate compliance with the principle of fault. Consequently, each body must consider the proportionality of imposed sanctions for doping cases."

It added, in section 1.5 (Conclusion; para 143, pp 54-55):

"The right to impose a sanction is limited by the mandatory prohibition of excessive penalties, which is embodied in several provisions of Swiss law. To find out whether a sanction is excessive, a judge must review the type and scope of the proved rule violation, the individual circumstances of the case, and the overall effect of the sanction on the offender. However, only if the sanction is evidently and grossly disproportionate in comparison to the proved rule violation and if it is considered as a violation of fundamental justice and fairness, would the panel regard such a sanction as abusive and, thus, contrary to mandatory Swiss law."

With respect to the significance of Advisory Opinions MacLaren stated[9]:

"Through the Advisory procedure, the CAS is able to give opinions on legal questions concerning any activity related to sport in general. Under Rule 60 of the Code (of Sports-related Arbitration) any questions of law or general interpretation related to sport may be submitted to the CAS for resolution. [...] For the Advisory procedure, the questions do not have to be fact specific; and thus, can raise and deal with general principles of law and how they may apply to sport. For instance, there have been Advisory Opinions on the

8 Cf., David 2008, p. 168 et seq.

9 CAS Advisory Opinions, in Blackshaw et al. 2006, pp. 180–181.

> application of lex mitior, jurisdiction to establish rules, and proportionality in determining sporting sanctions."

Turning to European law, the application of the proportionality principle was also recognised by the Court of Justice. See, forexample, the Meca-Medina case and Majcen v. European Commission, C-519/04. Ground 48 was as follows:

> "Rules of that kind [in this case, anti-doping rules] could indeed prove excessive by virtue of, first, the conditions laid down for establishing the dividing line between circumstances which amount to doping in respect of which penalties say be imposed and those which do not, and second, the severity of those penalties."

9.3.1.1 Dutch Association Law

As stated above, the issue of proportionality should also be considered on the basis of the standard of reasonableness and fairness relating to the membership relationship stated in section 2:8 of the Netherlands Civil Code. The text of the section was as follows:

> "A rule governing the relationship between them by law, custom, statutes, regulations or decision shall not be applicable in so far as it is unacceptable according to standards of reasonableness and fairness in the given circumstances."

The provision is an imperative rule of law and, furthermore, the relevant statutory provision is not excluded in the KNBB regulations. The Committee must therefore apply this rule of law.

The KNBB was an association residing in the Netherlands and it was therefore subject to Dutch association law. The defendant was a Dutch citizen residing in the Netherlands and, when the sample was taken, he was participating in a competition in the Netherlands. The membership relationship and the relevant conduct were entirely within the domain of Dutch law. Dutch law therefore applied exclusively.

The doping regulations were a component of the regulations of the KNBB. These regulations were a component of the membership relationship between the defendant and the KNBB. The application of those regulations implied that the appeals committee must base its considerations on the principle of reasonableness of section 2:8 of the Netherlands Civil Code, which also governed that membership relationship, and all the more because an explicit appeal had been made to that principle (by reference to proportionality).

The provision that required a minimum penalty of an ineligibility period of 2 years must guide the considerations of the appeals committee unless that rule "is unacceptable according to standards of reasonableness and fairness in the given circumstances." In that case, the rule in question must, by law, not be applied. The appeals committee, in a limited examination, was of the opinion that this unacceptability was a factor in this case, taking all the circumstances of the case into consideration. The reader is referred to Section 9.3.1.2 "Grounds for Consideration" *infra*.

9.3.1.2 Grounds for Consideration

After the application of the proportionality principle, the appeals committee came to the conclusion that the ineligibility period of 2 years imposed by the disciplinary committee was excessive. In so doing, the appeals committee took the following facts and circumstances into consideration:

a) "The defendant had not been found positive previously.
b) Cocaine was not a performance-enhancing substance in billiards. The sports doctor and doping expert Harm Kuipers had stated (Dagblad de Stentor, 6 September 2006) that the use of cocaine had no performance-enhancing effect for an athlete whatsoever. 'Certainly not for a billiards player. This is a sport requiring coordination and cocaine is of no use in that respect. Alertness is enhanced, but only for a very short time. Indeed, coordination is rapidly adversely affected, as is the capacity to take decisions quickly. Athletes who use cocaine may have a problem, but it's not a doping problem.'
c) The presence of cocaine in the urine of an athlete in an *out-of-competition control* did not constitute a violation of the Doping Regulations. The appeals committee concluded from this that the WADA also accepted that the use of cocaine did not provide athletes with any advantage other than immediately after use. In this case, there were 3 days between the use of the cocaine and the competition in which the defendant participated.
d) On the basis of the account of the defendant, which the committee considered to be credible, the appeals committee found in this procedure that it was a fact that the cocaine was taken unthinkingly in the context of the defendant's nightlife and that there was no question of any link to sports performance.
e) There was no intention to enhance performance and so there was also no intention to acquire an unfair and irregular advantage with respect to competitors.
f) Although it was the case that the defendant did not admit the violation in good time, or at least not in accordance with the Doping Regulations in the correct way prior to the results of the analysis and the charge, the defendant did not make any secret of the recreational use. He has frankly admitted using the substance and did so again during the hearing, seated alongside his father with a contrite expression. The KNBB was also visibly uncomfortable with its own draconic and implacable regulations. Its representative at the hearing was clearly embarrassed about the situation, but he had no choice. There had been a case recently in another sport of a 'spontaneous' admission of cocaine use which was evidently inspired by a sample being taken shortly after cocaine had been used. That strategic honesty—in the light of the prospect of discovery—was found to be grounds for halving the penalty. The defendant had not had routine experience with doping controls targeting cocaine use, by contrast with the reluctant repentant who was clearly motivated by strategic considerations. In all reasonableness, the defendant should not suffer a worse fate than that fellow-user.[10]
g) The defendant had also admitted his cocaine use in public. This could be seen from publications in the press and on various billiards websites. In this respect, the defendant contrasted favourably with numerous other athletes who, when confronted with a positive result, denied using prohibited substances regardless of the facts. With his public admission, and his expressions of regret about what had happened, the defendant had made a contribution to the discussion about this problem for, in particular, younger

[10] The *Instituut Sportrechtspraak* is here referring to the *Yuri van Gelder* case decided by the Disciplinary Commission of the Royal Dutch Gymnastics Union on 22 October 2009. Yuri van Gelder won the European and world champion's titles (rings) in 2005, 2008 and 2009 and 2005, 2006 and 2007 respectively.

billiards players. The publicity relating to this case had inflicted considerable damage on the defendant's good name, fame and reputation, and what was even worse in a matter that should have remained private (also from the point of view of the WADA ideology) if use had been established out of competition.

h) The defendant had stated that he did not know that the traces of cocaine would still be apparent in his urine after 3 days. Particularly when elite sports were involved, it was of course the responsibility of the athlete to be informed about the effect of the substances on the prohibited list. However, this did not absolve the sports associations from their responsibility in this respect. Article 22 of the Doping Regulations was very clear in this respect. Without wishing to suggest that there had been any significant shortcoming in the information provided by the KNBB, the appeals committee did believe it was justifiable to conclude that this information might have left something to be desired, at least in terms of the punishability and traceability of this forbidden substance. In the view of the appeals committee, the defendant was a serious athlete who, if he had been able to oversee the consequences of his cocaine use, would have been in a better position to resist the temptation.

i) The general goal of doping regulations in the field of sports was to combat doping in order to ensure fair competition and it included the need to ensure that all athletes had the same chances and to safeguard their health. The KNBB's aim—following in the footsteps of WADA—of setting punishments for the presence in the body of a series of substances was based on this general objective. Banning cocaine, a substance which did not enhance sporting, or at least billiards, performance was therefore, in the opinion of the appeals committee, difficult to describe as conducive to that aim. At the same time, the detection and prosecution of the presence of this substance led in this case to a serious infringement of the privacy of the defendant which was therefore not justified by the core aim of the fight against doping in sports. The infringement of privacy was all the more disproportional in consequence and the ineligibility period coming on top of that should be all the shorter in order to attain a reasonable proportionality."

In summary, the appeals committee, in a limited examination, considered the outcome of a rule that required a penalty of an ineligibility period of 2 years to be imposed for this violation to be disproportional and the result to be unacceptable in the sense of section 2:8 of the Netherlands Civil Code. This was supported by the grounds stated with respect to CAS decisions and European law. In this case, therefore, the rule and its result must not be applied. Instead, the appeals committee, after having taken all the circumstances into consideration and given the fact that the defendant had already received a substantial punishment, considered an ineligibility period of 1 year after the date of the initial decision to be reasonable.

9.3.1.3 Comment

(1) According to the website of the Netherlands Doping Authority, cocaine belongs to the doping category S6. Stimulantia. Cocaine may be used to improve the athelete's performance, because tiredness is dissipated and alertness temporarily stimulated. However, the use of cocaine may considerably damage a person's health. So, cocaine fulfils two out of three criteria which are applied when the decision is taken to put a substance on the doping list, that is (possibly) improving performance and (possibly) being harmful to health. The third criterion is: "contrary to the spirit of sport"; many people are of the opinion that this is true also for cocaine, a social or party drug. In competition a sportsperson is controlled with regard to all doping categories, but out of competition he or she is not tested with regard tot he doping categories S6. Stimulantia, S7. Narcotica, S8. Cannabino and S9. Glucocorticostero. The main reason to test with regard to these substances only in competition is their short-term effectiveness. If these subtances are used well in advance of competition, the sportsperson will not benefit from them in competition.

(2) As to the substantial aspects of the case, in my opinion, this is a clear case in which formalities had to be set aside. Generally speaking, it must be possible to impose a less severe penalty in appeal, reconsidering a case and taking all relevant circumstances into account, not only the formal legal ones but also possible aspects of (natural) justice which are not of a formal nature. It is the task of a judge and tribunals to do justice to the facts and circumstances of a case. A judge in a free, democratic society can never be expected to administer justice in a way he cannot reconcile with his conscience as a human being and citizen. Offenders must be treated fair and human. The closed, rigid sanctions system of the WADA Code is forced and even absurd. It is a purely defensive system which in not in conformity with the character of disciplinary law. One of the main purposes of the administration of disciplinary law is to take pedagogically, educationally useful measures which are effective from a societal perspective (society at large argument, on the micro—sporting—and macro levels). In *Meca-Medina*, the European Court of Justice makes the *ratio* of doping law explicit, which is not the case in the WADA Code or in the Doping Regulations of het *Instituut Sportrechtspraak* which follow the WADA Code, since in both a preamble is missing (this underlines the rigid- and closedness of the WADA Code which gives reasonable "society at large" arguments or other prayers for relief no chance).[11] Re-education of is not feasible, if not all circumstances of his or her case are being considered. A defendant must get the feeling that his arguments and explanation of the facts are really taken into account; otherwise, he or she will not have a cooperative, understanding attitude, once having been sentenced. The re-educational nature of

[11] Paragraph 43 of Meca-Medina reads in full: "As regards the overall context in which the rules at issue were adopted, the Commission could rightly take the view that the general objective of the rules was, as none of the parties disputes, to combat doping in order for competitive sport to be conducted fairly and that it included the need to safeguard equal chances for athletes, athletes' health, the integrity and objectivity of competitive sport and ethical values in sport." In the preamble of the UNESCO Anti-Doping Convention (and previously in similar terms, in the preamble of the Council of Europe Anti-Doping Convention) it reads: "Conscious that sport should play an important role in the protection of health, in moral, cultural and physical education and in promoting international understanding and peace," "Concerned by the use of doping by athletes in sport and the consequences thereof for their health, the principles of fair play, the elimination of cheating and the future of sport," "Mindful that doping puts at risk the ethical principles and educational values embodied in the International Charter of Physical Education and Sport of UNESCO and in the Olympic Charter" and "Mindful also of the influence that elite athletes have on youth.".

disciplinary law is particularly relevant, when it in fact is about amateur sport like in the present case. The defendant was sponsored, but not dependent on playing billiards for his income. A suspension of 2 years is not reasonable. It was questionable whether the defendant, a young very talented player ("the new Jaspers," as he was called),[12] would return to competition after this period of time. On the opposite, having been banned from competitive sport he might even become a regular drug user. So, the consequences of a disproportionate time penalty would be detrimental to the athlete and his sport. The aim of the sanction - to make clear that the recreational use of drugs may have consequences in doping law, in particular also because it is not "sportsmanlike" - could be achieved as effectively by imposing a penalty for a much shorter period (three or six months) combined with an official, conditional warning that recidivism would automatically lead to a 2 years suspension. The imposition of sanctions must be tailor-made. A two-year suspension would not communicate an appropriate message of condemnation to the receiver under the mitigating circumstances and really contribute to the prevention of recidivism. Apart from that, the question could be asked whether the use of social drugs (and excessive drinking and smoking/nicotine) would not better be combated under sporting disciplinary law independently from doping.

(3) However, in the opinion of the Netherlands NADO, the decision of the *Instituut Sportrechtspraak* was fundamentally incorrect. Having sympathy for the *Instituut*'s approach and the human considerations they bring forward, acceptance of these considerations would imply that the harmonisation of doping policy as it is laid down in the WADA Code would become almost an illusion, the Netherlands NADO observed. This became even more relevant now that the verdict was made by the Appeals Committee of the most important tribunal of The Netherlands in disciplinary matters. Therefore, the NADO had decided to submit the case to CAS.

(4) It is true that the CAS has applied the proportionality principle in exceptional cases, reducing fixed penalties The CAS did this before as well as after the adoption of the WADA Code in 2003 (in particular in Meca-Medina, Puerta). An Advisory Opinion of the CAS (FIFA and WADA) is of a general purport (R60 CAS; see also MacLaren, *supra* Section 9.3.1) and in Puerta reference is made to the fundamental reasoning on proportionality in FIFA and CAS. One of course might argue that it would be foreseeable that in an appeal in the Zuijkerbuijk case the CAS would come to a different conclusion than the *Instituut Sportrechtspraak*'s Appeals Committee, but this would not be absolutely certain beforehand because—as far as I know—the CAS was never confronted with a similar case before (and apart from the fact that the CAS is not obliged to apply the *stare decisis* principle in its decision-making). The "proportionality cases" of the CAS did concern the absence of (a plausible level of) fault or negligence, but the facts in those cases were indeed quite different. Why should it be expected that in *Zuijkerbuijk* the CAS would

[12] Dick Jaspers is a Dutch professional billiards player, who was world champion (three-cushions) in 2000, 2004 and 2011.

automatically use an *a contrario* reasoning, because the previous "proportionality cases" and *Zuijkerbuijk* were not similar (absence of analogy)?

9.3.2 *Appeal: Court of Arbitration for Sport (CAS)*

CAS 20091A/2012 Doping Authority Netherlands (hereafter: "NADO") (appellant) v. Mr Nick Zuijkerbuijk (respondent) (Sole Arbitrator: Mr. Manfred Peter Nan, The Netherlands), Lausanne, 11 June 2010.

On the principle of proportionality the CAS award in *Zuijkerbuijk* reads in full as follows (paras 65–79):

> "[T]he determination of the period of ineligibility necessarily requires the Sole Arbitrator to consider the issue of proportionality.
>
> The sanction must be proportionate. The issue is whether the Sole Arbitrator can impose a lesser period of ineligibility then is prescribed by Article 38.1 ISR Doping Regulations, knowing that the requirements for reduction as mentioned in Articles 39-42 ISR Doping Regulations are not met.
>
> NADO argues that DAC 'has not applied the doctrine of proportionality as developed by CAS, or at least has not applied this doctrine correctly in accordance with CAS case law. It has not established circumstances that make this case truly exceptional, and it has not (correctly) applied the criteria established in CAS case law on applying proportionality in doping cases.'
>
> The Athlete argues that a 2 years period of ineligibility is *'out of proportion'* and *'would apply to structural use of doping, especially when meant to enhance performance.'* The Athlete argues that DAC *'acknowledged the draconic and uncompromising nature of the applicable doping regulations, justifiably calling upon the principle of proportionality.'* DAC has reduced the ineligibility period imposed to 1 year, stating that after application of the proportionality principle an ineligibility period of 2 years is excessive, disproportional and also unacceptable in the sense of section 2:8 of the Netherlands Civil Code. In this regard, DAC refers in its Decision to facts regarding the Athlete, namely (a) *that he has not been found positive previously, (d) the cocaine was taken unthinkingly [...], (e) there is no intention to enhance performance [...], (j) he has frankly admitted using the substance [...],* (g) *the defendant has also admitted his cocaine use in public [...], (h) he did not know that the traces of cocaine would still be apparent in his urine [...].* In its Decision DAC also states that *(b) cocaine is not a performance-enhancing substance in billiards [...], (e) the presence of cocaine in the urine of an athlete in an out-of-competition control does not constitute a violation of the Doping Regulations [...], (j) there has been a case recently in another sport of a 'spontaneous' admission of cocaine use [...]. That [...] was found to be grounds for halving the penalty [...]. In all reasonableness, the defendant should not suffer a worse fate than that fellow-user [...].* Furthermore, DAC finds in its decision that *(h)* the information provided by the sports association KNBB with reference to the *punishability and traceability* of cocaine has left something to be desired. Finally, DAC holds that *(i) banning cocaine [...] is difficult to describe as conducive to the aim of combat doping.*
>
> The WADC and the ISR Doping Regulations, considerably restrict the application of the principle of proportionality. Whether an Athlete has never tested positive before in his sporting career is relevant only for determining the applicable range of sanctions as mentioned in Articles 38 and 45 ISR Doping Regulations. The Athlete's age, that he took the prohibited substance unthinkingly and not with the intention to enhance performance,

the question of whether taking the cocaine metabolite had a performance enhancing effect, the (not timely) admission, the admission in public, his unawareness of the traceability of cocaine, the fact that the presence of cocaine in the sample of an Athlete in an out-of-competition control does not constitute a violation of the Doping Regulations or the peculiarities of the particular type of Sport, are not—according to the WADC—matters to be weighed when determining the period of ineligibility. The purpose and intention of the WADC is, inter alia, to make the fight against doping more effective by harmonising the legal framework and to provide uniform sanctions to be applied in all sports, These rules, for instance, do not distinguish between amateur or professional athletes, old or young athletes or individual sport or team sport.

DAC's reference to an anonymous case in another sport and their opinion that banning cocaine is difficult to describe as conducive to the aim of combat doping do not justify a departure of the mandatory rule. DAC also mentioned in its Decision that the information provided by the sports association KNBB with reference to the punishability and traceability of cocaine has left something to be desired. Although Article 22 ISR Doping Regulations provides *that the association board is required to inform members about the content and operation of these regulations [...]*, it is not the duty of the Sports association to warn athletes against the use of cocaine (or its metabolite). While it is certainly desirable that a sports association should make every effort to educate athletes about doping, it is principally the sole duty of the individual athlete to ensure that no prohibited substances enter his body.

Article 10.2 WADC and Article 38.1 ISR Doping Regulations provides for a uniform sanction of an ineligibility of 2 years for first offences. The only possibility for the athlete to reduce this fixed sanction is by evidence of exceptional circumstances (Article 10.5 WADC and Article 40 and 41 ISR Doping Regulations). If the Sole Arbitrator denies the existence of exceptional circumstances, it has, under the WADC and ISR Doping Regulations, no other choice than to apply the sanction of a two year suspension.

The consequences of this abstract and rigid approach of the WADC when fixing the length of the period of ineligibility in an individual case may be detrimental or (in rare cases) advantageous to the athlete (see for instance CAS 2002/A/376 Baxter v/FIS). Insofar as the WADC prevents specific circumstances to be taken into account for the benefit of the athlete, the admissibility of such provisions is often questioned.

However, CAS case law and various legal opinions confirm that the WADC mechanisms are not contrary to human rights legislation. In the case CAS 2004/A/690 (Hipperdinger v/ATP), the Panel found that the athlete had not established either 'No Fault or Negligence' or 'No Significant Fault or Negligence.' In this case, in which the Panel upheld the 2 years suspension, the Panel cited with approval the decision of the Swiss Federal Court in N, et al. v/FINA (W. v/FINA 5P.83/1999). This latter case involved positive doping tests by four Chinese swimmers. The appeal concerned the CAS award upholding the swimmers' suspension. The award was rendered prior to the adoption of the WADC. One of several claims raised by the swimmers on appeal was that the CAS award failed to comply with the principle of proportionality. The amount of banned substance was very low, yet the suspension handed down could possibly end the swimmers' careers. The Swiss Federal Court held that under the applicable FINA Anti-Doping Rules, the appropriate question is not whether a penalty is proportionate to an offence, but rather whether the athlete is able to produce evidence of mitigating circumstances. Furthermore, the issue of proportionality would only be a legitimate issue if a CAS award constituted an infringement of individual rights that was extremely serious and completely disproportionate to the behaviour penalised. The Court found that the 2 year suspensions in question were only a moderate restriction on the athletes, because the suspensions resulted from a proven doping violation under rules that had been accepted by the athletes. In the result, the Court held that the 2 year suspensions handed down without examination of proportionality did not constitute a violation of the general principles of Swiss law.

The Sole Arbitrator refers also to CAS 2005/A/847 H. Knaus v/FIS and CAS 200S/A/830 G. Squizzato v/FINA. In this latter case the Panel considered: 'The Panel recognizes that a mere uncomfortable feeling alone that a 1 year penalty is not the appropriate sanction cannot itself justify a reduction. The individual circumstances of each case must always hold sway in determining any possible reduction. Nevertheless, the implementation of the principle of proportionality as given in the World Anti-Doping Code closes more than ever before the door to reducing fixed sanctions. Therefore, the principle of proportionality would apply if the award were to constitute an attack on personal rights which was serious and totally disproportionate to the behaviour penalised [...].'

In continuation, the Sole Arbitrator takes also in account the Advisory Opinion delivered by CAS in relation to the implementation of the WADC into the FIFA Disciplinary Code (CAS 2005/C/976 & 986 FIFA & WADA), in which the Panel held that the principle of proportionality is guaranteed under the WADC.

Furthermore, in the opinion by Prof. G. Kaufmann-Kohler-Antonio Rigozzi and Giorgio Malinvenu *(Legal Opinion on the Conformity of certain Provisions of the Draft World Anti-Doping Code with Commonly Accepted Principles of International Law, dated* 26 *February 2003),* the rigid system of fixed sanctions in the WADC considerably restricts the doctrine of proportionality, but is nevertheless compatible with human rights and general legal principles. These experts justify this characteristic by citing the legitimate aim of harmonising doping penalties.

Whether the conclusions to be drawn from these experts are correct in such finality can be left unanswered here (see also CAS 2004/A/690 Hipperdinger v/ATP and CAS 200S/A/847 Knaus v/FIS); for the case at hand does not require an in-depth discussion of the issue. The mechanism of fixed sanctions according to the WADC is incorporated into the ISR Doping Regulations. At least in the opinion of the Swiss Federal Tribunal, sports bodies can limit in their rules the circumstances to be taken into account when fixing sanctions and thereby also restrict the application of the doctrine of proportionality. However, in the opinion of the Swiss Federal Tribunal, the sport associations exceed their autonomy if these rules constitute an attack on personal rights, the nature and scope of which is extremely serious and totally disproportionate to the behaviour penalised. In the Sole Arbitrator's opinion, this threshold has not been exceeded in the present case. The Sole Arbitrator holds that a 2 years period of ineligibility is not out of proportion, excessive or disproportional.

This opinion is not contrary to the standard as set out in section 2.8 of the Netherlands Civil Code. This provision implies that a judging body is not allowed to apply a rule when the result of the application of that rule will be unacceptable. As said above, the application of the mandatory rule of a 2 years suspension is not unacceptable according to standards of reasonableness and fairness in the given circumstances.

For these reasons, the Sole Arbitrator decides that the Athlete is sanctioned with a period of ineligibility of 2 years."

9.3.2.1 Comment

No comment. This is a case of zero tolerance. Or, possibly: what is the usefulness of appeal, if in cases like *Zuijkerbuijk* there is not any room for *Einzelfallgerechtigkeit* ("casuistry" in the sense of a case-by-case approach and philosophy)? At first instances, at the national level one gets the feeling as a judge or arbitrator that one fulfils the role and function not of a human being and citizen, but of a stamping machine, acting as a counter clerk. An oral hearing giving a real. non-virtual opportunity to be informed about who is the defendant and why he or she did what he or she did etc. etc., becomes useless and superfluous under the circumstances.

9.4 Summary and Conclusion

(1) The WADA—institutionally—and the WADA Code—instrumentally/materially—have a sui generis character. In a pure formal sense, they are private legal instruments, but in fact they are a mixture of public and private (or private and public) elements. Their nature might be called semi-public (from the international governmental perspective) or semi-private (from the perspective of international organised sport). As such, they are separate phenomena in sports law, in a doctrinarian sense. The international community of states directly participates in WADA and its decision-making. Regional intergovernmental organisations such as the Council of Europe and the European Union participate indirectly in WADA (the European members of the Foundation Board are designated half by the Council of Europe and half by the EU). WADA is funded equally by the Olympic Movement on one hand and public governments on the other. Governments have on an equal basis taken part in the unanimous adoption of the initial WADA Code and its amended successor version of 2007. Through the introduction of the UNESCO Anti-Doping Convention states have endorsed the WADA Code in fact twice.

The WADA and WADA Code may be considered a global norm-setting model for other major problem areas in international sport like the fight against fraud and corruption. The introduction of public international agreements (treaties) is a first step to "juridify" such problems on an interstate level (see, for example, in particular the Anti-Football Hooliganism and Anti-Doping Conventions of the Council of Europe). Without the direct, explicit support of the international (or regional) community of states it is impossible to tackle major problems like football hooliganism, doping or fraud and corruption properly. States have the funding and the means (police enforcement and judicial measures). States in these circumstances must be the "double partners" of sport. The UNESCO Convention does not only have the same function as the Council of Europe Anti-Doping Convention, but then on a global level, it supports WADA and its Code directly. Hybrid organisations of the WADA type might be established—on a permanent, institutionalised basis—for the purpose of combating wrongs and abuses in the sporting world (and also beyond).

(2) What is the practical consequence of the close linkage between the international community of states and the WADA Code? The practical consequence is that what might be considered generally recognised principles of disciplinary law and procedure[13] are as such neglected as norms of a hierarchically superior order in relation to what initially were mere sporting rules which in fact are the laws of a subculture. In his PhD of 2006 at Erasmus University Rotterdam, Soek has come to the conclusion that the disciplinary law concerning doping violations must be

[13] Cf., on the international plane, "the general principles of law recognized by civilised nations" as a source of public international law in Article 38(1)(c) of the Statute of the International Court of Justice.

considered as pseudo-criminal law.[14] This would bring the general principles of criminal and criminal procedural law into the realm of disciplinary law in sport. The Dutch billiard social drugs case (*Zuijkerbuijk*) is a concrete example of the practical consequence of the close linkage between the international community of states and the WADA Code, in particular with regard to the application of the proportionality principle.

In this matter, states obviously have passed the Rubicon. It would be interesting to undertake an international comparative "state practice" research into the question whether and how states (governments) have weighed the general interest of the fight against doping in sport and the fundamental/human rights of the athlete against each other. What governments have stated within the framework of intergovernmental bodies like UNESCO and the Council of Europe? What positions national parliaments have taken? What were the legal and policy considerations to accept, for another example the whereabouts reporting and unannounced out-of-competition control system which seriously affects the privacy of the athlete? What are the arguments for delegating the investigating powers of national police and prosecution to the private sports organisations like WADA and others?[15] There still are a lot of questions to be asked and responded to. Finally, It seems fair to cite here what for example the Netherlands Minister of Sport replied to written parliamentary questions on this issue in 2010:

9.4.1 Question

What is the legal position of the National Doping Code with regard to current legislation and international conventions, such as the European Convention on the Protection of Human Rights and Fundamental Freedoms (ECHR) and the Convention on the Rights of the Child (UNCRC)? In the event that parts of the code deviate from these conventions, which have been ratified by the Dutch government, is it not true that the text of the convention would have to take precedence? What implications would this have for the rules on doping controls and how do you perceive your own role in this?

9.4.2 Answer

The National Doping Code is based almost entirely on the World Anti Doping Code and, first and foremost, must be regarded as a code for and by the sporting

[14] Soek 2006, in particular at p. 401 (Final statement no. 1). See previously also, Soek 2002, pp. 2–3, 5–7. See in general on principles of Dutch criminal law: Doelder 1981.

[15] See, in particular Soek 2008, pp. 3–13.

world. In this respect, therefore, by taking part in sport an athlete accepts obligations arising from the doping code. Within this context of the law of associations—in this case, sports associations—the international conventions mentioned above have no direct horizontal effect in principle. After all, an athlete can always refrain from taking part in sport. When the Code was established in 2003 and revised in 2007, this basic principle was universally accepted.

Furthermore, a number of professors (Kaufman-Kohler et al.) with expertise in the fields of international law and human rights have reviewed the key provisions of the Code in light of the general principles of relevant international law and concluded that there are no inconsistencies.

The international context of anti-doping policy is a crucial factor when planning this policy in the Netherlands. Governments and the sporting world have deliberately agreed, at global level, that the anti-doping rules are the same for all sports and in all countries. As well as being necessary for the success of anti-doping policy, this harmonisation has also been achieved through international agreements. Our country cannot unilaterally withdraw from this, partly because, if it did, it would run the very real risk of sporting isolation.

This does not detract from the fact that the Netherlands is dedicated to achieving a lasting and proper balance between the anti-doping rules and the rights of athletes. Among other achievements, this commitment has led to the current consultation within the Council of Europe regarding specific rules within anti-doping policy for athletes under the age of 18. Lastly, the principle of protecting health—alongside that of fair play—is also particularly relevant to young athletes (a principle that is also established in the Convention on the Rights of the Child).[16]

References

Blackshaw IS, Siekmann RCR, Soek J (eds) (2006) The court of arbitration for sport 1984–2004. T.M.C Asser Press, The Hague

Casini L (2009) Global hybrid public-private bodies: The World Anti-Doping Agency (WADA). International Organization Law Review 6

David P (2008) A guide to the World Anti-Doping Code—a fight for the spirit of sport. Cambridge University Press, Cambridge

de Doelder H (1981) Toepassing en beginselen van tuchtrecht [Scope and Principles of Disciplinary Law]. Alphen aan den Rijn

Latty F (2007) La *lex sportiva*. Recherche sur le droit transnational. Leiden-Boston

Pound RW, Q.C. (2002) The World Anti-Doping Agency: an experiment in international law. In: International Sports Law Review, July 2002 - Issue 3/02

Soek J (2002) The legal nature of doping law. The International Sports Law Journal (ISLJ) 2:2–7

Soek J (2006) The strict liability principle and the human rights of athletes in doping cases. T.M.C Asser Press, The Hague

Soek J (2008) The Athlete's right to respect for his private life and his home. The International Sports Law Journal ISLJ 3-4:3–13

[16] *Aanhangsel Handelingen Tweede Kamer* [Annex to Parliamentary Proceedings] 2009–2010 No. 1999.

Chapter 10
Legal Aspects of Combating Transnational Football Hooliganism in Europe

Abstract 'Football hooliganism' is a concept which is not easy to define. For instance, in the media, to a variety of incidents the label of 'hooliganism' has been used in a rather indeterminate way. The concept is broad as well as diffuse. As for present purposes one can say that football hooliganism has to do with crowd disorder involving football supporters. This involves usually some kind of criminal activity occurring at, just before or after a football match. Disorderly behaviour connected with the game of football has occurred in some form in virtually every EU Member State. Due to the various international and European competitions involving both national and club teams and the resultant travelling of large numbers of supporters together with the associated social and often violent disorder, football hooliganism has a highly visible profile. This international dimension has made it necessary to approach security in connection with football matches in a way that extends beyond national borders. This contribution charts the legal measures of a general nature which have been taken with regard to transnational football hooliganism. Also, individual countries in Europe have taken measures to combat transnational football hooliganism. In this contribution the various types of international measures will be dealt with in due course as well as the pertinent jurisprudence of the Court of Arbitration for Sport (CAS) and decisions taken by the European Commission regarding ticketing in relation to safety aspects at football matches.

This is a updated version of Chapter 27 in: Simon Gardiner, Richard Parrish and Robert C.R. Siekmann (Eds), *EU, Sport, Law and Policy*, The Hague 2009, pp. 499–533. See also: 'Football Hooliganism with an EU Dimension: Towards an International Legal Framework', Final Report AGIS Programme 2003, The Hague, T.M.C. Asser Instituut, November 2004. *Law and Policy*, The Hague 2009, pp. 499–533.Query

R. C. R. Siekmann, *Introduction to International and European Sports Law*,
ASSER International Sports Law Series, DOI: 10.1007/978-90-6704-852-1_10,

© T.M.C. Asser press, The Hague, The Netherlands, and the author 2012

Contents

10.1 Introduction

'Football hooliganism' is a concept which is not easy to define. For instance, in the media, to a variety of incidents the label of 'hooliganism' has been used in a rather indeterminate way. The concept is broad as well as diffuse. The European Convention on Spectator Violence and Misbehaviour at Sports Events and in particular at Football Matches (1985) does not contain any elaborated definition of the concept. As for present purposes one can say that football hooliganism has to do with crowd disorder involving football supporters. This involves usually some kind of criminal activity occurring at, just before or after a football match. Most football-crowd disorder occurs spontaneously, but it might as well be prearranged by gangs who attach themselves to football clubs and arrange to meet, and fight, gangs from other clubs in the vicinity of a stadium, but sometimes far away from any stadium. Disorderly behaviour connected with the game of football has occurred in some form in virtually every EU Member State. It seems to be a near-universal and unfortunately inevitable phenomenon connected with the game.

Due to the various international and European competitions involving both national and club teams (World and European Championships, Champions League and UEFA Cup) and the resultant travelling of large numbers of supporters together with the associated social and often violent disorder, football hooliganism has a highly visible profile. This international dimension has made it necessary to approach security in connection with football matches in a way that extends beyond national borders.

This contribution charts the legal measures of a general nature which have been taken with regard to transnational football hooliganism. These are international non-governmental measures that are in particular the European football governing body UEFA's Safety and Security Regulations. There are also intergovernmental measures, in particular the above-mentioned European Convention on Spectator Violence and Misbehaviour at Sports Events and in particular at Football Matches, as well as the measures taken within the framework of the European Union. Under the terms of Article 29 of the EU Treaty, the European Union's objective shall be to provide citizens with a high level of safety within an area of freedom, security and justice by developing common action among the Member States in the field of police and judicial cooperation in criminal matters and by preventing and combating racism and xenophobia. Also, individual countries in Europe have taken measures to combat transnational football hooliganism. An important example are the international banning orders in England on the basis of special legislation (Football Spectators Act 1989, as amended by the Football Disorder Act 2000) in order to prevent the free movement of football hooligans abroad. In this contribution the various types of international measures will be dealt with in due course as well as the pertinent jurisprudence of the Court of Arbitration for Sport (CAS) and decisions taken by the European Commission regarding ticketing in relation to safety aspects at football matches.

10.2 UEFA Safety and Security Regulations

The UEFA currently has 69 European national football associations amongst its membership (in 'wider Europe,' that is beyond the EU). The UEFA Safety and Security Regulations (latest edition: 2006; formerly: Binding Safety and Security Instructions to the organisers of, and the associations and clubs participating in matches played in any of the UEFA competitions regarding precautionary measures to be taken to ensure safety and security in the stadium, and to prevent crowd disturbances) is a non-governmental document applicable to competitions to be played under the auspices of UEFA. They are based on Article 50(1) of the UEFA Statutes, stating that the Executive Committee shall draw up regulations governing the conditions of participation in and the staging of UEFA competitions. The Regulations govern the organisational measures intended to ensure safety and security in and around the stadium before, during and after every match in the competition concerned. They do not constitute an exhaustive list of the organisational measures to be taken by the match organiser and participating organisations and clubs, and do not affect the legal obligations arising from the applicable national legislation. The aim of the Regulations is to make the match organiser and participating associations or clubs aware of their duties and responsibilities before, during and after a match in order to safeguard the safety and security of everyone present, as well as of the stadium and its installations. In the general part of the Regulations separate provisions deal with the appointment of a security coordinator by each association and club, and the relationship of associations and clubs with supporters' clubs. The Regulations further consist of particular sections regarding match preparation measures, admission of spectators to the stadium, and spectator control at the stadium. Provisions on spectator segregation and crowd dispersal strategy, ticketing, screening and searching of spectators, distribution of alcohol, provocative action and racism *inter alia* are incorporated in the Regulations.

10.3 UEFA Disciplinary Regulations (Edition 2006)

Article 6 provides that (1) member associations and clubs are responsible for the conduct of their supporters; and (2) the host association or club is responsible for order and security both inside and around the stadium before, during and after the match. It is liable for incidents of any kind, and can be rendered subject to disciplinary measures and bound to observe directives. Article 11 provides that disciplinary measures may be taken against member associations or clubs if spectators invade or attempt to invade the field of play, objects are thrown, fireworks ignited, or if order and discipline in the stadium area are otherwise not guaranteed. The disciplinary measures which may be imposed against member associations and clubs are listed in Article 14 (warning, reprimand, fine, annulment of the result of a match, order that a match be replayed, deduction of points, awarding of a match by default, playing of a match behind closed doors, stadium closure, playing of a match in a third country, disqualification from competitions in progress and/or exclusion from future competitions, withdrawal of a title or award, withdrawal of a licence). It is added in para 2 of Article 14 that a fine shall be not less than CHF 500 (five hundred) and not more than CHF 1,000,000 (one million). According to Article 11bis any member association or club whose supporters engage in discrimination on grounds of colour, race, religion or ethnic origin or in any form of extremist ideological propaganda will incur a minimum fine of CHF 30,000.

10.4 The Court of Arbitration for Sport

An award from the Court of Arbitration for Sports (CAS) confirmed the exclusion of the Dutch team Feyenoord from the UEFA Cup, following riots instigated by Feyenoord supporters at the UEFA Cup match between the club and the French team AS Nancy.[1] The legal issue in this award is whether a club has strict liability

---

1 *Feyenoord Rotterdam v. UEFA,* 20 April 2007, CAS 2007/A/1217.

for the acts of people associated with that club, even if that club does not want to recognise these individuals as supporters of their team. Feyenoord tried to argue against UEFA's strict liability rule with regard to supporter misconduct. The strict liability rule states that a club is responsible for the conduct of their supporters, regardless of whether the club itself is at fault. Feyenoord tried to argue that their exclusion from the UEFA Cup tournament was unjustified since the supporters that were responsible for the misconduct in Nancy were not supporters of their team. Feyenoord argued that these individuals had just come to Nancy to misbehave and were not connected legally to the team itself. In the end, CAS denied Feyenoord's appeal.

Feyenoord, in its submission to CAS, contended that the club is not to blame for the riots in Nancy. It had warned AS Nancy about the risks of selling tickets freely around their stadium and that a large group of potential troublemakers (whether with or without tickets) were travelling to Nancy. Feyenoord further criticised the decision of the chief of police to give all supporters access to the stadium, with or without tickets. Finally, Feyenoord criticised the decision to place its rogue supporters in sections of the stadium adjacent to the sections of the stadium in which the 'official' Feyenoord supporters were seated, thus giving these hooligans the opportunity to mix with the fans that had bought a ticket for the game directly from Feyenoord, a perpetually volatile situation because this way it was impossible for the police and stewards to distinguish between 'good' fans and 'bad' fans.

Furthermore, Feyenoord claimed that the troublemakers were not supporters of the club under the definition given to the term supporters by UEFA. These troublemakers did not buy their tickets through Feyenoord, did not travel to the stadium under the guidance of Feyenoord, could not be identified from their appearance as Feyenoord fans, and some of them even had a stadium ban in the Netherlands. Feyenoord argued that nothing distinguishes these individuals as being Feyenoord fans and therefore Feyenoord cannot be held responsible for the behaviour of these individuals [2]. Finally, the team complained about the proportionality of the sanction of the UEFA Appeals Body. The punishment received means that Feyenoord will miss out on a lot of income that could have been generated in the following round(s) of the UEFA Cup tournament.

UEFA responded to Feyenoord's contentions, saying that it is not a question of who is at fault for the behaviour of the supporters. Feyenoord is responsible for the behaviour of its supporters, irrespective of what the club may have done to either prevent or encourage this behaviour. The rule is strict liability for a club regarding the behaviour of its supporters. This also means that the warnings and measures taken by Feyenoord are irrelevant to the liability question.

With regard to the definition of the term supporter, UEFA stated that there is no clear definition of who is a supporter of a club. UEFA stated that the term supporter is 'not linked only to race, nationality of the place of residence of the individual, nor is it linked to a contract which an individual has concluded with the national association or the club in purchasing a ticket.' UEFA then concluded that 'there is no distinction between official and unofficial supporters of a team.'

CAS started its deliberations by stating it has competence to deal with this case and that the rules applicable to this dispute are the relevant UEFA rules and regulations. CAS then ruled that 'disciplinary law implemented in [UEFA's] regulations and directives is essentially a tool which allows UEFA to create order within the organization and to assert statutory standards of conduct through sanctions imposed by specific bodies and to ensure their appropriate execution.' CAS goes on to conclude that Feyenoord is subject to UEFA's rules and regulations and more specifically the ones upon which the decision by the UEFA Appeals Body is based.

CAS points at Article 6 of UEFA Disciplinary Regulations, which provides that:

> 1. 'Member associations and clubs are responsible for the conduct of their players, officials, members, supporters and any other persons exercising a function at a match at the request of the association or club.
> 2. The host association or club is responsible for the order and security both inside and around the stadium, before, during and after the match. It is liable for incidents of any kind, and can be rendered subject to disciplinary measures and bound to observe directives.'

CAS pointed out that, according to this article, Feyenoord has strict liability for the behaviour of its supporters. The point of contention that remained, then, was which persons can be defined as being a supporter. CAS noted that UEFA intentionally did not define the term supporter. UEFA did not specify the term supporter in terms of race, nationality, place of residence of the individual, or whether that person has a contract with a club or association by buying a ticket for a certain game. Defining the term supporter would alleviate clubs of responsibilities for supporters it does not want to recognise for legal purposes. The disciplinary sanctions of UEFA would in such a case apply only to supporters the club want them to apply to, while this could have never been the purpose of UEFA.

CAS went on to state that by leaving the term supporter undefined, the reasonable and objective observer could determine someone is a supporter of a club. Determinants that can help the reasonable and objective observer come to this conclusion are the behaviour of the individuals concerned and where they are located in the stadium and their vicinity. CAS went on to point to their prior case law, in which they considered that Article 6 Disciplinary Regulations was perfectly valid. CAS especially points to one case, *PSV Eindhoven* v. *UEFA*, 3 June 2003, CAS 2002/A/423. In that case, PSV was punished for racist behaviour by its supporters directed towards players of the opponent in a match in the Champions League tournament.

In this case CAS in relation to rule 6 paragraph 1 Disciplinary Regulations stated:

> 'According to this provision UEFA members and clubs are responsible for any breach of the UEFA Regulations committed by any of those persons. There is therefore no doubt that, under this rule, member associations and clubs bear strict responsibility for

> the actions of third parties, who are nonetheless specifically identified. This rule leaves absolutely no room for manoeuvre as far as its application is concerned. UEFA member associations and football clubs are responsible, even if they are not at fault, for the improper conduct of their supporters ...'

CAS further acknowledged that by penalising the clubs, UEFA in essence aims to penalise the supporters for their conduct. UEFA does not have a direct way of penalising individual supporters and therefore focuses all measures on the one body they do have authority over—the teams. UEFA in this way tries to indirectly achieve its goal of controlling the behaviour of certain (groups of) supporters by penalising the club these fans support. The objective of Article 6, then, with regard to the behaviour of supporters is to deter and prevent violent conduct, not to penalise clubs for wrongdoings. The strict liability rule makes sense in this context given that the goal is to prevent the violent acts of the supporters, so it does not matter what actions the club itself took.

CAS went on to conclude that the supporters responsible for the problems surrounding the match between AS Nancy and Feyenoord could be identified as Feyenoord supporters and therefore the strict liability rule applied. The fact that Feyenoord took measures to prevent any disorder does not alter the liability of the club for the behaviour of its supporters. The fact that there may have been errors in the way AS Nancy handled ticket sales, the way the French police handled the situation by giving the troublemakers access to the stadium and enabling them to mix with the 'official' Feyenoord supporters, was all held to be irrelevant for this case. Feyenoord is liable for the conduct of its fans under Article 6 paragraph 1 Disciplinary Regulations. This needs to be distinguished from the liability the home team possibly has under Article 6 paragraph 2 of the Disciplinary Regulations as the host and the organiser of the match.

Feyenoord further appealed to CAS on the severity of the penalty. However, CAS first stated that according to Article 14 Disciplinary Regulations, disqualification from the UEFA Cup competition could be used as a possible penalty for violation of the Disciplinary Regulations. CAS went on to assess Feyenoord's claim that disqualification would be disproportionate to the offence committed. CAS stated that according to its case law, a 'sanction imposed must not be evidently and grossly disproportionate to the offence.' CAS came to the conclusion that UEFA was allowed to impose the heavy sanction of disqualification. In reaching this conclusion it took into account that the behaviour of the fans, (e.g., breaking a wall inside the stadium to reach the supporters of the opposing team, throwing projectiles towards individuals) could have been considered as serious offences by the UEFA Appeals Body. Furthermore, Feyenoord was a multiple offender with regard to supporter misconduct. UEFA regards recidivism as an aggravating factor in its Disciplinary Regulations. Over the past five years there have been 12 disciplinary cases against Feyenoord for supporter misconduct. Finally, a disqualification ensures that in the further course of the UEFA Cup season, there would not be any further incidents of supporter misconduct of Feyenoord's supporters. On these grounds, CAS ruled that the sanction imposed by the UEFA Appeals Body was not disproportionate to the offences committed.

10.5 Council of Europe

The Council of Europe was the first international, interstate organisation established in Europe after the Second World War. With 46 Members, the Council of Europe currently represents the image of a 'wider Europe.' The main objective of the Council of Europe is to strengthen democracy, human rights and the rule of law. The Council of Europe was the first international, intergovernmental organisation to take initiatives, to establish legal instruments, and to offer an institutional framework for the development of sport at European level. The extensive work of the Council of Europe on sport is evident through the main texts on sport, such as the European Sports Charter and the Code of Sports Ethics, the European Convention on Spectator Violence and the Anti-Doping Convention. The Council of Europe fights to control the negative aspects of sport, in particular violence and doping, through two sports Conventions which are binding legal instruments. Although particularly acute today, the problem of violence has been a matter of concern to sports officials for a very long time. As early as 1983, the Council of Europe expressed its determination to take action against the increase in violence, both on and off the field. The Heysel disaster gave added urgency to the Council of Europe's work in this field. Shortly afterwards, Member States set out to find the best means of combating violence and developing international cooperation. The events at Heysel required an urgent response; and it was in this dramatic context that the European Convention on Spectator Violence and Misbehaviour at Sports Events and, in particular, at Football Matches was signed in Strasbourg on 19 August 1985 (including all EU Member States; it has been ratified by all but two).[2] A basis for this was already available, that is a Recommendation of the Committee of Ministers of March 1984. Some 41 States have now ratified this Convention.

Although the Convention is in the first instance directed at preventing hooliganism at international (European) sports events, the States Parties undertake to take the measures described in the Agreement at certain national high-risk matches as well. As preventing and combating hooliganism at such matches strictly speaking do not require international arrangements, the Convention is mainly relevant for international matches.

This Convention provides governments with measures and remedies for the control, prevention and, where necessary, punishment of violence, as well as educational measures to prevent outbreaks of violence. The Parties to the Convention undertake, within the limits of their respective constitutional provisions to take the necessary steps to give effect to its provisions (Article 1). The Parties undertake to ensure the formulation and implementation of measures designed to prevent and control violence and misbehaviour by spectators, *inter alia,* by applying or, if need be, adopting appropriate criminal and/or administrative legislation regarding perpetrators, and they shall seek to ensure, where necessary by introducing appropriate legislation that stadium owners and public authorities

---

[2] Council of Europe European Treaty Series No. 120.

take practical measures at and within stadiums to prevent or control such violence or misbehaviour (Article 3).The Standing Committee which was established in the framework of the Convention, monitors compliance with set measures and issues practical recommendations. Among the principal measures recommended by the Convention are:

- deploying public order resources in stadiums and along the transit routes used by spectators;
- separating rival groups of spectators;
- strictly controlling ticket sales;
- excluding trouble-makers from stadiums and matches;
- prohibiting the introduction and restricting the sale of alcoholic drinks in stadiums;
- conducting security checks, particularly for objects likely to be used for violence;
- clearly defining responsibilities between organisers and the public authorities;
- designing football stadiums in such a way as to guarantee spectator safety.
- In addition to the Convention, numerous Recommendations have been adopted by the Standing Committee, covering the following aspects:
- ticket sales (efficient management of ticket production, sale and distribution of tickets, key factors for overall football match safety);
- identification and treatment of offenders;
- stewarding (reducing police numbers in football stadiums);
- efficient crowd management inside stadiums, taking account of spectator safety and security (clear definition of responsibilities, appropriate stadiums design, measures concerning the sale of alcoholic drinks, and so on);
- action against racism and xenophobia;
- police cooperation and information exchange;
- social and educational measures to prevent violence in sport.

In the context of the identification and treatment of offenders it was recommended by the Standing Committee to impede known violent fans from leaving the country, allowing if possible, temporary arrest, re-instating temporary border control, recognising national exclusion orders. Also Recommendations were made regarding police-cooperation by arranging for 'police spotters,' that is plain-clothes policemen from the visiting countries to assist the local police force in identifying potential troublemakers.

The Convention on Spectator Violence encourages close international cooperation among States and close cooperation among the relevant national sports authorities.

The Convention expressly points to the importance of international cooperation and judicial assistance in this area by, where appropriate and in accordance with the applicable international agreements (European Conventions on the Transfer of Proceedings in Criminal Matters, on Extradition, and on the Transfer of Sentenced Persons), (a) transferring proceedings against persons apprehended in connection with violence or other criminal behaviour committed at sports events to their country of residence, (b) seeking the extradition of persons suspected of violence or other criminal behaviour committed at sports events, and (c) transferring persons convicted of offences of violence or other criminal behaviour committed at sports events to serve their sentences in the relevant country (Article 5). The Standing Committee is the body responsible for monitoring the implementation of the Convention. UEFA and FIFA are both associated with the Committee's work. During major international championships—the World Cup, European Championships, and others—the Standing Committee sets up an ad hoc working group to assess the security measures adopted and, after the major event in question, to draw conclusions from the implementation of such measures.

10.6 European Union

On 29 May 1985, a disaster took place at the Heysel stadium in Brussels. Before the start of the UEFA Cup Final, British hooligans charged the section of the stand where there were mostly Italian supporters. A total of 39 people died and 670 people were injured. Liverpool and Juventus went on to play the Cup Final regardless. Afterwards, UEFA decided to ban British football clubs from European Cup tournaments for a period of 5 years and the Secretary-General of the Belgian football league was given a suspended prison sentence. Some 14 British hooligans were sentenced to 3 years' effective imprisonment.

The Heysel tragedy led to the European Community's first involvement in the fight against hooliganism. Before, hooliganism had been a relatively unknown phenomenon on the European continent. This section gives an overview of the involvement of the EU in the fight against vandalism and violence in sport, which has led to numerous European Parliament resolutions and some European Parliament reports and to several Council resolutions and decisions. The hard and soft law resulting from the decisions of the EU institutions will be briefly described, although the amount of hard EU law in this field is rather limited.

10.6.1 After the Heysel Tragedy

Two weeks after the Heysel stadium disaster, the European Parliament adopted two resolutions condemning the violence preceding the European Cup Final.[3] It condemned 'these violent crimes of a minority and their exploitation by fascist and extremist groups which promote chauvinist, racist, intolerant and aggressive

[3] Resolution of the European Parliament on the violence at the football-match in Brussels on 29 May 1985, 13 June 1985; Resolution of the European Parliament on the tragedy at the Heysel stadium in Brussels, 13 June 1985.

feelings.'[4] In later reports, resolutions and decisions, a similar connection was made between fascism, chauvinism and football hooliganism.

In the first of the resolutions, the Parliament furthermore called on the Commission to urgently propose a directive in this field for adoption by the Council. Such a directive had to guarantee that sporting events could take place in conditions which ensured the personal safety of both players and spectators. The resolution further proposed a ban on the sale of alcohol inside and near stadiums and called on the governments of Member States and sporting associations to launch a major information campaign to raise public awareness concerning the importance of fair play in sport and to support sporting associations in their struggle against violence at sporting events.

Finally, the resolution contained an instruction to the Youth, Culture, Education, Information and Sports Committee of the European Parliament. This Committee as soon as possible had to present an intermediate report on violence in sport, which in particular had to deal with the measures to be taken in the short term to avoid any repetition of violence in sport. In addition, the resolution proposed a public hearing, following which a final report would be prepared containing an inventory of the policy and legislation in the different Member States to combat violence in sport and including an investigation into the causes of the increase of violence in sport. Measures taken to combat this violence, however, should not prevent the organisation of European sporting events, especially among youth organisations.

The second resolution adopted after the Heysel tragedy among other things requested the Commission and the Council to submit practical proposals for a genuine European sports policy within the Community.[5]

10.6.2 The Larive Report on Vandalism and Violence in Sport

The intermediate report requested in the aforementioned resolutions was drafted by the Dutch liberal MEP Mrs Larive-Groenendaal. It referred to earlier proposals by several MEPs for resolutions on violence in sport.[6] In it, the urgent call for practical measures to combat vandalism and violence at football matches was repeated. These measures were to be taken at Community level, in close cooperation with governments and sports authorities. Furthermore, a balance had to be struck between strict measures to repress violence in sport and the maintenance of the fundamental values of our society (as the final part of the preamble stressed). The causes of this violence should also be dealt with.

[4] Resolution of the European Parliament on the violence at the football-match in Brussels on 29 May 1985, 13 June 1985, Para 1.

[5] Resolution of the European Parliament on the tragedy at the Heysel stadium in Brussels, 13 June 1985.

[6] Motion for a resolution tabled by Mr McMahon on hooliganism and violence by football supporters at European football matches (Doc. 2-734/84), motion for a resolution tabled by Mrs De Backer-van Ocken and others on violence in sport (Doc. 2-1661/84); motion for a resolution tabled by Mr De la Malene on the increase in acts of violence (Doc. 2-1692/84).

The report suggested preventive measures in seven fields: international coordination, the sale of alcohol, body searches, the construction of football grounds, ticket controls, arrangements for supporters and the provision of entertainment. First of all, international coordination before, during and after matches between government, local authorities, police forces, sports organisations and other bodies concerned had to be strengthened. It was considered particularly important that a prudent timetable should be drafted for sporting events for the transport and accompaniment of supporters. In addition, exchange of information had to take place in order to initiate an effective campaign to prevent violence. Secondly, a ban was proposed on the sale and consumption of alcoholic drinks and of drinks in cans or bottles inside and around stadiums. Thirdly, the report made clear that body searches of all supporters should be performed, and any weapons or objects which might be used as such should be confiscated, as should banners and flags bearing slogans inciting to violence.

Fourthly, the design and construction of football grounds had to be adapted in order to meet European standards. Holding international matches at grounds which do not meet these standards had to be prohibited. The standards in question would concern: (1) the removal of all inflammable material; (2) barriers between groups of supporters which are strong enough to withstand crowd surges; (3) more and segregated entrances/exits both to the stadium and between blocks of seating, enabling their opening and closing to be controlled in accordance with requirements; (4) improvements in audiovisual control systems using closed-circuit television, loudspeakers and corridors for movement between blocks.

A fifth field in which action was considered necessary concerned ticket sales. These sales had to be brought under strict legal control, with sanctions applying against 'ticket touts' selling tickets on the black market and against their customers. Another field of action was to include arrangements for supporters. These had to consist of the organisation and monitoring of travel arrangements for visiting supporters, the combined sale of tickets (travel and match), accompaniment of the supporters from the train or coach to the stadium and back and the imposition of a ban on alcohol during the journey. A final field of action concerned the provision of entertainment before, between and after sporting events, to prevent misbehaviour arising from boredom.

After listing these preventive measures against violence during football matches, the report called on the police to take further specific action. First of all, it suggested that a sufficient number of police forces have to be mobilised to combat violence around matches. Laws to combat drunkenness on the public highway and the carrying of weapons would need to be applied very strictly. Troublemakers (including foreigners) would have to be arrested at an early stage and be tried immediately. Stiffer penalties, alternative sentences and the payment or repair by the delinquents of the damage they caused were also considered necessary. In addition, the report urged for a legal stadium ban based on a European blacklist for persons convicted of criminal acts at previous matches. Finally, the clubs whose supporters committed the acts of violence would have to be punished as well. The report proposed that all these measures should be laid down in a Community

Directive, as the Parliamentary Committee which drafted the report considered this the only way in which the uniform application of the measures could be ensured. In addition, the report called for another Directive to take account of the work of the Council of Europe, which adopted a convention against spectator violence after the Heysel stadium disaster.[7]

The report also stated that a broader approach to the problem of football hooliganism was needed. Such an approach could be instigated if the European Ministers responsible for sport were to 'study longer-term measures which [would] ensure the harmonious development of sport in the Community by drawing up a genuine action programme.'[8] This programme had to comprise education programmes at schools and public information campaigns against extremism and campaigns to promote fair play in sport. Sporting facilities at schools and for the general public also needed to be improved. Another suggestion in the report was to promote contact between supporters of opposing teams preceding matches, in order to improve mutual understanding. Finally, the programme had to aim to establish appropriate training for police forces and the appointment of police liaison officers.

Another proposal was to draw up a code of conduct for the media in order to avoid any stirring up of aggression and chauvinist sentiments by them.[9] Freedom of movement for sportsmen and women was also expected to lead to a less nationalistic attitude during European sporting events. Finally, it was suggested that the Committee on Youth of the European Parliament draft a final report on the basis of a public hearing. This report would have to include a study into the causes of the increase of violence in sport, research into the exploitation of sport for commercial, political and criminal purposes and a comparative overview of relevant legislation in the Member States. However, it had to be prevented that measures to combat football hooliganism would impede the organisation of European amateur sporting events.

10.6.3 An Amended Resolution

On 11 July, the European Parliament adopted the resolution proposed by the Education and Sports Committee after amendments.[10] One amendment was that the resolution now proposed disciplinary measures against players who in the

---

7 The European Convention on Spectator Violence and Misbehaviour at Sports Events and in particular at Football Matches; the Convention was adopted on 19 August 1985 and entered into force 1 November 1985.

8 Interim Report drawn up on behalf of the Committee on Youth, Culture, Education, Information and Sport on Vandalism and Violence in Sport, 2 July 1985, Motion for a resolution on vandalism and violence in sport, Para 6.

9 Id., Para 8.

10 Resolution of the European Parliament on the measures needed to combat vandalism and violence in sport, 11 July 1985.

course of matches gave way to excesses of enthusiasm and behaviour, which could unduly arouse and provoke emotional reactions from the spectators. The amended resolution also urged UEFA and FIFA to be responsible in determining the stadiums where major matches would take place and to ensure adequate standards and safety measures. Apart from these amendments, the essential elements of the proposed resolution of the Education and Sports Committee were left intact.

Despite the fact that two Community Directives concerning the fight against vandalism and violence in sport had been called for, the Commission did not submit any proposals to this end. In a new Resolution in January 1988, the European Parliament expressed its regret and repeated its call for measures against football hooliganism. It added that a possible Framework Directive would have to include rules concerning the international coordination of measures (among which exchange of information) and the harmonisation of national measures, and would need to provide standards for stadiums. Some new measures were also proposed, such as the establishment of central national information points in all Member States. These information points would consult prior to all international sporting events so as to be able to adopt common measures. Exchange of information should facilitate the extradition and bringing to trial of hooligans. Finally, it was suggested that Member States should introduce a licensing system for sports stadiums (based on health and safety grounds). The Parliament further called on the Commission to collect information on the role of racist and extreme right-wing political organisations in the provocation of violent incidents during sporting events.

Preventive action, especially in the social sphere, also had to be pursued. Its objective would have to be to educate young people towards a new way of thinking, which rejects violence and regards sport as a means of meeting other people. Member States had to make greater use of information campaigns. Sport education at school and sporting facilities in general needed to be improved. Attention also had to be paid to the link between drug use in sport and violence. The resolution concluded with a call for a European action programme for the harmonious development of sport. Six years later, the European Parliament would repeat its call for European standards concerning security in football stadiums. In addition, it called for comparative research into the Member States' policies for preventing and combating football hooliganism.[11]

10.6.4 The 1996 Council Recommendation

During the 1990s, the Council of Ministers finally began to pay attention to the phenomenon of football hooliganism, which would ultimately even result in a (limited) number of binding decisions in this field. However, the first action by the

[11] Resolution of the European Parliament on the Community and Sport, 6 May 1994.

Council was to adopt a number of non-binding recommendations.[12] In April 1996 the Council of Ministers adopted a recommendation in which it advised the EU Member States to draw on the recommendations of the Standing Committee of the Convention concerning spectator violence of the Council of Europe.[13] Member States were further urged to use a common format for police intelligence reports on known or suspected groups of troublemakers. This format would facilitate the exchange of information between Member States. The annex to the Council recommendation contained a specimen of the suggested format. Reports would have to be exchanged quickly and effectively between the Member States, possibly by means of the network of correspondents concerning football hooliganism. In addition, Member States were advised to cooperate in the training of police: where appropriate, police officers should be encouraged to attend relevant training courses in other Member States. Police cooperation also had to be made possible before, during and after football matches. Requests for such cooperation would have to be submitted as soon as possible and no later than 4 weeks prior to the match. Finally, the Council of Ministers recognised the importance of stewards in this field, and recommended that the police should contribute to training programmes promoting close cooperation between stewards and police officers.

10.6.5 The Roth Report and the Resulting Resolution

In April 1996, German MEP Claudia Roth (Green Party) submitted her report on hooliganism and the free movement of football supporters.[14] The report concerned a thorough examination of the problems caused by football hooligans and possible measures to counter these problems. The report resulted in a resolution, which was adopted by the European Parliament on 21 May 1996.[15] The resolution started with some general points, among which a call on the EU Member States to respect the Convention of the Council of Europe concerning spectator violence. Concerning stadiums, the European Parliament

---

[12] Earlier recommendations of the Council (indirectly) relating to football hooliganism were the following. Council recommendation of 30 November 1993 concerning the responsibility of organisers of sporting events; Council recommendation of, December 1994 concerning direct, informal exchanges of information with the CCEEs in the area of international sporting events (network of contact persons); Council recommendation of, December 1994 concerning exchange of information on the occasion of major events and meetings (network of contact persons).

[13] Council Recommendation on Guidelines for Preventing and Restraining Disorder connected with Football Matches, 22 April 1996.

[14] Ausschuß für Grundfreiheiten und innere Angelegenheiten, Bericht über das Problem des Hooliganismus und die Freizügigkeit der Fußballfans, Berichterstatterin: Frau Claudia Roth, 25 April 1996.

[15] Resolution of the European Parliament on Hooliganism and the Free Movement of Football Supporters, 21 May 1996.

> '[took] the view that the absolute requirement to provide all-seater stadiums is excessive and that the installation of "cages" is dangerous and degrading and may give rise to violence; [took] the view, on the other hand, that women and children should be encouraged to attend sports events, with family enclosures.'[16]

Furthermore, the Parliament noted 'that the current file system and the exchange of data has resulted in the detention or expulsion of innocent persons.'[17]

After these general points, the Resolution formulated several recommendations concerning social and preventive policy, free movement of persons and police and legal measures. Concerning the first policy field, fan projects were regarded by the Parliament as an excellent means to prevent violence at sports events. Clubs, national associations, UEFA and FIFA should therefore provide financial support for these projects. Clubs should also try to involve supporters in the life of the club, in particular in important decisions. The European Parliament further called on the Commission to take action against football clubs which linked ticket sales to travel packages. It furthermore proposed that all supporters' clubs should appoint stewards to look after and accompany groups of supporters of their club to away matches.

It was further noted that measures to restrict the free movement of persons could only be directed at individuals whose past conduct indicated that they posed a genuine and serious threat to public safety. The nationality of any given supporter can never be a criterion based on which access to sports events is denied. However, under certain conditions, the organisation of a match may justify internal border controls, 'provided they would not exceed what is strictly necessary to respond to a serious threat to public safety and to protect the rights and freedoms of others.'[18] In this, the European Parliament aimed to strike a balance between different sets of rights: 'the rights of all people, including football supporters, to free movement within the European Union; the rights of those who want to attend football matches in a safe and secure environment; and the rights of those who live near to stadiums.'[19] Restricting access to stadiums can only take place in accordance with fundamental standards. Unfortunately, legal differences between Member States made it difficult to apply restrictions on attendance at matches in other Member States for persons convicted of football-related offences. Only supporters who had been convicted for such offences could legitimately be prevented from attending football matches.

Concerning police and legal measures, the European Parliament called on the Member States to adopt legislation providing appropriate penalties for individuals found guilty of football-related offences. These penalties had to include stadium bans for a specific period of time. Spectators committing offences must be tried in accordance with the law of the country where the offence was committed. In case

---

[16] Id., Para 9.

[17] Id., Para 10.

[18] Id., Para 28.

[19] Id., Para 29.

of international matches, police assistance also had to be provided by police officers from the country of the team playing away. In general, it was considered that international police information had to be improved, as well as the exchange of information. Football clubs themselves also had to take appropriate measures to prevent fans from intimidating players and supporters. Clubs which openly tolerated violence and race hatred had to be penalised. A final recommendation concerned rigorous security checks, which must be carried out at the entrance to and in the streets near stadiums.

The resolution concluded by calling for the inclusion of a provision on countering racism, anti-semitism and xenophobia in the Treaty on the European Union. The European Parliament also called for extensive research to be undertaken into the causes of hooliganism, the role played by extremist organisations among groups of supporters and the ways in which the media could help prevent hooliganism. It also called on the Council to consider a Convention on measures to combat football violence. This Convention could define the concept of 'high-risk fan' and lay down clear rules for the exchange of information between Member States (with the necessary legal protection).

10.6.6 Binding Measures

The first binding Council decision to impact the fight against football hooliganism was made in May 1997,[20] when the Council adopted a Joint Action with regard to cooperation in law and order and security. The decision was taken within the framework of the third Community pillar, which (at that time) comprised cooperation in the field of justice and home affairs. The Joint Action was one of the (binding) instruments available within this framework. It was intended to supplement existing bilateral and multilateral arrangements and was without prejudice to closer cooperation between Member States.

The first obligation following from the Joint Action concerned the mutual provision (by Member States) of information. This information was to be requested via central bodies, whether upon request or not. Information would be provided if 'sizable groups which may pose a threat to law and order and security are travelling to another Member State in order to participate in events. This information shall be supplied at as early a stage as possible to all Member States concerned, regardless of whether they are neighbours, including Member States of transit.'[21] This information was to include the fullest possible details concerning the group in question (overall composition and nature of the group: is it aggressive and is there any chance of disturbances?), routes to be taken and stopping-off

[20] Joint Action adopted by the Council on the basis of Article K.3 of the Treaty on European Union with regard to Cooperation on Law and Order and Security, 26 May 1997.

[21] Id., Art I(I).

points, means of transport and any other relevant information. For each of these categories of information it had to be indicated how reliable the provided information was. Finally, the provision of information was to be in compliance with national law.

Article 2 had a less binding character than the first Article of the Joint Action. It created the possibility to post liaison officers to other Member States upon their request. These officers would have an advisory and supportive function, without any special powers, and they would be unarmed. They were to provide information and carry out their duties in accordance with instructions from their home Member State and guidelines from the Member State to which they were seconded. The host Member State would ensure the protection of the liaison officers (para 1). The competent authorities of the host Member State had to determine the activities in which the liaison officers would be involved. Liaison officers must follow the guidelines of the aforementioned competent authorities (para 2). Article 3 concerned a basis for further cooperation in the field of law and order and security. Each Spring, the EU Presidency had to organise a meeting of heads of central bodies for law and order and security in the Member States. During these meetings matters of common interest would be discussed. Furthermore the heads of the aforementioned central bodies were to encourage the holding of exercises and exchanges and training secondments for their staff.

10.6.7 The Possibility of Stadium Bans

In its recommendation of 9 June 1997, the Council considered the possibility of stadium exclusions/bans for football hooligans.[22] In March 1997, an EU seminar on football hooliganism took place in Amsterdam. This seminar led to the conclusion that greater cooperation between police forces on specific issues to combat disorder connected with football matches was needed. In certain Member States, stadium exclusions were found to be an effective means. In some of those Member States the exclusion followed from civil law (i.e., bans imposed by football clubs), while in other Member States the ban was regulated under public law. Stadium exclusions in one Member State must also be effective in another Member State during European football matches. For this reason, the recommendation suggested that the responsible Ministers in the Member States should invite their national sports associations to examine how stadium exclusions imposed under national civil law could be applied to football matches in a European context. An annual report on the situation in the Member States concerning football hooliganism and an annual meeting of experts would also be useful. Special attention had to be paid to international networks of supporters' groups. A checklist of

---

[22] Resolution of the Council on preventing and restraining football hooliganism through the exchange of experience, exclusion from stadiums and media policy, 9 June 1997.

media policy for use by police authorities in the Member States was also considered desirable. This checklist would contain recommendations for a media strategy relating to international football matches and championships. Comparative research into the situation in the Member States could lead to a future Joint Action to be adopted by the Council.

10.6.8 The First Police Handbook

In June 1999, the Council adopted a resolution concerning a Handbook for international police cooperation and measures to prevent and control violence and disturbances in connection with international football matches (the Handbook was included in the annex to the resolution).[23] A revised version of the Handbook was adopted in 2001 and therefore the description of the 1999 Handbook given here will be brief. The full title of the Handbook was as follows: 'Handbook for international police cooperation and measures to prevent and control violence and disturbances in connection with international football matches, in which at least one Member State is involved either by participation in the match and/or by hosting the match.' The non-binding Handbook concerned a large number of recommendations in this field. The Handbook concerned the following topics:

- *preparations by police forces:* organising authorities and police forces had to involve police forces from participating countries in preparations, at an early stage;
- *organising cooperation between police forces:* organising authorities and police forces had to take into account requirements for the organisation of international police cooperation;
- *information management by police forces:* organising authorities and police forces had to take into account the requirements of police information management;
- *cooperation between police forces and stewards:* organising authorities and police forces had to call on the persons responsible for supervising fans from participating football associations for assistance in maximum cooperation;
- *checklist for media policy and communication strategy (police/authorities) relating to major (international) championships and matches:* police forces must make use of the media policy checklist provided by the Handbook;
- *requirements for admission policy and ticketing policy:* organising authorities must take into account the requirements for organisers in the area of admission policy, in particular by establishing a ticketing policy and ticket control and by separating rival groups of fans.

[23] Resolution of the Council concerning a Handbook for international police cooperation and measures to prevent and control violence and disturbances in connection with international football matches, 21 June 1999 (OJ C 196, 13/7/1999).

The Handbook further contained a list of documents previously adopted by the Council of the European Union.

10.6.9 The 2001 Handbook

The new Handbook from 2001 was adopted in a Council resolution to which it was annexed and replaced the 1999 Handbook.[24] The Handbook remained a non-binding document containing a large number of recommendation concerning information management by police forces, preparations by police forces, organising cooperation between police forces, cooperation between police forces and stewards, the role of the organiser and a list of documents previously adopted by the Council. Below, we will focus more closely on the recommendations provided.

10.6.9.1 Information Management by Police Forces

The exchange of information is 'of the utmost importance' to combat and prevent football- related violence. In order to achieve this, Member States were strongly recommended to establish a permanent national (police) football information point. This information point ideally had to be the 'central and sole' contact point for the exchange of information relating to football matches with an international dimension. Member State were free to decide to organise certain contacts in this field through the competent authorities, but the national football information point should at least be provided with a minimum of information. Moreover, it had to be avoided that the quality and efficiency of the activities of the national information point would be jeopardised by any separate exchange of information. Member States had to equip the information points with the necessary technical facilities to fulfil their tasks effectively.[25]

The football information point also needed to aim to facilitate international police cooperation. The information point could support the competent national authorities by addressing the necessary proposals or recommendations to these authorities regarding the policy to be followed by them on football-related issues. With a view to football matches with an international dimension, it was considered desirable if the information point had at its disposal an updated risk-analysis related to its own dubs and its national team. In addition, the information point was to be responsible for administering personal data regarding high-risk supporters in accordance with the applicable legislation. Finally, the information point would be

---

24 Resolution of the Council concerning a Handbook with recommendations for international police cooperation and measures to prevent and control violence and disturbances in connection with football matches with an international dimension, in which at least one Member State is involved, 6 December 2001 (OJ C 22, 24/1/2002).

25 Id., Chapter 1, Section I, I. Introduction.

responsible for the coordination of police information in connection with football matches, whereby it could extend this exchange of information to other law enforcement services responsible for safety or public order.[26]

The Handbook devoted much attention to the actual exchange of information between the national football information points. A distinction was made between general information and personal information. What was termed general information was made up of information defining the event in all its dimensions with particular attention to the security risks at the event (strategic information), information that could help make a correct analysis of the issues surrounding the event (operational information) and information allowing the persons in charge at the operational level to respond appropriately in connection with order and security surrounding the event (tactical information). Personal information referred to information concerning individuals who represented or might represent a danger to public order or to security in connection with the event or who might have been involved in incidents, with a view to preparing or taking the appropriate measures (mentioned as examples of these measures are stadium bans and photos of the persons in question). Personal information could only be exchanged if it served a well-defined goal, i.e., it had to contribute to the success of a specific mission. Use of such information was furthermore limited in time and scope.[27]

Concerning the chronological sequence of the exchange of information the Handbook distinguished between three stages: before the event (i.e., the football match or tournament in all its aspects), during the event and after the event. The national football information points of both the organising country and the supporting country would each have different tasks during these stages. The three stages did not always need to be strictly separated.[28]

The tasks assigned to the national football information point of the organising country before, during and after the event were the following (with the aforementioned distinction concerning general information (strategic, operational and tactical information) also applying here). Before the event the information point of the organising country could formulate the information requirements and send a request for information to national football information points in one or more other countries (strategic level). This had to concern matters such as the risk analysis concerning the fans of the team concerned, information on the team itself and its accompanying party (when there was a threat) and information concerning spotters. Information if possible also had to concern the applicable legislation and policy of the authorities of the organising country, information on the organisation of the event and identification of officials and police chiefs in charge. This information could also be made available to the other national football information points concerned by the event. At operational level, the national football

[26] Id., Chapter 1, Section I, III. Tasks with an international dimension.

[27] Chapter 1, Section I, IV. Exchange of police information, 1. (Kinds of information).

[28] Chapter 1, Section I, IV Exchange of police information, 2. (Chronological sequence of information exchange).

information point of the supporting country could be asked to supply information regarding the movements of normal and risk supporters, the participating team and its accompanying party, ticket sales and possible requests for the participation of police officers and of fan coaches, and information regarding general crime, including terrorism. Information concerning the organisation of security during the event (e.g., the integration of the spotters within the local security system, guidelines for fans) could also be provided to the information point of the supporting country.[29]

During the event the national football information point of the organising country could request confirmation of the information supplied by the information point of the supporting country, including an update of the risk analysis (operational level). According to the Handbook, this request had to be forwarded and answered via a system of liaison officers if such a system had been set up. At tactical level, the information point of the organising country could provide confirmation of the information supplied by having all the parties involved carry out checks on the spot. Proposals might then be made for adjusting the measures. General information regarding the possible return of fans that were expelled and/or refused entry must also be supplied to the national football information points of the country of origin and of the transit countries. If necessary, information regarding this return could also be provided by the information point of the organising country.[30]

After the event, the information point of the organising country could assess fan behaviour so that a risk analysis of visitors could be updated by the information point of the supporting country. The process of information exchange could also be evaluated (strategic level). At operational level the information point of the organising country could assess the operational usefulness of the information provided by the supporting countries and of the support supplied by the visiting country. In addition, it could supply factual information concerning the reported visitors and a description of the incidents. Information regarding possible arrests could also be exchanged, with the legal possibilities being taken into account.[31]

For the national football information point of the supporting country, the Handbook recommended the following tasks. Before the event it could on its own initiative supply all relevant information to the other national football information points concerned. In addition, it could supply the information point of the organising country with answers to the questions formulated and make use of the list of stadium bans, in conformity with the law (strategic level). At operational level, it could answer the questions asked, especially the questions concerning the movements of fans, the participation of police officers such as spotters and the sending of fan coaches. At tactical level, preparations to integrate the police

[29] Chapter 1, Section I, IV Exchange of police information, 2.a. (Task of the national football information point of the organising country), Para 1.

[30] Ibid., Para 2.

[31] Ibid., Para 3.

delegation could be initiated. During the event and at operational level, the information supplied could be updated and the movements and stays of the fans could be monitored by the information point of the supporting country.[32]

After the event the information point of the supporting country could adapt the risk analysis (strategic level). At operational level it could carry out an assessment with regard to the following issues: the exchange of information based on the factual information supplied by the national football information point of the organising country; the operational usefulness of the exchange of information; the strategic and operational information given in advance by the national football information point of the organising country and the spotters' work.[33]

Concerning the communication procedure between the national football information points of the differing countries, the Handbook contained the following recommendations. First of all, the contacts between the police services of the countries involved in an event had to be coordinated and, if necessary, organised by the national information points. In addition, the lines of communication and information facilities had to be clear to the supporting foreign police forces. If a system of liaisons officers was set up, the different police forces deployed throughout the championships or match had to communicate via the liaison officer appointed and seconded by the country in question. This officer could have responsibility for tasks relating to public order, violent football hooliganism and general crime, including terrorism, where this was connected with a particular football match or tournament. If in place, local football information points had to cooperate with the national football information point. The use of the native language was recommended. The communication between the national information points had to guarantee the confidential character of the exchanged information. The exchanged information could also be stored and consulted at a later date by other national football information points.[34]

Finally, four general rules concerning the exchange of information were recommended. First of all, the police force of the organising country had to shield the liaison officer of the supporting foreign police force from any contact with the media, if the liaison officer so desired. Secondly, the officer had to be stationed at the national football information point for championships spread over a number of days and in case of one-off matches in the host country concerned. Thirdly, the national information point of the organising country had to make arrangements to promptly channel information received from the foreign police team to the proper authorities within its own police organisation. It also had to appoint an information officer who would be attached to the support team responsible for reconnaissance or spotting. The officer would be a contact for the team leader and would be responsible for the proper channelling of information. Finally, the police forces of

---

32 Chapter 1, Section I, IV Exchange of police information, 2.a. (Mission of the national football information point of the supporting country), Paras 1 and 2.

33 Ibid., Para 3.

34 Chapter 1, Section I, IV Exchange of police information, 3. (Communication procedure).

the organising country had to ensure that there were no differences in the quality of information available at local and national level.[35]

The national football information point could also support the competent national authorities and local police services with regard to national or international football matches. Concerning national football matches the information point could coordinate the exchange of information and organise the spotters' work. In addition, it could ensure the exchange of information with third countries. The first appendix to the Handbook contained a format for this exchange of information.

10.6.9.2 Preparations by Police Forces

In case of football championships or matches with an international dimension, police forces of the countries involved in the event could support each other. The Minister responsible in the organising country had to send a formal request for support. Before sending this request the Minister would receive advice from the national police services. The request had to indicate the degree of support and its constituent elements and had to be made well in advance of an event. For international tournaments, the supporting foreign police team required at least 16 weeks' preparation time. A request for police assistance could only be sent to countries whose assistance contributed added value. This added value had to be considered in the light of a number of factors (such as professional experience of football-related violence, knowledge about risk fans and being able to provide information so as to avert disturbances of public order and security). International police cooperation had to ensure the safety of the event with the following aims: intelligence gathering, reconnaissance, spotting and bringing the crowd under police supervision. The police forces from the supporting countries would be responsible for providing an advance risk analysis, which had to be handed over to the organising country at least 2 weeks before the beginning of the game (or, in case of a tournament, at least 8 weeks before the tournament would start). This analysis had to determine in which of the four fields mentioned police cooperation had to be requested. Furthermore, spotters who were acquainted with them had to accompany risk fans where possible. After receiving a request the foreign police force would have to indicate as soon as possible the extent to which it could meet the request. Supporting police forces have to be given the opportunity to acquaint themselves with the organisation of police operations in the host country and to get to know the operation commanders who are responsible for the match days.[36]

[35] Chapter 1, Section I, IV Exchange of police information, 4. (General Rules).

[36] Chapter 2, Preparations by police forces.

10.6.9.3 Organising Cooperation Between Police Forces

The Handbook recommended making maximum use of the support that foreign police forces could provide. This support had to be part of the host police organisation's tactical plan. Therefore, foreign police forces had to be informed thoroughly (in a language they understood) about this tactical plan and had to be given the opportunity to attend briefing and debriefing procedures. The foreign police forces also had to be given the opportunity to become an explicit partner in the information structure (so that they could supply information as well as be informed). Finally, they had to be actively involved in the police deployment in the field.

The host police organisation had to guarantee the safety of the supporting foreign police officers. In addition, the police forces of the country from which the fans would come had to supervise risk fans from the start of their journey until they reached the country where the match was to be played. The supporting country had to forward the necessary information on these risk fans to the organising country, so that these risk fans could be prevented from entering the country (insofar as the local law allowed this). Countries, which have the legal possibility to prevent risk fans from travelling abroad had to take all the necessary measures to achieve this objective effectively and had to inform the organising country accordingly. Each country had to take all possible measures to prevent its own citizens from participating in and/or organising public order disturbances in another country. Furthermore, the host police organisation had to assign the police team from the supporting country at least one accompanying police officer (preferably familiar with football hooliganism and with the spotters' task and with sufficient language knowledge) to maintain operational contact with the team and make reports.[37]

10.6.9.4 Cooperation Between Police Forces and Stewards

Police forces and stewards' organisations had to work together on a complementary basis. Placing a senior official from the stewards' organisation in the command centre of the police forces had to be considered by the latter. Mutual provision of information by both organisations had to be organised effectively.[38]

10.6.9.5 Checklist for Media Police and Communication Strategy

The Handbook concluded by providing a detailed checklist for media policy and communication strategy (of the police forces and responsible authorities) relating

---

[37] Chapter 3, Organising cooperation between police forces.

[38] Chapter 4.

to major (international) championships and matches. The central strategic aim of the media policy had to be 'ensuring police authorities' cooperation with the media in informing the public at national and international level of forthcoming championships and preparations and providing those attending matches with appropriate police advice concerning their security.'[39] This media policy would be part of a communication strategy and had to demonstrate the supportive role of the police and the authorities in ensuring the festive nature of sporting events. An active media policy had to have the following aims, according to the Handbook:

- creating a positive public image for the policy pursued by police and authorities;
- promoting amenities for those attending matches and encouraging a sporting attitude on their part;
- discouraging misbehaviour by those attending: misbehaviour does not pay;
- informing the public of police measures and the steps, which would be taken in the case of disturbances.

Finally, the media policy had to convey the idea of overall control, suggest security and trust, make it dear that football hooliganism would be severely dealt with and had to ensure openness and transparency.[40]

Concerning the communication strategy, the Handbook recommended establishing relations with the media focusing on championships and matches. These relations had to be established well in advance of the events. The press services of police, local and national authorities and national and international football organisations had to cooperate in order to communicate an unambiguous policy to the media. Finally, arrangements had to be made for providing police information to all those concerned. This could be done through information folders and daily press offices and by setting up a special press office for the duration of championships. The recommendations on the communication strategy were followed by a long list of 'important topics for consideration,' among which timely preparation and planning.[41]

10.6.9.6 Role of the Organiser

The Handbook contained a number of requirements which the organisers of football events had to fulfil. Organisers had to take 'all the sufficient and necessary measures' to avoid disturbances of the peace. An overall approach between all the parties concerned was expected to lead to an efficient policy and for this reason cooperation between the organiser, the private parties involved, the authorities and police services was strongly recommended. Member States had to identify who

---

[39] Chapter 5, Checklist for media policy and communication strategy, I. Media Policy, Para 1.

[40] Ibid., Paras 2 and 3.

[41] Chapter 5, Checklist for media policy and communication strategy, II. Communication strategy.

was responsible as the organiser of the match and of a possible division of responsibilities if two or more bodies were. In order to maintain public order and safety, the authorities and police services concerned had to impose on the organiser prior minimal requirements, which they had to meet in order to organise national or international games. These requirements had to lead to a situation in which the organiser and other services concerned fully assumed their own responsibilities so that the police forces could concentrate on their principal task of maintaining law and order.[42]

The second appendix to the Handbook contained a checklist for the authorities and police services. The checklist consisted of a number of requirements, which could be imposed upon the organiser of the match. The requirements had to be in conformity with national law. Requirements concerned the appointment by the organiser of a safety officer (for the coordination of safety policy), safety standards with regard to infrastructure, the use of stewards and ticketing policy and control. Other requirements concerned stadium regulations (among which the civil law exclusions/bans), agreements to be concluded (with the authorities, police services and emergency services concerned) and a local charter to be concluded in order to guarantee the safety of all the supporters, local residents and other parties concerned.[43]

10.6.10 The Council Decision of 25 April 2002

In April 2002 the Council adopted a decision concerning security in connection with football matches with an international dimension.[44] It based this decision on Article 30(i)(a) and (b) and Article 34(2)(c) of the Treaty on European Union. Both these provisions are part of Title VI of the Treaty concerning police and judicial cooperation in criminal matters and aim to achieve the Union's objective of providing EU citizens with a high level of safety within an area of freedom, security and justice. Article 30 concerns common actions in the field of police cooperation among which operational cooperation (para i(a)) and the exchange of information (para i(b)). Article 34 concerns the process of decision-making in the third-pillar (which entails police and judicial cooperation in criminal matters). According to Article 34(2)(c), the Council can adopt binding decisions in this field. These decisions shall, however, not entail direct effect. The Council, acting by a qualified majority, shall adopt measures necessary to implement those decisions at the level of the Union. This means that the decision of 25 April 2002 is binding upon the Member States, but lacks direct effect.

---

[42] Chapter 6, Role of the organiser, Section I, Criteria with which the organiser should comply.

[43] Handbook, Appendix 2, Checklist concerning possible requirements to be met by the organiser.

[44] Decision of the Council concerning security in connection with football matches with an international dimension, 25 April 2002 (2002/348/JHA).

The decision gave binding effect to a number of recommendations from the 2001 Handbook on police cooperation, especially concerning the exchange of information. First of all, it made binding the recommendation that each Member State set up or designate a national football information point. The information point has to act as the direct, central point for exchanging relevant information and for facilitating international police cooperation in connection with football matches with an international dimension. Each Member State can also decide to carry out certain contacts on football-related aspects through the services competent for those specific aspects, but it should always supply the national football information point with a minimum of information. Member States have to ensure that their national information points are capable of fulfilling their tasks efficiently and promptly. The Council decision applies without prejudice to existing national provisions, in particular the allocation of powers among the different services and authorities in the Member States concerned.

Article 2 of the Council decision concerns the tasks of the national football information point. The information point is responsible for coordinating and facilitating the police information exchange in connection with football matches with an international dimension. This exchange may also involve other law enforcement authorities contributing to security or law and order in accordance with the distribution of powers in the Member States. Therefore, the information point is to have access to information involving personal data on high-risk supporters. This access should be in accordance with the domestic and international rules applicable. In addition, the information points must facilitate, coordinate or organise the implementation of international police cooperation in connection with football matches with an international dimension. Furthermore, for these matches national football information points will provide, at least at the request of another football information point in a Member State concerned, a risk assessment of their own country's clubs and national team. Finally, they can be responsible for providing assistance to the competent national authorities.

Before, during and after a football event with an international dimension, national football information points, at the request of a national football information point concerned or on its own initiative, will engage in mutual exchange of general information and personal data.[45] The general information exchanged shall comprise strategic, operational and tactical information. These concepts are defined as follows:

- *strategic information:* information specifying all aspects of the event, with particular reference to the security risks involved;
- *operational information:* information providing an accurate picture of proceedings in the course of the event;
- *tactical information:* information enabling those in charge of operations to take appropriate action for the purposes of maintaining order and security in connection with the event.

[45] Ibid., Art. 3.

The exchange of personal data has to take place in accordance with the domestic and international rules applicable. In this context, reference is made to the principles of Convention no. 108 of the Council of Europe and to a Recommendation of the Committee of the Council of Europe.[46] The exchange of personal data has to take place with a view to preparing and taking the appropriate measures to maintain law and order when a football event takes place. Such exchange may in particular involve details of individuals actually or potentially posing a threat to law and order and security.

National football information points must coordinate the handling of information on football matches with an international dimension.[47] They are to ensure that all the police services concerned receive the necessary information in time. After processing, information can either be used by a national football information point itself or be passed to the relevant authorities and police forces. The information point in the Member State hosting a football event must communicate, before, during and after the competition or match, with the national police force(s) of the Member States concerned. Where appropriate, this communication shall take place via the liaison officer(s) appointed and supplied by the Member States concerned. Liaison officers may be contacted in the subject areas of law and order and security, football-related violence and ordinary crime, where this is connected with a particular football match or tournament. Communication will take place in such a way as to preserve the confidentiality of data. National football information points are to communicate with each other in their own language with a translation in a working language common to both sides (unless they make other arrangements).[48]

10.6.11 The Council and Stadium Bans

In November 2003, the Council adopted a resolution containing a number of recommendations concerning stadium bans.[49] The Council invited Member States to examine the possibility of introducing provisions establishing a means of banning individuals previously guilty of violent conduct at football matches from stadiums at which football matches are to be held. In order to ensure compliance with orders imposing stadium bans, Member States must provide penalties in the

---

[46] Convention No. 108 of the Council of Europe of 28 January 1981 for the protection of individuals with regard to automatic processing of personal data and Recommendation no. R (87) is of the Committee of Ministers of the Council of Europe of 17 September 1981 regulating the use of personal data in the police sector.

[47] Decision of the Council concerning security in connection with football matches with an international dimension, 25 April 2002, Art. 4.

[48] Id., Art. 5.

[49] Resolution of the Council on the use by Member Stairs of bans on access to venues of football matches with an international dimension (OJ C 281, 22/11/2003).

event of non-compliance. Member States in which stadium bans are in force are also invited to consider the possibility of extending these bans to other Member States, so that banned supporters in one Member State are prevented from attending matches held in other Member States, taking into account any orders issued by these Member States. The resolution contains a similar request for sports organisations in case they are the parties to impose stadium bans. Exchange of information is to take place via the national football information points. Exchange of personal data must be in accordance with the relevant national and international legislation.

There are limits to the possibility to extend stadium bans, however. Member States in which football matches with an international dimension are held can only use the personal details of persons who have been banned in other countries in order to deny them access to stadiums (if national law permits this) or in order to take other appropriate measures to maintain law and order. The use and storage of personal data must be restricted to the football matches in relation to which the details were transmitted. Finally, Member States staging international matches are invited to ensure that their police forces establish the necessary contacts with the event's organisers and with the competent authorities or sports bodies having an interest in it, for the purposes of coordinated cooperation under the resolution, within their respective spheres of responsibility.

10.6.12 Ticketing

As a general matter, similar issues arise in cases concerning ticketing arrangements for sport events as in ticketing arrangements for other events. However, there are some characteristics as regards ticketing for sport events relating in particular to safety aspects such as the effective segregation of rival groups of supporters and the counterfeiting of tickets.

In assessing ticketing arrangements, the Commission has taken as its guiding principle that these arrangements should ensure that all consumers in the EEA have reasonable access to entry tickets. Particular attention has in past cases been paid to exclusive distribution agreements, territorial restrictions on ticket sales and restrictions in payment methods (credit card exclusivity).

In a Commission Decision of 20 July 1999 relating to a proceeding under Article 82 of the EC Treaty and Article 54 of the EEA Agreement, *1998 Football World Cup* (*OJ* 2000 L 5/55, Paras 105–114) it is stated that ensuring effective safety at football matches is essential and may, in particular circumstances, justify the implementation of special ticket sales arrangements by tournament organisers. Nevertheless, in order to determine whether and, if so, to what extent, security considerations may justly ticketing arrangements which would otherwise be deemed to infringe Community law (Article 82 EC Treaty concerns abuse by an undertaking of a dominant position within the common market), each set of arrangements must be considered on their individual merits in the light of an objective assessment of what is necessary to achieve reasonable security objectives. The principal concern of the Comité français d'organisation de la Coupe du monde de football 1998 (CFO) was to ensure, in compliance with the provisions of the 1985 Convention, that rival groups of supporters of teams participating in any given match were separated from one another in each of the World Cup stadiums. The CFO sought to achieve such a segregation through the allocation to national football federations whose teams were participating in a given match of tickets relating to seats located at opposite ends of the stadium. Thus, tickets reserved for rival groups of supporters were not sold blind by the CFO but were made available at a time when the identities of participating teams were known. Tickets sold blind by the CFO in 1996 and 1997 related to seats reserved for neutral spectators. The CFO sold such tickets exclusively to members of the general public able to provide an address in France, who were classified in relation to all matches as neutral spectators. The CFO has, however, previously referred the Commission to expert opinion which considers that consumers purchasing blind tickets generally are peaceful spectators who do not represent a specific security risk. Such an analysis appears reasonable, given that consumers purchasing such tickets are evidently doing so because they wish to attend a football match irrespective of the teams involved, and are not therefore motivated by their support for any particular team. It follows therefore that any consumer, regardless of nationality, purchasing entry tickets on a blind basis should not, in principle, be regarded as a supporter of any particular team for purposes of security. Accordingly, such consumers should not, in principle, be subject to arrangements relating to the segregation of rival groups of supporters as envisaged under the 1985 Convention. The obligation to provide a postal address in France, imposed on consumers wishing to purchase blind tickets from the CFO in 1996 and 1997, was therefore excessive and failed to contribute in any material way to maintaining or improving security at football matches. In its response to the Commission's Statement of Objections and during the oral hearing, the CFO sought to justify its discriminatory sales arrangements on security grounds. According to the CFO, if it had sold tickets in 1996 and 1997 to the general public throughout the EEA, supporters of participating teams are likely to have found themselves located in those parts of the stadium reserved for neutral spectators. That being so, the CFO considers that for the purposes of ticket sales in 1996 and 1997 it was unable to treat all spectators throughout the EEA as neutral without at the same time contravening the provisions of the 1985 Convention as well as the relevant guidelines, which required an effective separation of rival groups of supporters of participating teams. The CFO also argued

a. that it was not possible to sell tickets on a blind basis in 1996 and 1997 and to determine the placement of ticket holders at a later date when the identities of participating teams were known, and

b. that no comparison could be made between CFO sales in 1996 and 1997 to the general public able to provide an address in France and CFO sales in 1998 to the general public able to provide an address within the EEA, given that sales in 1998 took place after the group draw when the identities of participating teams in first-phase matches were known.

The CFO's argument that it could not have treated all members of the general public in the EEA in 1996 and 1997 as neutral is rejected. The 1985 Convention refers specifically to the need to ensure an effective segregation of rival groups of supporters through *(inter alia)* a strict control over ticket sales. While the CFO considered it necessary to treat all members of the general public other than those able to provide an address in France as a potential rival supporter in 1996 and 1997 for the purposes of ticket sales, such a policy was excessive because it failed to take into account the generally peaceful nature of consumers purchasing tickets at a time when the identities of participating teams are not known. As the CFO has itself previously confirmed, consumers purchasing tickets on a blind basis would not have represented a specific security risk. Thus, the CFO was wrong to have considered members of the general public who were unable to provide an address in France but who wished to purchase tickets from it in 1996 and 1997 as potential rival supporters for the purposes of security. In any event, even if consumers purchasing tickets on a blind basis could properly have been considered to represent a specific security risk (which is not accepted by the Commission), it is unlikely in the extreme that anyone, having purchased a ticket on a blind basis (thereby entitling admission to that part of the stadium reserved specifically for the neutral public) and having by chance found himself attending a match involving the participation of his home team, would be located next to or within the vicinity of supporters of the opposing team, given that at the very least the latter must also have been fortunate enough, having purchased tickets on a blind basis, to find themselves also attending a match involving the participation of their home team in that part of the stadium reserved for the neutral public. Hence, any risk that the CFO might have breached the terms of the 1985 Convention by implementing non-discriminatory sales arrangements in 1996 and 1997 was, in statistical terms, insignificant. In view of the, above, the CFO's supposed inability to determine the siting of blind ticket holders after the identities of participating teams became known, as well as its contention that sales arrangements implemented in 1998 cannot be compared with those adopted previously, are irrelevant for the purposes of this Decision. Reference then is made to the Commission Decision of 13 December 2002, Case 37932 *Cupido* et al. *v. UEFA, Euro 2000 and ISL Marketing AG.* According to this decision member associations were effectively obliged by UEFA rules to ensure that their ticket allocation was distributed among their own supporters. However, these rules do not appear to constitute conduct which breaches Article 82, for the reasons described below. In this context, the Commission first notes UEFA's justification for this requirement. UEFA considers *inter alia* that limiting the distribution of tickets by national associations to their own supporters is a measure taken to enhance security. The Commission considers that this is indeed a legitimate aim of ticketing policy. That security has been a problem at some international football matches in the past, and that segregation of spectators from different countries is an appropriate measure to attempt to tackle such problems is uncontentious, and in any case evident from, for example, the European Convention on Spectator Violence and Misbehaviour at Sports Events and in particular at Football Matches. Article 3 (4) of this Convention indicates that a very important means to achieve this segregation is ticketing policy, viz.

> 'The Parties shall seek to ensure, where necessary by introducing appropriate legislation which contains sanctions for non-compliance or by any other appropriate means, that, where outbreaks of violence and misbehaviour by spectators are to be feared, sports organisations and clubs, together with, where appropriate, stadium owners and public authorities, in accordance with responsibilities defined in domestic law, take practical measures at and within stadiums to prevent or control such violence or misbehaviour, including:
>
> (a) ...
> (b) to segregate effectively groups of rival supporters, by allocation to groups of visiting supporters, when they are admitted, specific terraces;
> (c) to ensure this segregation by strictly controlling the sale of tickets and to take particular precautions in the period immediately preceding the match;'

In this context, the Council of the European Union has also recognised that

> 'Ticketing policy should be given practical effect through ticket control in which: separation of fans is brought about through strict allocation of accommodation (seating) to spectators by means of tickets, so that location in the stadium is determined by the participating team supported by a spectator and/or the nationality of a fan, ticketing policy should be designed so that allocation and hence separation of rival fans cannot be bypassed.'[50]

With this in mind, the obligation on member associations to ensure that the tickets intended for their supporters are indeed allocated to these supporters is necessary for and proportionate to the security objective mentioned above.

Even if it were considered that UEFA, Euro 2000 or the national associations were in a dominant position, their refusal to supply tickets to tour operators does not constitute an abuse. Despite the refusal to supply tickets, it would be possible for tour operators to continue to compete with one another for the provision of travel and/or accommodation arrangements to the general public for Euro 2000 matches. Moreover, it has not been shown that tickets to the 2000 European Football Championships are indispensable to the economic activity of ticket agents, tour operators or corporate hospitality providers. The fact that some national associations decided to supply tickets to tour operators, whereas others did not, does not mean that dissimilar conditions were applied to equivalent

---

[50] Council Resolution of 21 June 1999 concerning a handbook for international police cooperation and measures to prevent and control violence and disturbance in connection with international football matches *(OJ* C 193, 24.6.1997, p. 1), Chapter 6 (2).

transactions with other trading parties, putting some tour operators at a competitive disadvantage. Because of the territorial restrictions on the sale of tickets through the national associations, which as noted above are justified for safety/security reasons, tour operators were obliged to sell tickets only to the supporters of the team of their own national association. This means that markets for tour packages involving tickets for matches of different countries are separate and national—a tour operator wishing to provide tour packages including tickets for Sweden's matches would not be in competition with tour packages including tickets for France's matches, irrespective of the policies of the national football associations in Sweden and France. Hence there could be no discrimination between tour operators of different countries.

The complainant cites the fact that the general public was not permitted to order more than two tickets per Euro 2000 match as a violation of EC competition law. The complainant claims that this restriction was particularly relevant to the general public in the Netherlands. It is unclear how and under what legal construction this rule could constitute an abuse. Article 5.2 of the Euro 2000 General Terms and Conditions applies this condition to all ticket sales. Moreover, the Commission notes that this condition arises from concerns expressed by the Dutch and Belgian governments in order, in their view, to avoid black market sales which could compromise their security arrangements. The Commission also notes that the Council of the European Union also considers that a maximum of two tickets per purchaser is necessary in the interests of public order and safety (Council Resolution of 21 June 1999, Chapter 6 (4) 13th sub-paragraph). The Commission considers that this rule is not disproportionate to the legitimate objective of ensuring safety at international football matches.

The complainants also take the view that the fact that the right of admission on a ticket could not be transferred to a third party (Article 5.8 of the Euro 2000 General Terms and Conditions) was contrary to EC competition law, and furthermore that this restriction was only applied to tickets bought by the general public in Belgium and the Netherlands. As with the Tule discussed in the previous paragraph, it is unclear how and under what legal construction this rule could constitute an abuse, even if different systems were used to ensure this non-transferability condition, depending on whether the tickets were distributed directly by Euro 2000 or to national associations, UEFA or sponsors. The Commission also notes that a non-transferability requirement is intimately linked with the limitation of two tickets per person, discussed in the previous paragraph, and is necessary to give that rule effect. Non-transferability is also referred to specifically by the Council of the European Union as necessary in the interests of public order and safety (Council Resolution of 21 June 1999, Chapter 6 (2) 2nd and 6th sub-paragraphs). The Commission considers that non-transferability of tickets is proportionate to achieving the legitimate objective of ensuring safety at international football matches.

10.6.13 Concluding Remarks

European cooperation in the fight against violence in sport was strengthened after the Heysel stadium tragedy in 1985. The European Commission has actively promoted the development of improved violence prevention for international sporting events, focusing on two key objectives:

- Establishing common standards on safety and public order through the exchange off experience and best practice between Member States;
- Enhancing operational cooperation related to the exchange of information on football supporters at risk, or likely to be violent, in accordance with data protection rules.

In this respect, Council Decision 2002/348/JHA of 25 April 2002 concerning security in connection with football matches with an international dimension[51] introduced binding obligations on the establishment in all Member States of national football information points. These information points were intended to improve cooperation and information exchange between police forces and other competent authorities combating football-related violence. The Evaluation Report on the implementation of this Decision concluded that the Member States should set up the relevant structures, which have since played an effective role in the exchange of important data among relevant services. To facilitate and bring uniformity to this cooperation, on 6 December 2001 a Council Resolution was adopted concerning a Handbook with recommendations for international police cooperation and measures to prevent and control violence and disturbances in connection with football matches with an international dimension, in which at least one Member State is involved.[52] The Handbook—a follow-up to a first version of 21 June 1999,[53] which consolidated in a single text the cooperation already under way in this area—was further updated and amended by Council Resolution of 4 December 2006.[54] Moreover, based on the experience of some Member States, on 17 November 2003 the Council adopted another Resolution on the use by Member States of bans on access to venues of football matches with an international

---

[51] OJ L 121, 8/5/2002; amended by Council Decision 2007/412/JHA of 12 June 2007; *OJ* L 155, 15/6/2007.

[52] OJ C 22, 24/1/2002.

[53] OJ C 196, 13/7/1999.

[54] OJ C 322, 29/12/2006; see also, for a further update, OJ C 165, 24/6/2010. See also, Council Resolution concerning a Handbook with recommendations for hosting major football and other sports events, in particular tournaments with more than one organising country, 3081st Justice and Home Affairs meeting, Luxembourg, 11 and 12 April 2011 (for example, with regard to football: EURO 2000 in Belgium and the Netherlands, EURO 2008 in Austria and Switzerland, and EURO 2012 in Poland and Ukraine). See also, Handbook for the cooperation between Member States to avoid terrorist acts at the Olympic Games and comparable sporting events, Doc. 5774/1/04 REV 1 ENFOPOL 14. .

dimension.[55] The Member States were invited to examine the possibility of introducing provisions establishing a means of banning individuals previously guilty of violent conduct at football matches from stadiums at which football matches are to be held. In order to ensure compliance with orders imposing stadium bans, Member States should supplement them with provision for penalties in the event of non-compliance. Each Member State in which stadium bans are in force is furthermore invited to consider the possibility of taking appropriate steps to ensure that orders issued domestically may also be extended to cover certain football matches held in other Member States and take into account orders issued by other Member States. If there are stadium bans in a Member State imposed by sports organisations, the competent authorities of this Member State are invited, where appropriate, to contact these organisations to examine whether such stadium bans issued domestically could be applicable to football matches which are to be held in other countries. Member States, where appropriate, will invite the sports organisations to exchange the information between themselves. Information on details of orders imposing stadium bans issued domestically should be transmitted to countries staging football matches with an international dimension via the national football information points established by Decision 2002/348/JHA. It is stated that nothing in this Resolution should be interpreted as departing from the principle that the exchange of personal data shall comply with the relevant national and international legislation on personal data protection. Any Member State staging a football match with an international dimension should use details of those covered by banning orders issued in other countries solely in order to deny them access to stadiums staging matches, where denial of access is possible under national law, or to take other appropriate measures to maintain law and order. The use and storage of personal data should be restricted to the football matches in relation to which the details were transmitted.

In Brussels, on 28 and 29 November 2007, the European Commission, in association with UEFA, hosted a high-level conference entitled, 'Towards a European Strategy against Violence in Sport.' More than 150 delegates from EU Member States attended the conference. In July 2007 the Commission Action Plan for Sport 'Pierre de Coubertin' was adopted as part of the Commission's White Paper on Sport. The high-level conference as one of the first actions in the Plan, in order to discuss measures contributing to prevent and fight violence and racism in sport events with stakeholders. Other actions within the framework of the prevention of and fight against racism and violence in sport include: promote, in accordance with national and EU rules applicable, the exchange of operational information and practical know-how and experience on the prevention of violent and racist incidents between law enforcement services and with sport organisations; analyse possibilities for new legal instruments and other EU-wide standards to prevent public disorder at sport events; strengthen regular and structured cooperation among law enforcement services, sport organisations and other

---

[55] OJ C 281, 22/11/2003.

stakeholders. The European Commission took up the idea of UEFA president, Michel Platini, and announced the relatively swift implementation of a European police force, which would attempt to eradicate violence in high-level sporting events. At a press-conference, the European Commissioner responsible for Justice, Freedom and Security, Mr Franco Frattini, announced that at the beginning of 2008 he would propose the funding for a European police training programme in order to set up Europol coordinated teams on the ground. These would consist of officers who are specially trained in the fight against violence in football stadiums and at other sporting events. European police forces had already successfully cooperated during the 2006 World Cup in Germany, he recalled. According to Frattini, the first police training module could see the light before the beginning of the Europe of nations championship in Austria and Switzerland. The Commissioner also proposed training European stadium security personnel that could be deployed at these events. He said that the free movement of violent supporters had to be limited to prevent them moving around. The Portuguese minister for the interior, Rui Pereira, whose country was current in the presidency of the EU, announced that on 14 December the European Council would be adopting conclusions that go in the direction of greater security in sport. That text would focus on better police coordination, information exchange on violent and racist supporters, European level recognition of legal decisions banning individuals from travelling and the creation of joint police teams from different member states in charge of operations at these international events.[56]

The above overview of EU involvement in the fight against football hooliganism shows that only a limited amount of binding measures have been taken at EU level in this field. Only two Council decisions have been consequential for Member States' policy in the field of football hooliganism. The first decision, a Joint Action in the framework of the third pillar, aimed to establish and reinforce the exchange of information between Member States in order to counter violence and vandalism committed by football supporters. The second decision led to the establishment of national football information points responsible for the exchange of information in this field. This decision gave binding effect to a number of recommendations from the two Handbooks adopted in earlier Council resolutions.

In other fields of action concerning football hooliganism only soft law exists in the form of resolutions and recommendations of the European Parliament and the Council. Several times already, it has been proposed to introduce stadium bans with international effect (for the first time just after the Heysel tragedy), but no binding provisions have resulted from this yet. The EU did not get involved in establishing safety standards for stadiums or ticketing arrangements either. The directives which were called for during the 1980s have failed to come into existence. Policy concerning the fight against football hooliganism is, however, in full development. The 2001 Police Handbook has proved to be an important document (from which important recommendations now have binding effect). All in all, it

[56] *Bulletin Quotidien Europe* (Agence Europe) of 30 November 2007, No. 9554.

can be concluded that the European Union has been quite active in this area over the past few years and it is expected that this will result in more hard law and cooperation against violence and vandalism in sport.

10.7 Summary and Conclusions

The main special intergovernmental (interstate) text which is relevant in the context of the combat against football hooliganism is the European Convention on Spectator Violence and Misbehaviour at Sports Events and in particular at Football Matches, of 19 August 1985, which was concluded in the framework of the Council of Europe to which all EU Member States belong. The other special international document is a non-governmental text, i.e., the UEFA Safety and Security Regulations (current edition: 2006).

The Council of Europe Member States undertake within the limits of their respective constitutional provisions to take the necessary steps to give effect to its provisions. The Parties to the Convention undertake to ensure the formulation and implementation of measures designed to prevent and control violence and misbehaviour by spectators, *inter alia,* by applying or, if need be, adopting appropriate criminal and/or administrative legislation regarding perpetrators, and they shall seek to ensure, where necessary by introducing appropriate legislation that stadium owners and public authorities take practical measures at and within stadiums to prevent or control such violence or misbehaviour.

According to the Convention, the Parties shall where appropriate, and in accordance with the applicable international agreements, consider: (a) transferring proceedings against persons apprehended in connection with violence or other criminal behaviour committed at sports events to their country of residence; (b) seeking the extradition of persons suspected of violence or other criminal behaviour committed at sports events; (c) transferring persons convicted of offences or violence or other criminal behaviour committed at sports events to serve their sentences to the relevant country.

The Parties to the Convention shall also cooperate closely on the matters covered by it and encourage similar cooperation as appropriate between national sports authorities involved. The Convention applies to national as well as international football matches in Europe. Within the framework of the Council of Europe and, in particular, this Convention, additional pertinent resolutions were adopted, and recommendations made.

At a bilateral level, the nation hosting a European Football Championship (Belgium/Netherlands 2000, Portugal 2004, Austria/Switzerland 2008) or a World Cup in Europe (France 1998, Germany 2006) currently attempts to work in close collaboration with its immediate neighbours, signing agreements to this end (temporary border controls, cross-border police intervention etc.).

The UEFA Safety and Security Regulations are binding instructions to the organisers of, and the associations and clubs participating in matches played in any of the UEFA competitions regarding precautionary measures to be taken to ensure safety and security in the stadium, and to prevent crowd disturbances. These instructions complement national and local legislation, as well as instructions issued by competent national administrative bodies. The UEFA Regulations apply also to FIFA competition matches played in Europe, which are delegated to UEFA; they do not apply to national football matches.

According to Article 6 of the UEFA Disciplinary Regulations (edition: 2006) member associations and clubs are responsible for their supporters. In the *Feyenoord Rotterdam v. UEFA* award, CAS as the Supreme World Court of Sport, confirmed the rule that clubs have strict liability for the improper conduct of their supporters even if they are not at fault. Article 6 obviously is not in conformity with a key principle of the rule of law, i.e., 'no punishment without guilt.' Soek has successfully defended the thesis that the disciplinary law concerning doping violations must be considered as pseudo-criminal law, that Article 6 of the European Convention on Human Rights (cf., para 2: 'Everyone charged with a criminal offence shall be presumed innocent until proved guilty according to law.' —*praesumptio innocentiae)* is applicable to disciplinary doping law, and that the application of the strict liability principle is contrary to Article 6 and should therefore be replaced by the Anscheinsbeweis.[57] *Mutatis mutandis* the same conclusions could be drawn with regard to the responsibility of clubs for the football hooliganism of 'their' supporters. Clubs are simply identified with their supporters, while accepted legal principles should in fact be examined to determine whether the conduct of their supporters, or those who purport to be their supporters, can be blamed on them. There is, however, normally no authority relationship whatsoever between a club and its supporters. Anonymity is a characteristic of supporters; opportunistic fans can also be found amongst the hooligans. In fact, Article 6 of the FIFA Regulations unjustifiably assigns supporters the same status as players, trainers, club members and others who are officially active for the club (for example attendants and volunteers). Is the misbehaviour indeed a consequence of neglect or carelessness on the part of the club? Has the club contravened any regulatory obligation? The abilities of clubs playing away matches abroad to control their own followers are extremely limited. It is precisely the hard core of agitators who are not supporter club members (with the official variant for whom clubs at least attempt to maintain a formal link by working together with them), but those travelling under their own initiative. The only thing a club like Feyenoord could have done initially was to request its own government to suspend 'Schengen' so that frontier checks could have taken place on the grounds of public order! Whether the national government would have contemplated this is another matter. In any case an essential question in this respect is whether the home club as match organiser did what was necessary to prevent problems. The underlying application of the strict liability principle can actually only be justified by means of

[57] 'The Strict Liability Principle and the Human Rights of Athletes in Doping Cases', The Hague 2006, *passim.*

order measures, aimed at protecting the sport of football. In such an interpretation, the relevant UEFA measures would not be aimed at the clubs themselves, even though they operate to their disadvantage. Such considerations also resound clearly in the CAS decision on *Feyenoord v. UEFA:* 'The strict liability rule makes sense in this context given that the goal is to prevent the violent acts of the supporters, so it does not matter what actions the club itself took.' CAS says that UEFA has no immediate possibility of punishing supporters for their misbehaviour and that this can therefore only occur via the clubs in question. Here UEFA clearly exceeds its authority as a disciplinary referee. There is a criminal court which can indeed act, and civil claims can be submitted by UEFA, FAs and clubs against misbehaving fans. A number of countries also have criminal, administrative and civil law offering the opportunity to impose stadium bans as future preventive measures. In Britain international travel bans can also be imposed. Applying the strict liability principle in the case of football vandalism in fact reaches further than in doping cases, where 'third parties' (see clubs in the case of football vandalism) are not automatically punished, but rather that the focus goes directly to the sportsperson suspected of drug use. Applying the strict liability principle in fact requires a statutory, legal foundation (ideally through a treaty). This also applies to the actual privacy violations in out-of-competition tests in doping cases, where 'home' may also be one of the whereabouts. In fact society ideally needs to have agreed through parliament that 'strict liability' is applied in sport, because this implies that a proper consideration of interests has occurred—the interests of the club (football vandalism) and sportsperson (doping) against those of the sport (no violence and fair competition). In the European Conventions covering football vandalism and doping (both from the Council of Europe), and in the UNESCO treaty against doping in sport, with which the WADA Code is linked, these issues can be arranged initially, because the national parliaments are also involved in approving treaties. Of course the issue is then how a careful consideration of interests turns out, where precisely the boundaries lie between what can and cannot be incorporated in light of 'sport specificity.'

This also brings us directly to the issue of the international banning orders on complaint, such as those which can be enacted in Britain. Parliament there emphatically endorsed the introduction of this phenomenon in the Football Disorder Act 2000. Here even European law (EU: freedom of movement, Council of Europe: human rights) was defied. And the result of the *Gough* case which set further preconditions for this (proportionality criterion) has not yet been overturned. Here the foreign policy interests of combating the 'English Disease' (the United Kingdom's good name) have not yet even been raised.

The involvement of the European Union in the combat against violence and vandalism in sport led to numerous resolutions of the European Parliament, some Reports of the Parliament and to a limited number of Council resolutions and decisions, all concerning specific fields of action. The amount of binding EU law in this field is rather limited. Only two Council decisions had consequences for the policy of Member States against football hooliganism. The first instrument, a Joint Action of 26 May 1997 (within the so-called Third Pillar) aimed at the exchange of information between Member States in order to counter violence and vandalism committed by football supporters. The other instrument, a Decision of 25 April 2002 (amended in 2007), led to the establishment of national football information points responsible for the exchange of information in this field. This decision gave a binding effect to a number of recommendations for international police cooperation and measures 'to prevent and control violence and disturbances in connection with international football matches, in which at least one Member States is involved either by participation in the match and/or by hosting the match' which had been adopted in the 2001 Handbook. An important decision that was taken by the Council more recently is the Resolution of a recommendatory character on the use by Member States of bans on access to venues of football matches with an international dimension, of 17 November 2003. In this Resolution, Member States in which stadium bans are in force are invited to consider the possibility of extending these bans to other Member States and should take into account orders issued by these Member States. The Resolution contains a similar invitation to sports organisations in Member states, which impose stadium bans. At the high-level Brussels conference of November 2007 on 'Towards a European Strategy against Violence in Sport' the creation of joint police teams from different Member States in charge of operations at international events as well as European level recognition of legal decisions banning individuals from travelling were announced. This recognition would be a logical step from the recommendatory Resolution of 2003 to a binding instrument (Framework Decision). In such a binding instrument Member States should also be obliged to guarantee the effective national implementation of stadium bans by means of the withdrawal of passports, controlled house arrest and/or a duty for stadium-banned persons to report at the police during match periods. The most far-reaching measure to prevent known or potential troublemakers to travel to match abroad is the withdrawal of their passports. However, it is not the position in all EU Member States that the authorities have the power to withdraw travel documents: in that case, the possibility might exist to remand a troublemaker in custody for the time the match will be played abroad. In some EU Member States the legislation provides for the possibility to forbid known or potential troublemakers to enter the country. There exist three types of stadium bans: based on criminal law (by court order), based on administrative law (by order of the police)—both with a duty attached to report to the police, and based on civil law.

Freedom of movement is extremely important in the framework of European integration. Freedom of movement to provide services exists within the Community on the basis of the EC Treaty. It appears from the decisions of the European Court of Justice that this freedom encompasses the freedom to receive services in another member state. Football supporters as recipients of services could certainly be compared to tourists, with the Court having established that they may be regarded as such. Also from the perspective of human rights freedom of movement is essential. The right to leave one's own country is one of the fundamental rights in the framework of the Council of Europe (Article 2 of the Fourth Protocol to the European Convention on Human Rights). Through the Schengen acquis which, following the Treaty of Amsterdam, was integrated into the EU framework, controls at the common internal borders have been abolished. On the other hand, freedom of movement has its counterpart in the enforcement of public order. European integration and enlargement lead to ever further fading boundaries, but this may not come at the expense of effective public order enforcement. The relevant treaty provisions (EC Treaty, European Convention on Human Rights, Schengen acquis) all allow for the possibility to make exceptions to the freedom of movement due to public order concerns or the prevention of crime.

The lessons that can be drawn with respect to freedom of movement on the one hand and public order on the other is that there is a need for common European rules (EU/Council of Europe) in order to prevent large contingents of football hooligans from visiting matches abroad. The legislations of the countries concerned should be better attuned to each other, on the basis of which a truly common policy might be conducted. If one country claims that it cannot stop 'its' supporters, believing the other country will not have to admit them, while the other country think that it does, an unclear situation exists. If furthermore, the receiving country does stop misbehaving fans, but does not try them and immediately expels them, this may be understandable, but there will be no guarantee that they will still be tried in their own country for their misdeeds. Travel prohibitions, the withdrawal of passports coupled with house arrest, a duty to report to the police during the international match or competition are all instruments that can give shape to a common European policy.

As to ticketing, in *1998 Football World Cup* the European Commission stated that ensuring effective safety at football matches is essential and may, in particular circumstances, justify the implementation of special ticket sales arrangements by tournament organisers. Nevertheless, in order to determine whether and, if so to what extent, security considerations may justify ticketing arrangements which would otherwise be deemed to infringe Community law (Article 82 EC Treaty concerns abuse by an undertaking of a dominant position within the common market), each set of arrangements must be considered on their individual merits in the light of an objective assessment what is necessary to achieve reasonable security objectives such as the segregation of rival groups of supporters by way of ticket allocation distributed by UEFA member associations among their own supporters and related to seats located at opposite ends of the stadium, non-transferability of tickets, etc.

Generally speaking, the UEFA Safety and Security Regulations and the European Convention on Spectator Violence and Misbehaviour at Sports Events and in particular at Football Matches are implicitly implemented or explicitly referred to in EU Member States' national legislation as well as pertinent national football rules and regulations respectively. The same applies to the EU Handbook for international police cooperation. The Council of Europe's Convention and the UEFA Regulations together form the general international framework for combating football hooliganism in Europe at large. Both pan-European organisations have by and large the 'same' national members, i.e., states as well as football associations. Additionally, as far as the European Union is concerned, the

Schengen acquis is of central importance in particular regarding the free movement of persons and possible exceptions thereto.

A final observation can be made with regard to the issue of the character of transnational European anti-football hooliganism law from the perspective of it being a part of international sports law. It is of a private/public nature—on the one hand consisting of pertinent UEFA regulations and CAS jurisprudence, on the other of a Council of Europe treaty and EU decision-making.

Chapter 11
International Sports Boycotts: Sport, Law and Politics

Abstract In this paper, from a historical perspective particular attention is paid to the unilateral sports boycott of the 1980 Moscow Olympic Games against the background of the Helsinki process of détente (CSCE) in Europe, the 1995 EU sports boycott of Nigeria, and the debate concerning the Olympic Games, China and human rights in The Netherlands in 2008. In this context, the Netherlands government's so-called Starting Points for 'Sport and Politics' are separately dealt with in detail.

Contents

R. C. R. Siekmann, *Introduction to International and European Sports Law*,
ASSER International Sports Law Series, DOI: 10.1007/978-90-6704-852-1_11,
© T.M.C. ASSER PRESS, The Hague, The Netherlands, and the author 2012

11.1 Introduction[1]

'International sports law' can 'in the narrow sense' be considered to be the rules of the sports world itself in relation to international activities in the area of sport. This 'autonomous' part of international sports law could be referred to using the term 'lex sportiva internationalis,' and, in principle, it encompasses both the rules of the IOC and international sport federations as well as those of NOCs and national associations. Strictly speaking, 'autonomous' international rules which relate to national sports should also be included. The concept 'international sports law' can also be extended beyond this central non-governmental part by including, on the one hand, public law in the sense of international law (and jurisprudence) relating to sport (both international and national sport) and, on the other hand, national law (and jurisprudence) relating to international sporting activities.

How public international law can be used to regulate sport? In this context, two aspects can be distinguished. On the one hand there is, naturally, existing law which forms a framework for international sporting relations; here the law is a general given, establishing 'limiting conditions.' What is of particular importance is the negative side of the case, the aspects which hamper the freedom of international sport. In this context, one should especially think of foreign athletes denied entry to a country due to their country not being recognised for political reasons. On the other hand, in relation to sport, the law can also be used in an ad hoc way to create a barrier to force a certain country to change its behaviour. Hereby, the use of the instrument of the sport boycott immediately comes to mind. The behavioural change desired may have a (partial) effect on the sport itself. The standard example is the earlier

[1] Cf., Siekmann (1996), pp. E1-3.

sport boycott of South Africa due to apartheid in sport.[2] Sport can, however, also be used for purely political objectives which are entirely unrelated to sport. Examples include the now withdrawn UN sport boycott of the Federal Republic of Yugoslavia, i.e. Serbia and Montenegro, in order to force the end of its involvement in the war in Bosnia; and, on a regional level, the EU boycott of Nigeria due to the execution of a number of human rights activists. In the former case, the sport boycott was based on a mandatory resolution of the Security Council (no. 757 of 30 May 1992) in accordance with Article 41 of the United Nations Charter, which stated, *inter alia*, that member states were obliged to implement the boycott in their own legal systems by denying athletes or teams representing Serbia and Montenegro from participating in matches on their territory.[3] In the latter case, on 4 December 1995, the European Union's Council of Ministers of Foreign Affairs resolved to adopt a 'common position' on the basis of Article J.2 of the Maastricht Treaty, which meant, *inter alia*, that all sporting contacts with Nigeria had to be broken by refusing to issue visas to official delegations and national teams.

Intergovernmental organisations, such as the UN, use public international law as a legal instrument for collective sport boycotts. These can involve both recommendations and mandatory resolutions, and be converted into national legal systems. In the event of 'one-sided,' specific sport boycotts, usually related to a single sporting mega-event and initiated by one state or group of states (for example, the boycotts of the Olympic Games in Moscow and Los Angeles), the legal instruments required for a state to force its own national sports world to join a boycott may be absent. If a government does not want to restrict itself to using political means, then ad hoc legislation should, if possible, be able to break through the autonomy of the sports world.

When the problem of 'sport and politics' is being discussed, people are referring to issues like these, which are played out at the level of interstate diplomacy and whereby states or intergovernmental organisations are, as it were, the opponents of the sports world in the form of the IOC, international federations and national associations. From a political perspective, a sport boycott is, in general, a suitable means of exerting pressure, as publicity and such like focussing on public opinion can have maximum effect, while, at the same time, within the range of coercive measures (weapons embargoes, economic boycotts etc.), the means itself has minimum severity. However, from the other perspective, the sports world feels it is being 'abused' for political purposes, as the effects of a sport boycott are extremely far reaching.

---

[2] Cf., Siekmann (1984).

[3] In 1992, Robert ('Bobby') Fischer won an unofficial rematch against Boris Spassky of the USSR, after having captured the World Championship title from him in a match in Reykjavik, Iceland, that was widely publicised as a Cold War confrontation. The 1972 match attracted more worldwide interest than any chess match before or since. The rematch was held in Yugoslavia, which was then under the UN embargo. This led to a conflict with the US government, which was also seeking income tax from Fischer on his match winnings, and he never returned to his native country.

The second aspect of the special use of public international law to regulate sport also involves the international community of states making use of its powers, but in this case it does so to introduce general regulations for certain problem areas without relating the regulations to a specific country. The signing of treaties is the pre-eminent legal instrument to give shape to these regulations. There is, therefore, a question of 'international legislation' in respect of sport. The most obvious examples are the UN Convention against apartheid in sports, and the Anti-football hooliganism and Anti-doping conventions adopted by the Council of Europe.

In this paper, from a historical perspective particular attention is paid to the unilateral sports boycott of the 1980 Moscow Olympic Games against the background of the Helsinki process of *détente* (CSCE) in Europe, the 1995 EU sports boycott of Nigeria, and the debate concerning the Olympic Games, China and human rights in The Netherlands in 2008. In this context, the Netherlands government's so-called Starting Points for 'Sport and Politics' are separately dealt with in detail.

11.2 The Boycott of the 1980 Moscow Olympic Games and Détente[4]

11.2.1 Introduction

On 20 January, 1980, President Carter of the United States, in an address to the chairman of the American Olympic Committee (USOC), insisted that the Committee suggest to the International Olympic Committee (IOC) that the 1980 Summer Olympic Games in Moscow be transferred, postponed or cancelled, unless all Soviet troops had been withdrawn from Afghanistan within a month. He made it clear that if the IOC did not accept these proposals, the United States would not send a delegation to Moscow. The President explained: 'We must make clear to the Soviet Union that it cannot trample upon an independent nation and at the same time do business as usual with the rest of the world.'[5] Within a week the presidential request to USOC received support in resolutions of the American House of Representatives and the Senate, which voted with 386 votes in favour and 12 against, and 88 votes in favour and 4 against respectively, that no American athletes should participate in the Moscow Olympic Games unless the Soviet troops had been withdrawn from Afghanistan by 20 February, 1980. This American reaction to the Soviet Union's invasion of Afghanistan on 27 December, 1979 marked the start of an international boycott against the Moscow Olympic Games.

All this took place 'under' the 1975 Final Act of Helsinki, which devotes one paragraph to international sporting contacts. The question which concerns us here

[4] See, Siekmann (1985), pp. 181–201; see also, Siekmann (2003), pp. 87–97.

[5] Department of State Bulletin, March 1980, p. 50.

is how a boycott such as that of the 1980 Olympic Games can be assessed in the context of detente between East and West and under international law. When answering this question, we can distinguish two aspects: an inter-governmental aspect concerning the position of 'politics' (assessment of the boycott in the light of the Final Act, paras 2–5) and a nongovernmental aspect concerning the position of 'sport' (assessment of the boycott in the light of the relation between 'sport' and 'politics' and in the light of the Olympic Charter, paras 6–10).

11.2.2 Sport and the Final Act of Helsinki

The paragraph on sport can be found in the so-called 'Third Basket' of the Final Act of Helsinki, which deals with cooperation in humanitarian and other fields under para 1: Human contacts sub g (Sport). The provision reads as follows:

> 'In order to expand existing links and co-operation in the field of sport the participating States will encourage contacts and exchanges of this kind, including sports meetings and competitions of all sorts, on the basis of the established international rules, regulations and practice.'[6]

As indicated at the beginning of the 'Third Basket,' the co-operation referred to there should be encouraged by the States 'irrespective of their political, economic and social systems' and 'in full respect for the principles guiding relations among participating States as set forth in the relevant document' This document can be found in the 'First Basket' under (1): 'Declaration on principles guiding relations between participating States,' One of these ten principles, which together form the so-called 'Decalogue,' concerns Co-operation among States (principle IX). In this the participating States confirm that organisations should fulfil a relevant and

[6] This subject was based on an East European (Bulgarian/Polish) proposal (Doc. CSCE/I/8 and CSCE/II/I/1/Rev. 1 of 5 July and 19 September, 1973 respectively. See Kavass et al. (1981), vol. I: Stage I—Helsinki 1973, resp. vol. V: Stage II—Geneva 1973–1975, pp. 375 et seq., resp. pp. 21, 4–6. During the CSCE follow-up meeting in Belgrade, a Bulgarian proposal was submitted on Co-operation in Sports, Doc. CSCE/BM/44- of 11 November, 1977 (see Granier (1980), p. 559. The word 'sport' as such does not appear either in the final document of Belgrade of 8 March, 1978 or in that of the follow-up meeting of Madrid. On the background to the paragraph on sport: 'The intention of the East European countries was to ensure that sporting contacts would help to reinforce friendship and mutual understanding between nations and to use these contacts to carry out the East European idea of detente, and in general to introduce political aspects into sports contacts, possibly by the creation of new European organizations. In contrast, the Western countries adopted the position that only existing ties and existing co-operation was under discussion, as well as contacts in accordance with existing procedures. The text of the Final Act is in fact restricted to existing ties and co-operation. Nor can the text be used for the organization of "political" sporting events.' (See "Conferentie over Veiligheid en Samenwerking in Europa; Helsinki–Genève–Helsinki 1973–1975" [Conference on Security and Co-operation in Europe; Helsinki–Geneva–Helsinki 1973–1975], published by the Ministry of Foreign Affairs of the Netherlands, No. 115 (The Hague 1976), p. 155.).

positive role in the co-operation, *inter alia*, in the humanitarian field including human contacts in the field of sport.

On the basis of the 'paragraph on sport' combined with the text of principle IX, it is possible to state:

a. that one of the objectives of the Final Act is to encourage detente through the co-operation between States, *inter alia*, in sporting activities;
b. that the States which signed the Final Act did not thereby agree to any strictly legal obligations (of public international law) with regard to sporting activities among themselves, not in the least because of the mere fact that the Final Act as a whole is not a treaty, but should be considered as a 'legally non- binding agreement.'[7] Moreover, the non-binding character ensues from the use of the word 'will' rather than 'shall' in the paragraph on sport;
c. that the paragraph on sport is aimed at extending contacts in the field of sport. The participating States have been assigned an active role in this. This implies that the participating States should, at the one hand, stimulate existing contacts, whenever this is necessary to maintain these contacts. At the other hand, the CSCE States should remain passive with regard to the existing contacts in the field of sport in the sense that they will not discourage them;
d. that the relevant provisions of the Final Act are not addressed directly to the sporting organisations so that these organisations have not accepted any formal obligations under the Final Act. On the other hand, one should not overlook the fact that the Final Act explicitly states 'that governments, institutions, organisations and persons have a relevant and positive role to play in contributing toward the achievement' of the CSCE aims (see principle IX).

A clear example of the way in which sporting organisations have started to play a role in the context of the Final Act can be seen in the series of agreements (protocols) between the central Western and Eastern European and Soviet sporting organisations on the initiative of the East, concluded particularly since 1975 and always for a period of five years.[8] These are agreements between, on the one hand, nongovernmental umbrella organisations, and, on the other hand, state organs. In the Protocol of 29 March, 1977 between the German Sports League (Deutscher Sportbund; DSB) and the Committee for Physical Education and Sport of the Council of Ministers of the USSR, implicit reference is made to the Final Act of Helsinki by the use of the wording 'on the basis of the established international rules, regulations and practice,' derived from the paragraph on sport.[9] With regard

[7] On the legal character of the Final Act, see van Dijk (1980), pp. 106–110.

[8] The Russian bibliography about the CSCE which appeared in Moscow in 1978 lists in volume II the agreements/protocols of the USSR with Australia, Sweden, France, Portugal, Greece, the Netherlands, Norway, Finland, Denmark and Italy. Apart from its agreement with the Soviet Union, the Netherlands have also made agreements with East Germany, Czechoslovakia, Poland and Bulgaria.

[9] In the Agreement concerning the principles of co-operation between the sporting organisations of the USSR and the Netherlands (Nederlandse Sportfederatie: NSF) of 23 June, 1976, the only

to the meaning of the words 'established international rules, regulations and practice,' we take from an official statement made by the DSB that in the negotiations with the Soviet Sports Committee this formulation, derived from the Final Act of Helsinki was meant explicitly to refer to the rules, regulations and practice of international sport- federations and other world sporting organisations.[10] Examples of these could be the Statutes of the Federation of International Football Associations (FIFA), and the Olympic Charter.

11.2.3 Assessment

If we now assess the boycott of the 1980 Moscow Olympic Games in the light of the above conclusions with respect to the paragraph on sport combined with principle II of the Final Act, the following remarks can be made. Seen in isolation, the appeal made by the Government of the United States and others to the sporting world not to participate in the Games is not in accordance with the Final Act. It is submitted that this appeal to boycott was in conflict with the aim of the Final Act to promote detente through cooperation, *inter alia*, in the field of sport. The existing contacts in the field of sport were actually even discouraged, rather than encouraged. In this particular case the sporting contacts were based on the Olympic Charter, i.e., the rules etc. which govern the Olympic Games. Thus the existing contacts in the field of sport were also interfered with, in conflict with principle IX of the Final Act.

As regards the (final) decision of part of the sporting world not to go to Moscow, it is submitted here that this was not in conflict with the Final Act as such. The National Olympic Committees (NOCs) which had to take the decision, were not as such signatories to the Final Act. Cases in which the sporting world were to decide on a boycott on its own initiative could therefore not be assessed in the light of the Final Act, unless any decisive intervention by the government could be demonstrated. In principle, government intervention is more likely in the East than in the West, when one considers that the national sports federations in the Soviet Union, for example, are founded and run by the above-mentioned Sports Committee, a state organ which falls under the Council of Ministers of the Soviet

(Footnote 9 continued)
reference made is to the cultural agreement between the two countries which ascribes a role to exchanges in the field of sport in the context of détente (See Annex D for the text of the Agreement). Text of the Agreement concerning the cultural co-operation between the Kingdom of the Netherlands and the Union of Soviet Socialist Republics of 14 July, 1967, in: Tractatenblad, 1967, No. 115 (see introduction and under Article 2 sub k). See also the Explanatory Memorandum for the parliamentary approval of the agreement, Bijlage Handelingen [Annex to Parliamentary Proceedings], II 1967/68—9337, No. 3. N.B. In the protocols some references are made to the European Sports Conference, which has taken place in alternate years since 1973 between central Western and Eastern sports organisations.

[10] Knecht (1980), pp. 51–52.

Union. In his thesis, Van den Heuvel made the following remark about the position of the Soviet NOC: 'We have already noted that the sports federations are subordinated to the National Sports Committee and there can be no doubt that the National Sports Committee is more important than the Soviet Olympic Committee, One can also assume that foreign sports policy is indicated by the National Sports Committee or by the Central Committee of the CPSU [Communist Party of the Soviet Union; RS] and that the Olympic Committee implements this policy. One cannot, therefore, consider the Olympic Committee of the Soviet Union to be independent in the sense that is considered essential in the Olympic Charter.'[11]

11.2.4 Afghanistan

Viewed in isolation, the appeal of the United States and others to boycott the Moscow Games was in conflict with the Final Act of Helsinki. However, it ought to be remembered that this appeal arose from the Soviet intervention in Afghanistan, In this case the violation of the Final Act (the invasion of Afghanistan) was answered with a violation of the same Final Act on another point (the paragraph on sport and, in this context, also principle IX). In the view of the parties that took the initiative in the boycott, the earlier violation concerned military intervention by the Soviet Union in Afghanistan, an independent sovereign State, which constituted a violation of the basic principles of the United Nations Charter and of international law; a violation of the prohibition of aggression that applies to the relations between States. In the Final Act the prohibition against aggression is laid down, in particular, in principle II of the 'First Basket,' also with regard to States which did not sign the Final Act, as, for instance, Afghanistan: 'The participating States will refrain in their mutual relations, *as well as in their international relations in general*, from the threat or use of force against the territorial integrity or political independence of any State' [author's emphasis added].

In this context the preamble of the 'First Basket' is relevant. This concerns 'Questions relating to security in Europe' where detente is called a process 'universal in scope,' and where the close link between peace and security in Europe and in the world as a whole is recognised, as well as the need for each of the participating States to make its contribution to the strengthening of world peace and security. In fact the invasion of Afghanistan violated many other principles of the 'First Basket,' in particular principle VIII concerning the right of peoples to self-determination, as well as principles I, III, IV, and VI (Respect for the rights inherent in sovereignty, Inviolability of frontiers, Territorial integrity of States, Non-intervention in internal affairs) (8) via principle X (Fulfilment in good faith of obligations under international law). These principles guiding the relations

[11] Van den Heuvel (1978), p. 48. N.B. The present chairman of the Soviet N0C is also the Minister of Sport.

between the participating States represent at the same time principles of public international law and were, therefore, applicable in the relations between the Soviet Union and Afghanistan (see explicitly so principle II).

11.2.5 Reciprocity

Is it possible to justify the fact that the invasion of Afghanistan was answered with an appeal by the United States and others to the NOCs to boycott the Moscow Olympic Games? Or should this appeal nevertheless be considered in this context as a violation of the Final Act and therefore of detente?

The Final Act says only that the participating States 'will pay due regard to and implement the provisions in the Final Act of the Conference on Security and Co-operation in Europe' (see principle X). At the end of the Final Act the section 'Follow- up to the Conference' states that 'The participating States declare [...] their resolve to continue the multilateral process initiated by the Conference: (a) by proceeding to a thorough exchange of views [...] on the implementation of the provisions of the Final Act.'[12] In the Concluding Document of the follow-up meeting in Madrid, no mention was made of contacts in the field of sport, nor of the boycott of the Olympic Games, let alone of the boycott as a reaction to Afghanistan.

As it is, the Final Act of Helsinki is not an agreement under international law (treaty), though it is an agreement in the sense of an 'accord.' In this context one may refer to the following statement made on behalf of the Government of the Netherlands to parliaments 'Although the undertakings given within the framework of the Final Act of Helsinki are not, strictly speaking, obligations in the sense of treaty law, the Netherlands has consistently maintained the view that the Helsinki accords would lose their point unless all the signatories to the Final Act made every effort to ensure proper implementation of the Final Act provisions [...]. The Helsinki accords are accords between thirty-five countries. The mere fact of defective implementation of some of the accords by one or more countries need not immediately be a reason for other countries to stop implementing them. However, a situation in which some countries do and others do not act in accordance with what was agreed at Helsinki cannot last indefinitely. If one or more countries were to continue to ignore aspects of the Final Act that are essential to detente, and other countries had to tolerate this, then there would be no question of real détente. The fact is that accords such as those of Helsinki are based on the assumption of reciprocity.'[13]

---

[12] Cf., the vice-chairman of the American delegation at the follow- up meeting of Madrid on 24 November, 1980, World Affairs, 1982, No. 4, p. 333 et seq.

[13] NYIL, 1981, pp. 167–168.

If reciprocity is then accepted with regard to the implementation of the Final Act of Helsinki, the 1969 Vienna Convention on the Law of Treaties, which aims at the codification and progressive development of the law of treaties (see the preamble), contains a provision which could be invoked by analogy, viz., Article 60, para 2, under (c); 'A material breach of a multilateral treaty by one of the parties entitles any party other than the defaulting State to invoke the breach as a ground for suspending the operation of the treaty in whole or in part with respect to itself if the treaty is of such a character that a material breach of its provisions by one party radically changes the position of every other party with respect to the further performance of its obligations under the treaty,' In the case under discussion the description of 'material breach' in para 3 under (b) of Article 60 is particularly relevant: 'the violation of a provision essential to the accomplishment of the object and purpose of the treaty.'

If 'Afghanistan' and the boycott appeal which was a reaction to it are assessed in the light of the provisions of Article 60, the following conclusion would seem justified by analogy: (1) that the Soviet Union (defaulting State) directly violated, *inter alia*, principles II and VIII of the Final Act, which can undoubtedly be considered to be a material breach because it attacked the very essence of detente (cf., object and purpose), thereby radically altering the position of all the other States with regard to the further implementation of their obligations under the Final Act, and (2) that this material breach can be considered as a ground for the United States and others to suspend the paragraph on sport and, in connection with this, principle IX, with regard to the Moscow Olympic Games (cf., suspending the operation of the treaty in part with respect to itself).

11.2.6 Sport and Politics

The final decision on the boycott of the 1980 Moscow Olympic Games was left to the NOCs* The NOCs were free to make this decision in two ways. In the first place, in law they would do no more than ignore an invitation to participate in the Games by a negative decision, i.e., in accordance with the rules of a non-governmental organisation, the IOC (Article 61 of the Rules of the Olympic Charter). There is actually no obligation for the NOCs, the only responsible authorities for the representation of their countries at the Games (Article 24b Rules), to participate in the Olympic Games. The issue concerned here was, therefore, a decision about entering the Games by 24 May, 1980 at the latest; this was the official closing date which was extended by the IOC to give the NOCs a further opportunity to enter the Games.

In the second place, the Western NOCs—for these were concerned in particular as the boycott was taken on American initiative with the intention that Western Europe especially would follow suit remained officially free in their final decision because the principle of autonomy of the sport federations applies In the Western world, i.e., the respect for the individual responsibility of the national sports organisations. In principle, sports organisations should decide themselves which international contacts they desire to maintain. Governments cannot make directives or give instructions in this matter. They can, however, make recommendations or requests. Sport and politics cannot be separated, but there are areas of separate responsibility. One government (and parliament) will exercise more political pressure in the world of sport than another. In the case of Moscow 1980, the Government of the United States, which took the initiative for the boycott, exerted most pressure. Thus the USOC was addressed by Vice-President Mondale on behalf of President Carter, in his capacity as honorary President of the USOC, at its meeting on 12 April, 1980, when by a vote of 1,604 to 797 the decision was taken not to participate in the Games.[14] On the contrary, most Western European Governments, which, with the exception of Great Britain, were not such enthusiastic supporters of a boycott, were initially inclined to emphasise the independence of the NOCs. France—the birthplace of Baron Pierre de Coubertin, the spiritual father of the modern Olympic Games was the leading proponent of this point of view. This attitude changed abruptly in most cases when it became known that the Nobel Prize winner, Andrei Sacharov, was banished to Gorky on 22 January, 1980. This was a violation of principle VII of the Final Act of Helsinki (respect for human rights and freedoms). At that point even Western Europe put pressure on the sporting world, without however exceeding the limits of the sports federations' autonomy. To give just one example, the Dutch Government was the first to announce that it would advise its athletes to boycott the Games, The Government had already decided not to give any financial support to the Dutch team for the Games. It withdrew a subsidy of Fl, 6,000, which the NOC had requested for the travelling expenses of an interpreter and for the costs of participating in the IOC meeting in Moscow, However, Prime Minister Van Agt emphasised that in view of the size of the sum, this would not have any consequences for the participation nor for the independence of the sports federations involved in participating in the Olympic Games, a point which was also stressed by the Government as such,[15] Nevertheless, it is submitted that this sort of decision, when viewed in isolation, is, like the appeal to boycott, in conflict with the Final Act (paragraph on sport).

In the event, the boycott of the Olympic Games was not a complete boycott, 81 out of 146 NOCs sent teams to Moscow, and in some cases athletes did not participate in particular events because the national sports federation concerned wished to boycott the Games, even though the NOC did not. This was possible, unlike the converse, i.e., the individual participation of athletes, teams or even entire sports federations, NOCs of 42 countries had declined the invitation to the

[14] Department of State Bulletin, May 1980, pp. 14–15.

[15] Aanhangsel Handelingen [Appendix to Parliamentary Proceedings], II 1979/1980, No. 568, p. 1111.

1980 Moscow Olympic Games explicitly; these can be regarded as the true boycott States, USOC, for example, decided not to participate because the President of the United States had declared that the national security of the country was being threatened by international events. This motive could in fact have justified administrative measures such as the withdrawal of passports and the refusal of exit visas to those going to the Olympics, The remaining twenty-three countries had simply not responded to the invitation; there were reasons other than the boycott itself, for example, financial reasons. Twenty-seven of the thirty-five States that had signed the Final Act of Helsinki participated in the Games, including eighteen Western European States, The Games were boycotted by the Federal Republic of Germany, Canada, Liechtenstein, Monaco, Norway, Turkey and the United States (the Vatican does not have a NOC).

11.2.7 The Olympic Charter

The NOCs formally could make their decisions freely. In fact, they were obliged to do so pursuant to Article 24 C of the Rules of the Olympic Charter: 'NOCs must be autonomous and must resist all pressures of any kind whatsoever, whether of a political, religious or economic nature.' The question is whether there were good reasons to respond to the appeal to boycott.

In my opinion, sport should listen to politics when the underlying reason for the proposed measures also affects the sport as such, i.e., when there are reasons 'of sport' for the boycott. A good example is the boycott of sports with South Africa. If, and to the extent that there is apartheid in sport in South Africa, there should be no contacts with that country in the field of sports. It would be possible, however, to have contacts with multi-racial (non-racial) sports federations In South Africa. This implies that not all sporting contacts with South Africa should be cut off, in contrast to the aim of the International Declaration against Apartheid in Sport (resolution of the General Assembly of the United Nations of 14 December, 1977, 32/105 M). If this would happen, the world of sport would be adopting a purely political position, unless one would take the position that fully integrated, non-racial sport is impossible under the system of apartheid. Racism in sport should therefore be combatted by the world of sport for reasons of principles of sport (cf., the Olympic principle of non-discrimination), but it cannot be the function of the world of sport to combat the apartheid system as such.

What are the implications of all this for the appeal to boycott Moscow 1980? The governments in favour of a boycott were of the view that the Olympic Games should not take place in a country that committed acts of aggression against and within a small neighbouring country (Afghanistan) and thus acted in direct conflict with the principles as laid down in the Charter of the UN. Cf., also Article 1 of the Olympic Rules: 'The aims of the Olympic movement are: [...]—to educate young people through sport in a spirit of better understanding between each other and of friendship, thereby helping to build a better and more peaceful world,—to spread the Olympic principles throughout the world, thereby creating international goodwill.' The Olympic movement therefore has idealistic aims which go beyond the world of sport itself.

Thus the Olympic Games—'universal in scope' with 146 member countries with NOCs—have to a certain extent political purposes. Cf., for example, the preamble of the Third Basket of the Final Act of Helsinki (including the paragraph on sport), which refers to the participating States' desire to contribute to the strengthening of peace and understanding among peoples. It is now possible to conclude that the appeal to boycott in reaction to 'Afghanistan' was not arbitrary. The underlying consideration was that cooperation, the aim of which should be the promotion of detente, would be difficult to achieve in the context of the Olympic Games, which were aimed at promoting peace, at a time when detente had received such a blow by a violation of peace made by the very country where the Games were to take place. The same applies in an assessment of the appeal to boycott in the context of the Final Act, by analogy with Article 60 of the Vienna Convention on the Law of Treaties (see *supra* section 11.2.5), the position of the United States and others had altered radically as a result of 'Afghanistan' (and 'Sacharov'), particularly as regards the Olympic Games.

There is yet another aspect in which holding the Olympic Games in Moscow was directly related to the Final Act of Helsinki, viz., that of 'human contacts.' Many people wished to use the sporting occasion in Moscow as an opportunity for discussing with the hosts the question of human rights, and in this way for promoting the process of detente from their side.[16] However, the preparations for the Games included measures designed to forcibly displace Moscow inhabitants in order to prevent the population of Moscow from having any contact with foreign visitors and athletes. For many people the banishment of Sacharov symbolised the impossibility of any true dialogue. Prominent Russian dissidents abroad, such as Ginzburg, Bukovski and Amalrik founded a pro-boycott committee on the day of Sacharov's banishment. In the Netherlands, the Committee on Olympic Games and Human Rights (COSEM), consisting of members of parliament and representatives of social sectors, also began to favour a boycott, having been against it previously.

Were the NOCs in the same position as governments with regard to the question of whether to participate because the Olympic Games have a detente character which entails to a certain extent political purposes? For the NOCs 'Afghanistan' as such was not a sufficient reason of sport to boycott the Games. (N.B. An example of a boycott based on principles of sport was the boycott of the 1976 Olympic Games in Montreal by twenty-nine African states because New Zealand, which maintained contacts in the field of sport with South Africa, had not been banned from the Games by the IOC). The NOCs merely had to ascertain whether, notwithstanding 'Afghanistan' and other events, the Games could take place as a normal sports event, and also as an opportunity for the sporting youth of the whole

---

[16] Cf., Guldenpfennig (1981), in particular see pp. 35, 134.

world to meet 'in a spirit of better understanding between each other and of friendship,' 'thereby helping to build a better and more peaceful world,' and 'thereby creating international goodwill.' It is submitted that these questions could be answered affirmatively, although perhaps with some hesitation. Quite independently of the question of Afghanistan, one reason for a boycott might have been the fear that in principle the host country would use the Games for propaganda for its political and social system etc., to reveal its superiority before the eyes of the world. This would have been in conflict with the Olympic Charter, see Instruction II (The Olympic Games are not for profit): 'No one is permitted to profit from the Olympic Games [...] all are determined that neither individuals, organizations or nations shall be permitted to profit from them, politically or commercially.'

11.2.8 National Representation

As stated above, I do not consider that 'Afghanistan' alone could have been a reason for the NOCs to boycott the Games in Moscow, However, there is another aspect that should be considered in this study. The Games are admittedly apolitical in the way they are planned, but on the other hand, there are provisions in the Olympic Charter which clearly contradict this basic assumption. One example of an apolitical provision is the following: the Games are entrusted to a city by the IOC (Article 4 Olympic Rules), However, this provision is contradicted by Article 64 regarding the opening ceremony: the head of state of the country concerned declares the Games officially opened. At the closing ceremony the flag of the host country is hoisted and the national anthem is played (Article 66). Another apolitical provision is that the Olympic Games are not contests between nations, and no scoring by countries is recognised (Article 46), In this context, Instruction I of the Charter deserves consideration: the IOC 'considers [...] as dangerous to the Olympic ideals [...] that certain tendencies exist which aim primarily at a national exaltation of the results gained instead of the realization that the sharing of friendly effort and rivalry is the essential aim of the Olympic Games.' This is in line with-the important Article 9: 'The Games are contests between individuals and not between countries.' However, in direct opposition to this, is the fact that:

- only nationals of a country may represent that country and compete in the Games (Article 8);
- the flags of the countries of the medal winners are hoisted while the national anthem of the country of the winner is played (Article 65);
- name-boards of the countries which are represented and their flags are carried at the opening and closing ceremonies. (N.B. During the closing ceremony the athletes may march behind the name-boards and flags of another country,

'without distinction of nationality united only by the friendly bonds of Olympic sport.')

In fact, participating in the Olympic Games has both the character of participation of a State in the Games, and of participation of athletes with a particular nationality representing the NOC of the State in question.[17] Thus, in taking their decision on the boycott, the Western NOCs had to consider that they would not only be a sports delegation in Moscow, but actually also a national representation vis-a-vis the head of State of the Soviet Union, while their governments certainly did not wish to be represented there. (N.B. The diplomatic representatives (ambassadors) of the Western States in Moscow were absent for the duration of the Games.) By the use of national symbols (flag, national anthem), this would also become obvious in Moscow. Strictly speaking, USOC and others had to take a decision with national consequences, whether or not it was in accordance with the foreign policy of the government. It should be remembered that the governments feared that if the Western States participated, the Olympic Games would be used by the Soviets as proof of the international acceptance of the policy carried out by the USSR (particularly as regards Afghanistan and Sacharov).

11.2.9 Depoliticisation

The eighteen Western European NOCs which refused to boycott the Games attempted to resolve the dilemma outlined above by a degree of depoliticisation or denationalisation of their own participation in the Games, On 3 May, 1930, they issued a declaration in Rome, stating the conditions under which they participated, the most important of which are that:

- on all occasions the flag of their delegations would be the Olympic flag;
- the national anthem would be the official Olympic anthem, [N.B, A rather cryptic article (Article 24 F) had been added to the Olympic Charter (Rules) during the Winter Games in February 1980 at Lake Placid, to make this possible.[18]

Moreover, a variety of ways was used in the Summer Games to avoid any form of national representation. Some NOCs even boycotted the opening and closing ceremonies, others used a nameboard with the name of the NOC rather than a

[17] Cf., the Decision of the Judicial Division of the Council of State on 12 June, 1980 in pursuance of the possible South African participation in the Olympic Games for the Handicapped (Paralympics) held in the Netherlands, NYIL, 1981, p. 349 et seq.

[18] Article 24 F. 'The flag [...] used by a NOC at the Olympic Games shall be submitted to and approved by the Executive Board of the IOC.' The Bye-laws to the Rules states '[...] NOCs may only make use of the Olympic flag [...] provided that they have the express approval of the IOC to do so.'.

nameboard with the name of the country (e.g., 'BOA' instead of 'United Kingdom'). In a formal sense this covered any moral obligations towards the delegation's own government. In fact, the condemnation by the government of the countries concerned of 'Afghanistan' and 'Sacharov' was publicly revealed by the NOCs in this way—though admittedly to a lesser extent than by the absent NOCs. However, the media obviously continued to refer to the NOCs in question by the name of their country. The 'country' still participated. However, it is submitted that this is a consequence with which the world of sport, as a sector of society, need not concern itself, if 'sport' is not to be completely politicised. It is actually rather difficult to conceive of any other form of organisation for international sport than a territorial organisation, i.e., by country and also by nationality, cf., Article 24 E of the Olympic Charter (Rules): 'The name of a NOC must reflect the territorial extent and tradition of that country.' Even the abbreviations such as USOC and BOA, which are not at first glance obviously connected to a particular country, actually stand for 'United States' and 'British' respectively, while NOC also stands for the Netherlands Olympic Committee.

Meanwhile, further consideration has been given to the question of depoliticising the Olympic Games after the problems in Moscow in 1980, The Greek president, Karamanlis, repeated a proposal first made in 1976 (Montreal) to hold the Games permanently in his country at a place with extra-territorial status, in the vicinity of Olympia.[19] This was, therefore, a proposal to denationalise the location rather than the participants. On 15 February, 1980, the European Parliament accepted a resolution about the Olympic Games in Moscow in support of this proposal.[20] The Consultative Assembly of the Council of Europe adopted a similar resolution on 26 September, 1980 (Resolution 738 on the Olympic Games and the outlook for their future, based on a report by M. Druon.[21] 'Nea Olympia' would have to be assigned international status, and it would have to be placed under the authority of the IOC. Prompted by Karamanlis' offer, Lord Killanin, the then President of the IOC, finally set up a special study commission. This commission concerned itself, *inter alia*, with preparing a draft convention on this matter between the Greek government and the IOC.[22] However, the Olympic Congress in Baden–Baden in September 1981 came to the following conclusions with regard to the future of the Olympic Games:

- The Olympic Games ceremonial should be maintained as in the 'Olympic Charter' (however, Article 24 F (Rules) remains valid as an escape clause at the time of writing);
- 'The Olympic Games should continue to be able to be held anywhere in the world.'

[19] At the same time the Mayor of Innsbruck offered his city as a permanent location for the Winter Games, which had been held there previously in 1964 and 1976.

[20] Official Journal of the European Communities, No. C59 of 10 March, 1980, pp. 57–58.

[21] Doc. 4585.

[22] Olympic Review (1980), p. 706.

11.2.10 The IOC

In his initial appeal to boycott, on 20 January, 1980, President Carter had insisted that the USOC propose to the IOC that it relocate, postpone or cancel the Games. What was the IOC's position? The IOC is the final authority on all matters relating to the Olympic Games (Article 23). The IOC chooses the city where the Games are to be held at least six years in advance. 'In the event of a breach of the Rules being committed or a failure to observe the duties and obligations that have been entered into, the IOC may, pursuant to Rule [...] 23 [...], withdraw the organization of the Olympic Games from the city and from the NOC concerned' (Article 51).

The IOC is completely autonomous in its decision-making process, vis-à-vis the NOCs: 'Members of the IOC are representatives of the IOC in their countries and not delegates to the IOC' (Article 12). [N.B. IOC members must be members of the NOC of their country (see the Model Constitution for an NOC as contained in the Olympic Charter, Article 111(b)(1))]; 'They may not accept from governments or from any organizations or individuals instructions which shall in any way bind them or interfere with the independence of their vote.' (Cf., Article 24 C with regard to the NOCs.)

Unlike the NOCs, which have a national representation, the IOC was able to adopt a completely neutral position with regard to 'Afghanistan,' i.e., not merely because there were no reasons of 'sport' for the boycott. Therefore, there was no need to make an implicit choice for or against the Western policy, based on the view that the invasion of Afghanistan constituted military intervention (as expressed in Resolution ES-6/2 of the General Assembly of the United Nations) or between this view and that of the Soviet Union, that the Government of Afghanistan had requested military assistance against foreign aggression on the basis of the 1978 Treaty of Friendship between the two countries, so that Article 51 of the Charter of the United Nations (collective self-defence) was applicable.[23]

At the IOC session at Lake Placid on 12 February, 1980, the IOC unanimously decided to reject the USOC request to relocate etc. the Games (all seventy-three members were present). A few days earlier, during the opening of the IOC session, Lord Killanin had made the following statement: 'Solutions to the political problems of the world are not the responsibility of sporting bodies such as the

[23] However, the IOC now has at its disposal a formal criterion of assessment based on international law in view of the contract that is made between the IOC and the organising NOC, as well as the city chosen for the Games. This is Article 5 of the model contract as contained in the Olympic Charter. (This article was not included in the 1979 version, though it is contained in the 1982 and 1983 versions.) It reads: 'If the country where the city is located at any time before the opening ceremony of the Games finds itself in a state of war or in a situation officially considered as one of belligerence, the IOC has the right, by simple notification addressed to [...] the NOC, to withdraw the Games from the city.' (author's emphasis added). This provision could, in fact, be considered as a modern variation of the classic Olympic principle of political truce. During the Games there was always a truce, and the organising city State was forbidden to wage war and the other city States were forbidden to declare war on it.

International Olympic Committee, but of the appropriate governmental organizations [...]. We have had to face many problems in recent years, for example, political problems in Germany and China, and racial discrimination in South Africa and Rhodesia. We have always sought to resolve these problems from a sporting point of view, in an effort to bring the peoples of the world together, without discrimination as to race, religion or politics [...] As I have repeatedly said, we have the greatest dislike of sport being made the target, when political, diplomatic and economic measures should be used by those with conflicting ideologies to resolve the differences.'[24] At the end of the IOC session, Lord Killanin made the following statement about the IOC contract with the Soviet NOC and the city of Moscow (a declaration which was unanimously approved by the IOC): 'The Games of the XXII Olympiad were awarded to the City of Moscow by the 75th Session of the International Olympic Committee, and an agreement was signed between the parties on 23 October, 1974 All preparations have been made in keeping with the terms of that agreement and consistent with the rules of the IOC.'[25]

11.2.11 Conclusion

How can a boycott such as that of the 1980 Moscow Olympic Games be assessed from the point of view of the Final Act of Helsinki of 1975?

The Final Act of Helsinki contains a paragraph on sport, a specific elaboration of principle IX of the Decalogue, concerned with the co-operation between the participating States in the field of sport. In my view, the appeal of the American and other governments to boycott the Games is in conflict with the paragraph on sport, which implies that the participating States will not discourage any contacts in the field of sport. However, I do consider that the appeal was totally justified as a reaction to 'Afghanistan,' a violation of almost the entire Decalogue and, unlike the non-implementation of the paragraph on sport, a violation of international law. With regard to the implementation of the Final Act, although a 'legally non-binding agreement,' it is submitted that reciprocity is applicable. By analogy, then, Article 60 of the Vienna Convention on the Law of Treaties could be applied to the appeal to boycott.

As regards the NOCs' decision whether or not to boycott after being appealed to, they were no more bound to the Final Act than was the IOC. The NOCs' decision vis-a-vis Moscow 1980 was a decision about entering the Games to be taken independently of their governments and the IOC.

The position of the governments which had appealed to their NOCs to boycott was based particularly on the consideration that one should not participate in the

[24] Olympic Review (1980), pp. 107–108.

[25] *Id.*, p. 110.

Olympic Games, which are aimed at the promotion of world peace, in a country which had recently committed an aggressive act. However, it is submitted here that only reasons of principle relating to sport can be a justification for a sport boycott, at least from the perspective of the sporting world. Racial discrimination in sport is an example of this type of reason. In the case under discussion, the NOCs need only have considered whether the Olympic Games could take place normally as a sporting event and an opportunity for young sportsmen of the world to meet in a spirit of better understanding between each other and of friendship, notwithstanding 'Afghanistan.' Personally, I would have answered this question affirmatively. However, this leaves out one important obstacle. National teams represent their countries in a visible manner by means of the national flag, national anthem etc.

The NOCs which participated in the Games against the advice of their governments visibly demonstrated that they were ignoring the foreign policy of their governments, although they had valid sporting reasons for doing so, I therefore consider that it was a correct decision that the eighteen Western European NOCs attempted to denationalise their presence in Moscow by leaving their national anthems and flags behind. Meanwhile the attempts to depoliticise the Games by creating 'Nea Olympia' have foundered. Thus in future the same sort of situation might arise as that of Moscow 1980. There does not seem to be any permanent solution. Even If anything like 'Nea Olympia' could ever be achieved (an utopia?), there might still be boycotts among the participating countries, although the IOC would be the host.

Meanwhile I consider that Article 24 F of the Olympic Charter (NOCs performing under the Olympic flag and anthem) was retained for a good reason, so that it can be applied when the need arises. Moreover, the Olympic Charter should, in my view, make it possible for individual athletes, teams and entire sports federations to participate in the event of a boycott by the national NOC (obviously under the Olympic flag and anthem). After all, the converse is also possible, when athletes etc. do not compete though the NOC does participate. In this context, it should be remembered, that: 'The Games are contests between individuals and not between countries' (Article 9 of the Olympic Charter).

11.2.12 Postscript

Now that most socialist countries on their turn have boycotted the Olympic Games at Los Angeles in 1984, the question may be asked how this boycott is related to the Final Act of Helsinki.

The first observation to be made is that the boycott was an independent decision by the Olympic Committee of the Soviet Union, The Government had not made any public, official appeal not to participate in the Games before. So, the Final Act was not violated, since the sports organisations did not assume formal obligations under the Final Act.

Secondly, the reasons put forward by the Olympic Committee of the Soviet Union for the boycott, only referred to the organisation of the Games. There was no reason given that, on its own, had no direct relation to the Games (cf., Afghanistan). The reasons put forward were gross violations of the Olympic Charter by the host country, i.e., the organising committee and the public authorities, as a result of which the participants' security was not guaranteed.

So, the boycott of Los Angeles was the opposite of the boycott of Moscow 1980, at least in a formal sense: no political, but a purely 'sports' boycott, i.e., based on the sporting world's decision and for technical reasons. Was that true in fact? In the Soviet Union the national sports federations of which NOCs are made up for the most part, are subordinated to a State organ, the Sports Committee. So, one may suppose that, as the Soviet national sports federations suggested the Olympic Committee not to participate in the Games at Los Angeles, they in fact implemented the Government's and Party's policy. If the decision to boycott was taken by the USSR in reaction to the boycott of Moscow 1980 four years earlier, this decision amounts to a reprisal, belated but—for that very reason—exactly proportionate. From the Soviet point of view this reprisal was justified: Afghanistan was a question of military assistance instead of intervention and therefore the US boycott of Moscow 1980 had been unlawful. However, if one starts from the lawfulness of the 1980 appeal to boycott as this author does, it was the boycott of Los Angeles 1984 that constituted a violation of the Final Act of Helsinki.

11.3 The Sports Boycott of Nigeria: Sports, Politics and Human Rights[26]

On the subject of international sports boycotts many discussions have taken place in this country, especially in the 1970s and 1980s. Sports contacts with South Africa were permanently on the agenda. In 1978, the participation of the Dutch national soccer team in the soccer World Championship in Argentina was questioned. In 1980 and four years later the Olympic Games in Moscow and Los Angeles suffered from boycotts. In 1993 the United Nations instituted a sports boycott against Yugoslavia 'minor.' The international practice match between the Netherlands and Nigeria has once again placed the problem of the relationship between sports and politics in the limelight. What is special about this case is that it involves a regional boycott, namely instituted by the European Union.

11.3.1 South Africa

UN resolutions (since 1971) displayed the tendency to aim to prohibit all sports contacts with South Africa. To begin with, only contacts with teams or sportsmen

---

[26] Cf., Siekmann (2008), pp. 121–124.

selected on racial grounds were discouraged. The International Declaration against apartheid in sports (1977) however, took the position that a completely integrated, non-racial exercise of sports in a country like South Africa could not exist under the apartheid regime and it was couched in binding terms. The Netherlands initially voted in favour of the resolutions and the government requested the national sports associations to abstain from 'racial' sports contacts. The International Declaration was not voted on by our country, as the government had to respect the autonomy of sports organisations and could not curtail the freedom of movement of Dutch nationals, that is to say, could not limit the freedom to leave one's country (see international human rights treaties: ICCPR, ECHR). The Netherlands could not agree with the proposition that each and every sports contact should be broken off, regardless of whether the sports organisation in question was founded on racial principles or not.

The application and interpretation of the non-racial criterium was further developed in practice. The government appeared to only accord political consequences to national sports representation. With regard to respecting the autonomy of the sports associations, the Paralympics case (judgments of the Administrative Law Division of the Council of State, 1980) illustrated the point that it may be impossible to separate sports from politics, but that the government is bound to respect the sports associations' own responsibility and, where necessary, needs to live up to its own responsibility.

In 1982, the government policy regarding sports contacts with South Africa was intensified. All sports contacts with South Africa were discouraged from then on, irrespective of whether racial or non-racial sports contacts were involved, or international or non-international sports representation. The political significance of sports contacts with South Africa became decisive. It was, however, still understood that the sports associations had to abide by the regulations of international sports organisations.

The Dutch Sports Federation (NSF) could agree to this government standpoint, which resulted in the sports associations being discouraged from engaging in friendly sports contacts with South Africa. International obligations, however, still had to be met.

Then, the Minister of Foreign Affairs formulated a visa policy which in reality ruled out in advance any sports contact with South Africans in the Netherlands. The NSF justifiedly protested this. The complete non-participation of South Africans could now, in fact, be forced by the government through visa policy. This was not in accordance with previously formulated policy, in which respect for the sports associations' autonomy and their international obligations were apparent features. The government consequently adjusted the criteria for granting visa so as to allow exceptions to the highly restrictive policy. World championships were excluded, whereby it had to be shown that a refusal of South African participation would result in the impossibility of the event ever being staged in the Netherlands again and that the damage thus incurred by the Dutch sports scene would be so great, that refusing South African sportsmen had to be considered disproportional.

The sports boycott of South Africa in the sports community itself ran parallel to the action of the United Nations. In 1970, the IOC expelled South Africa from the Olympic Movement. The international sports federations followed suit, either by expelling South Africa, or by prohibiting South Africa from taking part in world championships. The focus then shifted to the ‘indirect’ boycott: African states boycotted the Olympic Games in Montreal in 1976 because New Zealand, whose national rugby team had done a tour of South Africa, was participating.

The sports boycott of South Africa was based on recommendations of the General Assembly of the United Nations, and as such not legally binding on the Member States. The reason for the boycott lay in the flagrant and systematic human rights violations in South Africa as a result of the apartheid regime. The principle of non-discrimination is a fundamental principle in the sports world, too, which is enshrined in the Olympic Charter and the Statutes of the international sports federations. It is therefore a ‘sporting’ criterium to take measures against a national association violating this principle.

11.3.2 Serbia Montenegro

In 1992, a sports boycott was instituted against Serbia Montenegro, or Yugoslavia ‘minor,’ in addition to an economic boycott, because of the continued military involvement of that country in the hostilities in Bosnia. The UN Security Council in Resolution 757 decided that all states had to take the necessary measures to prevent participation by persons or teams representing Serbia Montenegro in sports matches in their territory. Here, the sports boycott was not due to the violation of human rights, but to military intervention in another country. The Security Council acted on the basis of Chapter VII of the UN Charter. This means that the Council should at least have established the existence of a threat to international peace and security (Article 39 UN Charter). Such circumstances entitle the Council to proclaim non-military enforcement action (sanctions) on the basis of Article 41 of the UN Charter, which the Member States of the UN are legally obligated to carry out.

It was not in connection to the sports boycott (which was exclusively aimed against national representation: for example, Yugoslavia was not able to participate in the European soccer championship in 1992), but because of the trade embargo that questions were asked in parliament in 1993 about the transfers of the Serbian FC Volendam players, Vukov and Stefanovic. From the Minister of Justice’s answers to these questions it emerged that the FIFA suspected that in transferring Serbian players in general, deals were made to have the payments run through private persons in other countries so as to circumvent the trade embargo, which also included financial transactions. This illustrates that a general economic boycott also stretches to include sports, insofar as financial transactions (professional sports is an economic activity) are involved.

The sports boycott of Serbia Montenegro was the second sport boycott in the history of the UN. It was motivated by reasons lying outside the realm of sports, as it concerned military intervention in a neighbouring country. Sport could not, however, escape its influence, as it concerned a binding boycott, which had, moreover, also been taken up by the European Union.

11.3.3 The 1980 Moscow Olympics

Collective boycotts are proclaimed by intergovernmental organisations like the UN (worldwide) and the European Union (regional; see hereafter on the sports boycott of Nigeria). 'Unilateral' sports boycotts, in contrast, are proclaimed by a state or *ad hoc* group of states taking the initiative by itself.

On 20 January 1980, president Carter of the United States in a message to the chairman of the American Olympic Committee (USOC) pressed for the Committee to propose to move the Moscow Summer Games to another location, to postpone them or to cancel them altogether, unless all Soviet troops would have withdrawn from Afghanistan within a month. He made it dear that, if the IOC would not accept this proposal, the United States would not send a delegation to Moscow. 'We must make clear to the Soviet Union that it cannot trample upon an independent nation and at the same time do business as usual with the rest of the world,' so president Carter explained. Within a week, the presidential request to the USOC found itself supported by resolutions of the House of Representatives and the Senate, which declared with overwhelming majorities that no American athletes should take part in the Moscow Games, unless the Soviet troops would have left Afghanistan by 20 February 1980. This American reaction to the Soviet invasion of Afghanistan (on 27 December 1979) heralded the beginning of an international boycott against the Moscow Summer Games.

As far as the Netherlands were concerned, the government announced that it would advise the sport community not to participate in the Games. The government had already decided to withdraw a subsidy requested by the NOC for travel expenses of an interpreter and the costs of participation in the IOC meeting in Moscow. The Dutch government stressed, however, that given the amount involved, this would have no consequences for actual participation in the Games, nor for the independence of the sports associations involved in taking part in the Games.

The military intervention by the Soviet Union in Afghanistan as such was not a 'sporting' reason for a boycott (cf. Serbia Montenegro). Yet, staging the Olympics in a country which is in a state of war is contrary to Olympic principles, dating back to classical antiquity, when arms were put down during the Games. The IOC is entitled to take the Games away from such countries. War in progess could therefore have been a 'sporting' reason for boycotting the Moscow Games. This fits in with the fact that the General Assembly of the United Nations always calls for the suspension of war anywhere in the world during the Games (as with regard to the recent Winter Games in Japan in connection to a possible attack by the United States on Iraq). The military intervention by the Soviet Union in Hungary in 1956 at that time caused the Netherlands to boycott the Games in Melbourne because the Soviet Union would be participating ('indirect' boycott).

Much commotion was caused in 1978 on the occasion of the participation of the Dutch national soccer team in the World Championship in Argentina because of the human rights situation in that country. The Dutch government abstained from taking position. The cabaret act of Freek de Jonge and Bram Vermeulen ('The Nation's Hope in Evil Times' [*Neerlands Hoop in Bange Dagen*]) vigorously tried for a boycott, among others with their show 'Out for blood' [*Bloed aan de paal*]. The Netherlands reached the final against the host country. If Rob Rensenbrink had scored in the last minute of regular playing time instead of hitting the post, the 'Orange' team would undoubtedly have struck a far heavier political blow to the general's regime of Videla and co. (by sporting means) than would ever have been attainable through a 'unilateral' boycott.

11.3.4 Sports Boycott of Nigeria

The sport boycott of Nigeria is based on the 'common position' of the Council of the European Union of 4 December 1995, in which the Council decides, among others, to impose the measure of suspension of all contacts in the area of sports with Nigeria through a refusal of visa to official delegations and national teams. On 28 November 1997 the boycott was extended by a year and the Council decided to issue certain guidelines for the implementation of the common position. Exceptions could be allowed by Member States, *inter alia*, for meeting obligations which had been entered into prior to the common position of 1995, especially for sports events organised under the auspices of international sport associations, such as the soccer World Championship in 1998 and practice matches already committed to, and the basketball World Championship in 1998.

The reason for this boycott may primarily be found in the continued human rights violations by the military regime in Nigeria. No 'sporting' motives are involved, however, unlike in the case of the sports boycott against South Africa due to apartheid within sport.

The common position was based on Article J.2 of the EU ('Maastricht') Treaty, which states that the Council may issue common positions in the field of foreign and security policy (CFSP). The Member States have to ensure that their national policies are in accordance with these positions (in the new Treaty of Amsterdam Article J.5 speaks of 'bringing about' instead of 'ensuring'). A common position creates no legal obligations for the Member States but contains a political commitment. With regard to Nigeria, no binding sanctions in the sense of Article 228a of the EU Treaty were laid down for the implementation of the common position. Article 228a, moreover, concerns economic boycotts of third states. An economic boycott may, however, also affect professional sports in particular. As economic boycott (oil boycott) was, however, explicitly rejected with regard to Nigeria.

The cabinet eventually decided to respect the obligations of the Royal Dutch Football Association [*KNVB*] regarding the international practice match against Nigeria and merely urged for the event to be conducted as plainly as possible. A few comments are in order here:

1. The obligations in question were entered into after 1995. The 'letter of the law' is unambivalent here. That the date of reference was allegedly 28 November 1997—the date on which the exceptions clause was adopted—is an assumption which is contrary to the EU decision. The fact that in particular France and Germany have nevertheless interpreted the provision as such, does not derogate from this conclusion.
2. It was politically agreed among the EU members that the visa weapon would be employed, if necessary, to prevent the occurrence of sports contacts at a national representation level. The Ministry of Foreign Affairs went no further than to ask France to territorially restrict the visa for the Nigerian selection to France alone, so the Netherlands might have refused the players. France, however, was not willing to do so. On the basis of the Schengen Treaty (for the abolition of border controls at the common outer borders) though, the Netherlands in my opinion could, and should, have independently decided that the Nigerian team would not be admitted for the purpose of playing the international practice match. The 'international relations' of a Schengen country may constitute a reason for refusing visa (Article 5, para 1(e), of the Schengen Treaty). As the sports boycott of Nigeria is in fact EU policy, it is therefore also Dutch foreign policy. The Netherlands politically committed itself at EU level to carry out this policy through means of visa allocation if necessary.

The government apparently did not make use of the visa policy on purely formal grounds. 'Schengen' would not have allowed for it, seeing that the border controls are relocated to the outer borders (in this case France). France too, however, is bound by the EU boycott. The fact that France wrongly interprets the date of reference for international practice matches should not have been a reason for the Dutch government to dispense with the consistent application of the sports boycott against Nigeria. The EU boycott decision is based on the Maastricht Treaty. 'Schengen' too, is a treaty which, however, does not prevail over the EU Treaty. All countries parties to it are also EU Member States. 'Maastricht' is of a later date than 'Schengen.' The adage *Lex posterior derogat legi priori* (laws of a later date enjoy prevalence over earlier laws) is also true for treaties. Apart from this, it must be dear that the CFSP ('second pillar' of the EU) which is being taken into account in 'Schengen' ('international relations') is principally of a higher order than the admittance policy (visa policy) which should be instrumental in character with regard to the CFSP. In addition to this, it is intended since the Treaty of Amsterdam (the successor to 'Maastricht') to eventually integrate 'Schengen' into the EU Treaty (third pillar: justice and home affairs). The government reacted rather formally in this matter: 'once they have been admitted to Schengen territory, there is nothing we can do.'

11.3.5 Starting Points for 'Sports and Politics'

In 1981, the NSF as the umbrella organisation to the sports community in our country, drafted the so-called 'Starting points for sports and politics' after consultations with representatives of the main political parties *CDA, PvdA, VVD* and *D66,* in which the NOC was also involved. The immediate cause for this had been the boycott of the Olympic Games in Moscow a year earlier. In the 'Starting points' it is established that there should be timely consultations between organised sports and the government on upcoming international sports meets. Through such consultations it can be prevented that the sports community is presented with a *fait accomplit.* The 'Starting points' have remained valid up until this day. The question whether the 'Starting points' were adhered to with regard to the Nigeria sports boycott, and the international practice match between the Netherlands and Nigeria of June last in particular, is therefore justified. And; with an eye to the future, do they offer a workable frame of reference for fruitful consultation on the international relations of the sports world?

In the first place, it has to be noted that the NOC*NSF, nor the KNVB was informed beforehand by the government that the European Union was going to decide to issue a sports boycott of Nigeria. The decision by 'Brussels' therefore came as a complete surprise to the sports community in 1995. This was the reason why the NOC*NSF at that time rejected the boycott. This principled standpoint is not derogated from by the fact that the Ministry of Welfare, Public Health and Sports informed the sports associations many times, once the boycott had been proclaimed.

In the second place, according to the 'Starting points' the Dutch government may ultimately find it desirable to render the opinion that representatives of the Dutch sports organisations should not subject themselves to political use and should not take part in certain sports manifestations. Thereby, especially large international sports events which would draw worldwide audiences were indicated, because they can become an easy target for nationalist tendencies and political lobbies. They could be used by the organising countries for the purpose of boosting their prestige. Especially when this occurs in countries with controversial regimes, this may lead to enormous tension, the 'Starting points' claim. This concerns: countries committing military aggression (see earlier: the 1980 Moscow Olympic Games, Yugoslavia 'minor'); countries subjected to a general international boycott (cf. South Africa, Yugoslavia 'minor'); countries where serious and systematic violations of human rights are taking place (cf. South Africa, Argentina); and countries in which the principle of universality is not upheld (tin example is the sports boycott of Israel). The EU boycott of Nigeria is an international boycott, albeit not a 'general' one in the sense of worldwide, but a regional one. Apart from this, there is no doubt that serious and systematic human rights violations have taken place and are still taking place in Nigeria. Nigeria was and is a country with a controversial regime.

In the third place, it is stated in the 'Starting points' that it fits in with Dutch society for political institutions to create the terms within which sports organisations may exercise their sports functions in accordance with their own responsibilities. In acquitting these functions, the sports organisations must bear in mind the responsibility brought about by the way in which society and sports are interrelated. According to the 'Starting points,' opinions on the undesirability of certain international sports contacts must be accorded more weight as government and/or parliament:

- show that the sportsmen concerned are used for political purposes outside our country. This was not the case with the international practice match between the Netherlands and Nigeria, nor will it be the case with the soccer World Championship, the 'large international sports manifestation' to which the match was actually linked;
- appear to maintain a certain political consistence, also based on a wide political majority (in the Second Chamber of parliament). From a human rights perspective, it is quite unclear why a sports boycott had to be issued against Nigeria in particular but not against other similar countries. Selective indignation? The reason may be found in the sporting achievements of the *Super Eagles*, the Nigerian national soccer team, Olympic champion in 1996. This implies prestige for the military regime, and this is where that regime may be struck. Had Nigeria only disposed of a mediocre team, no sports boycott would have been proclaimed. And, one may still wonder whether a 5-1 victory of the 'Orange' team over Nigeria is not in itself an equally harsh blow to the regime of the now late Abacha. In the same way, Rob Rensenbrink in 1978 could no doubt have dealt a heavy political blow to the Argentine dictator Videla. But of course you can never tell these things beforehand...
- second the opinion of an international political institution. This condition was met through the EU boycott.
- indicate if, and if so, which, means are being employed to attain the political goal. The Dutch sports community vigorously resists having to act as a spearhead of policy. It demands that a boycott always be part of wider policy, in which other social interests are equally involved. It is not fair that sports should be the only sector in society to have to make sacrifices. As far as Nigeria is concerned, further action only consists of the suspension of military co-operation and an arms embargo. An oil embargo could, however, not be decided on. Sports therefore seems to be disproportionally hit.
- have tested the measure for effectivity. As they themselves suffer the disadvantages, the sports world understandably demands guarantees each time that a particular boycott will in fact have the desired effect. The sports boycott of Nigeria is not effective, because the European Union has itself in 1997 still made an exception for participation of Nigeria in the soccer World Championship in France. In doing so, the EU has itself definitively undermined its own sports boycott. Cancelling the international practice match between the Netherlands and Nigeria would certainly not have fixed that.

- seriously take into account the interests of the sportsmen and the obligations flowing from the membership to an international sports organisation and possible other commitments meanwhile entered into (with European and World Championships, Olympic Games and the necessary qualifying matches these obligations will be greater than with friendly matches). The World Championship has at a later stage therefore been shown every consideration by the EU. The international practice match between the Netherlands and Nigeria was a non-compulsory, friendly match. In any case according to the letter of the EU decision, it still fell within the scope of the sports boycott, in which only commitments entered into before the start of the boycott in 1995 were taken into account. This had however already been compromised because the international practice match between Germany and Nigeria had been played on 22 April last whereby a later date of reference was claimed.

11.3.6 Conclusion

Everything considered, one may not reasonably maintain that the KNVB should have co-operated at any cost with the cancellation of the international match against Nigeria. Where lie the boundaries of sports' responsibility to society? In the first place, it should be established that sports itself should in any event exclude those countries that violate the principle of non-discrimination within sports itself. This principle returns in the statutes of all international sports federations. The by now classic example is apartheid in sports in South Africa. If such an intrinsic link between politics and sports is absent, sports are taken into an area where a balance should be drawn between the ways in which politics may use/abuse sports. What should be considered to be of more importance: how a regime violating human rights may abuse sports (propaganda), or: how the 'own' government may use sports by attaching a political function (boycott) to it thereby harming sports? One reaches the conclusion that the more serious the human rights violations and the greater the boost to prestige which a controversial regime may bring about through international sports contacts, the more reason there would be in principle for the sports community to consider breaking off such contacts.

International sports contacts may be used by politics for the purposes of propaganda. If Nigeria had not been allowed to take part in the soccer World Championship in France this would no doubt have been an effective boycott in terms of constituting a considerable loss of political prestige to the military regime. From a completely different perspective, sports may however also be abused by politics because other measures against a regime, such as an economic boycott, were rejected. Due to the overwhelming media attention at Olympic Games and soccer World Championships a sports boycott is an attractive instrument for politics, bringing with it little economic damage. Sports must, however, in practice be able to set the boundaries for its responsibility to society. If the sports world refuses to co-operate in a boycott, for example, because the reason for it lies outside sports (Nigeria), then politics should make up its own balance of interests in the framework of foreign policy to see whether the boycott should be enforced through visa policy. It should not be so that the authorities in such cases merely complain that the sports world is being 'uncooperative' and cannot be forced into co-operation, which is in itself correct (the government could indeed not have cancelled the international match; only the KNVB could have done that), but leaves their own political responsibility intact.

The international match between the Netherlands and Nigeria was eventually seized upon by Amnesty International and other organisations to stage actions against the human rights violations in Nigeria. The KNVB facilitated these actions in the Amsterdam Arena soccer stadium, among others through allowing a relevant advert of Amnesty's to appear in the programme, which evoked some protest from the representatives of the Nigerian soccer association. A TV commercial, rejected by the national commercial advertisement board [*STER*] but not by the commercial stations, showed a keeper just before a penalty is taken, who is then executed and drops down dead—a reference to the death sentences carried out in Nigerian soccer stadiums. This fact alone could, in my opinion, actually have provided a 'sporting' reason for the KNVB to cancel the game, given the direct link between human rights violations and sports in Nigeria. The actions by Amnesty International and co. have meanwhile shown that, even if an event is gone through with, it is still possible to bring human rights violations to the attention in a way directly related to that event. Sports associations can play a facilitating role in this.

11.4 The Olympics, China and Human Rights[27]

11.4.1 Introduction

Just as in 1978, when two well-known Dutch cabaret performers were the first to call for a boycott by the Dutch national football team of the FIFA World Cup held in Argentina, the present discussion about a possible boycott of the upcoming Olympic Games in Beijing was also initiated by a cabaret artist interested in football. In both cases, human rights violations by the host nation are taken as an argument in favour of a sports boycott. In the case of China, the issues specifically include use of the death penalty, the torture of prisoners, administrative detention,

[27] On 27 May 1988, the T.M.C. Asser Instituut for International law in The Hague, in co-operation with the Society for Sports and Law, held a round Table Session on this subject. During this conference introductions were held by, apart from the author of this piece, Mr. M. den Hond, LL.M, MA (director of political affairs of the Ministry of Foreign Affairs), Mr. A. Sterk, M.A. (policy staff member for international sports affairs of the Ministry of Welfare, Public Health and Sports; he sat in for Mr. R. Kramer, LL.M, deputy director for sports with the same ministry) and Mr. G. Wegener (head of international affairs of the NOC'NSF). The main outcome of this Asser Round Table was the mutually declared willingness on the parts of the government and the NOC*NSF to re-open the dialogue on the basis of an evaluation of the 1982 NSF 'Starting points for sports and politics' (see hereafter).

the violation of the freedom of speech (including freedom of the press) and religious freedom, the violation of minority rights and the intimidation and arrest of human rights activists. In addition, critics denounce the expropriation of land to free up space for the construction of facilities for the Games without offering satisfactory compensation. They also condemn the policy of the People's Republic with respect to Africa, pointing towards the Chinese support for the regime in Sudan (the Darfur question). The recent developments in Tibet, however (the protest demonstration and their violent suppression), formed the incidents that truly brought the debate about a possible boycott of the Olympic Games to the fore.

What does a comparison of 'China' and the case history and possible precedents from the past teach us with regard to international sports boycotts?[28] Who can take action in this context; and in which way; taking which action? What is possible, what is allowed? What is reasonable? To answer these questions, I will pass the various possible international and national actors/stakeholders in revue, starting with the United Nations, the European Union and the Dutch government on the one hand, the IOC, the Dutch National Olympic Committee (NOC*NSF) and the individual Dutch Olympic competitor (athlete) on the other. Of course, China's responses will also be included in this summary.

11.4.2 United Nations

Statements made by the Security Council offer no foundation for a (binding) collective sports boycott. There is no case of a military intervention in Tibet. Tibet is a part of China, not an independent state; it is not a member of the UN and is not recognised as such by the international community. In other words, non-intervention in a state's internal affairs should be the primary aim, unless the Security Council were to qualify China's actions in Tibet at the very least as a threat to international peace and security, in accordance with Chapter VII of the UN Charter. This, however, is purely theoretical—an unreal conjecture. There is nothing that would suggest such a decision being reached. Indeed, 'Tibet' is not on the Security Council's agenda. Furthermore, as a permanent member of this body, China would veto any resolution in this direction.

The violation of human rights in China is even less likely to inspire a UN boycott. According to the annual report dealing with human rights violations throughout the world (2007 edition), the United States no longer considers China one of the worst offenders in the area of human rights. While the situation is bad, some progress is being made, and there have been various major legal reforms. At present, the People's Republic falls under the category of authoritarian regimes

[28] Reference is also made to the section 'History' in Siekmann (1998), pp. 400–405, which is the first time the article is published in an English version.

that are experiencing economic reforms and rapid social reforms, but are not yet implementing democratic political reforms. However, according to human rights organisations like Amnesty International, things have actually worsened in the run-up to the Olympic Games.

UN Secretary General Ban Ki-moon has expressed his concern about the violence in Tibet, and called on China to practice restraint in this area. As has the US Secretary of State Condoleezza Rice, who has urged China to speak with the Dalai Lama, the Tibetan spiritual leader and political leader-in-exile, in order to arrive at a peaceful solution for the Tibet question. The Chinese Premier Wen Jiabao and the Dalai Lama have expressed their willingness to enter into dialogue under certain conditions. Speaking to the United States Congress in October 1987, the Dalai Lama had already dropped his demand for independence for Tibet (trading separation for more autonomy and a stop to 'cultural genocide'). The Dalai Lama does not begrudge China its Olympic Games and is consequently opposed to a sports boycott.

The current debate completely ignores United Nations Resolution 62/4, adopted by the General Assembly on 16 November 2007. This resolution, which deals with the Olympic Truce during the Games in Beijing[29] appears to offer a sports-related handle—for diplomatic actions at any rate that focus specifically on the situation in Tibet. This resolution also refers to the 'harmonious development of society' as one of the official objectives of the Chinese Olympiad, applauds the decision of the IOC to mobilise international sports organisations and the National Olympic Committees to undertake concrete actions at the local, national, regional and global levels to promote and strengthen 'a culture of peace and harmony based on the spirit of the Olympic Truce' and calls on all member states to cooperate with the IOC to use sport as an instrument to promote peace, dialogue and reconciliation in areas of conflict during and after the period of the Games. And finally, the UN Secretary General is also asked in general terms to take action in the context of this resolution. China, however, is of the opinion that it is the Dalai Lama who has disrupted 'the harmony between peaceable nations' in this Olympic year!

11.4.3 European Union

The European Union has expressed its concerns about the situation in Tibet. It would be possible in principle to organise a sports boycott in response to human rights violations in China. In all fairness this would be a disproportionate reaction, however, because there has been no sudden escalation of such violations recently. 'Tibet' is a different matter. It is currently being discussed whether the heads of state and government leaders of the EU member states should boycott the opening

---

[29] Reference is made to the text of the Resolutions dealing with the Olympic Truce in the section 'Documentation' in Siekmann (1998).

ceremony of the Games. France in particular (Sarkozy) has not ruled out this gesture in protest of the Chinese actions in Tibet.

11.4.4 The Netherlands

The Dutch Ministers of Foreign Affairs and Health, Welfare and Sports have expressed their concern about the situation in Tibet to their Chinese counterparts, using both 'silent diplomacy' and other channels. In practical terms, this means that the Netherlands is following the same route as the European Union and the United Nations. The crown prince, Willem-Alexander, who is also a member of the IOC and who operates under ministerial responsibility, expressed his concern on the website of the Dutch Royal Family about the developments in Tibet. In the prince's opinion, parties should strive for a peaceful solution that is characterised by respect for human rights and that takes the position of all communities into account.

11.4.5 IOC

According to the Olympic Charter (see 'Fundamental Principles of Olympism'), one of sport's purposes is to promote a peaceful society concerned with the preservation of human dignity. In this context, one can also turn to the aforementioned UN Resolution 62/4, which also refers to a decision made by the IOC regarding this matter. This justifies a public statement by IOC President Jacques Rogge, who expressed his serious concern about the situation in Tibet. He has also announced his intention to engage in 'silent diplomacy' in order to improve the human rights situation in China. The IOC is not the UN of sports, however: 'If we start involving ourselves in politics, we will impede all the people of the world in coming together through sport,' Rogge explained.

According to the Chinese government, people and organisations who take the Olympic Games as an opportunity to criticise the human rights situation in China are violating the Olympic Charter, which demands that the Games will not be used for political purposes.

*11.4.6 NOC*NSF*

On 14 March 2008, the NOC*NSF issued an official Statement regarding Beijing 2008 (for the full text, please refer to Annex I). The Olympic Games are also a platform for debate that is utilised by all sorts of non-sports-related parties in the run-up to the event, leading to public discussions about China that focus among others on political issues and human rights. The NOC*NSF itself also participates in such debates when they focus on sports. According to the Statement, 'various athletes, coaches and administrators will be making their own comments about

China. These statements are strictly in a private capacity and are evidence of these individuals' personal social involvement.' In this context, one can also consider the coach of the national swimming team, Jacco Verhaeren, and his pupil, triple Olympic swimming champion Pieter Van den Hoogenband, who appealed to the IOC to speak out on the human rights situation in China, as the individual athletes should not be burdened with the political discussions. Furthermore, the NOC*NSF Statement also says that in their own field, sports can make a difference, for instance with respect to labour conditions in the manufacture of the clothing and shoes worn by the Dutch Olympic Team (the 'Clean Clothes Campaign' combating child labour).

Erica Terpstra, President of the NOC*NSF, has stated that sport should not be politicised. Nevertheless, sport does not exist in a vacuum either; it is an integral part of society. In that context, she considers it pure gain that the Olympic Games have generated so much interest in the human rights situation in China (she made this statement during the public roundtable conference dealing with 'China, the Olympic Games and human rights,' which the Ministry of Foreign Affairs organised in The Hague on 17 January 2008). On a later occasion, the NOC*NSF President called on China to arrive at a quick, peaceful solution to the situation in Tibet, but added that everyone needed to leave the athletes alone—it is up to the political establishment to take up a position.

In 1982, the Netherlands Sports Federation (Nederlandse Sport Federatie (NSF)), the predecessor of the NOC*NSF, issued the document *Uitgangspunten sport en politiek* ('Principles with respect to Sports and Politics'), which was intended to serve as the basis for the organisation's dialogue with the Dutch government about possible sports boycotts etc. (for the full text, please refer to Annex II). This document is no longer effective. Nevertheless, it is interesting to assess the NOC*NSF's current position against these Principles. One of the assumptions of the former document was that the main issue would be sport-related contacts with countries with a 'controversial regime,' with particular emphasis on countries involved in military aggression (for example, the sport boycotts of the 'small' Yugoslavia, and the Moscow Olympics of 1980) or in serious and systematic human rights violations (for instance, the sport boycotts of South Africa and Nigeria). Preferably, the situation should also include a negative ruling by an international political institution like the United Nations. Do such criteria also apply to China with respect to its actions in Tibet and internal human rights violations? Tibet: there is no case of aggression (see above). Human rights: this criterion does not apply either (China has not been condemned by either the United Nations or the European Union on these points).

11.4.7 Individual Athlete

The Olympic Rules explicitly prohibit wearing politically charged symbols during the Games themselves or on Olympic locations (so no political statements; no

Dalai Lama armbands). We can refer here to the 'Black Power' salute made by the African American athletes on the podium during the Olympic Games in Mexico in 1968, which focused attention on the race problem in the US. The complete text of Rule 51 of the Olympic Charter states: 'No kind of demonstration or political, religious or racial propaganda is permitted in any Olympic sites, venues or other areas.'

In contrast with the other National Olympic Committees, the NOC*NSF does not impose any additional restrictions on the participants' freedom of speech. The participants are allowed to speak out both before, during and after the Games. The NOC*NSF allows the participants to express their personal opinions in interviews and weblogs. The athletes commit themselves in advance to respecting the Olympic Rules (which are in place throughout their appointment). Any athletes not adhering to the Olympic Charter can be suspended for the rest of the Games. These agreements have been set down in the standard contract that each Dutch Olympic athlete enters into with the NOC*NSF.

In response to written questions submitted by the Dutch parliament, the Ministers of Foreign Affairs and of Health, Welfare and Sports have stated in this context that while freedom of speech is universal, Dutch citizens will in principle have to adhere to the laws and regulations of the People's Republic during their stay on Chinese soil.

11.4.8 In Closing

At this point in time, a sport boycott of China on the occasion of the upcoming Olympic Games cannot be considered a viable option. There is no support whatsoever for such a measure within the international community. Indeed, there are virtually no points of departure (precedents) to be found in this area in historic cases of sport boycotts up to this point. While sports and politics cannot be taken as fully separate entities, in terms of international relations, the two do have separate responsibilities. There are no 'athletic' reasons to boycott Beijing 2008. In the case of the sport boycott of South Africa, for instance, the situation was quite different, because like any other community in that country, the South African athletic community could not disentangle itself from the consequences of apartheid as an explicitly codified system of racial segregation and discrimination. If politicians wish to take action in non-sports-related cases, however, they will have to use the legal instruments and other means that are at their disposal on their own authority, without relying—or indeed being allowed to rely—on the cooperation of the athletic community. Naturally, such co-operation can be expected if the regular or trade boycott has a general status and as such automatically encapsulates sports activities.

Sports should not be an excuse for politics, should not be elevated to the position of policy spearhead. The 'specificity of sport' in this area indicates precisely that sports have an emphatically non-political purpose. In democratic societies, this specific quality of sport (its autonomy) should enjoy maximum safeguarding by public authorities. In the case of China, statements made by our politicians and diplomats—whether or not expressed in public—would appear to be the only realistic option open to us to promote human rights in the context of the Beijing Olympiad. A 'political' boycott of the Games' opening ceremony by heads of state and government leaders could be a fitting gesture to spherically denounce the present situation in Tibet.

11.5 Annex 1

*11.5.1 Statement NOC*NSF Beijing 2008*

> 'This year, the Netherlands will be taking part in the Summer Olympic Games and the Summer Paralympics, which will both be held in China. The Olympics are the most glorious event in international sports. Dutch athletes and coaches and a large proportion of the Dutch public are eagerly looking forward to the Games.'

The NOC*NSF is responsible for sending out the Olympic and Paralympic Teams. The NOC was set up for this purpose in 1912. We are proud of this core task and we prepare ourselves as thoroughly as possible—a process of years in which we are supported by the Dutch government—to give the best possible performance during each new edition of the Games. Our aim is to earn the Netherlands a place among the top 10 (Olympics) and 25 (Paralympics) countries in the respective national rankings.

In 2001, Beijing was awarded this year's Games on the basis of the strong quality of its sport bid. For the Chinese, hosting the 2008 Games entails development in a wide range of areas. In the area of sports, the IOC oversees the arrangements, to ensure that the athletes in 2008 will be able to achieve maximum performance under optimum circumstances.

The Olympic Games are not only the largest multi-sports event in the world. For over a century, the Games have also helped different cultures to get to know one another better. The 2008 Games will be taking place in a country that has a rich diversity of cultures, both in the past and today.

11.5.2 Public Debate

China is 'unfamiliar,' and for many outsiders it is still unknown ground. There is widespread interest in the country as a result of the 2008 Olympics, and the event features prominently in many people's agendas. The Games are also a platform for debate that has been utilised by a variety of non-sports-related parties in the run-up to the event. Both in the Netherlands and abroad, this edition of the Games has given rise to a public debate about China. This debate centres on political issues, human rights, economic developments, the Chinese culture, norms and values, the environment, education, sports, etc.

The NOC*NSF is aware of the issues existing beyond the realm of sports and welcomes public debate about China. The NOC*NSF itself participates in such debates where they focus on sports, the preparations for the Games and our delegation. On what happens on the field, in the hall, on the road, in the arena, on the track or in the pool.

Various athletes, coaches and administrators will be making their own comments about China. These statements are strictly in a private capacity and are evidence of these individuals' personal social involvement.

11.5.3 Social Effects

Sports are all about the participation in and organisation of athletic activities. Sports have an influence within their own domain. Sports can also make a difference within their sphere of influence, for instance with regard to labour conditions in the manufacture of the clothing and shoes worn by the Dutch Team. Sports are also responsible for the participants' adherence to the rules and for honouring values such as mutual respect, solidarity and fair play within the sporting activity.

Outside its domain, sports have various valuable effects that derive from their practice and organisation. In the Netherlands, for example, sectors like health, integration and education all benefit from sports, which make ongoing investment in sports a very rewarding policy.

The 2008 Games will also have social effects. What the consequences of the Olympics for developments in China will be is difficult to determine at this stage, because such processes often take years to run their course.

In 2008, the Netherlands will be participating in the Games, which without a doubt will once again be impressive, challenging and innovative. Despite the great differences between our various societies, the rules on the field are the same for everyone. Athletes practice sports. With each other and against each other. That's what makes sports so great and so unique.

11.6 Annex 2

11.6.1 NSF 'Basic Principles Concerning Sport and Politics'

1. International sports organisations promote human contacts—irrespective of race or religion—which transcend political borders. The world of sport enables representatives from all countries to meet one another to an extent which is

hardly ever achieved outside sport. This may be regarded as a valuable tool in our struggle for more understanding among nations. However, it can be argued that large-scale international sporting events that attract spectators worldwide can easily become a target for nationalist tendencies and political interests. They can be used for purposes of prestige by the organising countries, and this can cause considerable tension, particularly if it happens in countries with a controversial regime.

2. It is appropriate within relations in the Netherlands that political bodies create conditions in which sports organisations can exercise responsibility in fulfilling their sporting functions. When fulfilling such functions, these sports organisations must give an account of the responsibility arising from the relationship between society and the world of sport. At international level it is appropriate that political bodies that bear national responsibility express an opinion concerning conduct in the field of sport, for example.
   With due regard for personal responsibility concerning sport, this opinion could imply that a certain course of action should not be pursued.
3. Generally speaking, it is acknowledged that certain actions cannot be enforced by international political bodies. International sports organisations, on the other hand, generally have the option of sanctions, which can serve to influence certain conduct on the part of their members.
4. The Dutch government and/or parliament may consider it desirable to express the opinion that representatives of Dutch sports organisations should refrain from taking part in actions of a political nature when participating in international sporting events.
   As a last resort, the Dutch government and/or parliament may consider it desirable to express the opinion that representatives of Dutch sports organisations should refrain from exposing themselves to political use and should refrain from participating in certain sporting events. These statements will carry more weight for sport if the government and/or parliament:

   - argue(s) convincingly that the sportsmen and sportswomen are being used for political purposes outside the Netherlands;
   - demonstrate(s) a certain political consistency partly based on a wide political majority; concur(s) with the opinion of an international political body;
   - indicate(s) whether any resources are being utilised to achieve the political objective, and if so, which resources are employed herein;
   - has/have tested the efficacy of the measure; taking due account of the sportsmen's and sportswomen's interests and of the obligations arising from membership in an international sports organisation and of any other obligations which have meanwhile been assumed. In the case of European and World Championships, Olympic Games and the necessary qualifying rounds, these obligations will be greater than in the case of friendly competitions.

5. The Dutch sports organisations will hold consultations at NSF level on future international sports meetings. Measures must also be taken to enable consultations to be held in good time between organised sport and the government

(Ministry of Culture, Recreation and Social Services and Ministry of Foreign Affairs). These consultations can prevent the parties concerned from presenting each other with *faits accomplis*. A structure will (gradually) have to be found for both types of consultation.

6. These consultations must be conducted solely in the case of sporting contacts in and with countries with a controversial regime. Such countries can be divided into the following categories:

   a. countries which carry out acts of military aggression against other countries;
   b. countries subjected to a general international boycott;
   c. countries where serious and systematic human rights violations occur;
   d. countries in which the universality principle is not enforced (e.g. refusing visas to potential participants).

7. During the ultimate decision-making, in which the relevant sports organisation's responsibility and the Dutch citizens' individual responsibility are respected, the arguments from the consultations held will be taken into consideration.

11.7 Summary and Conclusion

International sport boycotts can be subdivided into unilateral, 'one-sided' and collective ones. The boycott of the 1980 Moscow Olympic Games is an example of the first type. The boycott was not initiated within the framework of an intergovernmental organisation like the United Nations or the European Union, but the initiative was taken by a single state (the United States of America) in cooperation with its allies. Collective sports boycotts like that regarding *apartheid* in South Africa (UN) may be based on mandatory decisions, which oblige Member States to implement them nationally. The UN's legal foundation then still is Article 41 of Chapter VII of the UN Charter concerning non-military enforcement action decided on by the Security Council in order to maintain or restore international peace and security. In this context, as to the EU, in present times reference has to be made to the relevant provisions of the Lisbon Treaty. Title V of the Treaty on European Union (TEU) concerns the EU's external action, and in particular EU common foreign and security policy. It says that its action on the international scene shall be guided by the principles which have inspired its own creation, development and enlargement, and which it seeks to advance in the wider world: democracy, the rule of law, the universality and indivisibility of human rights and fundamental freedoms, respect for human dignity, the principles of equality and solidarity, and respect for the principles of the United Nations (cf., maintaining international peace and security, developing friendly relations among nations, international cooperation, respect for human rights) and international law. Where the international situation requires operational action by the EU, the Council shall adopt the necessary decisions which shall commit the Member States in the positions they adopt and in the conduct of their activity.

In the model Host state Contract (HCC) which is also applicable to the forthcoming 2012 London Olympic Games, Article 64 on Termination of Contract reads in full as follows (sub a and i):

> 'The IOC shall be entitled to terminate this Contract and to withdraw the Games from the City if the Host Country is at any time, whether before the Opening Ceremony or during the Games, in a state of war, civil disorder, *boycott, embargo decreed by the international community* or in a situation officially recognised as one of belligerence or if the IOC has reasonable grounds to believe, in its sole discretion, that the safety of participants in the Games would be seriously threatened or jeopardised for any reason whatsoever.' (italics added, RS)

Generally speaking, it should be added that collective economic boycotts or embargos of a general and mandatory nature will implicitly include professional sporting relations of a financial-economic nature. Another observation is that international sports organisations (IOC, IFs etc.) are bound by collective boycott decision via their host state, insofar as that state is a member of the intergovernmental organisation, worldwide or regional, concerned.

Additionally, it could be observed that the repetitive UN General Assembly resolutions on the Olympic Truce (since 1993)[30] can be considered conducive to a peaceful international political climate during the Games, 'war' being a possible reason for boycotting a host state (cf., the 1980 Moscow Olympic Games boycott).

In democracies, and being merely called upon, sport governing bodies are free in their decision to follow a non-mandatory international collective boycott decision or not. The same of course applies to unilateral recommendations and the like by their government or a group of states to which their government belongs. In the Western world, the principle of autonomy, i.e. the respect for the individual responsibility of national sports organisations, more or less obtains (in 'interventionist' countries somewhat less than in 'non-interventionist' ones where the State in principle is used to fully respect the autonomy of the sport governing bodies). Apart from that, national sport organisations cannot even refuse contacts for political reasons when it concerns the participation in international competitions other than so-called 'friendly games,' since their membership of the international federation (IF) may be suspended because of such refusal, or their organisation of the championship may be withdrawn by the IF which decision would be ideologically footed on the universality principle in conducting international sporting relations.

However, in my opinion, 'sport' should listen to 'politics,' when the underlying reason for the propose measures also directly affects 'sport' as such, in other words when there are also reasons 'of sport' for a boycott, for example in case of a

[30] See for the text of such resolutions, The International Sports Law Journal (ISLJ) 2008/1-2, pp. 128–132.

country where the organisation of sport openly is founded on racial or other discrimination. With regard to South Africa, this even led to a unique, general, 'public' and 'private' ban on any sporting relations, irrespectively from particular forthcoming events of minor or major importance. IFs naturally make themselves quite vulnerable, when their Statutes and Constitutions explicitly would contain solemn declarations which go beyond the world of sport itself and as such coincide with UN (and EU) basic principles.

Another vulnerable, weak point of the sporting world is the national representation issue. In fact, in particular national teams and delegations are seen as representing not only the national sport governing body, but even much more their country. It is a historical fact that sport is organised according to states' boundaries, and that 'nationals' represent their national sport governing body.[31] Moreover, national symbols like anthems and flags are used. If the national government (state) does not wish to be represented in the country which is to be boycotted, it is very difficult for the sporting world to neglect this wish. For the IOC and Ifs, the position is a bit easier because they *qualitate qua* are nationality-neutral. 'Depoliticisation' (no flags, no anthems etc.; also non-nationals-in-residence in teams and delegations that then would represent the national sport association/sport governing body concerned!) of course could be a means to counter this problem as much as possible, but in practice this seems to be a purely theoretical option in the world of today as it was in the world of the past.[32]

Both issues—the autonomy one and the national representation issue (cf., 'Ein Platz Prinzip,' a single national association per sport, national flags/anthems and country as well as participation of athletes based on legal nationality, 'passport')—are in fact of a 'sport-specific' type. Autonomy in principle would be an argument for making exceptions ('sport has nothing to do with politics'), but national representation points into the opposite direction ('sport and politics cannot be separated').

References

Dijk P van (1980) The final act of Helsinki—basis for a Pan-European system? Netherlands Yearbook of International Law (NYIL)

Granier JP (1980) Human rights and the Helsinki conference on security and cooperation in Europe: an annotated bibliography of United States government documents. Vanderbilt Journal of Transnational Law, vol. 13, Spring–Summer 1980, Number 2–3

Guldenpfennig S (1981) Internationale Sportbeziehungen zwischen Entspannung und Konfrontation—Der Testfall 1980. Cologne

Heuvel MP van den (1978) Sport in de Sovjetunie [Sport in the Soviet-Union]. Haarlem

[31] The European Court of Justice explicitly accepted this (sport-specific) sporting exception to the non-discrimination of EU non -nationals with regard to team sports in *Walrave and Koch*.

[32] See on the matter of possibly depoliticising the venue of the Olympic Games: Rich 2009.

Kavass II, Granier JP, Dominick MF (eds) (1981) Human rights, european politics, and the Helsinki accord—the documentary evolution of the conference on security and co-operation in Europe 1973–1975, New York

Knecht W Ph (1980) Der Boykott—Moskaus missbrauchte Olympiade. Cologne

Siekmann RCR (1984) Sportcontacten met Zuid-Afrika (Sporting relations with South Africa), NSF [Netherlands Sport Federation] publication No. 116. The Hague, June 1984

Siekmann RCR (1985) The Boycott of the 1980 Olympic games and Détente. In: Bloed A, van Dijk P (eds) Essays on human rights in the Helsinki process. T.M.C Asser Instituut, The Hague

Siekmann RCR (1996) Internationaal sportrecht (International sports law). In: Praktijk voor de Sportbestuurder—Suppl 51, Nov 1996

Siekmann RCR (1998) De sportboycot van Nigeria: sport, politiek en mensenrechten (The sports boycott of Nigeria: sports, politics and human rights), Internationale Spectator

Siekmann RCR (2003) The Sports Boycott of Nigeria. In: Korchia N, Pettiti C (eds) Sports et Garanties Fondamentales: violences—dopage/sports and fundamental guarantees: assault—doping. In: 7th international congress of the international association of sports law co-organised by the human rights training institute of the Paris bar association—Center Louis Pettiti, Paris 30 November–1 December 2000. Tours

Siekmann RCR (2008) The sports boycott of Nigeria: sports, politics and human rights. The international sports law journal (ISLJ) 1–2, pp 121–124. Previously published in: Korchia N, Pettiti C (eds) (2003) Sports and fundamental guarantees—assault—doping, 7th I.A.S.L. Congress Papers. Tours, pp 85–97

MIX
Papier aus verantwortungsvollen Quellen
Paper from responsible sources
FSC® C105338

Printed by Books on Demand, Germany